Consent

This volume presents a leading contribution to the substantive arena relating to consent in the criminal law. In broad terms, the ambit of legally valid consent in extant law is contestable and opaque, and reveals significant problems in adoption of consistent approaches to doctrinal and theoretical underpinnings of consent. This book seeks to provide a logical template to focus the debate. The overall concept addresses three specific elements within this arena, embracing an overarching synergy between them. This edifice engages in an examination of UK provisions, with specialist contributions on Irish and Scottish law, and in contrasting these provisions against alternative domestic jurisdictions as well as comparative contributions addressing a particularised research grid for content. The comparative chapters provide a wider background of how other legal systems treat a variety of specialised issues relating to consent in the context of the criminal law. The debate in relation to consent principles continues apace for academics, practitioners and within the criminal justice system. Having expert descriptions of the wider issues surrounding the particular discussion and of other legal systems' approaches serves to stimulate and inform that debate. This collection will be a major source of reference for future discussion.

Alan Reed is Associate Dean (Research and Innovation) and Professor of Law at Northumbria Law School.

Michael Bohlander is the International Co-Investigating Judge at the Extraordinary Chambers in the Courts of Cambodia.

Dr Nicola Wake is Associate Professor of Law at Northumbria University.

Emma Smith is a Lecturer in Law, and has a number of leading outputs in the areas of Criminal Law and Evidence.

Substantive Issues in Criminal Law

Series Editors:
Alan Reed and Michael Bohlander

Substantive Issues in Criminal Law presents a series of volumes that systematically address areas of the criminal law that are in need of reform or which belong to the core areas of law where doctrinal abstraction or greater analysis is required. One part of each book is dedicated to an in-depth look at the situation in the UK, with individual chapters analysing points of current interest. A second feature of each volume is a major comparative section of other domestic jurisdictions. These international contributions are written to a uniform research grid provided by the editors in order to ensure a maximum degree of ease of comparison. The key purpose of the series is to produce a major library of reference works to which all actors in the wider criminal justice and policy community in the UK and elsewhere will have recourse for academic, judicial and policy purposes.

Other titles in this series

General Defences in Criminal Law: Domestic and Comparative Perspectives
Edited by Alan Reed and Michael Bohlander with Nicola Wake and Emma Smith
ISBN 978-1-4724-3335-0

Participation in Crime: Domestic and Comparative Perspectives
Edited by Alan Reed and Michael Bohlander
ISBN 978-1-4094-5345-1

Consent

Domestic and Comparative Perspectives

Edited by Alan Reed and Michael Bohlander
with
Nicola Wake and Emma Smith

Routledge
Taylor & Francis Group

LONDON AND NEW YORK

First published 2017
by Routledge
2 Park Square, Milton Park, Abingdon, Oxon OX14 4RN

and by Routledge
711 Third Avenue, New York, NY 10017

Routledge is an imprint of the Taylor & Francis Group, an informa business

British Library Cataloguing in Publication Data
A catalogue record for this book is available from the British Library

Library of Congress Cataloging in Publication Data
Names: Reed, Alan (Matthew Alan), editor.
Title: Consent : domestic and comparative perspectives.
Description: Abingdon, Oxon ; New York, NY : Routledge, 2017. |
Series: Substantive issues in criminal law | Includes bibliographical references and index.
Identifiers: LCCN 2016020415 (print) | LCCN 2016020655 (ebook) | ISBN 9781472469953 (hardback) | ISBN 9781315573472 (Master e-book) | ISBN 9781317161929 (Web PDF) | ISBN 9781317161912 (ePub) | ISBN 9781317161905 (MobiPocket)
Subjects: LCSH: Consent (Law) | Sexual consent. | Consent (Law)–Great Britain. | Sexual consent–Great Britain.
Classification: LCC K5087.C6 .C66 2017 (print) | LCC K5087.C6 (ebook) | DDC 346.01/62–dc23
LC record available at https://lccn.loc.gov/2016020415

ISBN: 978-1-472-46995-3 (hbk)
ISBN: 978-1-315-57347-2 (ebk)

Typeset in Minion
by Apex CoVantage, LLC

Printed and bound in Great Britain by
TJ International Ltd, Padstow, Cornwall

Contents

v

Notes on contributors

Verity Adams: Verity graduated from the University of Durham with an Upper Second Class LLB (Hons) in 2012. Subsequently, in 2013, she completed the Bar Professional Training Course at Northumbria University and a Master in Jurisprudence at Durham. In 2013 Verity was also called to the Bar at the Inner Temple. Verity's LLB dissertation was a comparative study on the age of consent while her MJur considered the legality of humanitarian interventions. Currently reading for a PhD which focuses on the internationalisation of internal armed conflicts, Verity also tutors in criminal law, interscholastic mooting and criminal evidence at Durham. She is an Assistant Editor for the OUP International Courts of General Jurisdiction database and the postgraduate convenor of the University of Durham's Centre for Criminal Law and Criminal Justice. Verity co-convened the Centre's 2015 Postgraduate Conference titled 'Sexual Offences in the Criminal Justice System'.

Kai Ambos: Chair of Criminal Law, Criminal Procedure, Comparative Law and International Criminal Law at the Georg-August-Universität Göttingen, Germany (since May 2003).

Head of the Department of 'Foreign and International Criminal Law', Institute of Criminal Law and Justice at the University of Göttingen. Director of the Centro de Estudios de Derecho Penal y Procesal Penal Latinoamericano (CEDPAL) of Georg-August-Universität Göttingen. Judge at the Provincial Court (*Landgericht*) of Lower Saxony in Göttingen (since 24 March 2006); since 1 January 2015 delegated to the Higher Regional Court (Oberlandesgericht) Braunschweig. Dean of Students of the Faculty of Law at the University of Göttingen between April 2008 and 2010; responsible for the Master Programs 'MLE' and 'LLM' from April 2006 to June 2014.

Petter Asp: is Professor of Criminal Law at Stockholm University and the present holder of the Torsten and Ragnar Soderberg Chair in Legal Science.

Mirko Bagaric: is a professor at the Deakin Law School. He is the author or co-author of over 25 books and 100 refereed articles. He is the editor or co-editor of several law journals, including Australia's leading criminal law journal: *The Criminal Law Journal*. His main research areas are sentencing, evidence, substantive criminal law and moral and legal philosophy. He is also a practising lawyer.

Vera Bergelson: is a Professor of Law and Robert E. Knowlton Scholar at Rutgers University School of Law (USA).

Vera Bergelson specializes in criminal law theory. She has written about consent, provocation, self-defense, necessity, victimless crime, and human trafficking. Her book *Victims' Rights and Victims' Wrongs: A Theory of Comparative Criminal Liability* (SUP 2009) raises questions about comparative liability in criminal law.

Vera Bergelson has served as a chair of the Association of American Law Schools' Section on Jurisprudence. She is on the editorial boards of BdeF and Edisofer (Buenos Aires and Madrid) and *Law and Philosophy*.

Stefanie Bock: Dr Stefanie Bock is a senior research assistant of Ambos, Department for Foreign and International Criminal Law, University of Göttingen and an Assistant Professor at the same department. She has studied law at the University of Hamburg and holds a PhD in criminal law from the same University. Prior to taking up her current position, she has worked as a research assistant at the Universities of Hamburg and Göttingen and as an intern at the International Criminal Court. Her main fields of research are international criminal law, European criminal law and comparative criminal law.

Michael Bohlander: is the International Co-Investigating Judge, Extraordinary Chambers in the Courts of Cambodia; Chair in Comparative and International Criminal Law, Durham Law School.

Gavin Byrne: Dr Gavin Byrne is a Senior Lecturer at Birmingham Law School, University of Birmingham. Dr Byrne received a BCL from University College Dublin in 1999, an LLM by research from the University of Kent in 2001, and a PhD from Birmingham Law School in 2008. His major research interests are in Jurisprudence and Political and Legal Theory.

Manuel Cancio Meliá: México, DF, 1967. Licenciado en Derecho (= JD; Universidad Autónoma de Madrid), 1991; Doctor en Derecho (= PhD; UAM), 1997.

Research Fellow of the German Academic Exchange Service, 1992/1993, 1998; Alexander-von-Humboldt Research Fellow, 2002/2009. Dr *honoris causa* (Universidad Peruana los Andes, Huancayo, 2008; Universidad Nacional de Córdoba, Argentina, 2012; Universidad Nacional de la Amazonía Peruana, Iquitos, 2013). Corresponding member and Secretary of the Criminal Law Section of the Spanish Royal Academy for Jurisprudence and Legislation. He has been and is a member of and responsible researcher for a series of Spanish and European-funded research projects in Criminal Law and is a member of the advisory boards of several Spanish, Latin American and German journals on criminal law.

Full Professor of Criminal Law at the Universidad Autónoma de Madrid since 2008.

Among his works, monographs on victim's behaviour relevance in criminal law (*Conducta de la víctima e imputación objetiva* (1998, 2nd edn 2001)), on terrorism offences (*Los delitos de terrorismo: estructura típica e injusto*, 2010) and on the so-called 'enemy criminal law' (*Derecho penal del enemigo* (2nd edn 2006, together with G. Jakobs)), and his participation in several commentaries on the Spanish penal code are to be highlighted.

Other publications (books, chapters, articles, case discussions), regarding Criminal Law principles, Criminal Law legal dogmatics, compared Criminal Law studies, European Criminal Law and several single offences (sexual crimes, terrorism, personal injuries, crimes against the environment, organised crime), have been published in several European countries, most countries of Latin America, the United States, Turkey, Taiwan and China.

John Child: Dr John Child is a Senior Lecturer in Law at the University of Sussex, and co-founding Director of the Sussex Crime Research Centre. Prior to this, John was a Lecturer (2010–11) and Senior Lecturer (2011–13) at Oxford Brookes Law School. John's research interests focus on criminal law, both doctrine and theory. Within this field, John has published widely, including within *Legal Studies*, the *Criminal Law Review* and the *Northern Ireland Legal Quarterly*. John also co-authors the textbook *Smith and Hogan's Essentials of Criminal Law* with Professor David Ormerod QC.

Claire de Than: BA (Hons), LLB, LLM is Co-Director of the Centre for Law, Justice and Journalism at City, University of London, and Deputy Director of the Institute of Law, Jersey, having previously held appointments at two London University colleges. A graduate of Queen Mary, University of London, she is the author or co-author of more than 15 books, including de Than and Heaton, *Criminal Law* (OUP, 2013) and de Than and Shorts, *International Criminal Law and Human Rights* (Sweet and Maxwell, 2004). She has also published articles in a variety of national and international journals, including the *Modern Law Review*. Her research fields include criminal law, human rights law, media law, and disability law. She has advised several governments and many organisations on criminal law, human rights, and law reform issues, with specialisms in the law of British overseas territories and Crown dependencies and in the law of consent.

Susan S M Edwards: BA, MA, PhD, LLM, is a barrister, Door Tenant at 1 Gray's Inn Square, London, and human rights lawyer. She is a Professor and Dean of Law at the University of Buckingham. An activist and campaigner for women's human rights, LGBT, ethnic minority voice and voices marginalised in the world order, Susan is a member of Stop the War Coalition, Amnesty International, Peace and Progress, and the Bar Human Rights Committee, for which she wrote an export report on Witchcraft and Accusation in Nepal with the WHRIN. Susan has also acted as NGO with a wide range of international organisations. Whilst practising as a barrister Susan dealt with both criminal and civil matters in England and Wales. She is also a member of the EWI and has given expert opinion in criminal cases involving domestic violence where battered women have killed, and where they have been victims of assault; on the effects of domestic violence in duress in the criminal courts, the Criminal Cases Compensation Tribunal, and family cases; and, in wearing the *niqab* in court in criminal cases. Her books include *Female Sexuality and the Law* (1981), *Women on Trial* (1984), *Policing Domestic Violence* (1989) and *Sex and Gender in the Legal Process* (1996). She is a regular contributor to the *Criminal Law Review*, publishing 'The Strangulation of Female Partners' (2015) 12 *Criminal Law Review* 949. Most recently she was a contributor on women's issues speaking as a panellist at the Battle of Ideas 2015 'Rape Culture Myth or Menace' (YouTube), took part in the Sky debate on International Women's Day, and was a contributor to BBC Radio 4 'Unreliable Evidence' with Clive Anderson (7 September 2016).

Jesse Elvin: graduated from the University of London in 1994 with a BA in Law and Anthropology. He obtained an LLM from the University of London in 1995, and a PhD from the same institution in 2005. Before joining City, University of London, he taught at the London School of Economics and University College London. He has published in a number of journals, including the *Cambridge Law Journal* and the *Modern Law Review*, and is a regular conference speaker. His research and teaching interests include criminal law, tort law, and contract law.

Dimitrios Giannoulopoulos: Dr Giannoulopoulos' research provides cross-cultural analysis of foreign procedural and institutional frameworks of criminal justice, in their doctrinal and jurisprudential underpinnings, with a focus on the identification of indigenous cosmo-politan attitudes and local resistance to international pressures for human rights reform. Dr Giannoulopoulos holds a PhD from the Doctoral School of Comparative Studies at Sor-bonne University (Paris I), and has completed Master degrees in criminal law, criminal pro-cedure and criminology, in Athens, Aix-en-Provence and London. His comparative research concentrates on analyses of the criminal justice systems of England, France, Greece and the United States, but also extends to drawing analogies with other systems in the common law and civil law world (such as those of Scotland, Belgium, Italy, Canada, Australia or New Zea-land), and with developments at the international criminal tribunals, thus aiming to provide normative and empirical accounts of the criminal process, criminal justice reform and the internationalisation of criminal evidence and procedure. Key themes explored in Dr Gian-noulopoulos' research include improperly obtained evidence, telephone interceptions and electronic surveillance, police interrogation and suspects' rights in Europe and the United States as well as comparative counter-terrorism legislation after September 11. Dr Giannou-lopoulos has appeared on TV and has commented on current affairs for the BBC, the *Guardian* and the *Independent*. He has also offered consultation to policy and governmental experts in the UK and abroad.

Alisdair Gillespie: is Professor of Criminal Law and Justice and Head of School at Lancaster University Law School. His main research interests relate to the law of child sexual exploita-tion, particularly where it is facilitated by information and communication technologies, and much of his work relates to child grooming, child pornography, and child solicitation. Alis-dair is also an expert in cybercrime issues and has a particular interest in harmful conduct.

Mohammad Hedayati-Kakhki: Dr Mohammad Hedayati-Kakhki is a Senior Lecturer and an Honorary Fellow at Durham Law School and Greenwich School of Management in London. He was the Co-Founder and the Associate Director of the Islam, Law & Modernity (ILM) research group at Durham Law School and continues to act as a Special Advisor on matters concerning the Middle East and the Islamic world. He is also a Special Advisor to the Centre for Criminal Law and Criminal Justice at Durham University.

He qualified from Shahid Beheshti University in Tehran with a law degree, before moving on to complete a Master's in International Law at the University of Shiraz. He holds a PhD in Middle Eastern Politics and Law from Durham University and continues to teach at this University since 2009. Alongside teaching BSc, LLB and LLM modules, he continues his legal practice by acting as a Legal Consultant on Islamic law and jurisprudence.

Jonathan Herring: is a fellow in law at Exeter College, Oxford University and Professor of Law at the Law Faculty, Oxford University. He has written on family law, medical law, criminal law and legal issues surrounding care and old age. His books include: *Caring and the Law* (2014) *Older People in Law and Society* (OUP, 2009); *European Human Rights and Family Law* (Hart, 2010) (with Shazia Choudhry); *Medical Law and Ethics* (OUP, 2014); *Criminal Law* (OUP, 2014); *Family Law* (Pearson, 2015); and *The Woman Who Tickled Too Much* (Pearson, 2009).

Mark James: is Professor of Sports Law at Manchester Law School and one of the UK's leading sports lawyers. He specialises in the interaction between the criminal law and the ways that sport is played, watched and administered. His interest in this area began with his PhD, which focused on the role of consent and the criminal law in the regulation of sports injury disputes and the appropriateness of using the criminal law instead of governing bodies' disciplinary tribunals as a means of punishing violent play. Since then, his work has expanded beyond the confines of the playing arena to cover the regulation of football supporters, the policing of football-related disorder, the legality of football banning orders, the regulation of ticket touting and the criminalisation of public space around sporting mega-event venues, especially the Olympic Games. He is the author of Palgrave's *Sports Law* and an Editor of the *Entertainment and Sports Law Journal.*

Gerhard Kemp: Gerhard Kemp is Professor of Criminal Law and International Criminal Law at Stellenbosch University, South Africa, and advocate of the High Court of South Africa. He is a visiting lecturer in international criminal law at Nelson Mandela Metropolitan University, Port Elizabeth, and author of a number of books, chapters in books, and journal articles in the fields of criminal law, international criminal law, and transitional justice. He is editor-in-chief of the *African Yearbook on International Humanitarian Law* and serves on the advisory board of *Studies in Political Transition* (Peter Lang Edition). Gerhard is also a director of the Institute for Justice and Reconciliation, Cape Town.

Mario Maraver Gómez: PhD in Law (Universidad Autónoma de Madrid, 2007, Extraordinary Doctorate Award). Associate Professor of Criminal Law, Universidad Autónoma de Madrid (since 2011). Vice-Dean for Student Affairs at the Faculty of Law, UAM (since 2011). DAAD (German Academic Exchange Service)-Research Scholar in Bonn (2003) and in Hamburg (2010). His research activities have been aimed towards the general part of the criminal law (doctrines of causation and imputation, omission, negligence, complicity and culpability). He is author of a monograph on self-responsibility and imputation entitled *El principio de confianza en Derecho penal* (2009), as well as several articles and contributions in the field of criminal law.

Claire McDiarmid: is a Reader at the University of Strathclyde, Glasgow, specialising in criminal law. She has a particular interest in homicide and defences and has written, on provocation ('Don't Look Back in Anger: The Partial Defence of Provocation in Scots Criminal Law' in J Chalmers, F Leverick and L Farmer (eds), *Essays in Criminal Law In Honour of Sir Gerald Gordon* (Edinburgh University Press, 2010)) and on the *mens rea* of murder ('"Something Wicked This Way Comes": The *Mens Rea* of Murder in Scots Law' 2012 *Juridical Review*). She is co-author of *Scots Criminal Law: A Critical Analysis*, now in its second edition (Edinburgh University Press, 2014). She has also published on the age of criminal responsibility and on aspects of the Scottish children's hearing system. She has a particular interest in the criminal capacity of the child and in the difficulty for law in dealing with child criminals – individuals who are, simultaneously, vulnerable and in need of protection as children and, also, offenders.

R Murat Önok: born in 1979, is currently an assistant professor in the Law School at Koç University, Istanbul. Dr Önok's fields of research are criminal law, human rights law and international criminal law. He has also taught public international law and criminology. Dr Önok is the author of two books (*The International Criminal Court and its Historical Perspective* (Turhan, 2003), *The Crime of Torture, and its International Dimension* (Seckin, 2006)), and co-author of three textbooks (*Theory and Practice of the Special Part of Penal Law* (11th edn, Seckin, 2014), *International Criminal Law* (2nd edn, Seckin, 2014), *Handbook on Human Rights* (5th edn, Seckin, 2014)). He has also written five book chapters, including 'Penal Law' in *Introduction to Turkish Law* (6th edn, Kluwer International, 2011). Dr Önok is currently Vice-President of the Turkish Press Council, and serves as executive board member of the national branch of Transparency International, the Koç University Gender Studies Center (Koç-KAM), and the Center for Global Public Law (KÜREMER). He is also a member of the Criminal Procedure Law Training Commission of the Turkish Union of Bar Associations.

Suzanne Ost: is a Professor of Law at Lancaster University. Her main research interests are the legal and societal responses to child pornography, the sexual grooming of children and child sexual exploitation, more broadly health care/medical law and bioethics (particularly breaches of the sexual boundaries between doctors and patients and assisted dying), the impact of criminal law on bioethics and health care practice and law and literature.

Tanya Palmer: is a lecturer in Law and co-director of the Crime Research Centre at the University of Sussex. Prior to this, she held an ESRC post-doctoral research fellowship at the University of Bristol. Tanya's research interests are primarily in the legal regulation of sexual encounters, particularly through the substantive criminal law. She is the author of *Re-Negotiating Sex and Sexual Violation in the Criminal Law* (Hart, forthcoming) which advocates a rethinking of legal and ethical distinctions between sex and sexual violation centred around a concept of 'freedom to negotiate'. Tanya is also interested in developing novel socio-legal research methodologies that draw together theoretical, doctrinal and empirical work.

Raphaële Parizot: is a professor of private and criminal law at the University of Paris Ouest Nanterre La Défense, vice-president of the Association de Recherches Pénales Européennes (ARPE) and general secretary of the Archives de Politique Criminelle.

She is a Doctor in law from the Universities of Paris 1 Panthéon-Sorbonne and Ferrara; her PhD's thesis 'Criminal responsibility and organized crime. The symptomatic case of criminal conspiracy and money laundering in France and in Italy' was published in 2010.

She was a maître de conférences at the Ecole de droit de la Sorbonne (University Paris 1 Panthéon-Sorbonne) between 2007 and 2011 and a Professor at the University of Poitiers between 2011 and 2015.

She teaches criminal law (general and special part), criminal procedure, execution of the punishments, European criminal law, international criminal law, law for children and young persons, law and literature.

Her researches are focused on criminal law and procedure, especially in a perspective of comparative law and European law.

Anne Postma: is lecturer in criminal law and criminal procedure at the University of Groningen and deputy judge at the District Court of Noord-Nederland. The focus of his research is mainly on substantive criminal law. In this field of law he has published several papers and book contributions. His PhD thesis (Groningen, 2014) concerns a comparative analysis of co-perpetration.

Alan Reed: graduated from Trinity College, Cambridge University with a First Class Honours Degree in Law, and was awarded the Herbert Smith Prize for Conflict of Laws and the Dr Lancey Prize. Cambridge University awarded him a full Holland Scholarship to facilitate study in the United States and he obtained an LLM Masters of Law (Comparative Law) at the University of Virginia. After completion of the Law Society Finals Examinations he spent three years in practice in London at Addleshaw Goddard, and also acted as a Tutor in Criminal Law at Trinity College, Cambridge. He spent seven years as a lecturer in law at Leeds University, and then engaged as Professor of Criminal and Private International Law at Sunderland University. Since April 2012 he has acted as Associate Dean (Research and Innovation) in the Faculty of Business and Law at Northumbria University. Alan has published over 200 monographs, textbooks and articles in the substantive arena in leading journals in England, Australia, New York, Florida and Los Angeles. For the last 14 years he has been editor of the *Journal of Criminal Law*.

Emma Smith: is a Senior Lecturer in Law at Northumbria University, her research interests include Criminal Evidence and Substantive Crime. Emma is working towards her PhD, and is looking specifically at evidence of bad character and its admissibility within the criminal trial. Emma is a member of the Socio-Legal Studies Association, the Society of Legal Scholars, the Law and Society Association and the European Association of Psychology and Law.

John Stannard: is a graduate of Oxford University, and has been on the staff of the Queen's University of Belfast since 1977. He has written widely on criminal law topics in a variety of journals including the *Irish Jurist*, *Legal Studies*, and the *Law Quarterly Review*, and is the author of a textbook on Northern Ireland criminal procedure. He is a member of the Society of Legal Scholars, of the Irish Legal History Society and a Fellow of the Institute of Teaching and Learning. He is also a Past President of the Irish Association of Law Teachers.

G R Sullivan: Robert Sullivan is Emeritus Professor of Law at University College London. Previously he was Barber Professor of Jurisprudence at the University of Birmingham and Professor of Law at the University of Durham.

He is a leading scholar of criminal law. He has an international reputation as a specialist in the relationship between criminal law doctrine and theory, a form of scholarship which combines analysis of the primary sources of criminal law with the techniques of legal philosophy. He is co-author (with Andrew Simester) of *Criminal Law: Theory and Doctrine*, now in its fourth edition (Hart Publishing, 2010). This work integrates theory and doctrine across the domain of substantive criminal law. It has established itself as a major point of reference in academic writing, here and abroad, and has been cited in appellate courts throughout the world. Additionally, Robert has long-standing research interests in corporate criminal liability, large-scale commercial fraud and bribery. He is a leading authority on the complex issues of law and policy which arise in these fields.

Julia Tolmie: Julia Tolmie (LLB (Hons) (Auckland), LLM (Harvard)) is an Associate Professor at the Faculty of Law, University of Auckland. Prior to taking up her position with the University of Auckland in 1999 she was an academic on the Faculty of Law, University of Sydney for ten years. She has researched and published extensively on issues arising within criminal law, family law and feminist legal theory across a number of jurisdictions and has spent brief periods of time as a visiting scholar at the University of Ottawa, Golden Gate University and Berkeley University.

Magnus Ulväng: is Professor of Criminal Law at Uppsala University.

William Wilson: is Professor of Criminal Law at Queen Mary, University of London. He is the author of *Criminal Law: Doctrine and Theory* (5th edn, Longmans, 2003) and *Central Issues in Criminal Theory* (Hart, 2002).

Preface

We are pleased to be able to present the fourth volume of our joint cooperation in areas of substantive criminal law, following on from previous collections on Loss of Control And Diminished Responsibility, Participation In Crime, and General Defences. This volume forms part of a series called 'Substantive Issues In Criminal Law', which over the next few years will continue to systematically address areas of the criminal law in the UK that are in need of reform or which belong to the core areas of law where doctrinal abstraction or greater analysis is required. One part of each book will be dedicated to an in-depth look at the situation in the UK, with individual chapters analysing points of current interest. A second feature of each volume will be a major comparative section of, we hope, mostly the same foreign (and occasionally international) jurisdictions. These foreign contributions will all be written to a uniform research grid provided by the editors in order to ensure a maximum degree of ease of comparison. In this manner we intend to produce a major library of reference works to which all actors in the wider criminal justice and policy community in the UK and elsewhere will have recourse for academic, judicial, and policy purposes.

As with the previous volumes, we thank our contributing authors for their willingness to commit to such a time-consuming and demanding project, and for putting up with the manifold requests from the editors in the process of putting their manuscripts together into a coherent volume. We owe a debt of gratitude to Nicola Wake and Emma Smith, who provided cheerful, unflappable and above all meticulous and sterling support in the collation, proof-reading and formatting of the final manuscript. We could not have done it without them, nor the outstanding editorial support provided by Verity Adams, Katherine Parker and Beth Stuart-Cole.

We have endeavoured to state the law as in force in each jurisdiction on 31 January 2016.

Michael Bohlander*
Alan Reed
Phnom Penh; Northumbria

---

* The views expressed in this work are Michael Bohlander's own and do not represent those of the United Nations, the Royal Government of the Kingdom of Cambodia or the ECCC.

Introduction

The ambit of legally valid consent in extant law is contestable and opaque. A number of juridical precepts affirm that a freely given and sufficiently informed consent by a victim will preclude a defendant from inculpation; but counterfactually there are a distinct spectra of cases where consent is legally irrelevant. It is difficult to chart a via media between these juxtapositions. Moreover, concerns related to individual autonomy and state paternalism are often in conflict. Consent engenders a perspective that the autonomy of the other person is involved, and that if that person consents to the conduct there should be no offence. However, we can also identify an attitude of paternalism that is primordial in a number of leading judgments: the proposition that the criminal law should be used to protect persons from themselves. Legal moralism can also be adduced in that where conduct *per se* is viewed as immoral then the stigmatisation of legal censure is presumptively justified; wholly outwith the consensual nature of the act itself. Consent has developed in the UK in this regard in a solipsistic *ad hoc* manner, and haphazardly rather than in a coherent structure.

Extant law reveals significant problems in adoption of consistent approaches to doctrinal and theoretical underpinnings of consent. This has been exemplified by a plethora of recent jurisprudential authorities revealing varying degrees of confusion and vacillation. A variety of Law Commission proposals, although emboldening the debate, have yet to be adopted in any logical template.

The proposed chapter breakdowns and detailed abstracts of relevant content are set out sequentially below for consideration. In terms of the overall concept we have addressed three specific elements within this arena, embracing an overarching synergy between them. This edifice engages in an examination of UK provisions, with specialist contributions on Irish and Scottish law, and in contrasting these provisions against alternative domestic jurisdictions as well as comparative contributions addressing a particularised research grid for content.

The comparative chapters will provide a wider background of how other legal systems treat a variety of specialised issues relating to consent in the context of the criminal law.

The debate in the UK in relation to consent principles continues apace for academics, practitioners and within the criminal justice system. Having expert descriptions of the wider issues surrounding the particular discussion and of other legal systems' approaches will serve to stimulate and inform that debate.

In Chapter 1, 'Distinguishing Sex from Sexual Violation: Consent, Negotiation and Freedom to Negotiate', Dr Tanya Palmer argues that consent is not an appropriate or effective way to distinguish legitimate sexual activity from sexual violation. Consent is enmeshed with a particular notion of the Kantian liberal subject and as such is inapt to respond to the bodily, affective and relational aspects of subjectivity in general and sexual subjectivity specifically. To champion consent as the standard for legitimate sexual activity implies that sexual relations are inherently asymmetric, obscures the context within which agreements to engage in sexual activity are made, and overlooks the fluid and variable nature of sexual activity itself that renders it ill-suited to a consent framework. The chapter considers alternative models of sex and sexual violation based on notions of communication and negotiation. Drawing on these models alongside theoretical argument and original empirical data, a new framework of 'freedom to negotiate' is proposed. The standard of 'freedom to negotiate' does not prescribe the form or content that any negotiation must take. It emphasises instead the context in which sexual activity takes place, requiring that, at a minimum, all parties to sexual activity should have the space to negotiate both the fact and nature of their participation throughout the duration of that activity.

In Chapter 2, 'Relational Autonomy and Consent', Professor Jonathan Herring explores the role of consent in the criminal law from the perspective of relational autonomy. This perspective offers two important insights. The first is over the moral significance of consent. It will be argued that consent operates to enable one person to accept another's assessment of their well-being. However, the ability to accept that assessment depends on the nature of their relationship. The second is that consent cannot be understood as a single moment (a 'yes') but must be viewed within the broader context of their relationship.

In Chapter 3, 'The Relationship between Capacity and Consent', Claire de Than and Dr Jesse Elvin argue that under existing general legal principles, it is presumed that all adults have capacity to make wise and unwise decisions, including decisions about sexual behaviour, except where the statutory presumptions under ss 75 and 76 of the Sexual Offences Act 2003 apply. However there have been suggestions that the presumption of capacity should be reversed for sex offences in at least certain circumstances not covered by these presumptions. For example, Shlomit Wallerstein has claimed that, for the purposes of s 74 of the Sexual Offences Act 2003, the courts should take the default position that, a drunken consent is *not* consent 'where the woman is very drunk' (S Wallerstein, '"A drunken consent is still consent"- or is it? A critical analysis of the law on a drunken consent to sex following *Bree*' (2009) 73 *Journal of Criminal Law* 318, 342). Similarly, Georgina Firth has argued that 'the decision of the government to abandon further reform proposals [relating to sexual offences], such as a rebuttable presumption of non-consent where the victim is intoxicated, is a missed opportunity' (G Firth, 'Not an invitation to rape: the Sexual Offences Act 2003, consent, and the case of the "drunken" victim' (2011) 62 *Northern Ireland Legal Quarterly* 99). The authors critically evaluate such suggestions and examine their potential implications, not only in relation to sex offences but also in relation to other aspects of criminal law. They also look at the relationship between capacity and consent throughout criminal law in the light of the wider context of international human rights and disability law, since there is a growing view that capacity is a discriminatory concept which has no place in modern legal systems, and concerns have been raised both about inroads into the Art 8 right to consensual sexual expression in private and inconsistent application of capacity and consent principles by courts and carers. The chapter will conclude with a critical assessment of rival reform proposals for capacity and consent in criminal law.

Chapter 4, 'Attacks on the Mind and the Legal Limits of the Seduction Industry' by Dr John Child and Dr Gavin Byrne, explores consciously manipulated sexual 'consent' from legal, psychological, and philosophical perspectives. As a prism through which to explore these issues, the chapter looks at the lucrative 'seduction industry', with a particular focus on courses that purport to teach single men how to 'programme' women in the pursuit of sexual 'consent'. Sitting between the extremes of consent by hypnosis, and consent by charm, the authors ask whether (and how) the law should engage with such activity, and what, if anything, this phenomenon reveals about the nature of consent. Techniques of programmed consent are analysed over three parts. Part A discusses attacks on the mind in general terms, exploring the extent to which the law protects against mental manipulations. Part B focuses on the seduction industry, and the detail of the claims made about their techniques. Finally, in Part C, the authors discuss how the current law (in the sexual context at least) could be used to protect victims' mental integrity, whether the techniques attempted for programming consent are successful or not.

In Chapter 5, 'Consenting to Personal Injury', Professor William Wilson considers that outwith mercy killings few doubt that it is appropriate that victim's consent does not and should not affect the legality of intentional killings. Why is it then that it is widely thought that consent should affect the legality of the intentional causing of non-fatal harm, whether that harm be delivered in the course of an informal fight, in the course of sado-masochistic activities or otherwise? In this chapter, the author seeks to evaluate the present law of consent as it affects non-fatal offences against the person. The rationale for criminalising the consensual causing of personal injury is considered and areas of doctrine apparently at odds with this rationale and so in need of reform are identified.

Chapter 6 by Professor Susan Edwards is entitled 'Assault, Strangulation and Murder – Challenging the Sexual Libido Consent Defence Narrative'. In this chapter the author explores the way in which contemporary narratives of sexual libido and desire have informed legal argument in constructing a consent 'defence' in cases of non-fatal assault where such arguments might bolster mitigation of sentence or in fatal assault in rebutting a murder conviction, especially where strangulation is the method of violence used. The criminal law has long time established that consent, for whatever reason, including circumstances of private sexual conduct, cannot provide a defence to assault or murder. However, there are cases where the defendant who is charged with murder alleges that the deceased victim consented to the activity, which may include bondage, domination, sadism and masochism (BDSM), and in consequence he should not be criminally liable for murder, liable for manslaughter only. Such a defence is easily manipulated by the defendant especially where women die as a result of strangulation or asphyxiation. Since strangulation is both an habituated and a specific form of violence against women in both non-fatal and fatal assault such narratives put women's safety at considerable risk while exonerating very dangerous men.

In Chapter 7, 'Contributory Negligence and Consent', Verity Adams explains that consent-based offences are offences because the consent of the victim is absent. Consent may be absent for a number of reasons, including the use of force, threat or through mistake on part of the victim. It may also be absent because of voluntary intoxication. For the defendant, voluntary intoxication is not a defence if the offence is a basic intent offence: public policy does not allow him to argue absence of *mens rea* although in fact it is absent. However, the victim is not beset by such restrictions: a woman may plead absence of consent even if she became drunk voluntarily in the company of the defendant. This chapter will investigate whether and where the victim's behaviour may be classified as contributory negligence, a concept well-established in tort law, and what the effects on the offender's liability or sentence might be.

In Chapter 8, 'Caveat Amator: Transmission Of HIV and The Parameters of Consent and Bad Character Evidence', Professor Alan Reed and Emma Smith focus on whether so-called 'inducing-causes' can destroy the reality of consent in terms of transmission of HIV. A new dynamic is identified herein beyond the mechanistic fraud in the factum/inducement binary divide for consent vitiation related to non-fatal and sexual crimes. The culpability–onus nexus is blurred within extant law *vis a vis* criminalisation of transmission of HIV: the onus of disclosure applied to a defendant for rape does not apply to the threshold of non-fatal offence liability. Deception is transmogrified to operate as an inducing cause for one type of liability but not another without regard for the dangerousness/blameworthiness of the individual actor. The debate extends to consideration of bad character evidence, and defendant propensity, within the purview of the Criminal Justice Act 2003 reforms. Recent case law demonstrates that evidence of past behaviours can be utilised extensively as proof that the actor proceeded to sexual activity, irrespective of consent and, further, that multiple counts within one indictment can ultimately prove mutually supportive, where similar/extraordinary behaviours exist. A new framework is adduced to act as a cathartic panacea to current ills attached to criminalisation of HIV transmission, and problems attached to the intersection with fraud vitiating consent. A new template is needed to avoid the palpable inconsistencies that apply to consent as a defence or otherwise to non-fatal offence liability and sexual crimes, and outwith the illogical disclosure/overt deception stratified boundaries that now apply.

In Chapter 9, 'Deciding to Die and Help with Dying: What Can Be Done in England and Wales', Professor Bob Sullivan considers the decision of the court in *Nicklinson,* in which a majority of the Supreme Court accepted that adult, mentally competent persons have a legal right to commit suicide. Further, a majority of the court were open to the possibility that in certain circumstances to deny assistance in an act of suicide to a person competent to decide on suicide might constitute a denial of his or her right to commit suicide. Post *Nicklinson,* arguably a competent person can decide on suicide for any reason if he or she is to die without assistance from others. However if assistance is necessary and wanted, it is highly likely that the health and motivation of the suicidal person must be taken into account when judging the legitimacy of any assistance in dying.

It is argued that there is no general right to commit suicide and that even competent adults can be prevented from taking their lives by way of proportionate interventions from third parties. There should be legislation legalising assistance in dying for persons placed in particular circumstances. Persons in those circumstances should be able to give valid consent to assistance in suicide or to euthanasia.

Professor Alisdair Gillespie / Professor Suzanne Ost, in Chapter 10, 'The "Higher" Age of Consent and the Concept of Sexual Exploitation', clarify that it is often said that the age of consent in England is 16 but that is not strictly true. Whilst the ordinary age of consent is 16, there has since 2000 been a higher age of consent for certain sexual activities. Originally this was where there was thought to be a position of trust (Sexual Offences (Amendment) Act 2000) but it then was extended to other forms of exploitation, including prostitution and child pornography.

This chapter considers this issue of the higher age of consent and attempts to consider whether it is truly protecting children or whether it is an example of a paternalistic society governing what sexual activities a 16- or 17-year-old child can engage with and/or who their sexual partner is. An analysis will be made of the types of situations where the higher age is engaged and why it is not engaged in other exploitative issues (such as employment). It will also consider whether these restrictions can be justified or whether it may infringe the child's right to a sexual identity.

In Chapter 11, 'Consent in Sport', Professor Mark James notes that the courts have often stated that the contacts made between athletes during participation in sports deserve special treatment by the law in order to preserve their many beneficial characteristics. The difficulty faced by athletes, sports administrators and the criminal justice system is that despite the longevity of this exceptional position, the scope of the partial exemption offered to interpersonal sporting contacts remains unclear. Acceptable conduct has been defined by reference to sports' rules and customs, the foreseeability of injury, degree of harm caused and the availability of disciplinary sanctions for the perpetrator. This uncertainty is caused by the lack of appellate-level direction on the definition of consent in sport and is compounded by contradictory public policy approaches and the many *obiter dicta* statements made by the judiciary about sport when discussing consent in other contexts. This chapter will examine the evolution of the sporting exemption and the problems caused by this lack of definitional precision by examining the tests that have been proposed by the courts over the last 150 years and the impact that this has had on the relationships between athletes, the governing bodies of sport, the CPS and the criminal law.

Dr Claire McDiarmid, in Chapter 12 entitled 'Finding Free Agreement: Consent in Sexual Offences in Scots Law', explains that much of the Sexual Offences (Scotland) Act 2009 came into force (without retrospective effect) on 1 December 2010. Hitherto, the position in Scots law was that the meaning of consent was regarded as obvious, commonsensical and unelucidated: 'the word "consent" ha[s] no special meaning in law but require[s] to be given its normal meaning' (*Marr v HM Advocate* 1996 SCCR 696 at 699 per Ross LJC). The 2009 Act introduced a statutory definition: 'free agreement' (s 12) together with six situations in which consent is deemed to be absent (s 13). Through an examination of reported cases under various sections of the 2009 Act, this chapter will identify the current meaning of 'consent' in Scots law. This is not a straightforward enterprise: no reported appeal case has, as yet, been required to consider the definition of 'free agreement'. Rather, an attempt will be made to piece together the current position on this issue from an examination of reported cases in which an absence of 'consent' was required for conviction – with reference to the pre-existing law as appropriate.

In Chapter 13, 'Consent in Irish Law', Dr John Stannard examines the general principles on consent in Irish criminal law. The chapter provides a timely reappraisal of the domestic position in light of a major new report recently published by the Irish Law Commission.

The domestic chapters are complemented in Part II by chapters on several foreign jurisdictions which were written to a common research grid, in order to allow a maximum of comparability between them. They set out the basic doctrine of the law on consent and, where appropriate, aspects of special interest. They will thus allow domestic lawyers to get a quick overview of the salient issues in these countries, which may also aid in efforts of law reform and in the evaluation of parallel domestic concepts on a more general level.

Part I

1

Distinguishing sex from sexual violation

Consent, negotiation and freedom to negotiate

Tanya Palmer

INTRODUCTION

Consent has become the dominant paradigm in legal and lay discourses for distinguishing sex from sexual violation. However, consent-based models of sexual offending are flawed in a number of respects. The first two parts of this chapter explore respectively the reasons why consent has been embraced as a framework for evaluating sexual encounters and the problems with this framework, concluding that consent is not an appropriate standard by which to distinguish sex from sexual violation. The third part of the chapter introduces negotiation as a potential alternative framework, focusing on two specific law reform proposals put forward by Lois Pineau and Michelle Anderson. This work offers valuable insights for rethinking the sexual offences so as to better reflect the reality of sexual encounters, but also reproduces some of the problematic aspects of consent frameworks. The final part of the chapter draws on these models alongside original empirical data to develop a concept of 'freedom to negotiate'. This is proposed as a viable basis around which to reframe sexual offences law.

CONSENT AS THE DOMINANT PARADIGM IN SEXUAL OFFENCES LAW

Consent is the primary dividing line between sex and sexual violation in English and Welsh law. It was recognised as a crucial element of the crime of rape as far back as the mid-nineteenth century,[1] and has become increasingly central to sex offences law, having been included within the first statutory definition of rape in 1976[2] and enshrined as the pivotal element of rape and sexual assault in the Sexual Offences Act 2003.[3] More recently, the European Court of Human Rights has affirmed that all non-consensual sex, not just that involving physical violence, is rape.[4] Numerous legal scholars have endorsed the definition of rape and sexual

---

1 *R v Camplin* (1845) 1 Cox 220; see also *R v Bradley* (1910) 4 Cr App R 225, in which it was held that the burden lies with the prosecution to prove that the victim did not consent.
2 Sexual Offences (Amendment) Act 1976, s 1(1).
3 Sexual Offences Act 2003, ss 1–4.
4 *MC v Bulgaria* (2005) 40 EHRR 20; Joanne Conaghan, 'Extending the Reach of Human Rights to Encompass Victims of Rape: *M.C. v Bulgaria*' (2005) 13 Feminist Legal Studies 145.

assault as non-consensual sexual activity and have explored in detail the specific form consent has taken and should take in sexual offences law.[5]

The legal reforms which have placed consent at the centre of sexual offences law have been widely embraced in large part because they emerged as a progressive shift from previous constructions of rape and sexual assault. Earlier definitions of rape emphasised physical force on the part of the perpetrator and resistance on the part of the victim, neither of which are required under a consent-based definition.[6] The latter therefore protects a greater number of people from having sexual activity imposed upon them against their will and has thus been broadly – though not universally – welcomed by feminist and women's movements.[7] At the same time, situating consent as the marker of legitimate sexual activity provides a basis for resisting the criminalisation of sexual acts that fall foul of conservative Christian sexual morality, eg anal sex and/or sexual activity between two or more men. Hence consent has also been championed by the gay rights movement and other sexual minorities.

Despite academic and popular support for the consent paradigm, sexual offending remains a highly problematic area of criminal law and criminal justice. Rates of victimisation are consistently high, whilst reporting and conviction rates are low.[8] In addition, reforms to the substantive law have not prevented factors other than consent – such as the infliction of physical injuries, the status of the relationship between the complainant and the accused, and the behaviour of the complainant after an alleged rape – from influencing the judgements of actors at every stage of the criminal process.[9] These difficulties are often interpreted as resulting from the relevant actors failing to properly apply consent to the facts; the status of consent itself as the dividing line between sex and sexual violation frequently goes unchallenged.[10] This perception that consent is not being properly understood underpinned the introduction of a statutory definition of consent in the Sexual Offences Act 2003,[11] as well as calls for consent to be included in sex education programmes at both school and university

---

5 See, for example, Douglas Husak and George Thomas, 'Date Rape, Social Convention and Reasonable Mistakes' (1992) 11 Law and Philosophy 95; Jennifer Temkin and Andrew Ashworth, 'The Sexual Offences Act 2003: Rape, Sexual Assault and the Problems of Consent' (2004) Criminal Law Review 328; Sharon Cowan, 'Choosing Freely: Theoretically Reframing the Concept of Consent' in Rosemary Hunter and Sharon Cowan (eds), *Choice and Consent: Feminist Engagements with Law and Subjectivity* (Routledge 2007); Catherine Elliott and Claire de Than, 'The Case for a Rational Reconstruction of Consent in Criminal Law' (2007) 70 The Modern Law Review 225; Vanessa Munro, 'Constructing Consent: Legislating Freedom and Legitimating Constraint in the Expression of Sexual Autonomy' (2008) 41 Akron Law Review 923; Michelle Dempsey, 'Victimless Consent and the Volenti Maxim: How Consent Works' (2013) 7 Criminal Law and Philosophy 11.

6 Vanessa Munro, 'From Consent to Coercion: Evaluating International and Domestic Frameworks for the Criminalization of Rape' in Clare McGlynn and Vanessa Munro (eds), *Rethinking Rape Law: International and Comparative Perspectives* (Routledge 2010).

7 ibid.

8 Ministry of Justice, Home Office and Office for National Statistics 'An Overview of Sexual Offending in England and Wales' (2013).

9 Liz Kelly, Jo Lovett and Linda Regan, 'A Gap or a Chasm? Attrition in reported Rape Cases' (Home Office Research Study 293, Home Office Research, Development and Statistics Directorate, 2005).

10 But see for example Catharine MacKinnon, *Towards a Feminist Theory of the State* (Harvard University Press 1989) and Victor Tadros, 'Rape Without Consent' (2006) 26 Oxford Journal of Legal Studies 515 for problematisation of the concept of consent itself.

11 Sexual Offences Act 2003, s 74.

level.[12] It is, however, far from clear that all those advocating a consent-based definition of sex and sexual violation are using the term 'consent' in the same way.

Consent is an ambiguous concept. There is a lack of consensus as to whether consent consists of a mental state or some external performance;[13] and even within these broad categories consent could consist of a range of mental states including actual desire, ambivalence, acquiescence and submission, or be constituted by a variety of actions including physical initiation, verbal agreement, or by a lack of action, ie a failure to say 'no' or resist. In addition, the extent to which different forms of coercion, deception and lack of mental competence can invalidate consent are hotly contested.[14] I do not, however, propose to develop a clearer definition of consent. By contrast, I submit that consent is not an appropriate standard by which to distinguish sex from sexual violation.

CONSENT IS INADEQUATE TO DISTINGUISH SEX FROM SEXUAL VIOLATION

Kants ethics – cannot treat ones as a means to an end. Putting indiv in a cate of objects.

Consent is not an appropriate or effective way to distinguish legitimate sexual activity from sexual violation, for four key reasons. First, consent is enmeshed with a particularly individualistic notion of the Kantian liberal subject and as such is inapt to respond to the bodily, affective and relational dimensions of sexual encounters. Second, consent models support a construction of sexual encounters as inherently asymmetric and unequal. Third, the variable and amorphous nature of sexual activity is poorly-suited to a consent framework. Fourth, consent obscures much of the relevant context within which agreements to engage in sexual activity are made.

Consent represents a liberal understanding of subjecthood

The consenting subject is arguably the epitome of the rational liberal subject.[15] Consent is effectively the granting of certain rights over oneself to another; it plays a central role in liberal discourses of the self as a mechanism by which autonomy is exercised. In the specific context of sexual offences, it functions as the gatekeeper of bodily autonomy, a power to control or limit access to one's body. This framework invokes a Cartesian dualism in which the mind is viewed as the locus of the self, while the body is merely property owned by the self or the vessel in which the self is housed.[16] Autonomy is then constructed as a cognitive process of reflection and rational choice. As such it obscures the central role that sensation, emotion, bodily realities and relationships with others play in guiding human decision-making, particularly in the area of sexuality.[17] This has several negative results.

---

12 See for example Sally Weale, 'Sex Education Should be Mandatory in All Schools, MPs Demand' *The Guardian* (London 17 February 2015) <http://www.theguardian.com/education/2015/feb/17/sex-education-mandatory-all-schools-mps-demand> accessed 6 October 2015; University of Sussex Students' Union, 'I Heart Consent Campaign' *University of Sussex Students' Union* <http://www.sussexstudent.com/campaigns/i-heart-consent/> accessed 6 October 2015.

13 For an overview of this debate see Cowan (n 5).

14 See discussion in Alan Wertheimer, *Consent to Sexual Relations* (Cambridge University Press 2003).

15 Vanessa Munro, 'Constructing Consent: Legislating Freedom and Legitimating Constraint in the Expression of Sexual Autonomy' (2008) 41 Akron Law Review 923.

16 Nicola Lacey, 'Unspeakable Subjects: Impossible Rights: Sexuality, Integrity and Criminal Law' (1998) 11 Canadian Journal of Law and Jurisprudence 47; Cowan (n 5).

17 See Tanya Palmer, *Renegotiating Sex and Sexual Violation in the Criminal Law* (Hart, forthcoming) for a fuller discussion.

First, the abstract disembodied form of autonomy with which consent is associated leads to a misunderstanding of the wrong of sexual violation. When framed as non-consensual sex, the wrong of rape tends to be understood as a violation of the will, in contradistinction to the body. The removal of choice is certainly one of the wrongs of rape, but it does not fully capture the wrong of this and related offences. Rape is an experience in which bodily contact and physical sensation in combination with the cultural and personal meanings of that contact creates a profound and unique sense of violation. Sexual offence laws that promote a disembodied conception of autonomy are therefore seriously misguided in that by characterising rape and sexual assault as wrongs against the mind, they obscure both the wrong against the body and the extent to which mind and body converge.[18] This misunderstanding of the wrong of rape can also lead to an underestimation of the harms of rape, particularly in cases where physical violence and injury are relatively minimal.[19]

Second, as a threshold requirement for intimate physical contact, consent emphasises the policing of bodily boundaries. As such, consent models are associated with a competitive conception of autonomy as isolation or exclusion, through which individuals are encouraged to jealously guard their own interests against those of others rather than taking an interest in each other's desires.[20] Within this framework potential sexual partners are logically understood as threats (who may violate one's bodily boundaries if one's non-consent is not enforced), or obstacles (whose consent must be obtained in order to proceed with one's own desires) rather than collaborators in the creation of a mutually satisfying experience.

Third, the twin emphasis in the liberal autonomy-consent framework on rationality and boundedness (both psychic and physical) sets a threshold for subjecthood that facilitates the exclusion of some categories of people from its remit. Those who supposedly lack stable physical boundaries – eg gay men, all women, and persons with disabilities[21] – cannot have their boundaries protected, while those deemed to lack a rational will – eg children and individuals with learning difficulties – cannot have their will respected. The sex life of these individuals cannot be easily accommodated within a consent framework and can thus be subject to a separate ethical and legal regime with a different set of rules. An illustration of this can be seen in the proliferation of specific offences against mentally disordered victims under the Sexual Offences Act 2003.[22] The ostensible neutrality of consent, and liberal subjectivity in general, thus masks its uneven operation in practice.

Consent implies an asymmetric interaction

Consent is inherently asymmetric.[23] Framing an interaction as consensual suggests that one party makes a suggestion or request, to which another party can either consent or object.[24]

---

18 Cowan (n 5); see also Ann Cahill, *Rethinking Rape* (Cornell University Press 2001) 197.
19 See for example Donald Dripps, 'Beyond Rape: An Essay on the Difference Between the Presence of Force and the Absence of Consent' (1992) 92 Columbia Law Review 1780.
20 Jennifer Nedelsky, 'Reconceiving Autonomy: Sources, Thoughts and Possibilities' (1989) 1 Yale Journal of Law and Feminism 7, 12.
21 Lacey (n 16), 115.
22 Sexual Offences Act 2003, ss 30–44; for discussion of these offences and their relationship to consent see Tanya Palmer, 'State Control of Consensual Sexual Behaviour Through the Sexual Offences Act 2003' in Alan Reed, Chris Ashford and Nicola Wake (eds), *Consent and Control: Legal Perspectives on State Power* (Cambridge Scholars Publishing, 2016) (forthcoming).
23 MacKinnon (n 10); Victor Tadros 'No Consent: A Historical Critique of the Actus Reus of Rape' (1999) 3 Edinburgh Law Review 317.
24 Robert Veatch, 'Abandoning Informed Consent' (1995) 25 *Hastings Center Report* 5, 5.

Consent is therefore a minimal, reactive form of participation. In the specific context of sexual activity, a consent framework implies that sex always involves one (active) person doing something to another (passive) person.[25] Thus two parties to an encounter are not equally situated. A party who does not want to engage in sex is always at a disadvantage because the consequences of not persuading the other to respect one's interests are far more serious.[26] Moreover, the differentiated positions of 'initiator' and 'responder' that a consent framework implies are not equally available to all. The distribution of these roles is shaped by strong cultural associations between masculinity, penetration, and sexual assertiveness, even aggression, and between femininity, passivity and openness or violability.[27]

The uneven burden on the parties is compounded in the context of a criminal investigation and trial. Assuming it is proven that relevant sexual activity between the parties took place, a conviction for rape or sexual assault hinges on two key questions: did the complainant consent? Did the defendant reasonably believe the complainant was consenting? Both invite an inquiry into the complainant's bodily comportment: did they say or do anything that could be reasonably interpreted as consent? Thus it is the complainant, rather than the defendant, whose actions are investigated. This tendency to 'put the victim on trial'[28] can be extremely traumatising, and has been likened to a 'second rape'.[29]

Distinguishing sex and sexual violation on the basis of consent envisages a question and answer model, whereby one person sets the terms of the interaction and the other can only accept or reject them; it 'does not envision a situation the woman controls being placed in, or choices she frames'.[30] The restrictiveness of this way of thinking is illustrated by the well-used feminist slogan 'no means no', and the more recent variant, 'yes means yes'. Both phrases emphasise a woman's right to have her sexual choices respected and challenge a host of lingering myths about female sexuality in a snappy and memorable form. Nevertheless, in centering the right to give or withhold consent, these slogans still position women as answering a question; they do not consider a woman doing the asking. Nor do they make room for the more radical possibility of reciprocity or co-production of sexual experience. As such, they demonstrate the limits of the binary structure of sexual participation presupposed by the consent model. In reality, sexual encounters often develop organically and mutually, without the parties taking on fixed active or passive roles.[31] Thus, while consent is clearly absent from the worst sexual encounters it will also be absent in the most positive sexual encounters jointly instigated by mutually active partners, because both partners are in a state beyond consent, a state of active involvement and participation rather than reaction or submission.[32]

Consent presupposes an act with clear, fixed parameters

Consent works well for activities that are very specific in form, and/or where any variability is controlled by one party. So, for example, I can consent to a standing order arrangement

---

25 Ngaire Naffine, 'Possession: Erotic Love in the Law of Rape' (1994) 57 The Modern Law Review 10.
26 MacKinnon (n 10), 174.
27 Nicola Gavey, *Just Sex? The Cultural Scaffolding of Rape* (Routledge 2005).
28 Tadros (n 10), 517.
29 Lee Madigan and Nancy Gamble, *The Second Rape: Society's Continued Betrayal of the Victim* (Lexington Books 1991).
30 MacKinnon (n 10), 174; for a similar argument see Wendy Brown, *States of Injury* (Princeton University Press 1995).
31 Cowan (n 5).
32 David Archard, *Sexual Consent* (Westview Press 1998).

whereby my bank transfers a fixed amount of money from my account to my landlord each month to cover my rent. The parameters of this arrangement are established in advance and, provided I am informed of and capable of understanding the terms, it makes sense to say that I consent to them. If I want the arrangement to stop, I can withdraw my consent. Consider another scenario in which I lend my car to a friend. Here again, there will be some pre-defined parameters. Some of these will be explicitly agreed, such as the dates and times during which she will borrow the car. Others may be implicit, for example it will likely go without saying that I do not consent to the vehicle being used for criminal activity. There will nevertheless be some uncertainty in this scenario. I may not know which specific roads my friend will drive on or the exact distance she will cover. To the extent of this uncertainty I am putting myself – or rather my car – in her hands. By consenting I grant her permission to make choices within the agreed parameters. Does consent to sex operate in the same way?

One view of sex, which David Archard has termed the 'climactic model',[33] holds that 'full sex' consists of penetrative intercourse and (penile) ejaculation, and relegates any other sexual activity to the category of foreplay. On this account, consent to sex operates much like consent to a friend borrowing my car. The key parameters have been specified in advance, and by giving consent one party hands control to the other to do whatever they choose within those parameters. In the car-borrowing scenario the finer details of where, how far and how fast my friend drives the car are all part of one overarching act of borrowing the car, which has been consented to. If sexual consent operates in the same way, any other sexual touching occurring around the same time as the penetration is counted as part and parcel of one seamless act of sexual intercourse. Archard rightly condemns this model, on the basis that it falsely implies that non-penetrative sexual activity cannot be enjoyed for its own sake and because it underpins the claim that consent to any form of sexual intimacy is consent to penetrative intercourse.[34]

Seemingly at the other end of the scale are models such as the Antioch Sexual Offense Policy of the 1990s, which required explicit verbal consent to every 'level' of sexual activity.[35] Under this policy, sexual consent operates more like my banking example. Consent is granted explicitly and for a very specific action, which must cease if consent is revoked. The policy was widely mocked and dismissed as unromantic, unrealistic, and requiring far too much of participants in sexual activity.[36] However, critiques of the policy tend to focus on the requirement of verbal consent, and in doing so mask a deeper flaw. The policy shares the same fundamental problem as the climactic model: it imagines that sex can be broken down into discrete acts. The Antioch policy divides sexual activity into much smaller units, but the underlying approach is the same. Both frameworks construct sex as constituted by individual acts that are fairly definite in form and uniform in character, such that autonomous participation in those acts can be exhausted by the giving or withholding of consent.

In reality, sexual activity is nebulous, variable and mutually produced. As a result, it is ill-suited to a consent framework. Breaking sex down into distinct acts, as per Antioch, does little to address the fact that parties to a sexual encounter need to be able to express something more than mere willingness (or lack of willingness) to participate. They also need to be able to negotiate the quality of that encounter, to express concepts such as 'faster', 'harder',

---

33 For a critique of the climactic model see Archard ibid 22–24.
34 Archard ibid.
35 Antioch College, 'The Antioch College Sexual Offense Policy', in Leslie Francis (ed), *Date Rape: Feminism Philosophy, and the Law* (The Pennsylvania University Press 1996).
36 For discussion see Matthew Silliman, 'The Antioch Policy, a Community Experiment in Communicative Sexuality', in Leslie Francis (ed), *Date Rape: Feminism Philosophy, and the Law* (The Pennsylvania University Press 1996).

'that hurts', 'touch me here'. This kind of communication appears peripheral under a consent framework, yet it is central to real world sexual communication.[37]

A consent framework decontextualises sexual encounters

A focus on consent can obscure relevant circumstances within which the sexual activity takes place and the reasons why an individual has ostensibly 'consented'.[38] Although a considerable body of literature has explored the way conditions such as coercion, deception and lack of capacity may invalidate an ostensible consent, this debate has operated within fairly strict parameters. The primary focus has been direct interpersonal coercion, deception or inducement at or immediately prior to sexual activity, and individualised medicalised diagnoses that would disrupt a person's capacity to consent. This limited focus finds expression in the conclusive and evidential presumptions regarding consent and in the specific offences against mentally disordered adults contained within the Sexual Offences Act 2003.[39]

At the same time, feminist and other critical scholarship that highlights the extent to which supposedly consensual choices are shaped by pervasive social and structural forces is often reductively presented as a claim that women's consent is meaningless under patriarchy.[40] Between these two poles of totalising patriarchal dominance and almost unfettered free choice, lies the reality of sexual agency. Thus the relevant context for evaluating the validity of consent extends beyond the immediate surrounding conditions in the moment that a decision is taken. It also includes the specific interpersonal dynamic of the parties and the backdrop of the various social structures, chiefly gender, against which they operate.[41]

The need to contextualise sexual consent in this way is particularly significant when considering its operation within abusive intimate relationships. In relationships characterised by 'coercive control', men entrap their female partners through a complex web of techniques including violence, isolation, intimidation and control of material resources.[42] This constraint at the individual level is further supported by structural constraints on women's autonomy, particularly the default consignment of women to the domestic sphere.[43] In a relationship of this nature, a woman's liberty is so constrained by her partner that her opportunity to make meaningful choices about many aspects of her life, particularly as they relate to her relationship with her partner, is reduced almost to nothing. However, a consent-based inquiry which extends only as far as the moments immediately preceding sexual activity may obscure more diffuse, unspoken threats of violence and deprivation and find that there was ample opportunity for the victim to refuse sexual activity or simply leave. Only an inquiry into the broader context of the relationship would reveal that there is nothing simple about leaving.[44]

---

37 Melanie Beres, 'Rethinking the Concept of Consent for Anti-Sexual Violence Activism and Education' (2014) 24 Feminism and Psychology 373.

38 MacKinnon (n 10) 177; Tadros, 'No Consent' (n 23); Tadros, 'Rape Without Consent' (n 10) 530; Cowan (n 5).

39 Sexual Offences Act 2003, ss 75–76 and 30–44 respectively.

40 See eg Archard (n 32); for an overview of the literature see Munro 'Constructing Consent' (n 5).

41 Gavey (n 27); Jennifer Nedelsky, *Law's Relations: A Relational Theory of Self, Autonomy and Law* (Oxford University Press 2012); Palmer, *Renegotiating Sex and Sexual Violation* (n 17).

42 Evan Stark, *Coercive Control: How Men Entrap Women in Personal Life* (Oxford University Press 2007) especially Ch 7.

43 ibid 211; thus, Stark's theory cannot be straightforwardly mapped onto abusive relationships that do not feature a male abuser and female victim, ibid 391–397.

44 ibid Ch 4; see also Sandra Horley, *Power and Control: Why Charming Men Can Make Dangerous Lovers* (Vermillion 2000) 90–102.

A high proportion of rape and sexual assault is committed by current or former partners of the victim, and yet this subset of offending has proved persistently difficult to bring within the ambit of the criminal law. Abusive relationships are thus a particularly salient example of the dangers of abstraction that accompany frameworks of sexual offending based on consent. They are however only an illustration of a general need to evaluate the legitimacy of sexual encounters in their interpersonal, social, structural and temporal contexts.

Summary: Consent is not an appropriate mechanism for distinguishing sex from sexual violation

Despite its broad appeal, consent is not fit for purpose when it comes to the complex task of distinguishing sex from sexual violation. As I have detailed above, consent calls to mind a rather mechanical exchange between parties abstracted from their social context and interpersonal history. One proposes a sexual act, the other rationally considers it, and either accepts or rejects it. If the proposal is accepted, the initiating party performs the act. This image is a world away from the ongoing process of reciprocal interaction that is the substance of most (if not all) non-violating sexual encounters. As a result, the concept of consent has significant limitations as a tool for evaluating the legitimacy of sexual encounters. It is ill-equipped to make sense of sexual activity involving parties who are incapable of either giving or withholding consent, and it fails to make sense of the many forms sexual coercion can take beyond specific immediate threats.

Despite its inadequacies, consent remains preferable to previously dominant ethical frameworks that restrictively defined sexual violation as sexual activity imposed via physical force, and/or adopted a conservative sexual morality under which non-marital and non-heterosexual sex are viewed as illegitimate. With this in mind, consent may be best thought of as a 'transition concept . . . that appears on the scene as an apparently progressive innovation, but after a period of experience turns out to be only useful as a transition to a more thoroughly revisionary conceptual framework'.[45] In what follows, I explore the possibilities for a more radical conceptual framework.

NEGOTIATION AND COMMUNICATIVE SEXUALITY

Lois Pineau's path-breaking text 'Date Rape: A Feminist Analysis', published in 1989, introduced the concept of 'communicative sexuality' as a means of refocusing attention from snap-shot moments of consent or resistance on the part of a woman to 'a reading of whether she agreed throughout the encounter'.[46] Pineau's central premise is that non-communicative sex, ie where the woman does not instruct her partner how and where to touch her and he does not ask, will most likely not be enjoyable for her, and it is therefore unreasonable for either the man having sex with her or a jury evaluating the scenario after the fact to believe that she consents.[47] This does not rule out consent in the absence of ongoing communication between the parties to a sexual encounter, but sets up a presumption against it, such that the man would have to be certain (and able to explain why he was certain) that she was, in fact, consenting and had a reason to do so other than reluctant acquiescence to the man's

---

45 Veatch (n 24), 5.
46 Lois Pineau, 'Date Rape: A Feminist Analysis' (1989) 8 Law and Philosophy 217, 231; see also Francis (n 35).
47 In this passage I specifically refer to male perpetrators and female victims in keeping with Pineau's formulation ibid.

'high pressure' tactics.[48] Subsequently, an emerging body of literature, both academic and non-academic, has explored similar themes to Pineau, whilst not necessarily building on her ideas explicitly.[49] A pertinent example is Michelle Anderson's proposed 'negotiation model', under which explicit verbal communication, or rather its absence, would be central to the definition of rape in criminal law.[50]

A framework for sexual offending based around communication or negotiation holds considerable potential for decentring consent and related notions of sexual encounters as asymmetric proposals of discrete, well-defined acts, and in its place emphasising the relationality, mutuality and fluidity of sexual encounters. By emphasising reciprocal dialogue, a negotiation standard encourages individuals both to articulate and engage with their own desires and to pay attention to those of their partner. Moreover, communicative sexuality more closely maps the way that sexual activity is agreed in practice than consent does – it is often through ongoing active participation, directing and shaping of the activity that individuals express their willingness to engage in a sexual act, as opposed to a one-off moment of agreement or refusal.[51] Understanding non-violating sexual encounters as produced through a process of negotiation and ongoing communication also provides greater scope than a consent framework for considering the context in which agreement about a sexual practice was reached, though realising this potential creates some tensions, explored below.

An additional advantage of communicative sexuality is that it places the spotlight on the defendant's, rather than the complainant's, conduct. In Anderson's words, 'Instead of asking, "What did she let him do?" the Negotiation Model asks, "Did the person who initiated sexual penetration negotiate with his or her partner and thereby come to an agreement that sexual penetration should occur?"'[52] Pineau similarly advocates asking the defendant whether he thought the complainant was enjoying the sexual activity. If not, why was it reasonable for him to think she agreed to it? If yes, how did he know? Did he ask her what she liked? Did they discuss contraception? What desires did she communicate and how?[53] Thus in a rape trial, the central question would focus on the behaviour of the accused. A negotiation standard would therefore address several of the problems with consent identified above. Nevertheless, attempts to operationalise communicative sexuality within the criminal law reveal some weaknesses.

Reformulating sexual offences law around negotiation requires decisions to be made about what exactly will satisfy the negotiation condition and which acts need to be negotiated. For Anderson, verbal negotiation is essential so that silence cannot be taken as consent to sex. Her concern is that existing consent models place the onus on the victim to verbally or physically resist their attacker, an unfair requirement given that victims of rape are often paralysed by fear.[54] In Anderson's view, affirmative consent requirements cannot solve this problem, because consent to other forms of sexual intimacy, eg passionate kissing or petting,

---

48 ibid 230.

49 See for example Cowan, (n 5); Thomas Macaulay Millar, 'Toward a Performance Model of Sex' in Jaclyn Friedman and Jessica Valenti (eds), *Yes Means Yes: Visions of Female Sexual Power and a World Without Rape* (Seal Press 2008); Rachel Kramer Bussel, 'Beyond Yes or No: Consent as Sexual Process' in Friedman and Valenti (eds), *Yes Means Yes: Visions of Female Sexual Power and a World Without Rape* (Seal Press 2008)

50 Michelle Anderson, 'Negotiating Sex' (2005) 78 Southern California Law Review 1401.

51 Pineau (n 46); Cowan (n 5); Beres (n 37).

52 Anderson (n 50) 1423.

53 Pineau (n 46) 240–241.

54 Anderson (n 50) 1405.

can be taken as consent to intercourse, so that once a person willingly engages in some sexual activity, they acquire the responsibility to clearly communicate any objection to sexual penetration. However, conscious of the criticisms of the Antioch Policy which required verbal consent to every level of sexual activity (above), Anderson stresses that her negotiation requirement only applies to penetrative sex, and creates an exemption for parties who have 'established a context in which they could reliably read one another's non-verbal behavior to indicate free and autonomous agreement'.[55] Applying these parameters has the effect of privileging penetrative sex and long-term relationships, despite the prevalence of sexual violation within relationships. A more fundamental problem, however, is that the requirement of explicit verbal negotiation shifts the focus back to episodic moments of agreement or refusal, with all the problems this entails for existing models of consent.

By contrast, Pineau's proposal emphasises the need for continuing alertness by each party to the others' desires, and calls for evidence of *ongoing* communication to establish the legitimacy of a sexual encounter, as opposed to evidence of a specific moment of agreement. Unlike Anderson, Pineau does not specify that communication must be verbal, and this is what allows for a more fluid understanding of negotiation. Pineau does not share Anderson's concerns about participation in one act of sexual intimacy being taken as consent for another because, as she demonstrates, there is scope for non-verbal forms of communication about sex that are reasonably clear, such as guiding another party's hand to the place one wishes to be touched.[56] Nevertheless, it is tolerably clear that in some instances individuals will need to use explicit words to negotiate their participation in a sexual encounter without misunderstanding, but the need for this is idiosyncratic and cannot be straightforwardly mapped on to the nature of the sex act or the length of the relationship, as Anderson suggests.

Nevertheless, Pineau's formulation of communicative sexuality also has some problems. Like Anderson, she does not fully exploit the potential of a negotiation framework to widen the contextual lens through which consent is evaluated. She does extend the focus of the enquiry to cover the duration of the sexual activity, whereas consent models, and even Anderson's negotiation model, are interested primarily in the moments immediately preceding a specified sexual act (unless there is clear evidence of the complainant later revoking consent). However, Pineau states that any prior behaviour or reputation of the parties should be excluded from the inquiry, and that, 'All that matters is the quality of communication with regard to the sex itself'.[57] Fixing the parameters as such is in order to exclude irrelevant evidence of the complainant's sexual history from the enquiry. However, in doing so Pineau also excludes evidence of previous abuse by the defendant that may be relevant to understanding the quality of the complainant's communication at the relevant moment.

In addition, the essence of Pineau's proposal is that, 'Where communicative sex does not occur, this establishes a presumption that there was no consent'.[58] This reverses the burden of proof, such that the defendant is required to prove that the complainant did in fact consent despite the likely unsatisfying nature of the sex.[59] I share Pineau's concerns about the tendency for rape victims to be 'put on trial' themselves, as detailed above. However, the burden of proof exists to protect defendants against the illegitimate infringements of their liberty by the state, and should not be abandoned lightly. Moreover, in requiring the defendant to prove

---

55   ibid 1425; for a similar approach see Tadros, 'Rape Without Consent' (n 10) 529 and 541; Archard, (n 32) 25–27.

56   See further Pineau, 'A Response to My Critics' in Francis (n 35) 96–98.

57   Pineau (n 46) 242.

58   ibid 242.

59   ibid 233.

that the complainant consented (provided the presumption has been triggered), Pineau's formula retains a focus on the complainant's behavior – did she or did she not consent? Thus the presumption approach involves a significant erosion of the presumption of innocence, with minimal gain for complainants. Communicative sexuality and negotiation offer a promising starting point for rethinking sex and sexual violation, but the weaknesses identified suggested further revisions are necessary, as I explore in the following section.

FROM NEGOTIATION TO 'FREEDOM TO NEGOTIATE'

Negotiation and communicative sexuality provide a useful starting point for rethinking sexual offences law so as to pay attention to the interactive and processual nature of sexual encounters. Nevertheless, these ideas need further development to provide a viable alternative to consent. In this final section I consider how the concept of negotiation might be developed in order to overcome its weaknesses. This development is informed by data from an original qualitative study into understandings of sex and sexual violation.[60]

Who is responsible for negotiating sexual activity?

Communicative sexuality is distinctive because, in theory, it treats ongoing reciprocal interaction as the paradigm form of legitimate sexual activity, rather than an asymmetric model of initiation and acceptance.[61] Pineau specifically seeks to challenge discourses of seduction and submission which normalise male sexual aggression and female reluctance.[62] Similarly, Anderson is concerned that 'girls' are 'too often trained to acquiesce to male desire' rather than being treated as 'human being[s] whose desires and boundaries matter'.[63] Both authors contest the idea that a dynamic of male initiation and female passivity, whereby a man may carry out his sexual desires unless and until his female partner resists, should be acceptable. In order to delegitimise this kind of interaction, they propose additional obligations on the initiator to verbally ask first and/or to maintain communication throughout the encounter to ensure that the other party is consenting. However, models which attach additional requirements to the initiation of sexual activity arguably reify an active–passive construction of sexual interaction, and are poorly equipped to deal with sexual encounters that do not fit this mould.

This can be illustrated using a sexual experience reported by Rosa, a lay volunteer I interviewed for a study of understandings of sex and sexual violation.[64] Rosa described an experience within an 'unhealthy' relationship, which she initially described as 'not quite rape':

ROSA: There was one particular afternoon, he came back in a foul mood, and I knew he was gonna hit me, and I didn't wanna get hit, um, so I just jumped his bones instead. And it wasn't making love, it wasn't sex. It was a really hard brutal fuck. I'm sorry for being blunt here, I was just bouncing up and down on his lap. And it was, it was almost vicious, I didn't hit him, he didn't hit me, but I, I, I knew he had to let that anger out, and I didn't want to get hit. Um, so I just, I hate saying this, rode him for all I was worth. Just in a, it

---

60　For a detailed discussion of the methodology and findings of this study, see Palmer, *Renegotiating Sex and Sexual Violation* (n 17).

61　Cowan (n 5).

62　Pineau (n 46).

63　Anderson (n 50) 1438.

64　For further analysis see Palmer, *Renegotiating Sex and Sexual Violation* (n 17).

was almost like I was the one going, 'I'm gonna fuck you!' I thought, although physically he was inside me, as far as the emotional power struggle went, and the control, I was fucking him. And it stopped him hitting me. Um, and it was one of the most powerful and intense experiences I've ever had, *I would never like to repeat that ever again.* The sex was amazing! But the fact that I had to instigate it in that way, to stop him from hitting me, absolutely appalling and dreadful.

TANYA: And, I mean you started off as describing it as 'not quite rape' but as 'having sex against your will'

ROSA: Yeah, 'cause if I, if I didn't do that, if I didn't – excuse my French – if I didn't *fuck* him the way I did, he'd have ended up hitting me and hurting me.

TANYA: And in terms of –

ROSA: And so I just had this really rough sex with him to avoid him hitting me. And as far as I'm concerned, yeah it was powerful, it was mental, but it was rape! I didn't wanna have sex with him, but more than I didn't wanna have sex with him I didn't want him to fucking hit me again!

Both Anderson and Pineau's constructions of communicative sexuality have limited utility in a situation of this nature.

If this scenario is analysed using Pineau's model, the central issues are, was it reasonable for Rosa's partner to think she enjoyed the sex? And if not, was it reasonable for him to nevertheless think she was consenting? Pineau assumes that it is not reasonable to think a woman is enjoying sexual activity in the absence of communication with her partner. However, in this scenario, Rosa's own admission that 'the sex was amazing!' (despite also being 'appalling', 'dreadful' and unwanted) and the fact that she 'jumped his bones', would make it very difficult to argue that it was unreasonable for her partner to think she enjoyed the sex. Even if the lack of communication was taken as sufficient evidence for a presumption of non-consent, it would also be fairly easy to rebut this presumption given that she initiated the sexual activity. By insisting that 'all that matters is the quality of communication with regard to the sex itself',[65] Pineau excludes evidence of the wider history of violence and abuse within which that sexual act took place, and its effect on Rosa's ability to make a free choice. While Pineau's model would struggle to recognise Rosa's experience of violation, under Anderson's model she would potentially be constructed as the viola*tor*.

Anderson's negotiation model specifically requires a person initiating sexual penetration to first verbally negotiate and gain explicit verbal agreement. Assuming that this includes a person initiating the sexual penetration of their own body (Anderson is unclear on this point), a person in Rosa's position who initiates penetrative sexual activity without negotiating first, would have committed an offence of rape. Arguably, Rosa could be saved by Anderson's exception whereby explicit verbal negotiation is not required if the parties have established a context within which they can reliably read each other's non-verbal signals. It does seem to be the case that Rosa could read her partner's body language, however what she 'read' in it was not 'I am agreeing to have sex with you' but rather 'I am going to hit you if you don't find some way to diffuse the situation.' This hardly seems to be what Anderson envisaged with this exception.

Both models struggle to make sense of the encounter between Rosa and her partner because they assume an initiator–responder model of sexual interaction. The strategy of placing additional burdens on the initiator of sexual activity has the undesirable consequence of

---

65 Pineau (n 46) 242.

reinforcing the idea that one person takes the lead in sexual encounters and as a result falls back into many of the same traps as existing consent models, by constructing sex as an asymmetric interaction characterised (at least in Anderson's case) by neatly delineated acts that can be agreed to or refused. In addition, models of communicative sexuality that focus narrowly on the form and content of the negotiation between the parties repeat consent's mistake of abstracting sexual encounters from their wider context. The wrongful aspect of the scenario described by Rosa is not the lack of communication on the part of either party, but rather the surrounding circumstances in which the sexual activity is initiated – something that is obscured by a focus on the negotiation between the parties immediately prior to and throughout the duration of the sexual activity. The question of whether this particular incident should be classed as criminal sexual violation would require a fuller enquiry into the behaviour of Rosa's partner both at the time of the sexual activity and earlier in the relationship, and the extent to which this constrained Rosa's choices at the given time. There is no room to ask these questions under a model that only examines negotiation at the time of the sex.

Negotiation and the 'room to say no'

Verbal negotiation is central to Anderson's distinction between sex and sexual violation because her aim is to counteract existing consent models under which silence is treated as consent. Anderson rightly draws attention to the problems inherent in expecting a party who is unwilling to engage in sexual activity to bear the burden of expressing dissent. However, requiring individuals initiating sexual activity to first verbally discuss it with their intended partner would not necessarily make it any easier to say 'no' rather than 'yes' to the proposed sexual activity. Both the tone of the negotiation and the context in which it takes place can render a verbal proposal oppressive.

The tone in which desires are communicated can have a significant impact on how they are received. A verbal request can be spoken in such a way as to make it clear that there is only one acceptable answer, while a different tone of voice would transform it into a sincere question. Similarly, while physical contact with another person can be forceful, can restrict freedom and can prevent resistance, physical touch can also be initiated tentatively, in such a way as to invite another party to respond freely. The tone of communication (inviting rather than insisting) is therefore more important than the form it takes (verbal rather than physical) in terms of preventing situations where one party unwillingly submits to sexual activity through lack of choice. The context in which sexual negotiation takes place is similarly important for ensuring it is genuinely free negotiation.

In a focus group with domestic violence support workers, Eve described the way that cultural expectations might restrict a person's options when negotiating sexual encounters:

> [I]n the 80s . . . there was no room to say no really to sex. And I'm pretty certain it's the same now. There was no way of justifying saying no. 'Cause there was the pill and then there was the coil, condoms, blah blah blah, the whole thing about society, our society, was that we were sexually liberated. Which meant actually we had to put out.[66]

Eve's reference to the 'room to say no' suggests that in the context she describes the problem is not so much a lack of verbal communication, but the location of that communication within a cultural environment that restricts women's freedom to express their desires

---

66   For further analysis see Palmer, *Renegotiating Sex and Sexual Violation* (n 17).

openly. Within such a context the initiation of verbal communication regarding a proposed sex act could appear less like an attempt at open dialogue and more like a demand. Eve here is focused on broad socio-cultural contexts of sexual interaction. These intersect with the narrower context of specific interpersonal relationships that can also restrict an individual's freedom to say 'no' where sexual communication is set against a backdrop of past abuse. I therefore advocate a shift in emphasis for communicative sexuality, placing the focus on the surrounding circumstances within which negotiation occurs, rather than on the content of the negotiation itself.

It would be unfair to claim that communicative sexuality models take no account of context whatsoever. Anderson explicitly states that, 'Force, coercion, or misrepresentations by the actor would be evidence of a failure to negotiate.'[67] Anderson's model could therefore be understood as consisting of two requirements: A requirement that the parties reach an explicit verbal agreement to engage in the sexual behaviour, and a requirement that both parties are free to negotiate the terms of that agreement. Without the freedom to negotiate, explicit verbal agreement is meaningless. A person may say 'yes' to an offer of sexual penetration, but if the other party is holding a gun to their head at the time, the subsequent intercourse will still be an instance of sexual violation. What happens if, instead, we take away the requirement of explicit verbal agreement?

If two or more parties to a sexual encounter all feel able to openly express their desires and their boundaries, but choose not to do so verbally, is it right to say that any of those parties has violated the other(s)? I submit that sexual penetration unaccompanied by verbal negotiation is not, of itself, an appropriate target for criminalisation. Instead, the focus of the criminal law should be on sexual activity which is unilaterally imposed on a person who lacks the opportunity, the freedom or the ability to refuse to engage in, or to actively participate in shaping, the sexual encounter. This would cover situations where a person's refusal is ignored, as well as situations when a person is prevented from expressing refusal in the first place. Central to the legitimacy of a given sexual encounter should be the creation and maintenance of a space within which negotiation can freely take place.

Freedom to negotiate: A possible way forward for law reform?

Consent is not an effective mechanism with which to distinguish sex from sexual violation. Negotiation and communicative sexuality represent a move in the right direction, but they focus too heavily on the form and content of negotiation and marginalise the context in which it takes place. I propose a standard of 'freedom to negotiate' as an alternative framework for sexual offences law. The core of the proposal is a restructuring of the existing offences of rape and sexual assault under ss 1–4 of the Sexual Offences Act 2003. These offences relate to different categories of sexual activity, but share a common *actus reus* element, that the designated sexual activity takes place without the victim's consent. It is submitted that the requirement of non-consensual sexual activity should be replaced by an *actus reus* element of sexual activity performed on a person who lacks the freedom to negotiate their participation in that activity.

It could be argued that this requirement is already incorporated in the definition of consent under s 74 of the 2003 Act, which provides that 'a person consents if he agrees by choice, and has the freedom and capacity to make that choice.' The law already prohibits sexual activity with a person who lacks the freedom to choose. In fact, replacing consent with freedom

---

67 Anderson (n 50) 1407.

to negotiate involves a radical reframing of the relevant inquiry. The central questions for identifying criminal sexual violation are no longer about the actions of the complainant – did they consent? Or did they do anything which could give rise to a reasonable belief in their consent to sex? These are replaced with questions about the behaviour of the defendant: did they do anything to restrict the complainant's freedom? Did they make the complainant feel like their wishes would not be respected? Did they ignore the complainant's words or body language? Changing the central questions in this way has important practical and symbolic consequences.

In terms of practical consequences, reframing rape and sexual assault law around a concept of freedom to negotiate would benefit both victims and suspects in the investigation and trial process. A freedom to negotiate model puts the focus where it should be: on interrogating the defendant's behaviour in context, rather than primarily scrutinising the complainant's behaviour to ascertain whether it gave rise to a reasonable inference of consent. In addition, it provides greater scope for victims to articulate on their own terms the ways in which their freedom to negotiate sex was constrained within the context of the particular relationship and the particular encounter in question, rather than requiring them to categorise their experience as strictly consensual or non-consensual, a framework which may not easily map onto their experiences. Under freedom to negotiate, the prosecution would be required to produce evidence demonstrating that the victim's freedom to negotiate their role in the sexual activity was constrained, and showing how the defendant either contributed to or took advantage of this constraint. This would mitigate the tendency to 'put the victim on trial' as the prosecution would not need to prove an absence of consent, which in practice often requires evidence of sufficient resistance by the victim.[68] At the same time however, the presumption of innocence would be preserved as there would be no implicit or explicit reversal of the burden of proof requiring the defendant to prove that they did communicate sufficiently with the victim, as Pineau advocates.[69]

Symbolically, introduction of a freedom to negotiate model would mark a significant shift in the way sex and sexual violation are conceptualised. The proposed formulation frames sexual encounters as dynamic processes of interaction rather than discrete, easily divisible events. It emphasises the relational, affective and embodied dimensions of sexuality and provides greater scope to take account of context and the power relations between the parties when evaluating a given sexual encounter. As such it more closely maps the messy reality of sexual encounters than an abstract consent standard. The linguistic break with consent and the unfamiliarity of the new terminology would also provide an opportunity for public discussion and consideration of the parameters of ethical and legal sexual activity. By contrast, efforts to reframe consent or re-educate people about its meaning are obstructed by the considerable conceptual baggage that that term carries and the proliferation of existing meanings with which it is associated.

The model which I have outlined here is presented as a starting point for rethinking the distinction between sex and sexual violation in criminal law. There are of course numerous details that remain to be developed and which there is not scope to explore here. Some of these questions are familiar. Like consent, consideration must be given to the kinds of force, coercion or deception that would restrict a person's freedom to negotiate, and the extent to which this freedom must be restricted in order to attract criminal liability. In this area, a freedom to negotiate model would in principle broaden the lens through which coercion can be

---

68 Munro, 'From Consent to Coercion' (n 6).
69 Pineau (n 46) 224.

considered, to look beyond direct and explicit threats immediately prior to the sexual activity. The vexatious issue of the *mens rea* of rape would remain, but the terrain of the debate would be relocated. Instead of oscillating between reasonable and honest belief in consent, discussion would now focus on whether a defendant must have intentionally, knowingly, recklessly or negligently restricted the victim's freedom to negotiate, or exploited existing restrictions on the victim's freedom. A subjective *mens rea* standard might be more palatable where it relates to a defendant's awareness of constraint and coercion as opposed to belief in consent. More radically, a freedom to negotiate model would also provide a basis for rethinking the relationship between rape and sexual assault and many of the other offences contained within the Sexual Offences Act 2003. This model foregrounds power disparities between the parties that prevent one individual from negotiating their participation in sexual activity. As such, it calls into question whether separate offences against children[70] or against mentally disordered adults[71] address a different form of sexual violation from rape and sexual assault, and whether there is a clear rationale for these additional offences.

CONCLUSIONS

Despite its broad appeal, consent is not an appropriate or effective way to distinguish legitimate sexual activity from sexual violation. Consent models invoke the abstract, disembodied, rational subject of liberal discourse and emphasise the policing of bodily boundaries as opposed to the relationality and intersubjectivity of sexual encounters. Consent is therefore useful for conceptualising asymmetric proposals and agreements to discrete acts, but poorly suited to evaluating dynamic interactions between parties, absent clear fixed parameters, which constitute the bulk of real-world sexual encounters. Consent models also have limited capacity for taking account of the contexts within which sexual activity is negotiated. Reframing the distinction between sex and sexual violation around a concept of negotiation or communication addresses many of these problems in theory, by constructing sexual encounters as ongoing processes of reciprocal interaction rather than episodic moments of consent or refusal. However, adopting a narrow focus on communication immediately prior to and during sexual activity reproduces several of consent's flaws. A concept of freedom to negotiate, which is informed by negotiation models as well as by original empirical research, is proposed as the basis for a radical rethinking of sexual offences law. At its core, freedom to negotiate emphasises the context in which sexual activity takes place, requiring that, at a minimum, all parties to sexual activity should have the space to negotiate both the fact and nature of their participation throughout the duration of that activity.

---

70 The Sexual Offences Act 2003, ss 5–29.
71 The Sexual Offences Act 2003, ss 30–44.

2

Relational autonomy and consent

Jonathan Herring

INTRODUCTION

It is generally accepted that the role of consent in the criminal law is closely tied to the right to autonomy. However, the notion of autonomy is itself contentious and has multiple meanings.[1] This chapter will explore the role of consent in the criminal law from the perspective of relational autonomy. This offers three important insights. The first is that relational autonomy emphasises that obtaining consent is a relational matter. It is not just a matter of what the victim said or did, but should be understood as a communicative exercise between the two parties. Second, the relational aspect means that a defendant relying on a victim's consent has responsibilities towards that victim. Third, it will be argued that the moral work that consent does is to enable the defendant to accept the victim's assessment of their own well-being. However, whether an apparent consent can be taken by a defendant as the victim's assessment of their well-being depends on an appreciation of the character of the victim, the nature of their relationship and the broader social context.

CONSENT AND AUTONOMY

Consent in the criminal law is typically tied to the notion of autonomy. The standard approach goes something like this:

If V has consented to the act of D, D cannot have committed a crime, because V has not been wronged. V has not been wronged because V has the right to decide what should or should not happen to her body as an aspect of her personal autonomy. If she consents to D touching her, then out of respect for her autonomy, we should permit the touching and not outlaw that activity (unless we can point to the interests of a third party who are impacted by the activity). To criminalise D for touching V with V's consent infringes her autonomy. It fails to respect her autonomy because it involves the criminal law in declaring that V has been harmed, when in fact V consented to the activity. Surely V knows better than the state what is or is not 'a harm' to her.

---

1 See also Jonathan Herring and Michelle Madden Dempsey, 'Rethinking the Criminal Law's Response to Sexual Penetration: On Theory and Context' in Claire McGlynn and Vanessa Munro (eds), *Rethinking Rape Law* (Routledge 2010).

Similarly if D touches V without her consent a wrong has been done. We should respect V's decision not to be touched without her consent. If the law did not acknowledge a crime, again the law would be being paternalistic. It would be assuming the state knew better than V whether a touching was good for her or not.

On this understanding of consent, consent is something the victim gives to the defendant: a kind of 'get out of jail free card', which, once received, permits the defendant to perform the act. The primary issues of controversy over consent in the literature focus on the victim's state of mind when providing the consent: was the victim too afraid / mistaken / pressurised / ignorant to give effective consent?[2]

This approach to autonomy is, however, based on one particular understanding of autonomy. In this chapter I want to explore the concept of relational autonomy and consider what implications adopting it might have for the criminal law on consent.[3] I will start by setting out the traditional understanding of autonomy before exploring the alternative version of relational autonomy, before concluding with an assessment of the significance for the law of adopting a relational autonomy approach.

THE TRADITIONAL MEANING OF AUTONOMY

The traditional version of autonomy is based on a claim that that individuals should be allowed to make decisions for themselves and that those decisions should be respected by others, unless the decision involves harming someone else. Ronald Dworkin is commonly quoted for explaining why autonomy is seen as important:

> Recognising an individual right of autonomy makes self-creation possible. It allows each of us to be responsible for shaping our lives according to our own coherent or incoherent – but, in any case, distinctive – personality. It allows us to lead our own lives rather than be led along them, so that each of us can be, to the extent a scheme of rights can make this possible, what we have made of ourselves. We allow someone to choose death over radical amputation or a blood transfusion, if that is his informed wish, because we acknowledge his right to a life structured by his own values.[4]

This traditional conception of autonomy is linked to a whole set of other values: self-sufficiency, self-sovereignty, moral independence, self-government, pluralism and liberty.[5] Indeed, so understood, autonomy might be seen as the most important legal right. It is about allowing us to choose what happens to us, rather than others making those decisions for us.

The significance of this approach to autonomy is seen in the values of law. As explained above, it is commonly used to explain why consent is so important in the criminal law; in short, because people should be allowed to do what they want with their bodies. Obviously much more could be said about the traditional version of autonomy, but my focus is on a competing understanding: relational autonomy.

---

2 Eg Joan McGregor, *Is it Rape?* (Ashgate 2005); Alan Wertheimer, *Consent to Sexual Relations* (Cambridge University Press 2003); Peter Westen, *The Logic Of Consent* (Ashgate 2004); Franklin Miller and Alan Wertheimer (eds), *The Ethics of Consent* (Oxford University Press 2010).

3 I draw on Jonathan Herring, *Relational Autonomy and Family Law* (Springer 2014) and Jonathan Herring, 'Consent in the Criminal Law: The Importance of Relationality and Responsibility' in Alan Reed, Michael Bohlander, Nicola Wake and Emma Smith (eds), *General Defences in Criminal Law* (Ashgate 2015).

4 Ronald Dworkin, *Life's Dominion* (Vintage 1993) 224.

5 Martha Albertson Fineman, *The Autonomy Myth* (New Press 2004) ch 1.

RELATIONAL AUTONOMY

The concept of relational autonomy rejects the traditional individualised concept of autonomy.[6] Catriona MacKenzie and Natalie Stoljar,[7] two leading proponents of the concept, explain its essence:

'relational autonomy' is an umbrella term, designating a range of related perspectives ... premised on a shared conviction that persons are socially embedded, that agents' identities are formed within the context of social relationships and shaped by a complex of intersecting social determinants, such as race, class, gender, and ethnicity.

Exploring it further, I would suggest the following three features are key aspects of relational autonomy.

First, human beings are in their nature relational. Our understanding of ourselves and the world around us emerges through our relationships with others from our earliest days. Who we are, what we want and where we want to go are all defined in terms of our relationships with others. As Jennifer Nedelsky[8] writes:

Relationships are central to people's lives – to who we are, to the capacities we are able to develop, to what we value, what we suffer, and what we are able to enjoy.

Second, our decisions are relational. This means that we cannot be free to 'live our lives as we choose' because we are constrained by the responsibilities, realities and relationships that embed our lives. Most choices we make require the cooperation of others and will impact upon them. Indeed we often make decisions based on the sharing of ideas, hopes, and plans with others. That is why it is rare for a person to make a decision on their own. They will consult, negotiate and discuss the decision jointly with those affected, and with those they are in relationship with. As Brent Slife and Frank Richardson[9] put it:

[W]e do not, indeed cannot, construct meanings to live by on our own, individualistically, without sensitively and responsibly coordinating our action, reflection, and creative imagination with that of other people.

Third, relational autonomy recognises the importance of relational obligations. It rejects the view that obligations flow from autonomy: that we are only subject to obligations that have been voluntary obligations. The obligations attached to parenthood, for example, arise not from a specific choice of an individual, but from the relationship that exists. The obligations we are under are generated through our relationships and the needs of others. This might be thought to create a tension between the freedom supported by autonomy and the restrictions of responsibilities, but responsibilities are an inherent part of relationships; and if relationships are what we want as part of our flourishing, then we take the obligations that go with them. For example, many people choose to formalise their relationships with marriage. Responsibilities come with marriage, but these are part

---

6 For a full account see Herring, *Relational Autonomy and Family Law* (n 3).
7 Catriona MacKenzie and Natalie Stoljar (eds), *Relational Autonomy* (Oxford University Press 2000) 4.
8 Jennifer Nedelsky, *Relational Law* (Oxford University Press 2012), 1.
9 Brent Slife and Frank Richardson, 'Is Gergen's Relational Being relational enough?' (2011) 24 Journal of Constructivist Psychology 304.

of the choice that is made in getting married. Indeed part of the appeal of marriage is the responsibilities that come with it.

This emphasis on responsibilities as an inherent part of autonomy should come as no surprise. Our lives are not marked by freedom, but by our obligations to others; not by living with no thought for others; but seeking to promote the well-being of those we love. For most people it is obligations to children; friends or relations who are dependent on us, or wider social causes, which mark out what is most precious for our lives. We seek not freedom and self-determination for ourselves, but the flourishing of those we love.

DISTINGUISHING RELATIONAL AND TRADITIONAL AUTONOMY

Much more could be said about relational autonomy, and to acknowledge some of the powerful criticisms that have been made of it, but for now I want to emphasise how a relational approach to autonomy differs from traditional understandings of autonomy. Three points should be emphasised:

The relational nature of choice

Traditional autonomy focuses on the question 'what does person X choose?' We should accept their answer at face value. We should not look behind it to explore whether it is justified. That is a back door to paternalism because once we look too deeply at the choice anyone makes we can find flaws. Nor should we use the interests of others to justify an interference in that choice, unless there is direct harm to them. Such an approach imagines that we can look at an individual's choice, outside the context of their relationships. So doing it promotes individualism.

The traditional approach incorrectly represents people as isolated individuals and so fails to resonate with the lived-in experience of people's lives and adequately promote relationships or protect people within them. By asking 'what is it you want' and elevating the importance of a person's choice, downplays the importance of individual's relational understandings of themselves and attaches no weight to the responsibilities that can flow from relationships. The emphasis on autonomy speaks to and respects the language of the selfish person.

Relational autonomy, by contrast, recognises that autonomy is not simply a matter of what you want. Few people make decisions based solely on their own interests. They quite properly take account of the interests of others.

The relational nature of self

Relational autonomy is highly sensitive to the way in which our relationships constitute identity and are integral to autonomy. So it is not, as traditional autonomy, would have it, that we form our goals for our life and then seek to use our relationships to pursue those goals. In a relational approach, autonomy emerges *within* and *because* of relationships.[10] Our goals are formed by and within the context of our relationship and in a context in which talk of using a relationship to achieve one's goals makes no sense because identities become fused. This means that an attempt to ascertain whether someone has capacity and what their autonomous wish is can only properly be made if assessed within the context of their relationships. A capacity test should therefore consider whether an individual, with the support of the family

---

10 Nedelsky (n 8) 1.

and friends, is able to make a decision.[11] What a person wants will be tied up with what others want. It can only be determined after discussions with those to whom they are especially interconnected. It is, if you like, a group decision, not an individual one.

The relational context of the decision

A third distinction is that relational autonomy perspective is far more aware than traditional autonomy of the way relationships can impair autonomy. It realises that 'our decisions' are in fact decisions reached within a relational context and so not straightforwardly ours. It is, therefore, peculiarly alert to the difficulties in determining the extent to which someone's decision may be the result of manipulation at the hands of others. The challenge is then to define how we determine which relationships a model of autonomy should promote and which it should regard as destructive of autonomy. The concern in particular is that a person in an oppressive relationship or member of an oppressive group will internalise the values of the group reducing their own self-worth and trust.[12] As Susan Sherwin and Meghan Winsby[13] write:

> For agents to be autonomous, they must be able to resist the options that help to sustain their own oppression. To ensure that conditions are such that the exercise of a reasonably high degree of autonomy is possible, it is sometimes necessary to try to correct limitations inherent in the background conditions of each person's social location.

Feminists have been particularly astute to the way that women can be defined by male-dominated society and take on the expectations and views expected of them.[14]

For relational autonomy, then, it is not simply a matter of did the victim say 'yes' or 'no' but an assessment of the relational context within which they said what they said. Whether those relationships were enabling the victim to have values of themselves, and respected them as mutual partners to the relationships. It is sensitive to claims that although the victim said 'yes' this was not their genuine consent, but the product of oppressive relationships.

RELATIONAL AUTONOMY AND THE NATURE OF CONSENT

So, what does relational autonomy have to say about consent in the context of criminal law? To answer that question I need to explain why it is that consent is 'morally transformative'.[15] In a previous book in this series,[16] I have explained my understanding of consent, which builds on the work of Michelle Madden Dempsey.[17] I will not repeat in detail what was said there, save to provide a brief outline.

---

11 Carolyn Ells, Matthew Hunt, Jane Chambers-Evans, 'Relational Autonomy as an Essential Component of Patient-centered Care' (2011) 4 International Journal of Feminist Approaches to Bioethics 79.
12 Nedelsky (n 8) 112.
13 Susan Sherwin and Meghan Winsby, 'A relational perspective on autonomy for older adults residing in nursing homes' (2011) 14 Health Expectations 182.
14 Nedelsky (n 8) 54.
15 Alan Wertheimer, 'Consent to Sexual Relations' in Franklin Miller and Alan Wertheimer (eds), *The Ethics of Consent* (Oxford University Press 2010).
16 Herring, 'Consent in the Criminal Law: The Importance of Relationality and Responsibility' (n 3).
17 Michelle Madden Dempsey, 'Victimless Conduct and the Volenti Maxim: How Consent Works' (2013) 7 Criminal Law and Philosophy 11.

Consent becomes relevant when D's act will wrongfully harm V's well-being thereby rendering the act a *prima facie* wrong. That requires the actor D to provide a reason justifying acting the way he or she acted. Consent can operate as providing a justifying reason. It gives D an option to decide to set aside the reasons against acing in a particular way which rest in V's well-being. Consent does that by allowing D to assume that the act is not all things considered contrary to the well-being of V. That is because D is permitted to rely on V's assessment that the act is overall in V's best interests. In effect where consent is effective Michelle Madden Dempsey claims that D is entitled to say:

> This is [V]'s decision. He's an adult and can decide for himself whether he thinks the risk is worth it. In considering what to do, I will assume that his decision is the right one for him. After all, he is in a better position than I to judge his own well-being. And so, I will not take it upon myself to reconsider those reasons. Instead, I will base my decision of whether to [harm] him on the other relevant reasons.[18]

This then is the 'work' of consent. That is why it gives D permission to set aside the reasons against harming V. That also explain what consent is. It must be sufficient to allow D to conclude that V has made an effective assessment of what is in her best interests, which D can accept.

This way of understanding consent is consistent with and can build upon a conception of consent based on relational autonomy. I will bring out several specific points of significance.

RESPECTING THE AUTONOMY OF V

It encourages an attitude of respect for the autonomy of the victim. It does not treat consent as a 'green traffic light' that permits D to proceed, without questioning. Rather D must make sure that V has made a proper assessment of her best interests. It acknowledges that what a person wants in the heat of the moment may not represent a genuine assessment of their well-being; a true expression of autonomy. Simply because V has said 'yes' will not be enough for D to be satisfied that V has undertaken an adequate assessment of their own well-being.

Catriona Makenzie and Wendy Rogers argue to be able to exercise autonomy and make an assessment of our own well-being we need to be the following:[19]

- *Self-determining*: being 'able to determine one's own beliefs, values, goals and wants, and to make choices regarding matters of practical import to one's life free from undue interference. The obverse of self-determination is determination by other persons, or by external forces or constraints.'[20]
- *Self-governing*: 'being able to make choices and enact decisions that express, or are consistent with, one's values, beliefs and commitments. Whereas the threats to self-determination are typically external, the threats to self-governance are typically internal, and often involve volitional or cognitive failings. Weakness of will and failures of self-control are common volitional failings that interfere with self-governance.'[21]

---

18 ibid 20.
19 Catriona Makenzie and Wendy Rogers, 'Autonomy, vulnerability and capacity: a philosophical appraisal of the Mental Capacity Act' (2013) 9 International Journal of the Law in Context 37.
20 ibid.
21 ibid.

- *Have authenticity:* 'a person's decisions, values, beliefs and commitments must be her "own" in some relevant sense; that is, she must identify herself with them and they must cohere with her "practical identity", her sense of who she is and what matters to her. Actions or decisions that a person feels were foisted on her, which do not cohere with her sense of herself, or from which she feels alienated, are not autonomous.'[22]

The relational autonomy advocated in this chapter requires that D respects V's autonomy in a meaningful way. To be sure that V has an understanding of all the relevant facts and is self-governing, self-determining and authentic in the way Mackenzie and Rogers outline. Only then can D rely on the 'consent' as a reasonable assessment by V of V's well-being.

It is true that the extent to which D can be expected to determine whether or not V's decision is richly autonomous will vary depending on the nature of the encounter. If the parties are strangers, the nature of the act and the severity of the harm and the circumstances of their interaction will determine whether it is appropriate for D to take the stranger V's current consent as being sufficient as an assessment of their well-being. A stranger asking the person next to them to scratch their back may be taken to consent with a minimum of assessment by their neighbour. However, if a person with a troubled mental history asks their friend to cut off their leg, much more will be required of the friend before consent can be found.

A central aspect of truly respecting the other person's autonomy is acknowledging the straitjacket of the law's approach which tries to restrict a determination of a victim's state of mind as either a 'yes' or a 'no'. In cases where the victim has consented to an act which is otherwise a *prima facie* wrong the attitude of the victim is normally far more complex than either of these two words. Their consent will relate to a particular act, in a particular context, with a particular individual, within a particular relationship. The problem with the law's 'yes or no' attitude is that it is not properly listening to the victim and seeking to ascertain what the victim wants. Nicola Lacey,[23] writing in the context of sexual behaviour, highlights the problems in simply asking whether the victim consented to 'the act'. She writes, discussing consent in the sexual context:

> The victim's consent responds to power by conferring legitimacy, rather than shaping power in its own terms: consent is currently understood not in terms of mutuality but rather in relation to a set of arrangements initiated, by implication, by the defendant, in an asymmetric structure which reflects the stereotypes of active masculinity and passive femininity.

That point can operate in many other contexts in which one person is planning to do an act which is a *prima facie* wrong to another. Proper respect for autonomy requires more than making a demand and limiting the other person's response to either yes or no. It can be a politician's favourite trick to claim 'you are either for us or against us', a trick that forecloses a range of more nuanced positions.[24]

A person who is genuinely interested in what the other person wants and is seeking to determine what their assessment of their well-being will be looking for more than a yes or no. Indeed, we would be rightly suspicious if a defendant who was wishing to do a *prima facie*

---

22 ibid.
23 Nicola Lacey, *Unspeakable Subjects* (Hart Publishing 1998).
24 See eg President Bush's remarks on the War on Terror: CNN on-line , 'You are either with us or against us' 6 November 2001.<http://edition.cnn.com/2001/US/11/06/gen.attack.on.terror/> accessed 18 December 2015.

lawful act was only seeking to discover if the victim said yes or no. Martha Nussbaum[25] has set out the ways that objectification can occur despite consent. These include instrumentality (where the objectifier treats the other as a tool for his or her purposes); violability (where the objectifier treats the other person as something that lacks boundary integrity and that it is 'permissible to break up, smash, break into')[26] and denial of subjectivity (where the objectifier treats the other as something whose experiences and feelings do not need to be taken into account). As she notes these can all occur in a case where the victim might on the traditional account have 'consented'. The relational autonomy approach advocated here would be inconsistent with these attitudes. A person seeking to determine whether the victim has made a full assessment of their own well-being and seeking to respect that would not have any of the kind of attitudes described by Nussbaum. Rather they would be seeking to adopt the approach Catriona Mackenzie describes, in a medical context:[27]

> The principle of respect for autonomy ... gives rise to an obligation to try to empathically engage with the other's experience, to imagine what the other person's situation is like for her, given her cares, values and concerns. In the context of patient care, it requires carers and medical staff to try to understand, from the patient's perspective, her experience of illness, or of particular treatment options.

RESPONSIBILITIES

Implied with what has been said under the previous heading is a further claim. Not only must D truly respect V's autonomy, V has a responsibility to take reasonable steps to enable V to exercise autonomy and to ensure they are doing something that does not impede autonomy.

It must be recalled we are dealing with a situation where D is planning to do an act which is a *prima facie* wrong to V. They are always free not to act in that way, but if they decide to commit the wrong, relying on the consent of V, then they have responsibilities to ensure that the consent is effective in the way explained above.

In relying on consent D has the responsibility of giving V the time, information and freedom from pressure to provide that consent. Where D has used deceptions, pressure, manipulation or exploitation in order to obtain consent, this is inconsistent with D properly relying on consent as an expression by V of their assessment of their well-being. He has not been respecting the right to bodily integrity that gives V the right to determine for themselves whether an act is in their well-being. Similarly, the fact that V is so intoxicated she cannot indicate her views or can give only a muddled version of them, of course, provides D with no justification for wronging V; indeed that is a particularly strong case of where D has no good reason for wronging V.

It may be helpful to ask: does the interaction indicate that D was seeking to let or enable V to make a free, informed decision about what was in her best interests or was D lying, threatening, pressurising V? The use of deceptions, pressures, manipulations and the like indicate that D was not seeking to use consent in the way promoted in this article, as an assessment by V of their well-being.

Looking at the context of sexual relations, asking these kinds of questions puts the practise of 'seduction' in a new light. Seduction has been defined as 'the offering of something that is desired,

---

25 Martha Nussbaum, 'Objectification' (1995) 24 Philosophy and Public Affairs 249.
26 ibid 357.
27 Catriona Mackenzie, 'Relational Autonomy, Normative Authority and Perfectionism' (2008) 39 Journal of Social Philosophy 512.

to persuade; duress, coercion, or compulsion uses negative reinforcement, the threat of something that is feared, to persuade'.[28] This is the very opposite of the kind of approach advocated here.

In the model proposed, D has an obligation to ensure that V has made an effective assessment of V's well-being. Consent is not a bauble, which D must grab in any way he can. D must have a particular attitude towards V – one that seeks to enable V to exercise her autonomy.

Imagine V is mistaken about a fact, when 'consent' is given, for example she thinks D belongs to a profession or is unmarried. If D knows that V is mistaken and V would not have reached the same conclusion, D cannot take that consent. Quite obviously the work of consent as we have described it cannot be achieved where V is mistaken. D cannot take V's consent as an assessment of V's well-being because D knows that V would not think the act would promote V's well-being if she knew the truth. So, where D seeks to play a dangerous sport with V, but realises that V does not know the danger of the sport, then D cannot say 'I assume V decided that the fun in the sport was worth the risk.' The consent that V has offered: 'I consent to this safe sport' is not consent to the dangerous sport.

THE RELATIONAL NATURE OF CONSENT

The approach advocated in this chapter shows that consent is not properly understood as simply a matter of what was V's state of mind. Rather it asks what D was entitled to understand and interpret about V's state of mind from what was said or done. In particular this encourages D to take reasonable steps to determine what V wants and to ensure that she understands what is proposed fully.

Relational autonomy acknowledges that consent must be seen in the context of the relationship between the parties. Anne Donchin[29] explains:

> Any tenable conception of personal autonomy is bound to be subject-centered; but a social conception that is relational will take into account the need for a network of personal relationships to develop and sustain competencies necessary to act as self-determining, responsible agents.

To take a simple example, I could not make a decision about raising our children without discussing the issue with my partner, enabling us to reach a joint decision. I will rely on her input and she will rely on mine. Our joint input, in informational and advisory terms, will produce the decision.

So it will be in a case of consent to sex or bodily harm. Each party will have things to contribute to the decision whether to engage in harmful behavior. This may involve the provision of information; the removal of pressures; giving time or offering emotional support. An effective decision will require both D and V to play their part. If D fails to do that, it will not be an autonomous decision. V will have been let down in the decision-making process. D cannot take V's assessment as an accurate one of her well-being if a key part of the decision-making process (D's involvement) is missing.

That said, it is important to appreciate that the relationship between D and V will determine what is expected from each other in the decision-making process. The expected involvement of a professional advisor may be very different from an acquaintance who asked for

---

28 Lucinda Vandervort, 'Sexual Consent as Voluntary Agreement: Tales of "Seduction" or Questions of Law' [2013] New Criminal Law Review 143.

29 Anne Donchin, 'Autonomy, interdependence, and assisted suicide: Respecting boundaries/crossing lines' (2000) 141 Bioethics 187, 192.

advice in a social situation. The expected involvement of a casual sexual partner may be very different from a spouse. And so on.

ACKNOWLEDGING EACH OTHER'S VULNERABILITY

We need to acknowledge our mutual vulnerabilities. There is ample evidence that we are bad decision makers. Jennifer Drobac and Oliver Goodenough[30] in their analysis of the psychology of decision-making list the following requirements for rational use of information:

  (i) parties with stable, well-ordered preferences;
 (ii) choices that are fully voluntary and unconstrained;
 (iii) relatively equal, and ideally complete, information;
 (iv) relatively equal bargaining power and experience;
  (v) sufficient cognitive capacity to evaluate the transaction and to exercise voluntary control over the conflicting factors and emotions involved;
 (vi) the absence of monopoly power or other distortions of the market;
(vii) the presence of good faith and absence of fraud in both parties; and
(viii) a level of consequence for a mistake that is not disastrous to the party.

The authors, after examining the latest neuroscience and psychology suggest that few people have capacity to consent.[31] They are not alone in their analysis. Neil Levy[32] refers to a wide range of psychological studies which reveal 'fallibilities of human reasoning' (including 'myopia for the future', 'motivated reasoning' and 'biases' in 'assessing probabilities . . . exacerbated . . . under cognitive load'). He concludes that human beings are, under a variety of conditions, systematically bad reasoners, and many of their reasoning faults can be expected to affect the kind of judgements that they make when they are called upon to give informed consent.

But, note, this works two ways. While the defendant must acknowledge the ways in which the victim's consent may be flawed, so too must the defendant appreciate the ways in which their own assessment of whether there is valid consent is potentially flawed. We hear what we want to hear. We like to think we know better than others what is good for them. We want people to like us and to agree with what we want.

Consent, then, must to be treated by both parties with an awareness of their vulnerabilities. The approach advocated in this chapter seeks to do this. It is line with what Kim Atkins argues:

> Respect for autonomy is an acknowledgment of the limitations of our knowledge of other people and a willingness to incorporate that understanding into our worldviews. When we respect autonomy we don't simply observe another's freedom from a distance, as it were; we accede to our fundamental fallibility and epistemological humility. It is in recognition of the fact that we cannot experience from another's perspective that we normally refrain from judging what will make another's life good *for them*.[33]

---

30 Jennifer Drobac and Oliver Goodenough, 'Exposing the Myth of Consent' (2015) Indiana Health Law Review, Forthcoming; Indiana University Robert H. McKinney School of Law Research Paper No 2015–3. Available at SSRN: <http://ssrn.com/abstract=2559341> accessed 18 December 2015.

31 ibid.

32 Neil Levy, 'Forced to be Free? Increasing Patient Autonomy by Constraining it' (2014) 40 Journal of Medical Ethics 293.

33 Kim Atkins, 'Autonomy and the Subjective Character of Experience' (2000) 17 Journal of Applied Philosophy 71.

But, more than that, it encourages us, in our interactions with others, to seek to engage with them accepting their values.

SOCIAL PRESSURES

A particularly significant aspect of appreciating our mutual vulnerabilities is to acknowledge how we are subject to societal pressures. Feminist writing has done much to show how societal pressures impact on women's sense of self. Feminism is 'centrally concerned with freeing women to shape their own lives' and to 'define' themselves 'rather than accepting the definition given by others (men and male-dominated society, in particular)'.[34]

This is particularly relevant in relation to consent in the sexual context. Catherine MacKinnon[35] argues:

> The problem with consent-only approaches to criminal law reform is that sex, under conditions of inequality, can look consensual when it is not wanted at the time, because women know that sex that women want is the sex men want from women. Men in positions of power over women can thus secure sex that looks, even is, consensual without that sex ever being freely chosen, far less desired.

The claim here is certainly not that women cannot make a rational decision about sex. Rather, the decision must be seen in the surrounding social, economic and relational background. In a survey for the children's charity, the NSPCC,[36] it was found that 44% of teenage girls felt guilty saying no to a request for sex from their boyfriends. Of those who had experienced unwanted sex, 55% thought the event was partly their fault.

The pressures can also come from the emotional context of the relationship. Again writing in the sexual context Robin Morgan[37] writes:

> [T]he pressure is there, and it need not be a knife blade against the throat, it's in his body language, his threat of sulking, his clenched or trembling hand, his self-deprecating humour or angry put-down or silent self-pity at being rejected. How many millions of times have women had sex 'willingly' with men they did not want to have sex with?

And the individual pressures with in the relationship will reflect broader social pressures. As Ngaire Naffine[38] argues:

> [R]ape is a crime whose setting is a society where women are expected to repress their desires, where they are expected to want what a man wants, where women's sexual wishes are actively (though never completely) suppressed or rendered mysterious or incredible whenever they cease to fit the possessive form.

---

34 Susan Boyd, 'Motherhood and Autonomy in a Shared Parenting Climate' in Jackie Jones, Anna Grear, Rachel Anne Fenton, Kim Stevens (eds), *Gender, Sexualities and Law* (Routledge 2011) 121.

35 Catherine MacKinnon, 'A sex equality approach to sexual assault' (2003) 989 Annals New York Academy of Sciences 265.

36 BBC News Online 'Girls reveal abuse by boyfriends', 2015 <http://news.bbc.co.uk/1/hi/uk/4366167.stm> accessed 18 December 2015.

37 Robin Morgan, 'Theory and practice: Pornography and rape' in Laura Lederer (ed), *Take Back the Night: Women on Pornography* (William Morrow 1980) 134.

38 Ngaire Naffine, 'Possession: Erotic Love in the Law of Rape' (1994) 57 Modern Law Review 10, 34–35.

The social context includes not just pressures on women, but also assumptions about masculinity. Michael Kimmel notes: boys are taught to try to get sex; girls are taught strategies to foil the boys' attempts. 'The whole game was to get a girl to give out', one man told sociologist Lillian Rubin: 'You expected her to resist . . . but you kept pushing. Part of it was the thrill of touching and being touched, but, I've got to admit, part of it was the conquest, too. . .' 'I felt as if I should want to get it as often as possible', recalled another. 'I guess that's because if you're a guy, you're supposed to want it.'[39]

Much more could be said about the cultural background against which sexual encounters take place. What I hope to show is that simply asking the question 'did the victim consent?' closes off the context within which the encounter takes place. An approach that fails to appreciate the pressures on the parties and the relationship between them, the fears of what might or might not happen, the awareness of the lack of effective criminal sanction in cases of rape, is one that cannot claim to be truly seeking to protect sexual autonomy.

CONCLUSION

This chapter has explored the concept of consent through the lens of relational autonomy. It has argued that we cannot simply reduce consent to being a question of whether the victim has said 'yes' or 'no' to the defendant causing harm. The responsibilities that arise from a relationship mean that the defendant before harming the victim must determine that the victim has made an effective assessment that the act will be in their best interests. This requires the defendant to look carefully at the decision that V has made and be as satisfied as is reasonable that the expression reflects a proper assessment by V of their well-being. It also requires the defendant to takes reasonable steps to enable V to be able to make an effective assessment of their well-being. That may be giving V the information they need to make a properly informed decision; giving V time and space to decide; and the support they need to do this.

The approach acknowledges that we are vulnerable. We acknowledge the vulnerability in others, that their apparent consent may not match a genuine assessment of their well-being, but be based on mistake; be the result of flawed reasoning; or not reflect their deepest values. However, the defendant must recognise their own vulnerabilities. The desire to hear what they want to hear; to be paternalistic towards others and impose on them what we think they may want; or to use prejudicial assumptions about others in our assessment of what they want.

Of course, the precise details of how this works out will depend on the nature of the relationship between the parties. What a patient might expect from a doctor will be very different from what someone might expect from a partner in an orgy, for example.

The relational autonomy recognises the mutual responsibility the parties owe to each other. We must not harm others without being sure their consent is a full assessment of their best interests. If we do not have that we must refrain from the harmful act. After all, walking away will never be directly harmful. The law on consent needs to develop in a way which is far more respectful of each other; recognises our mutual vulnerably and our responsibilities to seek out what the other person genuinely wants.

---

39 Michael Kimmel, *The Gender of Desires* (SUNY Press 2011) 5.

3

The relationship between capacity and consent

Claire de Than and Jesse Elvin

INTRODUCTION

> Most people faced with the decision whether or not to have sex do not embark on a process of weighing up complex, abstract or hypothetical information... There is a danger that the imposition of a higher standard for capacity [than basic understanding] may discriminate against people with a mental impairment.[1]

Under existing general legal principles, it is presumed that all adults have capacity and freedom to make wise and unwise decisions, including decisions about sexual behaviour, except where statutory provisions such as the presumptions under ss 75 and 76 of the Sexual Offences Act 2003 apply.[2] However there have been suggestions that the presumption of capacity should be reversed for sex offences in at least certain circumstances not covered by these presumptions. For example, Shlomit Wallerstein has claimed that, for the purposes of s 74 of the Sexual Offences Act 2003, the courts should take the default position that "'a drunken consent is *not* consent" where the woman is very drunk.[3] Similarly, Georgina Firth has argued that 'the decision of the government to abandon further reform proposals [relating to sexual offences], such as a rebuttable presumption of non-consent where the victim is intoxicated, is a missed opportunity.'[4] We will critically evaluate such suggestions and examine their potential implications, not only in relation to sex offences but also in relation to other aspects of criminal law. We will also look at the relationship between capacity and consent throughout criminal law in the light of the wider context of international human rights and disability law, since there is a growing view that capacity is a discriminatory concept that has no place in modern legal systems, and concerns have been raised both about inroads into the right under Article 8 of the European Convention on Human Rights (ECHR) to consensual sexual expression in private and inconsistent application of capacity

---

1 *A Local Authority v TZ (No 2)* (2014) EWCOP 973, (2014) MHLO 72 (Baker LJ).
2 Sexual Offences Act 2003. This is discussed in more detail below.
3 Shlomit Wallerstein, "'A Drunken Consent is still Consent"- or is it? A Critical Analysis of the Law on a Drunken Consent to Sex Following *Bree*' (2009) 73 Journal of Criminal Law 318, 342.
4 Georgina Firth, 'Not an Invitation to Rape: the Sexual Offences Act 2003, Consent, and the Case of the "Drunken" Victim' (2011) 62 Northern Ireland Legal Quarterly 99.

and consent principles by courts and carers. The chapter will conclude with a critical assessment of rival reform proposals for capacity and consent in criminal law.

THE CURRENT APPROACH TO CAPACITY AND CONSENT

We will begin with an analysis of the current criminal law approach to capacity and consent so that the debate that follows can be better understood in its context. The first point to note here is that 'Consent, or rather the absence thereof, is an element in many crimes of different natures.'[5] For instance, lack of consent is an element of the first four offences under the Sexual Offences Act 2003: rape, sexual penetration, sexual assault, and causing a person to engage in a sexual activity.[6] Similarly, absence of consent is an element of burglary, since this offence requires that D entered a building or part of a building as a trespasser.[7] Secondly, it is important to bear in mind that consent is relevant as a defence to a variety of criminal charges: for example, under ss 47, 20 and 18 of the Offences Against the Persons Act 2003.[8] A third point to note is that there is no core concept of consent within criminal law: 'English law has developed separate concepts of consent, depending upon the context and the type of offence in question.'[9] As one of us has argued elsewhere, this is a fundamental problem with the law: 'the law on consent risks being a patchwork of statute and ad hoc case law, without any overarching principle to deal with new situations and different offences'.[10] Part of this fundamental problem is the lack of a unified theoretical approach to the concept of capacity. It is clear that the notion of capacity underpins the concept of consent in all areas of criminal law. Furthermore, as we stated above, it is clear that it is presumed that all adults have capacity to make wise and unwise decisions, including decisions about sexual behaviour, except where certain statutory provision such as the presumptions under ss 75 and 76 of the Sexual Offences Act 2003 apply. However, 'The difficulty is how to determine when a person has sufficient capacity.'[11] There is no single definition, and the courts do not necessarily consider this matter in detail even when it is of central importance.

As the authors of Smith and Hogan note, cases such as *Burrell v Harmer*[12] make it clear that certain matters such as age or mental capacity are 'a potential impediment to the giving of effective consent' at common law,[13] but also highlight 'the relative superficiality of the English criminal courts' approach to . . . fundamental questions underlying the issue of consent'.[14] In *Burrell*, the court determined that two boys aged 12 and 13 were unable to appreciate the nature of tattooing, and could therefore not give consent to it, but this simply raises the question: 'in what sense did they not understand it?'[15] Given that capacity is a specific element of the definition which is employed, it is unfortunate that there is no definition of 'capacity' as this term is used in s 74 of the Sexual Offences Act 2003 for the purposes of Part 1

---

5 Catherine Elliott and Claire de Than, 'The Case for a Rational Reconstruction of Consent in Criminal Law' (2007) 70 Modern Law Review 225.

6 Contrary to ss 1–4 of The Sexual Offences Act 2003.

7 Theft Act 1968, s 9(1). For further analysis of the way in which the concept of consent is relevant in relation to property offences, see Elliott and de Than (n 5) 229–230.

8 *R v Brown* [1994] 1 AC 212.

9 Elliott and de Than (n 5) 229.

10 ibid 225.

11 ibid 239.

12 *Burrell v Harmer* [1967] Crim LR 169.

13 David Ormerod, *Smith and Hogan's Criminal Law* (13th edition, Oxford University Press 2011) 629.

14 ibid.

15 ibid.

of this Act. 'The statutory definition of consent [in s 74] refers to the idea of capacity and the explanatory notes simply state that a "person might not have sufficient capacity because of his age or because of mental disorder".'[16] Judges have, by necessity, attempted to expand and clarify the meaning of capacity in s 74: the Court of Appeal has stated that the test for capacity to consent to sexual relations should be 'necessarily informed by the definition and guidance contained in sections 2 and 3 of the Mental Capacity Act 2005',[17] although the 2005 Act does not apply to consent to sex, since nobody can consent to sex on another person's behalf. Section 3 of the 2005 Act states that the relevant factors for capacity are the ability to understand, retain and use relevant information, and to communicate a decision. However, 'That [the 2005 Act informs the test] is not to say that a jury will not need to be directed in strict accordance with the language used by and steps to be adopted in accordance with proceedings brought pursuant to the 2005 Act.'[18] Moreover, the courts will not necessarily draw upon the approach to capacity under the Mental Capacity Act 2005 in other contexts: 'It remains to be seen to what extent the criminal courts will draw upon the definition [in the 2005 Act].'[19] In *Re MAB,* Munby LJ held that the level of understanding necessary for consent to sex is necessarily low:

> Crucially, the question is whether she (or he) lacks the capacity to understand the sexual nature of the act. Her understanding need not be complete or sophisticated. It is enough that she has sufficient rudimentary knowledge of what the act comprises and of its sexual character to enable her to decide whether to give or withhold consent.[20]

In *MM,* he added that the relevant capacity 'depends on a person having sufficient knowledge and understanding of the sexual nature and character of the act and of the reasonably foreseeable consequences of sexual intercourse . . . it does not depend on an understanding of the consequences of sexual intercourse with a particular person'.[21] The question of capacity is decision-specific, in the sense that it must be based on the person's ability to make a particular decision at a particular time, and is not a judgment of their ability to make decisions in general.[22] A good thing too, since the medical reality of a person's capacity is that it may be highly variable and dependent upon many intricate factors.[23]

There has been variance between the civil and criminal courts as to the detail of the test for capacity to consent to sex: in some cases, members of the House of Lords seemed to use a person-specific capacity test.[24] For example, according to Baroness Hale, it is 'difficult to think of an activity that is more person- and situation-specific than sexual relations. One does not consent to sex in general. One consents to the act of sex with this person at this time

---

16 Elliott and de Than (n 5) 239, quoting Explanatory Notes to the Sexual Offences Act 2003 (Office of Public Sector Information 2003) [139].
17 *R v A(G)* [2014] EWCA Crim 299 [19].
18 ibid.
19 Ormerod (n 13) 630.
20 *Re MAB; X City Council v MB* [2006] EWHC 168 [74] (Lord Munby LJ)
21 *Re MM (An Adult)* [2007] EWHC 2003 [87].
22 *PC and NC v City of York Council* [2013] EWCA Civ 478
23 We have written about the legal myth of an 'on–off switch' of capacity elsewhere, in Claire de Than and Jesse Elvin, 'How Should Criminal Law deal with People who have "Partial Capacity"?', in Alan Reed, Nicola Wake, and Ben Livings (eds), *Mental Condition Defences and the Criminal Justice System: Perspectives from Law and Medicine* (Cambridge Scholars Publishing 2015) 295–317.
24 *R v C* [2009] UKHL 42.

and in this place.'[25] However, that conflates capacity and consent; consent is indeed person-specific, but capacity is not. In *LM v Liverpool City Council*,[26] Sir Brian Leveson confirmed that the civil courts and criminal courts are using different tests because they necessarily approach the issue of capacity from different directions; civil courts such as the Court of Protection are concerned with prospective assessment of an individual's decision-making abilities and hence their freedom, whereas the criminal courts act retrospectively in judging whether a particular defendant's conduct, in particular circumstances, has contravened legal standards. Given that the consequences of, for example, the Court of Protection finding that a person lacks capacity to consent to sex can be extreme, resulting in denial of contact with a long-term partner and 24-hour supervision, a cautious approach to capacity in civil cases is necessary from a human rights perspective. Ironically, human rights have not even been mentioned in some of the Court of Protection capacity cases,[27] and hence applying those cases even loosely in criminal law could be disastrous. But it is not the job of the criminal courts to bubble-wrap people in order to safeguard them from potential future crimes, and so the proper question in that context is whether the complainant did consent to the specific act at the specific time. Hence using the Mental Capacity Act outside its intended context may cause significant difficulties for criminal courts, and violate both individual human rights and sexual autonomy. However, using *different* tests for the same concept, when two or more versions of the test may apply simultaneously to the same person, may also have unfortunate consequences. This has been seen with *Hinks*,[28] where D could be guilty of theft of property to which she had gained title under civil law. We have explored elsewhere a parallel issue in relation to clashing principles of civil and criminal law and argued that the way forward is consistency[29] but via targeted reform rather than one branch of law simply adopting principles developed in another without fully considering their implications.

So, in sum, the relationship between capacity and consent is vital under current English criminal law but is disputed, variable, complex and subject to contradictory calls for reform: some argue that the threshold of capacity before consent is permitted in criminal law should be much higher, particularly in the context of sexual offences;[30] others argue that it should at least be consistent and coherent.[31] We will argue in this chapter that there are strong grounds for reference to capacity to be removed from legal definitions of consent altogether.

SHOULD THE LAW BE MORE PATERNALISTIC?

Criminal law adopts a paternalistic approach by drawing certain limits to the validity of consent: any consent given by children[32] or by adults deemed to lack mental capacity[33] is legally vitiated by specific statutory sex offences, and there is a presumption that such consent is invalid in

---

25 ibid (Baroness Hale) [24].
26 *LM v Liverpool City Council* [2014] EWCA Civ 37 (Sir Leveson)
27 Eg *D v AB* [2011] EWHC 101, which had clear potential arguments about the right to respect for private life under Article 8 of the ECHR, and discrimination.
28 *R v Hinks* [2000] UKHL 53
29 Claire de Than and Jesse Elvin, 'Mistaken Private Defence: The Case for Reform' in Alan Reed and Michael Bohlander (eds), *General Defences in Criminal Law: Domestic and Comparative Perspective* (Ashgate 2014).
30 Eg Wallerstein (n 3), whose views are considered below in detail.
31 Elliott and de Than (n 5).
32 Sexual Offences Act 2003, ss 5–8.
33 ibid, ss 30–33.

relation to adults with communication disorders.[34] Similarly, criminal law draws limits to the validity of consent in the context of the Offences Against the Person Act 1861.[35] This paternalistic aspect of the law is both controversial and highly complex. As the Law Commission has noted in relation to non-fatal offences against the person, 'The law concerning the effect of consent on liability for crimes of violence is extremely complicated and is the subject of a copious academic literature.'[36] Many, if not all, commentators believe that this area of the law is far from ideal. As Ormerod has put it in discussing the legal limits on the validity of consent, 'the law is in a dreadfully confused and unsatisfactory state.'[37] One clear criticism here is that one of the leading cases in this area, *Brown*, is too paternalistic: dealing with a group of sado-masochists charged under ss 47 and 20 of the 1861 Act, the majority of the House of Lords held that 'The activities of the appellants ... went far beyond the sort of conduct contemplated by the legislature in the foregoing statutory provisions and ... [thus] they were unlawful even when carried out in private.'[38] Criticising this decision, Nicholas Bamforth argues: 'If a presumption in favour of respecting a person as a sexual agent is adopted, given the misery caused by regulation of consenting sexual activity, it becomes clear that consenting sado-masochistic activity should be protected.'[39] There is indeed a strong line of case-law from the European Court of Human Rights on the right to consensual sexual activity in private, discussed below,[40] some of which now contradicts the approach taken by the latter court to the *Brown* case itself in *Jaggard, Laskey and Brown v UK*.[41] However, an alternative view is that the reasoning of the majority is admirable in so far as it provides 'support to the position that a drunken consent ought not be a valid consent.'[42] Wallerstein disagrees 'with the decision in *Brown* as far as it is justified by reasons of conventional conservative morality and public policy',[43] but agrees with Lord Templeman's view in the majority in *Brown* that consent is 'dubious or worthless'[44] where 'drink and drugs were employed to obtain consent and increase enthusiasm'.[45]

Her view is:

> [T]hat this reasoning is similarly applicable to the case of a drunken consent to sex ... The technical ability of the victim to refuse (ie the fact that she is conscious and able to talk) is insufficient to ensure the existence of real consent in such cases because of the effects of alcohol. In such circumstances sexual intercourse degrades the victim and humiliates her as can be seen from accounts of such victims after they sober up (their perception and feeling of being raped).[46]

Wallerstein explains that her use of female pronouns when referring to the victim or the complainant is simply 'for the sake of convenience ... [and that] the argument is similarly

---

34 ibid, s 75(2)(e).
35 *Brown* (n 8).
36 Law Commission, *Reform of Offences against the Person: A Scoping Consultation Paper* (Law Com No 217, 2014) 2.55.
37 Ormerod (n 13) 637.
38 *Brown* (n 8) 247 (Lord Jauncey).
39 Nicholas Bamforth, 'Sado-Masochism and Consent' [1994] Criminal Law Review 661, 663.
40 At 47.
41 *Laskey, Jaggard and Brown v UK* [1997] 24 EHRR 39.
42 Wallerstein (n 3) 337.
43 ibid 339.
44 *Brown* (n 8) 235 (Lord Templeman).
45 ibid 236.
46 Wallerstein (n 3) 338.

applicable to complainants and victims of both genders'.[47] Her focus is on the concept of capacity. She criticises the observation of the Court of Appeal in *Bree* that 'drunken consent is still consent' for the purposes of sexual offences.[48] In this case, the Court held that capacity to consent may evaporate before loss of consciousness, but that a complainant who has 'consumed even substantial quantities of alcohol . . . [may nevertheless remain] capable of choosing whether or not to have intercourse'.[49] Wallerstein's view is that *Bree* does not go far enough to protect people who are vulnerable through intoxication. Referring to the published view of one of us, she states:

> Jesse Elvin argues that the problem with *Bree* is that the court's position did not distinguish between voluntary and involuntary intoxication, but that, in so far as the judgment applies to voluntary intoxication, it is uncontroversial. Contrary to this position, it is submitted that the general rule (and the default position) even with regards to voluntarily intoxicated complainants should be that a drunken consent should not be recognised as valid consent.[50]

Following her view, a drunken consent would generally not be consent for the purposes of sexual offences. However, she argues that the law should recognise prior consent to the specific sexual activity that took place, if such prior consent was given and not withdrawn at any stage.[51] At the outset, it must be stated here that Wallerstein is plainly correct in at least one sense: her analysis shows that the view that a drunken consent is still consent is controversial even in relation to voluntary intoxication. Nonetheless, this does not mean that the rest of her analysis is unproblematic. It would be wise to begin by clarifying her position. Her view is that a person may lose capacity in this context even where he or she retains knowledge or understanding of the proposed activity and its potential consequences if this person's 'decision-making processes are distorted in ways that negate her ability to reject the offer'.[52] This is a much higher standard than that applied currently by either the civil or criminal courts, and directly conflicts with the ethos of the Mental Capacity Act 2005, which has universal presumed capacity as its starting point. However, it is not clear precisely what she means by this: her view of capacity does not accord with those of either the medical profession or the legal tests. It must be different from the 'agrees by choice' aspect of consent under s 74 of the Sexual Offences Act 2003, since otherwise there would be no need to categorise the issue as one of capacity. Yet a person who is unable to reject an offer does not agree by choice, so perhaps when she talks of loss of capacity she simply means absence of consent. She points out that alcohol can cause disinhibition,[53] and claims that 'a drunken person who has lost her "brakes" and is unable to stop herself from acting out of character does not have capacity to consent'.[54] However, she also states: 'acting "out of character" under the influence of alcohol is not merely the result of loosening the brakes, but rather it is a result of changes . . . in thought processes and behaviour.

---

47   ibid 344.
48   *R v Bree* [2007] EWCA Crim 256 [32].
49   ibid [34].
50   Wallerstein (n 3) 322–323, referring to Jesse Elvin, 'The Concept of Consent under the Sexual Offences Act 2003' (2008) 72 Journal of Criminal Law 519, 524; Jesse Elvin, 'Intoxication, Capacity to Consent, and the Sexual Offences Act 2003' (2008) 19 King's Law Journal 151, 152–153.
51   Wallerstein (n 3) 335.
52   ibid 332.
53   ibid.
54   ibid 333.

It is the alcohol that gives consent to intercourse and not the woman who has consumed it.'[55] Ultimately, Wallerstein's view seems to be that people who are acting 'out of character' because of intoxication are 'really drunk' and lack the capacity to consent even if they have knowledge and understanding of the proposed activity. But surely the issue is whether they consented as a matter of choice; it is very difficult to justify blurring the boundaries of capacity and argue for the expansion of legal presumptions of incapacity at precisely the same time as disability law is seeking to eliminate presumptions of incapacity from law.[56]

Wallerstein's argument contradicts the clear assertion of the right to make unwise decisions in both the Mental Capacity Act 2005 and human rights law. In *Ivison v UK*, the Commission found that even when a person is underage and vulnerable, their autonomy rights must be respected unless there is a real and immediate risk to their life or safety, for example from the criminal acts of a third party.[57] Thus the state does not owe a duty to take pre-emptive measure to prevent risks from materialising: 'although she was underage and thus vulnerable, this did not give the authorities carte blanche with regard to coercive or more draconian care measures. Considerations of her own individual autonomy cannot be excluded.'[58] A state will only clearly have a duty to protect a vulnerable person against risks which they have not chosen to run, and so the positive autonomy to run risks and make bad decisions generally outweighs the negative autonomy to be protected from harm. Thus, denying capacity on the basis of being 'really drunk' would raise major human rights concerns as a disproportionate measure with criminal sanctions attached. There are further unfortunate implications of Wallerstein's view – when both parties are really drunk, they may be found to have committed offences against each other, even if they do not see themselves as having been harmed in any way! Further, when only one party is really drunk and 'acting out of character', it is possible that this party may be liable as a secondary party for any offence committed by the other one.[59] This approach would also apply to non-sexual offences: eg under the 1861 Act.

These are not the only problems with Wallerstein's view; on the contrary, there are four other significant difficulties with it. First, the focus upon whether a party was so drunk that he or she acted out of character is of concern from a feminist perspective, since it suggests that the jury should routinely consider evidence about the complainant's sexual history where the complainant was intoxicated. The problem with this is that this evidence could be used to inappropriately discredit the complainant, since studies show that 'victim respectability is a critical variable'[60] and 'it has long been recognised that information about the victim's sexual history can have an impact on juror's decisions, undermining her credibility and leading to acquittal of the defendant'.[61] Secondly, it is not clear what harm Wallerstein is proposing to address. She claims that where the complainant is really drunk 'sexual intercourse degrades the victim and humiliates her as can be seen from accounts of such victims after they sober up (their perception and feeling of being raped)'.[62] However, she also says:

> What about the woman who on re-evaluation is happy with the consent she had given, even if this consent is invalid? If the above analysis is correct, rape has been committed;

---

55 ibid 334.
56 Examined in detail below at 45–48.
57 *Ivison v UK* Application no 39030/97, 16 April 2002.
58 ibid.
59 *R v Gnango* [2011] UKSC 59.
60 Jennifer Temkin and Barbara Krahé, *Sexual Assault and the Justice Gap* (Hart Publishing 2008) 45.
61 ibid.
62 Wallerstein (n 3) 338.

the woman was unable to consent. This is similar to the situation where a 13-year-old girl consents to sex with an adult and when confronted later on claims she is happy with her decision.[63]

This suggests that adults are similar to children in this context, in that they cannot necessarily determine what is in their best interests, and that their accounts are invalid if they are claiming to be happy with their drunken decisions. She acknowledges the argument that there is a distinction between adults and children in this context, and that others may argue that 'when an adult woman sobers up, she regains her full faculties and is best placed to judge if any harm was done to her'.[64] Nonetheless, she still seems to believe that adults who are happy with their drunken sexual decisions are victims, albeit victims who have a right to determine that a prosecution would be inappropriate: 'although a crime has been committed (ie she had been *wronged*), there is insufficient reason for the State to act against the will of the victim'.[65] An obvious problem with this reasoning is that it raises the question, how has a woman been wronged in this context, if she is happy with her decision? Unfortunately, Wallerstein does not address this important issue.

Another major problem with Wallerstein's position is that it is self-contradictory in places. She claims that really drunk people lose their brakes, yet she also asserts that 'Rejection while being drunk should be recognised as valid although the person lacks capacity to consent in similar situations'.[66] The difficulty here is that she does not explain how such rejection is possible if the complainant 'has lost her "brakes" and is unable to stop herself from acting out of character'.[67] She states that 'It is the alcohol that gives consent to intercourse',[68] but she also implies that alcohol may lead to rejection when she says that a drunken rejection should be recognised as a valid 'even if this rejection is driven by alcohol alone'.[69]

Despite the difficulties with Wallerstein's position, Georgina Firth agrees with her that 'the statement [in *Bree*] that "drunken consent is still consent", is too simplistic and is problematic for several reasons'.[70] Firth's view is that 'it could be argued that the court's focus on positive autonomy sends out the wrong message and fails to recognise the vulnerability of victims whose choices may be impaired by their alcohol intake'.[71] However, it is not clear to what extent Firth actually agrees with Wallerstein. Firth thinks that it is a myth that women 'become more sexually promiscuous when drunk',[72] whereas Wallerstein's analysis seems to be premised upon the belief that this is the case, since Wallerstein argues that 'really drunk' people have 'lost their brakes'. Firth claims that she agrees with Wallerstein that a definition of consent 'should take into account that heavy drinking can distort a person's decision-making to the extent that it negates her ability to give meaningful consent'.[73] However, Firth concludes: 'This would make clear to the jury that knowledge and understanding are integral to consent'.[74] This does not seem to be in line with Wallerstein's definition of capacity, since

---

63 ibid 336.
64 ibid.
65 ibid.
66 ibid.
67 ibid 330.
68 ibid 334.
69 ibid 336.
70 Firth (n 4) 111.
71 ibid 112.
72 ibid 113.
73 ibid 116.
74 ibid 116.

Wallerstein explicitly states that the definition of capacity has to be wider than this.[75] Rather, it seems to be almost identical to the published view of one of us,[76] notwithstanding the fact that Firth rejects this view:

> Elvin suggests that a possible definition could state that the complainant does not have the capacity to consent where her knowledge and understanding are so limited that she is not in a position to decide whether to agree. However, I would prefer a slightly wider definition which could more clearly encompass those who had been drinking heavily … namely victims who were so drunk that they were vomiting, and possibly unable to walk unaided and talk coherently.[77]

Firth's proposed definition of capacity would make it clear that those who are so drunk that they are vomiting and unable to walk unaided or talk coherently lack the capacity to consent. It appears that Firth would also introduce a rebuttable presumption of non-consent 'dealing with self-induced intoxication'.[78] However, all of this is compatible with the view that a complainant 'does not have the capacity to consent when his or her knowledge and understanding are so limited that he or she is not in a position to decide whether to agree'; ie Elvin's published view,[79] and the approach taken by the Mental Capacity Act 2005, and in the Court of Protection and criminal appeal cases cited above. Does the current law actually need to change in order to accomplish Firth and Wallerstein's goals? We would argue that the focus has been diverted wrongly from (absence of) consent to (absence of) capacity to consent. The legal issue in the relevant sexual offences is not whether a person was able to consent; it is whether they actually did consent, and whether the defendant lacked a reasonable belief in consent. We should concentrate efforts on a workable definition of consent rather than using capacity as a 'gatekeeper' that avoids the crucial legal questions. The presumptions in ss 75 and 76 of the Sexual Offences Act 2003 are about absence of consent and absence of reasonable belief in consent – they are not presumptions about capacity.

It seems reasonable to state that, where knowledge and understanding are concerned, 'it is the victim's state and not the means by which it is achieved that is important in determining the point at which consent is negated'.[80] However, as we shall see, there is an important limitation on such an argument, since it will conflict with disability and human rights law where the victim's 'state' includes a disability.

INTERNATIONAL HUMAN RIGHTS AND DISABILITY LAW

We have argued elsewhere in the context of the defence of insanity that some aspects of English criminal law's approach to issues of capacity require a rethink in order to comply with the UN Convention on the Rights of Persons with Disabilities (UNCRPD),[81] and that it would be unfortunate indeed to increase the criminal law's reliance on concepts of capacity at a time when human rights law is moving in the opposite direction; in that chapter we stated briefly that the case-law on capacity to consent raises serious human rights concerns.

---

75 Wallerstein (n 3) 332.
76 Elvin (n 50) 522.
77 Firth (n 4) referring to de Than Elvin (n 29) 155.
78 Firth (n 4) 118.
79 Elvin (n 50) 522.
80 Firth (n 4) 118.
81 De Than and Elvin (n 23).

The present chapter is an appropriate opportunity to examine such arguments in greater depth and detail, focusing upon capacity and consent as elements relevant to offences[82] and defences[83] in criminal law.

There is a growing view that capacity is a discriminatory concept that has no place in modern legal systems. It is necessary to distinguish mental capacity, which is the practical ability to make decisions, from legal capacity, which is the legal ability to exercise rights and to have one's actions recognised by law. Mental capacity is a very variable and subjective concept about which there is little agreement:[84] much time is spent in Court of Protection cases arguing over whether a person has sufficient cognitive abilities for English law to regard them as capable of making a decision, and many capacity decisions are reversed on appeal or show basic differences between medical and legal opinions on what capacity is.[85] What the law regards as an 'on–off switch' in reality fluctuates from day to day, mood to mood, and may depend as much on who is conducting the assessment as cognitive or psychosocial factors about the person being assessed. The consequences of a finding that a person lacks mental capacity to make a particular decision can be brutal: in the context of consent, the desire to protect them from possible sex offences may lead to them being put under 24-hour surveillance, and/or prevented from seeing a long-term partner.[86] Such consequences conflict directly with the clear requirements of Article 12 of the UNCRPD: a finding that a person's mental capacity is limited must never be used as a reason for denying them legal capacity; legal capacity includes the rights to give and to deny consent. As noted by the Committee on the Rights of Persons with Disabilities,[87] the scope and extent of the legal changes required by Article 12 of the UNCRPD have not been fully understood by signatory states: 'Indeed, there has been a general failure to understand that the human rights-based model of disability implies a shift from the substitute decision-making paradigm to one that is based on supported decision-making.'[88] In other words, all branches of law need to move away from the presumption that people with disabilities, whether physical or mental in nature, cannot make their own decisions, and towards making all possible efforts to support them in the decision-making that is their right. If it is possible via, for example, education or provision of information in formats suitable to a person's disability, to support them in making a decision, then there is a duty to do so under Article 10 of the ECHR, which combines with Article 12 of the UNCRPD to require far more efforts than are currently made at state level to provide support for decision-making for persons with disabilities. 'State parties must holistically

---

82　Such as sex offences and property offences.

83　The status of consent as a defence is unclear; for example, in relation to assault and battery, it has never been definitively stated whether consent prevents there being an *actus reus* or whether it operates as a defence, as the present authors have argued in their submission responding to Law Commission (n 36).

84　See Harry Kennedy, 'A General Theory of Mental Disorder and Consolidated Mental Disability Legislation: Commentary on the Mental Capacity and Guardianship Bill 2008' (2008) 14 Medico-Legal Journal of Ireland 51.

85　See for example *IM v LM and Liverpool CC* (n 26); *Derbyshire CC v AC, EC and LC* [2014] EWCOP 38.

86　See for example *A v H* [2012] EWHC 49, where an autistic woman was effectively banned from having sex by being put under 24/7 supervision.

87　General Comment No 1: Article 12: Equal recognition before the law, 11th sess, UN Doc CRPD/C/GC/1, 19 May 2014. <http://daccess-dds-ny.un.org/doc/UNDOC/GEN/G14/031/20/PDF/G1403120.pdf? OpenElement>accessed 29 October 2015.

88　ibid 3.

examine all areas of law to ensure that the right of persons with disabilities to legal capacity is not restricted on an unequal basis with others.'[89] The right to give consent for intimate relationships is specifically listed, as are other situations where consent is legally relevant.[90] The status of 'person with a disability' must never be used as grounds for denying the right to give consent for intimate relationships; English law does so routinely in relation to mental capacity, 'mental disorders' and to physical disabilities which affect communication. In order for the latter to be implemented in English law, many aspects of civil and criminal law and procedure would require substantial reform, and the criminal offences under discussion in this chapter do not comply with the requirements of Article 12. Hence the issue is, and should always be, whether a person has made a decision: if they have then the law should uphold it. If they have not, and they have a disability, then they must be supported in all possible ways towards making their own decision. When the impact of Article 12 is added to the relevant case-law on the ECHR, the urgency of a fundamental rethink becomes all the more pressing. Autonomy, dignity, independence, choice, the right to information that supports decision-making, and equality of everyone's rights, are themes that run throughout human rights law.

The right to consensual sexual expression in private between adults is clearly established as an aspect of Article 8 of the ECHR, the right to respect for private life, family life, home and correspondence. In a string of cases, the European Court of Human Rights has held that Article 8 protects sexual autonomy, dignity, forming and maintaining personal relationships and allowing them to develop normally. For example in *Pretty v UK*[91] the Court stated that 'Elements such as sexual life fall within the personal sphere protected by Article 8 . . . Article 8 also protects a right to personal development and the right to establish and develop relationships with other human beings and the outside world.' The rights protected go beyond sex lives, and include, essentially, a human right to have fun in a person's preferred ways, with others or alone, as long as they are not hurting others.[92] These rights may only be limited by the state if the state has a legitimate aim such as preventing crime or upholding the rights of others, and if the measures taken are a proportionate response to a pressing social need. In *ADT v UK* and *Dudgeon v UK* the Court stated that there would need to be very strong reasons to justify regulating consensual sexual acts (and other intimate acts) carried out in private.[93] Further, the state must take action to enable people to exercise their sexual autonomy rights, for example by passing laws or providing resources. Where existing legislation prevents a person from expressing themselves sexually, there may well be a violation of Article 8, as in *X v UK*.[94] So, it can now be said that there is an equal right for all adults to consensual sexual activity in private, including the right to choose what relationship their conduct has to reproduction, and whether it is linked to any relationship or intimacy. There are also similar rights to non-sexual fun. Hence the emphasis on capacity in English criminal law risks violating the sexual and non-sexual autonomy rights of people who are deemed to lack mental capacity, and then treated differently from others by the law.

The relationship between consent, capacity, education and information is also very important in terms of human rights and disability law. Article 10 of the ECHR protects freedom of expression rights and the public right to know; the latter includes the right to receive

---

89 ibid 7.
90 ibid 8.
91 Application No 2346/02, European Court of Human Rights, 29 April 2002.
92 *Laskey, Jaggard, and Brown v UK* (n 41).
93 European Court of Human Rights 21/7/2000 and European Court of Human Rights [1981] ECHR 5 respectively.
94 Case no 7215/75, European Court of Human Rights 1978.

information about sex, contraception and so on.[95] There is hence a strong argument of a duty on the state to provide education and support so that people can make their own decisions about their private lives. Given that in many cases capacity can be enhanced or created by education and information tailored to the needs of the individual recipient, Article 10 could be used to bolster the arguments for law reform and support decision-making to which we now turn under the United Nations Convention on the Rights of Persons with Disabilities.

But the human rights issues relevant to this chapter do not stop there. Some specific sexual offences deny the legal capacity of persons with disabilities, and hence directly conflict with Article 12 of the United Nations Convention on the Rights of Persons with Disabilities. Article 12(2) states that those with disabilities must be allowed to enjoy legal capacity on an equal basis with all others. According to Article 1, the meaning of 'persons with disabilities' includes 'those who have long-term physical, mental, intellectual or sensory impairments which in interaction with various barriers may hinder their full and effective participation in society on an equal basis with others'. Hence a criminal offence that treats a person differently because of their disability violates Article 12. It is indefensible in the twenty-first century to have criminal offences that violate both the autonomy rights of a person who consents to sexual activity and the UNCRPD. Yet a twenty-first century statute, the Sexual Offences Act 2003, does both. In the context of rape,[96] assault by penetration,[97] sexual assault,[98] and causing a person to engage in sexual activity without consent,[99] the evidential presumptions under s 75(2) apply. The effect of the evidential presumptions is that, if any of the fact patterns in s 75(2) occurs, then it is rebuttably presumed that the complainant did not consent, and that the defendant did not reasonably believe in consent.[100] Hence, it is presumed that a sex offence has occurred. One of the fact patterns relates specifically to physical disability: s 75(2)(e) applies the evidential presumptions where 'because of the complainant's physical disability, the complainant would not have been able at the time of the relevant act to communicate to the defendant whether the complainant consented'. Thus, it is presumed to be a sex offence against a person with a physical disability affecting communication[101] if they have sex with another person. This provision is fraught with difficulties from a human rights perspective. It obviously goes against the ethos of Article 12 of the UNCRPD, as interpreted by the UN High Commissioner above; it places a burden on a person with such a physical disability in relation to sexual activity and sexual expression with others, potentially criminalising loving behaviour; it may lead to intrusive questioning of people who clearly have mental capacity to consent to sexual activity, and such questioning would appear to violate the right to respect for private life and human dignity. Take a scenario as an example: Alfred suffers from otosclerosis, a disease of the ear bones. As a result, he is now severely deaf in both ears and experiences vertigo, but he is still articulate enough to make his living as a

---

95 *Open Door and Dublin Well Woman v Ireland*, (14234/88) [1992] ECHR 68 (29 October 1992).
96 Sexual Offences Act 2003, s 1.
97 ibid, s 2.
98 ibid, s 3.
99 ibid, s 4.
100 ibid, s 75(1): 'the complainant is to be taken not to have consented to the relevant act unless sufficient evidence is adduced to raise an issue as to whether he consented, and the defendant is to be taken not to have reasonably believed that the complainant consented unless sufficient evidence is adduced to raise an issue as to whether he reasonably believed it'.
101 Which will presumably include motor disabilities, since consent or its absence may be communicated in many ways. This would fit the approach taken by Toulson J in *Hulme v DPP* [2006] EWHC 1347 (Admin): a person is unable to communicate a choice if they are physically able to speak but unable to effectively do so in the way that someone of his age and not suffering from his disabilities would have done in similar circumstances. This is a logical interpretation, but one which clashes with disability rights law.

motivational speaker. D, who knows of Alfred's disability in general terms, makes a sexual suggestion to him at the same time as touching his hip. D's conduct is presumed to be sexual assault under s 3, and it is presumed that D has the *mens rea* and Alfred does not consent to the touching. The law does not first seek his opinion on the matter before changing the legal nature of his behaviour and relationships, which is an insult to his sexual autonomy. To avoid that changed legal status, he must communicate consent expressly, with evidence; there is no such burden on people who lack disabilities that affect communication. The same legal presumptions would apply where D silently approached and kissed a blind person, if D was aware of this person's condition, on the basis that the blind person would not be able to reject the proposed kiss in advance. But nobody routinely checks the capacity (or alcohol levels) of adults who are about to embark upon sexual encounters; it is only people with disabilities or in whom a capacity issue is suspected, who are subjected to testing and evaluation. Yet much sexual behaviour is not a methodically pre-planned process: it is instinctive, and, as noted by the Court of Appeal in *IM v LM*, 'the notional decision-making process attributed to the protected person with regard to consent to sexual relations should not become divorced from the actual decision-making process carried out in that regard on a daily basis by persons of full capacity'.[102] The process in question is 'largely visceral rather than cerebral, owing more to instinct and emotion than to analysis'.[103] As seen in the quote from *TZ* that introduced this chapter, there are clear dangers in raising the cognitive and/or communicative standards for capacity. It matters not that a criminal prosecution is unlikely in such a scenario; all persons with disabilities must be able to enjoy legal capacity, including capacity to consent to sexual activity, on an equal basis with others, which is plainly absent from s 75(2)(e). There are also other scenarios where the risk of criminal prosecution is real, and is having a chilling effect upon the human rights of persons with disabilities: the law does not currently allow any workable method by which deaf-blind adults may be given sex education, since physical contact would be required in contravention of (eg) s 3 of the 2003 Act, and that is a situation crying out for reform. We hence propose a simple amendment that would remove all the above objections: the deletion of 'because of the complainant's physical disability' from s 75(2)(e). The provision would then be disability-neutral, as are the other five fact patterns that lead to rebuttable presumptions in the remainder of s 75(2).

But other sexual offences discriminate on an even more fundamental level. Sections 30–32 of the 2003 Act are offences where the victim is a person with a mental disorder impeding choice. The use of the phrase 'mental disorder' is a giveaway that these offences do not operate in tandem with contemporary medical professional diagnoses, since it adopts the meaning from s 1 of the Mental Health Act 1983 'any disorder or disability of the mind'. A mental disorder impeding choice is one which leads to the complainant being likely to be unable to refuse the sexual activity, either by lacking the capacity to choose whether to be involved in the sexual activity or by being unable to communicate refusal.[104] These offences are protective in nature, and of course there is a human rights-based duty to protect vulnerable persons from imminent danger. Such a duty to protect will, by its nature, run headlong into the sexual autonomy rights of people with mental disabilities. However, there is no pressing need for these offences, since a person who is unable to choose whether to be involved in sexual behaviour does not consent within the general definition under s 74 of the 2003 Act. If these offences were deleted from the 2003 Act in order to comply with Article 12 of the UNCRPD, there does not appear to be anyone whose behaviour would be decriminalised in a manner that would violate C's

---

102 Kennedy (n 84) *IM v LM and Liverpool CC* (n 26) [80].
103 ibid [81].
104 See, ss 30(2), 31(2) and 32(2) of the Sexual Offences Act 2003 for an even wordier explanation.

rights. Some of the other sexual offences involving persons with mental disorders, although well-intentioned from a protective or safeguarding perspective, inhibit the Article 8 ECHR right to sexual expression of persons with disabilities, as well as conflicting with Article 12 of the UNCRPD. For example, ss 38–41 create a series of offences where a care-worker engages in sexual activity with,[105] or incites or causes sexual activity by,[106] or commits sexual activity in the presence of,[107] or causes the watching a sexual act by,[108] a person with a mental disorder. These offences are committed regardless of consent and capacity to consent; hence a consenting act between adults with mental capacity is criminalised because one of them has a disability which may have no effect whatsoever on capacity and consent. There are clear issues with both Article 8 of the ECHR and Article 12 of the UNCRPD in that respect. Some of these offences[109] potentially criminalise behaviour such as a care-worker arranging for a consenting sex worker, or an existing partner, to visit a person in their care, at the instigation of the person whom the law sees as a victim. They also potentially criminalise sex education for people with mental disabilities who live in care-homes; s 73 of the Act provides a form of sex education defence to various offences under the Act, but it only applies where the victim is a child under 16. The reality is that many people with disabilities do not receive adequate sex education as children, since they fall outside the scope of compulsory sex education in schools. To criminalise the provision of sex education for adults clearly goes against the human rights imperatives discussed above and is surely not what Parliament intended, or would have intended had it given thought to the matter. In short, these offences treat people differently because of their disabilities, and hence violate the (directly enforceable) Article 8 ECHR rights to sexual expression and information, and the (not yet directly enforceable, but international pressure is mounting) requirement of universal legal capacity under Article 12 of the UNCRPD.

REFORM

We would like to conclude this chapter by proposing reforms to address the concerns that it has raised and discussed. It is not possible to reconcile all the above needs for reform with a single proposal; rather a suite of changes is necessary in order to give effect to the requirements of human rights and disability law, and to find a better mechanism for dealing with 'drunken consent'. Specific references to disability or capacity in the 2003 Act should be removed, on the grounds discussed above in relation to the UNCRPD and the ECHR; this would affect not only the communication-related presumption in s 75(2)(f) but also the definition of consent in s 74 and would require the abolition of the specific 'mental disorder' offences discussed above. There is no imperative to reform the offences which specify children as victims, since being a child is not a disability, it is a universal condition.

Moving on to the effects of intoxication, Wallerstein's and Firth's arguments about the unreality of consent when C is very drunk could be met by a very different reform from those that they propose: a higher or more detailed requirement for consent, while removing the reference to capacity from s 74. Rather than stating that being very drunk means that a person is incapable of making a decision, we could require more evidence as to a decision having been made. Although references to capacity in Wallerstein's and Firth's proposals do not raise the Article 12 UNCRPD issue directly, since being very drunk is not a disability, they do conflict

---

105   ibid, s 38.
106   ibid, s 39.
107   ibid, s 40.
108   ibid, s 41.
109   ss 38 and 39 of the Sexual Offences Act 2003 do not require acts to be done for the purpose of D's sexual gratification; ss 40 and 41 do.

with it indirectly in two separate ways. Firstly, alcoholics will be 'persons with a disability' under Article 12, although not under the Equality Act 2010; and, secondly, as noted in the quote that began this chapter, raising the standard for capacity risks discriminating against people with disabilities indirectly, since they may find it a harder test to satisfy than others. We would argue that, in situations such as those that Wallerstein and Firth are discussing, an affirmative consent definition poses far fewer problems than adding new forms of legal incapacity. Part of California's affirmative consent bill for college campuses,[110] 2013–14, could be inspiration for a more rights-compliant definition of consent to sex than the sum total of ss 74, 75 and 76 of the Sexual Offences Act 2003. According to the Bill:

> 'Affirmative consent' means affirmative, conscious, and voluntary agreement to engage in sexual activity. It is the responsibility of each person involved in the sexual activity to ensure that he or she has the affirmative consent of the other or others to engage in the sexual activity. Lack of protest or resistance does not mean consent, nor does silence mean consent. Affirmative consent must be ongoing throughout a sexual activity and can be revoked at any time. The existence of a dating relationship between the persons involved, or the fact of past sexual relations between them, should never by itself be assumed to be an indicator of consent.[111]

This would meet the concerns about drunken 'consent', since in the situations used as examples by Firth above, the affirmative consent standard would not be met. The issue is correctly labelled as one of voluntariness and the expectation of evidence that D checked at every relevant stage for consent, not one of capacity. In at least some situations, a case could be made for going further with the expectations of consent: an 'enthusiastic consent' threshold could apply to any situations where serious physical or psychiatric harm was likely as a result of D's actions. Hence the controversial line of cases since *Brown* would have a single coherent policy to apply, and the equally controversial line of cases on 'deemed consent'[112] would have a different resolution. Jaclyn Friedman's explanation of enthusiastic consent is framed in terms of consent to sex, but could equally be applied to offences against the person or to those property transactions where consent is relevant. 'Consent isn't a question. It's a state. If, instead of lovers, the two of you were synchronized swimmers, consent would be the water. It's not enough to jump in, get wet and climb out – if you want to swim, you have to be in the water continually. And if you want to have sex, you have to be continually in a state of enthusiastic consent with your partner.'[113] Hence when an activity is initiated by an adult C, who remains enthusiastic throughout, their consent should be valid.[114] The simple statement in the last sentence would require substantial changes of law and practice throughout criminal and civil law in relation to capacity and consent. But substantial changes are necessary if English law is to do more than pay lip-service to the UNCRPD and related human rights standards.

---

110 Senate Bill No 967, 'Student Safety: Sexual Assault' (2013–14).

111 ibid.

112 Eg *Jones* (1986) 83 Cr App R 375; *Aitken* [1992] 1 WLR 1066; *Richardson and Irwin* [1999] CA; see the discussion throughout Elliott and de Than (n 5).

113 Jaclyn Friedman, blogpost, <http://amplifyyourvoice.org/u/Yes_Means_Yes> accessed 29 October 2015. See further Jaclyn Friedman and Jessica Valenti, *Yes Means Yes: Visions of Female Sexual Power and a World Without Rape* (Seal Press 2009).

114 Since enthusiastic consent is an enhanced version of affirmative consent, requiring a free and voluntary affirmative consent, neither form will exist where C has been deceived as to the nature of the activity, the identity of D or any other relevant factor.

4

Attacks on the mind and the legal limits of the seduction industry

Gavin Byrne and John Child*

The seduction industry aims to teach men how to be more successful at attracting women. It is global and highly lucrative. The ultimate aims of its clients vary. Some wish to find a partner for a long-term and monogamous relationship, others simply wish to have sex with as many women as possible. A wide variety of products are available to assist in these goals. A range of handbooks exist; some are bestselling and a part of mainstream culture. It is not at all unusual to see the authors of these books interviewed on daytime or primetime television. One even had his own reality television show in which contestants were coached in 'the art of the pick-up' on VH-1.[1] For the more serious aspiring Casanovas, one could attend a seminar, pursue an online course, or even sign up for one-to-one 'in-field training' from a self-styled 'pick-up artist' or PUA: Ross Jeffries, discussed below, charges $24,997 for seven days of private tuition.

In such a competitive market and with so much at stake, it is unsurprising that there should be a plethora of different approaches to seduction on offer. In addition, each of these approaches tackles the issue in minute detail, addressing different parts of social interaction. For our purposes, we can divide seduction training into two components.

The first component might be best described as focusing on *what women want*. This aspect teaches men how to dress, groom, behave and speak in a way that is considered desirable. Lists of ice-breakers, or 'openers', are provided as a way of approaching women for the first time. There are detailed strategies provided for how to deal with common obstacles such as a rival suitor or an overprotective friend. There are also step-by-step instructions on how to tell if a woman is interested, what to do if she is, and even how to exit with good grace if she is not.

A second component to the seduction industry might be best described as *making women want*. Our focus in this chapter will be this, second, aspect, and how it relates to programmed consent. By this we mean 'consent' to sexual activity gained through techniques such as neuro-linguistic programming (NLP) and hypnosis. Such techniques have been developed

* We would like to thank Robin Pickard for his research assistance. We would also like to thank Dr Tanya Palmer, Professor Jo Bridgeman and Dr Hans Crombag for their helpful comments. The usual disclaimer applies.

1 *The Pick Up Artist* (3Ball Productions) was hosted by Erik Von Markovic, aka 'Mystery'. It ran for two seasons from 2007 to 2008.

(in the context of seduction) and marketed by PUAs such as Ross Jefferies,[2] as a means to control the sexual desires of women and to program their sexual consent.[3] In this way, such techniques have the potential to undermine (or at least attempt to undermine) a woman's mental and sexual autonomy.

In spite of the prevalence of the seduction industry in mainstream culture, and despite the potential gravity of the harms risked, these issues are yet to receive extensive legal attention. In this chapter, we analyse techniques of programmed consent over three parts. In Part A we discuss attacks on the mind in general terms, exploring the extent to which the law protects against mental manipulations. In Part B we focus on the seduction industry, and the detail of the claims made about their techniques. Finally, in Part C, we discuss how the current law (in the sexual context at least) could be used to protect victims' mental integrity, whether the techniques attempted for programming consent are successful or not.

PART A. ATTACKS ON THE MIND

The most well-known (and, arguably, the most serious) subset of sexual offences depend in very large part upon demonstrating the non-consent of a victim (V) to sexual activity with (or under the control of) a defendant (D).[4] The central role of V's non-consent in such cases has been described as a form of 'moral-magic',[5] transforming the individual and social good of consensual sexual activity into a serious criminal wrong.[6] However, despite the vital role of consent within such offences, the legal problems encountered within its definition and application are depressingly familiar. Thus, it is important to place our current discussion of programmed consent within this literature.

The focus of this chapter, programmed consent, engages with the potential for an apparent communication of consent to be deemed legally ineffective. Within the current literature, this has been explored in relation to two main areas. First, we have cases where V lacks the capacity to consent because she is unable to make a reasoned decision (eg due to mental illness).[7] Secondly, we have cases where V has capacity to consent, but her apparent consent is invalid because it is the product of fraud or duress.[8] Both of these areas have been highly contested academically and in the courts.[9] However, although there is some overlap between our current investigation and both of these areas, the potential for programmed consent does not fit neatly into either category: a programmed V *may* lack capacity to consent, but this is not due

---

2 Ross Jeffries, *Secrets of Speed Seduction® Mastery: How to Master the Art and Science of Getting Any Woman into Bed in 20 Minutes or Less* (Ghita Services Inc. 2010); Ross Jeffries, *How to Get the Women You Desire into Bed* (Jefferies Publishing 1992).

3 Almost all sexual offences are gender-neutral, both in terms of defendant and victim. The seduction industry is aimed squarely at a male audience, so this chapter employs male pronouns for defendants and female pronouns for victims.

4 Sexual Offences Act 2003, ss 1–4.

5 Heidi Hurd, 'The moral magic of consent' [1996] Legal Theory 121.

6 For an alternative view, contending that all sexual penetration is *prima facie* wrongful, see Michelle Madden Dempsey and Jonathan Herring, 'Why sexual penetration requires justification (2007) 27(3) Oxford Journal of Legal Studies 467.

7 Where D lacks the capacity to choose to consent, any expression of consent will be legally ineffective and will be caught within the *actus reus* of ss 1–4 of the Sexual Offences Act 2003. In practice, however, ss 30–37 are more likely to be charged.

8 The most extreme cases in this category are covered by conclusive presumptions of non-consent (Sexual Offences Act 2003, s 76) and evidential presumptions (Sexual Offences Act 2003, s 75).

9 See, for example, the recent flurry of cases concerning consent gained by deception. Karl Laird, 'Rapist or Rogue? Deception, Consent and The Sexual Offences Act 2003' (2014) Criminal Law Review 492.

to any mental illness or naturally occurring infliction; she *may* have been unduly manipulated, but this will not necessarily involve fraud or duress. It is therefore important to analyse the legal position of programmed consent on its own merits.

ATTACKS ON THE MIND AND THE CRIMINAL LAW

There has been a long history of extreme claims being made about the power of techniques such as NLP, subliminal or non-conscious priming and persuasion, hypnotism, and so on. However, in almost every case such claims have been discredited as outright hoaxes and/or by failures to replicate their (ostensibly) supportive experimental evidence under controlled laboratory conditions.[10] Notwithstanding, a lot of money has been spent by people who want to believe that techniques of this kind can help them quit smoking or to be more successful in their lives.

The law has shown a clear scepticism whether there is a genuine need for protection in this area. There has been civil regulation, but an absence of criminal law.[11] However, there have been occasions, particularly in relation to hypnosis, where exaggerated claims have triggered a criminal law response. We see this, for example, in the current automatism rules where hypnotic suggestion or trance is almost universally included as a paradigm of involuntariness, allowing the drone-like subject of hypnosis to avoid liability for any crimes committed whilst under the power of the hypnotist.[12] The problem here is not the fact of a legal response, but rather the isolation of that response to deal exclusively with an exaggerated stereotype of hypnosis,[13] leading to its lack of use in practice.[14] Where a subject is hypnotised, but not rendered into a trance, their legal position is uncertain.

Criminal law's scepticism concerning claims about mind intervention and control is also shared within the psychology literature. However, crucially, the latter does not adopt the all-or-nothing approach we see in the law. Rather, despite recognising the unreliability of many of the more extreme claims,[15] and despite difficulties in methodology[16] (and ethics[17]) when

---

10   See, for example, James Vicary's claims in 1957 to have increased food and drink sales in a local cinema through subliminal persuasion. Erin Strahan et al, 'Subliminal priming and persuasion: Striking while the iron is hot' (2002) Journal of Experimental Social Psychology 556. More generally, see Stéphane Doyen et al, 'Behavioural priming: It's all in the mind, but whose mind?' (2012) 7(1) PLOS ONE; Dermot Lynott et al, 'Replication of "Experiencing physical warmth promotes interpersonal warmth"' (2014) 45 Social Psychology 216; Anil Seth et al, 'Measuring consciousness: relating behavioural and neurophysiological approaches' (2008) Trends in Cognitive Sciences 314.

11   The Hypnotism Act 1925, for example, simply deals with the licensing of venues for hypnotism performances. For the regulation of subliminal messages, see Timothy Morton, 'From the sublime to the ridiculous: hidden messages in computer games under English law' (1997) Computer and Telecommunications Law Review 49.

12   *R v Coley* [2013] EWCA Crim 223, [19]–[22]. See also the US Model Penal Code, 2.01(2)(c).

13   Graham Wagstaff, 'Hypnosis and the law: Examining the stereotypes' (2008) Criminal Justice and Behaviour 1277.

14   In their recent review of automatism the Law Commission has maintained references to hypnotism as a paradigm of automatism, but their consultation reveals only a single case where hypnotism was raised in this way (and this was unsuccessful). Law Commission, *Insanity and Automatism: A Discussion Paper* (2013) [B.165].

15   Wagstaff (n 13).

16   Anil Seth et al, 'Measuring consciousness: relating behavioural and neurophysiological approaches' (2008) Trends in Cognitive Sciences 314.

17   William Coe et al, 'Experimental and ethical problems of evaluating the influence of hypnosis in antisocial conduct' (1973) Journal of Abnormal Psychology 476.

it comes to testing those claims, there is a general consensus that various mind intervention techniques *do* have an impact upon the practical reasoning of a subject. The content of this consensus is rather modest. Subliminal priming can enhance or consolidate wants that are already apparent, but does not appear capable of controlling the actions of a subject;[18] hypnosis shows effects on a subject's frontal lobe, impacting their capacity to engage in critical thinking, but does not lead to uncontrolled movement;[19] and so on. Despite their relative modesty, where such techniques are employed without the authorisation of V, they still represent a threat to individual autonomy, a threat that warrants the attention of the criminal law.

Another common theme within the psychology and neuroscience literature is the understanding that techniques for mental intervention and control will become increasingly effective in the future, and a concern about where this might lead. The refinement of existing techniques and/or development of new techniques involving electronic, genetic and/or pharmacology-induced stimulation of select regions of the brain at cellular or even molecular levels holds the potential for much more precise and complete control in the future.[20] There has also been (and is likely to be) similar progress in the testing used for understanding what type and degree of intervention has taken place.[21] The progress in psychology in this area (both current and future) is often accompanied by concern, precisely because of the lack of legal protection. This includes the issue under discussion pertaining to programmed sexual consent, but extends to the potential for techniques of mental intervention and control to be used in unethical advertising, and even political brainwashing.[22] In this way, the case for increased protection through the criminal law is even more apparent, and has been acted upon in some other jurisdictions.[23]

It has been contended that the criminal law in this jurisdiction should recognise a specific right to mental self-determination, and create specific criminal offences to protect it. In a wide-ranging paper by Bublitz and Merkel in 2014, the case for offences of this kind is made convincingly.[24] The authors highlight a range of ways in which mental intervention is currently possible and/or is likely to become possible in the future, including the use of various drugs (eg causing hunger or thirst outside a restaurant), subliminal priming, electronic brain stimulation, and so on. Stressing the fundamental need for protection, they state:

> Mental self-determination is not just a right granted (or denied) by legal orders. It is among the basic assumptions on which liberal legal orders are built.[25]

---

18 Strahan et al (n 10) 566.

19 John Gruzelier, 'Redefining hypnosis: Theory, methods, and integration' (2000) Contemporary Hypnosis 51.

20 Steven Krasner, 'Behaviour control and social responsibility' (1962) American Psychologist 199, 201–2; Herbert Kelman, 'Manipulation of human behaviour: An ethical dilemma for the social scientist' (1965) Journal of Social Issues 31; Nicole Vincent, 'Neurolaw and direct brain interventions' (2014) Criminal Law and Philosophy 43.

21 Anil Seth et al, 'Measuring consciousness: relating behavioural and neurophysiological approaches' (2008) 12(8) Trends in Cognitive Sciences 314.

22 Kelman, (n 20); Jan Kristoph Bublitz and Reinhard Merkel, 'Crimes against minds: On mental manipulations, harms and a human right to mental self-determination' (2014) 8(1) Criminal Law and Philosophy 51.

23 For example, the French offence of Abuse of Ignorance or Weakness: Article 223–15–2.

24 Bublitz and Merkel (n 22). This article was published within a special issue of *Criminal Law and Philosophy* exploring the legal implications of mental interventions. The other papers are not directly relevant to the current discussion, but provide an interesting view of the (potential) future in this area.

25 ibid 62.

Beyond the general support within their paper for criminalising attacks on the minds of others, Bublitz and Merkel also highlight a useful distinction between direct and indirect brain intervention. Direct brain interventions are those which bypass V's thought processes entirely and work directly upon the physiology of the brain. Examples of this include the use of mind-altering drugs, surgical or electronic stimulation of the brain, and so on. Where D directly attacks the mind of V in this manner, the case for criminalisation is relatively straightforward: although V *may* not have suffered physical injury, their mental self-determination has been totally bypassed.[26] Direct interventions of this kind are peripheral to the focus of this chapter (ie the methods of programmed consent employed by PUAs), but we would certainly echo Bublitz and Merkel's conclusions that criminal offences should be put in place to protect victims from this form of intervention.

More relevant to our discussion is the potential criminalisation of indirect (or socially reinforced[27]) interventions. This category includes NLP, subliminal priming and hypnosis. Indirect attacks aim to impact V's thought processes, but without physical or chemical intervention on the brain itself. In many ways indirect attacks of this kind are indistinguishable from direct attacks: their engagement with V's critical faculties may be minimal (eg with V's unconscious mind only), and the outcome impacts upon V may be exactly the same.[28] Moreover, unless one takes a dualist stance on mind-brain relations, indirect interventions are also expected to alter biological processes, blurring the line between direct and indirect interventions even further. However, as Bublitz and Merkel highlight,[29] the criminalisation of indirect mind interventions would require additional elements within the construction of a crime. This is because, once we accept that interventions of this kind are not likely to result in automatism in V, and once we instead focus on more limited forms of control or manipulation, our indirect attack offence risks the criminalisation of 'legitimate' forms of manipulation such as advertising, and even political or religious discourse. Indeed, any interaction between human beings is capable of impacting their future behaviour and choices. Any new offence would therefore have to include an additional normative filter, requiring *undue* or *improper* intervention for example.[30]

PROGRAMMED SEDUCTION

Having discussed mental interventions and criminalisation in general terms, it is now useful to focus on the subset of attacks most relevant to this chapter: programmed consent. Whilst this area is not discussed within Bublitz and Merkel's paper, we believe that it warrants particular attention for three main reasons. First, unlike many of the more theoretical attacks discussed above, the seduction industry shows us that men are *currently* attempting techniques for manipulating and programming consent. We discuss the specifics of this in Part B below. Secondly, although psychology literature challenges the stereotype that hypnosis leads to a subject's automatic (entranced) obedience, it does support the idea that such techniques can disrupt V's reasoning processes. Thus, the particular dynamics between a PUA and his so-called 'target', combining hypnosis and other intervention techniques with assertive and sexually confident interaction, provides the ideal setting for such techniques to

---

26 ibid 69, 73.
27 Term employed in Krasner (n 20) 199.
28 Vincent (n 20) 46.
29 Bublitz and Merkel (n 22) 69–70.
30 ibid 70–75.

be most effective.[31] Thirdly, whereas Bublitz and Merkel lament the lack of criminal law protection and criticise the criminal law's focus on body rather than brain, the sexual offences are notable for not conforming to this general rule. This final point requires some unpacking.

Unlike most other non-fatal offences against the person, sexual offences are not defined in relation to physical harms suffered by V. Rather, as we highlighted above, the central wrong within offences of rape (s 1, Sexual Offences Act 2003), assault by penetration (s 2, Sexual Offences Act 2003), sexual assault (s 3, Sexual Offences Act 2003), and causing a person to engage in sexual activity (s 4, Sexual Offences Act 2003), is the fact that D's conduct is not consented to by V. Our focus for these offences, therefore, is the *mind* of the victim. Of course this has not always been true, and older cases have tended to conflate questions of non-consent with physical displays of resistance, but the focus of the current law on V's mental state is now clear.[32] Consent is defined in s 74 of the Sexual Offences Act 2003: 'a person consents if [s]he agrees by choice, and has the freedom and capacity to make that choice'.

The focus within this definition on 'choice', 'freedom', and 'capacity', provides a potential for legal protection of the mind, a potential that is absent from almost all other areas of criminal law.[33] Where V's choice to consent is programmed by another, it is important to ask whether such intervention undermines V's freedom and capacity to choose, even where this control is not complete.[34]

We return to the discussion of sexual offences and consent in Part C. It is in this part that we explore the potential application of these offences to PUAs who attack (or attempt to attack) V's freedom and capacity to choose.

PART B. THE SEDUCTION INDUSTRY

The part of the seduction industry relevant to this chapter suggests that it is possible to manipulate (and thus program) a woman's emotions and desires, through a variety of techniques, with the explicit and sole aim that she will 'want' to have intercourse with the practitioner of these techniques. These aspects are based upon NLP in particular, which is heavily influenced by Milton Erickson's pioneering work in the use of hypnosis in therapy. As the name suggests, neuro-linguistic programming purports to program (or control) thought processes, via speech. It is described as a form of 'hypnopsychology', and it was first popularised as a means of self-help in the 1970s. NLP claims that it is possible to make a person more assertive, confident and better at communication by programming one's own brain (or that of a subject in therapy) to respond in positive ways emotionally to various words.

---

31 Wagstaff (n 13) 1280.

32 *R v McFall* [1994] CrimLR 226; *R v Malone* [1998] All ER 176. Ian Leader-Elliott & Ngaire Naffine, 'Wittgenstein, rape law and the language games of consent' (2000) Monash University Law Review 48.

33 In fact, this area has attracted feminist critiques that it is *too* concerned with the mental and not with the body. For example, Nicola Lacey, 'Unspeakable subjects, impossible rights: Sexuality, integrity and criminal law' (1997) Women: A Cultural Review 143.

34 Despite a number of conclusive and evidential presumptions of non-consent within The Sexual Offences Act 2003, and despite the focus of consent on the mind of V, none of these presumptions apply straightforwardly to attacks on V's mind. The closest we have is an evidential presumption set out in, s 75(2)(f) of the Act relating to the non-consensual drugging of V. However, this presumption is not based on the drugs impact on V's mind, but rather on its potential for stupefying V or enabling D to overpower her. It is unclear why this presumption was isolated to the physical impacts of the drug rather than its mental impacts, but this is certainly an area that could be usefully reformed in the future to increase the protection of V's freedom to choose.

When NLP became popularised, industry was quick to pounce. If it is possible to program a desired emotional response into one's audience, there are clear advantages in sales, marketing, customer service, and contract negotiation. Even if the term itself has not been used, or has largely died out, many leading brands and industries have coached versions of these techniques as part of staff training.[35] NLP itself is a multi-billion dollar industry, in spite of persistent academic and popular scepticism. The NLP academy claims to have trained over 50,000 people worldwide in these techniques and a core skills diploma can be yours for £1,999. So-called 'life-coaching' and a plethora of guides and techniques to self-improvement, from quitting smoking to conquering phobias, have their roots in NLP.

The modern seduction industry was born when Ross Jeffries first saw the possibilities in NLP for becoming more successful with women. A central idea in seduction techniques that are based on NLP is that a man can program 'any woman' to wish to have sex with him, simply through the power of his voice and words, within 'twenty minutes or less' of meeting her.[36] It is claimed that one can use NLP to bypass the part of a woman's brain that deals with rational decision-making, logic and resistance to suggestion, and directly appeal to the subconscious, emotional parts of the brain. One can thereby program the responses that one wishes to elicit. It is said that by putting a woman into a 'trance' state in this way, '[i]nstead of dates that end up with a polite peck on the cheek, you'll end up taking it as far as you want to go, regardless of how the woman felt about you before you used these techniques on her'.[37]

ROSS JEFFRIES AND NEURO-LINGUISTIC PROGRAMMING

If it really is possible to bypass conscious decision-making on the part of a woman, this sounds a lot like bypassing consent itself. Indeed, in a chapter titled 'How to use hypnosis to get your date into the sack', Jeffries wrote the following in 1988:

> One last caution before I lay out this technology. In some states, rape is defined as 'intercourse of a woman, by a man, by force, threat of force, or OTHERWISE WITHOUT CONSENT'. In some states, if you get the date drunk, and fuck her while she's passed out, you could find yourself facing a rape rap. Likewise for hypnosis. I am not an attorney, and am not giving you legal advice, but I warn you here and now of the possible consequences and am not about to be held responsible if you get slapped with charges. YOU USE THESE METHODS AT YOUR OWN RISK (And I wouldn't have to give this disclaimer/warning if these methods did not work as well as they do).[38]
>
> *(emphasis in the original)*

Later in the same chapter, he talks of how to 'bypass all of a woman's conscious resistance to screwing you'.[39] In the following chapter he opens with the claim that 'we have all heard the nonsense about how "no means no"'.[40]

---

35 BMW, Diners Club, American Express and Fiat have each used NLP as part of staff training.
36 This claim comes from the subtitle in Jeffries' *Secrets of Speed Seduction* (n 2). A huge caveat must be applied; the seduction industry is rife with outlandish claims about what various techniques can do. It is beyond the scope of this paper to address whether NLP actually works.
37 Jeffries (n 2) 59.
38 ibid.
39 ibid 60.
40 ibid 71.

It should be noted at this point that Jeffries has distanced himself from that particular publication on the basis that it does not reflect 'who he is now'. He has even attempted to prevent further publication. Jeffries' personal rejection of this early, slender volume is irrelevant to our investigation for two reasons. First, the 'technology' referred to, above, is still at the very core of his Speed Seduction® technique, that he continues to teach and that has spawned hundreds of imitators. He has no qualms with using testimonials as to the successful application of his earlier work in order to promote later publications. The more recently published *Secrets of Speed Seduction® Mastery* contains a watered down, more vague disclaimer at the start for any actions by those that have learned this method.[41] Jeffries' recantation appears to be limited to some of the coarse vocabulary used; he no longer refers to himself as 'the guru of gash' and his website encourages 'respect for yourself and the women you enjoy', though there remains plenty of unfortunate language when one delves deeper.[42] Secondly, and much more importantly, we are not targeting Jeffries individually. Jeffries is 'the undisputed father of modern seduction'.[43] Many have earned more money or become more famous, but no pick-up artist has been anything like as influential. The self-published *How To Get The Women You Desire Into Bed* has been referred to as the Bible of the seduction industry. Every modern course in the industry borrows at least some of these techniques and our concern is with this element of the broader industry, rather than a witch-hunt of its pioneer.

Not all NLP-based aspects of the seduction industry are part of our investigation. Much of this approach focuses on self-improvement in order to portray confidence, communicate more effectively and overcome common anxieties involved in approaching women or asking someone out on a date. Instead we will focus on those techniques that are said to use hypnosis as a means of bypassing conscious decision-making and generating sexual arousal. In this regard, there are three key steps. These are likely to each be used more than once in the course of a 'seduction', and their order might vary depending on the circumstances. In what follows we provide the basics, while trying to avoid some of the nuances and more complicated jargon.

1. Eliciting the preferred representational system

A fundamental notion in NLP is that we each have different 'maps' for understanding and experiencing the 'terrain' of the real world that we encounter. Each person's map is different, but we each have a preferred representational system. Some prefer to experience and remember things visually, some orally, some aurally and others kinetically (through touch). In NLP-based seduction techniques, it is vital to identify the preferred representational system of the woman in question, in order to unlock her sub-conscious mind. One way of doing this is to engage the woman in a conversation about some pleasant, ideally 'exciting', memory. Jeffries claimed at one point that 'nine times out of ten', if you ask a woman to tell you about something exciting that has happened to her and use the correct tone of voice, the story will be an erotic one. This claim may seem dubious, but it need not be true. Something as simple and innocuous as an enjoyable vacation would work. As the woman recounts this story, her preferred representational system should become clear, but the man should ask questions that will help in its discovery. So if a woman describes a beach holiday, for example, the man should

---

41 Jeffries, *Secrets of Speed Seduction* (n 2) i.
42 Success story videos on the site include titles such as 'From rock bottom to moist pink abundance' and '51 Year Old Man Bangs over 90 Chicks', see <http://www.seduction.com/wallofproof/> accessed 2 August 2015.
43 Neil Strauss, *The Game: Penetrating the Secret Society of Pick Up Artists* (Regan Books 2005) 38.

ask questions about which feelings or sensations she particularly enjoyed. If she responds by talking about the feeling of warmth on her skin and the sand beneath her feet, her preferred representational system is kinetic. On the other hand, if she talks about the sight of sunshine glistening on the ocean and clear blue sky, her preferred system is visual. If she responds by talking about the sound of the swash and backwash of the ocean, it is aural, and so on. More daringly and more directly, one might even enter into a conversation about how the woman has felt in the past when she met a boyfriend for the first time or when she looks at a movie star upon whom she has a crush, and to key into how she expresses those feelings.

2. Patterns

Eliciting the preferred representation system will take place early on in the conversation, while the woman is talking. When the man talks he must use a number of 'patterns'. This may happen before, after, or preferably both before and after the preferred system has been determined. The purpose of a pattern is to induce a trance-like state in the woman, via specifically designed story-telling. It is important that this is done subliminally. A cardinal rule for Jeffries is that one must never tell a woman that one is capable of inducing such a state. Instead of talking about oneself, it is better to present the story (ie pattern) as though recounting something that has happened to a friend or that one has read or seen on television. In this way, it is said, one can bypass the parts of the mind that generate suspicion and resistance. The normal guards are lowered if the story is at a distance, so one might introduce it as something that happened to 'my friend, Tim' or in a television documentary that one has seen. The story should be very sensually rich so as to arouse a sensory response in the woman. It should also involve various, subliminal words that are really little more than double-entendres, but appear perfectly innocent in context.

A favourite of Jeffries (and through his influence, PUAs worldwide) is 'The Discovery Channel Pattern'. This involves claiming that one has seen a documentary on what makes the ideal rollercoaster ride at funfair attractions. As a pattern, it affords the opportunity to the man to talk in rich, sensual terms, perhaps with the knowledge in advance of the woman's preferred representational system. So if the woman is kinetic, one can emphasise the feeling of anticipation and excitement aroused when one feels the rollercoaster in its ascent, the sense of wild abandon when it reaches its climax, and the rush as it speeds onwards to more and more fun later on. If the story is told well, with the correct use of the voice, the woman will be emotionally transported to those sensations; she will actually imagine being on a rollercoaster and the feelings that it evokes. It also allows one to mention terms like 'attraction', 'feeling', 'excitement', 'arousal', 'climax' and even 'getting off', in an apparently innocent context. While the conscious mind might have put up resistance to discussion of such things in a sexual context during a conversation with a recent acquaintance, it will not do so in a discussion of rollercoasters. The subconscious mind, Jeffries and others suggest, will still make the connection. So even if the woman is only conscious of idle, relaxed chit-chat, the notion of sexual intercourse has been planted into her subconscious mind. The idea is that she is already being sexually aroused without knowing it.

3. Anchoring

During steps one and two, the man should use 'anchoring'. An 'anchor' is some physical marker, which is introduced during the creation of a desired response in the woman. These anchors are to be repeated throughout the conversation. So if the man were to rub his chin, during the sensual parts of the story when a woman is (unwittingly) revealing her representational system, he should perform the same gesture, at the relevant time, during the various patterns that he uses over the course of their conversation. If a trance state is correctly induced, the woman will experience the same sensual pleasure as she remembered in her story and imagined in his, any time the gesture is used thereafter. So by simply rubbing his chin, the man can put the woman in this aroused state at his will.

Once these three steps have been followed, there is a wide variety of ways to proceed to intercourse using this mind-manipulation. Space prohibits a full explanation of the various other techniques that can be employed. These include methods to get around 'last-minute resistance' by 'freezing out' a woman who refuses sex, thus associating negative emotions with that refusal. It also includes subliminal 'command words'. One could link the rollercoaster story to arousal by saying something innocuous such as 'when you are really attracted to someone, you feel the same way'; the idea being that the subconscious will hear the command 'feel the same way' and thereby respond with a flood of those sensations and emotions. This even extends to using deliberate mispronunciation to issue a command – a crude, but well-known example from Jefferies is to use what appears to be the phrase 'below me', but actually issue the command 'blow me'. In a trance state, it is claimed, the unconscious mind will make the woman respond to this command.[44]

All of the literature, online courses and YouTube seminars in this area are, of course, directed squarely at men. There are thus virtually no accounts of these interactions from the perspective of a woman who has been manipulated into sexual intercourse in these ways. It seems clear, however, that the woman in question will not feel so 'out of it' as to be unaware of what is happening or unable to remember the incident; this system does not produce a disso-ciative state. Popular stereotypes about hypnosis, highlighted in Part A, do not apply here; the woman in question does not stare at a pendulum then 'do her master's bidding'. Instead, the notion is that these techniques will enable a man to implant the desire to have sex with him into the mind of a woman. As Jeffries puts it, 'whatever you can get a woman to imagine for herself, is going to be perceived as her own thought . . . you are throwing your own thoughts into her head'.[45] The woman's conscious mind will feel that she has made a deliberate deci-sion, while in fact the man has programmed her to have that desire in the first place, and then programmed and commanded her to act on it.

PART C. LEGAL RESPONSES TO PROGRAMMED SEDUCTION

Having discussed the potential for legal protection against unauthorised mental interven-tions in general, and having discussed a particular set of techniques within the seduction industry, this part of the chapter brings the two areas together. It is here that we discuss the potential application of the law on sexual offences. In doing so, we split our discussion between two potential avenues. First, we explore the potential for liability where the tech-niques of the PUA work as intended, where D gains 'consent' through mental manipulation and programming. Secondly, we explore the potential for liability where these techniques are not successful, or where their impact on V cannot be proven.

Successfully programmed consent

Where D successfully gains 'consent' to sexual activity through the use of techniques such as those discussed in Part B, we ask whether this consent is legally valid, and whether D should

44 For a good, eye-witness account of Jefferies successfully using these techniques, see Strauss *The Game* (n 43) 45–47.

45 Jeffries, *Secrets of Speed Seduction* (n 2) 16.

be liable for sexual offences under ss 1–4 of the Sexual Offences Act 2003. There are two questions of consent within these offences. First, we must ask if the successfully manipulated V is consenting in fact (part of the *actus reus* of the offences). Secondly, we must ask if it is possible in these circumstances for D to have a reasonable belief that V is consenting (part of the *mens rea* of the offences). We explore each in turn.

On the first question (ie whether V consents), it is important that we focus on the mind of V and the wording of s 74 of the Sexual Offences Act 2003: does D's successful mind intervention undermine V's 'freedom' and/or 'capacity' to 'choose' to engage in sexual activity? The answer, we contend, is yes. This is because freedom to choose, at its minimum, must include the uncontrolled use of one's practical reasoning. Genuine choices about sexual consent will include a variety of factors (eg pleasure, financial gain, family, etc), and some of these may influence V to make unwise decisions that she might later regret, but at least this is a choice that *she* has made. Where V's mental processes are compromised to even a limited (but appreciable) extent, and where such compromise was not authorised by V, we are not dealing with choices that V has made. Interestingly, even those writers advocating that hypnotised movement should be described as action (ie not automatic) have still expressed support for this more limited position. We see this in William's example of Cesare, a fictional character who is mentally controlled by Dr Caligari and used by him to commit murder:[46]

> suppose Caligari had said, 'You agree to do it?' and Cesare, in his somnambulistic state, had said 'Yes, I agree to do it.' Cesare would not have actually agreed to do it: that is not an act that in this state he can perform. The explanation is to be found in his dissociation from considerations that essentially bear on his doing so. In this state, he cannot summon up, for instance, thoughts that would relate the killing to the rest of his life.[47]

Of course, the ultimate question about the validity of V's consent (as with Cesare's intention to kill) will have to consider the *degree* of D's intervention; the more minor the intervention, the more responsible V will be for her choices. Thus, if we consider the techniques summarised in Part B, the relevant question is not the number of 'patterns' or 'anchors' used, but rather the impact of these on the mind of V. Inevitably, this becomes a question of fact for a jury.

The second *mens rea* question is more straightforward. This is partly because of the extremely wide drafting of the relevant provisions in the Sexual Offences Act 2003 on *mens rea* as to consent, requiring only for D to have lacked an objectively reasonable belief that V was consenting.[48] In this way, even where D believes that V was consenting, (ie where he believed that she expressed a free and competent choice to consent), D will not avoid liability unless that belief was reasonably held. Where D's deliberate aim is to program (or at least disrupt the normal mental processing) of V's mind, then his aim is in direct opposition to V's ability to make a free and competent choice to consent. There is clearly such a deliberate aim (to program V) on the part of anyone employing the highly specific NLP-based seduction techniques discussed in Part B. Thus, D is very unlikely to believe that V is consenting in the relevant way, and even where he claims to have had such a belief, that belief could scarcely be described as a reasonable one.

---

46 Bernard Williams, 'The actus reus of Dr Caligari' (1994) 142 University of Pennsylvania Law Review 1661. The example is taken from Robert Wiene's 1919 film *The Cabinet of Dr Caligari*.

47 ibid 1671.

48 For rape, see the Sexual Offences Act 2003, s 1(1)(c).

Having established the likelihood for D to have committed a sexual offence in these circumstances, it is also appropriate to consider associative liability. Our question here is whether those teaching and/or publicising these techniques within the seduction industry may be prosecuted for the same offences as D, but as secondary parties?[49] The answer in most cases, again, is surely yes. Complicity liability does not require the aider or abettor (X) to have had a significant or causal impact on the actions of D. Rather, it is sufficient for X to have provided some assistance or encouragement, for that conduct to have been intentional, and for X to have at least foreseen the chance that D might go on to complete the relevant offence.[50] Crucially, this last element does not require X to recognise that D's conduct will amount to a sexual offence (ignorance of the law is no excuse). It merely requires that X had foreseen that D might employ the techniques, and that they might impact V's consent. Where promoters and PUA authors are making money from teaching about these techniques, one would assume that they at least foresee the chance that they might work. As noted in Part B, we even see explicit awareness of this via the use of disclaimers of liability. Of course, such disclaimers have no legal force.

Set out in these terms, the case for liability under the current law appears to be a strong one. However, it is useful to highlight two factors that will potentially make prosecutions problematic. Both relate to the question of whether V's consent is legally effective.

The first potential problem originates in the psychology literature, and the claim within certain studies that hypnosis cannot cause (or even influence) people to act against their will. In a series of studies by Coe, Kobayashi and Howard for example,[51] hypnotised and non-hypnotised participants were asked to sell heroin as a favour for the lead investigator (not knowing that the request was part of the study). The study found that hypnotism had no effect on a participant's willingness to engage in the illegal conduct (ie could not cause participants to act against their will), with the study even showing a slightly increased acceptance among the non-hypnotised group.[52] Similar doubts have also been raised as to NLP and subliminal persuasion.[53] If the techniques discussed in Part B could be shown to have no scientific basis whatsoever, then clearly those techniques will not have undermined V's consent. As discussed in Part A, it is likely that such techniques will be developed further in the future, and effects may (at that stage) be found,[54] but the current psychology literature remains problematic for prosecution purposes.

The second and related problem, also emanating from psychology, relates to the difficulty of measuring the effects of techniques such as NLP and hypnosis. Even where individuals are hypnotised under controlled conditions, different behavioural or neurophysiological measures designed to assess a subject's level and state of consciousness are not entirely reliable, and can often yield contradictory findings.[55] In the context of a criminal trial, which examines past (non-clinical) events, the lack of a reliable measure will be particularly troublesome. This is because the prosecution must prove beyond reasonable doubt that D successfully manipulated and/or programmed V's consent on the specific previous encounter.

---

49 Secondary liability is provided by the Accessories and Abettors Act 1861, s 8.
50 *Carter v Richardson* [1974] RTR 314.
51 William Coe et al, 'Experimental and ethical problems of evaluating the influence of hypnosis in anti-social conduct' (1973) Journal of Abnormal Psychology 476.
52 The study took account of variables such as the participant's individual moral stance in relation to drugs.
53 Anthony Pratkanis and Elliot Aronson, *Age of Propaganda: The Everyday Use and Abuse of Persuasion* (Owl Books 1992).
54 Current research does not support effects beyond chance level.
55 Anil Seth et al (n 21) 314.

This problem is exacerbated in the context of the scenarios outlined in Part B. Patterns are deliberately constructed so as to take the form of normal social interaction. Even evidence of standard pattern use will not be conclusive of their impact on V's mind. These problems may be overcome (or at least mitigated) over time as our ability to measure the effects of hypnosis and NLP improves. Currently it provides a significant obstacle to prosecution.

The problems identified in the previous paragraphs do not justify or mitigate the actions of men within the PUA community who attempt to use techniques such as NLP and hypnosis to undermine the sexual choices of women. Therefore, although they represent obstacles to prosecution, the case for criminal law intervention remains a strong one. With this in mind, a more promising route to prosecution may lie within the inchoate offences: offences that focus on the criminal ambitions of D, as opposed to the impacts of their conduct. Bublitz and Merkel have also highlighted this in relation to potential general offences of mental manipulation.[56]

Attempted programmed consent

In addition to the substantive sexual offences discussed above (ss1–4 of the Sexual Offences Act 2003), each offence can also be committed in an inchoate form. Inchoate offences, such as attempt,[57] may be particularly useful in this context. Where D's efforts to program the consent of V are unsuccessful, attempts liability provides one of the only routes to potential liability. And even where D's efforts are successful, charging D with an attempt offence avoids the problems of proof highlighted at the end of the last section. Essentially, attempts liability focuses on (and blames) D's conduct in trying to program the consent of V, avoiding psychologically controversial questions about the impacts of that attempt on V's mind. In other words, if D were to go through the steps outlined in Part B, culminating in a subliminal 'command' for V to sleep with him, D could still be liable even if V is unaffected (or the effects on V cannot be proved).

So does D commit an attempted sexual offence when he tries to program V's consent? First, to satisfy the *actus reus*, it must be proven that D's conduct went beyond mere preparation towards the commission of the substantive offence,[58] or did so on the facts as D believed them to be.[59] In this regard, it might be argued that a conversation between D and V would not be sufficiently proximate to the forms of sexual activity proscribed within the substantive offences to be 'more than merely preparatory'. Eliciting a preferred referential system, delivering a pattern and even anchoring do not necessarily involve any sexual activity. Indeed, patterns are often designed to appear entirely innocuous and devoid of sexual content. This argument, however, does not work. There is a strong line of precedent in relation to sexual offences that allows for attempts liability from the moment of confrontation.[60] For example, this would be the case where D physically restrains V prior to sexual contact. As noted in Part A, attacks on the mind should be treated no differently. D physically confronts and restrains V in order to prevent resistance. D runs patterns, anchors and programs V in order

---

56 Bublitz and Merkel (n 22) 74.
57 Criminal Attempts Act 1981, s 1.
58 ibid s 1(1).
59 ibid s 1(2).
60 *R v MH* [2004] WLR 713; *R v Dagnall* [2003] EWCA Crim 2441; *R v Paitnaik* [2000] 3 Arch News 2; *Attorney General's Reference (No 1 of 1992)* [1993] 96 Cr App R 298, [1993] 2 All ER 190; For discussion, see Christopher Clarkson, 'Attempt: The conduct requirement' (2009) 259 Oxford Journal of Legal Studies 25.

to prevent resistance. Indeed, 'overcoming' various forms of 'resistance', in the form of conscious decision-making, are recurring themes in the literature. D's conduct satisfies the *actus reus* of attempt through confrontation by way of attack on V's mind. Of course, in a case in which sexual activity ensues, the requirement of moving beyond mere preparation is clearly satisfied.[61]

The next question is whether, at the moment of confrontation, D has gone beyond mere preparation towards *non-consensual* sexual activity. This need not, however, lead us back to the problems of proof discussed in the previous section. Rather, even if D's attempts at NLP and/or hypnosis will have no impact on V's mind, as long as D intends and/or believes that they will, his conduct will satisfy the *actus reus* on the facts as he believes them to be (ie as an impossible attempt). Thus, as long as D performs the sort of techniques discussed in Part B, and does so in the belief that these techniques have some prospect of success, the *actus reus* of the attempt offence will be satisfied.

Beyond the conduct requirements for attempts liability, D must also hold the required *mens rea*. This is satisfied where D acts with the intention to complete the relevant sexual activity (ie within ss 1–4 of the Sexual Offences Act 2003), and intends/knows that V will not consent to that activity.[62] Where D is using techniques of NLP and/or hypnosis to seduce V, an intention to gain sexual contact is likely to be straightforward to prove. Demonstrating intention or knowledge as to V's non-consent should also be relatively easy. V's consent requires freedom and capacity to choose. D is specifically aiming to bypass conscious decision-making in order to program V to make the choices that he desires. On this basis, D must (in law[63]) be intending to undermine V's consent. Attempts liability appears to be satisfied.

Aside from those who put these techniques into practice (D), issues arise relating to those who teach, promote or publicise these techniques (X). In relation to such individuals, in cases where D is not straightforwardly liable for a substantive offence, the most appropriate charge would be inchoate assisting or encouraging under s 46 of the Serious Crime Act 2007. This offence does not require D to have committed a substantive sexual offence, or even to have completed an attempt. In this sense, X's liability here does not rely on the conduct of D at all, unlike complicity liability discussed in the previous section.

The *actus reus* of s 46 of the Serious Crimes Act 2007 requires X to have completed an act capable of assisting or encouraging D to commit one or more offences (ie in this case, one or more sexual offences).[64] The drafting here casts the net of liability very widely. X's act need not assist or encourage D in fact, as long as it is *capable* of doing so: thus, there is no need to show that anyone was actually influenced by X. Equally, there is no need to tie X's conduct to the assistance or encouragement of any one offence: as long as X's conduct is capable of assisting or encouraging one of a number of sexual offences (eg ss 1–4 of the Sexual Offences Act 2003), the *actus reus* is satisfied. In terms of *mens rea*, X must believe that his conduct will assist or encourage D to complete the act element of one or more of the substantive offences (ie believe that his conduct will assist or encourage D to engage in sexual activity with V);[65] X must believe that D will complete the act element of one or more of the substantive offences

61 In such a case the prosecution may nonetheless elect to charge D with an attempted sexual offence to avoid the issues of proof discussed above, for example the difficulty of measuring the impact on V's mind after the event.
62 Criminal Attempts Act 1981, s 1(1).
63 D may not categorise his own conduct as attempting to undermine V's consent, but by trying to control her ability to choose this is exactly what is happening.
64 The Serious Crimes Act 2007, s 46(1)(a).
65 The Serious Crimes Act 2007, s 46(1)(b)(ii), s 47(4)(b).

(ie believe that D will engage in sexual activity with V);[66] and X must be at least reckless as to whether D, when engaging in that sexual activity, will do so without V's consent and with the *mens rea* required for liability.[67] Although s 46 is (overly) complex in its construction, none of these elements would appear problematic for a prosecution to prove in the current context.[68] Ironically, Ross Jeffries' attempts to avoid liability may have the converse effect: his disclaimers demonstrate sufficient belief and appreciation of each element listed.

For those people making money from advertising and teaching PUA techniques such as NLP and hypnosis, there are very few routes available for avoiding liability under s 46 of the Serious Crimes Act 2007. One option for X would be to deny that techniques such as NLP and hypnosis are capable of having any impact on V's mind (ability to choose freely) whatsoever. This could be presented as a denial of *actus reus* (ie X does not assist or encourage non-consensual sexual activity because the techniques discussed do not facilitate such activity), or as a denial of *mens rea* (ie X is not even reckless as to D acting in the absence of V's consent because X does not foresee the possibility of the techniques working). Such denials would be problematic for X. Particularly where X is making money on the basis that he or she is teaching or advertising valid techniques, public denial that the techniques work and that X ever believed that they could work would be very bad for business. Indeed, such a denial could potentially lead to liability for fraud by (previous) false representation. The only other option open to X would be to rely on the defence of 'acting reasonably' set out in s 50 of the Serious Crimes Act 2007. However, this defence would require X to convince a jury that helping or encouraging men to program the sexual consent of women is reasonable. This would be (and should be) extremely difficult.

CONCLUSION

The criminal law generally should pay more attention to the potential for mental as well as physical attacks against the person. The potential for mental interventions and manipulations, both direct and indirect, are present dangers, and ones that are only likely to increase over time. Thus, it is important to have criminal law protection in place to protect victim's mental integrity as the science develops.

Nevertheless, as this chapter demonstrates, the law is already well equipped to protect the mental integrity of the potential victims of sexual offences. Crucially, this protection extends to attacks that use NLP and hypnosis. A host of further important issues are now raised. Prominent among these is the question of enforcement. Even if the criminal law is capable of finding liability in this area, should this be taken forward by public prosecution? We believe that it should, though a full exploration of this issue is not possible in the current chapter. Where the wrong of a criminal offence is located in a defendant's willingness to use another person against their will, and where the law is designed to protect a victim's right and freedom to choose, we believe that all conduct engaging this wrong should be treated equally. The law on sexual offences has already made great strides in this regard over the last few decades. Just as the law has come to dismiss rape myths and to recognise that non-violent

---

66 ibid, s 46(1)(b)(i), s 47(4)(a).

67 ibid, s 47(5).

68 For an overview of the *mens rea* requirements, see John Child and David Ormerod, *Smith and Hogan's Essentials of Criminal Law* (14th edition, Oxford University Press 2015) ch 11.4. For discussion, see John Child, 'Exploring the mens rea requirements of the Serious Crime Act 2007 assisting and encouraging offences' (2012) Journal of Criminal Law 220.

submission still falls short of positive consent, the full (and practically enforced) protection of a victim's mind cannot (and should not) be far away.

Equally importantly, we have also set out the potential for prosecution of defendants who assist or encourage others to attempt such techniques. Whether this prosecution takes the form of complicity or inchoate assisting or encouraging, there is a clear case to be made that these activities are criminally wrongful. Taken at its very best, this limb of the seduction industry is simply a lie to make men more confident when talking to women, making genuine consent more likely. However, even here, teaching men that confidence comes through attempted manipulation that removes choice from woman is dangerous, and its promulgation should be carefully managed.

If we take sexual offences seriously as violations of sexual autonomy as opposed to the simple infliction of harm, then mental manipulations (or attempts at such manipulations) are just as serious as physical manipulations. This is not the time to be sentimental about traditional ideas of seduction and masculinity. Techniques such as NLP and hypnosis are not displays of charm; they are attacks on mental and sexual integrity.

5

Consenting to personal injury

William Wilson

INTRODUCTION

Clearly there is room, within contemporary society, for people to consent to the infliction of injury. Body alteration, in one form or another, is a topical example. It is a paradigm example of enjoying the fruits of living in a free society. What does having autonomy mean if not that we are entitled to spend our hard-earned cash having a nose-job, our ears or navel pierced, or 'I love mum' tattooed on our forearm? But there is also room for criminalising consensual harm-causing activities, for example euthanasia, duelling, or prize-fights, which may harm public as well as private interests. Somehow a balance must be struck between individual autonomy and wider public interests. As yet the principles that would inform this balance have not been adequately weighed in the courts and this paper seeks to elucidate how this balance should be struck.[1]

Criminal doctrine draws a conceptually rather fragile distinction between contacts where the essential nature of the activity is innocuous, for example, intercourse, cuddling, or kissing, and those where it is harmful, either in its nature or in its potential as in fighting, sports, tattooing or rough horseplay. For the former, absence of consent is constitutive of the offence. For the latter, consent operates extra-definitionally by way of a defence. Although the fact of this separation might seem incoherent,[2] there is a point to it. This can be best appreciated by analysing the moral logic of the structure of non-fatal offences and what this means for the system of defences.[3] This structure divides non-fatal offences into crimes against autonomy and crimes of violence, a division which is a direct juridical representation of a corresponding distinction made at the social level. In rape or common assault this logic is uncontroversial. It is wrong to kiss, lay hands on, or have intercourse without the other's consent. And it is wrong precisely and solely because the contact is unwelcome – it is an attack on the victim's autonomy. This explains why rape, common assault, and false imprisonment are constituted as crimes and torts also, in the absence of proof of physical

---

1 See generally David Kell, 'Social Disutility and Consent' (1994) Oxford Journal of Legal Studies 12.
2 Alan Norrie, *Punishment, Responsibility, and Justice: A Relational Critique* (Oxford University Press 2000) 164.
3 See Kenneth Campbell, 'Offences and Defences' in Ian Dennis (eds), *Criminal Law and Criminal Justice* (Sweet and Maxwell 1987).

injury. Such wrongs may be aggravated by physical injury but they are not constituted by it. The wrong in wounding or inflicting grievous bodily harm, by contrast, is the wrong of hurting people. This is compounded no doubt where the hurt is unwelcome but the wrong may be constituted notwithstanding. Good human beings do not stab each other, shoot each other, or beat each other. Hurting people is wrong and it does not automatically become permissible if it is consented to.[4]

One of the core tasks for any community living under the rule of law is to communicate, with maximum moral clarity, basic norms of behaviour and their moral rationale.[5] The bifurcation does this. 'Do not attack a person's autonomy.' 'Do not hurt people.' Defences are then superimposed onto this template to provide further guidance as to the circumstances justifying deviations from the basic moral prohibition. This enables the nature of the deviation to be filtered for social acceptability. We cannot generally tolerate a law whose **offence elements** require the court to decide on moral or political grounds whether a person's action is lawful or not. This must be a technical determination, as it is in rape. But we still need a law that permits doctors to perform life-saving surgery with the patient's consent or where the patient lacks capacity to give consent, while at the same time prohibiting the surgery if they do not consent or giving a consensual lethal injection to a terminally patient.[6] We need a law that permits tattooing and ear-piercing but prohibits gratuitous violence. The law's technique for squaring this circle and allowing a moral / political evaluation ultimately to determine lawfulness is to render all cases of intentional harm-causing '*prima facie* wrongdoing' subject to defeasance where the fact of the victim's consent affects the community's judgement as to its wrongfulness. A similar analysis can be marshalled to account for the extra-definitional nature of self-defence. We do not say that no human value is challenged when citizens use violence to counter violence – something 'untoward' still happens when a person injures or kills another in self-defence.[7] We say rather that while the value is challenged the context permits the resort to force as a necessary evil in a society that values individual autonomy.

The reference made above to the conceptual fragility of the distinction comes about when we try to pin down an uncontroversial test for determining whether the essence of an activity is 'harmless', where consent negates the *actus reus* and 'harmful', where it does not. After all even kissing and intercourse can be harmful if entered into with sufficient gusto or if a participant is suffering from an infectious disease. Is what distinguishes kissing and cuddling from consensual fighting, sado-masochism, and so on, the nature of the activity, the absence of hostile[8] or evil[9] intent; the absence of a purpose to hurt; the absence of foresight of harm, or the objective unlikelihood of harm? On the occasions that the Appeal Courts have had the opportunity of answering this question answers have manifested little consistency or internal coherence. Typical is *Attorney General's Reference (no 6 of 1980)* where the Court of Appeal

---

4 See George Fletcher *Rethinking Criminal Law* (Open University Press 1978) 770–771; William Wilson, 'Is Hurting People Wrong?' (1992) Journal of Social Welfare and Family Law 388c.

5 Anthony Duff, 'Rule violations and wrongdoings' in Steven Shute and Andrew Simester (eds). *Criminal Law Theory: Doctrines of the General Part* (Oxford University Press 2002) 47, 51–56.

6 Exceptionally however it will not be as with dishonesty in theft. In recent years this has prompted challenges under the European Convention on Human Rights.

7 Fletcher (n 4) chapter 6.

8 As was suggested in *Collins v Willcock* [1984] 3 All ER 374.

9 The position adopted in Scots law. See, for example, *Smart v HM Advocate* (1975) JC 30 and discussion thereon in Pamela Ferguson and Claire McDiarmid *Scots Criminal Law: a Critical Analysis* (Dundee University Press 2009) 258.

held that consent was immaterial in a case of an informal fight between two youths resulting in physical injury. Lord Lane CJ ruled that it was not in the public interest 'that people should try to cause or should cause each other actual bodily harm for no good reason'.[10] Presumably worded to ensure that participants to such a fight should not escape liability simply on the ground that the resultant injuries exceeded the parties' expectations; the statement is clearly too broad to act as a general principle. There is no requirement, in this formulation, that the activity should actually cause harm. 'Trying' is enough. But if harm is caused there is no requirement that this should be intended. That it happens is enough. In *Boyea*[11] the unacceptable breadth of this principle was exposed. The case involved vigorous sexual activity that got out of hand rather than the intrinsically aggressive acts characterising *A-G's Reference*. In his summing up the judge, while accepting that the defendant neither intended nor foresaw any harm resulting ruled that 'consent cannot be a defence where the indecent assault consists of things done which the jury decides was intended *or likely to cause* bodily harm'. The Court of Appeal agreed.[12] Quite apart from the implications the decision had for sexual freedom, it made no serious attempt to delineate, for the benefit of future cases, the boundaries between the lawful and the unlawful.

Boyea is one of a number of cases where injury was sustained in the course or robust sexual activity. In *Slingsby*, where the victim died of septicaemia following extremely vigorous consensual anal 'fisting', a more principled approach was adopted. Judge J withdrew the case of constructive manslaughter from the jury on the basis that the activities were consensual, accidental, and therefore were also lawful. They could not be rendered unlawful simply because injury had been sustained even if injury was objectively likely.[13] In *Meachen*, on similar facts but without death resulting, the Court of Appeal came to the same conclusion but hinted strongly that consent would not be operative in such a case if physical injury was a foreseen outcome. This hint occurs in the course of the following remark:

> We agree with the comments made by the late Professor Sir John Smith on this decision (Slingsby): 'The offence alleged was manslaughter by an unlawful and dangerous act. It was essential for the prosecution to prove that the injuries were caused by an unlawful act, a battery. Because no injury was intended (or, indeed, foreseen) and V consented to the acts done, the judge held that there was no battery.' It is respectfully submitted that this is right. In Donovan and in Brown the injuries were intended and consent to the intentional inflection of injury was held to be no defence. Here there was no question of consenting to injury because the parties contemplated no injury.[14]

By implication, if injury had been contemplated, different considerations might apply. This poses a separate issue of principle which dogs this area of doctrine and that was exposed in the cases of *Dica* and *Konzani*[15] that individuals should be permitted to take risks, even extreme risks, with their physical safety if this is incidental to an otherwise lawful and permitted act.

---

10   *Attorney General's Reference (no 6 of 1980)* [1981] QB 71, 719.
11   *Boyea* [1992] Crim LR 574.
12   ibid.
13   *Slingsby* [1995] Crim LR 570.
14   *Meachen* [2006] EWCA Crim 2414 [40] (Thomas LJ)
15   *Dica* [2004] 3 All ER 593 (CA); *Konzani* [2005] EWCA Crim 706.

A LITTLE HISTORICAL CONTEXT

These issues of principle reflect a doctrinal ambiguity present since the case of *Coney*.[16] The decision concerned the lawfulness of prize-fights, which at that time attracted huge crowds with attendant disorder and lawlessness and which was widely considered a serious threat to public order. The case is noteworthy for the genuine attempt made by all the judges to reconcile the private and public interests involved; the private interests that individuals have in self-determination; the public interests of protecting people from unnecessary harm, maintaining public order and the discouragement of other practices contrary to defined public interests. Hawkins J, in acknowledging this conflict, made the point that the scope for the prosecution of private interests can only take place within the context of the criminal law's overall function. In his analysis, public interests outweighed private interests only when the public stand to be adversely affected by the conduct concerned.[17] Given the disorder commonly generated by prize-fights, it is hardly surprising where, for him and his brethren, the balance of convenience fell. Cave J and Lord Coleridge CJ expressed similar views.[18] Stephen J, however, hinted at a wider and more authoritarian basis for the decision. This is that gratuitous violence is wrong in itself rather than because it is conducive to public disorder although it is only where the injury caused is serious that the state takes ownership of the wrong.[19]

Taken together with the cases on duelling and maiming *Coney* emerges as authority for the proposition that where physical harm is deliberately perpetrated this constitutes a distinct wrong over which the state is entitled to take ownership if the interests affected have a public dimension not reducible to any wrong suffered by the individual. If the activity is 'harmful' in this way, it is unlawful and cannot be consented to. Feinberg has enumerated these public interests in the specific context of duelling. They include the knock-on economic and social effects to family, colleagues, employers and employees and, significantly more indirect 'social' harms; as he puts it:

> [r]espect for life would diminish; socially useful forms of competition would be avoided for fear of fatal complications; arrogant bullies would terrorise all social intercourse; general insecurity would increase. These results harm the interests of everyone. . . . In short . . . (it) would be a contract that is very much against the public interest.[20]

It is with this in mind that *Coney* is best understood, that is, as adding prize-fights to the existing limited contexts (duelling and maim) within which corporal hurt may not be inflicted, and the public interest reasons for it. Half a century later, in *Donovan*, a radically different approach is met. The appellant beat a girl of 17 with a cane for purposes of sexual gratification. The beating was consensual. Upholding the conviction Swift J said 'it is an unlawful act to beat another person with such a degree of violence that the infliction of bodily harm is a probable consequence, and when such an act is proved, consent is immaterial'.[21] The upshot is that while *Coney* held that consensual infliction of physical injury is unlawful *if it*

---

16 Coney (1882) 8 QBD 534.
17 ibid 553.
18 *Coney* (n 16) 567.
19 ibid 549. As Lord Lowry, for the majority, later acknowledged in *Brown* [1993] 2 All ER 75, Stephen J accepts without reservation in *Coney* and in his Digest of the criminal Law, the basic idea that consent is a defence to assault occasioning actual bodily harm 'even when considerable force is used'.
20 Joel Feinberg, *Harm to others: the moral limits of the criminal law* (Oxford University Press, 1984) 221.
21 *Donovan* [1934] 2 KB 498.

is contrary to the public interest *Donovan* concludes that the consensual infliction of physical injury is unlawful *because it is* contrary to the public interest. It is the fact that a person has *deliberately* inflicted physical harm that makes the act contrary to the public interest and so unlawful for Swift J. It is the fact that prize-fights are socially subversive in a manner described in Feinberg's analysis of duelling that makes it contrary to the public interest and so unlawful for the judges in *Coney*.[22]

Donovan ushered in a significant doctrinal fault line which has yet to be eradicated for the simple reason that it is itself a product of a fundamental moral ambiguity at the heart of doctrine and, indeed, at the heart of everyday thinking about right and wrong, and apparent in the reasoning of Stephen J in *Coney*. It can be stated as follows: On the one hand the law encapsulates and reflects a moral principle that prohibits the deliberate harming of another person unless, as in self-defence or cases of necessity, it can be justified. On the other hand it also encapsulates and reflects a principle, both moral and political, that people should be free to do what they like with their lives and bodies and it is wrong for other individuals or the state to compromise that autonomy unless, again, there are compelling reasons for so doing. In both cases the public interest is invoked but in the one case the notion of the public interest is authoritarian and inquires whether society is prepared to tolerate as an exception a particular harmful activity, thus requiring a positive justification. In the other it is essentially libertarian, inquiring whether there are pressing reasons of public concern that require this activity to be singled out for special control.

THE PRESENT LAW

The case-law that has developed since *Donovan* reflects this absence of theoretical clarity. Instead, the legality of consensual activities causing physical harm is determined by category. The question in each case is whether the activity concerned falls within a privileged exception to the general prohibition against causing physical injury. This approach is articulated by Lord Lane CJ in *Attorney Generals Reference (no 6 of 1980):*

> It is not in the public interest that people should try to cause, or should cause, each other actual bodily harm for no good reason. Minor struggles are another matter. So, in our judgment, it is immaterial whether the act occurs in private or in public; it is an assault if actual bodily harm is intended and / caused. This means that most fights will be unlawful regardless of consent. Nothing which we have said is intended to cast doubt upon the accepted legality of properly conducted games and sports, lawful chastisement or correction, reasonable surgical interference, dangerous exhibitions, etc. These apparent exceptions can be justified as involving the exercise of a legal right, in the case of chastisement or correction, or as needed in the public interest, in the other cases.[23]

In fact, however, this statement understates the tension between the libertarian and authoritarian strands immanent within the case-law and how it is suppressed. This case-law expresses a basic template for understanding and evaluating the attitude of the criminal law to consensually caused physical injury that transcends the formal category-based approach. By this template acts and activities intended to cause physical injury are *prima facie* unlawful and require an affirmative justification such as that uncontroversially available in cases

---

22 *Coney* (n 16) 507.
23 (n 10) 719.

of reasonable surgery (*Donovan*).[24] Acts and activities not intended to cause physical injury are, correspondingly, *prima facie* lawful and are not rendered unlawful simply by virtue that the resulting physical injury was likely (*Slingsby*). Neither *Slingsby* nor *Meachen* satisfactorily address the case of activities foreseen to involve the risk of physical injury. In this case, the principle struggling for dominance, reflected in the outcome of cases such as *Dica* and *Konzani*,[25] is that the activity should remain lawful so long as no weighty public policy reasons count against the activity – the premise underpinning recklessness as a fault element. These public policy reasons have not been articulated except, partially, in the case of lawful sports but should take account, as will be explained later, not only the undesirability of causing unnecessary physical injury but also, as is implicit in the concept of recklessness, matters such as the likelihood that the risk will materialise, the degree of harm threatened, the nature and social utility of the activity, the vulnerability of the victim, the potential for exploitation and the consequences for privacy and autonomy if the act were to be criminalised. In the remainder of this chapter I shall be examining the case-law to see how far this template is adhered to and how, if at all, it can be improved upon.[26]

INTENTIONALLY CAUSED INJURIES

A. Fighting and fisticuffs

The case of fighting and fisticuffs present the clearest evidence of the intellectual impoverishment of this branch of doctrine. While in *Coney* the signal importance of the public interest was conceived largely in terms of public order and was largely consistent with the freedom-respecting harm to others principle, in *Donovan* it is subsumed under questions of public tolerance.[27] This approach was continued in the case of the *Attorney General's Reference (no 6 of 1980)*. Here the Court of Appeal rejected the argument that because absence of consent was of the essence of battery it was also of the essence of the s 47 charge. It was held that liability depended upon whether the context justified the infliction of injury. This in turn depended upon whether the activity from which the injury arose was in the public interest. The Court of Appeal concluded that it did not, and was not. In the words of Lord Lane CJ it was not in the public interest 'that people should try to cause or should cause each other actual bodily harm for no good reason'.[28] Put another way 'We don't like so you don't do it.'

The question answered here, it should be noted, is not whether there were public interest reasons in favour of *criminalising* the activity, specifying what those interests may be but the altogether less challenging question (for the state) whether there were public interest reasons in favour of *rendering the activity lawful*. In other words, the burden of justifying a paradigm case of self-determination (resorting to fisticuffs rather than to lawyers) is placed on the

---

24 Donovan (n 21). In Scotland a comparable approach is used to distinguish between lawful and unlawful consensual activities resulting in harm. The legality of consensual activities resulting in harm is unlawful if accompanied by an 'evil intent'. Doctors and boxers lack evil intent for what they do and so are immune from prosecution. Ferguson and McDiarmid suggest that the 'evil intent' doctrine is simply another way of introducing the *Attorney General's Reference (no 6 of 1980)* policy considerations present into the equation (n 9).

25 (n 11).

26 The Crown Prosecution Service policy statement on prosecuting the transmission of sexually transmitted disease states that consent is not a defence to the intentional transmission of such disease.

27 A rare example of the opposing approach is to be found in *Wilson* (1996) 2 Cr App Rep 241.

28 (n 10).

individual rather than the state. As Feinberg observes this is contrary to the ethic of minimal criminalisation:

> If criminal prohibition of their conduct is to be justified by the harm principle, it must be on the ground that it is necessary to prevent harm to public interests'. Further all the public interests that may be involved (must be identified) and the source of the weight they have.[29]

No such analysis occurred in *Attorney General's Reference (no 6 of 1980)*, leaving doctrine with no clear basis for characterising the range of activities the legality of which are constituted by consent nor for settling future cases. Lord Lane CJ simply compared the social value of the activity with that of the exceptional categories, such as sports and games, where the activity concerned was uncontroversially of social benefit. This led to the unsurprising conclusion that the activity was not conducive to the public interest.[30] This is hardly a cogent doctrinal analysis. As we shall see, for example, the accepted legality of 'properly conducted games and sports' is better explained by the libertarian strand to doctrine – do not criminalise without good reason – rather than the authoritarian one – do not permit without good reason.[31] In this context the anomalous case of boxing would have been a more pertinent category to consider.[32] The immunity extended to boxing is unlikely to have derived from any judgment that boxing was 'a right' or 'needed in the public interest' but more likely was an accidental outcome of *Coney*. By justifying the criminalisation of prize-fights on public order grounds the ground was prepared for boxing to gain the immunity – offered lawful sports generally. This immunity is libertarian – it is contrary to the public interest to restrict people's freedom to play games and takes risks.[33] The public interest considerations for boxing, however, should stand or fall with the authoritarian approach characterising disorganised fighting where the causing of physical injury, as with boxing, is its own reward. The usual basis for distinguishing the unlawful prize-fight or disorganised fisticuffs from the lawful boxing contest or sparring is that boxing is part of everyday culture. It is a 'character-building' activity structured by rules,[34] unlike, say, an orgy[35] or street fight, where rules are subjugated to the passions.[36] If this is the true basis for the immunity it hardly passes scrutiny. As Lord Mustill put it:

> That the court is in such cases making a value-judgment, not dependent upon any general theory of consent is exposed by the failure of any attempt to deduce why professional boxing appears to be immune from prosecution. For money, not recreation or personal improvement, each boxer tries to hurt the opponent more than he is hurt himself, and aims to end the contest prematurely by inflicting a brain injury serious enough to make the opponent unconscious, or temporarily by impairing his central nervous system through a blow to the midriff, or cutting his skin to a degree which would ordinarily be well within the scope of section 20. The boxers display skill, strength and courage, but nobody pretends that they do good to themselves or others.

---

29 (n 10) 222.
30 (n 10) (Lord Lane CJ).
31 See *Pallante v Stadiums Pty* [1976] VR331; *Barnes* [2004] EWCA Crim 3246.
32 See generally David Ormerod and Michael Gunn, 'The Legality of Boxing' (1995) 15 Legal Studies 181.
33 East's Pleas of the Crown (1803), vol 1, ch V, 268–270 [41] and [42].
34 *Pallante* (n 31).
35 Inaccurately as it turns out; (n 32) 190–192.
36 *Cf Brown* (n 19) (Lord Mustill) 108–109.

The onlookers derive entertainment, but none of the physical and moral benefits which have been seen as the fruits of engagement in manly sports. I intend no disrespect to the valuable judgment of McInerney J in *Pallante v Stadiums Pty. Ltd.* (No 1) [1976] V.R. 331 when I say that the heroic efforts of that learned judge to arrive at an intellectually satisfying account of the apparent immunity of professional boxing from criminal process have convinced me that the task is impossible. It is in my judgment best to regard this as another special situation which for the time being stands outside the ordinary law of violence because society chooses to tolerate it.[37]

SADO-MASOCHISTIC SEX

That same society, via the majority judges in *Brown*, has chosen also not to tolerate sado-masochism. A group of homosexuals were prosecuted for having joined together for the purpose of engaging in consensual sado-masochistic activity, which had resulted in significant harm to the various participants. The charges were laid under both s 47 and s 20 of the Offences Against the Person Act 1861. The case did nothing to remove the fault line ushered in by *Donovan*. Indeed it dramatised it, by exposing a deep ideological division between their lordships. In reaching its decision the majority had no truck with the argument that since no wrong was done to the individuals the state had no business interfering.[38] Affirming *Donovan*, it concluded that the issue to be decided was not whether there were good reasons to *criminalise* the consented-to activity – the minority libertarian approach – but whether there were good reasons to *exempt* it from the standard prohibition against inflicting physical injury. This anti-libertarian sentiment is the basis for the widespread condemnation which *Brown* elicited. But unfortunately there was more to criticise in the majority opinion than this. None of the three majority opinions managed to untangle the features of violence and sexual expression. They seemed heavily influenced by moral disapproval. This is evident even in the opinion of Lord Templeman who makes the best attempt. Approving Lord Lane CJ's statement in *Attorney General's Reference (no 6 of 1980)* he said:

> [i]t is not in the public interest that a person should wound or cause actual bodily harm to another for no good reason . . . Thus in the absence of a good reason the victim's consent cannot amount to a defence . . . the satisfying of sadomasochistic desires cannot be classed as a good reason.[39]

Despite these signals of moral intolerance to sexually unorthodox practices, Lord Templeman's opinion, overall, is rooted in something deeper. For him, the objection to sado-masochism is not specifically that it is a form of sexual deviance. It is not specifically that it involves the infliction of injury. Rather it is that the infliction of pain and injury was the purpose of the activity rather than incidental to it and this is an attitude to be discouraged. 'Society is entitled and bound to protect itself against a cult of violence. Pleasure derived from the infliction of pain is an evil thing. Cruelty is uncivilised.'[40]

---

37 ibid, 266.
38 The strong complaint offered by Chrisje Brants in 'The State and the nation's bedrooms' in Peter Alldridge and Chrisje Brants (eds), *Personal Autonomy: the Private Sphere and the Criminal Law* (Hart Publishing 2001) 115.
39 *Attorney General ref No 6 of 1980* [1981] QB 715.
40 (n 10) 237.

There are two basic points of distinction between Lord Templeman and the minority. The first reduces to the way that 'harm' is conceptualised. The minority accepts that public interests can be harmed by consensual violence but only if they have a direct public impact. Such an impact might result from the fact that they take place in public and cause offence or breach public order. Alternatively, it might result from the fact that the injuries suffered were sufficiently serious to require medical treatment and thus the expenditure of public money. Lord Templeman, by contrast, insists that the public interest is not exhausted by such concerns. 'Moral harms' can be committed as well as more direct harms. The only difference between them is that the former take more time to become apparent, by which time it may be too late for the state to do anything about it.[41] The community has a stake in preventing the possible emergence of such cults where the infliction of injury is its own reward and the degree of injury uncertain.[42] Allow people to indulge a taste for (consensual) torture and it may not be long before the taste can be equally or better satisfied where consent is absent. Accordingly, the potential 'moral harm' to individuals and/or the community involved in consensual sado-masochism for sexual gratification 'trumped' the individual's presumptive right to (sexual) autonomy.[43] This argument transcends the unfocused moralism characterising Lord Devlin's attack on Wolfenden.[44]

At large in Lord Templeman's opinion there is, moreover, the core of a more compelling *moral* justification for criminalisation implicit in the statement 'cruelty is uncivilised'. This is that our humanity demands that we as individuals value and respect other animals, whether non-humans, implicit in the prohibitions against hunting and cruelty to animals, or humans, implicit in both forms of offences against the person. This respect cannot be reduced to acting in service to another's wants, needs or desires. There is more to showing respect for humanity than this. For example, we do not think this a very good justification for permitting consensual cannibalism, the consensual mutilation of beggars for earning purposes, or a free market in body parts from living human beings. It is not simply the potential harmfulness or corruptive potential of sado-masochistic violence that is under the spotlight but more specifically the attitude that accompanies it. This attitude, referred to below in connection with body alteration, is the attitude of thinking of the human body as a commodity to be dealt with like other commodities – to be bought, sold, damaged, altered, exploited or otherwise used as a resource. It is an attitude that opponents frequently bring to bear in decrying the legality of state action in relation to capital punishment:

> the primary moral principle (is) that the state, even as it punishes, must treat its citizens in a manner consistent with their intrinsic worth as human beings – a punishment must not be so severe as to be degrading to human dignity. . . The fatal constitutional infirmity in the punishment of death is that it treats 'members of the human race' as nonhumans, as objects to be toyed with and discarded. It is thus inconsistent with (that moral principle). . .[45]

---

41 For another example of the muddy waters engulfing the liberal's and moralist's sense of what is properly criminalised see Suzanne Ost, 'Criminalising fabricated images of child pornography: a matter of harm or morality?' (2010) 30(2) Legal Studies 230.

42 This argument was not enthusiastically received in the European Court of Human Rights which nevertheless upheld the decision on other grounds: *Laskey, Jaggard and Brown* v *UK* [1997] 24 EHRR 39.

43 See on this point Peter de Marneffe, 'Sexual Freedom & Impersonal Value' 2013 Criminal Law & Philosophy 7 (3):495–512; Antony Duff, 'Harms and Wrongs (2001) Buffalo Criminal Law Review 13.

44 See generally Lord Patrick Devlin, *The Enforcement of Morals* (Oxford University Press 1965).

45 *Gregg* v *Georgia* 428 US 153 (1976) (Mr Justice Brennan, dissenting). See further Jenny Waldron, 'How law protects dignity' (2012) 71(1) Cambridge Law Journal 200.

The criminalisation of the possession of extreme pornography is also commonly justified in this way.[46] In Duff's view, this is a public wrong even when it occurs in private in that it is a serious violation of the respect that we owe each other, and thus (a denial, at least implicitly) 'of the moral status of those who are their objects'. He considers two other cases where the conduct is less 'straightforwardly harmful', but because it 'seriously violates the dignity of those subjected to it (or taking part in it), even if they freely consent to it', potentially justifies criminalisation. These are 'dwarf-throwing', and (less enthusiastically) 'provides the only morally plausible (but still inadequate) basis for the notorious decision in the sadomasochist case of *Brown*'.[47]

Why then 'inadequate'? Presumably for Duff it is because, if we take out of account moral distaste for sado-masochistic practices, we are left with an activity that far from degrading the participants may lead to a heightened sense of identity, reciprocity and/or mutuality – the same kind of mutuality, reciprocity and identity that is routinely advanced as a justification for intrinsically violent nature of games such as rugby, ice hockey and other contact sports. What would rugby be without the scrum and the bone-crunching tackle, whether for spectator or participant? No such mutuality can be claimed for activities such as dwarf-throwing or organ donation for reward but with genuine sado-masochism it is core.

Lord Templeman's principled distinction between incidental harm and violence that is 'its own reward' fits neatly, therefore, with the categories of 'reasonable' surgery, tattooing, lawful sports and decisions such as *Slingsby* and *Meachen* but is ultimately implausible. There appear to be double standards operating in the field of consensual violence. On the one hand violence in the course of achieving sexual fulfilment – surely a key ingredient in general human happiness – is unlawful if not incidental to a 'legitimate' sex act.[48] On the other hand boxers can bludgeon one another to death in the course of an organised boxing match for no better reason, apparently, than that there is a referee on hand to ensure fair play, there is a winner and a loser, and it makes a lot of spectators very happy to witness the spectacle.[49] If public tolerance alone dictates the legality of consensual activities causing harm it behoves the judges to construct a coherent principle, immunised from the influence of moral populism, dictating when and why the limits of toleration are reached.

It also fits, again contentiously but for different reasons, with the case of *Wilson* in which a man branded his female partner on the buttocks with a hot wire.[50] In this case a number of discrete circumstances were taken into account in declaring its lawfulness. These included

---

46 Criminal Justice and Immigration Act 2008, s 63. Extreme pornography is defined as involving: 'an act which threatens a person's life, an act which results, or is likely to result, in serious injury to a person's anus, breasts or genitals, an act which involves sexual intercourse with a human corpse, or a person performing an act of intercourse or oral sex with an animal (whether dead or alive) and a reasonable person looking at the image would think that any such person or animal was real.' See Clare McGlynn and Erika Rackley, 'Criminalising Extreme Pornography: a Lost Opportunity' (2009), Criminal Law Review 245; Erica Rackley and Clare McGlynn' Prosecuting the possession of extreme pornography: a misunderstood and mis-used law' [2013] Criminal Law Review 400; Susan Easton, 'Criminalising the possession of extreme pornography: sword or shield?' (2011) 75(5) Journal of Criminal Law 391.

47 Antony Duff, 'Towards a Modest Legal Modernism' (2014) 8 Criminal Law and Philosophy 217–235, 232.

48 'One cannot help but question whether the fact that *Dica* allows consent to the risk of grievous bodily harm whereas *Brown* does not is because of the court's explicit assumption that the risk of HIV is just one of those risks that (normal) sexual intercourse incurs.' Sharon Cowan, 'The Pain of Pleasure: Consent and the Criminalisation of Sado Masochistic "Assaults"' *Edinburgh School of Law Research Paper No 2013/04*.

49 Nicholas Bamforth, 'Sado-Masochism and Consent' [1994] Criminal Law Review 661–665.

50 *Wilson* [1996] 2 Cr App R 241

the fact that these were private activities within an established relationship. This is not really pertinent. If privacy is a right it is a right for all irrespective of the relationship. It included also the fact that branding was closely analogous to tattooing, which is a tolerated category. The contentious issue here concerns the number of key factors that are skated over and that are central to any public interest determination. The first is how to distinguish cases where the causing of pain and injury, as with rough sex and as was alleged here, are incidental to the activity and where, as with sado-masochism, are constitutive of it. As Tolmie inquires:

> When does a sexual experience that involves 'nibbling and biting' cross a line and become a sado-masochistic sexual experience? Is 'fisting' a 'vigorous sexual activity' (i.e. sex), or sadomasochistic sex, for example. Does sexual intercourse involving penetration become sado-masochistic if the penis is used aggressively and causes pain or hurt, or does the fact that the activity involves penetration of a vagina by a penis mean that it is by definition sex and can never be sadomasochistic sex?[51]

If there are no principles dictating how to assign an activity to a given category, the process of assignment is inevitably and fundamentally flawed. People who engage in consensual activity causing harm should know in advance when consent is relevant and when it is irrelevant. The second factor is the fact that power differentials typically exist between individuals of different genders, wealth, age and status who get caught up in violence. The presence of these power differentials are enough for some to question whether consent is a robust enough concept to do what a caring tolerant community would wish it to do; namely to ensure that those who submit to violence are not exploited and those who perpetrate it are not dehumanised. These kind of questions are present but far less clamant in cases where the parties are at arms' length, as in the case of surgery, tattooing and body alteration, where the very fabric of the relationship is founded on consent. The fact of these differentials has long informed criminalisation debates about prostitution and domestic and sexual violence and are at the forefront of current public disquiet about people-trafficking. The merit of the current consent template – activities intended to cause significant pain and/or injury are unlawful unless there is an affirmative justification – is that factors such as these are placed centre stage where otherwise they might be ignored. It is with this in mind that Herring argues:

> I would not support a reversal of *Brown* and a straight-forward legalisation of sado-masochism … all the leading cases on sadomasochism … demonstrate how easily domestic violence can be portrayed as consensual sex.[52]

We could go further. Consider again consensual fisticuffs. If this were to be decriminalised, how would cases where two genuine equals decided to settle their differences by fighting be distinguished from cases where one of the parties is bullied or otherwise pressured into taking part?[53]

These kinds of considerations were played out in the case of *Emmett*,[54] where the kinds of injury, suffocation and setting alight the woman's breasts with lighter fuel, inflicted on the (predictably) female partner, if consistent with heightening the erotic pleasure of the

---

51 Tolmie.
52 Jonathan Herring, *Great Debates in Criminal Law* (Macmillan, 2015) 87.
53 A matter which Feinberg (n 20) does not consider, although he makes the point strongly in connection with duelling.
54 *Emmett* [1999] EWCA Crim 1710.

donor in the encounter could less easily pass muster in the case of the donee. Distinguishing *Wilson* as a tattooing case the Court of Appeal approved the following statement of the trial judge: '(t)he degree of actual and potential harm was such and also the degree of unpredictability as to injury was such as to make it a proper cause for the criminal law to intervene.' True enough, but the more pertinent point surely is that the context – male inflicts an uncontrolled measure of pain and injury on his female partner – compromises severely the notion of mutuality for which consent acts as proxy. Suffocating is one thing – it is known to heighten the sexual pleasure of the recipient. But wherein lies the mutuality in setting your partner's breasts alight with lighter fuel and what notion of consent is capable of constituting this mutuality?[55] And if no knock down answer to this question is forthcoming what wrong is done the participants by declaring 'The community you rely on to support you and protect you from harm and exploitation considers that this activity carries too much potential for disguised domestic violence, to you and others like you, to be safely permitted?'[56]

CAUSING PAIN AND INJURY FOR ENTERTAINMENT

A recent addition to the range of contexts within which pain and injury is caused with the victim's consent is the TV 'reality game show'. Cooper and James describe one such show, the *Human Dartboard*, in which participants propel darts at the exposed buttocks of other participants, eliciting in the process squeals of pain from the human dartboard and squeals of delight from the audience. Their purpose in identifying this new category is to use it as a basis for questioning the present category-based mechanism for determining the legality of consensually caused injuries. Adopting the template used in this paper they argue that since the pain and injury is intentionally caused the activity must be illegal unless supported by an affirmative justification. They conclude that there is no obvious justification that can be offered in support on the basis of analogy with the existing categories. It has no therapeutic value such as offered by reasonable surgery. And it has no cultural value as offered by cosmetic surgery, circumcision, and tattooing or body alteration. They conclude:

> It seems that painful entertainment is not readily analogous to any of the existing lawful exemptions. Indeed, painful entertainment appears to have more in common with activities like sadomasochism and dueling, which are unlawful. It might be that if an exemption is to be found at all, it could only be explained in the same way as the anomalous boxing exemption; because society, at present, chooses to tolerate this kind of activity.[57]

This is a reasonable if incomplete conclusion. Boxing is anomalous because it involves the deliberate infliction of potentially life-threatening injuries. It is also analogous since it shares many of the same ingredients – a controlled environment, an audience and a degree of mutuality between the participants. If its legality were to be tested in the courts these similarities together with the absence of the glorifying gladiatorial trappings, and the low levels of potential injury would likely render the case against criminalisation more compelling than the authors are prepared to concede. The overall point the authors make however cannot

---

55 Natalie Nenadic, 'Sexual Abuse, Modern Freedom, and Heidegger's Philosophy' (2011) 27 Social Philosophy Today 111–126.

56 *Cf* Pamela Ferguson, 'Reforming Rape and Other Sexual Offences' (2008) 12 Edinburgh Law Review 307.

57 Simon Cooper and Mark James, 'Entertainment – the painful process of rethinking consent' [2012] Criminal Law Review 188, 196.

be faulted and that is that the category of pain and injury for entertainment is a hard case whose legality should be informed by a clear norm of application rather than, as at present, dealt with in the piecemeal casuistic fashion characterising cases such as *Brown*, *Emmett*, and *Wilson*. This norm, they propose, is that the intentional causing of injury (or pain) should be presumptively unlawful where that harm arises in the course of an activity and/or in circumstances not tolerated by society. So far, so uncontroversial. Where I would part company with the authors is in their recipe for ensuring that what is and what is not adjudged to be beyond the pale of social tolerance is rooted in principle and immunised from the influence of moral populism. On this the authors simply recommend parliament to be formally assigned the role of determining society's limits of toleration in consultation with appropriate agencies. This is, I would suggest, both unrealistic – parliament is quick to criminalise but slow to decriminalise or rationalise[58] – and, in any event, a recipe for moral populism through the back door. The common law has its own resources for determining whether an activity is reasonable and so lawful or unreasonable and so unlawful. These resources, as shall be argued below, should be put to the new challenge of providing common and principled boundaries.

REASONABLE SURGERY AND BODY ALTERATION

The field of surgery is possibly the most troubling example of the absence of any guiding principles governing consent to physical injury.[59] English law suffers, in this regard from the same sloppy conceptualisation that dogs the Scottish notion of 'evil intent'. Of course doctors doing what is clinically necessary for therapeutic or palliative purposes lack 'evil intent' and their actions are in the public interest but this does not exhaust the inquiry as to the proper limits of consent. Beyond these core functions a considerable range of non-therapeutic surgeries are recognised as lawful, extending far beyond what the patient needs for 'her own' medical benefit. Thus circumcision,[60] sterilisation, cosmetic surgery, and organ donation are all capable of being lawful although it could hardly be claimed that all examples are necessarily in the patient's best interests or otherwise necessary.

In *Airedale v Bland* Lord Mustill implied that the surgeon's immunity is not absolute, again without attempting to explain its limits or the principles dictating these limits.

> If one person cuts off the hand of another it is no answer to say that the amputee consented to what was done ... How is it that consistently with the proposition just stated, a doctor can with immunity perform on a consenting [person] an act which would be a very serious crime if done by someone else? The answer must be that bodily invasions in the course of proper medical treatment stand completely outside the criminal law. The reason why the consent of the patient is so important is not that it furnished a defence in itself but because it is usually essential to the propriety of treatment.[61]

In other words, it is not because the patient gives consent that the surgery is lawful but because, assuming the patient does consent (or the surgery is necessary), proper surgery

---

58 A topical example is the parliamentary rejection of the Assisted Dying Bill in September 2015, despite the support of the overwhelming majority of society.

59 See, generally, The Law Commission Consultation Paper, *Consent in the Criminal Law* (Law Com No 139, 1995) Part VIII.

60 In the case of minors the consent of both parents is necessary for non-clinically necessary procedures such as circumcision (*Re J (a minor) (Prohibited steps order: circumcision)* (1999) CA.

61 *Airedale v Bland* (1993) AC 789.

is in the public interest. A telling indicator of the conceptual fragility of the relevance of consent as it affects surgery is the routine 'mantra' attached to the category, that is, 'reasonable' (or 'proper') surgery. I use the word 'mantra' here to convey the fact that, although it is used invariably to qualify what renders surgery lawful, there are no cases, to my knowledge, where the notion of reasonableness in this context is properly explored and analysed. The likely reason for this is the cultural power exercised over the concept by the medical profession. Another example is the incorporation into criminal law of the principle of civil liability whereby a doctor cannot be held accountable for conduct and decisions that conform to those accepted at the time by a responsible body of medical opinion.[62] In the civil law, where the rights and liabilities of individuals must be fairly balanced, this pragmatic decision makes sense. Decanted into criminal doctrine it is more subversive, since it places the governance of the principle that doctors should do no harm not merely within the hands of the medical profession but in the hands of a discrete moral community within the medical profession. Judicial reluctance to question the propriety of standard medical practice in engaging in the more controversial non-therapeutic surgeries is arguable indicative of a criminal justice system content to sweep the ethical dirt under the legal carpet. In short, the public interest renders the surgery lawful not because it is beneficial to the patient, not because it does not set back the patient's interests, but because it is not in the public interest to circumscribe the activities (and conscience) of doctors and gainsay their notion of proper reasonable surgery.

This issue is of increasing importance. In contemporary culture we are witnessing moves towards what some might see as the commodification of the human body. The medical profession is at the forefront of this cultural change. Organ transplant surgery has created a market for organs; body parts can be bought and sold for reward. Cosmetic surgery has latterly become seen as a means of self-expression and an opportunity to remedy the vagaries of nature rather than to reverse the accidents of fate. Perhaps the ultimate expression of this cultural shift is the practice of body alteration on those suffering body dysmorphic disorders.[63] This is a condition whose sufferers experience a morbid dissatisfaction with the appearance of their body. Sufferers frequently seek cosmetic surgery and other related treatments to improve what they perceive as their 'flawed' appearance. It becomes a compulsion. Surgery does little more than feed the compulsion without addressing the underlying cause.[64] The governing bodies of the medical profession understand this to be an underlying psychological problem, rather than, as with gender identity disorder, a more fundamental existential problem, for which gender reassignment surgery is a recommended and effective treatment. Accordingly the National Institute of Clinical Excellence (NICE) guidelines on body dysmorphic disorder recommend only two treatments: cognitive behaviour therapy and serotonergic anti-depressant medication. Nevertheless it is widely acknowledged, even within the medical profession, that some surgeons are prepared to operate even in the absence of prior non-surgical therapy and in the face of the substantial body of research that indicates that, at best, only a very small proportion of patients stand to gain any lasting benefit from such surgeries.[65] As Elliot argues in connection with the notorious limb amputations performed by Robert Smith in Falkirk upon patients with body dysmorphic disorder, such surgery goes

---

62 *Bolam v Friern Barnet Hospital Management Committee* [1957] 1 WLR 582, 587.

63 See generally Tali Nakshoni and Moshe Kotler, 'Legal and medical aspects of body dysmorphic disorder (2007) 26 (4) Medical Law 721.

64 David Veale, 'Outcome of cosmetic surgery and "DIY" surgery in patients with body dysmorphic disorder' (2000) Psychiatric Bulletin 24, 218–221.

65 Katherine A Phillips, 'Surgical and non-psychiatric medical treatment of patients with body dysmorphic disorder' (2001) Psychosomatics 42, 504–510.

much further than currently accepted forms of surgical body modification, since it turns a physically normal patient into an impaired one and this is both ethically improper and, for any number of obvious reasons, against the public interest.

The general picture that emerges from this category is that, far from being organised to ensure the legality of surgery where reasonably needed in the patent's interests, the law expresses a pragmatic libertarianism that permits surgeons to do their patient's bidding, effectively unchecked. This reflects the wider immunity extending beyond the medical profession to include other practitioners of body alteration such as tattooists and body piercers. Such activities are intrinsically injurious; they cannot be done without the infliction of both pain and injury, and there are clearly public interest arguments in favour of restricting the legality of the more extreme forms of tattooing or body-piercing. Tattooing, for example, although it may be expressive of personal autonomy, the level and nature of consent necessary to reconcile private and public interests is never questioned. In some sections of society, young persons often undergo tattooing simply to conform to culturally-generated expectations and peer group pressure. In such contexts it may be argued that a tolerant and civilised society has a duty to consider not only the freedom of individuals to choose to adorn themselves but also the nature of the tattoo, the power of the underlying social determinants and the un-freedom that will necessarily follow from exercising that freedom. In cases of facial or whole-body tattoos, for example, the consequences are a changed social identity that is effectively irreversible.

Perhaps it is only a matter of time before a challenge is raised in the courts. In principle, the legality of non-therapeutic surgery performed by doctors whose oath requires them to 'do no harm', should be settled consistently with the accepted juridical basis for all consensual hurts, namely that intentionally causing people unnecessary harm requires affirmative justification. Such a justification is available already in the case of Gender Identity Disorder but no serious medical evidence supports the use of surgery for those whose condition is rooted in an ungrounded hatred of their own body.

SUMMARY

The message presented so far is that to understand and evaluate the present law of consent in non-fatal injuries it is necessary to view the criminal law as a structured negotiation between two moral principles. These are the principle of autonomy and the principle of 'do no harm'. These principles do not collide in the case of assault, battery and rape. Respect for autonomy demands only that individuals do not, without the victim's consent, interfere with that autonomy. There is no countervailing reason. Where physical injury is inflicted, however, victim's consent does meet a countervailing reason, namely the separate moral principle informing crimes of violence, and that hurting people is wrong. The fact that the victim consents does not expunge this wrongfulness but it does make the causing of physical injury easier to justify. The criminal law has no business forcing to behave morally unless we wrong another person or our community and the wrong committed to is serious enough to justify the state taking ownership of that wrong. Harms that are consented to, even if, as with whole-body tattoos, they may set back the interests of those affected, do not generally justify state coercion since the individual is not wronged by virtue of her consent. State coercion in such circumstances requires defined public interests to be set back. In limited circumstances state coercion in connection with consented to physical injury can be justified in the absence of harm to public or private interests on the basis that the activity concerned is immoral. By immoral in this context we mean not simply that it offends moral sensibilities since this could itself involve unjustified interference with autonomy. We mean rather immoral in the sense that the activity contradicts the very basic moral principle that informs the whole of the law of offences against the person – that as members of a human community we should treat others with the respect due to human beings. Do not hurt them, do not exploit them and do not deceive them and so on. This principle explains why, with good reason, therapeutic surgery is lawful; with (less) good reason why non-therapeutic surgery that conforms to professional norms is lawful and why tattooing and body piercing is lawful; and with (little) good reason why boxing is lawful.

UNINTENTIONAL INJURIES

The categories above purport to follow an organisational template that holds that the intentional infliction of physical injury is unlawful irrespective of consent unless it passes the public interest test. I have sought to cast doubt on the cogency of this template since an investigation of the categories themselves disclose a different approach that is predominantly libertarian. 'Victim' consent in practice is enough to constitute lawfulness except in the cases of fighting and sado-masochism that the courts consider to be gratuitous violence and so unlawful irrespective of consent. This leaves the law in an unsatisfactory state. Public interests may be involved in cases where violence is not intended for its own sake and little attempt has been made to analyse why the public interest test differs according to whether injury is the incident or purpose of the activity and how they can effectively be distinguished. Low level sado-masochism in private is criminalised while extremely dangerous sexual practices and harmful surgical practices go unpunished, ironically in the name of privacy and autonomy.

In the corresponding case where pain and injury are foreseen but not intended the lawfulness of the activity does not hang on whether an affirmative justification can be identified but whether there are compelling reasons of public policy justifying the criminalisation of the relevant practice.[66] All the privileged activities not involving the deliberate infliction of injury referred to by Lord Lane conform to this template and in the remainder of this chapter I shall explain why this should be the template for the majority of cases involving consensual injury. Here again, however, there is an absence of comprehensive analysis as to why consensual activities causing foreseen harms are and should be permissible.

One area where this has been essayed is in the field of sports. Beginning with the category of lawful sports and games, and leaving boxing aside, many of the more dangerous practices, including deliberate violence, which occur on our football, rugby and cricket fields are lawful.[67] In *Barnes* the Court of Appeal emphasised the libertarian basis for the immunity in quashing the conviction of the defendant who, in the course of an amateur football game, had broken the victim's leg with a late tackle. The Court concluded, quashing the conviction, that resort to the criminal courts should be exceptional and should require a sufficiently grave breach of rules that resort to criminal proceedings was appropriate rather than the game's own internal disciplinary system:

> In making a judgment as to whether conduct is criminal or not, it has to be borne in mind that, in highly competitive sports, conduct outside the rules can be expected to occur in the heat of the moment, and even if the conduct justifies not only being penalised but also a warning or even a sending off, it still may not reach the threshold level

---

66 *Brown* (n 19).

67 ibid 'Even when violence is intentionally inflicted and results in actual bodily harm, wounding or serious bodily harm the accused is entitled to be acquitted if the injury was a foreseeable incident of a lawful activity in which the person injured was participating.' 231, per Lord Templeman.

required for it to be criminal. That level is an objective one and does not depend upon the views of individual players. The type of the sport, the level at which it is played, the nature of the act, the degree of force used, the extent of the risk of injury, the state of mind of the defendant are all likely to be relevant in determining whether the defendant's actions go beyond the threshold.[68]

Barnes upholds the generally accepted view that the lawfulness of an act causing physical injury is constituted not only with respect of those contacts that are lawful within the rules of game but also to those illegitimate contacts that are considered inevitable constituents of the game as it is played.[69] The immunities assigned to this category have a different rationale than that for boxing – namely that the taking of risks and engaging in dangerous pursuits is a normal human activity and should be criminalised only if the risk-taking is contrary to public policy, which in sport it clearly is not. It is inappropriate for a free society to punish harms committed unintentionally in moments of rash enthusiasm, where the harnessing and channelling of such enthusiasm is both the point of the game and the point of *playing* games. Likewise dangerous exhibitions such as knife-throwing and trapeze work may be consented to, despite the dangers they involve. No obvious public benefit is effected by such activities but a free society would surely be diminished by their criminalisation.

The participation of the parties in the relevant sport or game is deemed to commit them to any contact and its outcome that a player 'might reasonably be regarded as having accepted by taking part in the sport.' In motor racing one assumes this includes death. Whether the legality is truly a matter of whether the party expressly or impliedly consented to the risk is not, however, clear, as can be seen in Lord Woolf's insistence that the criminal law's threshold for intervention is 'an objective one (that) does not depend upon the views of individual players'.[70] Clearly, retaliatory punches and kicks are unlikely to be deemed lawful whether or not consented to, since, unlike boxing blows, such contacts evince no respect for structured rule-following. On the other hand, the statement does not say that absence of presumed consent necessarily elicits the conclusion that the threshold for intervention has been reached. So 'eye-gouging', stiff-arm tackles and collapsing the scrum in rugger, 'over-the-top' tackles in football, and bowling bouncers and fast high full tosses in cricket may still be deemed, in theory, *not* to have breached the threshold, even where the culture of the game breeds the inference that some players consider such actions to be beyond the pale. The libertarian would approve. Even where individual interests are wrongfully set back the state must hesitate before taking ownership of that wrong if the public interest is better served by allowing the sport's governing body to police and enforce its own norms. As Husak insists, the fact that someone has seriously wronged another is a necessary condition of state punishment but not a sufficient one.

> [t]he State must not only have good reason to restrict a person's freedom of action but also good reason to censure and punish people who, rightly or wrongly, reject that reason as a reason to comply with the law.[71]

Also recognised as an activity for which valid consent can be given to dangerous risk-taking is what has been termed 'horseplay'. This has been deemed lawful, even where the degree of

---

68 *Barnes* [2004] EWCA Crim 3246 (Lord Woolf CJ) [15].
69 *Billingshurst* [1978] Crim LR 553; *cf Bradshaw* (1878) 14 Cox CC 83; *Moore* (1898) 14 TLR 229.
70 *Cf* Simon Gardiner, 'The Law and the Sports-field' [1994] Criminal Law Review 513.
71 Douglas Husak, *Overcriminalization: The Limits of the Criminal Law* (Oxford University Press 2008).

harm to which the participants are exposed is severe. So, in *Jones and Others*, the Court of Appeal ruled that a defence of consent could be raised to a charge of s 20 where the defendants concerned were boys who had caused others a broken arm and a ruptured spleen, during the course of rough horseplay. It is important to remember what is at issue. Obviously the injuries themselves were not consented to. Moreover, in law, they *could not be* consented to. If the boys had said to the victim, 'we are going to break your arm and rupture your spleen. How about it?' the victim's consent, if he had been fool enough to grant it, would have been ineffective. The decision is, rather, that it is *nevertheless* in the public interest for people to be free to engage in certain activities that involve a risk of serious injury to other people so long as the point of the activity is not to realise that risk.

Strictly speaking, therefore, the legality of such activities, as in the category of lawful sports, is not solely fed by the presence of either express or implied consent. The case-law indicates that what is necessary is that the aggressors believe the victim to be consenting,[72] and the victim understands that the purpose is not hostile.[73] This is implicit in the case of *Jones* and also in *Aitken*.[74] In the former the defendants had thrown their victim into the air and failed to catch him. In *Aitken* the defendants, as a 'prank', had doused their fellow officer's flying suit with spirit and had set light to it. In neither case was there evidence of consent sufficient to, say, negate the *actus reus* of rape. In effect, the judges in both cases were saying 'you have to put up with a bit of rough and tumble if you are a "lad"' – an unfortunate qualification of the principle of autonomy, particularly if you are thinking of joining the armed forces.

The approach in *Aitken* is, however, consistent with the basic template governing crimes of violence discussed earlier. While intended harms are *prima facie* unlawful and in need of affirmative justification, foreseen harms are not *prima facie* unlawful.[75] The fact that the individual affected consents to the risk of harm does not settle the question. Their lawfulness also depends upon a finding of recklessness on the part of the defendants, which requires consideration of whether the risk taken was reasonable. This is the best, if not only possible, explanation for the point made strongly in *Dica*[76] and *Konzani* that informed consent is an answer to a charge under s 20 the Offences Against the Persons Act 1861 based on the reckless transmission of HIV. Given that play, horseplay and sexual relations are a core feature of our humanity it follows that, whatever dangers accompany a particular act, their legality can only be settled by a judgment as to their reasonableness; a judgment which no doubt over time will vary with cultural mores and social priorities. In short, the legality of taking risks with the health and safety of others should be a question for the jury, not the judge.

CONCLUSION

The problem with the category-based approach is that it seems to come unstuck in the face of novel situations. As can be seen in the sexual context there are fine lines to be drawn between vigorous sexual activity to which consent is a defence and sexually motivated sado-masochism to which it is not, likewise between boxing and disorganised fighting, between branding and

---

72 *Quaere* whether recklessness as to consent will suffice.
73 *Griffin* (1869) 11 Cox CC 402.
74 *Cf Aitken* (1992) 95 Cr App R 304; *Jones* (1986) 83 Cr App R 375.
75 'A person acts recklessly with respect to – (i) a circumstance when he is aware of a risk that it exists or will exist; (ii) a result when he is aware of a risk that it will occur; and it is, in the circumstances known to him, unreasonable to take the risk'; *Re J (A Minor) (Prohibited Steps Order: Circumcision)*; CA 22 DEC 1999.
76 *Dica* and *Konzani* (n 15).

tattooing, between cosmetic surgery and body alteration. As Tolmie insists, the overriding problem is that placing a particular activity into a pre-existing category involves a process of reasoning that is necessarily arbitrary and piecemeal. It results in cases outcomes which are lacking in moral neutrality. Clearly, therefore, the category-based approach to consent should be replaced with something more principled that centres upon the act under scrutiny rather than the category it falls into. Tolmie's solution is that consent should presumptively render the infliction of harm, of whatever degree of seriousness, lawful whether intentionally or recklessly inflicted. Then, in all cases, without reference to the category the activity fell into, the court would be required to examine the facts and the context of the particular case to see whether public policy would be advanced by criminalisation. In this way 'full expression can be given to the reasons for allowing/disallowing consent in the first place'.[77]

This is not my preferred solution. For the reasons stated earlier the case of deliberately inflicting injury has to be singled out for special attention. Because the prohibition against hurting people is a core moral value, any act in defiance of that core value must be subjected to particular scrutiny. The presence of victim's consent makes the act easier to justify but does not justify it. Too many considerations surround acts of deliberate violence to make it simply an issue of privacy or human rights. The potential for disguised domestic violence, particularly against women, is one. The potential for financial or other exploitation of the vulnerable is another. The fact that certain acts of violence are unpredictable in their consequences is another. The nature of the criminal trial is another. Should the female partner in *Emmett*, assuming for the moment that her consent was compromised in some way, have to give evidence to substantiate what for her was far worse than she had envisaged and a gross abuse of power?[78] Should it presumptively count against a conviction, if a participant to a fight happened to die, that the fight was consensual? His family and community will likely think not and crucially it will not be easy, in the absence of witnesses, to know the truth of the matter. Finally, the consequences for the community of muddying the clear moral waters that the prohibition sustains will be jeopardised if the rightness or wrongness of an act is dictated not by this prohibition but by the fact that the individuals themselves decide not to be bound by it.

Against these public concerns we must balance privacy and human rights. People should not be denied any freedom of the private sphere permitted to others with different preferences. Some want tattoos. Some want piercing for ornament. Some want piercing for pleasure. Some want a face-lift. Some want to be front row forwards. Some want to be professional pugilists. The principles governing the legality of the various activities should be the same. The state should not criminalise actions unless no other response is sufficient. The Law Commission's solution[79] is that individuals should have the right to consent to any injury falling short of serious disablement.[80] This would include controversial contexts such as sado-masochism[81]

---

77 Tolmie.

78 This seems to have happened in the Suffolk Crown Court in *Lock* (2013) see *The Independent* can be found at <http://www.independent.co.uk/news/uk/crime/gardener-cleared-of-assault-after-fifty-shades-of-grey-inspired-sadomasochistic-sex-session-8461714.html> accessed 8 January 2016; Ferguson (n 56).

79 Roger Leng, 'Consent and Offences against the Person Law Commission Consultation Paper No 134' (1994) Criminal Law Review 480; Law Commission Consultation Paper, *Consent in the Criminal Law* (Law Com No 139 1995).

80 See generally Stephen Shute, 'The Second Law Commission Consultation Paper on Consent: Something Old, Something New, Something Borrowed: Three Aspects of the Project' [1996] Criminal Law Review 684; David Ormerod and Michael Gunn, 'The Second Law Commission Consultation Paper on Consent: Consent – A Second Bash' [1996] Criminal Law Review 694.

81 Law Com No 139 (n 79) 10.52.

as well as those already provided for under the present law. Unorganised fighting should remain unlawful as long as the activity falls clearly outside the context of 'undisciplined, consensual horseplay'.[82] In cases of sports injuries it further proposes that liability should be dependent upon the injury suffered being seriously disabling, the aggressor being aware of the risk of such injury and that the risk taken be an unreasonable one to take in the context of the activity taking place. The view taken here is that the more measured solution is to draw the boundaries of permissible injury more precisely and at varying levels, depending upon whether the injury was aimed at for its own sake – for example, sado-masochism – fighting, boxing (low level) – was incidental to recreational/lifestyle activity, for example, contact sports, cosmetic surgery and body alteration, sexual activity (higher level), or was incidental to therapeutic surgery (highest level). This harm tariff has the merit, also achieved by the Law Commission, of creating the degree of clarity and consistency necessary to ensure the law's communicative function is satisfied. But in deciding the legality of the act the court should be required to unpick the notion of reasonableness in all contexts to ensure that full weight is given to the various interests, public and private, which may be affected. These include, of course, the degree of force used, the extent of the risk of injury, the unpredictability of the injury, and the motive of the defendant. But they must include also contextual matters such as the cultural, or other, value of the activity, the potential for exploitation or oppression and the respective power of the parties. Taking sado-masochism as an example a person who visits a specialised 'spanking clinic' is more likely be exploring her own autonomy than someone sucked into a life of sado-masochism by an ardent partner.[83] The commercial sphere, it is sad to say, is a rather less compromised place than the private sphere of the home.

---

82 ibid, 14.19.
83 The underlying theme of the popular erotic novel by E L James (Erika Mitchel) *50 Shades of Grey* (Arrow 2012). Tolerance of such activities 'at arm's length' may have been the reason why the jury at Suffolk Crown Court acquitted the defendant after he had reenacting, with this female partner's consent, a particularly grueling session based on the above novel. The couple had met on a website for fetishists and had subsequently enjoyed a long sado-masochistic 'love affair'. It was what they had in common and so constituted their mutuality. See (n 78).

6

Assault, strangulation and murder – Challenging the sexual libido consent defence narrative

Susan S M Edwards

There may be deeper affinities than we as yet understand between the 'total freedom' of the uncensored erotic imagination and the total freedom of the sadist. That these two freedoms have emerged in close historical proximity may not be a coincidence. Both are exercised at the expense of someone else's humanity.'[1]

INTRODUCTION

In this chapter my intention is to explore the way in which the narratives of sexual libido and desire have informed the consent 'defence' in cases of non-fatal and fatal assault and more recently especially where strangulation is the method of violence used. The criminal law has for a long time established that consent, for whatever reason, including circumstances of private sexual conduct, cannot provide a defence to assault or murder. However, there are cases where the defendant who is charged with murder alleges that the deceased 'victim' consented to the activity that formed part of the sexual encounter that led to death and in consequence he should not be criminally liable for murder. The criminal law has permitted exceptions to the general rule that consent cannot be a defence to physical harm. These exceptions have been driven by social policy but are restricted to, for example, particular contact sports, including boxing.[2]

The question that forms the discussion in this chapter is the place, if any, of consent as a defence or in mitigation in regulating and punishing harms that follow sexual acts between two or more allegedly consenting parties when followed by non-fatal or fatal harm. In this chapter I explore the manipulation by the defendant of a sexual consent narrative in assault and fatal assault and especially where women who die at the hands of men are strangled and asphyxiated. While bondage, domination, sadism and masochism (BDSM) contenders argue that there should be a legal space for sexual violence in the sexual encounter[3] and that partners who engage in sexual acts, including erotic asphyxia, do so from true consent and choice, the concern is that the defence contention that the victim/deceased consented to the violent

---

1 George Steiner, *Language and Silence* (Faber 2010) 114.
2 See *Brown* [1993] 2 All ER 75 [HL]; *Brown* [1994] 1 AC 212.
3 See for example, The Spanner Trust, (an organisation set up to lobby for change to the law on consensual sado-masochistic activity) <http://www.spannertrust.org/> accessed 12 October 2015.

acts (in such cases) is a claim that cannot be reliably tested by the courts. The BDSM narrative is being appropriated by defendants to disguise what is essentially cruel and misogynist conduct as a strategy to manipulate trial and sentencing outcomes. Whilst there are instances where single men[4] have died following auto-erotic asphyxia, the death of women in heterosexual relationships is particularly worrying because of the prevalence of strangulation as a specific form of violence against women in both non-fatal and fatal assault.

REGULATING HARMS

The underlying principle or norm that has regulated this area of human conduct relies on the harm justification for intervention in the private sphere. Here the Millsean tenet has prevailed, in so far as it is generally agreed that the law has no proper place in the regulation of human conduct unless it can be established that harm to others is occasioned. JS Mill in his essay *On Liberty*[5] stated as follows:

> The only freedom which deserves the name, is that of pursuing our own good in our own way, so long as we do not attempt to deprive others of theirs, or impede their efforts to obtain it. Each is the proper guardian of his own health, whether bodily, or mental and spiritual. . . . The only purpose for which power can be rightfully exercised over any member of a civilized community, against his will, is to prevent harm to others. His own good, either physical or moral, is not a sufficient warrant.[6]

Within the criminal law where individual harm is caused to another the motive of sexual libido within a consensual practice has never constituted a sufficient public policy reason to provide an exception to the general rule. What is significant however is the changing landscape with regard to both the appearance of and shift in perception of this sexual narrative. Narratives of consent to sexual harms including BDSM, conduct which Foucault refers to as 'spirals of power and pleasure',[7] once regarded almost universally as expressions of sexual perversion and cruelty,[8] are practices now described by some as 'transgressive sexuality'. These narratives of BDSM are entering the criminal law with greater frequency as part of defence submissions and considered by judges in trial and appellate courts where arguments of consent to BDSM are being presented as part of a defence or in mitigation of sentence. The case of *Brown*[9] and *Coutts*[10] (in England and Wales) are two such cases where the defendants' case at trial relied on arguments of sexual consent to BDSM. In *Brown*, the House of Lords importantly ruled that consent could not establish a defence to assault and in *Coutts* the jury rejected the defendant's case that death by asphyxia was an accident and the sexual activity causing it consensual. The case of *Brown* involved a number of homosexual men who

---

4 See Michael Hutchence (1997) <http://news.bbc.co.uk/onthisday/hi/dates/stories/november/22/newsid_4006000/4006205.stm.> accessed 12 October 2015; See David Carradine reported by Brian Orloff, 'David Carradine Died of Accidental Asphyxiation' (*People*, 2 July 2009); See also Roger Byard, Steven Hucker, and Robert Hazelwood, 'A comparison of typical death scene features in cases of fatal male and female autoerotic asphyxia' (1990) Forensic Science International 48, 113–121.

5 John Mill, *Essay on Liberty* (1st edition, Shields C 1958) 1859.

6 ibid 16, 68.

7 Michael Foucault, *The History of Sexuality vol 1* (Pantheon Books 1978).

8 Richard von Krafft Ebing, *Psychopathia Sexualis* (Rebman London 1901).

9 *Brown* (n 2).

10 *Coutts* [2006] UKHL 39; [2007] 1 Cr App R 6.

engaged in harming each other as part of the sexual activity between them, including genital torture to the buttocks, anus, penis, testicles and nipples as well as wounding and branding. The defendants were charged and convicted (notwithstanding their alleged consent) of assault occasioning actual bodily harm (Offences against the Person Act 1861, s 47) and grievous bodily harm (Offences against the Person Act 1861, s 20). Whilst the practices were deliberate, the prosecution no doubt concluded that proving intention might be difficult since the primary objective of the defendants was to heighten sexual excitement and to satisfy a sado-masochistic libido not to harm *per se*.

In *Coutts* the victim died in the course of strangulation, choking and asphyxia. The defendant said that such harm was agreed to by the victim to increase her sexual arousal. The defendant's account did not convince the jury and a verdict of guilty to murder was returned at trial and also on a retrial.

SEXUALISING HARM

Evidence of bondage, domination, sadism and masochism in sexual conduct has been long established in authoritative works, for example of Krafft-Ebing,[11] Havelock Ellis[12] and Montgomery Hyde.[13] The philosophical writings of Nietzsche[14] have also been pre-occupied with sadism and cruelty,[15] as have the pornographic novels and plays of de Sade.[16] These several discourses have been detailed and critiqued in the writings for example of Georges Bataille,[17] Michel Foucault[18] and Gilles Deleuze.[19] Angela Carter[20] in her critique of de Sade explores how these narratives are culturally determined and how a male-dominated society produces a pornography of universal female acquiescence. BDSM practices considered peccadillos throughout the late twentieth century[21] are being positioned by some as sexual lifestyle choices. Anne McClintock points out that these practices are both theatre and part of the social subculture of fetishism.[22] A report in 1990 conducted by the Kinsey Institute found that 5–10% of the US population 'engages in sadomasochism for sexual pleasure on at least an occasional basis, with most incidents being either mild or stage activities involving no real pain or violence.'[23]

Yet the risks and dangers of these practices cannot be ignored. BDSM in massage parlours and as part of sexual services[24] was a concern of the Policy Advisory Committee (The

---

11 Richard von Krafft Ebing, (n 8); See also Richard von Krafft Ebing, *Psychopathia Sexualis* (Wet Angel Books; Revised edition 2006); See also Anne McClintock, 'Maid to Order Commercial Fetishism and gender power' in Anne McClintock (ed), *Social Text* (Duke University Press 1993) 87–116, 89.

12 Havelock Ellis, *Studies in the Psychology of Sex* vols 1–7. (F.A. Davis and Company 1930).

13 Montgomery Hyde, *A History of Pornography* (A Four Square Book 1966).

14 Friedrick Nietzsche, *The Will to Power* (Weidenfeld and Nicholson 1968).

15 See Jonathan Glover, *Humanity A Moral History of the Twentieth Century* (Yale University Press 2012) 11.

16 For example see Donatien Alphonse François de Sade, *Juliette* (Grove Press 1968) (originally published 1757).

17 Georges Bataille, *Visions of Excess Selected Writings 1927–1939* (University of Minnesota 1985).

18 Michael Foucault (n 7).

19 Gilles Deleuze, *Masochism: Coldness and Cruelty & Venus in Furs* (Zone Books 1989).

20 Angela Carter, *The Sadeian Woman* (Virago 1979) 20.

21 See Stephen Marcus, *The Other Victorians* (Corgi 1969).

22 McClintock (n 11).

23 June Reinisch and Ruth Beasley, *Kinsey New Report on Sex* (St Martin's Press 1990) 162–3.

24 See Susan Edwards, 'Selling the Body, Keeping the Soul: Sexuality, Power, the Theories of Prostitution' in Sue Scott and David Morgan (ed), *Body Matters* (The Falmer Press 1993) 89; See also the Cynthia Payne Trial in Gloria Walker and Lynn Daly, *Sexplicitly Yours: The Trial of Cynthia Payne* (Penguin 1987) 66; See also Claude Jaget (ed), *Prostitutes: Our Life* (Falling Wall Press 1980) 105–108.

Criminal Law Revision Committee, Prostitution: Off Street Activities 1985).[25] On men leaving sado-masochistic premises the committee reported:

> [t]he nuisance to the public involved men being seen leaving the premises showing obvious signs of injury or distress, behaving indecently, vomiting in the vicinity and depositing offensive litter (such as soiled and bloodstained linen) in nearby litter bins ... the men who visit such places do so with the deliberate purpose of subjecting themselves to torture, humiliation and pain.

Despite the fact that the experience of those working in 'sexual services' pointed to the fact that it is men who desire sadism, the feminist writings of Andrea Dworkin[26] have consistently argued that these sadistic practices are a patriarchal atrocity against women. Reichian analysis would argue that sadism is part of the attitude of men and the product of destroyed sexuality.[27]

Sado-masochism 'theatre', 'freedom' or violence has been aided and facilitated by pornographic scenarios that rely for the most part on narratives of violence and sadism, masochism and cruelty.

Such realities and representations have invaded the mainstream and become part of the genre of commercial 'fiction',[28] media and 'entertainment'. For example in 2002 Madonna sings and performs in the music video for the film 'Die Another Day'[29] title track. Madonna is clad in a tight-fitting vest, her breasts and nipples protruding, she is bruised, writhing and sexualised. Her torturers submerge her head in a tank of water before they strap her down in an electric chair. This torture is routinely practised on men and women in dictatorships as Glover[30] details. This format of representation with its fusion of violence and sex, so redolent of de Sade's work, typifies the violent pornographic genre. It is conceived of and produced to entertain. Of course, Madonna, magically escapes. As we all know, in the real world of torture escape is pure fiction. Nonetheless Jenny Colgan writing in the *Scotsman*[31] asks:

> Have you seen the Madonna video for the Die another Day theme song? It's fabulous. She's great in it, playing both her evil twin and someone about to get killed on an electric chair. She's sexy, she looks terrific and she brings real drama to what is, in the end, just a promotional video.

Amnesty International documents the reality – such captives do not escape, nor are they set free. They disappear and die. As Dworkin recognised there is no atrocity in war that the pornographers have not based their scenarios upon.[32] Certainly the BDSM narrative of domination, subjugation and infliction of harm is a redolent feature of patriarchy. The sado-masochism narrative has historically fixed women as masochistic, enjoying and desiring

25 The Criminal Law Revision Committee, *Prostitution: Of Street Activities* (Cmnd 9688, 1985) para 3.8, 161.

26 Andrea Dworkin, *Pornography men possessing women* (The Women's Press 1981).

27 Wilheim Reich, *The Invasion of a Compulsory Sex Morality* (Condor 1972).

28 EL James (Erika Mitchell), *Fifty Shades of* Grey (Vintage 2011).

29 <https://www.youtube.com/watch?v=BfvD_brrrTc> accessed 2 October 2015.

30 Jonathan Glover (n 15) 11.

31 Jenny Colgan, 19 November 2002 <www.scotsman.com/news/the-way-the-week-went-jenny-colgan-1–629885> accessed 23 December 2015.

32 Andrea Dworkin (n 26) 144.

subjugation. Andrea Dworkin identified this habituated trope in the heterosexual pornographic scenario observing that 'male orgasm is linked to inequality'.[33] The tropes of women as masochistic, as Andrea Dworkin has argued, rely on the representation that 'Whatever you do to her she will enjoy it'.[34] Kathleen Barry[35] warns that sado-masochism is forcing a woman against her will.

Criminal law encounters the sadist perpetrator who commits violence upon an unwillingly victim and on a victim he describes as willing. The question for the criminal law is whether consent to such activity can ever be a relevant consideration.[36] Some would claim that where BSDM is part of consensual sexual activity the law should not interfere. Disturbingly, such arguments are found in defence submissions. Such representations operate within a sexual space that is still unequal. Male sexual violence against women has often been presented in the legal narrative as an equal playing field, ie as 'rough sex' or 'vigorous sexual activity'[37] (Slingsby below). This has harmed women making them responsible for their own demise. 'Part of the feminist legal theory project must include inquiry into how legal reasoning transforms the embodied imaginings from male lives into the "objective" form of doctrine which passes for the "normative".'[38]

THE CRIMINAL LAW

The question of whether a consent to non-fatal assault (excluding rape) within a sexual context vitiates a charge of assault has been considered by the criminal courts for several decades, and has been the subject of consideration by trial and appellate judges in England and Wales and also Anglo-American jurisdictions[39] in recent years. The law in England and Wales, the US and Canada is unequivocal, consent is not a defence to sado-masochistic assault.

Whilst consent is no defence, in 2013, at Ipswich Crown Court, a 'not guilty' verdict was returned in the trial of Steven Lock[40] who was charged with assault causing actual bodily harm. He had begun a relationship with a female complainant that included sado-masochistic role play. He went on to abuse her beyond the limits to which she had consented. She suffered bruising to the buttocks and neck. He chained her 'like a dog' to his bedroom floor and whipped her repeatedly with a rope. He said that she had consented. He said in his evidence that he had got the idea from *Fifty Shades of Grey*.[41] In Canada, in *JA*[42] the defendant

---

33 Andrea Dworkin, Omnibus 'Pornography 1991' <https://www.youtube.com/watch?v=L9j7-zZks08> accessed 31 October 2015; See also Andrea Dworkin, 'Against the Male Flood: Censorship, Pornography, and Equality' (1985) 8 Harvard Women's Law Journal 1, 26; See also <http://pzacad.pitzer.edu/~mma/teaching/MS110/reading/feminism&pornography_pp19–38_94–120.pdf> accessed 13 October 2015.

34 Dworkin (n 26).

35 Kathleen Barry, *Female Sexual Slavery* (New York University Press 1979) 209.

36 Igor Primoratz, 'Sexual Morality: Is Consent Enough?'(2001) 4(3) Ethical Theory and Moral Practice 201–218.

37 *Slingsby* [1995] Crim LR 570.

38 Judith E. Grbich, 'The Body in Legal Theory' in Martha A. Fineman, Nancy S. Thomadsen (eds), *At the Boundaries of Law: Feminism and Legal Theory. Volume 1* (Routledge 1991).

39 See Jian Ghomeshi case <http://www.independent.co.uk/news/people/jian-ghomeshi-accused-of-new-physical-and-sexual-abuse-allegations-9828378.html> accessed 2 November 2015.

40 Gardener cleared of assault after Fifty Shades of Grey-inspired sadomasochistic sex session *Independent. co.uk* (22 January 2013) <http://www.independent.co.uk/news/uk/crime/gardener-cleared-of-assault-after-fifty-shades-of-grey-inspired-sadomasochistic-sex-session-8461714.html> accessed 23 December 2015

41 EL James (Erika Mitchell) (n 28).

42 (2011) 2 SCR 440; 2011 SCC 28 (CanLII).

(JA) claimed that the complainant (KD) had agreed to being choked. After being choked KD lost consciousness and the defendant committed sexual acts upon her. When she regained consciousness she found that her hands were tied behind her back and JA was inserting a dildo into her anus. KD made a complaint to the police two months later. In her statement she said that she had consented to the choking but not to the sexual activity that had occurred when she lost consciousness. As she was in a custody dispute with JA over their son she felt pressured to withdraw the original allegation. However, the case went to trial and JA was subsequently convicted of sexual assault. He appealed. The appeal court, by a majority, allowed the appeal and set aside the conviction. On appeal to the Supreme Court of Canada the court ruled that consent in advance cannot be given, concluding that, 'Parliament viewed consent as the conscious agreement of the complainant.[43] In the US in *People v Jovanovic*,[44] a doctoral student engaged in internet discussion of BDSM interests with a female student (Rzucek). They arranged to meet for a meal and then went back to his apartment. The complainant alleged that 'Jovanovic tied her up, violently raped and sodomized her, struck her repeatedly with a club, burned her with candle wax, and repeatedly gagged her with a variety of materials.'[45] She was bitten and had an object inserted into her rectum. After 20 hours she managed to escape and went to the police. She said in her evidence that they had agreed on a safe word that she would say when she wanted the conduct to stop but Jovanovic ignored her pleas. Her screams could be heard by others within the vicinity. Jovanovic was found guilty of assault, sexual assault and kidnapping and sentenced to 15 years to life in prison. The Court of Appeals (the majority concurring) reversed all the convictions ordering a new trial on evidentiary grounds that the trial judge had erred in invoking the rape-shield law, denying the jury access to evidence regarding Rzucek's interest in sado-masochistic activity. The Court of Appeals said that, consent, while available as a defence to the charges of kidnapping and sexual assault, was irrelevant to the assault charge. Jovanovic refused to plead guilty to a misdemeanour and charges were subsequently dropped against him.

ENGLAND AND WALES – THE CASE-LAW HISTORY

Probably one of the earliest reported trials in England and Wales involving sado-masochism was that of *R v Donovan*;[46] this is suggested by the fact that counsel in legal argument did not refer to any similar cases as authority so we can assume that the matter had not previously been adduced before the criminal courts. In this case, the defendant had induced a young woman of 17 to accompany him to his garage where he beat her with a cane 'in circumstances of indecency . . .. It appeared that the appellant was addicted to a form of sexual perversion.'[47] He was found guilty of both indecent assault and common assault and sentenced to 18 months' imprisonment. He appealed on several grounds, *inter alia* that consent provided a defence to a charge of indecent assault. The Crown in its submission contended that flagellation for the purpose of sexual gratification cannot provide a defence to indecent

---

43 ibid (McLachlin).

44 *People v Jovanovic*, 95 NY 2d 846 (2000).

45 *Dr. Oliver Jovanovic, Plaintiff, v The City Of New York, Detective Milton Bonilla, Shield No 61, Individually And in his official capacity, New York County Assistant District Attorney Linda Fairstein, Individually and in her official capacity*, Defendants. No 04 Civ. 8437(PAC).Sept. 28, 2010. 2010 WL 8500283.

46 *R v Donovan* [1934] 2 KB 498; see also for commentary Lorena Leigh, 'Sado-Masochism, Consent, and the Reform of the Criminal Law' (1976) 39(2) The Modern Law Review 130–146.

47 *Donovan* (ibid) 502.

assault. The Crown's case was that she had gone with the defendant because 'she was compelled or induced by fear to do so'.[48] (It is of note that the language used in this case formed part of the ruling in *R v Olugboja*.[49] The Court of Appeal when considering consent in 1934 was well aware that if consent was induced by fear then it was not freely given. Such reasoning later formed the basis of s 74 of the Sexual Offences Act 2003). The defendant's case was that she went with him willingly. Medical evidence reported seven or eight marks on her body and concluded that she had sustained a 'fairly severe beating'. The Court of Appeal quashed the conviction on the basis of a misdirection and ruled that violence even if with consent for the purposes of sexual gratification is unlawful.

The consent narrative in BDSM surfaced again in later decades. In empirical research I conducted on rape trials in 1980 in the London, Manchester and Birmingham courts, in one particular case where two brothers were charged with rape and the complainant had suffered bruising to the face and lip, the defence submission was that the victim had been asked to be hit, saying 'hit me hit me I'm kinky', although disputed by the prosecution.[50] The question of whether consent to violence in the course of sexual activity could negate a charge of assault was considered authoritatively by the House of Lords (HL) in the case of *Brown*,[51] Lords Templeman, Jauncey and Lowry (affirming) and Lords Mustill and Slynn (dissenting). The HL considered whether sado-masochism fell into a special category of acts, like duelling and prize-fighting, and whether restricting the general principle of consent as a defence under these circumstances was in the public interest. The trial judge, Judge Rant at the Central Criminal Court asserted:

> This is not a witch-hunt against homosexuals . . . nor is it a campaign to curtail the private sexual activities of citizens of this country. Much has been said about individual liberty and the rights people have to do what they want with their own bodies but the courts must draw the line between what is acceptable in a civilised society and what is not.[52]

The appellants' case was that over a 10-year period they had willingly participated in sexual violence. These acts of violence were committed to film and it was the discovery of the film that led to the subsequent police investigation. Neither the Court of Appeal, nor the House of Lords viewed the videotapes. Lord Mustill said 'the House has been spared'. Lord Templeman reasoned that there was a difference between incidental violence and violence inflicted for the indulgence of cruelty: 'I am not prepared to invent a defence of consent for sadomasochistic encounters which breed and glorify cruelty and result in offences.'[53] Lord Lowry was of the opinion that sado-masochistic homosexual activity cannot be regarded as conducive to the enhancement or enjoyment of family life or conducive to the welfare of society. The courts could not give these activities a 'judicial imprimatur'. Lord Jauncey asserted, 'there is nothing in ss 20 and 47 to suggest that consent is either an essential ingredient of the offences or a defence thereto.'[54] It was not, he said, in the public interest. Lord Mustill considered at length judicial analyses of the relationship between violence and consent in a range of diverse

---

48   ibid 503.
49   *Olugboja* [1982] QB 320.
50   Susan Edwards, *Female Sexuality and the Law* (Martin Robertson Oxford 1981) 166 nb 23.
51   *Brown* (n 2).
52   ibid.
53   ibid 84.
54   *Brown* (n 2) 91.

human conduct, from prize-fighting and sparring (*Coney*,[55] *Young*[56] and *Orton*[57]) to ice hockey (*Ciccarelli*[58]) and the chastisement of children, to beatings inflicted with a cane for the benefit of the aggressor's sexual gratification (*Donovan*[59]). The HL decision provoked criticism from campaigning groups and also from within academia.[60]

There were further criminal cases where the act of violence against a complainant was presented as part of consensual erotic sex between equals. In *Boyea*[61] the defendant was convicted of indecent assault. He had inserted part of his hand into the complainant's vagina causing her bodily harm. She said she passed out after the incident. The extent of the violence inflicted went far beyond the risk of minor injury to which, if she did consent, might have constituted a defence. The Court of Appeal granted an appeal against a six-year sentence of imprisonment, reducing the term to four years. In this case although consent was not raised by the defence, the judge in his summing up raised it, as did the Court of Appeal. The trial judge said this:

> In some cases where an indecent assault is alleged whether the person complaining of the assault consented to what was done becomes a crucial issue in the case because in many cases where an indecent assault is alleged consent to what was done by the person complaining of the assault is a complete defence. In a case where consent is a complete defence to the charge it is for the prosecution to satisfy the jury that the person complaining of the indecent assault did not consent; it is not for the defence to prove that there was consent by the complainant.[62]

More significantly perhaps were the remarks of the Court of Appeal:

> [t]he court must take into account that social attitudes have changed, particularly in the field of sexual relations between adults. As a generality, the level of vigour in sexual congress which was generally acceptable, and therefore the voluntarily accepted risk of incurring some injury was probably higher now than it was in 1934.[63]

The Court of Appeal went on, 'Moreover, it was inconceivable that she would have consented to the injuries which were in fact inflicted on her.'[64]

---

55 *Coney* (1882) 8 QBD 534.
56 *Young* (1866) 10 Cox CC 371.
57 *Orton* (1878) 39 LT 293.
58 *Ciccarelli* (1989) 54 CCC (3d) 121 (Canada).
59 *Donovan* (n 46) 498.
60 Nicholas Bamforth, 'Sadomasochism and Consent' [1994] Criminal Law Review 661 [663]; Sharon Cowan, 'The Pain of Pleasure: Consent and the Criminalisation of Sadomasochistic "Assaults"' in Andrew Ashworth and Eric M Clive, *Essays in Criminal Law in honour of Sir Gerald* Gordon (Edinburgh Studies in Law) (English University Press 2010) [133]; Matthew Weait and Rosemary Hunter, 'Commentary' on "R v Brown"' in Rosemary Hunter, Claire McGlynn and Erika Rackley (eds), *Feminist Judgments: From Theory to Practice* (Hart Publishing 2010) [252]; Marianne Giles, 'R v Brown Consensual Harm in the Public Interest' (1994) 57 Modern Law Review 101, 104.
61 *Boyea* [1992] Crim LR 574.
62 Reported in Susan Edwards, *Sex and Gender in the Legal Process* (Blackstone Press 1996) 353.
63 ibid 353.
64 ibid 353.

Wilson[65] involved a consensual act of the branding of a husband's initials on the buttocks of his wife with a hot knife. The defence in a spectacular demonstration of the power of the performative utterance[66] said it amounted to no more than 'personal adornment.'

It was held not to be an offence since it did not amount to s 47 of the Offences Against the Person Act 1861. The court, not wishing to interfere between husband and wife, accepted the defence's argument that this act was very different from *Brown*, amounting only to branding. The Court of Appeal said 'We share the judge's disquiet that the prosecuting authority thought it fit to bring these proceedings.'[67] In *Emmett*[68] the complainant's head was covered with a plastic bag tied at the neck with a ligature whilst the defendant engaged in oral sex with her. The complainant was deprived of oxygen to the brain and sustained subconjunctival haemorrhages in both eyes and petechial bruising to the neck. The defendant also poured lighter fuel on her breasts and set it alight such that she lost consciousness and suffered burns that later became infected. The defendant was sentenced to nine months' imprisonment on each count consecutive, the sentence being suspended for two years. It was held that consent was no defence and his appeal against conviction dismissed. In *Meachen*,[69] in an attempt to bolster a claim that his violence and her injury was consensual the defendant in his evidence said 'you enjoyed yourself didn't you'. The complainant suffered injuries to her rectum and lower bowel during an assault when she was unconscious following having consumed alcohol and being drugged with a date rape drug, GHB. The injury was so severe that a colostomy was performed and the complainant was fitted with a colostomy bag. The defendant, who claimed the victim consented, was convicted of grievous bodily harm with intent and sentenced to ten years' imprisonment, upheld on appeal.

The 'vigorous sexual activity' narrative frequently used to rebut allegations of rape[70] is also used to normalise violence. In the case of *Slingsby*[71] the victim died of septicaemia. The appellant had sexual intercourse with her, buggered her, and penetrated her vagina and anus with his ringed hand, inflicting the injuries from which she died. The Crown alleged that the defendant was guilty of manslaughter; although the prosecution accepted that the activity, if consensual, would not amount to an assault or any other crime. It was held that consent to injury did not arise because all they were considering at the time was 'vigorous sexual activity'. The judge ruled that the defendant could not be found guilty since 'fisting' was not an unlawful or dangerous act! On this ruling the Crown offered no evidence and the judge entered a verdict of not guilty. Of course, the Court was not able to hear the victim's evidence. Section 2 of the Sexual Offences Act 2003 creates an offence of penetration where the complainant does not consent, and fisting would fall within that section.

DEAD AND ASPHYXIATED

In several cases where women die following strangulation the defence argument is either that both parties engaged in erotic asphyxia to which the deceased had consented or else strangulation or pressure to the neck was part of the accused's 'love making' or 'sexual embrace' and that what had occurred was a tragic accident. Since strangulation is a common method

---

65 *Wilson* [1996] 3 WLR 125.
66 John L Austin, *How to do things with words* (Cambridge, MA: Harvard University Press 1962).
67 *Wilson* (n 65) 128E.
68 *Emmett* (1999) (unreported, 18 June 1999), CA, No 9901191/ZZ, 1999); *The Times* (15 October 1999).
69 *Meachen* (2006) Court of Appeal (Criminal Division) [2006] EWCA Crim 2414.
70 *Sampson* [2001] EWCA Crim 154.
71 *Slingsby* (1995) Crim LR 570.

of killing a female partner[72] the argument that the deceased engaged in erotic asphyxiation and therefore consented to the strangulation is an allegation easily made and difficult to refute. Considering strangulation and asphyxiation as a method of killing, from 1987 to 2006 (n = 1960) women partners were killed by men and of this number 28% of female partners were strangled or asphyxiated by men.[73] More recent statistics for 2012–13[74] and 2013–14[75] similarly show that when men killed female partners/ex-partners, in 27% and 24% respectively, strangulation[76] is the killing method. In some cases there is evidence of the reliance on erotic asphyxia as part of part of a defence strategy. However, the frequency of the use of erotic asphyxia as a defence and in mitigation in trials for murder is unknown since it is only when such cases are appealed that such details are reported in the law. Furthermore, there may be some cases where erotic asphyxia is alleged that do not proceed to trial. To illustrate this possibility Milroy and Beckman[77] reported a case of same-sex erotic asphyxia that, although it proceeded to the trial stage, was discontinued prior to the jury hearing the evidence. In this particular case two men were engaging in intercourse during the course of which the older partner requested that his neck be squeezed, the pressure applied by his partner occurred over a period of approximately two minutes. The body of the man being squeezed suddenly went limp. His partner attempted resuscitation but this was unsuccessful. The Crown had to decide whether to proceed with a prosecution on the basis of unlawful act manslaughter or on the basis of gross negligence. The prosecution decided to proceed on the grounds that the behaviour of the defendant amounted to gross negligence. The case was not in the end put before the jury, the judge accepting that there was no case to answer.

Of cases that do go to trial the difficulty of contesting a defence submission which relies on accident following erotic asphyxia is illustrated in the following cases. One of the earliest reported cases raising a defence of erotic asphyxiation was that of *Sharmpal Singh*.[78] Here, the accused killed his wife while she was in bed. The defence called no evidence at the trial but made an unsworn statement stating that, on the night in question, he had intercourse with his wife, he pressed on her neck and throat and chest during what was described as a 'sexual embrace':

---

72 See Susan Edwards, *Policing Domestic Violence* (Sage 1989); Susan Edwards, *Sex and Gender in the Legal Process* (Blackstone Press 1996) 368–370; Susan Edwards, 'Ascribing Intention – The Neglected Role Of Modus Operandi – Implications For Gender' (1999/2000) 4(3) Contemporary Issues in Law 235–256; Susan Edwards, 'Abolishing Provocation and Reframing Self Defence – The Law Commission options for Reform' [2004] Criminal Law Review 181; Susan Edwards, 'Descent into Murder: Provocation's Stricture – The Prognosis for Women Who Kill Men Who Abuse Them' (2007) 71(4) Journal of Criminal Law 342; Susan Edwards, 'Anger and Fear as Justifiable Preludes for Loss of Self-Control' (2010) 74(3) Journal of Criminal Law 223.

73 The data set under analysis supplied to me by the Home Office Statistical Department with kind permission.

74 Office for National Statistics <http://www.ons.gov.uk/ons/rel/crime-stats/crime-statistics/focus-on-violent-crime-and-sexual-offences—2012–13/rpt–chapter-2—-homicide.html?format=print>#tab-Method-of-Killing> 14 accessed 23 July 2015.

75 See Office for National Statistics Chapter Two *Violent Crime and Sexual Offences* Homicide ONS date 12 February 2015 <http://www.ons.gov.uk/ons/dcp171776_394478.pdf> 13–14; See also *Focus on Partner/ ex partner Homicide* http://www.ons.gov.uk/ons/rel/crime-stats/crime-statistics/focus-on-violent-crime-and-sexual-offences—2012–13/rpt–chapter-2—-homicide.html?format=print>#tab-Focus-on-Partner-Ex-Partner-Homicides> accessed 23 July 2015.

76 See Office for National Statistics Chapter Two *Violent Crime and Sexual Offences* Homicide ONS <http://www.ons.gov.uk/ons/dcp171776_352260.pdf> 14 accessed 23 July 2015.

77 Christopher Milroy MD and Michael Beckman QC, 'Murder, manslaughter or nothing' – 147 New Law Journal 1736.

78 *Sharmpal Singh* [1962] 2 WLR 238.

'their Lordships of the Board understood that expression to mean no more than that the handling of the throat and the pressure on the chest were part of the love-making or bodily movements that went with the sexual act'.[79] At the end of the case the trial judge said this:

> Whether it was during intercourse or whilst Ajeet was just lying in her bed, to strangle one's wife is murder, be it to stifle her complaints because she objects to intercourse, or refuses to submit to it, or even, she having consented to intercourse, the accused strangled her to gratify his lust.

Counsel for the appellant argued that a verdict of manslaughter should not have been returned unless it is proved that the accused knowingly acted with reckless disregard for his wife's safety. The Privy Council said, 'It is possible that, as the Court of Appeal thought, the accused was "applying pressure in an excess of sadism to frighten or torment her, or to overcome resistance"'.[80] The appeal was dismissed and manslaughter upheld.

Of cases that do go to trial the difficulty of contesting a defence that relies on the defence of consensual erotic asphyxia is illustrated in the following cases. In *Williamson*,[81] a defence of manslaughter was accepted by the Crown. The defendant's case was that he and the deceased had engaged in mutual partial asphyxiation in order to heighten sexual arousal. Neck compression, he said, was part of their sexual activity, which he described as 'pseudo-masochistic'.[82] He had also smothered his girlfriend with a pillow because, he said, to quieten the noise she made during intercourse. A sentence of four years was reduced to three on appeal. The Crown's pathologist stated that the cause of death was asphyxia. The pathologist said that sexual practices involving mutual asphyxiation were recognised in the medical profession as being practised and as being highly dangerous and a number of deaths had occurred during such activity. Dr Paul on behalf of the defence expressed the same view. On appeal it was submitted that the defendant and the deceased 'had been deeply attached to each other'. Significantly perhaps, the appellant had a number of previous convictions including convictions for violence: assaults on the police; wounding with intent; common assault; and assault occasioning actual bodily harm. The appeal court issued a note of warning, 'Anyone indulging in that form of conduct that thereby causes a death will be very likely to receive a substantial sentence of imprisonment in the future.'[83] Williamson as it turned out was a very dangerous man and especially a high risk to women. Following his release he went on to abuse other women and to kill his mother.[84] In *Niall Duncan Mcdonald against Her Majesty's Advocate*[85] the appellant was charged with murdering his wife. The defendant's case was that the incident had begun as a consensual sexual encounter. He said:

> At this point my arms were round Mandy's throat because that's the way we normally love sort of thing . . . then, I am not sure of the time span, maybe two minutes, Mandy's noises stopped . . . I withdrew the whip and realised Mandy wasn't moving I might have

---

79 ibid 241.
80 ibid 245.
81 *Williamson* (1994) 15 Cr App R (S) 364,365; *Williamson* (1993) Times, 19 October; See also Susan Edwards (n 72) 393, 413.
82 Susan Edwards (n 72) 365.
83 Susan Edwards (n 72) 367
84 ibid 354.
85 *Niall Duncan Mcdonald against Her Majesty's Advocate* [2004] SCCR 161.

slapped her face to try and get her round. At that point I tried to give her the, the kiss of eh, life. There was nothing.[86]

The defendant appealed and the appeal court finding no fault with the judge's ruling upheld the appeal against conviction.[87] In *McCarry and Waters*,[88] manual and ligature strangulation resulted in death. McCarry's case was that asphyxia was consensual to increase the deceased's sexual pleasure[89] and death was an accident. The Crown was permitted to adduce evidence of McCarry's non-sexual violence, including strangulation, towards former sexual partners as bad character evidence. This was said to be admissible under s 101(1)(d) of the Criminal Justice Act 2003 on the ground that it was relevant to an important issue between the defendant and the prosecution.[90] The prosecution established that in fact McCarry had a long history of strangling women during sexual intercourse[91] and a propensity to strangle women.[92] His grounds for appeal against a conviction for murder were refused. In *Sacket*[93] the appellant killed his girlfriend by manual and ligature strangulation holding her in a head-lock and strangling her possibly with her thong. The defence claim was that the defendant had been 'play-fighting'. The judge considered the seriousness as 'particularly high' and a 25-year minimum term was handed down and upheld on appeal.

CONTESTING THE SEXUAL PLEASURE MISOGYNIST STRANGULATION REPRESENTATION

The danger of this misogynist narrative[94] to women as a group is all too apparent from the above cases. Luce Irigaray argues that in sexuality the reality is that the woman is an 'obliging prop for the enactment of mans' fantasies'.[95] The erotic asphyxiation narrative is a redolent feature in pornographic representation and its availability and legality was challenged following the killing by Graham Coutts of Jane Longhurst. In *Coutts*,[96] Graham Coutts was the partner of the girlfriend of the deceased. On 14 March 2003, Jane Longhurst was strangled to death by him. Her body was found 'with a ligature made from a pair of tights tied twice around the neck, with a knot on the right-hand side'.[97] The expert pathologist(s) for the prosecution and the defence agreed that the cause of death was compression of the neck by a ligature, causing asphyxiation. The prosecution expert considered vascular strangulation

---

86 ibid.
87 *HM Advocate v Rutherford* [1947] JC 1, HC the accused was charged with murdering a woman by strangling her. He stated in evidence that: 'she had repeatedly asked him to strangle her to death', that he had put his necktie round her neck and that he had pulled it and pulled it again on her telling him to get on with it.
88 *Robert George McCarry, Paul Waters* [2009] EWCA Crim 1718; *Toby William Norris* [2004] EWCA Crim 2800.
89 ibid [6] [11] [36] [37].
90 ibid [31]. (They were each sentenced to life imprisonment for the murder and to other concurrent terms of imprisonment for the other offences. Upon an Attorney General's reference, this court increased the recommended minimum periods before release from the life imprisonment to 24 years for McCarry and 18 years for Waters.)
91 ibid [16].
92 ibid [20].
93 *Sacket* [2012] EWCA Crim 3229.
94 See Jane Caputi, *The Age of Sex Crime* (The Women's Press 1988); Deborah Cameron and Elizabeth Frazer *The Lust to Kill* (Polity 1987).
95 Luce Irigaray, *This Sex which is not one* (Ithaca 1986) 25.
96 Coutts (n 10).
97 Coutts (n 10) [3].

or respiratory strangulation the most likely mechanisms causing death within about two to three minutes, considering vagal inhibition to be less likely. By contrast, the defence expert considered vagal inhibition the most likely explanation, with death occurring possibly within one to two seconds. The expert opinion was instructive in buttressing the competing claims of murder and manslaughter, respectively adduced. In his defence, Coutts claimed that the deceased had engaged in consensual erotic asphyxial sex and the death was an accident:

> He had put his hand around her neck, and she had squeezed his hand to tighten his grip. He had then, with her consent, tied a pair of tights round her neck and tied a knot in them. At some point he had closed his eyes and released the tights. He did not know how the deceased had died.[98]

The case for the Crown was that he had murdered the deceased in order to obtain sexual gratification. Evidence was adduced that he was in the habit of visiting websites that related to sex and violence containing images of asphyxiation, strangulation, rape, torture and violent sex and that the day before the deceased's death he had logged on to a website 'Death by asphyxia' for approximately an hour and three quarters. For the Crown it was disclosed during the trial that Coutts was in fact a habitual strangler having strangled (none fatally) several of his partners during the course of sexual activity with them. One former girlfriend said that he 'placed his hand around her neck, before and during intercourse, and had used tights and knickers around her neck'.[99] Another said that he had tied a stocking around her neck during intercourse. His current partner said he had indulged in what he called 'breath control play'. Coutts himself said he had been 'fascinated' by women's necks for about 20 years. The jury did not accept his defence that the victim had consented and returned a verdict of murder. He appealed on the grounds that the he had been denied the opportunity of an alternate verdict. The House of Lords agreed on the point that he had been denied the opportunity of an alternate verdict which was put before their Lordships as a point of law of public importance and a retrial was ordered. At retrial, he was convicted of murder and sentenced to a 26-year minimum term. Coutts' interest in strangulation instigated law reform regarding the possession of extreme violent pornography. Following agitation for reform, s 63 (7)(a) of the Criminal Justice and Immigration Act 2008[100] was introduced, making it illegal to possess 'an extreme pornographic image'[101] that included 'an act that threatens a person's life', punishable with up to three years in prison.

---

98   Coutts (n 10).

99   ibid.

100 An image is 'extreme' if it falls within Criminal Justice and Immigration Act 2008, s 63(7) and is 'grossly offensive, disgusting or otherwise of an obscene character' (s 63(6)). Section 63(7) of the Criminal Justice and Immigration Act 2008 states that an image falls within that subsection if it: portrays, in an explicit and realistic way any of the following – (a) an act which threatens a person's life, (b) an act which results, or is likely to result, in serious injury to a person's anus, breasts or genitals, (c) an act which involves sexual interference with a human corpse, or (d) a person performing an act of intercourse or oral sex with an animal (whether dead or alive).'

101 Criminal Justice and Immigration Act 2008 ss (2)–(8) set out the definition of 'extreme pornographic image'. In order to be considered pornographic, an image must be of such a nature that it must reasonably be assumed to have been produced solely or mainly for the purpose of sexual arousal. Whether this threshold has been met will be an issue for a jury to determine. Subsection (6): An extreme image is one which is grossly offensive, disgusting or otherwise of an obscene character and which depicts one of a list of acts set out in subsection (7). These are explicit and realistic portrayals of: acts which threaten a person's life; this could include depictions of hanging, suffocation, or sexual assault involving a threat with a weapon; acts which result in, or are likely to result in, serious injury to a person's anus, breasts or genitals; this could include the insertion of sharp objects or the mutilation of breasts or genitals; acts which involve sexual interference with a human corpse; or a person performing an act of intercourse or oral sex with an animal. The people and the animals portrayed must appear to a reasonable person to be real.

The Criminal Justice and Immigration Act 2008 was preceded by a Consultation Paper in 2005 on *Possession of Extreme Pornography*, proposing four new offences that became law. However, the provisions fell short of what the campaigners had intended leaving scenes of rape relatively untouched by legislation. In fact, since 2002 the film industry was left relatively unfettered and the British Board of Film Classification (BBFC)'s trend of licensing films for R18 certification consolidated their approach of non-interference. *Irreversible* – a film with a nine-minute rape scene – was granted a certificate in March 2003. When the film was shown in Cannes, 250 people walked out. The position of the BBFC was that a shocking or unpleasant viewing experience, provided the violence did not suggest that the victim enjoyed it or deserved it, is not sufficient grounds in the UK for censorship of material intended for adult consumption. So where does the BBFC stand on gratuitous violence. It seems to rely, for its non-interference, on the belief that people will find it shocking that it is on 'the aversion effect', which was indeed the very same belief turned into a defence argument that saved the publishers of otherwise pornographic material from being convicted under the Obscene Publication Act 1959. The US Meese Commission, in their review of pornography in 1986, reached this conclusion: 'Substantial exposure to sexually violent materials as described here bears a causal relationship to anti-social acts of sexual violence and, for some sub-groups, possibly to unlawful acts of sexual violence.'[102]

The objective of s 63 of the Criminal Justice and Immigration Act 2008 was to bring to justice those who possessed 'extreme pornographic images', which also included sexually violent assault and strangulation. Yet any examination of the reported case-law reveals that the cases reaching the appeal courts involve sex with animals, which commentators have argued are not acts that threaten a person's life – the primary purpose of the section.[103] Indeed since 2011 my own perusal of prosecutions under s 63 of the Criminal Justice and Immigration Act 2008 reveals that they continue to be brought in connection with child pornography and/ or bestiality.[104] The new provision continued to fail to give effect to what was intended and scenes of rape and violence against women and strangulation were not brought before the courts. This lacunae has been partly addressed with regard to rape as pornography by the introduction of s 37 of the Criminal Justice and Courts Act 2015, amending s 63 of the Criminal Justice and Immigration Act 2008 to prohibit the possession of an extreme pornographic image if it portrays, in an explicit and realistic way, either of the following – 'the non-consensual penetration of a person's vagina, anus or mouth by another with the other person's penis, or by another with a part of the other person's body or anything else, and a reasonable person looking at the image would think that the persons were real'. However, even within this amendment the sexualisation of strangulation remains absent. Of course it could be argued that such imagery could fall into s 63(7)(a) of the Criminal Justice and Immigration Act

---

102 US Attorney General's Commission on Pornography, Report of the Commission on Obscenity and Pornography (Meese Report, 1986 Vol 1) 325.

103 Susan Easton, 'Criminalising the possession of extreme pornography: sword or shield?' (2011) 75(5) Journal of Criminal Law 391–413; see also Andrew D Murray, 'The Reclassification of Extreme Pornographic Images' (2009) 72(1) Modern Law Review 73–90; Imogen Jones, 'A Beastly Provision: Why the Offence of "Intercourse with an Animal" Must Be Butchered' (2011) 75 Journal of Criminal Law 528–544.

104 See for example *MH; R v Ping Chen Cheung, Smith*, [2013] EWCA Crim 167; *Williamson* [2011] EWCA Crim 2002; *Wilde* (Nicholas John) [2010] EWCA Crim 1985; *AG's Reference (No 70 of 2012), Daffin* [2012] EWCA Crim 3119; *Lewis (Simon Richard)* [2012] EWCA Crim 1978; *Oliver (Phillip)*[2011] EWCA Crim 3114; *Filor (David John)* [2012] EWCA Crim 2788; *Wilkins (Paul)* [2012] EWCA Crim 1653, *Edwards (Neil)* [2012] EWCA Crim 1263; *Wakeling (Derek Arnold)* [2010] EWCA Crim 2210; *R v Sinclair (Stephen)* (2010)[2010] EWCA Crim 175; *L (A)* [2013] EWCA Crim 215; *Clark (Oliver)* [2012] EWCA Crim 1707; *Hathaway (Brian David)* [2012] EWCA Crim 825; *David Robert Reed Twist* [2012] EWCA Crim 760.

2008 as 'an act that threatens a persons' life. However such representations are yet to come before the courts to be tested.

What needs to be done now is a recognition of the dangers in the BDSM narrative and the dangers of asphyxiation. Websites and pornographic images need to be challenged in the courts.[105] The prosecution need to fully implement s 21 of the Offences Against the Person Act 1861 which provides:

> Whosoever shall, by any means whatsoever, attempt to choke, suffocate, or strangle any other person, or shall by any means calculated to choke, suffocate, or strangle, attempt to render any other person insensible, unconscious, or incapable of resistance, with intent in any of such cases thereby to enable himself or any other person to commit, or with intent in any of such cases thereby to assist any other person in committing, any indictable offence, shall be guilty of felony, and being convicted thereof shall be liable . . . to be kept in penal servitude for life.

Notwithstanding, strangulation has rarely formed part of an indictment.[106] Where the BDSM narrative may persuade juries to return not guilty verdicts, as was the case in Stephen Lock (above),[107] or else where a victim is killed and a manslaughter verdict returned then judges have discretion in sentencing, as in *Sacket*.[108] The Criminal Justice Act 2003, s 143(1) provides, 'the court must consider the offender's culpability in committing the offence and any harm which the offence caused, was intended to cause or might foreseeably have caused'. The first consideration is the gravity of the *actus reus* expressed in 'any harm'. The second consideration provides for a number of states of mind in setting out degrees of culpability from the lower threshold of 'might foreseeably' right up to the threshold of just below legal intention. This provision was considered in *Ellerbeck*.[109] where the defendant had strangled his wife, killing her (although he did not rely on erotic asphyxia). The Court of Appeal refused an appeal against an eight-year sentence, concluding that the potential for injury is plain, handing down a very important judgment with regard to strangulation:

> the judge, also in passing sentence, made the point, at p 6, that on an objective assessment of the facts, the potential for serious injury to be caused by what the Appellant did is plain. This is important because remarks of that sort properly reflect s 143 in directing attention to the consequences and to the potential harm which was risked by manual strangulation of the wife's neck.[110]

Other jurisdictions, such as some US states,[111] have criminalised strangulation in itself regardless of its part in the commission of other crimes. The jurisdiction of England and Wales might consider doing likewise. It is regrettable that the Law Commission in its Report

---

105 I ask why this site has not been banned <http://www.dangerandplay.com/2011/12/26/how-to-choke-a-woman/>accessed 9 November 2015.

106 See *Moura* [2009] EWCA Crim 1891.

107 *Lock* (n 40).

108 *Sacket* (n 93).

109 *Ellerbeck* [2010] EWCA Crim 905.

110 ibid [13].

111 In the US, most federal states have made strangulation a specific felony, and increased sentencing. See <http://www.ndaa.org/ncpa_state_statutes.html> accessed 4 May 2015. For a comprehensive overview of all US states measures.

'Offences Against the Person'[112] does not consider this problem of strangulation. The Law Commission of New Zealand in March 2016 set out their recommendation for law reform in this area in 'Strangulation: The Case for a New Offence'.[113]

Male violence against women and the ubiquity of grabbing a partner's neck must always be very carefully scrutinised. As to the question of erotic asphyxia there is no evidence that it heightens women's sexual libido but there is evidence that men routinely use strangulation as a method of assault, that it is a trope and a reality in pornography, that women die in the course of it and that it is part of the misogyny narratives. Andrea Dworkin recognised that women die in the course of the debate some would like to have.[114]

---

112 Law Commission, *Reform of Offences Against the Person* (Law Commission Report No 361 November 2015).

113 See New Zealand Law Commission, 'Strangulation: The Case for a New Offence' (Law Com Rep 138, 2016) available at <http://www.lawcom.govt.nz/sites/default/files/projectAvailableFormats/NZLC-R138. pdf>.

114 Dworkin (n 26, 32).

7

Contributory negligence and consent

Verity Adams

INTRODUCTION

It is an oft-told tale; a person wakes in the morning with a ringing head, the taste of alcohol in their mouth and hazy memories of mistakes made. Regardless of gender, many a person may have found themselves in the position of having drunk too much and having made choices they would otherwise have never made: telling a best friend what they really think of their partner, getting an unfortunate tattoo, or having sex they regret in the light of day. Some mistakes are, of course, far worse; Magistrates' and Crown Courts are filled with defendants who, whilst drunk, have committed offences varying from minor public order offences to serious offences against the person. Though many of these defendants would argue that they would have never committed the offence if they had not been intoxicated, criminal law has long rejected intoxication as a defence. Whilst intoxication may result in a defendant not possessing the necessary *mens rea* for specific intent offences, it fails to negate the *mens rea* necessary for basic intent offences. The retention of *mens rea* for basic intent offences is a matter of practical necessity. Understandably, where a person chooses to partake in alcohol or drugs, thereby lowering their inhibitions and 'cast[ing] off the restraints of reason and conscience', and commits an act they may never have soberly committed, they must still be held accountable.[1] To do otherwise would be to allow a slew of criminal acts to go unpunished and to enforce a worrying notion that drunkenness is a state in which any act is permissible.[2]

There exists, however, a possible tension within criminal law. Whilst a defendant is deemed culpable for their actions on the basis of having made, at the very least, an initial decision to lower their inhibitions through the use of drugs or alcohol, consent given to sexual acts by a person who voluntarily becomes intoxicated may be vitiated. Though the law holds responsible the intoxicated defendant, the law does not consider the same to apply to those who make the same choice and engage in similarly regrettable actions of a sexual nature. There is no doubt that the issue of drunken consent is a complex one. Arguments exist regarding the concern that

---

1 *DPP v Majewski* [1977] AC 443, 474.
2 The issues of public perception and manageable policy are both predominant in discussions concerning intoxication as a defence. As Bugg notes, there is a need to 'address immediate social policy demands . . . this is a story of the tension between "principle and policy"', Stuart Bugg, 'Intoxication and Liability: A Criminal Law Cocktail' (1984) 5 Auckland University Law Review 144, 145; *Majewski* ibid 474–475.

a woman who is intoxicated is considerably more vulnerable to a male partner; concerns over a culture where men prey upon intoxicated women are legitimate ones and should be addressed.[3] Any situation in which a person deliberately takes advantage of another's incapacitated state to elicit a favourable response to sexual overtures would demonstrate serious moral deficiencies.[4] However, invalidation of consent due to intoxication can be a blunt principle and may fail to take into consideration a variety of issues, including but not limited to: how the complainant became intoxicated and what role the defendant had to play in their intoxication; the level of intoxication of the defendant themselves (where both parties are equally voluntarily intoxicated, arguments regarding a deliberate act of 'preying' may be less forceful); and the gender of both individuals (discussion relating to drunken consent tends to revolve around a heteronormative scenario with a male as the aggressor and a female vulnerable party).[5]

This chapter investigates to what degree such a tension exists and whether the tension may be alleviated or addressed to some extent. This is done with reference to a possible classification of contributory negligence, and the effect such a classification would have on the offender's liability or sentence. Accordingly, the basis of contributory negligence and the manner in which it affects both liability and compensation in tort law are considered, along with whether the principle has been extended into criminal law.[6] The laws on intoxication, both

---

3 Studies have shown that, for example, there is a particular culture around this type of behaviour at universities; see Antonia Abbey, 'Alcohol-Related Sexual Assault: A Common Problem among College Students' (2002) 14 Journal of Studies on Alcohol 118; Emily Voller, 'Sexual Assault and Rape Perpetration by College Men' (2009) 25(3) Journal of Interpersonal Violence 457. See also the research by Martin and Hummer which noted that alcohol was a 'weapon against sexual reluctance' and that it provided a 'major tool . . . to gain sexual mastery over women', Patricia Yancey Martin and Robert A Hummer, 'Fraternities and Rape on Campus' in Pauline B Bart and Eileen Geil Moran (eds), *Violence against Women: The Bloody Footprints* (Sage Publications 1993) 122. Nevertheless, it should be noted, as commented by Finch and Munro, that 'this research does not indicate . . . the extent to which this misuse [of alcohol] is composed of spiking a victim's drink with alcohol without her knowledge as opposed to encouraging her to drink in the hope that she will be more amenable to intercourse or taking advantage of her self-induced intoxication', Emily Finch and Vanessa Munro, 'Intoxicated Consent and the Boundaries of Drug Assisted Rape' (2003) Criminal Law Review 773, 780.

4 Nicholas Dixon, 'Alcohol and Rape' (2001) 15 Public Affairs Quarterly 341, 349.

5 There exists a tendency to view the question of consent and sexual offences against adults through a heteronormative, patriarchal lens. For example, the headlines of news reports relating to reports/guidelines on consent show a conflation of consent and women, not consent and people generally: Gordon Rayner and Bill Gardner, 'Men must prove a woman said "Yes" under tough new rape rules' (*The Telegraph*, 28 January 2015) <http://www.telegraph.co.uk/news/uknews/law-and-order/11375667/Men-must-prove-a-woman-said-Yes-under-tough-new-rape-rules.html> accessed 28 November 2015; Richard Marsden, Ian Drury and Stephanie Linning, 'Men will have to prove a woman said "yes" in tough new rules for police investigating date rape' (*The Daily Mail*, 29 January 2015) <http://www.dailymail.co.uk/news/article-2930819/CPS-launches-crackdown-rapist-pray-drunk-women-tightened-laws-stop-suspects-using-social-media-help-cover-tracks.html> accessed 28 November 2015; 'New guidance to be issued to all police forces and prosecutors will require rape suspects to convince the authorities that a woman consented to sex' in Katie Grant, 'Campaigners hail DPP's tough new rape guidelines as "huge step forward"' (*The Independent*, 29 January 2015) <http://www.independent.co.uk/news/uk/crime/campaigners-hail-dpps-tough-new-rape-guidelines-as-huge-step-forward-10009595.html> accessed 28 November 2015; Arthur Martin, 'Courts "should assume women can't consent to sex when drunk": Rape report's controversial proposal' (*The Daily Mail*, 2 June 2015) <http://www.dailymail.co.uk/news/article-3108406/Courts-assume-women-t-consent-sex-drunk-Rape-report-s-controversial-proposal.html> accessed 28 November 2015.

6 A similar study has been undertaken in particular relation to causation in tort and criminal law; see, Sally K Cunningham and Gemma Turton, 'Causing Controversy: Interpreting the Requirements of Causation in Criminal Law and Tort Law' (Society of Legal Scholars Criminal Justice Conference, Nottingham 2014).

with regard to the liability of the defendant and the consent of the complainant, are then examined in greater detail. Finally, the chapter evaluates whether contributory negligence may play a role within intoxicated consent cases and, if so, how.

Before such analysis is undertaken, it is important to define what is meant by "intoxicated consent" in this chapter. Only those situations where consent is given expressly or implied through actions, whilst the complainant is voluntarily intoxicated, are considered in this chapter. Consent is not considered to have been given where it is obtained through the threat or use of force, coercion or deception. In such circumstances it is clear consent has not been given. Furthermore, in cases where a defendant administers a substance to the complainant so as to incapacitate them, any sexual activity that occurs as a result of the complainant's inability to refuse such advances (either through stupefaction or unconsciousness) is not considered to be consented to.[7] Finally, where the complainant is unconscious, or wavering between unconsciousness and consciousness, whether due to their own voluntary intoxication or not, consent is incapable of being given.[8] In any of the noted circumstances, the intoxication of the complainant is not considered a contributing factor to any action taken by the defendant. In any of the above circumstances, culpability lies solely with the defendant, with the 'activity in question [being] both legally unproblematic and easily condemned'.[9]

CONTRIBUTORY NEGLIGENCE

Tort law

Tort law serves to provide some sort of remedy to an injured party through first the imposition of liability on the wrong-doing party (or parties) and then, further, through the award of damages to the injured party; much like criminal law it 'can be viewed as a system of ethical rules and principles of personal responsibility for conduct'.[10] While in some cases there will be a clear distinction between the wrong-doer(s) and the injured party, there are circumstances in which the lines are blurred. This can occur where the injured party may also be considered a wrong-doer as their actions partially contributed to the harm they suffered. Initially, the law remedied this complication by allowing fault (irrespective of the level of fault) on the part of the plaintiff to exclude any liability[11] on the part of the defendant.[12] As noted in *Cayzer, Irvine & Co v Carron Ltd*, 'the rule of law is that if there is blame causing the accident on both sides, however small that blame may be on one side, the loss lies where it falls'.[13] This approach was amended by the Law Reform (Contributory Negligence) Act 1945, which stipulated that:

> Where any person suffers damage as the result partly of his own fault and partly of the fault of any other person or persons, a claim in respect of that damage shall not

---

7   Emily Finch and Vanessa E Munro, 'Juror Stereotypes and Blame Attribution in Rape Cases Involving Intoxicants: The Findings of a Pilot Study' (2005) 45 British Journal of Criminology 25, 25.

8   ibid.

9   ibid.

10   Peter Cane, *The Anatomy of Tort Law* (Oxford University Press 1997) 1.

11   *Butterfield v Forrester* (1809) 11 East 60, 103 ER 926.

12   Jenny Steele, *Tort Law* (3rd edition, Oxford University Press 2014) 270.

13   [1849] 9 App Cas 873, 881. It should be noted that there existed a modifying principle: the doctrine of last opportunity. This served to allow the plaintiff to recover damages where the defendant could have avoided the harm at the time of injury whilst the plaintiff could not; see *Bridge v Grand Junction Ry* (1838) 3 M & W 244 and *Davies v Mann* (1842) 10 M & W 546.

be defeated by reason of the fault of the person suffering the damage, but the damages recoverable in respect thereof shall be reduced to such extent as the court thinks just and equitable having regard to the claimant's share in the responsibility for the damage.[14]

Under this regime there is apportionment of responsibility on all parties who took part in creating the circumstances in which the plaintiff was harmed. Recognition of the plaintiff's part in the injury does not serve to remove blame from the other party(ies) involved (who may often hold the majority of the blame for the injury incurred); nor does it put the blame on the plaintiff. The act in effect 'enable[d] . . . loss to be apportioned in accordance with the ordinary ideas of fairness'.[15]

In the case of *Nance v British Columbia Electric Railway Co Ltd* Viscount Simon clearly outlined the requirements for fulfilling the partial defence of contributory negligence, stating that 'all that is necessary to establish such a defence is to prove . . . that the injured party did not in his own interest take reasonable care of himself and contributed, by this want of care, to his own injury'.[16] Thus, two requirements must be fulfilled in order for contributory negligence to be raised and blame to be apportioned appropriately. First, it must be shown that the plaintiff failed to exercise reasonable care to avoid being hurt.[17] In determining what constituted failure to exercise reasonable care, Lord Denning argued it was a matter of foreseeability and that 'a person is guilty of contributory negligence if he ought reasonably to have foreseen that, if he did not act as a reasonable, prudent man, he might be hurt himself'.[18] In *Froom v Butcher* Denning again addressed the issue, stating 'contributory negligence is a man's carelessness in looking after his own safety'.[19]

Secondly, there must be evidence that the failure to exercise reasonable care contributed to the damage suffered by the plaintiff. Logically, only those actions, or omissions, by the plaintiff that had a direct contribution to the damage suffered may be considered in apportioning responsibility. In determining what constitutes a contributing factor the court considered 'What faults were there which caused the damage?' and made a clear distinction between 'causes' and the 'circumstances in which, or on which, they operate'.[20] In the case of *Jones v Linox Quarries*, Jones had chosen to ride on the back of a vehicle (something expressly prohibited by his employer). The vehicle was involved in an accident, negligently caused by the vehicle's driver, and Jones was crushed. Jones attempted to argue that, though there had been a risk of falling off the vehicle, the risk of being crushed could not be attributed to his sitting on the back of the vehicle. Such a reading was rejected by the court as it was 'too fine a distinction' to make.[21] Though it would be the case that Jones' decision to ride on the back of the vehicle would not be a contributory factor, but a mere matter of circumstance, were a huntsman to have accidentally shot him, on the facts his sitting on the vehicle caused him to

---

14 Section 1(1) of the 1945 Act.

15 Glanville Williams, 'The Law Reform (Contributory Negligence) Act 1945' [1946] 9(2) Modern Law Review 105, 105.

16 [1951] AC 601; [1951] 2 All ER 448, 611.

17 Though generally speaking this is an objective test, as Horsey and Rackley note, 'the law does allow for some modification of this objective standard, eg in relation to children'; see *Probert (A Child) v Moore* [2012] EWHC 2324 (QB) in Kirsty Horsey and Erika Rackley, *Tort Law* (3rd edition, Oxford University Press 2013) 270, fn 28.

18 *Jones v Livox Quarries* [1952] 2 QB 608, 615 (*Jones*).

19 [1976] QB 286, 291.

20 *Jones* (n 18) 616.

21 ibid 617.

be in a dangerous position 'in which his injuries [were] made worse by reason of his position than they otherwise would have been, then his damage is partly the result of his own fault'.[22]

Once it is found that there has been both a failure to exercise reasonable care and that that failure contributed to the harm suffered by the plaintiff, 'the damages recoverable ... shall be reduced to such extent as the court thinks just and equitable'.[23] While it may be that, generally speaking, the reduction is limited, the primary purpose is to acknowledge the contribution of the plaintiff in the damages, as opposed to absolving the defendant of all responsibility. It is for this reason that a finding of 100% contributory negligence cannot occur, for to do so would suggest not that there are multiple parties contributing to the damage which occurred, but that a single party (the plaintiff) is responsible.[24]

What is of paramount importance in understanding contributory negligence is that it does not operate to provide the defendant with an excuse for their actions; nor does it serve to place blame at the feet of the plaintiff. Instead it attempts to recognise a plaintiff's contribution to their damage to ensure the plaintiff does not evade all and any responsibility while also recognising the defendant's primary role in the harm occurring. This can be seen with reference to cases of contributory negligence where a plaintiff has accepted a car ride from an intoxicated person. In such cases, there is no doubt that primary responsibility for the harm to the plaintiff, and blame, lies with the person who sat behind the wheel of a car and chose to drive whilst intoxicated. Any accident that occurred as a result of their intoxication is their fault and to say otherwise would be illogical. It has to be acknowledged, however, that a person who chooses to accept a ride from an intoxicated driver fails to exercise due care in ensuring their own safety. Where there is no compulsion to accept a ride, the failure of the passenger to refuse to get in a car with someone who is obviously incapable of driving safely must be acknowledged. This does not exclude blame on the part of the driver, but merely recognises the risk the passenger took and accordingly holds them responsible for that risk to a limited extent. This sentiment was noted in *Meah v McCreamer* where Woolf J found 'there was an obvious risk in accompanying the Defendant in that motorcar' and that such risk must be acknowledged through the reduction of damages.[25]

Criminal law

Contributory negligence does not, *per se*, exist within criminal law. Currently, there is no defence known as contributory negligence; nor, in sentencing, does any defence serve to reduce the sentence by percentages. However, the partial defence of loss of self-control does act in a way reminiscent of the principle of contributory negligence. Loss of self-control, previously provocation under the common law prior to the enactment of the Coroners and Justice Act 2009, operates to reduce a charge from murder, with a mandatory life sentence, to voluntary manslaughter, with sentencing wholly at the discretion of the sentencing judge. The principle behind the original partial defence of provocation was based on the combination of two factors: first, there exist situations in which the actions of another (initially this related primarily to sexual infidelity) may cause a normal man to act in a manner falling outside of reasonable conduct. The partial defence of provocation sought to 'accommodate

---

22 ibid.
23 Law Reform (Contributory Negligence) Act 1945, s 1(1); Christopher Kennedy and Matthew Snarr, 'Intoxication and Inebriation: Another Late Night' [2015] Journal of Personal Injury Law 84, 85.
24 *Pitts v Hunt* [1991] 1 QB 24, 49.
25 [1985] 1 All ER 367, 371.

human emotion'[26] and acted as a 'concession to human frailty'.[27] Secondly, murder was punishable by death and thus the partial defence was created to allow defendants to evade the death penalty, instead leaving their punishment to judges to determine.

The justification behind loss of self-control remains predominantly the same, though with less of a focus on the protection of one's 'honour'; instead shifting to acknowledging that in particular circumstances the actions of the victim may justify, to some extent, the actions of the defendant, whilst not accepting the latter's actions as acceptable.[28] As Norrie notes, 'the law condemns the act both for the wrong done and the loss of control, but still extends a compassionate hand to the actor . . . the loss of self-control and its consequences are condemned, but the weakness it represents is viewed with sympathy'.[29] When considering some of the examples where the partial defence is applicable, especially in respect of domestic abuse, it becomes obvious that there is a clear policy rationale for accepting that judicial discretion in (reducing) sentencing is appropriate in particular circumstances, whilst still condemning the use of violence. In the case of *Ahluwalia* the defendant had suffered ten years of violence, humiliation and abuse at the hands of the victim; on at least one occasion the victim had attempted to kill the defendant, and had repeatedly threatened to kill her.[30] On the day the offence occurred, the victim told the defendant to leave and threatened to beat her and burn her with a hot iron if she did not leave him alone.[31] Later that evening, considering the victim's threat, the defendant threw petrol and a lit candle into the victim's bedroom causing him to die from burns sustained.[32] Though the partial defence of provocation was made out,[33] due to the *Duffy* requirement that the loss of control be 'sudden and temporary', the new loss of self-control requires no such temporal determination and thus the defendant may have been able to use the partial defence successfully, in particular under the limb of 'fear of serious violence'.[34] In such cases there is a strong argument for why there should not be the imposition of the full penalty for murder. While the killing of another person is not an acceptable method of leaving an abusive relationship (nor an acceptable reaction in general, barring cases of self-defence) it becomes understandable why a person in Ahluwalia's position may have acted in the manner she did. It is this understanding, neither acceptance nor condonation, that fuels the desire to provide the opportunity for more lenient sentencing. The same could be said for other situations in which a person loses control – though the act of losing control is not one which should be encouraged, there are circumstances in which it is understandable that a person lost the restraint that would normally prevent them from acting violently. In these instances it is unlikely that it would serve the purposes of sentencing outlined in the Criminal Justice Act 2003 to sentence the defendant for murder.[35]

---

26 Chris Morgan, 'Loss of Self-Control: Back to the Good Old Days' (2013) Journal of Criminal Law 119, 120.

27 Barry Mitchell, Ronnie Mackay and Warren Brookbanks, 'Pleading for Provoked Killers: In Defence of *Morgan Smith*' (2008) 124 Law Quarterly Review 675, 683.

28 Morgan (n 26).

29 Alan Norrie, 'The Coroners and Justice Act 2009 – Partial Defence to Murder (1) Loss of Control' (2010) Criminal Law Review 275, 279.

30 [1992] 4 All ER 889, 891–892.

31 ibid 892.

32 ibid 893–894.

33 ibid 896.

34 *Duffy* [1949] 1 All ER 932, 932; Coroners and Justice Act 2009, s 55(3).

35 The purposes of sentencing are listed under s 142(1) of the Criminal Justice Act 2003: '(a) the punishment of offenders, (b) the reduction of crime (including its reduction by deterrence), (c) the reform and rehabilitation of offenders, (d) the protection of the public, and (e) the making of reparation by offenders to persons affected by their offences'.

Cases involving domestic abuse are not the sole ambit of loss of self-control. The qualifying triggers under s 55 include not only a 'fear of serious violence',[36] under which arguably most domestic abuse cases would fall, but also 'things done or said which ... constituted circumstances of an extremely grave character, and ... caused D to have a justifiable sense of being seriously wronged'.[37] The inclusion of an 'anger' trigger allows for the partial defence to operate in situations where 'the defendant had a legitimate ground to feel strongly aggrieved ... to the extent that it would be harsh to regard their moral culpability for reacting as they did in the same way as if it had been an unprovoked killing'.[38] These situations, under English and Welsh law, are no less deserving of the understanding afforded in cases of domestic abuse.

As noted earlier, though loss of self-control (provocation) was not incorporated into criminal law on the basis of an application of contributory negligence, Nelson opines that 'similar to the contributory negligence doctrine ... the paradigmatic facts ... do not involve the prototypical innocent victim, rather there are arguably moral wrongs committed by all parties involved in the crime – both victim and perpetrator'.[39] Thus, whilst no claim can be made to the inclusion of contributory negligence doctrinally within criminal law, it is clear that, at the very least, some core principles may be transferred.[40]

INTOXICATION

Under criminal law, intoxication is separated into two different categories: involuntary and voluntary intoxication. Irrespective of whether intoxication was voluntary or involuntary, intoxication does not operate as a defence within criminal law.[41] The law treats the two categories differently in their relevance to whether the defendant possessed the necessary *mens rea* for an offence. Whilst involuntary intoxication may allow a defendant to persuade a jury that they lacked *mens rea* for a crime, irrespective of whether the crime is one of basic or specific intent, the same cannot be said of voluntary intoxication.[42] The difference in treatment may be most strongly related to the fact that, where a defendant is involuntarily intoxicated, they made no choice to take a substance which would lower their inhibitions or 'impair [their] perception and judgment so that [they] may fail to be aware of facts, or ...

---

36 Coroners and Justice Act 2009, s 55(3).

37 ibid, s 55(4).

38 Law Commission, *Partial Defences to Murder: Final Report* (Law Com No 290, 2004) 3.68.

39 Nelson refers to the partial defence of provocation under United States law, which, in basic principles, is similar to the English loss of self-control; Camille A Nelson, 'A Consideration of Mitigatory Criminal Defences and Racism-related Mental Illness: Provocation' (*Race, Racism and the Law*) <http://racism. org/index.php?option=com_content&view=article&id=1561:mitigatorycriminaldefenses&catid=136& Itemid=155&showall=&limitstart=6> accessed 28 November 2015.

40 In an expanded study of the role of contributory negligence in the criminal law, consideration should be made to the fact that policy reasons exist which suggest a direct transplantation of civil law principles into the criminal law may be problematic. In *Wacker* [2003] QB 1207 the Court of Appeal had to consider whether the principle of *ex turpi causa* was applicable within criminal law. It was noted, at 1216, that to allow a defendant to argue that they could evade responsibility for the deaths of others, due to negligence, on the basis of joint engagement in criminal activity 'would be unacceptable in civilised society' and that the 'very same public policy that causes the civil courts to refuse the claim points in a quite different direction in considering a criminal offence'. Accordingly, policy concerns must always be borne in mind when determining whether a civil principle may effectively be incorporated into the criminal law.

41 Michael Allen, *Textbook on Criminal Law* (12th edition, Oxford University Press 2013) 164.

42 ibid.

foresee results of [their] conduct, of which [they] would certainly have been aware, or have foreseen, if [they] had been sober'.[43] Conversely, a defendant who voluntarily consumes a substance and becomes intoxicated makes a choice to use a substance that they know may 'cause [them] to cast off the restraints of reason and conscience' and accordingly may be held far more responsible for any actions they commit whilst in that inebriated state.[44]

For the purposes of this chapter, the involuntary intoxication of the defendant is not considered; instead, the focus is on the law in relation to how voluntary intoxication operates with respect to the defendant's *mens rea* and how the voluntary intoxication of the complainant, in sexual offences, affects any consent given.

Intoxication of the defendant

As much as it is generally accepted that substances (such as alcohol) lower one's inhibitions, it is also a generally accepted fact that, whilst intoxicated, a 'person's perception and judgment' may be impaired 'so that he may fail to be aware of facts, or to foresee results of his conduct'.[45] This universally acknowledged fact has resulted in a need for intoxication to play at least some part in determining culpability for criminal offences. Though there is a strong policy desire to avoid any possible suggestion that intoxication provides a good 'excuse' for criminal behaviour due to the damaging message this could send, there is also a need to maintain the requirement of the fulfilment of the necessary *mens rea* of an offence. The prevalence of alcohol-related crime would, if nothing else, make the inclusion of a defence of intoxication untenable.[46] At the same time, it is similarly untenable to suggest that the law can presume a person held the necessary direct or oblique intent for the commission of, for example, murder where they obviously lacked the intent by virtue of their intoxication.

It is for this reason that intoxication instead operates neither to provide a defence, nor to assume that *mens rea* is not fulfilled. The intoxication doctrine performs a slightly different role in that it becomes operative where a defendant 'seeks to argue that as a result of intoxication [they] lacked the necessary *mens rea* for the offence'.[47] Where a person has the intent for an offence but is also intoxicated then the intoxication is irrelevant. For example, a woman finds out her wife is cheating and decides to kill her; however, she does not think she can do so sober and whilst waiting for her wife to return home (at which point she will shoot her), drinks to steady her nerves. Though the defendant may be intoxicated at the point of shooting her wife, she shoots and kills with the intent of murdering her wife. Her intoxication proves no difficulty for the *mens rea* of murder. In cases where a person does not have the necessary *mens rea*, as a result of their intoxication, the lack of *mens rea* may result in an acquittal. Where the offence is a specific intent offence, voluntary intoxication that results in the defendant not being able to form the necessary *mens rea* will result in an acquittal. If the offence is a basic intent offence, voluntary intoxication that results in the defendant not being able to form the necessary *mens rea* will not result in an acquittal where the defendant would have had the necessary *mens rea* if sober.[48] For example, a member of a gang is returning

---

43 David Ormerod and Karl Laird, *Smith and Hogan's Criminal Law* (14th edition, Oxford University Press 2015) 353.

44 *Majewski* (n 1) 474.

45 Ormerod and Laird (n 43).

46 In a recent study it was found that 53% of violent crime was alcohol related, Office for National Statistics, 'Chapter 5: Violent Crime and Sexual Offences – Alcohol-Related Violence' (12 February 2015) 7.

47 Rebecca Williams, 'Voluntary Intoxication – A Lost Cause?' (2013) Law Quarterly Review 264, 267.

48 Jeremy Horder, 'The Classification of Crimes and the General Part' in Antony Duff and Stuart Green, *Defining Crimes* (Oxford University Press 2005).

home from the pub, having become very drunk; whilst walking home he sees a member of an opposing gang and to scare him begins to shoot randomly into the air and street, in the process killing an innocent bystander. He claims that, in his drunkenness, he did not realise anyone else was on the street and that, by randomly firing, he would hit another person. A charge of murder would be unlikely to succeed because the man's intoxication prevents *mens rea* from forming and such *mens rea* cannot be assumed.[49] Conversely, a charge of manslaughter is likely to be successful because although the man may not have appreciated his recklessness whilst intoxicated, he would have appreciated the risk if sober. As noted by Spencer, intoxication thus 'operates for the benefit of the prosecution . . . wherever the doctrine applies, its function – sole function – is to treat the defendant as if he acted with *mens rea* when, in fact, he did not'.[50]

This ability to 'construct' intent in cases where no such intent exists is one which is primarily born out of necessity.[51] As noted above, it would be inconceivable to allow those who act unlawfully due to their drunkenness to avoid punishment, even in situations where they knew that their drunken selves may act in an unlawful manner. This may not seem necessarily problematic in a scenario involving a person who has never committed a crime before and very rarely drinks but, whilst drunk, has done something that they would normally never have done. In such a situation some may even sympathise with the offender that they should be given the benefit of the doubt – after all, "everybody makes mistakes". However, the same principle would have to apply to all individuals who commit crime whilst intoxicated. This includes people who regularly become intoxicated (through drink or drugs) and commit acts of criminal damage, become violent, act recklessly, and so on. The same sympathy is unlikely to arise for an individual who has, countless times before, become intoxicated and committed crimes. What might be considered an 'unfortunate mistake' in the first example becomes a worrying pattern of behaviour in the second. It is for this reason that the law finds that intent can be constructed, even if technically it did not exist, for 'a mind rendered self-inducedly insensible . . . through drink or drugs, to the nature of a prohibited act or to its probable consequences is *as wrongful* a mind as one which consciously contemplates the prohibited act and foresees its probable consequence'.[52] Such behaviour is considered so harmful that 'the element of guilt or moral turpitude is supplied by the act of self-intoxication reckless of possible consequences'.[53] Thus, the necessary *mens rea* can be constructed in basic intent offences, thereby preventing defendants from evading liability due to intoxication. Sexual offences have been determined to be basic intent offences; as such, the intoxication doctrine can be used to construct the intent of a defendant where they claim to have been too intoxicated to realise that no consent existed.[54] Accordingly, where a defendant has become involuntarily intoxicated and wrongly believes consent is being given, the law can presume their knowledge of a lack of consent based on the fact they would have knowledge of the lack of consent had they been sober.[55]

49 *Woollin* intent is unlikely as the death or serious injury of the bystander may not be a virtual certainty. *Woollin* [1999] AC 82.

50 Andrew Simester, 'Intoxication is Never a Defence' (2009) Criminal Law Review 3, 4.

51 ibid 10.

52 *Majewski* (n 1) 479.

53 ibid 498.

54 *Heard* [2008] QB 43; *Woods* (1982) 74 Cr App R 312.

55 For a critical analysis of the categorisation of sexual assault as a basic intent offence see: Ben Fitzpatrick, 'Sexual Assault: Intoxication' (2008) Journal of Criminal Law 16; Rebecca Williams, 'Voluntary Intoxication, Sexual Assault and the Future of *Majewski*' (2007) Cambridge Law Journal 260; Alan Reed, 'Intoxication and Sexual Assaults' (2007) Criminal Lawyer 1; Antje du Bois-Pedain, 'Voluntary Intoxication and Sexual Assault Contrary to s 3 of the Sexual Offences Act 2003' (2007) Archbold News 4.

Intoxication of the complainant in sexual offences

Under the Sexual Offences Act 2003 consent is valid only if a person 'agrees by choice, and has the freedom and capacity to make that choice'.[56] A rebuttable presumption of the complainant not having consented also exists where 'the complainant was asleep or otherwise unconscious at the time of the relevant act'.[57] There is no test or specified threshold within the Sexual Offences Act at which point consent is no longer valid due to intoxication. In order to determine if consent is valid, one must look instead to ss 74 and 75. Initially, in the proposals made in *Setting the Boundaries*, the issue of intoxicated consent was dealt with, at least to some extent. It was proposed that, within the rebuttable presumption triggers, the trigger of 'too affected by alcohol or drugs to give consent' would be included.[58] Its inclusion was made on the basis that, in such circumstances, a person would be unable to give 'free agreement' and thus, even where consent had been given, it would be presumed invalid.[59] This inclusion would not have necessarily clarified the law on this matter; there still existed the issue of the point at which a person becomes 'too affected' and the manner in which this would be measured. The proposal was rejected and in the Government's White Paper, *Protecting the Public,* there was no inclusion of intoxication.[60] Without clear legislative guidance it became an issue for the courts to determine. The matter was considered, with some finality, in the case of *Bree (Benjamin)*.[61]

Bree and the 19-year-old complainant were both part of a group that went out drinking one evening; both the complainant and Bree had a considerable amount to drink. The complainant remembered little of being taken to her home by Bree but did remember being continually sick in her bathroom. The defendant looked after her and washed her hair, though the complainant asserted that she lost consciousness at this point. She stated that she next remembered the defendant on top of her and penetrating her, which she had not consented to. Originally, the prosecution's case was that the complainant was unconscious and therefore incapable of giving consent to the defendant; however, over the course of the trial the prosecution acknowledged that the gaps in the complainant's memory were not from unconsciousness but from having 'blacked out' due to drinking. Bree claimed that the complainant was conscious throughout the night and that, after having been sick, she had become considerably more alert and sober and was not so drunk as to be incapable of consenting; any sexual activity took place consensually and the complainant was enthusiastic and willing throughout. The defendant was found guilty of rape and appealed on the basis that the trial judge had failed to direct the jury properly on the matter of drunken consent.

The court was tasked with determining the point at which intoxication may vitiate any consent obtained; thus, the question remained as to the point at which a person becomes so intoxicated that their choices are no longer 'free' and made with the necessary 'capacity'. The court noted the issue of intoxicated consent was one that the courts had addressed in the past. In *Lang* it was stated that 'there is no special rule applicable to drink and rape. If the issue be, as here, did the woman consent? The critical question is not how she came to take the drink,

---

56 Sexual Offences Act, s 74.

57 ibid, s 75(1) and (2)(d).

58 Home Office, *Setting the Boundaries: Volume I* (HMSO 2000) xii, recommendation 6.

59 ibid 19.

60 Home Office, *Protecting the Public: Strengthening Protection against Sex Offenders and Reforming the Law on Sexual Offences* (White Paper, Cm 5668, 2002).

61 [2008] QB 131 (CA (Crim Div)).

but whether she understood her situation and was capable of making up her mind'.[62] The issue was again addressed by the Court of Appeal in *Malone*, where the Court noted 'submitting to an act of sexual intercourse, because through drink she was unable physically to resist though she wished to, is not consent'.[63] The issue of intoxicated consent, however, was not one that had arisen since the enactment of the new Sexual Offences Act 2003. Accordingly, the Court had the task of determining under the new legislation the point at which consent may no longer be valid. Only one case, unreported, was noted by the Court to have dealt with the issue of intoxicated consent; though in *Dougal* the prosecution offered no evidence, counsel for the prosecution stated to the jury that 'a drunken consent is still a consent'.[64] The Court, in considering the phrase 'drunken consent is still consent', noted that the law in relation to the intoxication of defendants, found that 'a drunken intent is still an intent'[65] and though 'the phrase lacks delicacy ... properly understood, it provides a useful shorthand accurately encapsulating the legal position'.[66] In fact, the Court went further to note that, in the same way that 'drunken consent is still consent', a 'drunken man who intends to commit rape, and does so, is not excused by the fact that his intention is a drunken intention'.[67] It was consequently found that

> if, through drink (or for any other reason) the complainant has temporarily lost her capacity to choose whether to have intercourse on the relevant occasion, she is not consenting ... however, where the complainant has voluntarily consumed even substantial quantities of alcohol, but nevertheless remains capable of choosing whether or not to have intercourse, and in drink agrees to do so, this would not be rape.[68]

While the Court does clarify that 'drunken consent is still consent' there is little guidance on when evidence could be used to determine the point at which a person's intoxication becomes so profound that they become incapable of consent. It has been suggested that by looking at the facts in *Bree* a high threshold is found; the complainant was sick and by her own evidence 'blacking out'.[69] Though, on the particular facts, the case of *Bree* did not set a clear, high threshold for capacity to consent when intoxicated, the court's failure to provide any clear guidance on ways in which to determine capacity is troublesome. The concept of 'capacity' is not particularly well-developed; although often terms, for example 'intent', are left to the jury to be given their ordinary meaning, the issue of capacity is far more inconsistent in interpretation and understanding than intent. A person's understanding of what capacity means may differ substantially; for example, one juror may consider capacity in what they deem to be a 'legal' context (capacity in relation to contracts), while another may view capacity as a far more practical consideration based predominantly on actions. In a survey of barristers' perspectives on the Sexual Offences Act 2003 and alcohol-related rape cases, a particular issue of concern was the lack of an 'objective standard that you can

---

62 [1975] 62 Cr App R 50, 52.
63 [1998] 2 Cr App R 447, 452.
64 (CC, 24 November 2005).
65 The Court of Appeal referred to the principle in *Sheehan* [1975] 1 WLR 739.
66 *Bree* (n 61) 139–140.
67 ibid 140.
68 ibid.
69 Shlomit Wallerstein, '"A Drunken Consent is Still Consent" – or is it? A Critical Analysis of the Law on a Drunken Consent to Sex Following *Bree*' (2009) Journal of Criminal Law 318.

put the person against and say at that point, they're so drunk that they cannot consent'.[70] Though in the same study there was a clear belief that further legislative guidance on capacity would be unhelpful, the lack of objective standards was noted by some as being of particular concern.[71]

Preconceptions surrounding intoxicated consent

It is at this point that some consideration of the preconceptions around sexual offences and intoxicated consent is made. As noted previously, it can be found that there is a bias in mainstream media, and in academia, to discussing sexual offences against adults and consent in relation to women. When reforms to sexual offences laws are proposed or when guidelines regarding consent are made, the media predominantly reacts in relation to the effects on women, and on men in relation to their interaction with women. This may be a result of a historical tendency of the law to fail to protect women from male oppressors;[72] women have historically been divorced from rights over their bodies.[73] Only recently has it been recognised in law, for example, that a husband does not have sexual rights over his wife and accordingly that marital rape is unlawful.[74] Conceptions of sexual assault have tended to revolve around the vulnerability of women, the ability for men to overpower women purely by virtue of their greater strength, and men's ability to intimidate women;[75] in turn, this has seeped into discussion of consent.[76]

In general, marginalising other groups of victims, particularly failing to consider the vulnerability of non-heteronormative groups, is dangerous when discussing sexual offences as it only continues past discrimination against these groups. However, this type of stereotyping of the 'attacker' and 'victim' can be particularly concerning when discussing issues such as intoxicated consent. Constructing intoxicated consent around a model of male oppression and female suppression leaves room not only for further victimisation[77] but also of unfair burdens on particular gender groups.[78] It further fails to acknowledge that the world no

---

70 Clare Gunby, Anna Carline and Caryl Beynon, 'Alcohol-Related Rape Cases: Barristers' Perspectives on the Sexual Offences Act 2003 and its Impact on Practice' (2010) Journal of Criminal Law 579, 588.

71 ibid 599.

72 Susan Brownmiller, *Against Our Will: Men, Women and Rape* (Ballantine 1975).

73 Kathryn Kish Sklar and James Brewer Stewart, *Women's Rights and Transatlantic Antislavery in the Era of Emancipation* (Yale University Press 2007) 132.

74 *R v R* [1991] 3 WLR 767.

75 A Vinsel, 'Rape: A Review Essay' (1977) 3 Personality and Social Psychology Bulletin 183; Rochelle Semmel Albin, 'Psychological Studies of Rape' (1977) 3(2) Signs 423.

76 See for example the work of Ehrlich and its predominant consideration of interpretation of consent by a woman: Susan Lynn Ehrlich, *Representing Rape: Language and Sexual Consent* (Routledge 2001). See also the article by Finch and Munro which slips into heteronormative considerations of consent with the female always being placed in the position of victim: Emily Finch and Vanessa E Munro, 'Breaking Boundaries? Sexual Consent in the Jury Room' (2006) 26(3) Legal Studies 303.

77 An American study showed increased rates of sexual assaults against those who identify as LGBT: Emily Rothman, Deinera Exner and Allyson Baughman, 'The Prevalence of Sexual Assault against People Who Identify as Gay, Lesbian, or Bisexual in the United States: A Systematic Review' (2011) 12(2) Trauma Violence Abuse 55.

78 Framing discussions of consent on the presumption of the male as the aggressor risks increased ostracism of male victims (the concept of a male victim of alcohol-related rape, particularly if the aggressor is a woman, is almost unheard of) and risks placing an unfair assumption of aggression on those who are legally 'male' but do not identify as such, a group already victimised sexually; 'Lesbian, Gay, Bisexual, Transgender & Queer Community' (*WCSAP*, 7 May 2015) <http://www.wcsap.org/lesbian-gay-bisexual-transgender-queer-community> accessed 27 November 2015.

longer functions in a binary gender system; those who fail to identify with a particular gender or those who are in transition and thus identify with one gender while legally are another fall outside of such discourse.[79]

It is therefore important to divorce the law from gender-biased and heteronormative conceptions of how consent operates; understandings of the law on intoxicated consent should not come from the idea that men use alcohol to target women and obtain sexual gratification – they should instead revolve around the concepts of autonomy and capacity (gender- and sexual-orientation neutral concepts). To do otherwise would be to allow for stereotypes surrounding sexuality to seep into the law; for example, the erroneous belief that gay men are hypersexual, promiscuous and likely always to consent, or the stereotype that a man is happy about any sexual encounter, irrespective of consent, because he 'got laid'.[80] For example, in a study undertaken in the United States it was found that men are more likely to have been a victim of a sexual assault while intoxicated.[81] Such stereotypes are harmful and risk alienating true victims; at the same time, they also risk labelling genders on the basis of preconceptions.[82] Consequently, when considering intoxicated consent, the primary concern should be on whether the intoxication was self-induced and whether the decision made was one that was made with the necessary capacity and freedom as stipulated under the Sexual Offences Act.

CONTRIBUTORY NEGLIGENCE IN RELATION TO SEXUAL OFFENCES

As was previously noted, contributory negligence does not, *per se*, operate within criminal law. Nevertheless, contributory negligence has, in some ways, been incorporated through the partial defence of loss of self-control. There is always some reticence in applying a model of attribution of responsibility to the victim in criminal law; logically, to allow any responsibility or condemnation of the victim may detract from the seriousness of the offence and the need to make the perpetrator understand why their actions are wrongful.[83] In some circumstances, however, there may be a variety of reasons (including discouraging reckless behaviour on the part of the complainant) for recognising that, at least in some way, the victim has contributed to the end result, even if this recognition in no way exculpates the defendant or legitimises the offence carried out.[84] This is particularly evident in cases where both the defendant and complainant are equally voluntarily intoxicated. Though the law would hold the defendant

---

79 Standing Together against Domestic Violence, 'Domestic Violence and LGBT Relationships' (*Standing Together*, 2010) <www.standingtogether.org.uk/fileadmin/user . . . /pub-LGBT-factsheet.pdf> accessed 29 November 2015.

80 Karen G Weiss, 'Male Sexual Victimization: Examining Men's Experiences of Rape and Sexual Assault' (2010) 12(3) Men and Masculinities 275.

81 Reported in Weiss, *ibid* 284.

82 Weiss notes that 'norms of masculinity (and shame for not conforming to those norms) may especially help to explain men's greater reluctance to report sexual victimization incidents perpetrated by women' which should considered in tandem with the fact that 'while 99 percent of women are sexually victimized by men . . . 46 percent of men [are] victimized by women', ibid 284–286.

83 See (n 90) on victim blaming.

84 This view was shown to be a prominent one in Finch and Munro's jury study. It was found that 'in the majority of cases in which the victim had voluntarily ingested either alcohol or recreational drugs, participants were in broad agreement that she ought to bear some responsibility for the subsequent intercourse. There was a degree of divergence amongst participants as to the consequences of attributing responsibility to the victim', Finch and Munro (n 7) 30–31.

culpable irrespective of his intoxication, the complainant's consent may be vitiated – a situation that may be deemed unfair in the public's eye.[85]

It has been suggested that the failure of the Government to include reference to intoxication under the triggers to the rebuttable presumption in the White Paper *Protecting the Public* was, in effect, a 'nod' to the doctrine of contributory negligence. Temkin and Ashworth note the initial proposal, *Setting the Boundaries*,

> further recommended that the list should include the situation where C was 'too affected by alcohol or drugs to give free agreement'. This proposal was not adopted in *Protecting the Public* and section 75(2)(f) is considerably narrower, since it relates only to situations where C's intoxication is patently blameless. Whilst contributory negligence has no place in the criminal law, it is apparent that such ideas had an influence on the Government's thinking.[86]

The inclusion of a form of contributory negligence within sexual offences could be achieved in one of two ways. First, similar to how the partial defence of loss of self-control operates to result in manslaughter,[87] an offence of sexual assault occasioned through invalid intoxicated consent could be created.[88] Defendants found guilty on an alternative charge of this nature could either be sentenced under similar guidelines to those existing for the correlating offence or under guidelines that take into consideration the various factors peculiar to intoxicated consent cases. In the first scenario the separate offence would operate merely to amend the label attached to the offence.[89] In the second, the alternative guidelines would allow for sentencing that is appropriate for a wider variety of situations. For example, this could include cases where a complainant has shown sexual interest in the defendant (this could be engaging in sexual contact like kissing or touching) but thereafter became heavily intoxicated to the point of invalidating consent. The complainant may still be conscious, participating to a limited extent, or even actively consenting, yet their consent may have been found to lack the necessary capacity. In such cases, though the defendant *should* have recognised the complainant's inability to give valid consent due to intoxication, the defendant's engagement in sexual acts is not done irrespective of the complainant's consent, *per se*, and failure to recognise the complainant's state of intoxication is not necessarily a matter of deliberate manipulation. The law already includes partial defences that acknowledge contributory actions whilst still punishing the offender; the provision of a lesser offence (which is primarily for purposes of sentencing) allows for such acknowledgement, provides recognition of the harm done by the defendant and does so in a clearly structured manner.[90] By including an alternative offence there is a clear structure within the law, similar to the structure of murder and manslaughter.

---

85 ibid, 32.

86 Jennifer Temkin and Andrew Ashworth, 'The Sexual Offences Act 2003: (1) Rape, Sexual Assaults and the Problems of Consent' (2004) Criminal Law Review 328, 339.

87 As opposed to murder, Jonathan Herring, *Criminal Law* (6th edition, Oxford University Press 2014) 237.

88 This could also be similar to the American system of degrees of offences (whereby offences are ranked on the basis of severity and intent – murder being a prime example).

89 Finch and Munro (n 7) 31.

90 The issue of 'victim blaming' can often be seen to be a consideration in any form of criminal application of 'contributory negligence'. As this chapter does not consider the sociological or criminological merits of amending the law on consent to sexual activity through the inclusion of contributory negligence, the issue of victim blaming is not considered. For discussion of the effect victim blaming has on the law see: Susan Edwards, '"Provoking Her Own Demise": From Common Assault to Homicide' in Jalna Hanmer and Mary Maynars (eds), *Women, Violence and Social Control* (Macmillan Press 1987); Joshua Dressler,

Secondly, contributory negligence could function similar to the manner in which it operates in civil law. Sentencing guidelines could introduce fixed reductions in sentence or have invalid intoxicated consent operate as a discretionary mitigating element when particular factors are present. This would operate in much the same way as discounts are awarded for pleading guilty early; a particular percentage of the overall sentence could be reduced so as to take into consideration a variety of additional factors.[91] Similar to the first possibility, the provision of specific sentencing guidelines would primarily affect the level or type of punishment meted out. Unlike creating an alternative offence, there would be no official portioning of responsibility on the complainant; consequently, this may be a more effective method of introducing contributory negligence.

CONCLUSION

It is evident that there does exist, to some extent, a tension in the law regarding the treatment of intoxication. Intoxication (irrespective of the level) fails, in cases of criminal behaviour, to vitiate criminal liability – rightly so, as to allow persons to blame their drunkenness for poor behaviour would set a disturbing and unsustainable precedent for reckless behaviour. In contrast, intoxication can vitiate the consent of a person to sexual activity even where that consent is clearly made – the person consenting is deemed to be incapable of choosing to act in a particular way and thus cannot agree to engage in sexual activity. As noted in the introduction, this chapter aimed to see if any possible tension could be resolved or limited through the application of a form of contributory negligence. The purpose of such incorporation (irrespective of the manner) would be to attempt to mirror more accurately other areas of the law dealing with intoxication while providing the necessary punitive measures against defendants.

'Provocation: Partial Justification or Partial Excuse?' (1988) 51(4) Modern Law Review 467; Kevin D McCaul and others, 'Understanding Attributions of Victim Blame for Rape: Sex, Violence and Foreseeability' (1990) 20(1) Journal of Applied Social Psychology 1; Eliana Suarez, 'Stop Blaming the Victim: A Meta-Analysis on Rape Myths' (2010) 25(11) Journal on Interpersonal Violence 2010; Amy Grubb and Emily Turner, 'Attribution of blame in rape cases: A review of the impact of rape myth acceptance, gender role conformity and substance use on victim blaming' (2012) 17(5) Aggression and Violent Behaviour 443; Sarah Becker and Justine Tinkler, '"Me Getting Plastered and Her Provoking My Eyes": Young People's Attribution of Blame for Sexual Aggression in Public Drinking Spaces' (2015) 10(3) Feminist Criminology 235; Rebecca Hayes, Katherine Lorenz and Kristin A Bell, 'Victim Blaming Others: Rape Myth Acceptance and the Just World Belief' (2013) 8(3) Feminist Criminology 202; Kate Fitz-Gibbon, 'Provocation in New South Wales: The need for abolition' (2012) 45(2) Australian & New Zealand Journal of Criminology 194; Danielle Tyson, 'Victoria's New Homicide Laws: Provocative Reforms or More Stories of Women 'Asking for it'?' (2012) 23 Current Issues in Criminal Justice 203.

91 Such factors could include, but are not limited to:
  - the defendant's involvement in the complainant's drinking (was the defendant actively encouraging or berating the complainant to drink?);
  - the complainant's willingness to drink (was the complainant drinking only to please the defendant?);
  - was the defendant drinking with the complainant?;
  - the defendant's level of intoxication (only in relation to whether the defendant was profiting from a marked contrast in sobriety between the defendant and the complainant);
  - whether the defendant deliberately approached the complainant as a result of their intoxication (was the complainant already considerably intoxicated at the point of meeting the defendant?, was there only a short period of time between meeting the complainant and the defendant committing the sexual offence?).

Without doubt there exist concerning behaviours around consent and intoxication; there are serious problems with the use of alcohol in 'loosening up' people in order to engage in sexual activity that is not necessarily consensual and taking advantage of individuals who are incapacitated by drink or drugs.[92] Drinking to excess is a problem that plagues any criminal justice system and makes those who act in this fashion particularly vulnerable to wrongdoing (whether sexual or not). Just as the law may hold those who act unlawfully while intoxicated responsible in some cases, it can be argued that so must the law acknowledge irresponsible behaviour caused by intoxication. That does not diminish the injury done to complainants, just as contributory negligence within the civil law does not diminish the harm done to victims: it merely acknowledges the diverse origins of the harm.

Incorporation of contributory negligence into the criminal law for this purpose could limit some of the tension surrounding intoxication and would arguably do so with the least negative impact on the way in which sexual offences operate. Whether such an incorporation would in fact be welcomed is very much another question.

---

92 Finch and Munro (n 7) 31.

8

Caveat Amator
Transmission of HIV and the parameters of consent and bad character evidence

Alan Reed and Emma Smith

Deceit and violence – these are the two forms of deliberate assault on human beings. Both can coerce people into acting against their will. Most harms that can befall victims through violence can come to them also through deceit. But deceit controls more subtly, for it works on belief as well as action. Even Othello, whom few would have deemed to try to subdue by force, could be brought to destroy himself and Desdemona through falsehood.[1]

INTRODUCTION

Feinberg, in a seminal article published three decades ago in *Ethics*,[2] considered the parameters of consent as a defence to what otherwise would be presented as a criminal harm. At the definitional core the defence, within supererogatory contextualisations, was viewed through a legal prism of justification.[3] The conclusion adduced was consent should properly be classified as a justification in that it demonstrated that the contested conduct was a legally permissible thing to do, not something legally prohibited.[4] The corollary, however, is that intentional or reckless infliction of harm on another person, even one who may consent, undermines society as a whole and such conduct should, generally speaking, be outlawed, unless there are special circumstances that may justify it.[5] In this sphere the criminalisation of the transmission of HIV and other communicable sexual diseases, either via non-fatal offence legislation, or alternatively as a sexual crime (rape) where fraud vitiates consent, raises fundamental questions about the function and purpose of criminal law as a tool of

---

1   Sissela Bok, *Lying: Moral Choice in Public and Private Life* (Pantheon Books, 1978) 18; and see Joseph H. Beale Jr, 'Consent in the Criminal Law' (1895) 8 Harvard Law Review 317, 321: 'A seeming consent extorted by force or terror differs from consent obtained by fraud. In the latter case the mind is deceived into agreement; in the former, the body is forced to act without a real agreement of the mind.'
2   Joel Feinberg, 'Victims' Excuses: The Case of Fraudulently Procured Consent' (1986) 96 Ethics 330.
3   ibid 370–371.
4   ibid; see generally, Alan Wertheimer, 'What is Consent? And is it Important' (2000) 3 Buffalo Criminal Law Review 557; Donald A. Dripps, 'Beyond Rape: An Essay on the Difference Between the Presence of Force and the Absence of Consent' (1992) 92 Columbia Law Review 1780; and Deborah Tuerkheimer, 'Sex Without Consent' (2013) 123 Yale Law Journal 335.
5   See generally, Dennis J Baker, 'The Moral Limits of Consent as a Defense in the Criminal Law' (2009) 12 New Criminal Law Review 93.

social control.[6] It has also highlighted the ability and suitability (or inability and unsuitability) of criminal law to regulate an intimate and fundamental aspect of an individual's private life.[7]

In broader terms, the ambit of legally valid consent in criminal law, beyond transmission of HIV, is also contestable and opaque.[8] A number of juridical precepts affirm that a freely given and sufficiently informed consent by a victim will preclude a defendant from inculpation;[9] but counterfactually there are a distinct spectra of cases where consent is legally irrelevant.[10] It is difficult to chart a via media between these juxtapositions. Moreover, concerns related to individual autonomy and state paternalism are often in conflict.[11] The latter indicia plays a crucial, but often forgotten, role within sentencing inculcations in this arena. Consent engenders a perspective that the autonomy of the other person is involved, and that if that person consents to the conduct there should be no offence.[12] However, we can also identify an attitude of paternalism that is primordial in a number of leading judgments: the proposition that the criminal law should be used to protect persons from themselves.[13] Legal moralism can also be translucent in that where conduct *per se* is viewed as immoral then the stigmatisation of legal censure is presumptively justified; wholly outwith the consensual nature of the act itself.[14] Consent principles have developed in this regard in a solipsistic *ad hoc* manner, and haphazardly rather than within a coherent structure.[15]

A powerful isomorphic relationship correlates between academic propositions and legislative determinations *vis a vis* types of fraudulent conduct that are legally problematic in

---

6 Lisa Cherkassky, 'Being Informed: The Complexities of Knowledge, Deception and Consent when Transmitting HIV' (2010) 74 Journal of Criminal Law 242; and see generally, Alan Reed, 'An Analysis of Fraud Vitiating consent in Rape Cases' (1995) 59 Journal of Criminal Law 310.

7 See generally, Samantha Ryan, 'Reckless Transmission of HIV: Knowledge and Culpability' [2006] Criminal Law Review 981; Mitchell Davies, 'R v Dica: Lessons in Practising Unsafe Sex' (2004) 68 Journal of Criminal Law 498; Matthew Weait, 'Knowledge, Consent and the Transmission of HIV' (2004) 154 New Law Journal 826; and Matthew Weait, 'Knowledge, Autonomy and Consent: R v Konzani' [2005] Criminal Law Review 763.

8 Paul Roberts, 'The Philosophical Foundations of Consent in the Criminal Law' (1997) 17 Oxford Journal of Legal Studies 389; and see generally Vera Bergelson, 'The Right to be Hurt: Testing the Boundaries of Consent' (2007) 75 George Washington Law Review 165; and Donald A Dripps, 'For a Negative, Normative Model of Consent, with a Comment on Preference Scepticism' (1996) 2 Legal Theory 113.

9 Andrew P Simester, John R Spencer, GR Sullivan and Graham J Virgo, *Criminal Law: Theory and Doctrine* (5th edition, Hart 2013); and William Wilson, *Criminal Law: Doctrine and Theory* (4th edition, Longman 2011).

10 Outwith bespoke public policy considerations, where the harm inflicted by D upon V equates to actual bodily, or a higher threshold, then consent is inoperable as a defence: see Brown [1994] I A C 212; and Emmett (Stephen Roy), *The Times*, 15 October 1999 (CA).

11 Joel Feinberg, *Harm to Others* (Oxford University Press 1984) 26–27 articulates paternalistic justification of criminalisation: 'It is always a good reason in support of a prohibition that it is probably necessary to prevent harm (physical, psychological , or economic) to the actor himself and there is probably no other means that is equally effective at no greater cost to other values.'

12 See generally Heidi Hurd, 'The Moral Magic of Consent' (1996) 2 Legal Theory 121; and Lucinda Vandervort, 'Sexual Consent as Voluntary Agreement: Tales of 'Seduction' or Questions of Law? (2013) 16 New Criminal Law Review 143.

13 Feinberg (n 11) 27.

14 See Simester, Spencer, Sullivan and Virgo (n 9); and Wilson (n 9); and Joel Feinberg, *Harmless Wrongdoing* (Oxford University Press 1988) 20, 25.

15 See generally, Law Commission, *Reform of Offences Against the Person: A Scoping Consultation Paper* (Law Com CP No 127, 2014) (hereinafter The Scoping Paper).

securing consent to sexual intercourse.[16] Deontological categorisations have been promulgated, and highlighted, where consent is voided by deception: *non est factum* cases; physical difference cases; and false qualification precepts.[17] The fraudulent concealment of HIV status by an individual actor presents separate categorisation issues and challenges over appropriate criminalisation demarcations: manifestation of the transmission of a serious harm (non-fatal offence pathway); and risk of harm at point of sexual intercourse temporal individuation where D1 conceals status (rape and sexual crimes).[18] Rape by fraud within the penumbra of this latter individuation raises core questions about the nature of rape and whether a violence/deception dichotomy should prevail, the nature of the harm that is brought about, and the inculpatory boundaries that justify law's intrusion into sexual intimacies.[19]

A dialectic relationship prevails between courts and legislatures in criminalising rape by fraud in the wider sense, and arguably repronormative ideologies linger still today.[20] A primordial distinction has been distilled as to a consent given under a deception or mistake as to the *thing itself*, ie the act of sexual intercourse, and a consent to that act of sexual intercourse itself induced by deception or mistake as to a *matter antecedent or collateral thereto* (fraud in the inducement does not destroy the reality of the apparent consent; fraud in the factum does).[21] Under the first category there will be cases where the complainant is deluded into supposing that she is undergoing medical treatment, and the cases where in the dark she is induced to assume that it is her husband who is the man with whom she is having sexual intercourse. Within the second heading will come consent induced by fraudulent representations given by the individual actor as to matters such as his wealth, lack of sexual infections, or freedom to marry the complainant, or the promise to pay for the sexual services provided.[22] Chamallas has provided the following succinct review of the distinction:

> [I]n fraud in the factum ... the victim consents to the doing of act X and the perpetrator of the fraud, in the guise of doing act X, actually does act Y. [I]n ... fraud in the inducement ... the victim is fundamentally induced to consent to the doing of act X and the perpetrator of the fraud does indeed commit to act X.[23]

This chapter focuses on whether so-called 'inducing causes' can destroy the reality of the consent in terms of transmission of HIV.[24] A new dynamic is identified herein beyond the

---

16 Patricia J Falk, 'Rape by Fraud and Rape by Coercion' (1998) 64 Brooklyn Law Review 39.

17 See generally, Rebecca Williams, 'Deception, Mistake and Vitiation of the Victim's Consent' (2008) 124 Law Quarterly Review 132; Karl Laird, 'Rapist or Rogue? Deception, Consent and the Sexual Offences Act 2003' [2014] Criminal Law Review 492; and Simon Cooper and Alan Reed, 'Informed Consent and the Transmission of Sexual Disease: Dadson Revivified' (2007) 71 Journal of Criminal Law 461.

18 John Flaherty, 'Clarifying the Duty to Warn in HIV Transference Cases' (2008) 54 Criminal Law Quarterly 60; and Matthew Weait, 'Criminal Law and the Sexual Transmission of HIV: *R v Dica*' (2005) 68 Modern Law Review 121.

19 See generally, Jed Rubenfeld, 'The Riddle of Rape-by-Deception and the Myth of Sexual Autonomy' (2013) 122 Yale Law Journal 1372.

20 Jocelynne A Scott, 'Fraud and Consent in Rape: Comprehension of the Nature and Character of the Act and its Moral Implications' (1975) 18 Criminal Law Quarterly 312.

21 See *R v Harms* (1944) 2 DLR 61.

22 Williams (n 17) 153–157; and see Michael Bohlander, 'Mistaken Consent to Sex, Political Correctness and Correct Policy' (2007) 71 Journal of Criminal Law 412; and Laird (n 17) 495–498.

23 Martha Chamallas, 'Consent, Equality, and the Legal Control of Sexual Conduct' (1988) 61 Southern California Law Review 777, 831 n. 224.

24 See generally, Isabel Grant, 'The Prosecution of Non-Disclosure of HIV in Canada: Time to Rethink *Cuerrier*' (2011) 5 McGill Journal of Law and Health 7.

.hanistic fraud in the factum/inducement binary divide for consent vitiation related
ion-fatal and sexual crimes. In the context of non-fatal offences it is contended herein,
t informed consent on the part of V as to D's HIV status may provide an exculpatory
fence, wholly outwith D's malfeasant concealment, as the outcomes of the appellate
decisions in *Dica*[25] and *Konzani*[26] have identified. In terms of the definitional construction of non-fatal offences it has always been a matter of some debate and disagreement as
to whether or not the presence or absence of consent forms part of the *actus reus* of the
relevant assault offence or whether it is a separate and independent element that stands
outside of the conduct component of the offence.[27] If 'absence of consent' is regarded as
an ingredient of the conduct element of the offence then, if the assault is consented to, a
vital element is missing and there is no legal wrong of any kind.[28] If, however, consent is
seen as a defence falling outside of the *actus reus* then there remains a 'legal wrong' that,
in the circumstances existing at the time, may be justified by the consent of the victim.[29]
The majority of legal opinion seems to favour the interpretation that consent operates as
a defence outside the *actus reus* of the offence although there is considerable authority to
the contrary.[30]

In contradistinction, for sexual crimes, including rape, lack of consent sits squarely within
the conduct element of the offence(s), and is palpably inculpatory.[31] A novel schema has
thereby been created under extant law within the contextualisation of fraud and HIV transmission.[32] The judicial template provided now focuses on disclosure/non-disclosure by D
of HIV status, and separately whether overt/non-overt deception applies as a determinative
concomitant and the fraud in factum/inducement dichotomy is rendered nugatory. The second section of the chapter provides four postulations to illustrate the parameters of fraud
and HIV transmission in the context of non-fatal/rape criminalisation, drawing contemporary boundaries, and illustrating problems engendered relating to unknown justification
and appropriate culpability thresholds.[33]

Extant law is Janus-facing in terms of disclosure/deception categorisations, as Laird and
Ormerod have intimated.[34] The appellate decisions in *Dica*[35] and *Konzani*[36] established that
informed consent on the part of V may exculpate D from liability for what otherwise fits
within the gravamen of reckless transmission of grievous bodily harm (HIV), even in a

---

25 [2004] EWCA Crim. 1103; [2004] QB 1257.
26 [2005] EWCA Crim. 706; [2005] 2 Cr App R 14.
27 David Ormerod and Karl Laird, *Smith and Hogan's Criminal Law* (14th edition, Oxford University Press 2015).
28 ibid.
29 See generally, Paul H Robinson, 'Criminal Law Defenses: A Systematic Analysis' (1982) 82 Columbia Law Review 199.
30 See *Brown* [1993] AC 212 where the majority saw consent as a defence operating outside the *actus reus* of the offence, but in *R v K* [2001] UKHL 41, a contrary view was taken by Lord Hobhouse who expressed the view that absence of consent formed part of the *actus reus*. A similar view was taken by Laws LJ in *R v Andrews* [2003] Crim LR 477.
31 Ormerod and Laird (n 27) 820–821.
32 See generally, Russell L Christopher and Kathryn H Christopher, 'Adult Impersonation: Rape by Fraud as a Defense to Statutory Rape' (2007) 101 Northwestern University Law Review 75.
33 Ormerod and Laird (n 27) 823–824.
34 ibid.
35 [2004] EWCA Crim. 1103; [2004] QB 1257.
36 [2005] EWCA Crim. 706; [2005] 2 Cr App R 14.

situation where D has deliberately and wilfully concealed the infection.[37] Liability may ensue for reckless transmission (non-disclosure) without informed consent.[38] Basic non-disclosure of status, without further overt deception, does not transmute consensual intercourse to non-consensual, for the purposes of rape, but rather any potential liability falls under the Offences Against the Person Act.[39] More recently, however, in *McNally*[40] it was stated, albeit *obiter*, that a rape conviction may be appropriate, and consent vitiated, where the complainant 'directly' asks the defendant if he is HIV-positive, and he responds fraudulently.[41] Effective choice is removed, and the divide between fraud in the factum/inducement is obfuscated by novel overt deception (inducing cause) preconditions to intercourse.[42] The culpability–onus nexus is consequently blurred in the context of criminalisation of transmission of HIV; the onus of disclosure applied to a defendant for rape does not apply to the threshold of non-fatal offence liability.[43] Deception is transmogrified to operate as an inducing cause for one type of liability but not another without regard for dangerousness/blameworthiness of the individual actor.

Consent is an essential ingredient of sexual offences such as rape or sexual assault within all offence-definitional constructive elements of the offences; moreover, what the complainant did or did not genuinely consent to is often a live and contentious issue at trial.[44] The afore-mentioned offences require that the complainant does not consent to the relevant sexual activity and the defendant has no reasonable belief in consent.[45] A practical illustration of the operation of these requirements can be found in the case of *R (on the Application of F) v DPP* relating to conditional consent in the context of accedance, or otherwise, to a no ejacu-lation during penetration pre-condition.[46] The Divisional Court considered that one of the fundamental questions underpinning liability was as follows: 'Did the complainant consent to this penetration? She did so, provided, in the language of s. 74 of the 2003 Act, she agreed by choice, when she had the freedom and capacity to make the choice.'[47] Whilst there is some consideration of the defendant, the question with which the courts are most preoccupied is: to what did the complainant consent? Did she have a 'choice'? Indeed, this becomes even more important when deception is an issue at trial. Such postulations are considered within this chapter, both in the substantive criminal context, and also from an evidential perspective. The discussions will illustrate that the reforms to the admissibility of bad character evidence within the Criminal Justice Act 2003 have enabled the admission of bad character evidence in order to facilitate the making of a propensity inference, or support truthfulness between counts. Through the admission of bad character evidence, more specifically evidence of pro-pensity, it is possible to effect a partial shift in focus from whether the complainant would/did

---

37 See generally, Sophie Matthiesson, 'Should the Law Deal with Reckless HIV Infection as a Criminal Offence or as a Matter of Public Health?' (2010) 21 Kings Law Journal 123; and George Mawhinney, 'To be Ill or to Kill: The Criminality of Contagion' (2013) 77 Journal of Criminal Law 202.

38 Matthew Weait and Yusef Azad, 'The Criminalisation of HIV Transmission in England and Wales: Questions of Law and Policy' (2005) 10(s) HIV AIDS Policy and Law Review 1, 5–12.

39 Cherkassky (n 6) 245–247.

40 [2013] EWCA Crim 1051.

41 ibid [26]–[27] per Leveson L.J.

42 Alex Sharpe, 'Criminalising Sexual Intimacy: Transgender Defendants and the Legal Construction of Non-Consent' [2014] Criminal Law Review 207, 222.

43 Laird (n 17) 501.

44 See for example Jenny McEwan, 'Proving Consent in Sexual Cases: Legislative Control and Cultural Evolution' (2005) International Journal of Evidence and Proof 1, 1–3.

45 Sexual Offences Act 2003, ss 1, 3.

46 [2013] EWHC 945. See also *R v McNally* [2013] EWCA 1051.

47 ibid [26].

consent, to whether this defendant is the kind of/is likely to be the person that would commit such serious sexual offences, and this is addressed in the third section of the chapter.

The final part of this chapter proposes a new reform framework to act as a cathartic panacea to current ills attached to criminalisation of HIV transmission, and problems attached to intersection with fraud vitiating consent. A new template is needed to avoid the palpable inconsistencies that apply to consent as a defence or otherwise to non-fatal offences and sexual crimes, and within the illogical disclosure/overt deception boundaries that now apply. Proposals are adduced for bespoke legislation, establishing a structured offence hierarchy for transmission of HIV, and with a new focus on *mens rea* ingredients of *de novo* offences, and appropriate categorisation of blameworthiness and culpability. With regard to the use of bad character evidence, the chapter will consider the overall effects of the CJA 2003 reforms on admission and evaluate earlier claims that the new rules can prove favourable for the prosecution within the sexual offence trial. Recent case-law demonstrates that evidence of past behaviours can be put to extensive use in proving that a defendant is likely to have proceeded to sexual activity irrespective of consent and, further, multiple counts within one indictment can ultimately be mutually supportive, where sufficiently similar/extraordinary behaviours exist. This chapter concludes that greater admissibility of bad character is of fundamental importance as there is some scope for evidence of this nature to counteract pre-conceived ideas of what 'real rape'/rapists look like, though it is by no means a satisfactory counterfoil to the effects of such ideals.

TRANSMISSION OF HIV: THE NON-DISCLOSURE/ DECEPTION BINARY DIVIDE

The consent defence, as Robinson has asserted,[48] may be viewed through an offence modification prism serving to exculpate or to mitigate.[49] Focal import attaches to the culpability of the individual actor. The culpability–onus nexus, however has become blurred in the context of criminalisation of transmission of HIV.[50] Substantive precepts remain controversial where D is HIV-positive but conceals/fails to warn V of that fact, and potential inculpation may apply within either the gravamen of non-fatal offences, or potentially rape (sexual crime).[51] A paradoxical binary divide has been created in terms of informed consent to sexual activity as a defence or otherwise: 'we now have a situation where, in law, it may be possible for V to consent to D's act in one dimension but not consent to other facets of the act that, for the purposes of the criminal law, belong in a different dimension. This is the case even if V would have refused D's act *tout court* had she known the true position.'[52] Case-law on the disclosure/deception bifurcation received its apogee in the recent appellate decision of *McNally*,[53] reinforcing the dimensional nature of the sexual act. Four postulations are consequentially presented below to highlight the illogical parameters of fraud and HIV transmission inculpation, and the opaque ambit of conditional consent. The postulations emphasise the urgent need to reconceptualise culpability and blameworthiness via bespoke

---

48   Paul H Robinson (n 29) 212.
49   ibid.
50   Antje Du Bois-Pedain, 'HIV and Responsible Sexual Behaviour' (2005) 64 Cambridge Law Journal 540.
51   See generally, Matthew Weait, *Intimacy and Responsibility: The Criminalisation of HIV Transmission* (Routledge-Cavendish 2007).
52   Simester, Spencer, Sullivan and Virgo (n 9) 770–771.
53   [2013] EWCA Crim 1051.

de novo legislation, and correspondingly to focus appropriately on the actual 'wrong' committed by a 'dangerous' offender.[54]

> (i) *Scenario 1: D fails to inform V of his HIV status, and V subsequently contracts the disease. D is charged with the reckless infliction of grievous bodily harm.*
>
> (ii) *Scenario 2: D fails to warn V of his HIV status, and V subsequently contracts the disease. Contrary to Scenario 1, however, V, prior to intercourse, has received information from a third party extraneous source that D may potentially be infected with the virus.*

In addressing these postulations, if we focus not only on V, but also on the actor, not only on the result, but also on the act itself, we will see that extant criminal law has a strong deontological component. This was revealed in the appellate decisions of *Dica*[55] and *Konzani*.[56] In *Dica*, the defendant infected two sexual partners with the HIV virus, and had failed to disclose his condition (Scenario 1 – non-disclosure and grievous bodily harm). The Court of Appeal held that a sexual partner could not give effective consent to the risk of infection by merely consenting to sexual intercourse while in ignorance of D's condition.

In *Konzani*, the defendant who was HIV+ had sexual intercourse with several women from whom he concealed his condition. The women became infected with the virus as a result of the intercourse. The convictions for inflicting grievous bodily harm contrary to s 20 of the Offences Against the Person Act 1861 were upheld. Transmission of HIV was conceptualised as a physical act separate from the intercourse itself: 'consent to the sex had not been vitiated, only consent to the transmission of HIV'.[57] As Weait has articulated, a distinction may apply in that public policy intimates a different legal response to conduct which in terms of temporal and physical immediacy presents a risk of injury, as opposed to injury that is, 'more or less a foregone conclusion'.[58] In the former category, it seems clear that informed consent, where the victim knows that the defendant is infected, and has sexual intercourse aware of that fact, can act as a defence.[59] Equally, it is apparent that the defendant may plead the defence of consent in this dimension where he has an honest belief in the victim's consent, subject, as emphasised in *Konzani*, to the personal autonomy of the victim:

> [T]he principle of her personal autonomy is not enhanced if he is exculpated when he recklessly transmits the HIV virus to her through consensual sexual intercourse. On any view, the concealment of this fact from her almost inevitably means that she is deceived. Her consent is not properly informed, and she cannot give an informed consent to something of which she is ignorant. Equally, her personal autonomy is not normally protected by allowing a defendant who knows that he is suffering from the HIV virus which he deliberately conceals, to assert an honest belief in his partner's informed consent to the risk of transmission of the HIV virus. Silence in these circumstances is incongruous with honesty, or with a genuine belief that there is informed consent.[60]

---

54 See generally, Kriston L Isaacson, 'Rape by Fraud or Impersonation: A Necessary Addition to Michigan's Criminal Sexual Conduct Statute' (1998) 44 Wayne Law Review 1781.

55 [2004] EWCA Crim 1103; [2004] QB 1257.

56 [2005] EWCA Crim 706; [2005] 2 Cr App R 14.

57 Williams (n 17) 153.

58 Weait (n 18) 126.

59 ibid.

60 [2005] 2 Cr App R 14 [42].

The postulation in scenario (ii) above, circumnavigating non-disclosure/overt deception and unknown justification as a defence to reckless transmission of HIV (gbh), was considered, albeit *obiter* in *Konzani*.[61] The suggestion therein is that once the victim has sufficient awareness of conditional facts (HIV status) from extraneous sources, even where the condition is deliberately and wilfully concealed by D, this may transmogrify to risk of harm acceptance via V's informed consent/personal autonomy determination. In essence, an offence modification defence (consent) may prevail, outwith an examination of the culpability/dangerousness of the individual actor, where D behaves recklessly (overt deception), but in complete ignorance of the victim's level of awareness of his condition.[62] This contradicts the propensity/dangerousness analysis of bad character evidence and consent that is deployed subsequently in this chapter. The defendant benefits from an undeserved unknown justification defence that, arguably, is counterintuitive, and has been consistently rejected elsewhere:[63]

[W]e accept that there may be circumstances in which it would be open to the jury to infer that, notwithstanding that the defendant was reckless and concealed his position from the complainant, she may nevertheless have given an informed consent to the risk of contracting the HIV virus. By way of example, an individual with HIV may develop a sexual relationship with someone who knew him while he was in hospital, receiving treatment for the condition. If so, her informed consent. . . would remain a defence, to be disproved by the prosecution, even if the defendant had not personally informed her of his condition. Even if she did not in fact consent, this example would illustrate the basis for an argument that he honestly believed in her consent. Alternatively, he may honestly believe that his new sexual partner was told of his condition by someone known to them both. Cases like these, not too remote to be fanciful, may arise.[64]

The culpability–onus dichotomy appears out of kilter in *Konzani*, and it is counterfactual that an individual actor may rely on a defence in such circumstances, predicated in effect upon unknown justification.[65] It is one of the functions of the criminal law to convict and punish those who recklessly or intentionally inflect harm on other members of society yet in these circumstances (non-disclosure/overt deception), unlike other circumstances where the defence of consent operates, there appears to be no requirement that the defendant knew or genuinely believed that the victim was consenting to the risk. Where the defence of consent is to operate, it should surely be limited to those situations where it removes the defendant's culpability and blameworthiness because he is fully aware that the victim has knowledge of the risk at the relevant time, and is, therefore, consenting.[66] The offence modification defence

---

61 Samantha Ryan, 'Risk-taking, Recklessness and HIV Transmission: Accommodating the Reality of Sexual Transmission of HIV within a Justifiable Approach to Criminal Liability' (2007) 28 Liverpool Law Review 215.

62 See generally, Paul H Robinson, *Structure And Function In Criminal Law* (Clarendon Press 1997).

63 The focus on victim awareness or conduct raises the spectre of unknown justification exculpating a defendant from liability. General principles of criminal liability, since the fundamental decision in *Dadson* (1850) 175 ER 499, have been traditionally accepted as precluding reliance on such conceptual analysis. On the ambit and nature of this general principle, see Brian Hogan, 'The *Dadson* Principle' [1989] Criminal Law Review 679. This article is strongly in favour of the view that D should not be able to rely on unknown circumstances of justification.

64 *Konzani* [2005] 2 Cr App R 14 [44].

65 See generally, Kate Harker and Ellen Wright, 'The HIV Stigma: Duty or Defence?' (2015) 4(1) UCL Journal of Law and Jurisprudence 55.

66 See Weait (n 7).

of consent ought to apply in such a scenario, and not leave exculpation dependent upon the chance fact of whether or not the victim has any partial awareness, howsoever acquired, of his condition, and outwith reckless overt deception.[67] The defence of consent should not apply, via unknown justification, where there is an awareness on the part of D of a very real risk that the other party will suffer grave harm.[68] Penal sanctions should apply, and bespoke legislation is propounded below, to individuals who intentionally or recklessly subject others to a real risk of grievous harm through deliberate concealment.[69] Inculpation is apposite outwith the parameters of apparent informed consent or personal autonomy determinations, and the criminal law has a particularised function in this regard. This is conjoined with concepts of propensity that are analysed in the contextualisation of bad character evidence.

> (iii) *Scenario 3: D is HIV-positive and fails to reveal this condition to V (non-disclosure) prior to intercourse. Does the 'act' of intercourse become non-consensual for the purposes of rape? Is the sexual act reviewed through a different dimension with conditional consent attached to freedom from communicable infectious diseases?*

The postulations in scenario (iii) above were considered in *R v EB*[70] where, at issue, was whether an implied deception was operative that vitiated consent for the purposes of rape under s 74[71] of the Sexual Offences Act 2003, or constituted a conclusive presumption as to lack of consent under s 76[72] of that Act. D had approached V at a bus stop having been out socially with friends. They had, apparently, engaged in conversation and walked together to a nearby street. Sexual intercourse occurred, and it was disputed whether or not the act was consensual. At issue, *inter alia*, before the appellate court was the inclusionary nature of D's HIV status as a matter of evidence, and its import as a matter vitiating consent as an implied deception where D had withheld knowledge of this condition.

Their Lordships in *R v EB*, the leading judgement that of Latham LJ, were explicit that a dissonance applied between the offence of infliction of grievous bodily harm under s 20 of the Offences Against the Person Act 1861, and rape.[73] In terms of the former offence the reckless concealment of HIV status (see *Dica* and *Konzani*), and failure to inform V (informed consent),

---

67 Robinson (n 29).
68 Baker (n 5).
69 See generally, Claire Strickland, 'Why Parliament Should Create HIV Specific Legislation' (2001) 2 Web Journal of Current Legal Issues 5: and Carol L. Galletly and Steven D Pinkerton, 'Towards Rational HIV Exposure Laws' (2004) 32 Journal of Law and Medicine 327.
70 [2006] EWCA Crim. 2945; [2007] 1 Cr App R 29.
71 Section 74 contains the general definition of consent: 'For the purposes of this part, a person consents if he agrees by choice, and has the freedom and capacity to make that choice.'
72 Section 76 sets out a series of conclusive presumptions about lack of consent. It states:

> '(1) If in proceedings for an offence to which this section applies it is proved that the defendant did the relevant act and that any of the circumstances specified in subsection (2) existed, it is to be conclusively presumed –
>   (a) that the complainant did not consent to the relevant act, and
>   (b) that the defendant did not believe that the complainant consented to the relevant act.
> (2) The circumstances are that –
>   (a) the defendant intentionally deceived the complainant as to the nature or purposes of the relevant act;
>   (b) the defendant intentionally induced the complainant to consent to the relevant act by impersonating a person known personally to the complainant.'

73 [2007] 1 Cr App R 29 [15].

precludes D's ability to rely on V's consent to the risk of transmission. This preclusion applies, of course, unless V has received 'informed consent' of D's HIV+ status (partial risk awareness) through extraneous sources or third party information. In the latter scenario, however, of rape liability there is no mention in the conclusive presumptions contained within s 76 of the Sexual Offences Act 2003 of 'implied deception.' It was not for the courts through 'implicit judicial legislation' to read this into the Act. Moreover, HIV status, by itself and via non-disclosure, cannot operate to vitiate consent to the sexual act within s 74 of the Sexual Offences Act 2003 as a material dimension diversion. Representationally, the matter has been objectified as non-disclosure *per se*, rather than within the overt/covert deception imprimatur in failure to inform: 'the Court of Appeal refused to hold that non-disclosure was analogous to active deception.'[74] The consequentialist effect is to render nugatory any fraud in the factum/inducement debate in this contextualisation, and non-disclosure sits outwith fraud standardisations in a particularised template.[75] If V is infected, liability for reckless non-disclosure on the part of D may apply via non-fatal offence inculpation, and not as implied deception for rape:

> Where one party to sexual activity has a sexually transmissible disease which is not disclosed to the other party any consent that may have been given to that activity by the other party is not thereby vitiated. The act remains a consensual act. However, the party suffering from the sexually transmissible disease will not have any defence to any charge which may result from harm created by that sexual activity, merely by virtue of that consent, because such consent did not include consent to infection by the disease.[76]

(iv) Scenario 4: D is HIV-positive and engages in intercourse with V. D is directly asked by V whether he carries the virus, but explicitly lies to conceal the disease. Is consent vitiated for the purposes of rape liability within s 74 of the Sexual Offences Act 2003?

A dissonance applies between scenario (iv) above, and that presented earlier, in that explicit fraudulent concealment of HIV status applies to potentially vitiate consent, con-trasted and counterpoised with basic non-disclosure.[77] The consent provided is predicated and conditional upon freedom from communicable infection. A developing body of conditional consent juridical precepts have highlighted the more constrained parameters of valid consent to sexual activity, and vitiation where dependent on explicit factorisations such as condom use[78] or no ejaculation.[79] The jurors, as moral arbiters, are asked to consider whether the complainant has been deprived of the freedom to choose to engage in sexual activity subject to prescribed conditions.[80]

The decision in *McNally*[81] is significant within a new panoply of conditional consent artic-ulations. The defendant was a transgender male who conducted an online relationship with the complainant, and this interaction developed over a number of years. The denuded party

---

74 Laird (n 17) 501.
75 See Harker and Wright (n 65).
76 [2007] 1 WLR 1567 [17] per Latham LJ.
77 See Laird (n 17) 504–505; Harker and Wright (n 65).
78 *Assange v Sweden* [2011] EWHC 2849 (Admin.)
79 *R (on the Application of F) v DPP* [2013] EWHC 945 (Admin.); and see B [2013] EWCA Crim. 823 (impersonation over webcam).
80 See generally, Jonathan Herring, 'Mistaken Sex' [2005] Criminal Law Review 511; Hyman Gross, 'Rape, Moralism and Legal Rights' [2007] Criminal Law Review 220; and Bohlander (n 22).
81 [2013] 2 Cr App R 28.

considered McNally to be her boyfriend, and on numerous subsequent occasions oral and digital penetration occurred. The evidence presented suggested that V did not know that McNally was transgender, and that her true identity had been fraudulently concealed, with respective sexual acts occurring in the dark, and with utilisation of a strap-on dildo. McNally was charged with six counts of assault by penetration contrary to s 2 of the Sexual Offences Act 2003.

The appellate court in *McNally*,[82] upholding D's conviction, determined that consent was vitiated for the purposes of s 74, with active (overt) deception on the part of D.[83] A binary divide applied in the context of non-disclosure/deception for prospective review. A failure to disclose HIV status *per se*, as in *R v EB*, equated to basic non-disclosure (no sexual crime).[84] In contradistinction, the fraudulent concealment of that status, when directly asked by V, was equated by Leveson LJ in *McNally* to 'active deception,' consequentially vitiating consent within the parameters of s 74.[85] This distinction between 'active deception' and 'basic non-disclosure' is difficult to draw across a spectra of fraudulent vitiation of consent propositions, and where concealment may be covert: 'it is not entirely satisfactory that liability should turn on this distinction. It could be a matter of semantics whether the facts of a given case are framed as involving an "active deception" as opposed to a failure by D to correct an assumption that he knows C has made, such as that D is not HIV-positive.'[86] The dichotomy between active deception or non-disclosure is one that Sharpe has legitimately characterised as 'morally problematic'.[87] The binary divide more generally, in any event, between commission/omission liability in criminal law has proved enduringly problematic, and subject to academic dispute, and conflicted appellate decisions, as evidenced in *Evans (Gemma)*[88] where responsibilities/duties became blurred. Moreover, the categories of 'active deception', outwith HIV concealment, that may vitiate consent for sexual crimes within s 74 still remain open to solipsistic *ad hoc* development and recourse to judicial divining-rod determinations:[89]

> In reality, some deceptions (such as, for example, in relation to wealth) will obviously not be sufficient to vitiate consent. In our judgment, Lord Judge C.J.'s observations (in F) that, 'the evidence relating to "choice" and the "freedom" to make any particular choice must be approached in a broad common sense way,' identifies the route through the dilemma.[90]

The semantic line-drawing that applies to vitiation of consent for non-fatal offences/rape, *vis a vis* non-disclosure/deception implies a correlative judgement. The conjunction is normatively arbitrary, but not inherent in any statutory formulation.[91] One might argue against the distinction on either consequential or deontological moral grounds. No philosophical basis exists for the proposition that the template that judges the circumstances in which

---

82   ibid.
83   ibid.
84   Ormerod and Laird (n 27) 824.
85   [2013] EWCA Crim. 1051 per Leveson LJ.
86   Laird (n 17) 505.
87   Sharpe (n 42).
88   [2009] EWCA Crim 650; [2009] 1 WLR 1999; and see generally Glenys Williams, 'Gross Negligence Manslaughter and Duty of Care in Drugs Cases: R v Evans' [2009] Criminal Law Review 631.
89   [2013] EWCA Crim 1051 [26]–[27] per Leveson L.J. See generally George Syrota, 'Rape: When Does Fraud Vitiate Consent?' (1995) 23 University of Western Australia Law Review 334; and Neil Morgan, 'Oppression, Fraud and Consent in Sexual Offences (2006) 20 University of Western Australia Law Review 223.
90   ibid.
91   See Vanessa E Munro, 'On Responsible Relationships and Irresponsible Sex – Criminalising The Reckless Transmission of HIV: R v Dica and R v Konzani' (2007) 19 Child and Family Law Quarterly 112.

consent is vitiated can be different according to whether the case is one of sexual crime or one where the assault is non-sexual. The time is ripe for a fresh reappraisal of criminalisation of HIV transmission interposed with fraudulent concealment, and rectification of extant law via bespoke legislation. The cathartic panacea presented by new reform propositions is considered subsequently, but attention now turns to propensity in a consent context, aligned with bad character evidence principles as part of holistic reconceptualisations of defendant conduct and culpability.

BAD CHARACTER: ADMISSIBILITY PRE-CJA 2003

The presence (or lack thereof) of consent becomes a fundamental issue within sexual crimes, and it is herein that evidence of the defendant's antecedent history is adduced to substantiate the claim that the defendant is pre-disposed towards non-consensual penetration or sexual touching or, at the very least, is prepared to engage in sexual intercourse or touching irrespective of the presence of C's consent. It is obvious that the principal use for bad character evidence here is usually to demonstrate a relevant propensity on the part of D; such evidence can therefore possess a high probative value, but can also engender a high degree of prejudicial feeling towards the defendant.[92] In 2005, McEwan (echoed by Withey in 2007) propitiously recognised that the changes within the Sexual Offences Act 2003 and the Criminal Justice Act 2003 could effect both substantive (SOA) and evidential (CJA) changes to the law that may affect trials of serious sexual offences.[93] The complex mixture of common law and statute in the old system[94] had resulted in a situation whereby it was too difficult to admit evidence of a defendant's bad character but, controversially, imputations on the character of a witness were much easier to facilitate.[95] In the years preceding the Criminal Justice Act 2003, the issue was not whether the evidence was or was not evidence of bad character; considerations focused instead upon whether the misconduct evidence was admissible. Admissibility was only possible in a small number of circumstances, which chiefly included the following:

- Where the doctrine of similar fact evidence was applicable, enabling the jury to rule out coincidence due to the similarity of the conduct alleged with prior behaviours/offending.
- Where the Criminal Evidence Act 1898 made it admissible.
- Where the evidence was admissible on the basis that it formed part of the *res gestae*, and constituted 'background evidence'.[96]

---

92 This is one rationale behind the prohibition on propensity reasoning that beset the common law prior to the reforms in the CJA 2003. Referring to the *Makin* rule ('It is undoubtedly not competent for the prosecution to adduce evidence tending to show that the accused has been guilty of criminal acts other than those covered by the indictment, for the purpose of leading to the conclusion that the accused is a person likely from his criminal conduct or character to have committed the offence for which he is being tried' [1894] AC 57, 65), the court in *Boardman* acknowledged that the prevention of propensity reasoning was 'designed to exclude a particular kind of inference being drawn which might upset the presumption of innocence by introducing more heat than light'. *Boardman* [1975] AC 421, 452 as per Lord Hailsham.

93 McEwan (n 44), 1 proving consent; See also Carol Withey, 'Female Rape – An Ongoing Concern: Strategies for Improving Reporting and Conviction Levels' (2007) Journal of Criminal Law 54

94 Before the Criminal Justice Act 2003 was implemented, Part 11 in particular.

95 See as a starting point, the case of *Butterwasser* [1948] 1 KB 4, 7, in which it was held that a defendant who does not testify does not put their credit in issue and their shield against admissibility should, therefore, remain intact.

96 There is considerable overlap between this facet of the old law, and the present exceptions to the definition of bad character evidence under s 98(a), (b) Criminal Justice Act 2003. Section 27 of the Theft Act could also have made bad character evidence admissible in certain circumstances.

Under the Criminal Evidence Act 1898, the defendant enjoyed a shield against admission of his history unless he had cast imputations on the character of another, and it is noteworthy that a defendant could not lose his shield if he did not testify;[97] witnesses, on the other hand, could be subjected to 'gratuitous and humiliating irrelevant cross-examination in relation to misconduct'.[98] The Criminal Evidence Act 1898, s 1(3) prevented the admission of the defendant's character unless he had (or his counsel had) asked questions designed to put his good character to the court, or had attacked the character of a prosecutor/witness for the prosecution or the complainant. The similar fact doctrine served as an important exception to the over-arching exclusionary rule governing admissibility, and contained a gateway under which cross-examination on similar fact evidence was permissible, but was narrowly construed and was demarcated by the application of a 'catchphrase' to determine admissibility under its head.[99] The combination of common law and statute, as an holistic means of regulating the admissibility of such an important evidential category, proved too convoluted, propagating a fragmentation of the law, inefficiency and confusion; Murphy cogently highlighted:

No other area of the law of evidence is in such urgent need of real, effective reform. . . the criticisms have exposed, not merely disorganisation and uncertainty as to particular rules of law, but rather fundamental defects in the logic and policy of the law of character evidence.[100]

The concept of 'background evidence' is now represented by s 101(1)(c) of the Criminal Justice Act 2003.[101] Section 99 of the Criminal Justice Act 2003 abolished all common law rules governing the admissibility of bad character evidence in criminal proceedings and so the similar fact rule is no longer applicable, the same being true of background evidence[102] and of *res gestae*,[103] though commentators have argued that the similar facts doctrine has been replaced by s 101(1)(d) of the Criminal Justice Act 2003.[104]

---

97 See above (n 95).

98 Dr Louise Smail and Susan Ghaiwal, 'When the Past isn't Always Behind You . . . Bad Character Admission [2010] Health and Safety at Work 1, 1. This is, of course, subject to the restrictions in s 41 of the Youth Justice and Criminal Evidence Act 1999 or its predecessor, and would also fall within the remit of s 78 Police and Criminal Evidence Act 1984. A discussion of s 41 of the 1999 Act is necessary, but beyond the remit of the current piece which focuses mainly on defendant bad character.

99 See, for example, *Boardman* (n 92), and the later cases of *DPP v P* [1991] 2 AC 447, *DPP v H* [1995] 2 AC 596 which criticised the use of the term 'striking similarity' in *Boardman* ((n 92) 448).

100 Peter Murphy, 'Character Evidence: The Search for Logic and Policy Continues' [1998] International Journal of Evidence and Proof 71, 71–72; see also Jenny McEwan, 'Previous Misconduct at the Cross-Roads: Which "Way Ahead"?' [2002] Criminal Law Review 180.

101 Although it is hard to see where s 98(a) Criminal Justice Act 2003 ends and gateway (c) begins and the courts need to make clear when misconduct will be subject to the statutory scheme/safeguards and when it is will be subject to ordinary rules of evidence, Andrew Roberts, 'R v Sule (Sahid): bad character evidence – adducing previous incidents as motive for index offence' [2013] Criminal Law Review 504, 506. See, See *R v Tirnaveanu* [2007] EWCA Crim 1239; *R v McNeill* [2007] EWCA Crim 2927; *R v McKintosh* [2006] EWCA Crim 193, *R v Machado* [2006] EWCA Crim 837, *R v Saleem* [2007] EWCA Crim 1923; *R v Mullings* [2010] EWCA Crim 2820; *Sule* [2012] EWCA Crim 1130; *Rostami* [2013] EWCA Crim 1363 amongst others.

102 See now s 101(1)(c) CJA 2003.

103 See s 98 CJA 2003.

104 Whilst it is clear that 'gateway (d)' does indeed encompass similar fact evidence, the gateway itself is much wider than the similar fact doctrine itself, see further *Chopra* [2006] EWCA Crim 2133. As a starting point to this discussion, see Fitzpatrick who states that s 101(1)(d) Criminal Justice Act 2003,

BAD CHARACTER: ADMISSIBILITY POST-CJA 2003

Under the CJA 2003 evidence of bad character continues to be *prima facie* inadmissible as was the case at common law. Thus, where evidence falls within the statutory definition of bad character[105] it must meet one of the seven 'gateways' to admissibility before it can be admitted at trial. Subject to s 98(a) and (b), the Criminal Justice Act 2003 defines bad character evidence as 'evidence of, or of a disposition towards, misconduct'.[106] Misconduct is defined in s 112[107] and includes, as one would expect, the commission of an offence, and also 'reprehensible behaviour'. An effect of the reforms was that evidence could be excluded from the definition (for example, where it was central to the present charge as per s 98(a)–(b) CJA 2003) and was therefore more readily admissible before a jury. If evidence fits the definition of bad character in s 98,[108] then it must satisfy one of the gateways in s 101(1) of the 2003 Act before it will become admissible, some of which also have the potential to be widely construed.

Whilst the law regulating the admissibility of defendant bad character is more inclusionary in its ambit than the preceding regime, especially in the context of the admission of propensity evidence (s 101(1)(d) CJA 2003), an over-arching exclusionary rule is still in effect across the area. The exclusionary nature of the law regulating admissibility is evident in the wording of the Act, for example, s 101(1) dictates that, In criminal proceedings evidence of the defendant's bad character is admissible if, but only if – one of several 'gateways to admissibility' contained in subss (a)–(g) are met. The provisions immediately following s 101 of the Criminal Justice Act 2003 offer guidance on the limits of these gateways and there are a number of self-contained safeguards that sit in conjunction with corresponding gateways.[109]

The present analysis seeks to ascertain to what extent the evidential reform of the rules governing the admission of bad character might have increased the scope for conviction of defendants, and made the criminal justice landscape more accessible to rape complainants. In order to do so (having considered the problems with the complex and restrictive approach that characterised the law pre-2003) it would seem that there would need to be (and, as will

---

'is one of the most significant in the Act and its principal effect is to supplant the previous common law rules relating to the adduction in chief by the prosecution of so-called 'similar fact evidence'. Ben Fitzpatrick, 'Bad character: Criminal Justice Act 2003; Defendant's Previous convictions; Propensity' (2006) Journal of Criminal Law 6, 7. Consult further the work of Huxley wherein he argues as follows: 'it is clear that s 99 abolished rules as to the admissibility of bad character as those two words are defined by s 112. Though no authority is cited for admission of the evidence other than the 'common law' it can only be an application of the similar fact or extraneous act evidence principle. If so, although the common law rules relating to the admissibility of bad character evidence were expressly abolished by s 99(1), evidence of this kind remains admissible at common law. It follows that for the purpose of admissibility of evidence, bad character now has two meanings – one under the CJA 2003 (ss 98 and 112(1)) and another at common law. For admissibility purposes, statutory bad character must be distinguished from common law bad character'. Phil Huxley, 'Mental Gymnastics and Intellectual Acrobatics: the Meanings of Statutory and Common Law "Bad Character" (2011) Journal of Criminal Law 132, 135–136. Further, consider Gregory Durston, 'The Impact of the Criminal Justice Act 2003 on Similar Fact Evidence' (2004) Journal of Criminal Law 307; Sarah Brown and Beverley Steventon, 'The Admissibility of Bad Character Evidence' (2009) Coventry Law Journal 1, 6.

105 Section 98 Criminal Justice Act 2003.
106 Section 98 Criminal Justice Act 2003.
107 Section 112 of the 2003 Act defines 'misconduct' as 'the commission of an offence or other reprehensible behaviour'.
108 And does not fall within the exceptions in s 98(a)–(b) Criminal Justice Act 2003.
109 For example, s 101(3) CJA 2003 contains an exclusionary discretion based around fairness which pertains to gateways (d) and (g).

be shown subsequently, there was) a broadening of the scope for admission of bad character; this might enable relevant circumstances relating to propensity and/or consent to be put before the finder of fact. The authors will focus upon s 101(1)(d) CJA 2003,[110] which enables evidence of bad character to be used as evidence of a propensity towards engaging in particular behaviours, or to demonstrate that the defendant lacks credibility and may not be worthy of belief as per s 103 CJA 2003. Gateway (d) appears to be reflective of a perceived need for placing trust in the fact-finder, enabling a level of flexibility in interpretation that facilitates the provision of information pertaining to a defendant's history and trusting jurors to use it fairly.[111] The CJA 2003 embodies a significant departure from the previous regime's antipathy towards the use of propensity evidence to show guilt. Propensity evidence can be pivotal in trials for serious sexual offences, such as rape, as McEwan has identified:

> In the absence of serious violence, the law of evidence can do little to affect the operation of [rape] scripts, short of offering expert evidence on the nature of sexual assault. It does, however, have a role to play in determining to what extent the court will become aware of other factors *critical* to the fact-finder's perception of an encounter as 'real rape' or otherwise.[112]

The Criminal Justice Act 2003 provisions, as discussed further below, do offer a greater scope to prosecutors to adduce defendant bad character, especially where it is related to propensity, though it remains to be seen whether legislative changes have had a positive effect on trials of serious sexual offences. The existence of rape myths and the 'rape script' present an ongoing problem, as averred by Temkin and Krahé:

> stereotypical beliefs and attitudes about victims, perpetrators and the circumstances of sexual violence may affect the judgements of those involved at each stage of decision-making in the criminal justice process. . . When asked to describe a typical rape situation, many people are likely to conjure up an attack by a stranger on an unsuspecting victim in an outdoor location, involving the use or threat of force by the assailant and active physical resistance by the victim.[113]

Any attempts at legislative reform of evidential precepts will have to go some way to address the effects of the attitudes/myths that Temkin and Krahé propound. Where an allegation of rape is made and the trial process is underway, the complainant may be at a disadvantage from the start due to the circumstances surrounding the commission of the alleged offence, or the characteristics of the defendant themselves: The 'popular conception of the sex offender requires the defendant to appear disturbed and violent. An attractive and

---

110 Though it is acknowledged that other gateways can also have a significant effect, such as those that admit bad character evidence where it is compliant with s 101(1)(c) (important explanatory evidence), s 101(1)(f) (Correcting a false impression given by D) and s 101(1)(g) (where D has attacked the character of another) CJA 2003. These are beyond the remit of the current piece.

111 For example in the Criminal Justice White Paper, it is stated that 'We favour an approach that entrusts relevant information to those determining the case as far as possible', Criminal Justice White Paper *Justice for All* (Cm 5563, July 2002) 4.56.

112 McEwan (n 44) 4. Author's emphasis added.

113 Jennifer Temkin and Barbara Krahé, *Sexual Assault and the Justice Gap: A Question of Attitude* (Hart Publishing 2008) 31.

apparently respectable defendant therefore presents prosecutors with a problem.'[114] Though it is beyond the scope of the present chapter, the admission of evidence of good character could also present a problem here – a lack of evidence of sexual violence in a person's past does not indicate an absence of a propensity to engage in such behaviours, but a juror may take it as such, attributing disproportionate weight to good character evidence.[115] This might be addressed by adducing evidence of bad character where there is evidence of a propensity to sex offending'[116] or where the accused has given a false impression of good character.[117]

Case commentaries – Consent, propensity and bad character evidence

Withey recognised the incremental impact and embryonic nature of extant law in this arena: 'In relation to the new provisions governing the admissibility of the accused's bad character, s 101 of the CJA 2003 only became law in December 2004 and thus it is too early to adequately evaluate its impact on increasing bad character evidence in court'.[118] Later juridical precepts will allow us to gain some insight into how the CJA 2003 has impacted upon admissibility and the uses to which bad character evidence can be put at trial.

The courts initial reaction to the provisions were to read them deontologically and teleo-logically, for example, in *Hanson*[119] a narrow construction applied:

> There is no minimum number of events necessary to demonstrate... propensity. The fewer the number of convictions the weaker is likely to be the evidence of propensity. A single previous conviction for an offence of the same description or category will often not show propensity. But it may do so where, for example, it shows a tendency to unusual behaviour or where its circumstances demonstrate probative force in relation to the offence charged.[120]

This seemed to echo the need for similarity that categorised the similar fact doctrine, but remained sufficiently flexible to allow for the use of bad character evidence (even one single act of misconduct) where it carried sufficient probative force in the context of the case as a whole. Eleven years on, we are now well placed to assess to what extent evidence of propensity has been more frequently admitted in trials for serious sexual offences, and a number of appellate judgments are deserving of consideration in order to evaluate this factorisation. It is arguable that the outlook (at the point the CJA provisions were implemented) was positive in

---

114 McEwan (n 44) 22.
115 A particularly illuminating example can be found in the case of *R v Dizaei (Jamshid Ali)* [2013] EWCA Crim 88. See also the commentary of Brewis, Jackson and Stockdale who note that 'The Crown's inaccurate depiction of W's character gave the jury the misleading impression that they could assess the credibility of both parties from the standpoint that both were men of *good character* when, in fact, this was true only of the appellant.' Brian Brewis, Adam Jackson and Michael Stockdale, 'Case Comment: Bad Character and Potential Satellite Litigation' [2013] Journal of Criminal Law 110, 111.
116 McEwan (n 44) 22.
117 Though due to the necessarily limited scope of the present piece, the authors will not engage with s 101(1)(f) CJA 2003.
118 Withey (n 93) 84.
119 [2005] EWCA Crim 824.
120 ibid [9]. See also Withey, who argues that 'Section 101(1)(d) provides more scope for admissibility than the previous SFE rules because there is no requirement that probative value outweigh prejudicial effect. Evidence of only one conviction can now be admissible. This should increase the admissibility of an accused's bad character and in turn help to increase the rape conviction rate'. Withey (n 93) 71.

the sense that it was anticipated that more frequent admission of propensity evidence would fundamentally contribute to an increase in conviction levels.[121] Successive case-law will now be considered in this contextualisation.

Adducing bad character evidence under the CJA 2003

Immediately following the implementation of the Criminal Justice Act 2003, it became obvious quickly that evidence of a defendant's past behaviours would have an important part to play in the proving (or otherwise) of a lack of consent. The determination in *Somanathan*,[122] for instance, illustrated the potentially high probative value of evidence of past behaviours in the context of the criminal trial. The defendant was accused of rape, his having abused his position as a priest to gain entry to the home of the complainant wherein it was alleged that non-consensual intercourse took place on two occasions. The court heard evidence from three witnesses to the effect that during home visits by D (then working as a priest) they had received unwanted sexual advances from him at a time in their lives when they were vulnerable and alone – if another person was unexpectedly present, D would allegedly cancel any appointments upon becoming aware of another's presence.

The court ruled the evidence to be admissible under the gateways within s 101(1)(f) (the defendant had stated that he was of good character and had not been forced to leave his previous employ at another temple), (g) (he had alleged that the complainant and other witnesses in support had colluded and lied, concocting their allegations against him) and, potentially, (d) (as it demonstrated a relevant propensity). It was determined that 'the probative force of the evidence of I and V was considerable because, if accepted, it lent powerful support to what the complainant said about the appellant's technique'.[123] Ultimately, the similarity of *modus operandi* within the counts was suggestive of guilt.

The appeal in *Manister*[124] further illustrates the court's willingness to allow evidence of past sexual behaviours into the trial, which concerned alleged sexual assaults against a 13-year-old female. The appellate court ruled that evidence of a sexual relationship with a 16-year-old female was not reprehensible behaviour and therefore was not bad character evidence. The effect of this was to negate the requirement for the evidence to surmount the hurdles to admissibility within s 101(1) of the Criminal Justice Act 2003; therefore, provided the evidence was admissible at common law (and it was ruled it would be), it was admissible, the court ruling that to do so was not unfair and therefore did not warrant exclusion under s 78 of the Police and Criminal Evidence Act 1984.[125] This was so, because the s 99 CJA 2003 abolition of the common law admissibility rules applied to bad character evidence as defined

---

121 Withey, ibid.

122 [2006] 1 WLR 1885 [10] ongoing . . .

123 *Somanathan* ibid, [39]. See also *R v O'Dowds* [2009] EWCA Crim 905, in which case a prior conviction and further instances of sexual violence provide bad character evidence that ultimately helped to secure a conviction on the basis of a pattern of repeated similar conduct: the appellant striking up a friendship with a drug addict victim, supplying the victim with cannabis, recounting stories of violence committed against others, making sexual advances to the victim in her flat, and, after rejection of those advances, forcing her into sexual intercourse through fear. [48] The conviction was subsequently quashed due to case management issues – for further information on this, see D Ormerod, 'R v O'Dowd: Trial – Length of Trial – Whether Making Trial Unfair and Conviction Unsafe' [2009] *Criminal Law Review* 827, 828–829.

124 *Manister* (n 122).

125 ibid [95].

by s 98 of the CJA 2003 only, and therefore did not operate with regard to this evidence. As Roberts recognised:

> Determining whether conduct is to be considered 'reprehensible' is an intrinsically moral inquiry and *Manister* is illustrative of the divergence of views on the morality of lawful behaviour that are likely to be engendered. Without the touchstone of some objective measure of 'reprehensibility' the defendant who is subject to any illiberal moral views held by a judge, will be exposed to the moral prejudice of the jury, a prospect to which the 'old law' concerning bad character was acutely attuned.[126]

It is clear from case-law immediately following the implementation of the Criminal Justice Act 2003, that even the definition of bad character evidence can be open to interpretation in such a way as to facilitate admissibility.[127] Further, admitting bad character evidence to demonstrate propensity seemed to have retained an emphasis on similarity between behaviours/convictions, and where this can be demonstrated, it is evident that it is easier to admit propensity evidence, opening up the defendant to moral judgement by the jury. Whilst this may be the case, and it could be advantageous for the prosecution case, this should be read in line with the *Hanson* guidelines, which prohibits the use of bad character evidence to lend support to a weak case: 'Evidence of bad character cannot be used simply to bolster a weak case, or to prejudice the minds of a jury against a defendant.'[128]

The significance of bad character evidence in demonstrating consent – Then and now

The case of *X and Others*[129] is a particularly stark example of the growing emphasis on unusual/repetitive behaviours within the criminal trial. In *X and Others,* the complainant alleged that she had been subject to a harrowing series of sexual assaults, and had been raped. One defendant, X, had previously befriended the complainant, encouraged her to come to the address wherein the alleged sexual offences were carried out, and was ostensibly responsible for the assault by penetration alongside providing encouragement for an oral rape. X had previous convictions for causing or inciting a child under 13 to engage in sexual activity, false imprisonment, ABH and battery. The appellate court stipulated that:

> In X's case, Ms Hill contends that the underlying facts of the previous convictions were so shocking and unusual that they were bound to have an undue effect on the jury's approach to her case. They were shocking but, in our view, they were relevant to an important matter in issue between X and the prosecution, namely, whether the Complainant consented. The fact that only three years before, as a young girl, X, no doubt

---

126 Andrew Roberts, 'Evidence: Criminal Justice Act 2003 Part II – Bad Character Provisions' [2006] Criminal Law Review 433, 437.

127 For a thorough critique of these provisions see Roderick Munday, 'What Constitutes "Other Reprehensible Behaviour" Under the Bad Character Provisions of the Criminal Justice Act 2003?' [2005] Criminal Law Review 24 and James Goudkamp, 'Bad Character Evidence and Reprehensible Behaviour' [2008] International Journal of Evidence and Proof 116.

128 *Hanson* (n 119) [18].

129 [2012] EWCA Crim 2276.

for her own gratification, had pressured vulnerable victims to engage in sexual activity in her presence had a striking similarity to the facts of the instant case.[130]

The Court of Appeal, in *X*, were of the opinion that whilst the admission of the bad character was not unfair, the summing up was defective and, therefore, the character may have unduly influenced the jury. For this reason, the appeals against conviction were allowed. This does not change one of the key principles we can derive from *X*, which is that the court are prepared to rely upon 'single act propensity' where there is sufficient similarity between pre-existing and alleged behaviours following *Hanson*.[131] Indeed, as Munday has noted, for the court to allow the prosecution to rely upon single acts within an antecedent history, it would take evidence of distinctive or special behaviours such as a 'predilection for highly unusual sexual activity'.[132]

The relevant propensity equipoise has received recent consideration in *Ford*,[133] where the defendant was convicted of rape and sentenced to ten years' imprisonment due to a variety of aggravating factors, including the admission of his antecedent history and the use of alcohol to facilitate the commission of a sexual offence.[134] The defendant (D) and the complainant (K) met at a public house after K had parted company with her partner following a minor disagreement. K accepted a lift home in D's van and, on the way home, they stopped at a local recreation ground and engaged in sexual intercourse. D told the court that K did not appear to be in an intoxicated state, especially not to such a degree that she would have been unable to consent, and he believed the intercourse was consensual. K stated that she had little recollection of the events described and believed she had been drugged, alleging that D had opportunistically spiked her drink when she visited the lavatory, leaving her drink unattended. Expert evidence was provided to the effect that this could not be ruled out, given how quickly the kinds of drugs used in such circumstances move through the system. D, conversely, stated that K had instigated the sexual intercourse, her behaviour reflecting her earlier row with her partner, and that her present allegation emerged from her later regret at having been unfaithful.

Critically, for the purposes of the present discussion, in order to evidence the prosecution's assertion that K could not have consented, and D had no reasonable belief in consent, two convictions for sexual assault to which the defendant had pleaded guilty in July 2008 were used to demonstrate his disposition towards engaging in sexual intercourse in circumstances where consent is absent or unclear. The parties within these earlier offences were vulnerable females living in sheltered accommodation, and the prosecution sought to provide this information to the jury, asserting that the present complainant, 'had had sex with someone who did not have the mental capacity to consent'. The judge ruled the convictions to be capable of proving a relevant propensity, and that any potential unfairness would be

---

130 ibid [12].
131 *Hanson* (n 119).
132 Roderick Munday, 'Single Act Propensity' (2010) 74 Journal of Criminal Law 127, 136.
133 [2015] EWCA Crim 617.
134 The Court of Appeal were concerned by evidence that the defendant only bought two small glasses of wine for the complainant, who voluntarily purchased and consumed a number of drinks of her own accord. The sentence of 10 years was quashed on appeal against sentence and a period of eight years substituted instead, the Court of Appeal stating that there was insufficient evidence to substantiate the assertion that the defendant had used alcohol to enable sexual intercourse. This would otherwise have constituted an additional aggravating factor.

ameliorated by his decision to prohibit the prosecution from referring to the mental capacity of the earlier victims:

> the specific matter in issue between the defendant and the prosecution, to which the bad character evidence is capable of being relevant is whether, if the jury are sure [K] was incapacitated as she describes. . . the defendant went on to have sex with her regardless of whether or not she was consenting and/or was able to consent. . . In my judgment the previous convictions, showing an intent on the part of the defendant to proceed with sexual activity irrespective of the consent of the victim, is directly relevant. . . The previous convictions show the defendant *to be someone who has a propensity to indulge in sexual activity irrespective of the consent of his victim.*[135]

There is undoubtedly an element of common sense reasoning present in *Ford*. Admitting the relevant convictions, and omitting the mental capacity of the complainants, demonstrates a measured approach very much in keeping with the earlier precedents regulating the admissibility of bad character evidence, such as the *Hanson* requirements.[136] However, when a witness unexpectedly revealed that the defendant had engaged in sexual activity with someone who would have been incapable of consenting, the judge declined to discharge the jury – despite this rendering void his earlier reasoning regarding the admission of the antecedent history, and reducing unfairness for D. The defendant made a successful appeal against sentence on the basis that the Court of Appeal considered it incorrect for the judge to have found that D used alcohol to facilitate the offence as this was not substantiated on the facts. The appeal against conviction was unsuccessful, the court finding that the judge had balanced the risk, and carefully directed the jury. This positions this individuated precept within a long line in which the Court of Appeal have been reluctant to interfere with a conviction where the judge has provided a 'careful' or 'thorough' direction to the jury,[137] upon the assumption that jurors are capable of understanding the complex, detailed directions that are provided at trial. Such an assumption is not entirely in keeping with literature in the area.[138]

In *MD*,[139] the defendant was convicted of two counts of rape of girls aged 13 and 14. A single previous conviction for sexual assault was admitted under the provisions of the Criminal Justice Act 2003. *Hanson* previously warned of the dangers of relying upon a single act of propensity, though it was recognised that there were exceptions where it could be demonstrated that the behaviours exhibited within the counts were sufficiently similar/unusual or extraordinary to warrant admission. In the case of *MD* the court held as follows: 'The rapes as evidentially founded relied upon an individual of audacity, who was aware of a first rebuff but persisted, and who was careless of whether his victim consented. That is in common to all three offences – that in 2012, and those two indicted.'[140] It would seem, therefore, that not

---

135 [2015] EWCA Crim 617, [11]–[12] (author emphasis added).

136 Such as not using bad character evidence to bolster a weak case and having a focus on behaviour giving rise to a relevant propensity, *Hanson* (n 119) [18] . . .

137 See *Hanson* (n 119), *R v Norris* [2013] EWCA Crim 128; *R v Kelly* [2013] EWCA Crim 128 amongst others.

138 See for example Duncanson and Henderson, who note that judicial directions can confuse jurors, even when intended to dissuade them from applying rape myths during deliberations in a rape trial, as '[t]he complexity of judicial instructions compounds the difficulty the jury faces in cognitively digesting and remembering the content of the directions', K Duncanson and E Henderson, 'Narrative, Theatre and the Disruptive Potential of Jury Directions in Rape Trials' (2014) 22(2) Feminist Legal Studies 170.

139 [2015] EWCA Crim 837.

140 ibid [35].

only does a previous conviction found a propensity towards engaging in sexual intercourse irrespective of consent, but the similarity of behaviours is also capable of going to guilt. Further, in order to make the decision as to admissibility, the judge will rely upon (and assume correct and truthful under s 109 of the CJA 2003) the complainant's version of events and consider the events cumulatively:

> She thought the previous conviction unusual on its facts, he had forced himself upon a school teacher so as to take what he wanted. That in essence was what the Crown suggested he had done to D and to M. He was, the judge thought, completely oblivious as to whether they were consenting if the Crown's case were well made out and simply took what he wanted on each occasion, using sexual assault against each. The previous conviction was capable of establishing propensity to act in that way with females. . . he had done this before.[141]

On appeal, defence counsel submitted that there was insufficient similarity between the previous conviction for sexual assault and the two rapes. Counsel cited differences in age, removal of clothing, use of a weapon and persistent behaviours as being distinctive factors differentiating the bad character evidence from the present charge. In response, whilst the court conceded that some members of the judiciary would not have admitted the evidence, the rapes were evidentially founded on the audacity of the behaviour demonstrated, which was common to all three instances of sexual behaviours/violence. The evidence of sexual assault on a previous occasion, alongside the charges of rape, demonstrated collectively that the defendant was 'audacious, bold, reckless and persistent'[142] and happy to proceed to intercourse irrespective of consent and irrespective of whether any person could enter the room at any moment. Again, the court noted that there were 'sufficient checks and balances within her direction for justice to have been done'.[143] This case can also be viewed as a continuation of a line of case-law in which the courts have determined that charges can be cross-admissible.[144] Provided evidence is s 98 CJA 2003 compliant, bad character evidence, as regards the other count(s), and one of the requirements of s 101(1) of the CJA 2003 is met, this evidence can be admitted as bad character evidence capable of lending support to the other counts. The court in *Freeman* made clear that any requirement in previous case-law, for the jury to be sure of guilt in one count before using it as evidence to support another, created too restrictive an approach and should not be applied henceforth. Interestingly, the court put forth a disjunctive perspective:

> it may not always be helpful to concentrate on the concept of propensity when the nature of the evidence is such that, in itself, it is capable of being probative in relation to another count, in the sense that it makes it more likely either that the offence was committed (Chopra) or that this defendant committed the offence (Wallace).[145]

Applying *Freeman*, if we do not treat evidence of similar previous convictions as evidence demonstrating propensity, the similar nature of the behaviours is instead considered capable

---

141 ibid [24].
142 ibid [32].
143 ibid [34].
144 *Hanson* (n 119), *Chopra* [2006] EWCA Crim 2133, *Wallace* [2007] EWCA Crim 1760 and *DM* [2008] EWCA Crim 1544, *Freeman & Crawford* [2008] EWCA Crim 1863. For an enlightening and thorough discussion of cross-admissibility, see further David Ormerod QC, HHJ Martin Picton and Andrew Roberts, 'Bad Character Provisions and Their Application to Sexual Offences' in Pamela Radcliffe, Gisli H Gudjonsson CBE, Anthony Heaton-Armstrong, and David Wolchover, *Witness Testimony in Sexual Cases: Evidential, Investigative and Scientific Perspectives* (Oxford University Press, 2016) 89 onwards.
145 *Freeman* (ibid) [19].

of making the other counts more likely to be true. Multiple counts within one indictment may be mutually supportive of truth in this sense, provided sufficient similarity exists between them. Upon further consideration, the admission of a single previous conviction within a multi-count indictment does not embody 'single act propensity' in a *Hanson* sense, as (taking the case of *MD* as an example), the jury may be faced with one similar previous conviction *and* two cross-admissible counts of rape which might be construed as three instances of bad character evidence attributable to the present defendant. This can go some way in suggesting a relevant disposition on the part of the defendant in a trial for a serious sexual offence.

The aforementioned cases demonstrate a clear pattern when the principles are drawn together and viewed holistically. Where counsel seek to admit evidence of propensity under s 101(1)(d) of the CJA 2003 in trials for serious sexual offences, the courts will only do so where there is a discernible pattern of behaviour, or a similarity/peculiarity in the behaviour itself that makes it sufficiently unusual to warrant admission and support either the making of a propensity inference or an inference of truthfulness as regards other allegations that sit within the current trial. The common law rules regulating admissibility were abolished by s 99 of the CJA 2003, but we still place a significant amount of emphasis on similarity when admitting evidence through 'gateway (d)'.[146] Applying *Hanson*, it is easier to admit a similar pattern of behaviours as opposed to older, single convictions that may lack extraordinariness. Though it is far from impossible to adduce single instances of unusual behaviours;[147] there has been explicit recognition of the requirement for similarity by the judiciary and evidence of bad character has been inadmissible for want of it or due to age.[148] Evidence of character has been declared inadmissible where the courts have noted differences in the relevant factual scenarios (the previous fact-pattern, and the present allegation) despite the abolition of the need for a striking similarity that categorised the old law for a time.[149] However, where there is evidence of sufficiently similar behaviours prior to the present charge, and/or multiple counts within the trial, the jury can be provided with a great deal of evidence that may go some way in demonstrating the defendant's capability with regards to certain behaviours. It is the similarity of the behaviours that is advantageous from a prosecution perspective. Though the courts must be mindful of the prejudice the admission of bad character may invoke in jurors, greater access to information regarding the defendant's bad character may go some way in ameliorating any false impressions the jury may have of the defendant based upon the admission of good character, or pre-conceived ideas of the 'kind of person that commits a rape'.

---

146 See above, (n 104) for further commentary substantiating the argument that gateway (d) has replaced the doctrine of similar facts. It is beyond the scope of this chapter to undertake a comprehensive review of this.

147 See Munday's (n 132) discussion of single act propensity.

148 See further, *McGarvie* [2011] EWCA Crim 1414 [16]–[20] in which the court held that whilst 'striking similarity' is no longer the requirement, there does still need to be a degree of similarity. Though the age of the convictions admitted in this case meant that the appeal against conviction was successful. See also *R v PK; R v TK* [2008] EWCA Crim 434.

149 In *Benabbou* [2012] EWCA Crim 1256 the court did not think a conviction for rape could be properly admitted to substantiate a current claim of sexual assault or assault by penetration as the offences were different, and the prejudicial effect would be disproportionately high, [19] onwards. Also, in *Kumar* [2005] EWCA Crim 3549, applying similar fact principles, the court listed the similarities and dissimarities between the offences ([18], [19]) and stated that whilst the facts of both counts were 'just' ([21]) sufficiently similar, that there must be 'some identifiable common feature or features which amount to a significant connection going beyond mere coincidence before the evidence of one complainant may be regarded as supporting the truth of another' ([15]).

Viewed as a whole, the case-law cited illuminates the utility of bad character evidence as being capable of demonstrating 'what the lawyers call "a propensity and tendency to commit sexual offences"'.[150] What the admission of bad character facilitates is the making of a propensity inference or, it would appear following *Freeman*, an inference of truthfulness between counts or a level of similarity indicative that all counts were committed by the same person. In the case of trials for serious sexual offences, it is the making of an inference that this particular defendant is pre-disposed to rape or commit sexual assault/assault by penetration: presumably this is possible both where bad character evidence takes the form of previous convictions and where it takes the form of different counts in the same indictment. The judgment of the court in *Freeman* would suggest that cross-admissible counts necessarily enable an inference of credibility as regards other counts or that all counts are likely to have been committed by the same person and that person is likely to be the defendant.

INFERRING PROPENSITY

> The propensity inference has a number of variations, but in its archetypal form it amounts to the following: the defendant has committed this kind of misconduct on other occasions; the defendant's propensity for this type of misconduct led them to commit the charged offence.[151]

As Hamer clarifies, the probative value of the propensity inference falls to be determined by considering three components: (1) linkage of evidence and the (2) degree of singularity, both of which must be set in the (3) context of other evidence.[152] There will be sufficient linkage where the evidence can be linked to the defendant.[153] The degree of singularity requires a consideration of the prior instance of misconduct and the present charge and requires a connection between the two. Other evidence may provide context by suggesting a motive, or a degree of knowledge (amongst other things) that would enable commission and, in the context of this factorisation, a strong inference of propensity could be made.[154] The case-law previously discussed demonstrated that propensity evidence can link the defendant to the behaviour alleged in such a way as to increase the probability of guilt. Propensity evidence can highlight a proclivity towards particular behaviours in rebutting consent or, as Bagaric and Amarasekara explain, can form background/transaction evidence which 'is often admitted where it explains lack of complaint or absence of resistance by the complainant'.[155] There is potential for evidence of bad character to ameliorate the imbalance inherent in the jurors (perhaps unconscious) subscription to rape myths. For example:

> *D is known to C, as the two have mixed in similar social circles previously. D has been violent in C's presence in the past, punching a woman who rejected his advances on a night out, engendering a fear within C of D. One night, at a party, C is ambushed by D as she*

---

150 *Baker* [2012] EWCA Crim 1801 [10]. Despite the age of some of the conviction in this case, there were enough of them to support a propensity inference and the probative value outweighed the prejudicial effect.

151 David Hamer, 'The Structure and Strength of the Propensity Inference: Singularity, Linkage and the Other Evidence' (2003) 29 Monash Law Review 137, 138.

152 ibid.

153 This would seem to hold the most significance, in the view of the present authors, where the defendant denies *mens rea* but admits having engaged in the relevant conduct.

154 ibid.

155 Mirko Bagaric and Kumar Amarasekara, 'The Prejudice Against Similar Fact Evidence' (2001) International Journal of Evidence and Proof 71, 73–74.

enters the bathroom. D rapes C despite the fact that party-goers are just in the next room and could enter the bathroom at any moment. C tries to leave the room unsuccessfully, and does not resist for fear of further injury. D has previous convictions for the Assault Occasioning Actual Bodily Harm (the aforementioned punch) and for attempted rape, when he forced a co-worker, V, into the stationary cupboard two years previously. On that occasion, V was able to escape before the rape took place.

In this example, the evidence of bad character can be used in two ways:[156]

1   To demonstrate propensity to rape under s 101(1)(d): both the rape and the attempted rape involved an ambush, and took place in crowded places where there was a risk of being caught. Drawing from the patterns illustrated in the case studies above, the courts would be likely to admit such evidence due to the inherent similarities and the peculiarity/audacity of the behaviours shown.

2   The evidence of the previous conviction for ABH may be admissible under s 101(1)(c) of the Criminal Justice Act 2003, as it provides important background evidence explaining that the complainant assessed the situation and decided she would be safer were she to submit. This is inextricably linked to her knowledge of D's violent past. Such evidence may also be admissible under to s 101(1)(d) of the CJA 2003 as going to propensity as it is capable of showing that the defendant is violent in circumstances involving sexual advances by him, especially where they are rejected.

Whilst Bagaric and Amarasekara have alleged that the propensity inference is over-stated and may be more comparable to identity evidence in that it helps to identify D as someone who is likely to be guilty,[157] Redmayne has pinpointed the significance of propensity in his explanation of 'comparative propensity'. One significant advantage of the principle of comparative propensity is that it facilitates an understanding of the probative value of 'single act propensity' along with other uses to which bad character evidence may be put.[158] Redmayne's explanation is elegantly simple – the 'basic idea is that if D has a recent previous conviction, then he can be said to have a comparative propensity to commit similar crimes: he is more likely to offend than someone without a previous conviction.'[159] The more allegations are made, the more likely it is that the defendant has a propensity to commit offences of the kind charged.[160] This has also been referred to as coincidence reasoning[161] though Redmayne disputes the distinction. He points out, quite rightly, that there is an unavoidable element of

---

156   Both instances of misconduct constitute previous convictions and would therefore be s 98-compliant bad character evidence under the Criminal Justice Act 2003. The bad character evidence would need to surmount the gateways, and would have the best chance of admission under 'gateway (d)'.

157   See various analogies employed by Bagaric and Amarasekara in previous works (n 155) 85–86. They also argue that 'Similar fact evidence does not derive its relevance via some mystical 'propensity chain of reasoning'. Rather, it places the accused in a small class of the community that are willing to achieve their ends via the means now alleged and hence fits the accused in a further independent class which is relevant to the determination of guilt'.

158   Munday (n 132).

159   Mike Redmayne, *Character in the Criminal Trial* (Oxford University Press 2015) 113.

160   ibid, 115.

161   This is akin to the Doctrine of Chances, an Anglo-American concept, that has proven controversial due to some commentators' attempts to distance it from propensity reasoning. See Sean P Sullivan, 'Probative Inference from Phenomenal Coincidence: Demystifying the Doctrine of Chances' (2015) 14 Law Probability and Risk 27–50 and Paul F Rothstein, 'Comment: The Doctrine of Chances, Brides of the

propensity reasoning behind the argument that several complainants are unlikely to be mistaken in or concocting their allegations.[162] By reasoning that a complainant is not mistaken/ lying, this suggests that it was D who engaged in a pattern of relevant behaviours, and this pattern is capable of supporting a behavioural disposition – a propensity.

The increased scope for the admission of bad character evidence under the CJA 2003 (whether in the guise of evidence of propensity or of multiple counts capable of supporting the truth of one another) enables the prosecution to go so far as to highlight for the jury that D is a person who is *capable* of such behaviours, regardless of initial appearances. Further, where a pattern of behaviours is established, the jury may even consider themselves able to infer that this defendant is comparatively *more likely* to be guilty of the present alleged offence(s), whether D admits the conduct or not. This may serve to increase the chances of a conviction and may ameliorate, though it is unlikely to remove, the effects of pre-conceived ideas of what 'real rape' entails.

CONCLUSIONS

The primordial focus of this chapter has related to defendant conduct, their attitudinal beliefs as to consent or otherwise attached to sexual activity, and concomitantly the propensity relevance of bad character evidence. The culpability–onus nexus has become blurred in the context of criminalisation of transmission of HIV; as stated herein, the onus of disclosure applied to a defendant for the sexual crime of rape does not apply to the threshold of non-fatal offence liability. The binary divides created between disclosure/non-disclosure responsibilities, and covert/overt deception blameworthiness thresholds are illogical and indefensible. Further grist to the mill is added by recent novel developments on bad character evidence as part of overarching outcome determinateness when applied to consent more broadly. The time is ripe for a fresh reappraisal of HIV criminalisation precepts, and a far broader review beyond the recent Law Commission considerations within the delineated sphere of reform of offences against the person. A *de novo* bespoke legislative framework is required that is predicated on fair labelling. Rather than an inapposite attempt to shoehorn inculpatory conduct under the umbrella of reckless transmission of grievous bodily harm or rape the offence-definitional constructs ought to reflect the gravamen of the harm that actually occurs. Legitimate boundaries should be created that justify the intrusion of criminal law into consensual sexual intimacies.

A new offence ought beneficially to be promulgated to attach to conduct where an individual actor intentionally or recklessly places another in danger of contracting a serious transmissible disease without explicit informed consent as a justification, and the defined harm occurs. In essence, the defendant should not be able to rely on consent as an unknown justificatory defence where he knows that there is a significant risk that the other party will suffer grave harm. In terms of culpability more weight ought to be placed upon the defendant's fault as a primordial factor *vis a vis* inculpation or otherwise. The transmission of HIV is a physical act, demarcated from sexual intimacy itself, and with a focus upon actual risk of transmission of serious injury. The concomitant is that liability is predicated on the defendant placing another person in danger of contracting a serious communicable disease, intending that the other party contract the disease, or being reckless as to whether a significant risk exists that the other party contracts the disease. It is contended that the terms of this

---

Bath and a Reply to Sean Sullivan' (2015) 14 Law Probability and Risk 51–66 for a recent summation of such discussions.
162 Redmayne (n 159) 180–184.

new legislative response effectively focuses on D's fault, the unjustified risk of serious harm, and fair labelling.

The new classificatory offence system should delineate between actual transmission of HIV (intentional or reckless fault) and situations engaging the risk of significant harm, as set out above, with higher penal sanctions attached to the former. This ought to be conjoined with a separate offence that attaches to the act of sexual intimacy itself with fraudulent inducing causes, whether active or passive deception. In this context, as previously argued, it is important to revivify the former offence under s 3(1) of the Sexual Offences Act 1956 that was erroneously excluded from the Sexual Offences Act 2003 whereby: 'it is an offence for a person to procure a woman by false pretences or false representations, to have unlawful sexual intercourse.' The former maximum sentence was two years' imprisonment. A defendant who fraudulently deceives the complainant as to freedom from serious communicable disease, outwith disease harm transmission itself, falls squarely within this offence-definition construct, rather than rape. The offence, of course, would apply more broadly to other cases where deception vitiates consent beyond the parameters of HIV fraudulent concealment. The human dignity of the 'consentor' is fundamentally degraded, and significant personal harm caused that justifies the stated culpability threshold for liability. It is also justifiable that, as indicated, a fresh reappraisal occurs of the relevance of bad character evidence, and relational propensity appurtenant to consent within the sexual crime trial process.

There is a demonstrable efficacy in the use of bad character evidence in trials for serious sexual assault. It is a form of evidence that can go directly to guilt in the eyes of a juror, and can perhaps help to raise conviction rates. It might also help to rebalance the criminal trial to some degree; whilst jurors may be affected by a derogation from the rape script as previously discussed, evidence of bad character can elevate the probability of guilt in the eyes of the juror, and isolate the defendant.[163] Unfortunately, the admission of bad character evidence has its limitations and is affected by problems pertaining to juror decision-making processes, such as a lack of objectivity.[164] Two significant issues are relevant in this regard:

1   Bad character does not necessarily constitute a solid predictive base, and there is a need to be mindful of jurors inferring repetitious character traits where to do so is inappropriate. Heuristic reasoning processes can give rise to fast, 'frugal' decisions as to the probability of guilt based upon our everyday perceptions of behaviour and the continuity of character/personality.[165] 'Psychological research lends some support to the claim that we are not very good at recognising when patterns are due to chance',[166] and further, the utility of character as a predictive base requires a broader conception of what character is before it can be identified with certainty. As Park asserts, 'there is a great difference between predicting what might happen and finding out what did happen', citing 'inferential error prejudice' as a problem that leads jurors to attach disproportionate weight to bad character evidence in proving guilt.[167] Personality

---

163   See empirical studies suggesting that jurors are incapable of dealing with evidence of similar previous convictions objectively, whatever the offence category, for example, Sally Lloyd Bostock, 'The Effects on Juries of Hearing About the Defendant's Previous Criminal Record: A Simulation Study' [2000] Criminal Law Review 734.

164   ibid.

165   An excellent discussion of heuristic reasoning processes can be found in Daniel Kahneman, *Thinking Fast and Slow* (Penguin Books 2011).

166   Redmayne (n 159).

167   Roger C Park, 'Character at the Crossroads' (1997–1998) 49 Hastings Law Journal 717, 720–723.

theory requires that situational variants such as frequency, circumstantial similarity and temporal proximity is taken into account.[168] This is a problem that merits in-depth discussion that is beyond the scope of the present chapter. Suffice that, as Redmayne asserts, 'If character is fragmented, we should be wary of the notion of out-of-character actions, unless we have information about D's behaviour in similar situations to the present one'.[169]

2   Next is the problem of the rape myth, and the prevalence of a 'widely shared real rape stereotype'.[170] As Temkin and Krahé explain with regard to rape, 'There is probably no other criminal offence that is as intimately related to broader social attitudes and evaluations of the complainant's conduct as sexual assault. When confronted with an account of alleged rape, individuals tend to respond to it against the backdrop of their personal beliefs and understandings about gender relationships in general, appropriate role behaviour for men and women, and the rules and rituals of consensual sexual interactions'.[171] Considering how deeply embedded these social attitudes are considered to be, it is possible that the admission of bad character can only go so far in establishing consent or otherwise in trials for serious sexual offences.[172]

Whilst the effect of the Criminal Justice Act 2003 has been to enable the bad character evidence of persons to be used more frequently when establishing propensity,[173] the extent to which this can help to establish guilt, or raise conviction rates remains unclear and requires empirical testing. What we can see from our detailed review of recent case-law is that such evidence is now easier to admit, and propensity reasoning is consequently facilitated, albeit perhaps arising out of an imperfect normative understanding of character on the part of the fact-finder. This should be viewed as a positive development for the prosecuting authorities in rebalancing apposite gradations of admissibility, and a momentum shift towards appropriate equipoise in the trial process.

---

168   Situationism, interactionism, Trait theory amongst others. See ibid, 729.
169   Redmayne (n 159) 16. See also, Julian Baggini, *The Ego Trick* (Grantia 2011).
170   Temkin and Krahé (n 113) 31.
171   Temkin and Krahé (n 113) 33.
172   Though, contrast the arguments of Helen Reece to the effect that 'the regressiveness of current public attitudes towards rape has been overstated. The claim that rape myths are widespread may be challenged on three grounds: first, some of the attitudes are not myths; secondly, not all the myths are about rape; thirdly, there is little evidence that the rape myths are widespread. To a troubling extent, we are in the process of creating myths about myths' 'Rape Myths: Is Elite Opinion Right and Popular Opinion Wrong?' (2013) 33(3) Oxford Journal of Legal Studies 445, 445–447.
173   Which may be a worrying prospect from the perspective of the defendant.

9

Deciding to die and help with dying

What can and cannot be done in England and Wales

*G R Sullivan**

Two cases

(1) P is a student in his first term at university. His parents recently separated and his relationship with his long-term girlfriend ended instantly when she briskly informed him that she was seeing someone else. He received a bad fail mark and caustic feedback for his first essay. He decided to kill himself and would have done so by jumping from a balcony but for the return of his room-mate, who physically restrained him and called for assistance. P was compulsorily detained in hospital under the terms of the Mental Health Act 1983. He received effective therapy and is now enjoying university life.

(2) Q was a middle-aged man with motor neurone disease. He lived in fear of a protracted and frightening death, unmitigated by any form of palliation. While his wife was away visiting friends, he took a large amount of paracetamol. A written note clearly expressed his wish to die and his rejection of any life-saving intervention. When his wife returned she read his note and then called an ambulance. The comatose Q was resuscitated in hospital. Subsequently, he endured the form of death he most feared.

DECIDING TO DIE AND BEING HELPED TO DIE – A BRIEF PROPOSAL

Below is a brief proposal for a legal regime for regulating choices to die and assisting others to die. The proposal assumes that in some circumstances it is morally legitimate to choose to end one's own life and for registered medical practitioners to assist a person in realising a wish to die. Of course, these assumptions are contestable.[1] No attempt will be made to

---

* Thanks are due to Jonathan Rogers and Anne Sullivan for help with this chapter. The usual conditions apply.

1 Lord Steyn gives a fine summary of the contesting moral and ethical issues in play surrounding voluntary euthanasia and physician assistance in dying: *Pretty v DPP* (n 1) [54]. For persons whose moral stance is not primarily based on religious texts, the main objection to any liberalisation of the law is the fear that individuals dependent on the provision of care by family and others may feel pressurised or obliged to lift the care burden by dying, despite an underlying wish to live. This concern proved decisive for the large majority of MPs who recently voted down by 330 votes to 118 a private member's bill to provide

argue the moral case for the regime. All that will be said here is that this chapter is written from the perspective of one who believes that certain persons in dire straits should receive assistance in dying provided they have a 'voluntary, clear, settled and informed' wish to die.[2] Ideally, the assistance should take the form of assisting suicide or voluntary euthanasia, whatever is best suited to the circumstances and wishes of V. An important requirement is that V must have a 'settled' wish to die in the sense that it is most unlikely that V will change his or her mind about wishing to die whatever form of therapy is brought to bear. That would almost certainly be the case for Q in the second hypothetical case above. Contrast P in the first case. At the time of his suicidal state his resolve to die might well have been firm, and yet he was a suitable case for therapeutic intervention. He would fall outside the class of persons who, under the proposal sketched below, may lawfully receive assistance in dying.

The purpose of this chapter is to assess to what extent the details of the proposed legal regime are compatible with the current state of English and Welsh criminal law as it stands now and as it may be developed in the near future. The focus is exclusively on what the judges have decided and said and on what they might decide and say in the matters of assisted suicide and voluntary euthanasia. For England and Wales, it seems that there will be no legislative changes in these areas of law in the foreseeable future.[3]

The proposal

(1) V has no right to assistance in suicide or to voluntary euthanasia under the supervision of a registered medical practitioner, unless the High Court (Family Division) has made a declaration that V may receive help and support in dying from registered medical practitioners and their supporting staff. No such declaration shall be made unless the court is satisfied that V's wish to die is voluntary, clear, settled and informed.

(This part of the proposals envisages that court approval may be given for medical staff to assist V in dying either by his or her own hand or by way of voluntary euthanasia. There is some prospect that assistance in suicide may become available for some applicants to the high court[4] but approval of voluntary euthanasia in any circumstances appears to be a remote possibility.[5] Lawful assistance in dying if and when made available should require permission in each case given by the High Court and be medically supervised.)

---

physician assistance in dying for terminal patients suffering pain and distress with less than six months to live: Assistance in Dying Bill HC (2015–09) [2]. The same concern featured prominently in the decision of the House of Lords Committee on Medical Ethics not to recommend any change in the law relating to assisted suicide: HL Paper (1994–5) 26 cl 21(1).

2 The phrase is taken from the Assistance in Dying Bill ibid.

3 See (nn 1–2). But nothing is set in stone. On 5 October 2015, Governor Brown signed into law the Assistance in Dying Bill (California). That such a populous and heterogeneous state has taken that decision might well have influence beyond its boundaries.

4 The opinion that there is a prospect of judicial endorsement of physician assistance in dying is based on some of the judgments in the Supreme Court in *R (on the application of Nicklinson) and R (on the application of AM) v DPP* [2014] UKSC 38. See (n 22) and associated text.

5 In *Nicklinson* [2013] EWCA Civ 38 before the case reached the Supreme Court, arguments in favour of euthanasia were made but gained no traction. Before the Supreme Court argument was confined to physician assisted suicide and prosecution policy in relation to the offence of complicity in suicide.

(2) If V attempts to commit suicide, he or she should be immune from criminal liability in respect of the attempt.

(This provision accurately reflects the law as set down in the Suicide Act 1961 as amended, or so it will be argued. Argument is required because of some recent *dicta* delivered in strong language endorsing the idea that there is a right to commit suicide.[6] It is submitted that attempted suicide has merely been 'decriminalised' and that some suicidal acts can be lawfully prevented as in the case of P above.)

(3) Well-intentioned interventions on the part of D (a lay person) to prevent V from committing suicide (physical restraint; summoning medical and other emergency services) should not normally attract criminal or civil liability. This immunity should hold even in cases where V's wish to commit suicide is known to D to be 'voluntary, clear, settled and informed' and where D's intervention is resisted by V.

(If there is no right to commit suicide it follows that some particular acts of suicide may be prevented. The lawful status of preventive acts is of great importance for persons with close emotional ties to a suicidal person. Interventions by lay persons motivated by affection or a sense of duty should not attract criminal or tortious responsibility, save in exceptional circumstances. Of course, if, contrary to the view argued below, there is a right to commit suicide the legality of preventive interventions by lay persons and persons with duties to the public such as medical practitioners, paramedics, fire men and women, police officers and prison wardens becomes more problematic.)

(4) Any assistance by D to V in V's suicidal acts or any participation in a process leading to the voluntary euthanasia of V should continue to be criminalised.

(If at some future point in time the High Court develops a practice of permitting assistance in dying for persons with a settled wish to die, this should have no implications for persons acting of their own initiative.)

(5) D (1) (a medic, paramedic, police officer, etc)[7] should have immunity from criminal and tortious liability when intervening to stop V from committing suicide (physical restraint; imposition of medical or surgical treatment) unless he or she knows or should know that V's wish to commit suicide is voluntary, clear, settled and informed. If V falls within that class, any forceful intervention on the part of D (1) should be a crime and a tort unless D (1) was not at fault in being unaware that V was within the protected class or that the intervention was necessary to protect third parties from physical harm, shock or alarm.

---

6 *R v Nicklinson* [2014] UKSC 38 [255] [90] (Lord Neuberger); [200] (Lord Wilson): 'In law, the state is not entitled to intervene to prevent a person of full capacity who has arrived at a settled decision to take his own life from doing so. However, such a person does not have a right to call on a third party to help him to end his life.' There are also other references suggestive of an unqualified right to commit suicide but not in such clear cut terms (n 42).

7 If V is in prison or other forms of lawful custody those charged with his or her care or supervision are seemingly empowered to prevent any suicide attempt: *Reeves v Commissioner of Police for the Metropolis* [2000] 1 AC 360.

(In certain respects this part of the proposal may be more permissive of preventive medical interventions than the current law.[8] It is now well accepted that if V is mentally competent, she may refuse medical treatment for any reason or indeed for no reason at all. Refusal of treatment can be facilitated by an advanced directive.[9] Forced treatment of persons who have rejected treatment is criminal and tortious. Be this as it may, frontline emergency services will often send to hospital persons who have made clear their rejection of any life-saving measures but who have yet to die from their suicide attempt. The aspiration behind this limb of the proposal is to allow therapeutic interventions in cases such as P's despite his wish to die but to disallow therapeutic intervention in a case such as Q's. This will not be easy in practice: emergency service personnel should always be given the benefit of any reasonable doubt as to which side of the line the patient falls.)

(6) If V claims a voluntary, settled clear and informed wish to die, he or she may apply to the High Court (Family Division) for help and support in the process of dying. If satisfied that V does have a voluntary, settled, clear and informed wish to die the court should make a declaration that help and support in dying can be lawfully given by registered medical practitioners and supporting staff under their direction.

(The High Court has a long-standing jurisdiction to pronounce on the legality of proposed medical interventions by way of declaratory judgments.[10] If a decision is made to allow assistance in dying it is very likely that the court will set down criteria to assist in determining whether an applicant can be said to have a voluntary, settled, clear and informed wish to die.)[11]

(7) The help and support in dying supervised by a registered medical practitioner may take the form of assistance in suicide or voluntary euthanasia, whatever is best suited to the needs and wishes of V.

(The thought is that this limb of the proposal is right in principle: if a threshold decision is taken that V should be assisted in dying, the line between assisting suicide and voluntary euthanasia will not necessarily track any sustainable moral difference, particularly in cases where complex devices are set up to allow it to be said that the final act was that of the patient, even in cases of complete paralysis.[12] English courts are likely to persist with their insistence that assisting suicide is in different case from voluntary euthanasia, with the latter forbidden in all circumstances.)[13]

---

8 Arguably V has the right to refuse treatment for any reason or indeed no reason at all: *B (Adult refusal of medical treatment)* [2002] EWHC 429; *St George's Health Care Trust v S* [1998] 3 All ER 673. As a matter of practice treatment may be imposed to prevent V's suicide by assumptions that suicidal impulses are pathological and warrant confinement under the terms of the Mental Health Act 1983.

9 Mental Capacity Act 2005.

10 As in for example *Airedale NHS Trust v Bland* [1993] AC 789.

11 In *Nicklinson* [2014] UKSC 38 [205] Lord Wilson compiled a detailed checklist of factors the High Court might take into account when ascertaining whether an applicant petitioning for physician assisted suicide had a voluntary, clear, settled and informed wish to die.

12 Lord Neuberger saw merit in terms of staying the right side of the assistance in dying/euthanasia divide in a device invented by a Dr Nitschke which can be loaded with a lethal drug and be digitally activated by a pass phrase via an eye blink computer: *R v Nicklinson* (n 6); Lord Kerr and Lord Sumption saw less merit in the device.

13 *Nicklinson* (n 5).

(8) Assistance in suicide or participation in voluntary euthanasia by registered medical practitioners and supporting staff should continue to attract the current penalties for assisting suicide and murder if carried out without the authority of the High Court.

(9) Any prosecution for the offence of encouraging or assisting suicide must be consented to by the Director of Public Prosecutions.

(This is of course the current position which at least ensures that prosecutions for assisted suicide are very rare.)[14]

Why a proposal in these terms?

When considering the complex, and uncertain substantive law and procedural law[15] relating to suicide in England and Wales from a liberal, secular perspective, it is tempting to argue that any reform should maximise the personal autonomy of mentally competent agents. A thought along the lines of 'if V really wants to die let him die and if he wants help in dying give him help in dying' attracts as an uncluttered way forward. In terms of achieving precision and structure, it is more challenging to fashion a humane and principled regime offering assistance in dying to persons with a voluntary, clear, settled and informed wish to die but which also permits overriding the suicidal impulses of persons who may be restored to a life they wish to live. And, of course, there are a significant number of persons who would not accept either alternative. They would insist that no one should be helped to die whatever their condition and whatever their firm and settled wishes.

If we argue for full autonomy in the matter of choosing when and how to die, we must concede the legitimacy to some very drastic and sudden decisions. It is all too tempting in a case such as the student P to assert that wishing to jump here and now to a certain death from a balcony is a form of mental disorder. However P had his reasons, grounded in things that matter. He thought he had a settled home life, a loving girlfriend and a good intellect. The sudden deflation of these sources of well-being could well have convinced him that he had reached depths from which he could not emerge. Yet despair should not be confused with irrationality.[16] If he had given vent to his feelings by trashing his room or picking a fight with

---

14 *Richardson and another v Director of Public Prosecutions* [2014] UKSC 8 [254]. In the last nine years there has been only one prosecution for the offence of complicity in suicide, involving facts which established that D's involvement in V's suicide was malevolent and self-interested. Many hundreds of UK citizens have travelled to Switzerland and elsewhere with assistance from third parties rendered in England or Wales. Before the Supreme Court the Director of Public Prosecutions confirmed that she had no intention to change her policy of desisting from prosecution in such cases.

15 *R v Purdy* [2010] I AC 345. The potential impact of the clear terms of s 2 of the Suicide Act 1961 have been considerably baffled by interpretations of Article 8 of the European Convention for Human Rights which, as interpreted, requires publication of codes of practice which list the considerations the Director of Public Prosecutions takes into account when considering whether to prosecute the offence of complicity in suicide.

16 Studies consistently establish that a significant proportion of young adults and adolescents with strong suicidal impulses are legally competent decision makers in the sense that there is no psychosis and no clinical depression: Karen Hawton and Keith Rodham, *By Their Own Young Hand: Deliberate Self-harm and Suicidal Ideas in Adolescents* (Jessica Kinsley Publishers 2006); Genevra Richardson, 'Assessing Capacity in the Shadow of Suicide: What can the law do?' (2013) 91 International Journal of Law in Context 1.

his room-mate, he would have been held fully accountable for his wrongdoing,[17] albeit with mitigation of penalty. But choosing suicide is in a different case from damaging property or hitting people. Even if a suicide is based on a voluntary choice by a competent agent, it is not only the last choice the agent will make but a choice that, if realised, may radically change for the worse the lives of connected persons such as partners, children, and parents.[18] It is a decision that, sometimes, should be taken out of the hands of even mentally competent agents.

In practice, P's suicidal wishes might well be overridden by resorting to mental health legislation. Should he refuse a voluntary admission to a psychiatric hospital ward he might well be found mentally disordered and detained and treated in hospital in the interests of his health and safety.[19] From the protectionist stance taken here, no great objection is raised against this familiar procedure in cases such as P's. In large part this is because many interventions of this kind involving adolescents and young adults, destabilised by life events, are successful and lead on to lives unburdened by further suicidal thoughts.[20] With such gains in mind one might not be unduly worried if the notion of clinical depression is stretched in some instances to cover extreme but non-psychotic responses to personal setbacks. Contrast the case of P with Q, the middle-aged man with motor neurone disease. Assume that the burden of living with the prospect of a grisly death, together with the physical deterioration entailed by this condition, had induced a state of depression requiring strong psychotropic medication merely to get by day to day. If following his resuscitation, he had been made an involuntary patient on a psychiatric ward the admission would have been be fully congruent with the letter of the law, more so than in the case of P. However, what good would have come of it?

That voluntary and mentally competent adults should be free to decide things for themselves must be the default position for anyone of a secular, liberal, persuasion regarding any proposal to override decisions taken by competent agents. And that default position holds not merely for decisions taken after full and calm deliberation, but also for choices influenced by strong and in the moment influences, such as rage, euphoria, sexual excitement and drink. Let us introduce W, who was not sober, but still should have seen through the flattery of the attractive stranger and caught his flight, thereby avoiding a lot of grief for himself and for others. It would be wrong in principle, and quite hopeless in practice to legislate against such forms of foolishness. The same hands-off approach, entailing no resuscitation or coercive therapy, should apply to the case of Q, even though his suicide attempt would have been strongly influenced by his (fully rational) depression. How then in the light of the freedom allowed to W and Q can coercion be legitimately used in the case of P? To be sure no one can claim a right to commit suicide in such a public and dangerous way as in jumping from a balcony. Yet aside from restraining acts of that kind, should he be left to make his own decisions? If he accepts an offer of therapy, well fine; but if not leave it there – or so a libertarian liberal might argue.

Below a fuller argument favouring coercion in P's case and in cases of a kindred kind will be made. But before that we should consider the possibility that arises following *dicta*

---

17 However potent his emotionally charged condition was in provoking violent or destructive emotions it could not form the basis of any defence known to English criminal law: *R v Parker* [1977] 2 All ER 475; *R v Briggs* [1977] 1 All ER 475.

18 A parallel may be drawn with close family members of homicide victims who are included in the class of primary victims in the Article 2 jurisprudence of the European Court of Human Rights. Frequently, an act of suicide will not be merely a self-regarding act in the Millsian sense.

19 Mental Health Act 1983(as amended), s 2.

20 Keith Hawton (ed), *Prevention and Treatment of Suicidal Behaviour* (Oxford University Press 2005).

in *Nicklinson* that coercion in a case such as P's might now be suspect in terms of the law. The case also has important things to say about prosecution policy for the offence of assisted suicide, and the compatibility of the offence of complicity in suicide with the right to private life guaranteed by Article 8 of the ECHR. An examination of this decision will provide a basis for estimating to what extent the assistance in dying regime proposed above has been realised and may further be realised by the judiciary.

Nicklinson[21]

In *Nicklinson*,[22] the applicants sought a declaration from a nine-member panel of the Supreme Court that s 2 of the Suicide Act 1961 in proscribing assistance in suicide to persons in the circumstances of the applicants was incompatible with Article 8(1) of the European Convention for Human Rights. They argued that the Strasbourg jurisprudence had established an individual's right to decide by what means and at what point his or her life will end, provided he or she is capable of freely reaching a decision on this question and acting in consequence, is one of the aspects of the right to respect for private life within the meaning of Article 8 of the Convention. Additionally, the applicants sought a declaration that the published guidelines, provided by the Director of Public Prosecutions concerning the circumstances she would take into account in resolving whether to consent to a prosecution for the offence of assisted suicide, lacked clarity for persons in the circumstances of the applicants and should be amended. In the courts below, and in associated litigation, it was argued for the applicant Mr Nicklinson that assistance in dying taking the form of voluntary euthanasia should be permitted in his case. The argument did not prosper to any extent and was not put before the Supreme Court.[23]

The applicants suffered complete paralysis and thus were incapable of taking their own lives. The applicants were not facing any immediate or short-term death. There was a general acceptance that a 'blanket ban' on all forms of assistance in suicide would contravene the right to private life guaranteed by Article 8(1) of the Convention. Despite the unyielding terms of s 2 of the Suicide Act 1961 it was concluded that there was not a blanket ban on assistance in suicide because of the guidance on prosecutions for the offence provided in publicly available form by the Director of Public Prosecutions.[24] The Director conceded before the court that the published guidelines lacked clarity in some particulars, particularly in cases of participation by medical and kindred personnel, and indicated that she would amend the guidelines accordingly.[25]

The key issue in *Nicklinson* was whether it would be lawful to provide assistance in suicide to persons in the condition of the applicants. The applicants argued that to disallow assistance in suicide for persons in their circumstances, as s 2 did, was to deny them their right under Article 8(1), as interpreted by the European Court for Human Rights, to decide by what means

---

21 For an incisive analysis of this Supreme Court decision see Jonathan Rogers, 'Assisted Suicide Saga – the *Nicklinson* Episode' (2014) (7) Archbold Review 7. Dr Rogers takes the view that the undertaking given to the court by the Director of Public Prosecutions to include particular clarifications in the prosecution guidelines relating to assisted suicide makes any liberalisation of the applicable law unlikely.

22 *Nicklinson* [2014] UKSC 38.

23 See (n 5).

24 The Director of Public Prosecutions must give her consent to any prosecution for assisting suicide. In *Purdy* [2010] 1 AC 345, the House of Lords ruled that as a matter of law that the Director must give clear and publicised guidance about the circumstances when she would likely authorise a prosecution.

25 Lord Neuberger considered it inappropriate to give any order to the Director but indicated the courts powers could be invoked if the confusion was not resolved. *R v Nicklinson* (n 6).

and at what point their lives would end.[26] Baroness Hale and Lord Kerr agreed that persons in the circumstances of the applicants should enjoy exemption from the terms of s 2 and made the declaration the applicants sought. They were strongly of the opinion that assistance in dying can and should be given to persons in the applicant's circumstances, who understandably wished to die but who were unable to bring about their own deaths unaided.[27] Refusal of assistance in order to protect vulnerable persons who might feel compromised by any liberalisation of the law would be a disproportionate denial of the applicant's rights.

Lord Neuberger and Lord Wilson were highly sympathetic to the applicants and agreed that it would be much better if the applicant's entitlement to any assistance was grounded in law rather than resting on the practice of the Director of Public Prosecutions.[28] However, although the judgments lean heavily in favour of providing assistance in suicide in some particular circumstances they stayed their hands in issuing a declaration. They were mindful that at the time of the hearing, parliament was on the point of debating the Assistance in Dying Bill. They made clear that the courts would be open to future applicants in like cases if Parliament declined to make any exceptions to the general proscription on assisting suicide for persons who found themselves in the circumstances of the applicants.[29]

Lord Mance was open to the opinion that the absence of any exemptions from the sweep in s 2 of the Suicide Act might be Convention incompatible and challengeable in court but thought that Parliament was much the best place for debating and changing the law.[30] Lord Clarke and Lord Sumption did not rule out completely the possibility that to proscribe all tokens of assistance in suicide might give rise to Convention incompatibility and future applications to courts, but considered that any decisions by Parliament taken on matters arising in *Nicklinson* (including a decision not to allow assistance) would preclude any future applications to courts.[31] Lord Reed and Lord Hughes saw no role for courts rather than Parliament in deciding when if ever some exceptions to the ban on assisting suicide should be made.

In substance, *Nicklinson* decides nothing about persons in the helpless condition of the applicants seeking assistance in suicide. A declaration of incompatibility was asked for but, by a 7/2 majority, not given. Baroness Hale and Lord Kerr did what is to be expected of judges, namely to analyse the applicable law and then make a ruling, in their case a ruling that to deny assistance to the applicants contravened Article 8. The other judgments make rulings in the narrow sense of refusing to grant a declaration, but without explicitly ruling whether or not the denial of assistance to the applicants was compatible or incompatible with Article 8 of the Convention. This reticence to resolve on the day the key issue in the case was not so much based on a concern with the separation of powers, in a strict constitutional sense, but with deferring to Parliament as the best place for debating questions relating to the ending of life. This deference undermines the processes and rationale of the Human Rights Act 1998. If the majority had made a declaration of incompatibility relating to the refusal of assistance to the applicants, the letter of the law would still have stood: s 2 of the Suicide Act 1961 would have read as it reads now.[32] A majority declaration of incompatibility would have merely placed

---

26 The applicants were not protesting the existence of s 2 of the Suicide Act 1961 but the impact of the provision on their particular circumstances, a distinction not kept in sight by all members of the court.

27 *R v Nicklinson* (n 6) (Baroness Hale); [357] (Lord Kerr).

28 ibid [148] (Lord Neuberger); [202] (Lord Wilson).

29 The House of Commons has recently rejected An Assistance In Dying Bill that was confined to terminally ill patients (n 1).

30 *R v Nicklinson* [2014] UKSC 38 [186]–[187].

31 ibid [293] (Lord Clarke); [233] Lord Sumption).

32 Human Rights Act 1998, s 3(2)(b).

a legal onus on the government to make a considered response to the question of whether the terms of s 2 should be changed to allow assistance in dying to persons in like case to the applicants.[33] Within the terms of the Human Rights Act 1998, it is perfectly in order for the government to confirm the domestic law even though it accepts that in some of its applications the law will not be Convention-compliant. Rulings on the compatibility issue would have informed discussions within government and Parliamentary debates.

None the less, *Nicklinson* is not unimportant. Seven members of the Supreme Court accepted that Article 8(1)[34] as interpreted in the Strasbourg jurisprudence did confer a right for persons to decide for themselves by what means and at what point their lives would end (Lord Reed and Lord Hughes did not address the matter). That was the starting point for considering what restraints if any did Article 8(2)[35] and the applicable jurisprudence (which allows a wide margin of appreciation for member states) place on the provision of assistance in dying for persons who wished to exercise their right to die at the time and by the means of their choice.

That a right to die may be a right known to English law by way of the Convention comes as some surprise. Previously in *Pretty* the House of Lords took a different view.[36] But assume for now (and only for now) that there is such a right. Without question a consistent recognition of that right would bring change. Recall Q, the man with motor neurone disease who took an overdose and left a refusal of treatment note. The decision to resuscitate, legally suspect even at the time (in the light of the right of mentally competent persons to refuse all forms of medical and surgical treatment for whatever reason), would be even more dubious. The only route to lawful intervention would have been a reasonable assumption on the part of interveners that he was mentally incompetent. Indeed, he was very depressed. However, are we to refuse a right to die to persons who are made depressed for the reasons leading to a wish to die? And what of interventions preceding his taking of the pills. Can the pills be taken away? Should he be stopped from buying them? Should the pharmacy refuse to sell pills to him?

Overdoses are far from ideal as a way of exercising a right to die. If there is a right to die it is surely perverse to proscribe all forms of assistance in dying. *De facto*, and maybe even *de jure*,[37] assistance can be sought and received if one has the financial means and the ability to travel. Hundreds of people have travelled from the UK to Switzerland and other countries where assistance in dying is lawful. Not one prosecution for assisting in suicide has been brought in respect of these cases although there have been many instances where there has been clear evidence of assistance rendered in England or Wales by family and friends of the person travelling to die. During argument in *Nicklinson* the Director of Public Prosecutions announced in open court that this policy of abstaining from prosecution in cases of this kind would continue.[38] Furthermore, she also indicated that if a doctor gave direct assistance in

---

33 ibid, *s* 7.
34 Which provides that everyone has the right to respect for his private and family life, his home and his correspondence.
35 Which permits derogations from the rights conferred by Article 8(1). Of particular relevance in *Nicklinson* was the allowance made for public authorities to interfere with Article 8(1) rights for the protection of the rights and freedoms of others. Any derogation must be in 'accordance with law' a phrase of some significance in the light of *R (Purdy) v DPP* [2010] 1 AC 345.
36 *R v (Pretty)* [2002] 1 AC 800. There was unanimity for the view that none of the articles of the European Convention for Human Rights were engaged by the exceptional proscription of assistance in suicide or by the lack of notice concerning what forms of assistance might attract prosecution.
37 *R v Purdy* [2010] I AC 345.
38 *Richardson and another v Director of Public Prosecutions* (n 14) [254], [255].

dying in England or Wales to persons in like case to the applicants, a prosecution would be most unlikely.[39]

Plainly legislative intervention in the matter of assistance in dying (including voluntary euthanasia) is long overdue but seems a very unlikely prospect at present.[40] If there were to be a statutory scheme it is immodestly claimed that the best scheme would be something along the lines of the proposal outlined at the start of this chapter. The scheme is not based on any right to die that V can exercise at a time and place of his or her choosing. Only when a declaration is given by the court that help and support in dying can be provided is there legally based entitlement to die with assistance and only with assistance from a registered medical practitioner. A declaration may only be made if the applicant is proved to have a clear, settled and informed wish to die. Any person whose suicidal wishes may be deflected by therapy would not be entitled to assistance in dying. Indeed, it is contemplated that in suitable cases therapy may be non-optional.

All but two members of the Supreme Court in *Nicklinson* recognised a right to die at the time and by the means one chooses. This right arises from three decisions of the European Court of Human Rights involving applicants in dire straits in terms of health and well-being.[41] On the face of it this right could have some unsettling consequences if at large and not confined to persons whose lives are unbearable in ways that cannot be alleviated. Lord Sumption spoke trenchantly in terms of an unqualified right to die at one's own hand.[42] This is an over-reading of the relevant Strasbourg jurisprudence, which establishes a far more nuanced right that could be developed incrementally by English courts. That process will be assisted by seeking guidance from the High Court by way of *ex ante* declaratory judgments in respect of proposed forms of assistance in dying. The legitimacy of such assistance is recognised in the Convention jurisprudence. A statutory scheme would be better but a qualified right to die with assistance sensitively developed could offer something much better than the current dispensation. However, we cannot rule out the possibility that under English law there is an unqualified right to die at one's own hand but no right whatever to assistance in dying.

IS THERE AN UNQUALIFIED RIGHT TO DIE UNDER ENGLISH LAW?

Until very recently the answer to the question would have been unquestionably negative. The Suicide Act 1961 s 1 states that attempting suicide in no longer a crime but s 2 lays down in the clearest terms without any exceptions that assisting suicide is a crime, a serious crime, with a maximum penalty of 14 years. In *Pretty*, the applicant argued that she was entitled to guidance from the Director of Public Prosecutions regarding what assistance in dying she could receive from her husband without risk of his prosecution when the symptoms of her

---

39 In the unlikely event of the Director (in the absence of special aggravating features) consenting to prosecution of assisters of persons travelling abroad to die there is little doubt that after *Purdy* any prosecution would be found to be in breach of Article 8. Her statement concerning the unlikelihood of her consenting to the prosecution of a doctor giving direct assistance in dying in England or Wales was interesting. Her latest post *Nicklinson* guidelines (October 2014) on prosecuting assisting suicide fall far short of holding out immunity for doctors rendering direct assistance, however compassionate their motives.

40 *Pretty v DPP* (n 1).

41 *Haas v Switzerland* (2011) 53EHRR 33.

42 'In law, the state is not entitled to intervene to prevent a person of full capacity who has arrived at a settled decision to take his own life from doing so. However, such a person does not have a right to call on a third party to help him to end his life.' *R v Nicklinson* (n 6). There are also other references suggestive of an unqualified right to commit suicide but not in such clear cut terms; see [90] (Lord Neuberger) and [200] (Lord Wilson).

motor neurone disease became intolerable. In refusing, along with other members of the appellate committee of the House of Lords, to require the Director to give guidance, Lord Bingham said: 'while the 1961 Act abrogated the rule of law whereby it was a crime to commit (or attempt to commit) suicide it conferred no right on anyone to do so.'[43] The House of Lords was unanimous that no Convention rights were in issue and in particular that the right to life in the terms of Article 2 had no implications for questions relating to chosen ways of dying, that limitations on suicide and euthanasia did not give rise to inhuman and degrading treatment within the terms of Article 3 whatever the medical condition of the applicant and that a right to a private life guaranteed by Article 8(1) did not impinge on state regulation of suicide and euthanasia.

The European Court of Human Rights found that Mrs Pretty's desire to end her life did engage Article 8(1) of the Convention.[44] However, on the facts, the court found that the interference with her right under the terms of s 2 of the Suicide Act 1961 was justified under Article 8(2) because s 2, although of a blanket nature, was designed to safeguard life by protecting the weak and vulnerable. Moreover, the unyielding terms of s 2 were tempered by the provision of a maximum penalty and the requirement that the Director of Public Prosecutions must give consent to any prosecution for assisting suicide. For the Court this made for a system of enforcement and adjudication which allowed consideration of the details of the particular case to be balanced against the requirements of retribution and deterrence.

This judgment of the European Court of Human Rights in *Pretty* seemed to leave the English law of suicide pretty much intact. Subsequently in *Purdy*,[45] however, much was made of the fact that a desire on the part of V to end her life engaged the protection of private life under Article 8(1). The case-law developing Article 8 has created a 'quality of law' test requiring acceptable standards of clarity and consistency when unpacking what a right to private life entailed by way of legally protected interests. For the House of Lords this stricture required the Director of Public Prosecutions to issue detailed and public guidance on the factors that would influence a decision to prosecute and those factors that would militate against a decision to prosecute assistance in suicide (there have been three iterations of this guidance). If D, an assister of the suicidal V, is prosecuted in circumstances where the court considers that insufficient notice was given by the DPP of this possibility, proceedings would be in breach of Article 8(1).

In its own terms *Purdy* is radical. On the face of it, s 2 of the Suicide Act 1961 should satisfy any quality of law test concerned with clarity and consistency: it proscribes in clear terms all forms of assistance in suicide, irrespective of the reasons that prompted the assistance. The DPP, unprecedentedly, was made by order of the House of Lords to give detailed and public consideration to his future decisions relating to just one of the offences for which he had responsibility. This tells us that the offence is special and must be handled with kid gloves. But, the case is about protection of the vulnerable and pressured, rather than directly conferred, rights at large. It does not disrupt the formal law. Recall that, in *Pretty*, the fact that the DPP had to give consent to any prosecution for assisting suicide was the major reason for the European Court of Human Rights conclusion that s 2 of the Suicide Act 1961 did not contravene Article 8(1) of the Convention. At that time the DPP was not required to make public the grounds for any of his decisions. Post *Purdy*, s 2 would seem, as it were, even more Convention-compliant.

43 *R (Pretty) v DPP* (n 1) [35].
44 *Pretty v UK* (2002) EHRR 1 [67].
45 *R v Purdy* [2010] 1 AC 345.

Subsequent to *Purdy* there have been three important decisions of the European Court of Human Rights relating to assertions of a right to die and assistance in dying, namely *Haas v Switzerland*,[46] *Koch v Germany*,[47] and *Gross v Switzerland*.[48] In each case there is a finding that Article 8(1) of the Convention confers on every person within its protection who is 'free' to make the choice, a right to die. In each case the formulation of this right is in identical terms:

> an individual's right to decide by what means and at what point his or her life will end, provided he or she is capable of freely reaching a decision on this question and acting in consequence, is one of the aspects of the right to respect for private life within the meaning of article 8 of the Convention.[49]

Persons free to make the choice can choose the timing and manner of their death. In formulating this right the court had a particular concern with the avoidance of distressing and undignified deaths. The fact that a third party may have to be involved in enabling V to die does not prevent her from asserting her right to die under Article 8(1). Further, the court in *Koch* ruled that a spouse or partner of V closely involved in V's suffering is, in her own right, within Article 8(1). The decision in *Gross* is of particular interest. The applicant had no terminal condition but was so old and frail that, in the light of her quality of life, she wished to die. She could not obtain a lethal, prescription drug from her doctor because the legal position was not clear where death was not imminent from a specific medical condition. By a 4/3 majority there was a ruling that her state of anguish and uncertainty arising after making a serious decision to end her life made for a violation of Article 8(1) that could not be redeemed under the qualifications contained in Article 8(2).

With some confidence it can be said that a right to die, in the terms of a Strasbourg understanding of the right, is now a part of English law. In *Nicklinson* the seven Supreme Court judges who thought that changing the law relating to assisting suicide could at least be discussed in court and not only in Parliament took as their starting point the existence of a right to die in the Strasbourg sense. As already noted, Lord Sumption considered that this jurisprudence created a zone of complete autonomy for those who wished to end their lives.[50] This opinion receives some support from English case-law that endorses the right of any competent adult to refuse medical treatment for any reason or for no reason, however dire the consequences of refusal.[51] Whether this line of authority gives rise to a right to die for competent persons exercisable in all circumstances even when a medical intervention of a non-surgical kind would be lifesaving is not resolved. A key case is *Re B*[52] where V's right to refuse artificial ventilation was fully vindicated by the Court of Appeal. It would be perfectly natural to describe *Re B* as a claim for assistance in suicide: the applicant found her

---

46 *Haas v Switzerland* (2011) 53 EHRR 33.
47 *Koch v Germany* (2013) 56 EHRR 6.
48 *Gross v Switzerland* (2014) 58 EHRR 7.
49 *Haas v Switzerland* 53 EHRR 33 [51]; *Koch v Germany (2013)* 56 EHRR 6 [52]; *Gross v Switzerland* (2014) 58 EHRR 7 [59].
50 His words are worth repeating: 'In law the State is not entitled to intervene to prevent a person of full capacity who has arrived at a settled decision to take his own life from doing so. However, such a person does not have a right to call on a third person to help him to end his life.' *Nicklinson* [2014] UKSC 38 [255].
51 *B (Adult refusal of medical treatment)*; *St George's Health Care Trust v S* (n 8).
52 *B v NHS Hospital Trust* [2002] EWHC 429.

confinement intolerable and demanded that others remove the apparatus that kept her alive. For Lord Neuberger, what was granted to the applicant in *Re B* was more radical than what was sought in *Nicklinson*: 'in some respects a more drastic interference in that person's life and a more extreme moral step, than authorising a third party to set up a lethal drug delivery system'.[53] Yet what happened in *Re B* is blandly described in Butler-Sloss LJ's judgment as a lawful omission to provide further treatment, thereby evading any entanglement with s 2 of the Suicide Act 1961. This muddies the waters as to when it can be said that a decision to end one's life is a decision to commit suicide. To date, English civil law endorses no right to commit suicide. A failure to prevent a suicide can be an actionable wrong.[54] Whether there is a right to commit suicide in the untrammelled sense stated by Lord Sumption can only be answered following an appellate decision that directly takes on the question. It must be added that if Lord Sumption is correct that competent persons in England and Wales are fully entitled to commit suicide at any time and for whatever reason, it is remarkable for him to hold, as he does, that to give assistance in suicide remains unlawful under current English law.

What is clear is that the Strasbourg jurisprudence by itself does not give rise to an unqualified right to die. The three relevant cases give clear expression to a right to die and in *Gross* came to a decision that goes beyond anything decided in England or Wales to date. At the same time, the cases stress that a right to die is only given to for persons free to make that choice and, given the importance of this choice, official procedures are necessary to vet V's choice to die to ensure that V will act freely. The need for these procedures is also required by the unqualified right to life enshrined in Article 2, a right that requires signatory states to take proactive steps to save lives.[55] Judicial notice is taken of the fact that the vast majority of signatory states prioritise protecting life rather than allowing a right to die, and have stringent controls over assisting suicide. This requires a generous margin of appreciation for the legal regimes that member states have created to regulate life/death decisions.

This jurisprudence clearly allows judicial rulings legitimating assistance in dying to those with the freedom and competence to choose when and how they will die. But at the same time it places within the margin of appreciation life-saving restrictions on the choice to die. Recognition in *Nicklinson* of the reception into English law of a qualified right to die in the Strasbourg sense is important. Given the latitude that Strasbourg allows, how important this qualified right will prove is up to the English and Welsh judiciary.

WHAT NEXT?

Any discussion about the future must bear in mind the overwhelming rejection by the House of Commons of a bill allowing assistance in dying (not including voluntary euthanasia) for persons with terminal conditions entailing death in less than six months, who sought such assistance because of their pain and distress. Given the deference to Parliament understandably accorded to Parliament in *Nicklinson*, is it the case that the courts will now eschew any development of the law in this contested and emotive area of the law? After all the bill was less radical than the assistance in dying that Baroness Hale and Lord Kerr would have afforded to the applicants appearing before them, assistance that Lord Neuberger, Lord Mance and Lord Wilson considered might be made available by the courts at some future time. None of the applicants in *Nicklinson* were in a terminal condition.

---

53 *R v Nicklinson* (n 6) [94].
54 *Reeves v Commissioner of police for the Metropolis* [2000] 1 AC 360; *Corr v IBC Vehicles* [2008] 1 AC 884.
55 *Keenan v UK* 2001 II 35 EHRR 913.

Suppose that a health authority applies to the High Court for a declaration that the prohibition of assistance in dying to a person in like case to Mr Nicklinson (who starved himself after assistance was refused) contravenes Article 8 of the ECHR. There is no reason in law or constitutional propriety why a court should decline the jurisdiction to decide this question. If the court were to make the declaration sought by the health authority, s 2 of the Suicide Act 1961 remains intact. Any assistance would be an offence. The government of the day would be forced to decide whether to stand behind the domestic law or to change the law to comply with Article 8. Change might come, hopefully, for this writer, in the direction of travel set out at the beginning of this chapter. There can be no certainty about this. The legal and moral issues surrounding assistance in dying divide courts at the highest level. In *Carter and others v Attorney General of Canada and another*[56] The Supreme Court of Canada ruled that to deny assistance in dying to persons with painful and distressing conditions was to deny important human rights.[57] This ruling made void clearly stated provisions of the Canadian criminal code that proscribed assistance in dying in all circumstances. Contrastingly, the High Court of New Zealand in *Seales v Attorney General*[58] upheld the legality of an exceptionless ban on assisted dying.[59] All that can be said with any certainty is that seven of the justices in *Nicklinson* were closer in spirit to *Carter* than *Seales* but with differing degrees of intensity, and with differences too as to when it would be appropriate for courts to take jurisdiction on the legality of assistance in dying question. How this will cash out in any future litigation on the matter of assistance in dying at Supreme Court level and below is anyone's guess.

What is certain is that the current treatment of this contested and emotive issue in England and Wales is unedifying. Anyone with the financial means and the support of family and friends can travel to Switzerland to find assistance in dying.[60] The Director of Public Prosecutions has let it be known that she is very unlikely to prosecute any doctor practising in England or Wales who provides assistance in dying for compassionate reasons.[61] And yet the letter of the domestic law is unyielding. This cannot be satisfactory for anyone, whatever position they take, on the matters ventilated here.

---

56 *Carter and others v Attorney General of Canada and another* [2015] SCC 5.
57 In particular, the supreme court of Canada ruled that the right to life was engaged because the denial of physician assisted dying would force some individuals to end their lives prematurely for fear that they would be incapable of doing so at the point when suffering was intolerable.
58 *Seales v Attorney-General* [2015] NZHC 1239.
59 Essentially the high court ruled that no breach of human rights had occurred because the suffering and distress endured by the applicant arose from her medical condition (brain tumour) rather than anything done to her by a public authority.
60 *Richardson and another v Director of Public Prosecutions* (n 14).
61 ibid [255].

10

The 'higher' age of consent and the concept of sexual exploitation

Alisdair Gillespie and Suzanne Ost

The age of consent in England is 16. Except it is not always. It is ordinarily the age of 16 but, since 2000, there has been a higher age of consent (18) for certain sexual activities. Originally this was where there was thought to be a position of trust (Sexual Offences (Amendment) Act 2000), but it then was extended to other forms of exploitation, including prostitution and child pornography.

This chapter will consider the issue of the higher age of consent and consider whether it is truly protecting children or whether it is an example of a paternalistic society governing what sexual activities a 16- or 17-year-old child can engage in and/or who their sexual partner is. After a critical exploration of the age of consent, an analysis will be made of the types of situations where the higher age is engaged and why it is not engaged in other exploitative contexts (such as employment). We will also consider whether the criminal law's restrictions can be justified or whether they may infringe the older child's right to a sexual identity. We then engage with philosophical understandings of the concept of sexual exploitation and consider what the crux of the issue (justifying criminalisation) should be. Ultimately, we will argue that a higher age of consent can be justified in the context of exploitative relationships, with the existence of exploitation being ascertained through a consideration of the circumstances of the relationship rather than the relationship falling under a definitive statutory list.

AGE OF CONSENT

A useful starting point is to consider what an age of consent is and what its purpose is. It is often said that the age of consent in England and Wales is 16 but that is not strictly true. The age varies depending on the particular relationship between the parties engaging in sexual activity. Indeed it is this variance that forms the discussion of this chapter.

Consent?

The term 'age of consent' is itself controversial and it has been suggested that what is created is an 'age of liability' for the offender rather than an age of consent.[1] The context of this

---

1 Kieran Walsh, 'Images of Childhood, Adolescent Sexual Reality and the Age of Consent' in Helen Gavin and Jacquelyn Bent, *Sex, Drugs and Rock & Roll: Psychological, Legal and Cultural Examinations of Sex and Sexuality* (Inter-Disciplinary Press 2010) 47–58, 48.

comment is that the age of consent arguably has little to do with consent and is instead the establishment of an age at which the law decides that a child is allowed to have sex. This is a point that is taken up by other commentators.

Consent is ordinarily considered to be a concept that relates to self-determination,[2] the right to make self-governing decisions about one's life.[3] It is the capacity of an individual to give permission to do something that makes their consent valid.[4] In the context of sex, this would mean that they have the capacity to understand what sex is, what it means and the ability to decide whether they want to have sexual contact with another. However, capacity is a very subjective concept. It must vary between individuals because of their developmental differences. The significance of developmental capacity is reflected in the approach taken to consent to treatment and capacity in medical law when a doctor is faced with an older '*Gillick* competent' child. In such a case, the status-based presumption that children lack capacity is rebutted provided the child can establish that she has the requisite maturity to possess decision-making capacity.[5]

The age of consent cannot therefore realistically relate to the capacity of an individual. As capacity will differ between individuals, so will the age at which they are capable of making that decision. This has been considered to create problems for the law because it means that a clear statement of rule cannot be set out – 'you will not have sexual contact with a child under *n* years of age' – because, if it were based on capacity, that would not follow. Someone (*n-2*) may have the capacity to consent and yet someone else (*n+3*) may not. Of course, not everyone would agree that this is a problem. In the context of adult sexual assaults, there is similar variance. Different people will consent to different actions and thus an individual will need to ascertain that V consents before having sexual contact with him or her. Could it be said that the same should apply to some children? Is it not more appropriate that an individual wishing to have sexual contact with an adolescent[6] should ascertain whether the child understands the nature of the activity, any potential consequence (eg sexually transmitted diseases (STIs), pregnancy, loss of virginity, cultural or other societal factors) and ascertain their desire to connect sexually?

The current age of consent does not do this and therefore it realistically moves us away from *factual* consent and instead steers us towards *legal* consent. The age of consent means that a person under the prescribed age cannot, as a matter of law, give consent, irrespective of whether they have the capacity to make that decision and the desire to do so. The law not only fails to recognise that decision, it prohibits this decision from being acted upon. Anyone who has sexual contact with that child will commit a criminal offence.[7]

---

2 In the context of medical law, see, for example, the much-quoted statement from Cardozo J in *Schloen-dorff v New York State Hospital* (1914) 105 NE 92 that 'every human being of adult years and sound mind has a right to determine what shall be done with his own body; and a surgeon who performs an operation without his patient's consent, commits an assault' 93.

3 John Coggon and Jose Miola, 'Autonomy, Liberty and Medical Decision-making' (2011) 70 Cambridge Law Journal 523–547, 524.

4 'Law makes the power of individual choice legally contingent on competence. The right to make decisions in matters such as marriage, contractual relations, voting, testamentary disposition, and health care depends on being legally competent.' Susan Stefan, 'Silencing the Different Voice: Competence, Feminist Theory and Law' (1993) 47 University of Miami Law Review 763–815, 765.

5 See *Gillick v West Norfolk and Wisbech AHA* [1986] 1 AC 112 and *R (On the Application of Axon) v Secretary of State for Health (Family Planning Association intervening)* [2006] EWHC 37 (Admin).

6 In this chapter we do not propose to discuss the idea that a child of any age can consent as we believe such a contention is unarguable. Instead the discussion relates to children aged between 14 and 18 (14 being the youngest age often referred to as a potential age of consent).

7 See, most notably, the offences contained in ss 5–15 Sexual Offences Act 2003.

However, although the age of consent is supposed to render factual consent irrelevant it does not always do this. So, for example, under English law a person commits the offence of rape of a child if he has sexual intercourse with a child under the age of 13.[8] The offence is one of strict liability and it is therefore irrelevant whether the offender knew the age of the child or indeed whether the child gave factual consent. Whilst there is also the offence of rape,[9] which applies irrespective of the age of the victim, theoretically there should be no need to use the offence where the victim is aged under 13 because proving the offence under s 5 is simpler. For the offence of rape under s 1, it is necessary to prove an absence of factual consent[10] and also the fact that D did not believe that V consented.[11] Notwithstanding this fact and that the CPS charging guidance specifically states that s 1 should not be used,[12] there have been occasions when the offence of s 1 has been used even when the victim is aged under 13.[13] This would seem to suggest that even the law does not view the age of consent as being about consent but, rather, about the liability of the offender. By prosecuting rape, rather than the rape of a child, the law is admitting that factual consent is more important than legal consent and that the absence of factual consent is more serious than the absence of legal consent. There is logic to such a distinction but it does raise questions about whether this could create 'classes' of victims, especially if sentencing differs between the offences. This would be problematic where it was unclear whether a child factually consented meaning the prosecution would face a decision as to whether to accept a guilty plea in respect of the 'lesser' offence or to proceed to trial on the other.

Identifying an age

If, for simplicity, it is decided to have an age of consent (which is the pattern that most developed countries have adopted[14]) then the question becomes what age is chosen? And indeed how is that age chosen? The setting of the age of 16 as the (ordinary) age of consent in England and Wales occurred for reasons of political pragmatism rather than a considered societal response.

The first reference to an age of consent is arguably to be found in the first Statute of Westminster (1275) where a misdemeanour was created of ravishing 'a maiden within age' which Blackstone contended meant the age of marriage, then set at 12,[15] the offence applying to those victims under that age. In 1576 a felony was created of having carnal knowledge of a woman child under the age of 10.[16] There is some confusion over what this meant, with Hale contending it meant that the age of consent remained at 12 but that stronger punishment was imposed on those who abused a child under the age of 10 (as that was a felony). However, some countries who took their laws from England adopted a different approach and decided that the age of consent became 10 (in effect ignoring the Statute of Westminster).

---

8 Sexual Offences Act 2003, s 5.
9 Sexual Offences Act 2003, s 1.
10 David C Ormerod and Karl Laird, *Smith & Hogan's Criminal Law* (14th edition, Oxford University Press 2015) 852.
11 Save where one of the irrebutable presumptions of consent apply (see Sexual Offences Act 2003 s76).
12 See <http://www.cps.gov.uk/legal/p_to_r/rape_and_sexual_offences/soa_2003_and_soa_1956/#a16> accessed 30 October 2015.
13 See, for example *R v JM* [2015] EWCA Crim 1638.
14 Julia Rudolph 'Rape and Resistance: Women and Consent in Seventeenth-Century English Legal and Political Thought' (2000) 39 Journal of British Studies 157–184, 173.
15 ibid 178.
16 Benefit of the Clergy Act 1575.

The age then remained relatively stable until the nineteenth century when a series of stories in the *Pall Mall Gazette* describing how widespread child prostitution led to public disquiet, causing Parliament to act to increase the age of consent to 16.[17] However, there was no clear rationale for choosing the age of 16. It was not based on any scientific evidence, it was a reaction to what had happened and was an age that politicians compromised on. Similarly, when the age for (male) homosexual intercourse was set at 21 following the decriminalisation of consensual buggery,[18] the choice of age was not really the product of any scientific or sociological stance but was a political reaction to the decriminalisation and a belief that the youth and young persons should not be permitted to engage in such activity for fear of being corrupted.[19] In 1994, the age was reduced to the age of 18[20] even though this created a position whereby heterosexual and (male) homosexual sex were treated differently. Again, the age of 18 was a political choice/compromise[21] and not a reasoned decision. When the age of consent was finally equalised between homosexual and heterosexual acts[22] there was no real consideration of whether 16 was the correct age for the age of consent. That is, the age for homosexual activities was reduced to 16 to introduce equality, not because there was a rational argument for 16 being the appropriate age for consent.

One of the difficulties in this area is that identifying an age is, and always has been, difficult. There is no identifiable point at which we can point to someone and say 'child'. International law, or at least some parts of it, consider a child to be anyone under the age of 18.[23] However, it is unlikely that many 17-year-olds would be particularly impressed at being called a child. Also, we cannot suggest a 17-year-old is the same as a 17-month-old. The most obvious distinction between a child and adult would be puberty, particularly in respect of females. The onset of menses marks the point at which the female is able to bear a child. Historically this was often considered the point at which a girl became a woman[24] and it is perhaps one reason why the age of 12 was chosen in the Statute of Westminster. A difficulty with choosing puberty is twofold. The first is that the age at which a person goes through puberty differs between individuals. Perhaps this is not problematic since there are at least obvious signs a person has gone through puberty, although person A is not necessarily going to know whether person B has experienced the menarche. The second problem is that puberty is a physical transformation but there is nothing that indicates that a child is emotionally able to have sex. When 'childhood' is considered less as a physical issue and more of a social construct,[25] the emotional maturity and ability of a child becomes relevant, which returns us to capacity. Separate to these two problems is the fact that whilst puberty may act

---

17 Criminal Law (Amendment) Act 1885.
18 Sexual Offences Act 1967, s 1.
19 The age of 21 was chosen because at that time the age of majority was 21. Thus it was decided that homosexual acts were decriminalised between adults.
20 Criminal Justice and Public Order Act 1994, s 143.
21 Given the age of majority had been reduced to 18 in 1970 (Family Reform Act 1969, s 1) it is perhaps surprising that it took so long for the age to be reduced but it also demonstrates why 18 was chosen: homosexual acts remained decriminalised only when they involved adults.
22 Sexual Offences (Amendment) Act 2000, s 1.
23 See most notably, the *United Nations Convention on the Rights of the Child*.
24 A useful discussion on the place of puberty is given by Michael C Seto *Pedophilia and Sexual Offending Against Children* (American Psychological Association 2008) 4–6.
25 Margaret L King, 'Concepts of Childhood: What We Know and Where We Might Go' (2007) 60 Renaissance Quarterly 371–407, 402.

as a distinctive marker for females, there is no masculine equivalent to the menarche meaning puberty would be an even more problematic distinction for boys.[26]

If we set aside physical factors to decide who is a child then can the social sciences assist us with the question of what makes someone a child rather than an adult? The concept of childhood has long been considered a social construct and the late-nineteenth and twentieth centuries saw increasing focus on psychology and the belief that childhood could be explained through maturation by development.[27] However, the difficulty with this is that it returns us to subjectivity. Children develop at different rates and thus it can be questioned whether this assists us with identifying an age of consent because it brings us back to the difficulties of capacity discussed above.

Of course the pragmatic solution would be to adopt a compromise. A uniform age of consent brings simplicity. It is simple to understand for both children and adults. Whilst, of course, capacity remains important since without the capacity to consent there cannot be any factual consent, a uniform age is normally set at a point in time by which the majority of individuals of that age would have this capacity. It renders prosecutions slightly easier as it removes the issue of consent, something that has always been considered difficult to prove.[28] If the prosecution needed to not only address factual consent but also capacity then it is likely that their task would be considerably harder.

However the simplicity of adopting a uniform age of consent also causes the weakness of arbitrariness. The age chosen has to be a compromise and as it is a legal issue it becomes as much a question of politics as child development. Across Europe there is a broad range of ages of consent[29] although the most common ages are 15 and 16. Waites, in his excellent text on the age of consent, ultimately concludes that a uniform age is most appropriate but suggests the age of 14, although subject to a 'buffer' under the age of 16.[30] It is not our purpose in this chapter to consider the appropriate age, but it is submitted that if any reform is to be introduced it should be based on scientific understandings of the development of children.

A slightly different, but extremely relevant, question for us is whether there should be a single age of consent for all circumstances or whether we recognise that some situations require a different age. The logic of introducing two ages would be to recognise that children may have capacity to make decisions of consent in respect of situation x but might not have the capacity to deal with situation y. This perhaps recognises that the decision to have sexual intercourse with a child of the same age may raise very different issues to the decision to have sexual intercourse with someone in authority. To some, the question is superfluous as the sole issue should be whether someone has consented or not. However focusing exclusively on the existence or non-existence of consent carries with it two potential disadvantages. The first is that consent has proven a particularly difficult concept over the years to prove, particularly

---

26 Historically it was not uncommon for a 'boy' to become a 'man' after his first act of (heterosexual) intercourse (which would cause a logic loop if this was considered to be the marker for sexual consent) or, in some cultures, it could be their first hunt or kill.

27 Matthew Waites, *The Age of Consent* (Palgrave MacMillan 2005) 12.

28 For a good discussion on some of the problems that consent has proven (in general) see Clare McGlynn, 'Feminist activism and rape law reform in England and Wales: A Sisyphean struggle?' in Clare McGlynn and Vanessa Muno, *Rethinking Rape Law: International and Comparative Perspectives* (Routledge 2019) 139–153.

29 From 14 (Germany) to 18 (Malta).

30 Waites (n 27) 238. The 'buffer' is that decriminalisation occurs when the parties are within 2 years of each other when either party is below the age of 16. So for example, D (aged 17) could lawfully have sex with V (aged 15) but E (aged 20) could not lawfully have sex with W (aged 15).

in contexts that do not meet traditional stereotypes of non-consent.[31] Where there is ostensible consent then it is likely to be even more difficult to persuade a tribunal of fact that this ostensible consent was vitiated.[32] The second disadvantage is that it is more difficult to deter potential harmful contact by relying on consent. Creating a specific criminal offence that labels certain types of behaviour as criminal carries with it a degree of certainty and puts people on notice that such behaviour is considered illicit. Relying on the definition of consent however does not bring this clarity, not least because the average person is unlikely to be familiar with decisions of the courts.

Perhaps with these concerns in mind, as has been noted, England and Wales has adopted the position of having a 'higher' age of consent for some situations and it is to that which we now turn.

THE 'HIGHER' AGE OF CONSENT

The 'higher' age of consent applies to limited circumstances and it is necessary to briefly identify these circumstances and how they came to apply.

Sexual Offences (Amendment) Act 2000

The Sexual Offences (Amendment) Act 2000 was the culmination of legislative attempts that dated back to 1998.[33] As part of a process to equalise the age of consent between heterosexual and homosexual acts, the Sexual Offences (Amendment) Bill 1998 sought to introduce new offences of abuse of a position of trust.[34] However whilst the Bill was passed by the House of Commons it was rejected by the House of Lords (primarily due to resistance to the idea of equalising the age of consent). Reintroduced the following year, it was again rejected by the House of Lords. On its third passage through the House of Commons, the Parliament Act[35] was invoked and it received Royal Assent without the need to pass the House of Lords.

The reduction in age to 16 was discussed briefly above and is not strictly necessary to our discussion here. What is of interest however is that alongside reducing the age of consent for homosexual acts to 16, it introduced a new offence termed 'abuse of a position of trust'.[36] Much of the discussion that accompanied the reduction in the age of consent for homosexual acts concerned the belief that 16- and 17-year-old boys would be 'preyed' upon by older men.[37] One response to this concern was the new abuse of trust provision, although it should be noted that this applied equally to male and female victims.[38]

---

31 For example criminal law textbooks have long debated the matter of consent in the context of the perceived difference between a threat ('if you do not have sex with me I will sack you') and a promise ('if you have sex with me I will give you a pay rise') see for example Ormerod and Laird (n 10) 823.

32 See, for example, Louise Ellison and Vanessa Munro, 'Jury deliberations and complainant credibility in rape trials' in McGlynn and Munro (n 28) 281–293.

33 The 2000 Act was initially introduced in 1998. It was defeated in two parliamentary sessions and the Parliament Act 1911 was invoked to allow it to be given Royal Assent without it being passed by the House of Lords.

34 For a useful background on the Bill see 'The Sexual Offences (Amendment) Bill: "Age of consent" and abuse of a position of trust' (House of Commons Research Paper 99/4, 21 January 1999)'.

35 Parliament Acts of 1911 and 1949.

36 Sexual Offences (Amendment) Act 2000, s 3.

37 Waites provides a useful summary of the passage of the Act (n 27) 183–207.

38 Interestingly, little discussion was spent noting that older men could quite legally prey on 16- and 17-year-old girls or, indeed, older women could have preyed upon 16- and 17-year-old boys, although a rare mention was made by Baroness Gould of Potternewton (*Hansard, HL Deb*, vol 612, col 113 (11 April 2000)).

A position of trust was defined as follows:

- D looks after V in an institution by virtue of an order of a court.
- V is resident in accommodation pursuant to the Children Act 1989 and D is employed to look after such persons.
- V is resident in a hospital, a residential care home, community home or a home provided under the Children Act 1989 and D is employed to look after such persons.
- D looks after persons receiving full-time education at an educational institution and V attends that institution.[39]

It has been suggested that the phraseology of the 2000 Act is that it is the position of trust that is abused rather than a child[40] and this would seem to be the case. Section 3(1) criminalises sexual intercourse or sexual activity with a child under 18 'if . . . he is in a position of trust in relation to that person'. As the position of trust is defined as above, it follows that the emphasis of the action is not on whether D abused the trust of V but whether D was in a *position* whereby that trust could be abused. That may seem the same thing but it is very different. It is irrelevant whether D actually abused his position of trust over V, it is merely that he was in a position to do so.

The term 'abuse' has been the subject of some criticism, with Waites suggesting the term was used after pressure from feminists and child protection advocates.[41] The difference between 'abuse' and 'exploitation' is very interesting in terms of linguistics and it is something that we return to below, when we put forward an argument that English law has focused on the wrong concept and that 'exploitation' is a more pertinent concept to tackle this behaviour.

What is notable about these positions is that they were very restrictive in scope. For example, education seemed to have been covered but only if the student was in full-time education. Moreover, at the time the 2000 Act was in force, the age a child could leave school was 16, which potentially led to a loophole. Let us take two examples:

- V is taking A-level History and has become emotionally attached to his sixth form history teacher, Ms X. They eventually have sexual intercourse.
- V has left school and is working in a training scheme. As part of that she has to attend a secretarial qualification at her local sixth form college. During one of her sessions she becomes close to her instructor, Ms X, and ultimately has sex with her.

Is there any difference between these two examples? In both, V is being instructed by an adult – Ms X. In both situations V has sexual contact with Ms X, but only in the first example would an offence under the Sexual Offences Act 2000 have been committed.

Similar problems arose with other positions. So, for example, a position of trust exists for those who look after a child detained by order of the court (eg an officer within a young offender institution) but a probation officer would not be covered because the child is not in detention.[42] Yet a parole officer could have particular influence over a child, particularly where she is scared that she could be sent back to court for breaching a non-custodial

---

39 Sexual Offences (Amendment) Act 2000, s 4(2)–(5).
40 Waites (n 27) 191.
41 Waites (n 27) 192.
42 It is possible that sexual activity by such persons would be considered to breach the (common law) offence of misconduct in a public office but that is not recognised as a sex offence and also suggests that the 'victim' of the offence is the public office rather than a potentially vulnerable youth.

sentence. Likewise a doctor or nurse treating a patient in a hospital is covered by the law but a GP is not. Potentially a GP may actually be in a greater position of trust as it is possible they will know their parents or other members of the local society and may have had a longer-term relationship with the child.

Indecent photographs of children

Section 1 of the Protection of Children Act 1978 as amended states that it is, *inter alia*, an offence to take, make or distribute an indecent photograph of a child. For these purposes, 'child' is defined as 18,[43] which was increased from 16 in 2003.[44] The decision to increase the age of 'a child' for these purposes was taken ostensibly to comply with international law.[45]

The provision to increase the age was passed with little critical debate, with most simply taking it as read that it was necessary to ensure that children were protected. Much mention was made in Parliament of the disgusting nature of child pornography, including statements of revulsion at images that had been shown to Parliamentarians. However, what is not clear is whether such images included 16- and 17-year olds. Indeed it is probably more likely that such images would not have been included because the vast majority of child pornography involves younger children.[46] This point was picked up by some, although not particularly strongly. In the House of Lords, Lord Monson noted that the overarching purpose of the Act was to tackle paedophiles and yet they would not be interested in 16- and 17-year olds.[47] Setting aside the precise definition of a paedophile,[48] there is some merit to what was being said here. The mischief behind the Act was to tackle those who were taking or distributing images of children being abused and exploited,[49] and the strict liability approach to age was justified on the basis that it (ordinarily) documents a criminal act.[50]

Changing the age of 'a child' to 18 breaks this link to a criminal act. It is not necessarily a legal wrong to have sexual contact with a 16- or 17-year-old child. While this chapter will, in the next section, highlight some situations when such conduct would be illegal, the general rule is that sexual intercourse with a 16- or 17-year-old is not illegal. Therefore why create a situation in which two 16-year-olds can have sex with each other but not photograph each other? Lord Monson noted that there could be a justification for criminalising *commercial* photographs of 16- and 17-year-olds, but this is not what has happened. Instead Parliament chose to criminalise all photographs of 16- and 17-year-olds, even when they take them of themselves.

---

43 Sexual Offences Act 1967, s 1(1).

44 Sexual Offences Act 2003, s 45.

45 *Hansard*, HL Deb, 04 October 2000, vol 616, col 1566.

46 The Internet Watch Foundation estimate that c 80% of the images that they identify as child pornography involve a child who appears to be under the age of 10 (Internet Watch Foundation *Annual Report 2014*, 9).

47 *Hansard* (n 45).

48 Paedophile has a clinical definition which relates to the sexual attraction to pre-pubescent children: see Seto (n 24).

49 See MA McCarthy and RA Moodie, 'Parliament and pornography: the 1978 Child Protection Act' (1981) 34 Parliamentary Affairs 47–62.

50 A picture that shows any sort of sexual contact with a child under 16 would document a crime since the child cannot consent to that act. An image that simply shows the child posing naked or topless would not document a crime (as it is not illegal for a child to be naked). The criminalisation of simple nudity has been debated for some time (see Alisdair A Gillespie, *Child Pornography: Law and Policy* (Routledge 2011) 57; Suzanne Ost, *Child Pornography and Sexual Grooming: Legal and Societal Responses* (Cambridge 2009) 132–135.

One justification for increasing the age to 18 that was advanced by some NGOs concerned the maturity of adolescents and the permanent nature of images. The issue of maturity has already been raised in the context of the age of consent and it has been noted that it is difficult to base any decision on a uniform understanding of maturity as no such thing exists. Children and young people mature at different rates and there is no evidence to show that an 18-year-old is more mature than a 16-year-old. Whilst it is undoubtedly true that sexualised photographs are a permanent record[51] there are many other permanent dangers (or at least dangers with long-term effects) involved in sexual activity, including sexually-transmitted diseases and pregnancy, and yet there has been no (serious) call for the age of consent for sex to be increased. While it was not true at the time the decision was taken to raise the age of a child, the mischief behind the desire to increase the age – that 16- and 17-year-olds may naively allow people to take sexualised photographs of themselves – would now be protected by the new 'revenge pornography' laws.[52] The new law criminalises the disclosure of a private sexual photograph with intent to cause distress. Whilst there are some concerns over the extent of the new law,[53] it will broadly cover those situations where a person, in order to cause distress, discloses to another a sexual photograph of the victim.

Sixteen and 17-year-olds are taking sexualised photographs of one another, as indeed do adults.[54] The automatic criminalisation of photographs of those under 16 can be justified as it is the picture of an illegal act, but if it is not illegal for two 16-year-olds to have sex with each other, why should a picture of the same be criminalised? If it is a worry that the image will be leaked, the new offence would criminalise such conduct and therefore that protection is now offered.

Sexual Offences Act 2003

The Sexual Offences (Amendment) Act 2000 offences were repealed and replaced by the Sexual Offences Act 2003 (SOA). The new provisions cover two classes of offences: abuse of trust[55] and familial child sex offences.[56] It is not possible in a chapter of this size to consider the detail of these offences in depth and reference should be made elsewhere for critique of these provisions.[57] Also, for reasons of space we will not consider the familial offences as these raise subtly different issues. While both concern the 'higher' age, the justification differs between those relating to an abuse of a position of trust and those relating to prohibiting sexual contact with a family member. Focusing on the abuse of a position of trust allows greater

---

51 Research has demonstrated that once a sexualised image is released onto the internet then it is unlikely to ever be recovered because it will be downloaded, duplicated, mirrored and reposted: see Max Taylor and Ethel Quayle *Child Pornography: An Internet Crime* (Routledge 2003) 24.

52 Criminal Justice and Court Services Act 2015, ss 33–35. Arguably certain other laws (most notably s 1, Malicious Communications Act 1988; s 127, Communications Act 2003; and s 2, Protection from Harassment Act 1997 (see *AMP v Persons Unknown* [2011] EHWC 3454 (TCC) which, whilst a civil case, demonstrates a potential use of the 1997 Act)) would also apply but this new law is perhaps the most pertinent.

53 See, for example, Alisdair A Gillespie, '"Trust me, it's only for me": "Revenge Porn" and the Criminal Law' [2015] Criminal Law Review 866–880.

54 See, for example, Kath Albury and Kate Crawford, 'Sexting, consent and young people's ethics' (2012) 26 Continuum 463–473.

55 Sexual Offences Act 2003, ss 16–24.

56 ibid, ss 25–29.

57 The leading text on this area is Peter Rook and Robert Ward, *Rook and Ward on Sexual Offences* (4th edition, Sweet & Maxwell 2014).

scrutiny of these issues in the limited space but we acknowledge that there are concerns as to whether the familial offences criminalise conduct appropriately.[58]

The Sexual Offences Act 2003 widened the criminal liability in respect of an abuse of a position of trust. In essence it replicated certain offences against the child[59] but raised the age of a victim to 18. Peculiarly a lesser sentence is given for these offences,[60] which indicates that, despite the statutory wording (which suggests it applies to a victim of any age under 18), the offences should ordinarily only be used for victims aged 16 or 17.[61] This is perhaps confirmed by the fact that abusing a position of trust becomes an aggravating factor for the offences under ss 9–12,[62] despite the fact that the term is not actually defined in the Sentencing Council's guideline.

As with the Sexual Offences (Amendment) Act 2000, the term 'position of trust' is given a statutory definition through an inclusive list. The first four are the same as in the Sexual Offences (Amendment) Act 2000 although in terms of educational establishments there is no longer a requirement that the child is in full-time education.[63] Other positions within the Act would include:

- The provision of certain careers advice within educational establishments but only where the adult looks after the child on an individual basis.
- Where a child is accommodated by the local authority and the adult has regular unsupervised contact with the child.
- Where a person is employed to make a report on the child's welfare for the purposes of proceedings under the Children Act 1989.
- Where a person is engaged to become a personal advisor for the purposes of the Children Act 1989 and the adult looks after B on an individual basis.
- Those who look after a child who is the subject of a care or supervision order under the Children Act 1989.
- Where the adult has been appointed the *guardian ad litem* of the child and regularly has unsupervised access with the child.
- Where a child has been released from gaol or is under an order from a criminal court (ie the child is either on licence or under a community order) and the adult looks after the child on an individual basis.[64]

The Sexual Offences Act 2003 cured some loopholes, most notably the issue of a probation officer, but left many untouched or criminalised them in a partial way. For example, a number of these situations require the adult to be looking after the victim on an *individual* basis, which may not always be realistic, or where the adult has 'regular' unsupervised access to the child. It is not immediately clear why the position of trust is only triggered by unsupervised access

---

58 See, for example, John R Spencer, 'The Sexual Offences Act 2003: (2) Child and Family Offences' [2004] Criminal Law Review 347–360 and for a more general critique of criminalising familial abuse see, for example, James A Roffee, 'No Consensus on Incest? Criminalisation and Compatibility with the European Convention on Human Rights' (2014) 14 Human Rights Law Review 541–572.

59 Sexual Offences Act 2003, ss 9–12.

60 Compare, for example, sexual activity with a child (s 9, 14 years' imprisonment) and sexual activity with a child whilst in a position of trust (s 16, five years' imprisonment).

61 With the substantive offences in ss 9–12 being used for younger victims.

62 See Sexual Offences: Definitive Guideline (Sentencing Council 2013) 45–60.

63 Sexual Offences Act 2003, s 21(5).

64 Sexual Offences Act 2003, s 21(6)–(13) inclusive.

to a child and not also in those situations where there is supervised access. Presumably the thought was that supervised access means that the adult would not be in a position to influence the child inappropriately, but in the era of modern communication technologies this can no longer be said to be true. D may have supervised access to a child but if she then contacts the child through social media (or allows the child to contact her) and they interact in a sexual way subsequent to this, the wrong is equally present even though the offence may not be.[65]

An example of those situations that have been left untouched would include the situation of a GP having sexual intercourse with a 17-year-old patient discussed above.[66] As the Sexual Offences Act 2003 follows the logic of the Sexual Offences (Amendment) Act 2000 by providing a finite list, if an activity is not included on the list then it does not constitute an abuse of trust even if it is an exploitative relationship. For example, private tutors are not covered by this rule; so if a school teacher from another school is employed by a parent to provide additional tuition to their son for A-levels and that teacher then has sexual intercourse with the son, this would not be covered under the 2003 Act. There is, at the very least, a potential abuse of trust in such circumstances that the Sexual Offences Act provisions fail to address.

It has also been noted that if it was decided that criminalising ostensibly consensual sexual activities with 16- and 17-year-olds is correct,[67] criminalising it in the way that the Sexual Offences Act 2003 does is a peculiar way of going about it. Nine sections and four new offences were created and yet the substantive offences could have been used, simply raising the age of the victim when a position of authority or trust was identified.[68] However this would arguably not have resolved the key weakness of the offence, which is that by defining 'abuse of trust' in a finite way, obvious situations are missed. That perhaps means that the legislature should have focused on something different.

THE CONCEPT OF SEXUAL EXPLOITATION

It has been noted that the current method of protecting 16–18-year-olds is flawed. By focusing on the age of the child (as a consent issue), it becomes quickly impractical to think about and list every situation where there may be the risk of abuse or exploitation due to the misuse of authority. Instead of treating this as an issue of age, it may be preferable to consider refocusing attention away from (legal) consent to the concept of exploitation.

What is sexual exploitation?

Exploitation is a term often banded about but its utilisation is not commonly accompanied by an analysis of what exactly is meant by the concept.[69] That said, the meaning of exploitation has been scrutinised within philosophical literature, to which we now turn briefly. According to

---

65 Where the child is aged 16 or over then such conduct would not be captured by the so-called 'grooming' offences (Sexual Offences Act 2003, ss 14–15).

66 Whilst, of course, this would constitute serious professional misconduct for disciplinary purposes, it would not be addressed by the criminal law unless factual consent was in issue. See further Suzanne Ost and Hazel Biggs, '"Consensual" sexual activity between doctors and patients: a matter for the Criminal Law?' in Amel Alghrani, Rebecca Bennett & Suzanne Ost (eds), *The Criminal Law and Bioethical Conflict: Walking the Tightrope* (Cambridge University Press 2012) 102–117.

67 And it should be noted that not everyone agrees that it is: see, for example, Spencer (n 58) 356; Waites (n 27) 193.

68 Spencer (n 58) 59.

69 'Too often, uses of exploitation less explain than presuppose the conception applicable.' Rick Bigwood, *Exploitative Contracts* (Oxford University Press 2003) 1. We are concerned here with exploitation we morally disapprove of, rather than in a non-moral context. See Stephen Wilkinson, *Bodies for Sale: Ethics and Exploitation in the Human Body Trade* (Routledge 2003) 10.

Feinberg, '(e)xploitation in the usual pejorative sense is the *wrongful turning to some advantage by one party (A) of some trait or circumstances of another party (B)*'.[70] In common with similar understandings of the concept,[71] Feinberg's definition reveals how exploitation can amount to a violation of the humanity formulation of Kant's second categorical imperative, the ethical responsibility to treat individuals as ends in themselves, rather than merely as means to an end.[72] Put simply, the exploiter fails to respect the individual he exploits as a person.

Turning specifically to sexual exploitation, in 2003 the (then) Secretary-General of the UN defined sexual exploitation as 'any actual or attempted abuse of a position of vulnerability, differential power, or trust, for sexual purposes, including, but not limited to, profiting monetarily, socially or politically from the sexual exploitation of another'.[73] This definition captures profiting in some way from another's weaker position and emphasises elements of trust, vulnerability and an imbalance of power. Sexual exploitation constitutes particularly serious wrongful exploitation because of the trust that the level of intimacy involved in sexual activity so often entails.[74] Moreover, the breach of trust involved makes the effects of sexual exploitation particularly harmful.[75]

Respecting and not violating an individual's autonomy is an integral part of our recognition of them as a person. Hence, the wrong of violating autonomy that so often accompanies sexual exploitation is commonly emphasised. For instance, in Archard's words:

> sexuality is an area in which it is particularly important to treat one another as ends, that is to take into account and respect a person's wishes and beliefs. We are acutely aware of the dangers of failing to do so, and to that extent regard full, knowing, and considered consent as a prerequisite or at least ideal requirement of intimacy.[76]

It is thus unsurprising that consent is the tool by which we appraise whether a person engages willingly in sexual activity, albeit it is a much disparaged legal and moral means of assessment and we have already noted the difficulties raised by consent in the context of older children and varying levels of capacity. Moreover, the mere existence or lack of consent cannot be the only element scrutinised to ascertain whether both parties act in accordance with the aforementioned formulation of Kant's categorical imperative.[77] To return to one of our

---

70 Joel Feinberg, *The Moral Limits of the Criminal Law: Harmless Wrongdoing* (Oxford University Press 1988) 192 (our emphasis).

71 Robert E Goodin, 'Exploiting a Situation and Exploiting a Person', in Andrew Reeve (ed), *Modern Theories of Exploitation* (Sage 1987) 166, 182; Jonathan Wolff, 'Marx and Exploitation' (1999) 3 The Journal of Ethics, 105, 110–11.

72 Immanuel Kant, *Groundwork of the Metaphysics of Morals*. In Immanuel Kant and Mary J Gregor (ed), *Practical Philosophy: (The Cambridge Edition of the Works of Immanuel Kant)* (Cambridge University Press 1999) 37. See also Allen Buchanan, *Ethics, Efficiency, and the Market* (Rowman and Allanheld 1985) 87: 'to exploit a person involves the harmful, merely instrumental utilization of him or his capacities, for one's own advantage or for the sake of one's own ends.'

73 Secretary-General's Bulletin, 'Special measures for protection from sexual exploitation and sexual abuse' ST/SGB/2003/13. Available at: <https://cdu.unlb.org/Portals/0/Documents/KeyDoc4.pdf> accessed 7 February 2016.

74 David Archard, 'Exploited Consent' (1994) 25 Journal of Social Philosophy, 92, 99.

75 See Suzanne Ost, Breaching the Sexual Boundaries in the Doctor–Patient Relationship: Should English Law Recognise Fiduciary Duties?' (2016) 24, Medical Law Review 206.

76 See Archard (n 74).

77 Indeed, philosophical literature recognises that that one can consent and still be exploited. See eg, Wolff (n 71) 113. For an interesting view that where there is no consent, we would not commonly have exploitation, see Wilkinson 2003: 74.

earlier examples involving V and her instructor Ms X, both parties may consent, but V may do so because of Ms X's deliberate use of her more powerful position to make V feel that she cannot refuse Ms X's sexual advances, or to impede V's choice so that she considers consent to be her only option, or to make it very difficult in some other way for V to refuse. This might occur, for instance, in a situation of blackmail,[78] where Ms X threatens to send V's work to a particularly strict examiner if she does not have sex with her, or in a situation involving an inducement, where Ms X offers to provide V with private tuition in exchange for sex, for example. Such sexual exploitation is most likely to be present when there is an imbalance of power between the parties as there is between Ms X and V, and the '"powerful" person abuses the position of authority by inducing the "dependent" person into' sexual activity.[79] Whilst the circumstances may well be enough to cause us to question how real Y's consent actually is,[80] our moral objection is inextricably connected to the *way* in which consent is induced through Ms X's manipulation of her more powerful position, her exploitation of V.[81]

CRIMINALISING SEXUAL EXPLOITATION

How then can you capture an offence that criminalises sexual exploitation? The amended Sexual Offences Act 2003 purports to criminalise the sexual exploitation of a child although it does so only in respect of children who are prostituted and those who are involved in (child) pornography.[82] This is overly restrictive and is improperly worded. This is *not* sexual exploitation, this is a *type* of sexual exploitation.

We have argued that the Sexual Offences (Amendment) Act 2000 and Sexual Offences Act 2003 got into problems by providing a statutory list of what amounted to an abuse of trust. That is nonsensical as whether someone is in a position of trust (or, to adopt our logic, in an exploitative situation) will differ on the circumstances. Rather than providing a list of situations that are exploitative, with the obvious risk of such a list being under or over inclusive, we believe that it would be better to have a statutory test that is linked to a specific crime. In that way it is possible to ensure that the offence covers those who are being exploited, but does not include situations where no exploitation of a position or position of authority exists.

LEARNING FROM CANADA

English law could, in our view, learn lessons from Canada. Rather than adopt a list of situations that constitute abuse or exploitation, the relevant statutory provision instead adopts a single test. The legislation is set out in s 153 of the Criminal Code, which states:

> Every person commits an offence who is in a position of trust or authority towards a young person, who is a person with whom the young person is in a relationship of

---

78 See Ost (n 75) 213–214.

79 Phyllis Coleman, 'Sex in Power Dependency Relationships: Taking Unfair Advantage of the "Fair" Sex', (1988) 53 Albany Law Review, 95, 96.

80 Some have gone so far as to argue that in any situation where there is a relationship of 'power dependency', the weaker party's consent to sexual activity is always questionable. See Coleman ibid; Tom Allen, 'Civil liability for Sexual Exploitation in Professional Relationships' (1996) 59(1) Modern Law Review 56, 58.

81 See David Archard's conceptions of 'manipulated consent' and 'exploited consent': Archard (n 74): 94–94.

82 Sexual Offences Act 2003, ss 47–50 as amended by the Serious Crime Act 2015. For a discussion on whether these offences are needed see Alisdair A Gillespie 'Prostitution or abuse? The Sexual Offences Act 2003' [2005] Criminal Law Review 285–289, which remains a valid criticism as the new offences do not affect the basic structure of those that they replace.

dependency or who is in a relationship with a young person that is exploitative of the young person, and who:

(a) for a sexual purpose, touches, directly or indirectly, with a part of the body or with an object, any part of the body of the young person; or

(b) for a sexual purpose, invites, counsels or incites a young person to touch, directly or indirectly, with a part of the body or with an object, the body of any person, including the body of the person who so invites, counsels or incites and the body of the young person.[83]

This is a more comprehensive offence than the comparable English offences. The offence applies only to those aged 16–18[84] and covers all the sexually exploitative activity in a single offence rather than creating separate, overlapping offences (as the English offences do). Rather than list specific circumstances that are deemed to be exploitative in order to determine whether the relationship is appropriate, the judge is encouraged to consider specific points, namely:

(a) the age of the young person;

(b) the age difference between the person and the young person;

(c) the evolution of the relationship; and

(d) the degree of control or influence by the person over the young person.[85]

The latter factor is particularly interesting. It allows judges to look at the circumstances of the relationship and not whether it is included within a particular list. Applying this test, it is likely that relationships such as the GP example discussed above would be caught by the Canadian legislation. Clearly a GP would exercise a high degree of control or influence over a young person and any relationship between them is likely to be considered inappropriate and exploitative. What is more, it is difficult to see how any of the situations set out in the Sexual Offences Act 2003 would not also be captured by the Canadian law. The Canadian law would, as already noted, go further in its reach.

In the discussion of English law we noted that an employer/employee relationship would not be caught by the abuse of a position of trust laws. An employer/employee relationship is not automatically exploitative, but it certainly has the potential to be and offers a sexual exploiter the scope to exert a high level of coercion. Canadian law would recognise this. Nothing in s 153 *requires* the court to find that a relationship is exploitative; it simply *empowers* them to do so when the circumstances and context of the relationship are known. Where an employer is seeking sexual contact with an employee and makes an implicit or otherwise link to their future career, probation or promotion then that could be considered exploitative. Similarly, we presented the hypothetical private tutor who enters into sexual activity with a child assigned to him. The nature of this relationship means that it could well be exploitative, particularly where, for example, the tutor is aware that the parents believe that the child is under-performing educationally and are punishing the child for the same.

The flexibility of the offence under s 153 is illustrated by some of the cases that have been decided under it. In *R v O (CP)*[86] the offence applied where the father of a friend of the victim

---

83 Canadian Penal Code, s 153(1).

84 ibid, s 153(2). Until recently the age of consent in Canada was 14 and so older cases relate to 14-year olds.

85 ibid, s 153(1.2).

86 *R v O(CP)* (1993) 124 NSR (2d) 366.

had sexual contact with her when she had sleepovers at his house. The court held that the defendant was exercising authority over the child when she stayed at his house. This type of case would not be covered by the English offences and yet this is perhaps a classic example of when there may be *de facto* trust and an imbalance of power that would call into question the consent given by the child.

In *R v Edwards*[87] the offender was a dance-class instructor. He paid particular attention to a 14-year-old girl who attended his dance classes and ultimately he had sexual intercourse with her. The court was clear that this amounted to an exploitative relationship, not least because of the circumstances regarding how the defendant and victim knew each other. Under English law this would not be considered an abuse of a position of trust because it did not take place in an educational establishment that V attended.

A more troubling, but equally important, case is *R v G (C)*.[88] A 27-year-old man was living in a (shared) house when a 14-year-old girl who had ran away from home came to squat. He was aware of her age and that she had ran away from home and they had sexual intercourse daily. The child testified that the defendant was responsible for providing shelter to her and providing food etc. The Court of Appeal held that this was an exploitative relationship, partly due to the difference in age but also because V was undoubtedly dependent on D. It is unclear that a similar result would occur in England.[89] The only potential argument is that this is a case of child prostitution[90] although (a) this would be controversial[91] and (b) it is unclear whether such an argument would succeed.[92] It is submitted that it would be preferable and much more of an accurate reflection of the situation to adopt the approach adopted in Canada of simply considering it an exploitative relationship.

CONCLUSION

It is acknowledged that some people are not convinced that it is appropriate to operate two ages of consent. Some have argued that the abuse of trust provisions are unnecessary and were a political sop to those who were opposed to reducing the homosexual age of consent.[93] However we disagree. Waites has noted that while it is not possible to say that every child–adult relationship will be intrinsically harmful, such relationships are undoubtedly risky, and he suggests that this justifies an age of consent.[94] We would take this further and suggest that this logic justifies criminalising certain relationships between adults and young people over the ordinary age of consent. However the current (English) law operates on the basis that a limited number of certain defined relationships are *always* harmful and should be prohibited. Even if this could be proved, and it is less than clear that this is the case, it leaves a number of other abusive relationships unregulated. That does not protect vulnerable young

---

87 *R v Edwards* (2003) 172 CCC (3d) 313.
88 *R v G(C)* (1994) 90 CCC (3d) 76.
89 Obviously if V was 14 a substantive offence could be used, but for the purpose of the argument and focus of this chapter, it is meant that no liability would arise if V was 16.
90 Sexual Offences Act 2003, s 47 (see in particular, s 47(2)).
91 Partly because the term itself is problematic and pejorative (see Gillespie (n 83) 285) and partly because it is quite possible/likely that the child may not consider herself to being prostituted.
92 It is reliant on the prosecution proving that D made or promised payment, which could include the accommodation. On the facts of *R v G(C)* it does not seem that this would be easy to prove.
93 Spencer (n 58) 355.
94 Waites (n 27) 30.

people and there are simply too many exceptions because of the blunt way that the law currently operates.

England should learn from Canada and focus not on a list of positions but instead consider whether the actual relationship between the youth and the adult is exploitative. This will involve a number of factors but, at its heart, will be whether the adult has any undue control or influence over the youth. If they do then it can be legitimately questioned whether a child is truly able to give full, knowing and considered consent. Our objection to accepting that the child's consent is genuine is undoubtedly connected to the way in which it has been obtained by the adult's manipulation of power and exertion of control or influence, thereby undermining the capacity of the child to decide whether to engage in sexual activity. This is worthy of protection under the criminal law. To that extent a higher age of consent can be justified but not when applied uniformly. If the specific circumstances of the relationship are examined and evaluated and found to be exploitative then consent is likely to be vitiated and criminal liability can be justified.

11

Consent

Revisiting the exemption for contact sports

Mark James

INTRODUCTION

The courts have often stated that the contacts made between athletes during participation in sporting activities deserve special treatment by the law in order to preserve sport's many beneficial characteristics. The difficulty faced by athletes,[1] sports administrators and the criminal justice system is that despite the longevity of this exceptional position, the scope of the partial exemption provided to interpersonal sporting contacts remains unclear. Consensual conduct has been defined by reference to sports' rules and customs, the foreseeability of injury, the degree of harm caused, its acceptability to those involved with the game and the availability of sporting-disciplinary sanctions against the perpetrator. This uncertainty is caused by the lack of appellate level direction on the definition of consent in sport, which is compounded by contradictory public policy approaches and the many *obiter dicta* statements made by the judiciary about sport when discussing consent in other contexts. This chapter provides original insight into the evolution of the sporting exemption through its analysis of the problems caused by this lack of definitional precision. By examining the tests that have been proposed by the courts over the last 150 years and the impact that these have had on the relationships between athletes, the governing bodies of sport, the prosecuting authorities and the criminal law, a model for analysing sporting consent is proposed.

THE PROBLEM OF DEFINING CONSENT IN SPORT

It has long been accepted that there is something inherently good about sport, and in particular about participation in sport, that can justify what would otherwise be criminal assaults being held to be lawful, consensual activities.[2] Despite the longevity and provenance of such differential treatment, however, the precise scope of the sporting exemption and its underlying justifications has rarely been articulated in any depth by the courts. Thus, injurious contacts

---

1 'Athlete' is used here as a generic term to include participants in any sporting activity.
2 Michael Dalton, *The country justice* (Rawlins and Roycroft 1618) quoted in Dr Curtis Fogel, 'Ultra-Violence on the Pitch: Establishing a Threshold for the Intervention of Criminal Law in English Football' (2014) 2 Journal of Law and Criminal Justice 11; Michael Foster, *Crown Law* (3rd edition, Dodson (ed), 1792) 259.

performed in the name of sport fall within the 'unstable and contested'[3] area to which lawful consent might extend.

The few cases that do come before the courts are often uncontroversial applications of the law, in that they concern incidents of deliberate assaults unconnected with the actual playing of the sport in question, such as punching,[4] kicking,[5] head-butting[6] and biting.[7] The obvious illegality of such assaults has resulted in a lack of critical engagement with the scope of the defence as it so clearly does not apply on the facts of these cases.

This lack of critical engagement is compounded by there being very few cases that have had to consider the position of on-the-ball or during-the-play incidents and the need to distinguish between consensual challenges that are part of the playing of the game, consensual challenges that are within the sport's playing culture but punished by the governing body and challenges constituting criminal assault to which consent cannot extend. In the overwhelming majority of during-the-play incidents, any punishment imposed on the athlete causing the injury is determined by their sports governing body's disciplinary mechanism, not the courts. This in turn removes the opportunity for the law to clarify the scope of the defence and the appropriateness of resorting to an alternative dispute resolution process that effectively decriminalises sports assaults; a position that appears to be exacerbated where professional athletes are concerned.[8] For sports assaults, these hard cases are not so much leading to bad law, but to a situation where there is no adequate law to govern the dispute.[9] This unquestioning acceptance or assumption that sport is, at least for the most part, beneficial to society in general and athletes in particular, coupled with the lack of cases reaching the appellate level has left the associated jurisprudence confused, confusing and incomplete.

A further complicating factor is that the exemption granted to contact sports is often discussed at the same time as that which is granted to boxing and other combat sports. An intellectually satisfying justification of the law's position on boxing has been attempted on a number of occasions, but the result of these attempts has been either to leave a more confusing situation,[10] or the simple conclusion that combat sports represent a 'special situation' that society for the time being chooses to tolerate.[11] It is important to keep consideration of the legality of combat and contact sports separate. Their different aims, objectives, intentions and inherent risks result in different justifications for the existence of the respective exemptions that must be analysed independently of each other.[12]

---

3   Andrew Simester et al, *Simester and Sullivan's Criminal Law: Theory and Doctrine* (4th edition, Hart 2010) 749.

4   *R v Birkin* (1988) 10 Cr App R (S) 303.

5   *R v Garfield* [2008] EWCA Crim 130, 120.

6   *Attorney General's Reference (No 27 of 1993)* also known as *R v Piff* (1994) 15 Cr App R (S) 737, 120.

7   *R v Johnson* (1986) 8 Cr App R (S) 343.

8   Compare *The Football Association v Luis Suarez*, FA Regulatory Commission, available at: <https://www.google.co.uk/url?sa=t&rct=j&q=&esrc=s&source=web&cd=2&cad=rja&uact=8&ved=0CCYQFjABah UKEwjhm7PDi7DIAhVICBoKHVc2CXQ&url=http%3A%2F%2Fwww.thefa.com%2F~%2Fmedia%2 Ffiles%2Fpdf%2Fthe-fa-2012–13%2Fdisciplinary%2Fmr-luis-suarez – written reasons.ashx%3Fla% 3Den&usg=AFQjCNG_FbijZ9kJ41pANIVf9o4hIkoTPQ> last accessed, 7 October 2015; *Johnson* (n 7) where the biters received a 10-match suspension and six months' imprisonment respectively.

9   Glanville Williams, *The Sanctity of Life and the Criminal Law* (Knopf 1957) 105.

10 *Pallante v Stadiums Pty Ltd (No 1)* [1976] VR 331.

11 *R v Brown* [1994] 1 AC 212 (Lord Mustill) 265.

12 Michael Gunn and David Ormerod, 'The legality of boxing' (1995) 15(2) Legal Studies 181; Jack Anderson, 'The right to a fair fight: sporting lessons on consensual harm' (2014) 17(1) New Criminal Law Review 55; Jack Anderson, *The Legality of Boxing: a punch drunk love* (Routledge 2007).

Adding to this confusion, many of the leading non-sports cases that have considered the scope of the general defence of consent have made at least passing reference to the sports exemption. These judicial comments, which are at best *obiter dicta* and often little more than casual asides, have ensured that this lack of clarity has remained by either restating the assumption that sports are one of the 'well-established exceptions',[13] or by adding an unnecessary gloss to the existing body of comment.[14] The culmination of these uncertainties leads to an unwelcome opening position: the theoretical basis of the sports exemption, its scope, the types of conduct to which it applies and the boundaries of the overlapping jurisdictions of the criminal law and an apparently viable alternative punishment structure all require clarification.

THE UNDERPINNING JUSTIFICATION FOR GRANTING AN EXEMPTION TO SPORT

The rationale underpinning the encroachment of the criminal law into sports is that no particular section of society should be permitted to commit crime with impunity.[15] Although it is widely accepted that contact sports should be exempted from the normal operation of the law of consent, there is no satisfactory judicial explanation for why this should be the case. Indeed, the Court of Appeal has stated specifically that it is unnecessary to provide a separate jurisprudential basis for the application of the defence as it is grounded in public policy considerations.[16] The difficulty with the Lord Chief Justice's statement is that there is no attempt to define what exactly are those public policy considerations that can justify contact sports being treated exceptionally. Thus, the law is left open to the criticism that it is developing in accordance with the morality of the key players in the criminal justice system, instead of in a coherent and justified manner,[17] or conferring the power to 'license violence' on a private body.[18]

Historically, it was more common for justifications to be provided for the statutory prohibition of particular sporting activities. These 'unlawful games' statutes prohibited participation in tennis, football and other 'importune sports' on the grounds that they were vain, dishonest and idle activities that were associated with alcohol and gambling.[19] In contrast, the legality of sports evolves initially as a negative; they were lawful if they did not promote these vices. This approach is epitomised by the exemption granted to boxing being predicated on it not being prize-fighting,[20] rather than being based on a positive justification of its sporting, social and cultural merits.[21]

---

13 *R v Donovan* [1934] 2 KB 498 (Swift J) 508.
14 *Attorney-General's Reference (No 6 of 1980)* [1981] QB 715 (Lord Lane CJ) 719 Reference to 'properly conducted sports and games'.
15 Jack Anderson, 'No licence for thuggery: violence, sport and the criminal law' [2008] 10 Criminal Law Review 751, 252.
16 *R v Barnes* [2004] EWCA Crim 3246 (Lord Woolf CJ) para 11.
17 Amy Kerr, 'Consensual sado-masochism and the public interest: distinguishing morality and legality' (2014) 2 North East Law Review 51.
18 John McCutcheon, 'Sports violence, consent and the criminal law' (1994) 45(3) Northern Ireland Legal Quarterly 267, 273.
19 *Abbot v Weekly* (1665) 83 ER 357; 1 Lev 176' in Jack Anderson (ed), *Leading Cases in Sports Law* (The Hague: TMC Asser Press, 2013) 8.
20 *R v Coney* (1881–82) 8 QBD 534.
21 Anderson (n 12).

In what appears to be the earliest comment on an emerging exemption for sports assaults, a more positive approach based on the benefits associated with sports participation is provided by Dalton, who stated that anyone:

> [P]laying at Hand-Sworn, Bucklers, Football, Wrestling, and the like, whereby one of them receiveth a hurt, and dieth thereof within a year and a day; in these cases, some are of the opinion, that this is a Felony of Death: some others are of opinion, that this is no Felony of Death, but that they shall have their pardon, of course, as for misadventure, for that such their play was by *consent, and again, there was no former intent to do hurt, or any former malice, but done only for disport, and trail of Manhood.*[22]

Similarly, Sir Michael Foster wrote that 'manly diversions' such as wrestling and fighting with cudgels or foils are lawful because the participants are engaged only in 'friendly exertions' that develop their strength, skill, dexterity and physical activity and enable them to be fit enough to fight for their country. This is in contrast to activities such as prize-fights, which are claimed to serve no valuable purpose and encourage a spirit of idleness and debauchery.[23] Similar public policy claims for the health benefits of participation in contact sports could be made today (without the need for preparation for close-quarters military combat), though these are rarely articulated by the judiciary. This broadly liberal perspective, where the law accords the greatest possible liberty compatible with respecting that of others, appears at least tacitly to underpin these and later analyses.[24]

A changing socio-political approach to sports participation in the Victorian era saw an increasing acceptance of the physical, social and moral positives associated with an active lifestyle. Statutory protections for recreational spaces and public baths encouraged outdoor leisure pursuits, team sports and swimming.[25] If these social and legislative developments influenced judicial pronouncements on the acceptability of sports participation and the ability to consent to the contacts that were a necessary part of playing them, they were neither referred to by the courts nor were they made explicit in their judgments.[26]

From these very basic beginnings, the leading cases on sports assaults make very little attempt to clarify or develop further the justification for the exemption. In *Bradshaw*, Bramwell LJ was simply, 'unwilling to decry the manly sports of this country, all of which were no doubt attended with more or less danger'.[27] More commonly, the courts do not engage with the debate at all, accepting the existence of the defence, without further interrogation,[28] or dismissing the need to engage with further justification as the existence of the exemption is a matter of public policy.[29] Thus, the underpinning rationale for the existence of the exemption is neither fully nor explicitly articulated.

---

22 Dalton (n 2) emphasis added.
23 Michael Foster, *Crown Law* (n 2)
24 Nafsika Athanassoulis, 'The role of consent in sado-masochistic practices' (2002) 8(2) Res Publica 141, 142.
25 Anderson (n 19) 21.
26 A similar 'public benefit' justification underpins ss 3(1)(d) and (g) The Charities Act 2011, and its predecessors in charities law, which provide charitable status for the advancement of health and amateur sport respectively.
27 *R v Bradshaw* (1878) 14 Cox CC 83, 85.
28 *Attorney-General's Reference (No 6 of 1980)* (n 14) (Lord Lane CJ) 719.
29 *Barnes* (n 16).

The same is true of the leading consent cases not involving sport. Sport is simply considered to be a well-established exception,[30] with Lord Mustill considering that intuitive references to public policy are made to justify the legality of sports in substitution for developing further a theory of consent.[31] This position is exemplified by Lord Lane CJ, who held that injuries amounting to actual bodily harm that are inflicted in the course of 'properly conducted games and sports' can be consented to as they are in the (again undefined) public interest,[32] and Lord Jauncey who inferred that the presence of a referee reinforcing the formality of the activity was key to its legality.[33]

In the alternative, justification can be provided implicitly from a negative: consent does not extend to contacts in sport that are accompanied by an intention to cause serious harm,[34] or to engaging in acts of physical violence off the ball,[35] or to actions that are 'wholly unacceptable'.[36] This has been distilled into the pithy and much quoted judicial statement that sports do not provide athletes with a 'licence to commit thuggery'.[37] It appears that in these cases, the contacts do not fall within the sports exemption because they fail to provide any social benefit to either the protagonists or society at large, leaving the contacts that are considered to be more closely associated with the playing of the game in question imbued with an undefined social utility that renders them lawful.

A more comprehensive approach could have been expected when the defence of consent in criminal law was reviewed in both England and Ireland by the Law Commission and the Law Reform Commission, respectively. The Irish Law Reform Commission explained that participation in sporting activities promotes fitness and good health, discipline, teamwork and self-control.[38] There was no similar justification provided by the Law Commission in either of its two consultation papers, just an assumption, based on Foster, that the exemption is a good idea.[39] The Law Commission went so far as to state that courts would not have any difficulty in identifying which activities constituted sports and would, therefore, benefit from the exemption.[40] Further, it was proposed that the Sports Council should determine which activities ought to be classified as sports, again working from the presumption that sport possesses some inherent, but undefined, social utility.[41]

If the law failed to treat sport differently from other contexts in which interpersonal contacts occur, then contact sports could not continue in their current forms. Whether or not one considers such an approach to be in the public good on a personal level, it is unlikely that contact sports as a category of activity will be banned in their entirety.[42] It is possible,

---

30 *Donovan* (n 13) 508.
31 *Brown* (n 11) 264.
32 *Attorney-General's Reference (No 6 of 1980)* (n 14).
33 *Brown* (n 11) (Lord Jauncey) 238.
34 *Bradshaw* (n 27).
35 *R v Bowyer* [2001] EWCA Crim 1853.
36 *Garfield* (n 5).
37 *R v Lloyd* (1989) 11 Cr App R (S) 36.
38 Law Reform Commission, *Report in non-fatal offences against the person*, (Cmnd. 45, 1994) 274.
39 The Law Commission Consultation Paper, *Consent and offences against the person*, (Law Com, No 134, London: HMSO 1994) 10.1; The Law Commission Consultation Paper, *Consent in the criminal law* (Law Com No 139, London: HMSO 1995) 12.1.
40 ibid *Consultation Paper No 134*, 44.2.
41 The Law Commission, Consultation Paper, *Consent in Criminal Law* (n 39) 13.
42 Parliament has failed to outlaw boxing on numerous occasions. If this most extreme of contact sports cannot garner the support to be criminalised, then the likelihood of any contact sport (as opposed to combat sport) being declared unlawful is very unlikely.

however, that some sports, or at least some aspects of some sports, may at some future point be considered to be no longer acceptable to society and therefore no longer acceptable to the law. Therefore, the need for an exception for sports can be justified most easily on the grounds that these are activities that promote physical, social and cultural well-being by helping to develop athletes' fitness, good health, strength, skill, dexterity, self-control, teamwork, sense of fair play and community identity.

DIFFERENTIATING CONSENT IN SPORTS TO CONSENT IN OTHER CONTEXTS

When discussing a unified approach to defining consent, the sports exemption is often overlooked or at least marginalised.[43] This lack of engagement can be better understood if a number of distinguishing features are identified that explain how and why consent in sport is a very different construct to consent in other exempted activities.[44] Thus, before analysing the various formulations of the sports exemption that have been utilised by the courts, it is essential to address four distinctive elements of consent in sport that justify its exceptional treatment.

First, consent in contact sports is always implied from the athlete's participation in the particular game as there is no formal agreement entered into by them in advance of the contest.[45] This is distinct from, for example, the obtaining of written consent from a patient in advance of a specific medical procedure. McCutcheon goes further, stating that an athlete's consent is more accurately described as being attributed or deemed, as it is not something that can be challenged by the athlete once they have engaged with the game.[46]

Secondly, an athlete's consent is assumed to be informed, rather than being specifically informed.[47] All participants in a sporting activity have to be assumed to be at least generally aware of the rules of the game that they are playing, its objects, its inherent dangers and, in particular, the risk of being injured. These obviously vary from sport to sport, but the nature of the game itself will mean that athletes possess significant knowledge about the activity in which they are engaging, even where they have not been told specifically about each and every potentially injurious situation with which they may be confronted.

Thirdly, consent is to the risk of a range of known or anticipated outcomes or harms that can be caused by a specific act. Even where contact is intentional and with extreme force, for example a rugby tackle, it is impossible to say that the athlete has consented to specific injuries being caused to them. Instead, the reality is that athletes are running the risk of being caused one or more of a range of injuries, from bruising (highly likely) to death (highly unlikely) that result from participation; they do not consent to a specific harm being caused by a specific action on the part of the perpetrator. Significant confusion has resulted from discussions where there has been a focus on the type and extent of the injury caused.[48] It

---

43   Catherine Elliott and Claire de Than, 'The case of a rational reconstruction of consent in criminal law' (2007) 70(2) Modern Law Review 225; Ben Livings, 'A different ball game – why the nature of consent in contact sports undermines a unitary approach' (2007) 71(6) Journal of Criminal Law 534.

44   On the other exempted activities, see Simon Cooper and Mark James, 'Entertainment – the painful process of rethinking consent' [2012] 3 Criminal Law Review 188.

45   *Barnes* (n 16) [12].

46   McCutcheon (n 18) 281.

47   As is now required, wherever possible, before surgical procedures are performed on a patient, *Montgomery v Lanarkshire Health Board* [2015] UKSC 11.

48   The Law Commission Consultation Paper, *Consent and offences against the person* (n 39).

is essential that, when discussing the sports exemption, focus is maintained on the injury-causing act,[49] whether it is capable of being consented to and the associated *mens rea*, whilst not becoming entangled with the emotional responses to the degree of injury caused.[50]

Fourthly, and most distinctively, consent as it operates in respect of participants in contact sports, is defined objectively. Unlike every other situation where it is at issue, and in particular sexual offences,[51] consent in sport must be defined from an objective viewpoint, not subjectively from the victim's perspective or on their behalf.[52] The original discussion of the need for an objective approach is found in the Canadian case of *Cey*,[53] which has been extremely influential on the development of English law in this field. The court stated that because the presence of consent is a state of the injured party's mind, it is ordinarily a subjective matter; however, as there cannot be as many different definitions of consent as there are participants in a game, the scope of an athlete's implied or deemed consent must be determined according to objective criteria in order to ensure the necessary degree of uniformity to enable the game to take place.[54] An individual in a contact sport cannot subjectively opt out of contacts that are an inherent and/or necessary part of playing the game in question; a rugby player cannot refuse to be tackled, nor an ice hockey player to be checked. Instead, consent operates objectively on the basis of what is acceptable not to the individual athlete concerned but to the reasonable player of that sport. As sporting contests operate as a 'closed system' that is isolated from contacts with the world outside the playing arena, then everyone within that system must be judged by the same objectively defined standard. By undertaking an holistic appraisal of the circumstances in which the sporting injury occurs, the full, free and informed consent of all participants is applied multilaterally and conterminously to all participants.[55] This results in all participants in a game-system providing consent that is to the same level of interpersonal contact occurring, which in turn enables the contest to take place.

THE HISTORICAL DEVELOPMENT OF THE LEGAL TESTS

The earliest discussions of an emerging acceptance that contact sports needed to be treated differently are found in the commentaries of Dalton and Foster. Dalton states that an athlete's consent might extend to the harm caused by contacts that occur in the course of sports because there is no intent to do hurt to one's opponent.[56] Foster agrees with this interpretation of the law and builds on it by stating that in sports, there is no intent to cause harm to an opponent as the aim of the contest is to develop the strength, skill and dexterity of the participants through engagement in physical activity.[57] The common and enduring elements of these statements of the law are that consent extends to any contacts that are performed 'only for disport', but that this consent cannot extend to contacts accompanied by an intention to cause harm. The difficulty for the courts is the need to determine which contacts can be considered to be 'only for disport', or part of the game, and to which consent can extend.

---

49 Athanassoulis (n 24) 145.
50 See for example the comments on sado-masochism in Peter Murphy, 'Flogging live complainants and dead horses: we may no longer need to be in bondage to Brown' [2011] Criminal Law Review 758, 760.
51 Sexual Offences Act 2003, s 74.
52 The Law Commission Consultation Paper, *Consent and offences against the person* (n 39) [10.8].
53 *R v Cey* (1989) 48 CCC (3d) 480.
54 ibid (Gerwing JA) 490.
55 Livings (n 43) 546.
56 Dalton (n 22).
57 Foster (n 23).

Having determined the legality of the act in general terms, the court must then ascertain the *mens rea* of the defendant athlete to determine whether the particular act was legally capable of being consented to.

The first case to address these issues directly was *Bradshaw*, where the defendant footballer charged his opponent when challenging for the ball. The victim fell awkwardly and died from internal injuries. The judge directed the jury that:

> No rules or practice of any game whatever can make that lawful which is unlawful by the law of the land ... [I]f a man is playing according to the rules and practice of the game and not going beyond it, it may be reasonable to infer that he is not actuated by any malicious motive or intention, and that he is not acting in a manner which he knows will be likely to be productive of death or injury. But, independent of the rules, if the prisoner intended to cause serious hurt to the deceased, or if he knew that, in charging as he did, he might produce serious injury and was indifferent and reckless as to whether he would produce serious injury or not, then the act would be unlawful.[58]

Bradshaw leads us to four foundational principles. First, sports are lawful activities provided that their rules do not have as their object an obvious illegality. Although appearing to be a circular argument, *Bradshaw* ensures that as long as contact sports do not have as their specific objective the causing of serious injury or death, then the incidental contacts inherent in playing the game are lawful. Secondly, it should be inferred that athletes who are playing the sport in question in accordance with its rules are acting lawfully because, by doing so, they do not intend to cause serious injury or death to others. Conversely, those acting outside of the rules and with the intent to cause, or being reckless as to whether they will cause, serious injury or death are to be inferred to be acting criminally. Thirdly, it should be inferred that athletes acting in accordance with a sport's accepted practices, including some acts of foul play, are acting lawfully as by doing so they do not intend to cause serious injury or death. Conversely, athletes acting outside of those accepted norms by intending to cause, or being reckless as to whether they would cause, serious injury or death are acting criminally. Fourthly, consent cannot extend to intentionally or recklessly inflicted serious injury or death. Thus, consent extends to contacts that are allowed within the rules, or that are accepted practices or norms of the game, but not to the intentional or reckless infliction of serious injury or death.

The social utility of the activity as contrasted to the degree of harm caused underpinned the decision in *Coney*, where the legality of a prize-fight was at issue.[59] Cave J focused on the *mens rea* of the defendant athlete in much the same way as had Bramwell J in *Bradshaw*. He held that, 'a blow struck in anger, or which is likely or is intended to do corporal hurt, is an assault, but that a blow struck in sport, and not likely, nor intended to cause bodily harm, is not an assault'.[60] Once again, the assumption is that there is no intention to injure an opponent when playing sport and, if such an intention exists, then consent is inoperative.

Stephen J took the alternative approach by focusing more on playing culture by holding that where the athlete is not exposed to serious danger in the common course of things, then consent will be operative even when considerable force is used, in particular in the course of sports.[61] Whether or not a contact was 'in the common course of things' depended upon the

---

58 *Bradshaw* (n 27) 84.
59 *R v Coney* (n 20).
60 ibid 539.
61 ibid 549.

circumstances in which the contact took place, again enabling the court to examine a sport's rules, practices and norms when determining the legality of the injurious contact.[62]

After these seminal cases, there was little development in the law for over 100 years, though the terminology used by the judiciary often varied. These phraseological differences can be seen either as the courts saying the same thing in a different way, adding to or amending the earlier approaches. In reality, it ensured that there was a lack of jurisprudential consistency that had the potential to lead to confusion. In two of the few reported sports cases, *Moore* reiterated that football was a lawful game, but that anyone playing it must be careful to restrain themselves from causing bodily harm to other players,[63] whilst in *Billinghurst* the court stated that athletes consent to force from contacts 'of a kind which could reasonably be expected to happen during a game'.[64] When discussing the operation of consent in cases arising outside of sports, the Court of Appeal and House of Lords stated that contacts occurring during 'properly conducted games and sports' were lawful,[65] but that the law would not license brutality in the name of sport.[66] Although these comments were *obiter dicta*, they are important as they attempt to convey the same underpinning approach: that something about the formality and rules of a sport makes it different from other contexts in which injury is caused, and that undefined 'something' is worth protecting from the intrusion of the criminal law.

The two reviews undertaken by the Law Commission in the 1990s could have produced clear and useful guidance to sport; however, its approach was fundamentally flawed. By focusing on the legality of the degree of injury caused instead of the legality of the act that led to the injury, the Commission was making criminality contingent on the outcome. It is contrary to orthodox principles of the criminal law that the definition of an offence is predicated on the harm produced rather than on proof of the coexistence of the necessary *actus reus* and *mens rea*.[67] For example, a rugby player tackling an opponent with significant force but within the rules of the game, would appear to be acting with the victim's consent if no injury was caused, but criminally where injury or greater harm were caused. The correct approach, as it would be for a surgical procedure, for example, is that the injured party consents to the act, the tackle, regardless of the degree of harm ultimately caused, provided that the defendant does not intend to cause serious injury when performing the tackle.[68]

In contrast to the lack of consistency of the English approach at this time, Canadian Law was developing a much clearer exposition of the interaction between contacts sports, assaults and consent. Following the high profile prosecution of two National Hockey League professional ice hockey players, the Canadian courts have created a clear and pragmatic approach to consent in sport.[69] Although the cases of *Maki* and *Green* resulted in acquittals based on

---

62   See for example *R v Orton* (1878) 14 Cox CC 226, where it was held that what was originally a lawful sparring bout could become an illegal fight where the protagonists' state of mind changed from being one of trying to demonstrate superior skill, (within the playing culture), to intending to cause injury to the opponent, (outside of the rules and playing culture).

63   *R v Moore* (1898) 14 TLR 229 (Hawkins J).

64   *R v Billinghurst* [1978] Crim LR 553.

65   *Attorney General's Reference (No 6 of 1980)*, (n 14) (Lord Lane CJ) 719.

66   *Brown* (n 11) (Lord Slynn) 266.

67   For a more recent examination of the definitional problems associated with the assault offences see further, Law Commission, *Reform of Offences against the Person: A Scoping Consultation Paper*, Consultation Paper No.217 <http://www.lawcom.gov.uk/wp-content/uploads/2015/06/cp217_offences_against_the_person.pdf> accessed 9 October 2015.

68   Law Commission Consultation Paper, *Consent and offences against the person* (n 39) 10.18.

69   See further, Jack Anderson, 'Policing the sports field: the role of the criminal law' [2005] International Sports Law Review 25, 27; McCutcheon (n 18) 274–7.

the instinctive and unintentional nature of their actions,[70] the courts were quick to point out that there were limits on how far consent could extend. These limits were explored explicitly in the cases of *Cey* and *Ciccarelli*, involving a body check and a fight respectively, in ice hockey games.[71] The combined impact of these cases is that the courts must take into consideration a series of relevant circumstances to determine the scope of the players' implied consent and whether the injurious contact under consideration exceeds this. These include, but are not limited to: the conditions under which the game in question is being played; the nature of the act that forms the charge; the extent of the force employed; the degree of risk of injury; and the state of mind of the accused. This approach enabled the courts to determine objectively the kinds of contacts that could be consented to in the particular game being played and, in situations where that consent was exceeded, whether the defendant had the necessary subjectively defined *mens rea* to criminalise their conduct.

The pre-*Barnes* cases, and in particular the more overtly progressive approach of the Canadian courts, attempted to encapsulate something more than simply playing in accordance with the rules of the game. To define the law so restrictively is both impractical, because of the sheer magnitude of cases that would then become criminal, and fails to reflect the reality of athletes' consent; they both accept and expect that fouls will occur, that sometimes these fouls will be deliberate and that occasionally injury will result.[72] This requires something more than the rules alone acting as a means of clarifying the extent and type of consent and enforcing it,[73] by including of necessity some of the commonly occurring incidents of foul play. If sport has social utility, then it is the sport as a whole, including its normal attributes, incidents and inherent spirit that attract the protection of the law.[74]

Although lacking a consistent rationale, it is clear that each of these different judicial approaches are aiming at achieving the same goal; the determination of whether the particular contact is consensual and acceptable to the law, consensual but unacceptable, or not legally capable of being covered by consent. The resultant problem is that by developing a legal test with sufficient flexibility to protect socially beneficial injurious contacts, it runs the risk of being unworkably vague by allowing too much latitude to genuinely violent players.[75]

This has been addressed by making reference to the 'playing culture' of a sport and enables each of the circumstances discussed above to be considered in a contextually appropriate approach.[76] As something more than just the playing rules must be referred to, the playing culture can be seen as an expression of the consent deemed to apply to athletes: it is a means of clarifying the scope of their consent and enforcing it.

This concept draws on Williams' reference to a game's 'working culture' when he stated that, 'the players are even deemed to consent to an application of force that is in breach of the rules of the game, if it is the sort of thing that may be expected to happen during the game'.[77] Although not doing so explicitly, it can be seen that a game's playing culture is referred to inherently by all of the preceding cases and commentaries by the references made to contacts

---

70 *R v Maki* (1970) 14 DLR (3d) 164; *R v Green* (1970) 16 DLR (3d) 137.

71 *R v Cey* (1989) 48 CCC (3d) 480; *R v Ciccarelli* (1989) 54 CCC (3d) 121.

72 In stark contrast, some seek to interpret the law in such a way that anyone not playing by its rules cannot be said to be playing the game and is therefore acting criminally; Edward Grayson, *Sport and the Law* (3rd edition, Butterworths 2000) ch 6; app 6.

73 Athanassoulis (n 24) 148.

74 McCutcheon (n 18) 273.

75 ibid 275.

76 Mark James, 'The trouble with Roy Keane' (2002) 1(3) Entertainment Law 72.

77 Glanville Williams, 'Consent and public policy' [1962] Criminal Law Review 74, 80.

being in accordance with: disport and trial of manhood; manly diversions and friendly exertions; the rules and practices of a game; the common course of things; what is reasonably expected in the game; and properly conducted sports and games.

MODERN ATTEMPTS TO REDEFINE THE LAW

Prior to *Barnes*, there were three key issues that needed addressing by the courts: the continuing confusion over whether the criminal law should apply to sports; the concurrent jurisdiction over the resultant disputes claimed by the criminal law, civil actions in tort and sports' disciplinary tribunals; and the emergence of a much more sophisticated approach to sports injuries in negligence cases.[78]

Barnes provided the perfect opportunity to clarify the law on consent and its application to contact sports. The defendant performed what was described by the prosecution as a crushing, reckless challenge that was tantamount to stamping on the outstretched leg of the victim, seriously injuring his right ankle and tibia. The defence argued that this was a hard but fair sliding tackle and that any injury caused was accidental. In his summing up, Judge van der Bijl explained to the jury that the challenge would be criminal if it was 'so reckless that it could not have been in legitimate sport' or was 'over and above what is generally acceptable in a football game' and that they should concentrate on the 'quality of the challenge' in the context of a football match. The jury sought further clarification of these terms, which the judge attempted to provide by reiterating his previous explanations. *Barnes* was convicted and appealed, in particular on the grounds that the phrase 'legitimate sport' had not been explained adequately to the jury.

Lord Woolf CJ began his judgment by addressing the appropriateness of resorting to the criminal law to resolve sports disputes and the problem of concurrent jurisdiction.[79] He reiterated that sporting activities are in general lawful, but that prosecution should be resorted to only where the conduct was 'sufficiently grave' to be properly categorised as criminal. For the most part, however, it is 'undesirable that there should be any criminal proceedings' and recourse should instead be had to a sport's internal disciplinary proceedings and/or the civil law.[80] This position has been reinforced by the introduction of an agreement between the Crown Prosecution Service, Association of Chief Police Officers, Football Association and Football Association of Wales that locates primary jurisdiction for on-field assaults with the football authorities.[81]

On the main issue, the Court held that the concept of 'legitimate sport' was not of itself unhelpful, but that it had not been explained sufficiently by the trial judge.[82] Despite the case 'calling out' for the jury to be given help, the Court of Appeal did not provide that additional explanation and instead referred to actions that were, 'anticipated in a normal game of football', or were 'something quite outside what could be expected to occur' and were therefore

---

78 Mark James, 'Player violence and compensation for injury' in J Anderson, (ed), *Leading Cases in Sports Law* (Asser Press, 2013) ch 20.

79 *Barnes* (n 16) [4]–[5].

80 Such an approach is contingent on the robustness of a sport's disciplinary procedures. See Jack Anderson, 'Policing the sports field: the role of the criminal law' [2005] 2 ISLR 25 for a discussion of the mishandling of an incident by a governing body that resulted in a criminal prosecution.

81 *Agreement on the handling of incidents falling under both criminal and football regulatory jurisdiction*, art.5, available at: <http://www.cps.gov.uk/publications/agencies/football_agreement_30_09_2015.pdf> accessed 28 October 2015.

82 *Barnes* (n 16) [28].

'sufficiently grave' to consider prosecution. The Court provided no further explanation of any of these new terms in judging the inadequacy of the trial judge's use of 'legitimate sport'. The lack of a justification for the differential treatment of sport and the failure to provide a single, authoritative approach, remain key criticisms of *Barnes*, though the incorporation of the Canadian 'playing culture' approach to determine whether a challenge is lawful adds some clarity.[83] Perhaps the most confusing aspect of the case, however, was the refusal to apply its new approach to the facts before it, or to submit the case for retrial on the basis of the playing culture approach, which could have provided the necessary clarification of the law.

Subsequent commentators have attempted to provide that missing clarity. For example, Anderson argues that where the injuring player's conduct is within the bounds of what one would *reasonably foresee* as a physical hazard of the game, the violent act is authorised and will not expose the perpetrator to criminal liability. Conversely, participants cannot be taken to consent to injuries caused by intentional and/or reckless acts of violence or behaviour beyond that which is *ordinarily incidental* to the playing of the game in question.[84] On a more cautionary note, whilst the playing culture approach promotes prosecutorial discretion, certainty of approach is sacrificed,[85] a position that is exacerbated by each new court using new terminology to define the acceptability or otherwise of the injurious conduct.

A WORKABLE MODEL FOR CONSENT IN SPORTS LAW: IS IT ACHIEVABLE?

The failure of the English courts to provide a consistent framework for determining the scope of consent in contact sports has spawned a number of attempts to provide a working model. Sports-specific approaches have been developed by McCutcheon and Anderson. The former proposes that only injuries caused by intentional or reckless breaches of a game's 'safety rules' should be criminal.[86] By focusing on the intent to act dangerously by breaching a safety rule, rather than the intent to inflict bodily harm, a flexible test that acknowledges the fundamental characteristics of contact sports and the aims of the criminal law can be developed. The advantage of this approach is that criminality is determined by the act, not its consequences, subject to the residual power of the criminal law to declare unlawful any contacts that are contrary to the public interest. Anderson develops the principle of implied sporting consent by combining the approaches of *Cey* and its progeny and *Barnes* but requiring the court to take into particular consideration the playing culture of a sport and that actions 'in the heat of the moment' might not reach the required level of criminality.[87] Both approaches are sympathetic to the needs of contact sports and juries by providing more detail on how to determine the legality of a particular act through a contextual analysis based on the way that any given sport is actually played.

An alternative approach has been to develop typologies that distinguish between different levels of interpersonal contact that can be used as guides for determining the legality of a particular challenge. The most recent of these reviews previous analyses of 'sports violence' by dividing challenges into routine contacts, immoderate violence and ultra-violence.[88]

---

83 ibid [12]–[14].

84 Anderson (n 69) 31.

85 Ben Livings, '"Legitimate sport" or criminal assault? What are the roles of the rules and the rule-makers in determining criminal liability for violence on the sports field?' (2006) 70(6) Journal of Criminal Law 495, 501.

86 McCutcheon (n 18) 79–80.

87 Anderson (n 15) 762.

88 Fogel (n 2) 14.

Although providing detailed definitions of the different levels of interpersonal contact expected from participation in sport, and a compelling soundbite, these approaches add little to the playing culture theory. Challenges are deemed criminal only where the conduct is outside the safety rules and playing culture of the sport, committed recklessly or with intent and where serious long-term bodily harm results.[89]

A more generalist approach has informed attempts to reconstruct consent on a less category-based perspective. In her review of *Lee*,[90] Tolmie discusses a tripartite approach.[91] At the first level, the consent of the victim operates as a defence where the defendant intends or is reckless as to causing actual bodily harm. Secondly, there is a presumption in favour of consent operating as a defence where grievous bodily harm is intended or subjectively risked. For this category, the court must balance the personal autonomy of the injured person to choose to be harmed against any relevant public policy factors. Thirdly, consent is no defence where death is intended or subjectively risked. Where sport is being played in accordance with its playing culture, the vast majority of sports assaults would be consensual at level one. Level two contacts would be consensual where the playing culture of the sport was examined as part the public policy balancing exercise and had been adhered to. Although rare in contact sports, level three would justify conviction of those whose high risk conduct was outside of the playing culture of the sport.[92]

A compelling alternative approach would, in effect, change the burden of proof when determining the utility of an activity. At present, the defendant is required to justify that an activity ought to be exempted on the basis of public policy and/or social utility considerations. Where consensual activities are concerned, their lawfulness should be presumed unless the prosecution is able to provide persuasive reasons for their prohibition. Under this social disutility model, consent will be generally effective up to the level of grievous bodily harm.[93] Such an approach would render the majority of sports assaults consensual, but ultimately still makes legality contingent on the seriousness of the harm caused.

Without the final modifier, the social disutility model provides a sound theoretical justification for the treatment of contact sports. The presumption would be that all contacts performed in sport would be lawful, unless the prosecution could prove that they should be prohibited. To do this, reference would have to be made to the social benefits of sport and the playing culture of the sport in question. Only where the prosecution could prove that the stated benefits of sports participation were not achieved by a particular sporting activity, or that the injury-causing act was beyond the playing culture of the sport and was therefore outside the scope of the athletes' operative deemed consent, would conviction be appropriate.

CONCLUSION

Despite the universal acceptance that physical challenges performed as an integral part of participation in contact sports ought to be treated differently by the law, the underlying justification for this exceptional position has never been fully articulated. Further, the scope and extent of the exception granted to such challenges lacks clarity, in particular through the

---

89 ibid 24.

90 *R v Lee* (2006) 22 CRNZ 568 (CA).

91 Julia Tolmie, 'Consent to harmful assaults: the case for moving away from category based decision making' [2012] Criminal Law Review 656, 658. For a similar approach based on 'tolerated activities' see Simon Cooper and Mark James, 'Entertainment – the painful process of rethinking consent' [2012] 3 Criminal Law Review 188.

92 For example, the successful manslaughter case in *R v CC* [2009] ONCJ 249.

93 David Kell, 'Social disutility and consent' [1994] Oxford Journal of Legal Studies 121, 127.

use of constantly changing definitional terminology. A definitive list of what is and what is not acceptable, has not been developed and is in reality likely only to create further confusion. In its current form, the law is sufficiently flexible to deal with different acts, in different sports involving players of different standards. Regardless of the formulation used, however, the courts and commentators appear to be trying to conceptualise an instinctive reaction, perhaps best encapsulated by 'a sharp intake of breath,' to the unacceptability of a challenge to contemporary society.

The treatment of sport by the law can be justified by the approaches of all of the main sports law and generalist commentators on consent. Whether using a generalised uniformly applicable approach, or one that allows for a low threshold of harm coupled with exempted categories of activity as is currently the case, the key issue for athletes is to be able to determine which acts and which contacts can be consented to and which cannot. The development of the 'playing culture' concept from *Cey* and *Barnes* enables the lawfulness of sports contacts to be determined and to which an athlete can be deemed to consent. Criminality will, therefore, only attach to actions that deliberately or recklessly go beyond the playing culture of the sport in question.

Following the clarification of the law in *Barnes*, participants consent to the contacts expected from and accepted as necessary for the playing of that particular sport. Where that consent is operative, athletes voluntarily run the risk that injuries may be suffered as a result of such lawful contacts as these are dangers inherent in participating in that sport. The justification for this exemption is that sport is socially beneficial because it promotes health, exercise, teamwork and fair play. Further, as there is no social disutility in allowing consent to these acts, the burden of proof should be on the prosecution to demonstrate why a particular challenge, or aspect of a sport, is no longer achieving its socially beneficial claims.

12

Finding free agreement
The meaning of consent in sexual offences in Scots criminal law

*Claire McDiarmid**

INTRODUCTION

Sexual offending is an area in which the stakes are high. On the one hand, legal processes following on an initial allegation often cause distress to complainers.[1] On the other, the label of 'sex offender' is one of the most stigmatising that can be attached in contemporary society[2] and conviction should therefore not be brought about lightly.[3] It is clear that an integrated approach across a number of agencies[4] at the levels of policy, practice and law is required.[5] Within this matrix, the substantive criminal law is, at best, only one strand and it has been noted that isolated reform of its principles 'unhelpfully abstracts it from its complex courtroom context'.[6] Nonetheless, criminal law is still a fundamental element of that matrix and the importance of clear, well-publicised, workable definitions of individual sex offences is obvious. Central to such definitions in Scots law, as in other jurisdictions, is consent.

In law, the presence or absence of consent constitutes the dividing line between commission of a serious sexual assault and no crime at all. As such, it is a transformative concept and

---

* Reader, Law School, University of Strathclyde.

1 For example, a 22-year-old woman who was required to hold up in court the underwear she was wearing at the time of the alleged offence made a suicide attempt days later sparking a review by the then Scottish Justice Secretary: Auslan Cramb, 'Woman "had to Hold up Underwear in Rape Trial" *The Daily Telegraph* (London, 7 October 2011) 15. Research supports this view of the traumatising effects: see Michele Burman, 'Evidencing Sexual Assault: Women in the Witness Box' (2009) 56 Probation Journal 379.

2 See, for example, Daniel Marshall and Terry Thomas, 'Polygraphs and Sex Offenders' (2015) 179(26) Criminal Law & Justice Weekly 546.

3 See Laura Hoyano, 'Reforming the Adversarial Trial for Vulnerable Witnesses and Defendants' [2015] Criminal Law Review 107.

4 For example, the police as investigators and, frequently, first responders; the Crown Office and Procurator Fiscal Service as public prosecutors and Third Sector organisations such as Rape Crisis.

5 For an incisive overview of the current situation across these areas see Sandy Brindley and Michele Burman, 'Meeting the Challenge? Responding to Rape in Scotland' in Nicole Westmarland and Geetanjali Gangoli (eds), *International Approaches to Rape* (Policy Press 2011).

6 Sharon Cowan, 'All Change or Business as Usual?: Reforming the Law of Rape in Scotland' in Clare McGlynn and Vanessa E Munro (eds), *Rethinking Rape Law: International and Comparative Perspectives* (Routledge Glasshouse 2010) 165. The point is made in relation to the Scottish Law Commission's work on rape and other sexual offences, on which the current Scottish legislation is based.

considerable importance attaches – or certainly should attach – to it. Heidi Hurd has identified its role as 'moral magic'[7] – because it 'can function to transform the morality of another's
conduct – to make an action right when it would otherwise be wrong'.[8] For example, '[b]y
consenting to another's touch, one puts that person at liberty to do what it was antecedently
obligatory of her not to do.'[9] If properly and carefully defined and applied then, consent
brings together the parties to sexual activity before and during their encounter so that it
proceeds as agreed by, and understood between, them. Unfortunately, however, its treatment
in Scots law has often been superficial and minimal so that its transformative quality has not
been obvious.

This chapter traces the history and evolution of the concept in sex offences considering
particularly its theoretical shift from a word to be given its ordinary meaning, to (through the
work of the Scottish Law Commission) a model with its own statutory definition ('free agreement') in terms of the current law – the Sexual Offences (Scotland) Act 2009 (asp 9) ('the 2009
Act'). It will touch upon the way in which consent is now embedded within the crime of rape
and other sexual offences. Finally, it examines critically the (few) cases which have considered
the definition of consent since the 2009 Act came into force on 1 December 2010. Overall,
it argues that the law did metamorphose positively with the passage of this Act and that its
potential is evident however the pre-existing, rather unconsidered, approach still casts a long
shadow so that the full promise of the new legislative arrangements is not being realised.

THE EVOLUTION OF CONSENT IN SCOTS CRIMINAL LAW

Given the centrality of consent to the current law on sexual offences, it is helpful briefly to
trace its legal history. With regard to rape specifically, it is arguable that Scots law 'remained
problematically archaic'[10] for rather longer than the law in other jurisdictions in that it
continued largely to disregard the consent of the complainer altogether in establishing the
commission of, at least, the *actus reus* of the offence.

Rape was originally constituted by penile (only) penetration of the vagina (only), which
was carried out 'against the will' of the complainer. This required her utmost resistance as can
be seen from the explanation given, in 1844, by the Scottish institutional writer, Baron David
Hume, which, in 2002, the High Court of Justiciary took as '[t]he starting point in the history
of the law of rape'.[11] Hume defined it in these terms:

> The knowledge of the woman's person must be against her will, and by force. So that
> though she be carried off by violence at first, and even detained in some measure in
> a state of confinement and distress; yet, if in the end, being weakened in mind, and
> shaken with continual solicitation and importunity, she submit to the embraces of her
> companion without any use of threats or violence at the time, or recently before; this
> is not a rape, but a crime of a different though perhaps a still more base and flagitious
> description. The resistance must, therefore, be continued to the last; so that it is by main
> force only and terror that the violation is accomplished.[12]

---

7 Heidi M Hurd, 'The Moral Magic of Consent' (1996) 2 Legal Theory 121.
8 ibid 123.
9 ibid 124.
10 Cowan (n 6) 155.
11 *Lord Advocate's Reference No 1 of 2001* [2002] SLT 466, 4 (Cullen LJ-G).
12 Baron David Hume, *Commentaries on the Law of Scotland, Respecting Crimes* (vol I, 4th edition, The Law
Society of Scotland 1986, reprint 1844) 302.

This translated into the need for force (with the likely concomitant that the victim would be beaten), or, in relatively recent times, at least the threat of force.[13] Consent was not necessarily irrelevant even in the nineteenth century,[14] but the use of force, as demonstrating that the will had been overcome, was the critical factor.

In the case law of the late twentieth and the very early twenty-first centuries, these principles continued to apply. Consent was present in the case reports in that the accused's lack of an honest belief in the complainer's consent was a key element of the *mens rea*,[15] and, indeed, on occasion, some *obiter* comments might have suggested that its absence was definitive;[16] however the context was always that of overcoming the will and the crime was not constituted without evidence of this.

In contrast, the crime of indecent assault operated alongside rape. Because of rape's narrow definition, this separate offence – whether regarded as a crime in its own right[17] or as assault aggravated by circumstances of indecency – swept up many incidences of sexual attack including some involving no force but clear absence of consent on the part of the complainer.[18] Thus, consent constituted the dividing line between lawful behaviour (sexual touching to which both parties assented) and offending. While the courts applied some of the same principles across both crimes,[19] consent was central to indecent assault but not – or not necessarily – to rape.

The starkness, and limitations of the 'against her will' definition of rape were thrown into sharp relief in 2001 when a judge upheld a plea of no case to answer put forward by an accused in a rape trial on the basis that lack of consent was irrelevant if the accused had not employed force or the threat of force to overcome the complainer's will. This – rightly – generated outcry at the state of Scots law, particularly given that the complainer gave evidence that she had verbally stated her lack of consent by saying to the accused at the time of the incident 'No, stop, I don't want this'.[20] In response to the judgment, the Lord Advocate exercised his power to refer a point of law for clarification to the High Court of Justiciary.[21] His petition raised four questions for the court's consideration, including 'Did the trial judge err in holding that to have sexual intercourse with a woman without her consent is not rape?'[22]

A bench of seven judges was convened to deliver an authoritative judgment. By a majority of five to two[23] it determined that 'the general rule is that the actus reus of rape is constituted by the man having sexual intercourse with the woman without her consent'.[24] While it is submitted that this was, undoubtedly, the 'right' outcome in a moral and social sense, its

---

13 For example *Barbour v HM Advocate* [1982] SCCR 195.

14 See, for example, the terms of the indictment in *Charles Sweenie* [1858] 3 Irvine 109.

15 See, for example, *Meek v HM Advocate* [1983] SLT 280.

16 For example, 'the jury probably would have appreciated that if they held that the complainer was intoxicated and was for a period inclined to indulge in sexual intercourse which she soon regretted, that meant that she had consented, in which event there could be no question of the appellant being convicted of rape': *W v HM Advocate* [1995] SLT 685, 687 (Ross LJ-C).

17 See Timothy H Jones and Michael G A Christie, *Criminal Law* (2nd edn, W 1996) 9–19.

18 See for example *Young v McGlennan* [1991] SCCR 738.

19 For example an honest belief in the complainer's consent was sufficient to vitiate the *mens rea* of both crimes. There was no requirement for such a belief to be held on reasonable grounds. See *Peace v HM Advocate* [2003] SLT 419.

20 See Susan Lumsden, '"Rape Victim' Said: No Stop I Do Not Want This' *The Sun* (24 March 2001).

21 Criminal Procedure (Scotland) Act 1995 (c 46), s 123.

22 *Lord Advocate's Reference No 1 of 2001* (n 11).

23 Lords Marnoch and McCluskey dissenting.

24 *Lord Advocate's Reference No 1 of 2001* (n 11) 44 (Cullen LJ-G).

constitutional legality was questioned in the dissenting judgments[25] and the Scottish ministers referred the whole area to the Scottish Law Commission in June 2004. In January 2006, it produced its *Discussion Paper on Rape and Other Sexual Offences*[26] followed, in December 2007 by its *Report*[27] on the basis of which, in 2009, the Scottish Government passed the Sexual Offences (Scotland) Act 2009 (asp 9).

THE USE AND MEANING OF CONSENT AT COMMON LAW

Until 2009, in common with most other areas of Scots criminal law – for example, homicide, assault and theft – sexual offending was unlegislated and therefore defined in, and developed exclusively through, case law. Consent was not regarded as in any way technical or, indeed, as requiring any explanation whatsoever in a legal sense for a lay audience. This is clear from the response of both the trial judge and, subsequently the appeal court, to a question from a jury as to its meaning in a 1996 indecent assault case.[28]

The sheriff advised the jury as follows:

> The definition of consent is a common, straightforward definition of consent. It's the common English word given its normal meaning. And that I am afraid is it. Consent is consent. What does consent mean? Is that the only question you have? Thank you very much.[29]

The appeal court did, however, slightly expand:

> The important thing appears to us to be this, that the jury were obviously enquiring whether the word 'consent' had a legal or special meaning and what the sheriff did was to explain to them that it had no legal or special meaning, but that the word 'consent' simply had to be given its ordinary meaning. We recognise that the sheriff might have decided in the face of this request to use some synonym for consent and, for example, tell the jury that they must look for agreement, but we are not persuaded that it was necessary for her to do so. What was important was that she made it plain to the jury that the word 'consent' had no special meaning in law but required to be given its normal meaning.[30]

This then could be taken as the starting point in modern Scots law. It is chiefly of interest for how little consideration consent as a *concept* was deemed to merit and for the dismissive judicial response to the suggestion that it might be more technically defined.[31] Consent was one-dimensional. It was simply a word and it was not to be applied in any specialised way to

---

25 ibid 12 (Lord Marnoch); 4, 7, 16, 22 and 24 (Lord McCluskey). The separation of powers requires that judges only interpret and do not 'make' law.
26 Scottish Law Commission, *Discussion Paper on Rape and other Sexual Offences* (Scot Law Com DP No 131, 2006).
27 Scottish Law Commission, *Report on Rape and Other Sexual Offences* (Scot Law Com No 209, 2007).
28 *Marr* v *HM Advocate* [1996] SCCR 696.
29 ibid 699 (Sheriff Cowan) at the trial and quoted by Ross LJ-C.
30 ibid 699 (Ross LJ-C).
31 This is further borne out by the fact that the case is also covered in the *Justiciary Cases* and *Scots Law Times* series of reports but neither regards this definitional point as worthy of reporting. The SLT report [1996] SLT 1035 omits it altogether. The JC report states only that 'Their Lordships thereafter dealt with matters with which this report is not concerned' [1996] JC 199, 202.

the actual on-the-ground encounter between the parties. This is perhaps emblematic of one of the particular difficulties with consent in sexual offences in Scots law – that it seems to be more important to know (and for courts faced with consent issues to determine) whether or not it has been given than clearly to define it.

There is some evolution in the judicial approach in the Lord Justice-General's judgment in the *Lord Advocate's Reference*[32] where he stated that 'the absence of the woman's "consent" refers to a lack of active consent, as opposed to mere submission or permission'.[33] While this recognises that consent is something more than 'just a word', it is not unproblematic in that it rests to some extent in a model that suggests that the responsibility for consent within the incident under scrutiny rests with the complainer,[34] albeit that it does not diminish it to the near vanishing point of 'mere permission'.[35] It is from these beginnings, then, that the Scottish Law Commission's consideration of consent, which will now be considered, proceeded.

FINDING FREE AGREEMENT

In its *Report*, the Scottish Law Commission consistently refers to a consent 'model'[36] or to the 'concept of consent'.[37] This indicates that consent is more than a word. It also, helpfully, recognises that there is not one single model but a number to choose between.[38] Ultimately, the following was proposed:

> The model of consent which we proposed was an 'active' (or positive) type as opposed to a passive model. On an active understanding of consent to sexual conduct the basic principle is that both participants in sexual activity should respect each other's sexual autonomy and each is equally active in reaching agreement on their sexual relations. In determining whether agreement has been given to a particular sexual act a court or jury should look at the whole background circumstances. The primary question should be 'what did all the parties do to ensure that they participated in a fully consensual act?' The focus of enquiry would be not only on the behaviour of the victim but on the actions of the accused in the process of reaching agreement on consent.[39]

---

32 (n 11).

33 ibid [39] (Cullen LJ-G).

34 At the time, rape was a gender-specific crime in Scots law and the victim had to be female.

35 For discussion of models placing responsibility on one party, see Michelle J Anderson, 'Negotiating Sex' (2005) 78 Southern California Law Review 1401, 1404–1407; 1409–1421.

36 Scottish Law Commission (n 27) for example 2.1, 2.6, 2.10, 2.11 and 2.12.

37 ibid 2.6. It is interesting that, in its response to the Commission's *Discussion Paper* (n 26) the judges of the High Court of Justiciary took the view that consent was 'not a concept [but rather] (...) a matter of fact which we think can be readily understood by juries in a range of different circumstances' (Scottish Law Commission (n 27) 2.21); (n 17).

38 Reference is made to 'consent *models*' (emphasis added) ibid 2.6.

39 ibid 2.24. In fact, this paragraph summarises the approach put forward in the *Discussion Paper* (n 26) but the Scottish Law Commission did not depart from that in its final recommendations in the *Report*. It also noted these further advantages of such a model: 'However, a model which locates consent in the interaction between the parties avoids this problem [of relying on one party expressly verbalising their consent]. Giving consent is not simply a matter of making a particular verbal utterance. It is rather something which emerges from what the parties do and say to each other. The result is that the focus of attention is moved away from the victim, and towards what both parties did to bring about consent. In particular, it allows the law to adopt the position that if one person wants to have sex with another, and there is any doubt that the other person is consenting, then the obvious step to take is to ask' 2.27.

In its *Policy Memorandum* on the Bill preceding the Sexual Offences (Scotland) Act 2009 (asp 9),[40] the Scottish Government stated that it was 'persuaded by the [Scottish Law Commission's] conclusions on this issue and the approach taken to the definition of "consent" and associated issues in Part Two of the Bill is the same as that contained in the [Scottish Law Commission's] final report and draft Bill'.[41] This then passed into s 12 of the Act. Accordingly, the Scottish Law Commission's view of consent can be said to underlie the current law.

In theory, there are notable benefits arising from the adoption of this approach. As the *Report* states, both parties are now to be involved in freely agreeing with each other to undertake any relevant sexual activity rather than that responsibility resting solely on the (ultimate) complainer. The act(s) itself is to be considered embedded in the context of the whole 'background circumstances'. Application of this model requires not that a court should ask whether, at an exact, given moment in the course of a relationship or of an encounter that may have lasted hours, consent had been given[42] (a 'snapshot')[43] but rather that the act is situated within the overall actings of the parties over a period of time that led each to consider that 'free agreement' had been reached.[44] Consent is 'given', usually by only one party, the (ultimate) complainer. Agreement is 'reached' between both. Before proceeding to look at the application of this new concept of consent, it is important to clarify exactly how it has been incorporated into the 2009 Act.

THE SEXUAL OFFENCES (SCOTLAND) ACT 2009 (ASP 9)

The Sexual Offences (Scotland) Act 2009 (asp 9) now structures much of the Scots law on sexual offences. Indeed, it marks a departure even simply by its codification of many sexual offences[45] out of their case law roots and into statutory form. Consent is immediately central. Part 1 identifies and defines nine offences: rape (s 1); sexual assault by penetration (s 2); sexual assault (s 3); sexual coercion (s 4); coercing a person into being present during a sexual activity (s 5); coercing a person into looking at a sexual image (s 6); communicating indecently (s 7); sexual exposure (s 8); and voyeurism (s 9), which are constituted partly by their commission 'without another person ('B') [ie the complainer] consenting and without any reasonable belief [on the accused's part] that B consents'.

Taken out of context, this formulation – 'without B consenting' – might suggest a return to a model where the complainer takes sole responsibility for permitting (or not) the sexual activity. The use of the term 'consent*ing*' (rather than just 'consent') does, however, help to move the issue away from the 'snapshot' approach towards a recognition of the ongoing nature of the types of sexual encounters covered. Moreover, consent is now a defined term ('free agreement') in terms of s 12. This ought to mean that this definition is considered in

---

40 SP Bill 11 Policy Memorandum on Sexual Offences (Scotland) Bill [as introduced] (2008).

41 ibid 70.

42 The appeal in the case of *McKearney v HM Advocate* [2004] JC 87 was successful partly because the appeal court accepted that 'one view of the facts that the jury might have properly taken was that the sexual activity leading to full intercourse was a separate chapter of events from those involving violence and menacing behaviour on the part of the appellant' [34] (Lord McCluskey). This was despite the fact that all events took place over a single night.

43 See Sharon Cowan, 'Choosing Freely: Theoretically Reframing the Concept of Consent' in Rosemary Hunter and Sharon Cowan (eds), *Choice and Consent: Feminist Engagements with Law and Subjectivity* (Routledge-Cavendish (Glasshouse) 2007) 101.

44 This is similar to the 'negotiation model' propounded by Anderson (n 35) 1421–1427.

45 It is not a complete codification. For example, incest is covered by the Criminal Law (Consolidation) Act 1995 (c 9), s 1. It remains possible to prosecute for the common law crime of public indecency (see, for example, *McNair v Murphy* [2015] HCJAC 61).

all cases under ss 1–9 so that a nuanced legal understanding of its meaning emerges. After all, statutes regularly define terms of which citizens and lawyers might well think they know the meaning without further guidance. Examples include 'museum';[46] 'parent' (which has different meanings in different Acts);[47] and 'marriage'.[48] Where these concepts are of relevance in any case – and consent is immediately relevant to the nine sexual offences identified above – courts must engage the correct definition. They cannot fall back on their own 'common-sense' understanding. Defining 'consent' within the statute therefore invites consideration of the way in which that definition changes or adds depth to the term in a general sense and also requires that the meaning of consent as 'free agreement' is considered in individual cases.

Overall, then, this is now a critical element of the individual offences set down in ss 1–9, and s 13 goes on to provide an inexhaustive list of six situations in which consent is automatically deemed to be absent.[49] The Scottish Law Commission clearly envisaged that this legislation would be animated and refined by subsequent judicial decision.[50] It will therefore be interesting now to consider the way in which, and the extent to which, this has, in fact, happened.

THE POST-2009 DEVELOPMENT OF THE LAW

Writing in 2010 on the prospects for the Sexual Offences (Scotland) Act 2009 (asp 9), Sharon Cowan commented:

> it is not clear that much judicial contemplation or brow-furrowing will in fact occur over the meaning of 'free agreement'. Arguably courts will continue to operate with the 'common-sense' definition of consent that they have always used, without a philosophical foray into the precise meanings of 'freedom' and 'capacity'.[51]

In some respects, this was prescient. It is initially noticeable how few *reported* cases deal with these issues at all – only two seem to have cited the general 'free agreement' definition

---

46 Defined in the Air Weapons and Licensing (Scotland) Act 2015 (asp 10), s 40(1).
47 Defined in the Children (Scotland) Act 1995 (c 36), s 15(1) and, differently, in the Education (Scotland) Act 1980 (c 44), s 135.
48 Defined in the Marriage and Civil Partnership (Scotland) Act 2014 (asp 5), s 4.
49 Sexual Offences (Scotland) Act 2009 (asp 9), s 13 provides as follows:

(1) For the purposes of section 12, but without prejudice to the generality of that section, free agreement to conduct is absent in the circumstances set out in subsection (2).
(2) Those circumstances are:
  (a) where the conduct occurs at a time when B is incapable because of the effect of alcohol or any other substance of consenting to it,
  (b) where B agrees or submits to the conduct because of violence used against B or any other person, or because of threats of violence made against B or any other person,
  (c) where B agrees or submits to the conduct because B is unlawfully detained by A,
  (d) where B agrees or submits to the conduct because B is mistaken, as a result of deception by A, as to the nature or purpose of the conduct,
  (e) where B agrees or submits to the conduct because A induces B to agree or submit to the conduct by impersonating a person known personally to B, or
  (f) where the only expression or indication of agreement to the conduct is from a person other than B.
(3) References in this section to A and to B are to be construed in accordance with sections 1 to 9.
[In effect, A is the accused and B is the complainer.]

50 Scottish Law Commission (n 27) 2.60.
51 Cowan (n 6) 162.

of consent in s 12[52] and a further two cite directly s 13 and its situations of deemed lack of consent.[53] This certainly suggests that the new definitions have not occupied a great deal of judicial thought or innovation. Also, within this small number, there are instances where the issues surrounding consent appear to have grown or changed little beyond their common law characterisations.

Taking the Scottish Law Commission's model as the basis, remarks of the trial judge in a sexual assault case seem to come closest to capturing a meaning of free agreement as a dynamic arrangement between both parties but these are brief, of little value as precedent and given in the context of explaining to the jury how it was to determine if there was a reasonable belief on the part of the accused in the complainers' consent, rather than as a definition of consent as free agreement *per se*. Nonetheless, they are worth quoting:

> But a reasonable belief is not the same thing as an honest belief, the belief must be held on reasonable grounds. So how do you judge that? *Well, you look at what the facts tell you about the interaction between the victim and the accused, and a shared understanding of what was happening.*[54]

Free agreement on the Scottish Law Commission model *should* look at the interaction between the complainer and the accused and at their shared understanding (if any can be divined) of the events in which they were participating. Even this brief statement offers a relatively rich approach to consent. Other cases unfortunately seem to offer slimmer pickings in this respect. Cases citing s 12 (which provides that '*consent*' means 'free agreement'[55] will be considered first.

(a) Section 12 of the Sexual Offences (Scotland) Act 2009 (asp 9)

In *Van Der Schyff v HM Advocate*,[56] (another sexual assault charge) the term 'free agreement' appears only in a quote from the trial judge's charge to the jury summarising ss 12 and 13: 'Now, consent, let me tell you what the Act says in terms. It says, "consent means free agreement" and just so that we're in no doubt, it goes on to say "circumstances in which conduct takes place without free agreement".'[57] Here, then, free agreement is not used to contextualise the interaction between the parties or even to add nuance, depth or explanation to the term 'consent'. The case turned, essentially, on whether the jury accepted the complainer's evidence that, despite being roused from sleep and in a state of drink-enhanced drowsiness, she had not consented to any sexual touching, or whether it preferred the accused's account, which was that, at least, he had had a reasonable belief[58] in her consent.[59] The court stated the relevant issues as follows:

> The Crown had to establish, in terms of the statutory provision, and as the sheriff correctly directed the jury, that: the appellant had deliberately touched the complainer

---

52 *Mutebi v HM Advocate* [2013] HCJAC 142; *Van Der Schyff v HM Advocate* [2015] HCJAC 67.

53 *HM Advocate v Hutchison* [2013] HCJAC 91; *Drummond v HM Advocate* [2015] HCJAC 30.

54 *Dempster v HMA* [2012] HCJAC 140 [7] (Carloway LJ-C) quoting trial judge (emphasis added).

55 Italicisation and quotation marks in original.

56 *Van Der Schyff v HM Advocate* (n 52).

57 ibid [8].

58 At common law, the accused only had to hold a 'genuine' belief in consent. The Sexual Offences (Scotland) Act 2009 (asp 9) moved to the requirement of 'reasonable' belief.

59 *Van Der Schyff v HM Advocate* (n 52) [13]. The jury convicted the accused and that decision was upheld on appeal.

sexually (which is not in dispute); the complainer had not consented to the touching (which is what the complainer's evidence was); and the appellant did not reasonably believe that she had consented.[60]

This is a reasonable summary of the bald terms of s 3 of the Sexual Offences (Scotland) Act 2009 (asp 9) but it offers nothing in relation to deepening the legal understanding of consent. Other than using the 'free agreement' term, and referring to a reasonable (rather than a genuine) belief in consent on the accused's part, these categories are virtually unchanged from the way in which such allegations would have been conceptualised under the pre-existing common law. There will be difficulties with the Scottish Law Commission's free agreement model where two diametrically opposed accounts are given since it is rooted in the (mutual) reaching of that agreement; however there was certainly scope within this case to offer fuller discussion of the term thereby recognising its centrality to the post-2009 Act law.

The other case citing s 12 (and s 13), *Mutebi v HM Advocate*,[61] is also concerned with intoxicated consent,[62] an issue which the Scottish Law Commission addressed. In recommending that extreme intoxication on the complainer's part should constitute one situation in which consent is deemed automatically to be absent, it said:

> [such a provision's] particular value is that it sends a signal that anyone dealing with someone who is intoxicated is put on notice that that person may not be able to give consent to sex no matter what she says or does. The definition also helps in countering any social stereotype that people who are drunk, especially young women, are by that very fact consenting to sex and are to shoulder the full blame for any unwanted sex which follows (they are 'asking for it').[63]

In *Mutebi* the complainer was a 25-year-old female post-graduate student. In the early part of the evening she had been drinking in a friend's flat. She had later gone to a club where she had consumed more alcohol. CCTV footage of her leaving there showed her sitting on the pavement, scrabbling to find her dropped mobile phone and then walking away unsteadily. Her testimony about the subsequent sexual activity was that 'it was well possible that she had consented at the outset to intercourse; she could not remember one way or the other'.[64] Both of these pieces of evidence suggest extreme intoxication, which is, it would appear, exactly the state for which the Scottish Law Commission sought to provide some protection. In the end, however, the jury did not accept that she was 'incapable' of consenting. Accordingly, s 13(2)(a)[65] could not be applied to deem consent completely absent on the ground of intoxicated incapacity. The jury still returned a guilty verdict, which the accused appealed.

In addition to the evidence of the complainer's drunkenness, the further facts were that the accused was a stranger to the complainer. He testified that they were both drunk when they met, at some point on her journey from the club. They shared a taxi back to her flat. She had only two further memories of the night before waking to find the accused lying on top

---

60 ibid [13] (Carloway LJ-C).
61 *Mutebi* (n 52)
62 Sharon Cowan, 'The Trouble with Drink: Intoxication, (In)Capacity, and the Evaporation of Consent to Sex' (2008) 41 Akron Law Review 899.
63 Scottish Law Commission (n 27) 2.62; The Sexual Offences (Scotland) Act 2009 (asp 9), s 13(2)(a) contains the resulting provision (n 49).
64 *Mutebi v HM Advocate* (n 52) [2].
65 Sexual Offences (Scotland) Act 2009 (asp 9), s 13 (n 49)

of her. The first was of kissing him at the door of the close (or entryway) into her building. The second was of being in the bathroom of the flat. She stated that, subsequently, she woke up, naked in her own bed alongside the appellant who was also naked and who was lying on top of her penetrating her vagina with his penis. She told him 'no' and was then able to wriggle clear, estimating that he had continued in his actions for about 20 seconds after she indicated that she wanted him to stop. In these circumstances, having ruled out the application of s 13(2)(a), and knowing that the jury had, by its guilty verdict accepted that there was an absence of consent and of reasonable belief in its existence, there was certainly scope for the appeal court to examine the terms of s 12.

Instead, similarly to *Van Der Schyff v HM Advocate*, the term 'free agreement' is only stated once in the case report, and only as a technical definition, where it says '[s]ection 12 of the [Sexual Offences Act] 2009 Act [(asp 9)] provides that "consent" means "free agreement"'.[66] The appeal proceeded on the basis that the only point in issue was whether there was corroboration of the complainer's 'withdrawal of consent and the appellant's persistence in the sexual intercourse, knowing of the revocation of consent or recklessness as to whether it continued'[67] for the 20-second period following the complainer awakening. Thus, again, the issues seem to be pared back to resemble closely the way in which the pre-existing common law would have conceptualised the matter. The difficulty of corroborating the complainer's non-consent (though here it is now taken as *withdrawal* of consent,[68] implying that it is accepted that she initially consented), and the accused's knowledge of this, since each is personal to the complainer and the accused respectively, made common law rape hard to prove beyond reasonable doubt. The complainer's non-consent remains in issue under the current law but the Sexual Offences (Scotland) Act 2009 (asp 9) only requires no *reasonable* belief in consent on the accused's part. Thus, arguably, there is no need to know what he was actually thinking.[69] Reasonable belief means that it is what reasonable people would think which is significant. If it is not reasonable to believe that, in the circumstances, this complainer was consenting, then the fact that the accused *did* believe this to be so is irrelevant. The crime is still rape. The judgment in *Mutebi* does not clearly recognise this.

While the Crown also seemed to accept, in the end, that the issue had to be categorised as one relating to corroboration of non-consent and the accused's state of mind in relation to this, its approach held more promise for building the free agreement model which the Scottish Law Commission envisaged. It (the Crown) put forward seven factors each of which might have had something to contribute to an overarching view, in the context of the parties' whole encounter, as to whether there was free agreement to sex. These were, however, pled unsuccessfully, in pursuit of the Crown's claim that the appellant had no reasonable belief in the complainer's consent. The factors were: (1) the parties were not in a relationship; (2) the complainer was menstruating, wearing a tampon and therefore unlikely to want sex; (3) she was very intoxicated; (4) the complainer was distressed 'later in the day'; (5) the accused stole the complainer's phone and £170 as he left; (6) he left the door to her flat open on leaving;[70] and (7) the accused had given a number of differing accounts of the events of the night.[71] If

---

66 *Mutebi v HM Advocate* (n 52) [11] (Lord Brailsford).
67 ibid [13] (Lord Brailsford).
68 Sexual Offences (Scotland) Act 2009 (asp 9), s 15.
69 See Margaret Ross and James Chalmers *Walker and Walker: The Law of Evidence in Scotland* (4th edition, Bloomsbury Professional Ltd 2015) 6.7.2.
70 Though it was subsequently established that the door was broken and that he would not have been able to secure it without the key: *Mutebi v HM Advocate* (n 52) [3].
71 ibid [6].

the question is whether, over a 20-second period, any of these facts supports the contention that the accused knew that the complainer had withdrawn her consent then, clearly, as the appeal court decided, they do not.[72] If the question is instead, whether, over the whole period of the encounter, the parties reached free agreement to have sex, perhaps some are slightly more illuminating. For example, the facts that the parties were strangers, that she was under the influence of alcohol throughout and that she was menstruating[73] might suggest that more inquiry into whether she wished to have sex was required. (These facts might also assist in determining if the accused's belief in consent was reasonable, where that is couched as an objective inquiry detached from what he actually ('genuinely') thought.) Here, then, facts were presented to the court around which it could have built a more nuanced inquiry into the existence (or otherwise) of free agreement but ultimately, these were deployed in pursuit of a rather more common law query as to the accused's belief. It is important to recognise that the law has developed and changed from these older precepts.

(b) Section 13 of the Sexual Offences (Scotland) Act 2009 (asp 9)

Section 13 is a new departure for Scots law in that, for the first time, six sets of circumstances[74] are set out in which 'free agreement to conduct' is automatically deemed to be 'absent'.[75] Following the shift to the consent-based definition in the *Lord Advocate's Reference* in 2002 the law of evidence privileged 'forcible' rape, allowing *de recent* distress reported to others to be led as evidence of this form.[76] This was partly on the basis that, if the accused had had to use force, then he must have known that the victim was not consenting.[77]

Section 13 could be said to draw on this underlying notion that there are circumstances so clearly indicative of non-consent that they speak for themselves. These *include* the use, or threat, of violence[78] but another five now exist alongside:[79] the complainer's incapacity through intoxication; unlawful detention of the complainer; deception as to the nature or purpose of the sexual conduct; impersonation; and where consent is purportedly offered only by a person other than the complainer. It is certainly arguable, by analogy from the evidential position in relation to violence, that s 13 places all parties on notice that, if the accused has to resort to violence, or to detain, deceive, impersonate, accept the word of another person or take advantage of a state of intoxication then there is no free agreement. What is evident from the few cases mentioning s 13 is, however, that these factual scenarios are not easily evidenced and corroborated and the fact that they are set out in the legislation does not insulate them

---

72 ibid [13] (Lord Brailsford).
73 This issue of consent to sex while menstruating also arose in *Drummond v HMA* (n 53) where the complainer's evidence was that she gave this as a reason for not wishing to have sex. *Drummond* and *Mutebi* together at least suggest that an issue arises in these circumstances and, while it should not be assumed that no complainer would wish to have vaginal intercourse at such a time, it is not necessarily a neutral fact as to consent.
74 See (n 49) for the exact terms of s 13(2).
75 Sexual Offences (Scotland) Act 2009 (asp 9), s 13(1).
76 *F v HM Advocate* [2009] HCJAC 64. Distress has been applied more broadly than this, in circumstances where force was not used, as broadly corroborative of a lack of consent. See *Lennie v HM Advocate* [2014] HCJAC 103.
77 See Gerald H Gordon and Christopher HW Gane, *Renton and Brown Criminal Procedure* (6th edition, W Green & Son Ltd 2015) 24–71.
78 Sexual Offences (Scotland) Act 2009 (n 49), s 13(2)(b).
79 ibid, s 13(2)(a) and (c)–(f).

from either the exigencies of the law of evidence, or the way in which a jury may determine factual matters.

As discussed above, this can be seen in *Mutebi* where, despite at least some evidence of the complainer's extremely drunken state, the jury deleted from the indictment the Crown's charge that she was 'unconscious and incapable of giving or withholding consent'. While it accepted that 'she was under the influence of alcohol', this was not enough for s 13(2)(a) since the statutorily recognised circumstances require incapability.[80]

Similarly, in *Drummond v HMA*,[81] the accused was convicted at trial of charges of assault and rape. In relation to the latter, the Crown put in issue, in terms of s 13(2)(c), that '[t]he detention of the complainer was a relevant factor'[82] and recognised the seriousness of this allegation in its own right by bringing a separate charge of abduction, of which the accused was acquitted. Here again then, as in *Mutebi*, the jury negated much of the evidence of the s 13 circumstances.

Following his abduction acquittal, the accused went on to appeal his rape conviction on the basis that the trial judge should have upheld a plea of no case to answer. Because he did not directly appeal the conviction, however, the High Court was not constrained by the jury's findings but was required instead:

> to proceed on the basis of the Crown case, taken at its highest [which was] . . . spoken to not only by the complainer but also supported by circumstantial evidence from her friends, . . . that [she] had effectively been held captive over the period 23 to 29 October 2013.[83]

Nonetheless, the case turned on the fact that the complainer had both said 'no' to sexual intercourse and given a reason (menstruation) for not wanting sex. In other words, while the s 13 circumstance was considered to be of relevance in determining the no case to answer submission, in the end it was not decisive.

In effectively falling back on s 12 and 'free agreement' however, the court in *Drummond* does take a contextualised approach, more in line with the Scottish Law Commission's model. Indeed, in some respects, the court had little alternative in that it was dealing with a set of circumstances that took place over a six-day period.[84] As in *Mutebi* however, it gathers and applies the relevant facts in determining whether the accused had a reasonable belief in consent rather than in seeking directly to clarify free agreement.

The facts were that, on 23 October 2013, the accused attacked the complainer, with whom he was in a relationship characterised by the consumption of excessive quantities of alcohol, by punching and kicking to her head and body, knocking out a number of teeth and by incising a 2.5 cm wound in her neck. Her evidence was that he then detained her in his flat, locking all the doors and windows thus preventing her from leaving, which, in any event, she was too scared to do (though this formed the basis of the charge of abduction that was not upheld at trial). On 26 October, he asked her to have intercourse with him and she said 'no' stating that she did not want to because she was menstruating. She was also still visibly suffering from the effects of the assault. He proceeded to lie on top of her and penetrate her – these events forming the basis of the rape charge.

---

80 ibid, s 13(2)(a).
81 *Hutchinson* (n 53)
82 ibid [12].
83 ibid [14] (Carloway LJ-C).
84 23rd–29th October 2013.

Correctly, the court did not take a particularly 'snapshot' view of the moment at which sexual intercourse took place. Having taken into account the complainer's statement to the accused that she was menstruating, Lord Justice-Clerk Carloway went on:

> the complainer must have been in a visibly distressed state in terms of pure physical pain. She would therefore have been unlikely to have decided to give her free agreement to sexual intercourse with the person who had recently inflicted these injuries, whilst she was continuing to be detained by him at his flat, even if it cannot be said in absolute terms that such prior infliction of pain excludes consent in every possible case. It is legitimate to infer that the appellant, knowing of the complainer's state and that he had caused it, could not reasonably have believed that the complainer was proffering her consent.[85]

There is some evidence here of considering if free agreement was reached rather than merely determining if consent was given by the complainer at the instant of penetration in that the issue is embedded in its context. Instead of construing the matter solely as the accused's view of the complainer's thoughts on the matter ('was there any (reasonable) reason for him to think that she didn't consent?') it considers whether *anyone* would consider that they had freely agreed to have sex with another person in circumstances where that other person was still visibly injured and in pain as a result of an assault that they had inflicted.[86] The views of both the complainer and the accused are considered in the context of reaching a decision on whether or not to have sex. While, as noted above, one of the court's concerns is whether there is corroboration of the absence of a reasonable belief in consent, it is similarly interested in the issue of whether the complainer was consenting – which is the main site of the free agreement model. It is arguable that, in requiring only to determine if there was sufficient evidence to proceed to trial, and not, definitively, whether the crime of rape was established, the court was freed to apply a more reflective perspective on consent.

CONCLUSION

The Scots law on consent has significantly evolved in a relatively short period from a consciously undefined word,[87] through an otherwise unexplored requirement that it should be 'active'[88] to its current free agreement model[89] and its six situations of deemed non-consent.[90] Since consent is a defined term and all offences under ss 1–9 of the Sexual Offences (Scotland) Act 2009 (asp 9) require its absence, courts should be routinely considering the free agreement model and, indeed, there are some, promising, indications that they are contextualising the conduct of the parties, looking at sexual encounters and activities as a

---

85 *Drummond v HMA* (n 53) [19].

86 In *HMA v Hutchison* (n 53), the third reported case on s 13, the complainer made the similar point that 'it would be unlikely that any person would have consented to intercourse with the person, who had carried out [a serious] assault, on the very next day' [4] and the appeal court (who were dealing with a Crown appeal against a no case to answer determination on two charges of rape and one of abduction) determined that this was a view which a jury would also be entitled to take [4] (Carloway LJ-C). The appeal was upheld.

87 *Marr v HM Advocate* (n 28).

88 *Lord Advocate's Reference No 1 of 2001* (n 11) [39] (LJ-GCullen).

89 Sexual Offences (Scotland) Act 2009 (asp 9), s 12.

90 ibid, s 13.

whole and eschewing the 'snapshot' approach to a single moment at which the complainer must either have confirmed or refused her consent and the accused must have recognised this.[91] Equally, there is still a tendency to settle for common law categories[92] or to use the Sexual Offences (Scotland) Act 2009 (asp 9) concepts interchangeably with common law terms.[93] Even where facts arise from which a model demonstrating the presence or absence of free agreement could be constructed, these may instead be construed only as indicators (or otherwise) of the accused's reasonable belief.[94] Overall, the criminal law does have potential to reform approaches to sexual offending by disseminating clearly the circumstances in which consent is automatically absent and by promoting the negotiation of agreement between the parties. It is incumbent on those working with it to apply it so that that potential can be realised.

---

91 For example *Drummond v HM Advocate* (n 53); *Dempster v HM Advocate* (n 54).
92 For example, *Mutebi v HM Advocate* (n 52) does not clearly recognise the shift from the need for a genuine to a reasonable belief in consent.
93 See *Van Der Schyff v HM Advocate* (n 52) and *Mutebi v HM Advocate* (n 52) in both of which the jury is instructed that 'consent means free agreement'.
94 See *Mutebi v HM Advocate* (n 52) and *Dempster v HM Advocate* (n 54).

13
Consent in Irish law

John Stannard

The exercise of writing from a comparative perspective on any legal topic requires the existence both of similarities and of differences. Of similarities, because in the absence of such it is hard to draw any meaningful comparison; it is easier, after all, to compare two different kinds of cheese than to compare cheese to chalk. Of differences, because if there are none there is no need to draw any comparison in the first place. What makes the law of Ireland, both North and South, such a useful source of comparison is the fact that both jurisdictions have the same common law basis as do England and Wales, but have, especially south of the border, diverged to a significant extent from that jurisdiction. Such divergences may vary from topic to topic, as can be seen from the previous three volumes in this series. In relation to insanity, the old *McNaghten* Rules have been abandoned in favour of a statutory formulation on both sides of the border;[1] in relation to diminished responsibility, the differences are more marked in the South than in the North, especially since the passing of the Coroners and Justice Act 2009.[2] In relation to complicity, the law is much the same, but the scandals of recent years involving the treatment of children by clergy and other religious, again on both sides of the border, have highlighted the importance of the topic to a very significant extent.[3] And in relation to general defences, the continuing existence of the excessive defence doctrine in the South after its rejection, both in England and Wales and indeed in the country of its origin, again provides a very useful point of comparison.[4]

When one turns to the issue of consent one again sees a different picture. On the one hand, there are no major doctrinal differences, as in relation to insanity and the doctrine of excessive defence. Nor is the law the focus of any major debate at the level of public discourse, as in relation to complicity and the child abuse scandal. Differences there undoubtedly are, but

---

1 John Stannard, 'The View from Ireland' in Alan Reed and Michael Bohlander (eds), *Loss of Control and Diminished Responsibility: Domestic, Comparative and International Perspectives* (Ashgate 2011).
2 ibid.
3 John Stannard, 'Bishops in the Dock: Child Abuse and the Irish Law of Complicity' in Alan Reed and Michael Bohlander (eds), *Participation in Crime: Domestic, Comparative and International Perspectives* (Ashgate 2013) ch 14.
4 John E Stannard, 'In the Spirit of Compromise: The Irish Doctrine of Excessive Defence.' in Alan Reed, Michael Bohlander, Nicola Wake and Emma Smith (eds), *General Defences in Criminal Law: Domestic, Comparative and International Perspectives* (Ashgate 2014) ch 12.

it is not easy at first sight to see whether and to what extent they reflect any divergences of philosophy or of principle.

In the pages that follow we shall undertake a number of tasks. First of all, we shall look at those areas of Irish criminal law where consent plays a key role. Next, we shall consider the philosophy of consent and how it applies both in Irish law and on a more general basis. Given that in this area the law of Northern Ireland is identical to that of England and Wales, our focus throughout the chapter will be on Irish law south of the border, though for convenience we shall refer throughout to 'Ireland' and to 'Irish law'.[5]

THE EXISTING LAW

As in England and Wales, there are three main areas of criminal law where consent is a key issue, the first being non-fatal offences against the person, the second sexual offences and the third theft. We shall now consider each of these in turn.

(1) Non-fatal offences against the person

Prior to 1997 non-fatal offences against the person in Ireland were governed, as in England and Wales, by the common law and by the Offences Against the Person Act 1861.[6] Following a report by the Law Reform Commission in 1994,[7] this was replaced by the Non-Fatal Offences Against the Person Act 1997. Before we consider the relevant provisions of this legislation, it is worth looking more closely at the 1994 Report and at what it had to say about consent.

(a) The 1994 report

As might have been expected, the main recommendation of the Commission was that the common law offences of assault and battery,[8] together with ss 18, 20 and 47 of the Offences Against the Person Act 1861,[9] should be replaced by a three-tier structure of offences comprising simple assault,[10] assault causing harm,[11] and assault causing serious harm.[12] With regard to consent, the starting point for the 1994 Report was the *dictum* of Swift J in *Donovan*,[13] whereby it was an unlawful act to beat another with such a degree of violence that the infliction of bodily harm was a probable consequence, and that such unlawfulness operated to vitiate consent.[14] The upshot of all this was as in England and Wales, whereby consent always operated as a defence to assault and battery, but only in certain cases to offences involving the infliction of harm.[15] As we shall see, the Commission were happy to

---

5   Indeed, this is officially the correct term according to the Irish Constitution: *Ellis v O'Dea* [1989] IR 530 (Walsh J) 539, 540.
6   Law Reform Commission, *Report on Non-Fatal Offences Against the Person* (Law Reform Com No 45, 1994) [1.7]–[1.34]; Conor Hanly, *An Introduction to Irish Criminal Law* (Gill and Macmillan 2006) 258–259.
7   ibid.
8   ibid [9.52].
9   ibid [9.44].
10 ibid.
11 ibid [9.63].
12 ibid.
13 *Donovan* [1934] KB 496.
14 *Law Reform Com No 45*, 1994 (n 6) [9.131].
15 ibid [9.130].

retain the first branch of this rule, but were less sure of what to do about the second. Three broad approaches were considered in this connection. The first was to leave the present law unchanged; this was rejected on the grounds that it required the courts to characterise as an assault conduct that was in fact consensual.[16] The second was to allow consent as a defence to all acts of violence, however severe and whatever the circumstances of their occurrence; this too was rejected on the grounds that it involved too radical a shift in philosophy from that underlying the existing law, most notably the rule that consent was no defence to murder.[17] This left the third approach, which was to retain the criminal prohibition on the consensual infliction of bodily harm, whilst at the same time defining the offence so as to avoid any constructive or artificial characterisation of the relevant conduct as non-consensual.[18]

How then was this to be done? Again, three possible strategies were identified. One was to spell out in detail situations where the consensual infliction of bodily harm was or was not an offence; this however was rejected on two grounds, one being that such a list would be unduly rigid, and the other that it failed to deal with the objection that a person should not be allowed to compromise the human dignity of another person by seriously interfering with his or her bodily integrity even with his or her consent.[19] The second strategy considered was to do no more than state a general principle in reference to which the lawfulness or unlawfulness of the conduct would be determined; this too was rejected on the ground that it would be hard to articulate the public policy considerations that underlay the existing law in such a way as to remove a sense of vagueness and uncertainty.[20]

In the end, therefore, the Commission recommended a compromise approach whereby a statement of general principle would be supplemented by a non-exhaustive list of situations where the conduct would or would not be lawful, such as contact sports and necessary medical treatment.[21] The recommended principle was that a person who caused serious bodily harm to another with the other's consent should be guilty of an offence unless: (1) that harm was inflicted either with the purpose of benefitting another person or in pursuance of a socially beneficial function or activity; and (2) in either case, having regard to the intended beneficial purpose, function or activity, the infliction of that harm was reasonable.[22] The Commission also recommended that, where consent was a defence, the test should be whether it was freely given by a competent, informed person either expressly or by reasonable implication and not obtained by force, threat or deceit.[23]

(b) The 1997 Act

So to what extent were these recommendations implemented? The answer is only to a limited degree. In particular, though the Non-Fatal Offences Against the Person Act 1997 implemented the structural changes recommended by the Commission, the Act provided no general definition of consent, and little by way of guidance as to when it was a defence and when not. There are now four offences that need to be considered in this context.

---

16 ibid [9.132].
17 ibid [9.133].
18 ibid [9.134].
19 ibid [9.135].
20 ibid para 9.136.
21 ibid para 9.138
22 ibid para 9.140.
23 ibid para 9.143.

(i) Assault

The first of these is the statutory version of assault. Section 2(1) of the Act provides as follows:

> A person shall be guilty of the offence of assault who, without lawful excuse, intentionally or recklessly:
> (a) directly or indirectly applies force to or causes an impact on the body of another, or
> (b) causes another to believe on reasonable grounds that he or she is likely immediately to be subjected to any such force or impact without the consent of the other.

Here, as in English law, consent is clearly a defence, the only difference being that whereas in England and Wales this is set out by the common law, in Ireland lack of consent is expressly stated as an element of the crime in question.[24]

(ii) Assault causing harm

Next, we have assault causing harm. Section 3(1) of the Act provides as follows:

> A person who assaults another causing him or her harm shall be guilty of an offence.

Is consent a defence here? It was argued that it had to be, on the grounds that assault was an element of the offence, and assault could not be committed without proof of lack of consent on the part of the victim.[25] However, it was decided by the Supreme Court in *MJER v Dolny*[26] that the offences in ss 2 and 3 were separate and distinct, and that s 2 was not intended to define the concept of 'assault' for all purposes under the Act. Though the issue of consent was not directly to the fore – the case related to the validity of an extradition warrant – the result seems to be that the common law rules as to consent still apply in relation to s 3 as they do to s 4.[27]

(iii) Causing serious harm

Section 4(1) of the Act provides as follows: A person who intentionally or recklessly causes serious harm to another shall be guilty of an offence.

Since there is no reference to assault here, there can be no argument that lack of consent is an element of the crime. As noted above, the Act gives no general guidance as to when consent is a defence, but s 22(1) provides as follows:

> The provisions of this Act have effect subject to any enactment or rule of law providing a defence, or providing lawful authority, justification or excuse for an act or omission.

This would therefore seem to preserve the common law rules on consent in relation to this offence,[28] and indeed in relation to other offences in the Act for which no express provision is made.[29]

---

24 Hanly (n 6) 259.
25 ibid.
26 *MJER v Dolny* [2009] IESC 48 [13], affirming the judgment of Peart J in the High Court; see Sean Quinn, *Criminal Law in Ireland* (Longman) 26.05.
27 Non-Fatal Offences Against the Person Act 1997, s 22(1) discussed below.
28 Hanly (n 6) 260.
29 For instance assault causing harm under, s 3 of the Non-Fatal Offences Against the Person Act 1997. But it does not apply to offences such as assault (s 2) or false imprisonment (s 15), or other offences for which lack of consent is an essential element.

(iv) False imprisonment and a definition of consent

Finally, section 15(1), deals with false imprisonment. The significance of this offence in the present context is that, as with assault under s 2, lack of consent must be proved as an essential element of the offence. The Act provides a definition of consent in s 15(2), which reads as follows:

> For the purposes of this section, a person acts without the consent of another if the person obtains the other's consent by force or threat of force, or by deception causing the other to believe that he or she is under legal compulsion to consent.

Two things may be noted. The first is that it only applies 'for the purposes of this section'; it is not of general application. The second is that, though its provisions with regard to force and deception mirror the common law to some extent, they are more narrowly drawn; consent will therefore not be negated by threats that do not involve the use of force (for instance a threat to dismiss the victim from his or her job), nor will a deception in relation to an issue other than legal compulsion to consent. All of this makes s 15(2) of little value when it comes to investigating the general philosophy underlying the defence of consent in Irish law.

(2) Sexual offences

As far as sexual offences are concerned, the key areas to note in the present context are rape and sexual assault. Rape in Ireland is a common law offence defined by statute, whereas sexual assault is an umbrella term covering a number of discrete offences. Consent is a defence in both cases, but, as in the case of the other non-fatal offences against the person, it works in different ways. Note should be taken of the issue of the law regarding capacity to consent generally in relation to sexual offences, as this has recently been the topic of a major report by the Law Reform Commission.[30]

(a) Rape

Rape was and remains a common law offence,[31] but the current definition of rape is as set out by s 2(1) of the Criminal Law (Rape) Act 1981, which reads as follows:

> A man commits rape if,
> (a) he has sexual intercourse with a woman who at the time of the intercourse does not consent to it, and
> (b) at the time he knows that she does not consent to the intercourse or he is reckless as to whether he does or does not consent to it,
> and references to rape in this Act or any other enactment shall be construed accordingly.

Lack of consent, therefore, is an essential element of the crime of rape in Ireland no less than in England and Wales. The definition given in the 1981 Act is, of course, more or less the same as the definition set out in England in s 1(1) of the Sexual Offences (Amendment) Act 1976, and the old English cases on the point still continue to be relevant in Ireland.[32] General

---

30 Law Reform Commission, *Sexual Offences and Capacity to Consent* (Law Reform Com No 109, 2013).
31 Quinn (n 26) 30.07.
32 Hanly (n 6) 282–287.

guidance as to the meaning of consent in this context was given by Murray J in *The People (DPP) v C*, where he said:

> Consent means voluntary agreement or acquiescence to sexual intercourse by a person of the age of consent with the requisite mental capacity. Knowledge or understanding of facts material to the acts being consented to is necessary for the consent to be voluntary or to constitute acquiescence.[33]

There are several points to note in relation to this.

The first is that, despite the reference to 'acquiescence' by Murray J, it is clear that in Ireland, just as in England and Wales, there is more to consent than mere submission.[34] Indeed, this is made clear by s 9 of the Criminal Law (Rape) (Amendment) Act 1990, which reads as follows:

> It is hereby declared that in relation to any offence that consists of or includes the doing of an act to a person without the consent of that person any failure or omission by that person to offer resistance to the act does not of itself constitute consent to that act.

This applies not only to rape but also to sexual assault, and also to *any* offence that 'consists of or includes the doing of an act to a person without the consent of that person'.

Next, the consent must be to sexual intercourse. This reflects the common law rule that consent is vitiated by fraud as to the nature of the act.[35] Indeed, it has been suggested that a man would also be guilty of rape if he had intercourse with a woman knowing that she was under such a mistake, even though it was not induced by him,[36] and the Irish cases seem to bear this out.[37]

Though Murray J says that consent can only be given by a person 'of the age of consent' there is no fixed age in Irish law under which a woman's consent is regarded as invalid for the purposes of rape.[38] A man who has sexual intercourse with a young girl can be guilty of one of the offences under the Criminal Law (Sexual Offences) Act 2006[39] even where it was done with consent,[40] but though these offences are often colloquially referred to as 'statutory rape' they do not amount to rape as defined in s 1 of the 1981 Act. Rather, it has been suggested that the test is as laid down by the House of Lords in *Gillick v West Norfolk and Wisbech AHA*,[41] that is to say whether the girl in question had sufficient understanding of what was proposed to enable her to choose among different alternatives.[42] The same applies to mental capacity; though a man who has sexual intercourse with someone who is mentally impaired may commit an offence under ss 5 and 6 of the Criminal Law (Sexual Offences) Act 1993, it will not be rape unless the woman's state of mind was so impaired that she was incapable of exercising judgment.[43]

---

33 *The People (DPP) v CCA*, unreported 3 July 2001 (Murray J); see Hanly (n 6) 283; Quinn (n 26) 30.30.
34 *Olugboja* [1982] QB 320.
35 *Flattery* (1884) 15 Cox CC 579; *Williams* [1923] 1 KB 340.
36 *Papadimitropoulos* (1958) 98 CLR 249, 260.
37 See *People (DPP) v C* (n 33).
38 *Cf Harling* [1938] 1 All ER 307, 308 (Humphreys J).
39 See the Criminal Law (Sexual Offences) Act 2006, s 2(1) (girl under 15); s 3(1) (girl under 17).
40 ibid, ss 2(5), 3(7).
41 *Gillick v West Norfolk and Wisbech AHA* [1986] AC 112.
42 Hanly (n 6) 283.
43 ibid; *cf Lang* (1975) 62 Cr App R 50; *Bree* [2007] EWCA Crim 804 (intoxication).

It should also be noted that one key requirement of consent as defined by Murray J is 'knowledge or understanding of facts material to the acts being consented to'. Where such knowledge is absent, consent will be ineffective. When are facts 'material' for this purpose? According to the common law, there are two key considerations here, one being the nature of the act and the other the identity of the man. We have already seen how fraud or mistake as to the nature of the act may vitiate consent, but what about mistakes of identity? Section 4 of the Criminal Law Amendment Act 1885 provides that a man who induces a married woman to permit him to have connection with her by impersonating her husband is guilty of rape, but in *The People (DPP) v C*[44] the Irish courts recognised a wider principle. This was a case where a man got into bed with a woman and had sexual intercourse with her. She consented to this being done in the belief that he was her partner. His conviction for rape was upheld by the Court of Criminal Appeal, who said that where the man knew well that consent was given only because the woman concerned believed him to be another person, then he knew that there was no consent by the woman to having sexual intercourse with him.[45] This extends the principle in s 4 by showing that it applies to partners as well as to husbands, and also to cases of mistake as well as to cases of fraud.

Finally, even where the woman does not in fact consent, the man will still not be guilty of rape unless he knew that she did not consent or was reckless as to that fact. This reflects the English law prior to the Sexual Offences Act 2003 as laid down in *DPP v Morgan*;[46] a man cannot be guilty of rape if he honestly believed that the woman consented to the act. Note that there is no requirement, as in England, that the belief be a reasonable one,[47] though the presence of absence of reasonable grounds for such belief is a matter to which the jury must have regard in considering whether he so believed.[48]

(b) Sexual assault

Sexual assault in Irish law is not so much a single offence as an umbrella term covering a number of different offences of varying degrees of gravity. The relevant provisions are to be found in ss 2, 3 and 4 of the Criminal Law (Rape) (Amendment) Act 1990.

First, we have s 2, which provides that the offences of indecent assault on a male person (formerly found in s 62 of the Offences Against the Person Act 1861) and indecent assault on a female person (formerly found in s 52 of the same Act), shall be known as sexual assault.[49] The case of *People v O'Connor*[50] laid down that it was not open to a jury to convict on a charge of indecent assault on a female where the person assaulted was shown to have consented to the act, and no doubt the same applies to sexual assault under the 1990 Act. However, s 14 of the Act goes on to say that such consent is no defence where the victim is under the age of 15.[51]

Next, we have s 3, which provides for the offence of aggravated sexual assault.[52] This means a sexual assault that involves violence or the threat of serious violence or is such as to cause injury,

---

44 *The People (DPP) v CCA* (n 33).
45 Quinn (n 26) 30.30.
46 *DPP v Morgan* [1976] AC 182.
47 Sexual Offences Act 2003, s 1(1)(c).
48 Criminal Law (Rape) Act 1981, s 2(2); *cf* Sexual Offences Amendment Act 1976, s 2(2).
49 Quinn (n 26) 30.44.
50 *People v O'Connor* [1949] 15 Ir Jur Rep 25; Quinn (n 26) 30.51.
51 ibid 30.52.
52 ibid 30.53.

humiliation or degradation of a grave nature to the person assaulted.[53] Since no provision is made for consent, the rules of the common law will presumably apply here, and given the way in which the offence is framed it is hard to conceive circumstances in which a court would hold it to be in the public interest for someone to be allowed to consent to this sort of activity.[54]

Finally, there is s 4, which on the face of it seems to contemplate rape. Rape under s 4 is defined in terms of a sexual assault that includes penetration (however slight) of the anus or mouth by the penis, or penetration (however slight) of the vagina by any object held or manipulated by another person.[55] Is consent a defence here? The use of the label 'rape' would suggest that it was, but given: (1) the definition of the offence in terms of sexual assault rather than rape, and (2) the clear differences between this offence and rape proper,[56] the better view would seem to be that the common law rules as to consent apply. The key question would then be whether the conduct in question involved actual bodily harm to the victim; if not, consent would be a defence generally (assuming the victim to be over the age of 15), but if it did, consent would be a defence only in cases where it was in the public interest to allow it as such.

(c) Capacity to consent

In some cases the consent of the victim will be disregarded on the grounds that he or she did not have the capacity to provide it. The issue here is not so much whether the victim gave his or her consent on the occasion in question; rather, the issue of consent is disregarded on the basis that the victim is a member of a particular class of persons who are deemed to require special protection. Irish law, in common with other legal systems, recognises two such classes, one based on age and the other on mental incapacity. Disregarding the victim's consent in such cases cuts both ways; on the one hand, the victim has the benefit of extra protection, but on the other he or she is effectively denied the opportunity of a sexual relationship.[57] This does not matter so much in relation to age, as this is only temporary, but in relation to mental capacity it is a very significant issue indeed, and it is this that was the focus of the Law Reform Commission Report of 2013.[58]

The current Irish law on the topic is set out in s 5 of the Criminal Law (Sexual Offences) Act 1993, which provides as follows:

(1) A person who
    (a) has or attempts to have sexual intercourse, or
    (b) commits or attempts to commit an act of buggery,
with a person who is mentally impaired (other than a person to whom he is married or to whom he believes with reasonable cause he is married) shall be guilty of an offence.

---

53 Criminal Law (Rape) (Amendment) Act 1990, s 3(1).
54 Were the facts of *Brown* [1994] 1 AC 212 to occur in Ireland, they would clearly fall within the scope of s 3 of the Criminal Law (Rape) (Amendment) Act 1990; indeed, the practice of sado-masochism – at least in its more serious manifestations – would almost require such conduct by definition.
55 Criminal Law (Rape) (Amendment) Act 1990, s 4(1); Quinn (n 26) para 30.56.
56 Thus whereas rape proper can only be committed by a man, rape under the Criminal Law (Rape) (Amendment) Act 1990, s 4 can sometimes be committed by a woman. In the same way, whereas rape proper involves conventional sexual intercourse, rape under s 4 involves other forms of penetration. However, both offences carry a penalty of up to life imprisonment.
57 See the Law Reform Commission, *Report on Sexual Offences Against the Mentally Handicapped* (Law Reform Commission No 33, 1990) 35.
58 Law Reform Com No 109, 2013 (n 30).

Mental impairment, in the context of the Act, is defined in terms of 'a disorder of the mind, whether through mental handicap or mental illness, which is of such a nature or degree as to render a person incapable of living an independent life or of guarding against serious exploitation'.[59] It is a defence for the accused to show that at the relevant time he did not know and had no reason to believe that the person in respect of whom he was charged was mentally impaired.[60]

The Law Reform Commission identified a number of problems in relation to this provision. In particular, it was both too wide and too narrow. Too wide, because it effectively barred any mutually consensual sexual relationship with a person with mental disability;[61] too narrow, because the protection conferred by s 5 was limited to sexual intercourse and buggery, and did not apply to other forms of sexual exploitation.[62] Instead, it was recommended that the blanket approach seen in s 5 should be abandoned and replaced with a functional test of capacity[63] depending on whether the person in question could choose to agree to the sexual act involved (including where he or she could so choose arising from the provision to him or her of suitable decision-making assistance) because he or she had sufficient understanding of the nature and reasonably foreseeable consequences of the sexual act involved.[64] Such a test would include a requirement that the person was able to weigh up relevant information in deciding whether or not to engage in the act in question,[65] and also that he or she was able to communicate his or her decision in some way, whether by talking, sign language or any other means.[66] These and other recommendations were set out in a draft bill attached to the report, but so far this has not been brought in.

(3) Theft

Prior to 2001, theft in Ireland was governed by s 1(1) of the old Larceny Act 1916,[67] which provided as follows:

> A person steals who, without the consent of the owner, fraudulently and without a claim of right made in good faith, takes and carries away anything capable of being stolen with intent, at the time of such taking, permanently to deprive the owner thereof...

Consent was therefore clearly a defence, but not in cases where the owner was induced to part with possession of the property by a trick[68] or by intimidation.[69] Where the owner intended to part with both possession and property in the goods the relevant offence was not larceny but obtaining by false pretences.

---

59 Criminal Law (Sexual Offences) Act 1993, s 5(5).
60 ibid, s 5(3).
61 Law Reform Com No 109, 2013 (n 30) 1.13.
62 ibid 1.18.
63 ibid 2.70.
64 ibid 3.31.
65 ibid 3.51.
66 ibid 3.60.
67 See generally J Paul McCutcheon, *The Larceny Act 1916* (Round Hall Ltd 1988).
68 Law Reform Com No 109, 2013 (n 30) 49. The essence of larceny by a trick was that the prosecutor intended to part with possession of the goods, but not with property in them: *Aikles* (1784) 1 Leach 294; *Russett* [1892] 2 QB 312.
69 Law Reform Com No 109, 2013 (n 30) 51; *McGrath* (1869) LR 1 CCR 205.

In discussing the potential reform of the law in this area the Law Reform Commission[70] considered whether or not to follow the approach taken in the Theft Act 1968 in England and Wales.[71] Section 1 of the Act, as is well known, did not include any reference to consent,[72] and one of the reasons why the Commission were reluctant to follow it was the confusion to which this omission had given rise.[73] In the end its recommendation was that the reference to lack of consent should be retained, but also the restrictions in relation to deception and intimidation.[74] The law is now to be found in s 4(1) of the Criminal Justice (Theft and Fraud Offences) Act 2001, which reads as follows:

[A] person is guilty of theft if he or she dishonestly appropriates property without the consent of the owner and with the intention of depriving its owner of it.

On the face of it, this seems fairly straightforward; if the owner consents, it cannot be theft, but if the owner does not consent it may be. However, s 4(2) of the Act goes on to qualify this by saying:

For the purposes of this section a person does not appropriate property without the consent of the owner if –
(a) the person believes that he or she has the owner's consent, or would have the other's consent if the owner knew of the appropriation of the property and the circumstances in which it was appropriated, or
(b) (except where the property came to the person as trustee or personal representative) he or she appropriates the property in the belief that the owner cannot be discovered by taking reasonable steps,
but consent obtained by deception or intimidation is not consent for these purposes.

It will be obvious from this that the concept of consent adopted in the Act is a strange one, in that it depends a great deal on the beliefs of both the accused and the alleged victim of theft. It is also both wider and narrower than that seen in other branches of the law, in the sense that it includes cases of honest belief, but excludes *all* cases of deception or intimidation, and not just those which are of a serious nature. In particular, s 2(2) of the Act provides as follows:

For the purposes of this Act a person deceives if he or she:
(a) creates or reinforces a false impression, including a false impression as to law, value or intention or other state of mind
(b) prevents another person from acquiring information which would affect that person's judgement of a transaction, or
(c) fails to correct a false impression which the deceiver previously created or reinforced or which the deceiver knows to be influencing another to whom he or she stands in a fiduciary or confidential relationship,
and references to deception shall be construed accordingly.

---

70 Law Reform Commission, *Report on the Law Relating to Dishonesty* (Law Reform Commission No 43, 1992).
71 ibid ch 15.
72 *Lawrence v Commissioner of Police for the Metropolis* [1972] AC 626, 633.
73 Law Reform Commission No 43, 1992 (n 70) 15.13–15.24.
74 ibid 36.45.

The upshot would seem to be that cases such as *Lawrence*[75] and *Gomez*[76] would be theft in Irish law just as in English law, but for a different reason. In England and Wales, they are theft because the definition of theft does not require lack of consent on the part of the owner. In Ireland, lack of consent must be proved, but in these cases the consent would be invalid because it was obtained by deception.[77]

THE PHILOSOPHY OF CONSENT

In deciding whether and to what extent consent should be a defence, the criminal law comes up against five principles, those of autonomy, paternalism, legal moralism, correspondence and fair labelling. In the section which follows we shall begin by describing the content of these principles, before considering how they may interact. We shall then see how this is reflected in Irish criminal law as it currently stands.

(1) The five principles

Obviously it is beyond the scope of the present chapter to try to analyse the five key principles in detail. Suffice it to say that the first two of these are centred on the victim, the third on the community in general, and the last two on the accused.

The principle of individual autonomy posits, in the words of Ashworth, that each person is responsible for his or her behaviour;[78] since individuals in general have capacity to make their own choices, the law should treat them as agents fully capable of choosing how to conduct their lives.[79] The corollary of this is that the criminal law should not deprive them of that choice without good reason; in particular, no one can rightly intervene to prevent a responsible adult from voluntarily doing something that will harm only himself.[80] On the basis of this principle consent, provided that it is freely and willingly given, will always be a defence.

The principle of paternalism, in contrast, asserts that the criminal law is entitled to intervene to prevent harm in general, including harm to the actor himself or herself;[81] in the words of Roberts, the state may be justified in using its most coercive powers to force a person to act or forbear to act against his will in order to promote his own self-interest and well-being.[82] On the basis of this principle the law may or may not allow consent as a defence, but it is justified in not doing so in cases where the conduct in question is harmful to the person concerned.

Similar claims are made by what Roberts terms 'legal moralism',[83] namely the principle that the law may legitimately criminalise conduct either on the ground that it is inherently immoral (Roberts terms this 'strict legal moralism'),[84] or because it will lead to drastic change in traditional ways of life, whether or not that involves harm or offence to the person

---

75 *Lawrence* [1972] AC 626.

76 *Gomez* [1993] AC 442.

77 *Hinks* [2001] 2 AC 241 is a more problematic case, as there was no proof there of either deception or intimidation.

78 Andrew Ashworth and Jeremy Horder, *Principles of Criminal Law* (Oxford University Press 2013) 23.

79 ibid 23–24.

80 Law Commission Consultation Paper No 139, *Consent in the Criminal Law* (Law Com CP No 139, 1995), Appendix C, by Paul Roberts C.43 (citing Joel Feinberg).

81 ibid C.44.

82 ibid C.58-C.59.

83 ibid C.70-C.71.

84 ibid C.70.

responsible or to others (he terms this 'moral conservatism'). On the basis of this principle the law may or may not allow consent as a defence, but is justified in not doing so in cases where the conduct in question infringes the principle.

In the context of the criminal law, one also has to have regard to the principle of correspondence.[85] As Ashworth argues, this is to be implied both from the principle of autonomy and that of the rule of law, and means that the defendant's intention, knowledge or recklessness relates to the proscribed harm.[86] What this means in the present context is that it is not enough simply to show that the victim did not consent; rather, the accused must also be shown to be aware at least of the possibility that this may be the case.

Finally, we have the principle of fair labelling. Under this principle the criminal law must try to ensure that it reflects key distinctions between kinds of offences and degrees of wrongdoing.[87] This means that even if it is clear that a person is guilty of some crime, he or she should not be convicted of crime A when his or her conduct would fall more appropriately into crime B, either because A is a more severe offence than B or because the harm targeted by offence B differs in some key respect from the harm targeted by offence A. The point here is that the key distinction between offence A and offence B may be the presence or absence of consent on the part of the victim, and this is something that the law must reflect.

(2) Interaction between the five principles

Our next question is how these principles interact.

- Since it is the criminal law we are discussing, the principle of correspondence is always relevant to the situation; unlike a situation, say, where a court is asked to decide in advance whether a person, P, may legitimately consent to something – as the philosophers would say, Ø – being done to him or her, the fact that it is a criminal case presupposes that Ø *has already been done*, and the issue is rather whether D, the defendant, should be convicted of the relevant crime on the basis of it.
- In a case where Ø involves neither harm nor a breach of morality, the only other principle is that of autonomy; in so far as P genuinely consented to Ø being done, the law has no reason to brand the conduct as being criminal.
- If on the other hand Ø involves harm to P or others, the principle of paternalism may restrict the extent to which P may consent to it even though there is no room for doubt as to the reality of that consent.
- Likewise, if Ø is considered immoral, the effectiveness of P's consent as a defence to the charge may be restricted by the principle of legal moralism.
- Finally, if Ø involves conduct that may fall within the bounds of more than one offence, P's consent may also be relevant to the question whether it is appropriate to convict D of the offence for which he or she is being tried rather than for some other.

(3) The five principles in Irish law

How does the Irish law on consent sit with regard to these five principles? As might be expected, there is no one consistent picture.

---

85 (n 78) 75.
86 ibid.
87 ibid 77.

In relation to non-fatal offences against the person, the approach of Irish law is said to be rooted in the right to bodily integrity, as set out in Article 40.3.2 of the Constitution and as cited by the Law Reform Commission in the opening paragraph of its 1994 Report.[88] Under Article 40.3.2 the state is under a duty by its laws to protect as best it may from unjust attack and, in the case of injustice done, to vindicate the person of every citizen; this means that the state must protect its citizens from dangers to health, albeit in a manner that is not incompatible or inconsistent with their rights as human persons.[89] The Commission goes on to point out that the state's duties in respect of the protection of the citizen's right to bodily integrity are primarily discharged by the adoption and enforcement of appropriate measures for the promotion and protection of public health and safety.[90] Injury resulting from negligence is almost exclusively the province of private law, the role of the criminal law is this field being limited to providing sanctions for persons who intentionally or recklessly cause harm to others.[91] It is clear that in the eyes of the Commission the law in this context must be seen in paternalist terms; as we have already seen, the option of making consent a complete defence by withdrawing the criminal sanction from all acts of violence, however severe and whatever the circumstances of their occurrence, once it could be shown that the victim consented to them, is specifically rejected on the ground that this would involve too radical a shift of philosophy from that underlying the existing law.[92] It is therefore not surprising that, in relation to non-fatal offences against the person, Irish law takes the approach adopted by Lord Lane CJ, whereby it is not in the public interest that people should try to cause, or should cause, each other actual bodily harm for no good reason.[93] It has been argued that issues of legal moralism play a part – albeit not explicitly – in deciding what amounts to a good reason in such cases,[94] but where no harm is involved, as in the case of simple assault, there is nothing to prevent the principle of autonomy having free rein, and this means that consent can be a complete defence as we have seen;[95] the principle of correspondence means that even an honest belief as to consent will suffice in a case of this sort.[96]

When it comes to sexual offences, somewhat different considerations apply. Whereas the non-fatal offences against the person (other than simple assault) are defined in terms of harm, this is not necessarily true of sexual offences; although it makes sense to say that people should not be allowed to cause actual bodily harm to one another without good reason,[97] this reasoning is less convincing in the context of sexual intercourse and other conduct of a similar nature not involving such harm.[98] This leaves the protection of autonomy as the

88 Law Reform Com No 45, 1994 (n 6) 1.1.
89 *Ryan v Attorney-General* [1965] IR 348.
90 Law Reform Com No 45, 1994 (n 6) 9.1.
91 ibid.
92 ibid 9.133.
93 *Attorney-General's Reference (No 6 of 1980)* [1981] QB 715, 719.
94 Louis Bibbings 'Boys will be boys: Masculinity and offences against the person' in Louis Bibbings and Donald Nicolson (eds), *Feminist Perspectives on Criminal Law* (Cavendish 2000) 231.
95 Hanly (n 6).
96 *Kimber* [1983] 1 WLR 1118.
97 ibid.
98 The assumption that sexual conduct is basically 'good' as opposed to actual bodily harm, which is 'bad', is challenged by Jonathan Herring and others, but is vigorously defended by Hyman Gross; see Jonathan Herring, 'Mistaken Sex' [2005] Criminal Law Review 511; Michelle Madden Dempsey and Jonathan Herring, 'Why Sexual Penetration Requires Justification' (2007) Oxford Journal of Legal Studies 467; Hyman Gross, 'Rape, Moralism and Human Rights' [2007] Criminal Law Review 220; Jonathan Herring, 'Human Rights and Rape: a Reply to Hyman Gross [2007] Criminal Law Review 228.

key consideration; as the Law Reform Commission says in its 2013 Report,[99] whilst every person has the right to express his or her sexuality, some lack the capacity to consent, whilst others are vulnerable to abuse or exploitation.[100] What this means is that while the presence of consent in this area of the law will clearly render lawful that which would otherwise be unlawful,[101] such a consent must be both genuine and informed, and this is reflected both in the 'functional' test propounded by Murray J in *The People (DPP) v C*[102] and proposed by the Law Reform Commission in its 2013 Report,[103] and in the rule that an apparent consent can sometimes be vitiated by fear or fraud.[104] On the other hand, Irish law, unlike the law of England and Wales, still gives full force to the principle of correspondence; under s 2(1) of the Criminal Law (Rape) Act 1981 a man can only be convicted if he knew that the other party did not consent or was reckless as to that fact,[105] and an honest belief in consent will be a defence in all cases.[106] Though this relates specifically to rape, there is no reason to suppose that the law is different in relation to the other sexual offences, at least where they do not involve the commission of actual bodily harm.

In relation to theft, the picture is again rather different. The principle of autonomy is reflected again here both in the requirement that the dishonest appropriation be without the consent of the owner[107] and in the proviso that this will not apply where such consent was obtained by threats or by deception;[108] the principle of correspondence is reflected in the defence of honest belief that the owner consented or would have done so if he or she had known of the appropriation and of the circumstances in which it took place.[109] There is a further principle at stake here, and that is the principle of fair labelling.[110] Whereas in the context of offences against the person consent basically operates to distinguish conduct that is criminal from that which is not, the same does not apply in the context of theft, where it may do no more than separate theft from some other offence of dishonesty.[111]

CONCLUSION

One of the requirements of a coherent system of law is that it should treat like cases alike and different cases differently. On this basis, one should not be surprised at the fact that Irish law – or indeed any other system of law – does not adhere to a single philosophy of consent, as the notion of consent can operate in so many different ways. On the contrary, to adopt such a one-size-fits-all approach would be to the detriment of the law. The purpose of this chapter has been to illustrate how consent operates in the particular context of Irish criminal law, but one is encouraged to hope that the insights generated in doing so will be of broader relevance.

---

99 Law Reform Com No 109, 2013 (n 30).
100 ibid 1.02.
101 ibid 2.02.
102 *The People (DPP) v CCA* (n 33).
103 Law Reform Com No 109, 2013 (n 30).
104 *Flattery* (n 35).
105 Quinn (n 26).
106 ibid.
107 Criminal Justice (Theft and Fraud Offences) Act 2001, s 4(1); Law Reform Commission No 43, 1992 (n 70).
108 ibid, s 4(2); Law Reform Commission No 43, 1992 (n 70).
109 ibid.
110 Ashworth and Horder (n 78) 77–79.
111 This is of course the key issue in cases such as *Lawrence* (n 75); *Gomez* (n 76); (to some extent) *Hinks* (n 77).

Part II

14
South Africa

Gerhard Kemp

1 GENERAL ISSUES

1.1 Conceptual foundations

1.1.1 *Philosophical and theoretical principles informing the law surrounding consent*

South African criminal law – under the influence of English law[1] as well as Roman-Dutch authorities and German commentaries[2] – recognises consent as a defence[3] or as a ground of justification.[4]

On the understanding that human beings are essentially autonomous, and able to freely waive legal rights if they so choose, the logical conclusion must be that consent to harm serves as an excuse: *volenti non fit iniuria*. This is, with some qualification, true in private law.[5] The question is whether such a liberal view of individual autonomy holds true for defences/justifications in criminal law as well. It appears that, while the law of delict and criminal law share the same basic point of departure, criminal law includes broader considerations beyond individual consent. These considerations can collectively be labelled as public interest considerations; and public interest here plays a more significant role than in the law of delict.[6]

Given the public interest in the harm done by unlawful acts in criminal law, the question is whether consent is relevant at all. Does public interest totally override individual autonomy? Relying on English law, and with reference to the authors Simester and Sullivan, Burchell noted that there are three basic scenarios in criminal law where consent comes into play: first, there are clear cases where it can be said that freely given and sufficiently informed consent

---

1 See in particular Jonathan Burchell, *Principles of Criminal Law* (4th edition, Juta 2013) 204–205.
2 Johannes Christiaan de Wet, *Strafreg* (4th edition, Butterworth 1985) 94–97.
3 Burchell (n 1) 205; Gerhard Kemp and others, *Criminal Law in South Africa* (2nd edition, Oxford University Press 2015) 134.
4 CR Snyman, *Criminal Law* (6th edition, LexisNexis 2014) 122–123.
5 Max Loubser and Rob Midgley (eds), *The Law of Delict in South Africa* (2nd edition, Oxford University Press 2012) 163.
6 Burchell (n 1) 204.

will preclude any finding of liability. Secondly, there are clear cases where consent is legally irrelevant. Thirdly, there are grey areas where the lack of guiding principles is exposed.[7]

With reference to *prima facie* unlawful acts rendered lawful as a result of the consent by the victim, the question is one of weight given to the consent in question. There appear to be a number of approaches in this regard. These are,[8] broadly speaking, the following:

- thorough-going liberalism;
- the absolute inapplicability of consent; and
- the middle course between the above two approaches.

To the extent that lack of consent is not in itself an element of the crime, the above three approaches to the role of consent in circumscribing the lawfulness of an act are about degrees on a spectrum. At the one end of the spectrum (thorough-going liberalism) the emphasis is on individual freedom of choice. The law should respect this choice and public morals or public interest should in principle not limit individual autonomy. At the other end of the spectrum, logically, is the absolute irrelevance of consent. Individual consent cannot justify or excuse the wrongfulness of the act. The terrain between the two polar positions is where criminal law theory has to find appropriate solutions. Three possible grounds for the differentiation between what would be considered valid and invalid consent are offered. These are: public policy, paternalism, and moralism.[9] There appears to be no single or even dominant ground for the differentiation between valid and invalid consent.[10] The dynamic, sometimes contradictory interplay between the different grounds put the courts in a difficult but unavoidable role as seekers of the most appropriate guidelines for the lawful bounds of consent in modern South African criminal law. Some of the contentious topics addressed in this chapter, including mercy killing, euthanasia and conduct like self-mutilation, illustrate the difficult task of finding a philosophically and theoretically sound set of principles to circumscribe the role of consent in criminal law.

1.1.2 Influence of feminist and queer theory

Section 9(3) of the Constitution of South Africa provides as follows: 'The state may not unfairly discriminate directly or indirectly against anyone on one or more grounds, including race, gender, sex, pregnancy, marital status, ethnic or social origin, colour, sexual orientation, age, disability, religion, conscience, belief, culture, language and birth.' Discrimination was the bedrock of the apartheid-system. Section 9 (the equality clause) can therefore be seen as one of the cornerstone provisions of South Africa's democratic Constitution.

Underlying[11] the equality clause of the Constitution, is a rich feminist and gay rights discourse.[12] Given the explicit recognition of gay rights in the Constitution it came as no surprise that some of the earliest decisions by the Constitutional Court concerned laws adversely

---

7   Burchell (n 1) 204, citing Antony Simester, John R Spencer, GR Sullivan and Graham J Virgo, *Simester and Sullivan's Criminal Law* (4th edition, Hart Publishing 2010) 749.

8   ibid, referring to the propositions made by Paul Roberts, 'The philosophical foundations of consent in criminal law' (1997) 17 Oxford Journal of Legal Studies 389.

9   ibid 205.

10 Kemp (n 3) 134.

11 Edwin Cameron, 'Sexual orientation and the Constitution: A test case for human rights' [1993] 110 South African Law Journal 450.

12 For an overview and a South African perspective, see Chapter 12 (Feminism and the law) and Chapter 13 (Gay and Lesbian Legal Theory) in Christopher J Roederer and Darrel Moellendorf, *Jurisprudence* (Juta 2004).

affecting the gay community. In *National Coalition for Gay and Lesbian Equality v Minister of Justice*,[13] the Constitutional Court invalidated the common law crime of sodomy and related statutory offences, decriminalising consensual sexual intercourse between gay men. In *Geldenhuys v National Director of Public Prosecutions*[14] provisions of the now repealed Sexual Offences Act, 1957, which set the age of consent for sexual intercourse at 19 years for homosexuals and 16 years for heterosexuals, were held to be unconstitutional. The Criminal Law (Sexual Offences and Related Matters) Amendment Act 32 of 2007 now sets the uniform and gender neutral age of consent at 16.[15]

The decriminalisation of abortion (to a large extent) as well as rape law reform that resulted in a definition that recognises gender vulnerabilities and power imbalances, should be seen as further manifestations of a decades-long feminist discourse. Many women in South Africa are still subjected to patriarchal family and traditional authority structures that undermine free choice and the voluntary basis of lawful consent. This means that many women have 'little control over decisions relating to sex and reproduction'.[16] The consent-based termination of pregnancy dispensation (considered in 2.1.3. below) as well as the inclusion of the element of coercion in sexual offences (considered in 2.3.1. below) are legislative attempts to address inequality and the vulnerability caused by gender discrimination as well as deep-seated cultural realities in South Africa. Some feminist commentators argue that the legislative reforms do not go far enough, or are inadequate in terms of the purported or stated objectives.[17]

1.1.3 Definition of informed consent

A number of cases – mostly concerning delictual liability – considered the meaning of 'informed consent' as a requirement for valid consent. In *Castell v de Greef*[18] the court identified a number of requirements for informed consent. This case concerned consent in the context of medical treatment. The court noted that South African law generally classifies *volenti non fit iniuria*, irrespective of whether it takes the narrower form of consent to a specific harm or the wider form of assumption of the risk of harm, as a ground of justification that excludes the unlawfulness or wrongfulness element of a crime or delict. The requirements for informed consent can also

---

13 *National Coalition for Gay and Lesbian Equality v Minister of Justice* 1999 (1) SA 6 (CC).

14 *Geldenhuys v National Director of Public Prosecutions* 2009 (2) SA 310 (CC).

15 It needs to be noted that consensual sexual intercourse between adolescents and where both parties are *under* the age of 16, has been decriminalised. Where one party is older than 16 and the other is under 16 but where the age difference between the two parties is not more than two years, sexual consensual sexual intercourse is also lawful. See *Teddy Bear Clinic for Abused Children and Another v Minister of Justice and Constitutional Development and Another* 2014 (2) SA 168 (CC), and the subsequent Criminal Law (Sexual Offences and Related Matters) Amendment Act, 5 of 2015.

16 Adila Hassim, Mark Heywood and Jonathan Berger (eds), *Health & Democracy* (SiberInk 2007) 357.

17 See Louise Du Toit, 'From consent to coercive circumstances: Rape law reform on trial' [2012] 28(3) South African Journal of Human Rights 380. The author points out that the 2007 Sexual Offences Act retained consent as a key element in the definition of rape in contrast with the South African Law Reform Commission's evaluation and ultimate recommendation that the element of consent be replaced with a more complex and nuanced notion of 'coercive circumstances'. By evaluating the surrounding coercive circumstances, a determination of *prima facie* unlawfulness can be made according to this view. The author argues that there seems to be a discrepancy between the preamble to the Act's mention of 'vulnerable persons', and the operative part of the Act's retention of the element of consent, which seems to be premised on sexual autonomy that exists and are in place for all individuals regardless of their gender and circumstances. As a result, consent, as retained in the Sexual Offences Act, has meanings that 'are deeply embedded in modernity's contradictory view of women's sexual autonomy'.

18 *Castell v de Greef* 1994 (4) SA 408 (C).

be applicable for purposes of consent in the context of criminal law. With reference to informed consent, the court put it in the context of the other requirements of lawful consent.

For consent to operate as a defence the following requirements must, *inter alia*, be satisfied:

(a) the consenting party must have had knowledge and been aware of the nature and extent of the harm or risk;
(b) the consenting party must have appreciated and understood the nature and extent of the harm or risk;
(c) the consenting party must have consented to the harm or assumed the risk;
(d) the consent must be comprehensive, that is extend to the entire transaction, inclusive of its consequences.[19]

The court in *Castell* stated that, for a patient's consent to constitute a justification that excludes wrongfulness of medical treatment and its consequences, the relevant practitioner is obliged to warn the patient consenting of a material risk inherent in the proposed treatment. A risk will be regarded as material if, in the circumstances of the particular case:

• a reasonable person in the patient's position, if warned of the risk, would be likely to attach significance to it; or
• the medical practitioner is or should reasonably be aware that the particular patient, if warned of the risk, would be likely to attach significance to it.[20]

'Informed consent' can be defined as an awareness and appreciation of the material facts concerning the act to which a person is consenting.[21]

1.1.4 Consent to risk or consent to outcome

In general, a person undertaking a risk would do so with the necessary knowledge, appreciation and consent regarding the risk.[22] For consent to be a defence, the complainant's consent must cover the harm 'that is the subject matter of the charge'.[23]

1.1.5 Revocation of consent

It was held by the Supreme Court of Appeal in *M*[24] that consent remains revocable, on condition that the act has not yet been committed. This means that the act must not have been completed. *Ex post facto* ratification of an unlawful act does not render the act lawful.[25] On the other hand, consent that rendered an act lawful cannot be revoked after the fact rendering it unlawful.

---

19 ibid 425.
20 ibid 426.
21 Kemp (n 3) 142. See also Patrick Van den Heever, 'The patient's right to know: Informed consent in South African medical law' (1995) *De Rebus* 53; Andra Le Roux-Kemp, *Law, Power and the Doctor-Patient Relationship* (VDM Publishing 2011) 81–103; Pieter Carstens and Debbie Pearmain, *Foundational Principles of South African Medical Law* (LexisNexis 2007) 687; Murray Earle, '"Informed consent": Is there room for the reasonable patient in South African law?' [1995] *South African Law Journal* 629, 630.
22 See the pre-union South African case of *Waring and Gillow Ltd v Sherborne* 1904 TS 340, per Chief Justice Innes at 344.
23 Burchell (n 1) 225.
24 1953 (4) SA 393 (A).
25 Snyman (n 4) 127.

1.1.6 Ownership and limits of consent

The basic point of departure is private autonomy. The ability to give consent rests with the private individual. The person giving the consent must have the mental capacity to do so. This means the person must have the capacity to know (a) the nature of the act and (b) have appreciation of the consequences.[26] It can be said that private autonomy, conditioned on the qualification of mental capacity, generally determines the ownership and scope of consent.

There are instances where public interest limits private autonomy. For instance, s 57(1) of the Criminal Law (Sexual Offences and Related Matters) Amendment Act provides that 'a male or female person under the age of 12 years is incapable of consenting to a sexual act'.[27] The child's mental capacity is not the issue; the issue is that children are regarded as a vulnerable group that needs to be protected. A fusion of public policy and paternalism creates here a justifiable limit on the ability to give consent.

1.2 Place of consent in the offence structure

Commentators discuss consent as a defence that affects unlawfulness.[28] It is accordingly treated under the topic of unlawfulness in the structure of general principles of criminal liability. Snyman utilises a schema in order to illustrate the role of consent as a justification:[29]

Crimes in respect of which consent may operate as justification:

(A) Crimes against specific individual:	*(B) Crimes against the community or the state:*
A.1 Crimes where absence of consent forms part of the definitional elements (eg the crime of rape)	Consent is no defence
A.2 Crimes where consent can never be a defence (eg the crime of murder)	
A.3 Crimes where consent is a ground of justification (eg the crimes of theft, and injury to property)	
A.4 Crimes where consent is sometimes a justification (eg the crime of assault)	

The above schema is, broadly speaking, useful to illustrate the role of consent in terms of the general principles of South African criminal law. The application of the principle with respect to certain offences reveals some nuance and makes it harder to frame consent in absolute terms. This is particularly the case with murder, where the role of consent in terms of the element of unlawfulness has seen some changes as a result of case-law on euthanasia, which is further explored in 2.1.2. below. The place of consent in the offence structure in

---

26 ibid 126.
27 32 of 2007.
28 Burchell (n 1) 205; Kemp (n 3) 134; De Wet (n 2) 94; Snyman (n 4) 123.
29 Snyman (n 4) 123.

South African criminal law is still under general unlawfulness, but within this structure it is clear that the role of consent is changing.

1.3 Form of consent

1.3.1 Declared or implied

The form of consent required will be determined by the context. In general, consent may be given either expressly or tacitly. There is in principle no difference between the effect of declared and implied forms of consent.[30] Legislation and standards set by case-law may require consent to be given in more formal, explicit formats. It is especially in the context of medical treatment that precedents of consent forms were developed in order to provide protection for both the patient and the medical practitioner or service provider. The most common generic precedents[31] are the following:

- confirmation informed consent protocol;
- consent to emergency operations on an adult who is contractually incompetent;
- consent to emergency operation on a minor whose parents or guardian cannot be found;
- generic consent to operation;
- consent indemnity and conditions of admission to a medical facility;
- consent to transfusion for blood or blood derivatives and refusal to permit the transfusion of blood or blood derivatives;
- the 'do not resuscitate' instruction form;
- specific patient consent information;
- health care proxy form;
- patient informed consent form;
- refusal to hospital treatment form;
- refusal to consent form.

It is important to note that while there is no qualitative difference between declared and implied forms of consent, mere submission is not enough to establish consent. It is not always easy to distinguish between implied consent and mere submission. In *Swiggelaar* the Supreme Court of Appeal noted that all the circumstances of a particular matter must be taken into account to determine whether passivity is proof of implied consent or whether it is merely the abandonment of outward resistance.[32] Power, gender and age are factors that can also play a role in determining whether passivity constitutes implied consent or whether it is more a question of submission.[33]

1.3.2 Presumed consent

Authors often deal with the topic of 'presumed consent' under the heading of '*negotiorum gestio*' (or, unauthorised administration). In essence, *negotiorum gestio* is the situation where someone intervenes on behalf of someone who is, due to some reason or other, not conscious

---

30 ibid 126.
31 Carstens and Pearmain (n 21) 905–906.
32 1950 (1) PH H61 (AD). This approach was followed by the Supreme Court of Appeal in, s *v*, s 1971 (2) SA 591 (A), 596.
33 S *v* S (n 25) 597.

or in a position to give consent. The consent provided on behalf of someone else will render the intervention lawful. The principles underlying *negotiorum gestio* were crystallised particularly in the context of medical law. A number of requirements have been identified:

- There must be a situation of emergency.
- The patient must be incapable of consenting. The point of departure is, again, individual autonomy. The question is not whether a person's refusal to receive, for instance, medical treatment is wise or not. The question is whether the person was in a position to give consent or not. Accordingly, the first requirement relating to the fact that there must have been an emergency cannot be isolated from the requirement that there must have been an impossibility of procuring the patient's consent.
- The intervention must not be expressly prohibited or against the patient's will. In so far as the wishes of a person are known, there should be no intervention against the known wishes of the patient.
- The intervention should, as a matter of principle, be intended to be in the patient's best interest.[34]

In addition to the requirements referred to above, one can note some general requirements for presumed consent to qualify as a defence. First, there must be reasonable (objective) grounds to assume that had the person affected by the conduct been aware of all the material facts, he or she would not have objected to the intervention. These reasonable grounds for assuming that the affected person would not have objected to the intervention must exist at the time of the commission of the relevant acts. Secondly, the intrusive acts should not go beyond what the presumed consent would have covered. Thirdly, it is not required that the intervention has indeed succeeded in protecting or furthering the interests of the affected person.[35]

Some suggest that motive may play an important role in determining the lawfulness or unlawfulness of the intervention. Motive alone is not enough, of course. Whether the intervention is lawful or not must still be evaluated with regards to the requirements mentioned above.[36]

1.4 Capacity to consent

The general principle is that a person on whose consent reliance is put must have the capacity to consent. This means the person must have (a) the mental capacity to know the nature of the act to which consent is given and (b) appreciates the consequences that may flow from the act. Mentally ill or mentally impaired persons, persons under the influence of alcohol or drugs, asleep persons or persons who are unconscious[37] are therefore regarded as incapable of giving valid consent.[38]

---

34 Carstens and Pearmain (n 21) 907–908.
35 Snyman (n 4) 128. The author defines 'presumed consent' as follows: 'If X commits an act which infringes the interests of another (Y), and X's act thereby accords with the definitional elements of a crime, her conduct is justified if she acts in defence of, or in the furthering of, Y's interests, in circumstances in which Y's consent to the act is not obtainable but there are, nevertheless, at the time of X's conduct reasonable grounds for assuming that Y would indeed have consented to X's conduct had she been in a position to make a decision about it', 127.
36 Burchell (n 1) 350.
37 *S v McLaggan* 2013 (1) SACR 267 (ECG). The court held that the accused in this rape case must have known that the complainant was asleep or unconscious and accordingly knew that the complainant had not consented to sexual intercourse. The accused was accordingly convicted of rape.
38 Snyman (n 4) 126; Burchell (n 1) 229–231.

The fact that a person is mentally ill is not an impediment *per se* to lawful consent. The test for capacity to consent is clinical and with reference to each intervention individually and at the relevant time of the act in question. A mentally ill patient is 'incapable of giving informed consent owing to a mental disorder, if a mental disorder prevents a patient from understanding what he or she consents to – if a mental disorder prevents a patient from choosing decisively; if a mental disorder prevents a patient from communicating his or her consent; or if the mental disorder prevents a patient from accepting the need for a medical intervention.'[39]

Section 3 of the Criminal Law (Sexual Offences and Related Matters) Amendment Act 32 of 2007 provides that 'any person ("A") who unlawfully and intentionally commits an act of sexual penetration with a complainant ("B"), without the consent of B, is guilty of the offence of rape'. It is clear from the statutory text that the element of unlawfulness will be excluded in cases where sexual penetration occurred with the necessary consent. Consent in this context means 'voluntary or uncoerced agreement'.[40] Section 57(2) of Act 32 of 2007 provides that 'notwithstanding anything to the contrary in any law contained, a person who is mentally disabled is incapable of consenting to a sexual act.'

In *S v Chinridze*[41] the appellant was convicted in a regional court of contravening s 3 of Act 32 of 2007 in that he had raped the complainant, a 15-year-old girl who was assessed by a psychiatrist as having an IQ of 60 or below. The psychiatrist found that the complainant was 'mildly retarded' and was unable to tell the time or do simple calculations. The appellant contended that the sexual intercourse had been consensual. The regional court rejected the appellant's contention that the sexual intercourse was consensual. The appellant was sentenced to 15 years' imprisonment. On appeal the court held on the evidence that the intercourse between the appellant and the complainant had not been consensual and that the appellant had been correctly convicted of rape. It is important to note that the court on appeal did not find that the complainant was a person suffering from a *mental disability*, as per s 57(2), read with s 1(1) of Act 32 of 2007. The central issue before the court, for purposes of determining whether the sexual intercourse amounted to rape, was the question of consent on the part of the 15-year-old complainant. The court took the following approach:

> The facts before this court indicate that the complainant resisted the advances of the appellant. There is also the corroboratory evidence of her brother who saw the appellant climbing off the complainant and who confirms the appellant threatened them not to talk.
>
> In considering the evidence of a complainant who was allegedly raped and who was suffering from some mental retardation, a court should consider whether there was both factual and/or legal consent – the former existing when a complainant subjectively or objectively desires to indulge in sexual intercourse, as compared to the latter where a complainant does not choose for herself to have sexual intercourse.
>
> This court is accordingly tasked with a twofold enquiry:
> (1) Was there consent as a matter of fact?
> (2) If yes, then the second enquiry is to ascertain whether there was legal consent (bearing in mind her mental retardation).

39 Carstens and Pearmain (n 21) 901.
40 Gerhard Kemp and others, *Criminal Law in South Africa* (Oxford University Press 2012) 317.
41 *S v Chinridze* 2015 (1) SACR 364 (GP).

If there were no factual consent then naturally the conviction must stand and the second enquiry should fall away.[42]

The court evaluated the evidence, including the testimony of the complainant, and came to the conclusion that, on the first question the answer has to be that there was no *factual consent* on the part of the complainant. The court proceeded to consider the second enquiry as well, in order to cover any possibility that the court could have been wrong on the first enquiry. With regard to the question of *legal consent*, and bearing in mind the mental retardation of the complainant (which is not the same as a clinically proven mental disability), the court concluded that 'the complainant was unable to differentiate between the meaning of the words "rape" and "sexual intercourse"'. The court also noted that, had the necessary enquiry been done in terms of s 1(1) of Act 32 of 2007, 'it is most likely that the complainant would have fallen within one of the four . . . categories, which would have suggested that there could not have been legal consent'.[43] Of course, the strict psychiatric test was not done or at least not presented as evidence in court, making it impossible for the court to establish whether the complainant was indeed suffering from a mental disability. For this case it was not necessary to rely on that determination, since, as stated above, the court was able to determine that there was no factual consent on the part of the complainant. The appeal was therefore dismissed.

The lesson from this judgment is clear: the absence or presence of factual and legal consent is often difficult to determine. Factual consent might even be more difficult to determine. But where there is evidence that suggests mental disability, the state must make sure that it complies with the strict test of s 1(1) of Act 32 of 2007. It will not be enough simply to present evidence (even expert evidence) that informs the court about the complainant's lack of intellectual abilities. The evidence must be in the form of psychiatric evidence proving that the complainant suffers from a form of mental disability that would trigger the absence of legal consent for purposes of s 57(2) read with s 1(1) of Act 32 of 2007.

The age of the person involved can also be important. Under common law, a child (girl) under the age of 12 could not give valid consent to sexual intercourse. The actual age of the girl and not her mental age was the determining factor.[44] The common law presumption is now superseded by s 57(1) of the Criminal Law (Sexual Offences and Related Matters) Amendment Act 32 of 2007 which provides that 'notwithstanding anything to the contrary in any law contained, a male or female person under the age of 12 years is incapable of consenting to a sexual act'. The incapacity to consent to sexual acts has been extended to male children as well.

Children under the age of 18 years cannot consent to a sterilisation, unless a panel of experts has also approved the procedure.[45] The panel of experts will normally only advise in favour of sterilisation of a person under the age of 18 in cases where the risk of pregnancy or eventual childbirth will constitute a real or material threat to the physical health of the patient.[46] Minors 14 years of age or older have the legal capacity to consent to general medical treatment, but parental consent is still necessary for medical operations. In the absence of parents or guardians, persons acting *in loco parentis* may give consent if the power to

---

42 ibid [20]–[22].
43 ibid [37].
44 Burchell (n 1) 229.
45 Section 3 of the Sterilisation Act 44 of 1998.
46 Carstens and Pearmain (n 21) 905.

consent was delegated by the parents/guardians. By law, the High Court, as upper guardians of minors, may also authorise medical interventions where appropriate.[47]

1.5 Consequences of mistaken consent

1.5.1 Mistake

Does a mistaken belief by the victim vitiate consent? It is often in the context of sexual offences that the question arises. If a complainant in a rape case mistook the accused for another person, causing her to have consensual sex with that person, it will be considered a case of *error in persona*. Such a mistake will nullify the consent. As a matter of principle, it is submitted that a mistake caused by fraud should generally vitiate the consent.[48]

1.5.2 Deception

In principle, consent obtained as a result of fraud or deception may nullify the consent. Error as to the nature of the conduct (*error in negotio*) and error as to the identity of a person participating in the conduct (*error in persona*) may affect the validity of the consent.[49] The common law principles, as developed in case-law, now also find expression in legislation, for instance the Criminal Law (Sexual Offences and Related Matters) Amendment Act. Section 1 of this Act provides for a list of circumstances that affect the validity of consent, including consent as a result of fraud and false pretences. Moreover, the Act also provides for instances where vulnerable persons, notably children, are induced to participate in sexual activities. Section 18 of the Act provides for the criminalisation of the sexual grooming of children. In particular, it is a criminal offence for someone to communicate with a child by any means from, to or in any part of the world with the intention of committing a sexual act with that child; further, it is an offence, having communicated with a child, to invite, persuade, seduce, induce, entice or coerce a child to travel to any part of the world in order to meet another person with the intention to commit a sexual act with the perpetrator or such other person. The internet and social media obviously provide many avenues and platforms for the commission of such acts of grooming. The deceptive acts by the perpetrator will not only vitiate consent but will also be criminal acts under the Criminal Law (Sexual Offences and Related Matters) Amendment Act.[50]

1.6 Mistake about consent

Putative consent, that is, the situation where the accused thought that the victim was consenting to the conduct, does not make the conduct lawful, but may, depending on the circumstances, affect the fault element. Fault, in the form of knowledge of unlawfulness, may be absent in a situation like this. The essential requirement is that the mistake must be *bona fide*.[51] South Africa does not have an equivalent statutory provision as in England, where s 1(1)(c) of the Sexual Offences Act 2003 provides that an accused person's mistaken belief in the existence of consent must be a reasonable belief. In the absence of an objective statutory requirement like in England, reliance is still put on case-law in order to determine what

---

47 ibid 902–903; Burchell (n 1) 230–231.
48 ibid 227.
49 ibid 223.
50 See also Kemp (n 3) 378–379.
51 Burchell (n 1) 231.

would be acceptable *bona fide* mistakes about the existence of consent. A crime like rape is a crime of intention. A *bona fide* mistaken belief regarding consent would exclude fault. The belief would not have to be reasonable. Of course, if the accused foresee the possibility that the complainant is not consenting and proceed with his actions regardless, he will have the necessary intention in the form of *dolus eventualis*, which is sufficient for sexual offences such as rape.[52] There will be no question of *bona fide* mistaken belief that could affect the element of fault, and there will at any rate not be consent to make the action lawful. Commentators on South Africa's Criminal Law (Sexual Offences and Related Matters) Amendment Act suggest that for putative consent to neutralise fault, three requirements should be met:

* Evidence of the mistaken belief must have an 'air of reality' about it.
* The accused must not be 'wilfully blind' or reckless as to whether or not the complainant consented.
* The relevant court must determine 'whether the accused took reasonable steps, in the circumstances, to determine whether consent was present'.[53]

It has to be said that the above submission, broadly based on the case-law of the Canadian Supreme Court, is not universally supported in South Africa.[54] The better way to deal with putative consent is probably to deal with it in specific statutory contexts, such as the English Sexual Offences Act, and with reference to an objective standard that is clearly defined.

2 SPECIFIC ISSUES

2.1 Consent and homicide offences

2.1.1 Mercy killings

For present purposes 'mercy killing' is understood to mean the situation where a person ends the life of another person, without the clear or explicit consent of that person, for humanitarian reasons. Where explicit consent is given, it will be a situation of 'assisted suicide', which is discussed below under 2.1.2.

The 'passive' termination of life, for instance when a life-sustaining treatment is terminated, may be justified and there seems to be broad jurisprudential support for 'passive euthanasia' in South Africa.[55]

---

52 ibid 232.

53 Dee Smythe and Bronwyn Pithey (eds), *Sexual Offences Commentary* (Juta 2011) [2.4.1.2].

54 Burchell (n 1) 232.

55 See *Clarke v Hurst NO and others* 1992 (4) SA 630 (D) on the termination of a life-support system of a patient in a persistent vegetative state. The court held that allowing a terminally ill person to die with dignity is not contrary to the legal convictions of the community (ie the general test for unlawfulness). For further commentary, see ML Lupton, *Clarke v Hurst NO, Brain NO and Attorney-General*, Natal (Unreported 1992 N): A living will, brain death and the best interests of a patient' [1992] 5 South African Journal of Criminal Justice 342; DF Dörfling, 'Eutanasie: Die Reg van die Curator Personae om Verdere Behandeling van 'n Pasient te verbied: 'n Nuwe regverdigingsgrond in die Suid-Afrikaanse reg' [1993] 2 Tydskrif vir Suid-Afrikaanse Reg 345; Neil Boister, 'Causation at the death? *Clarke v Hurst* 1992 (2) SA 676 (D)' [1993] 56 Tydskrif vir Hedendaags Romeins-Hollandse Reg 516; Sybrand A Strauss, 'The right to die or passive euthanasia: One American and the other South African: Two important decisions' [1993] 6 South African Journal of Criminal Justice 196; JL Taitz, 'Euthanasia and the 'legal convictions of society' in a South African context' [1993] 110 South African Law Journal 440.

More controversial is active forms of euthanasia, or mercy killing. The case of *S v Hart-mann*[56] is a good illustration of the different moral, philosophical and legal issues at stake. Hartmann was a medical doctor whose father, at an advanced age, was terminally ill and in great pain. Doctor Hartmann intervened and hastened his father's death by administering a fatal injection of pentothal (an anaesthetic) and was charged with murder. At his trial, he gave evidence that, before his death, he had asked his father if he wanted to 'sleep' and his father had vaguely nodded his head in approval. There was no clear or explicit instruction from his father, so the issue of declared consent was somewhat in dispute. Nevertheless, the court held that according to South African law, deliberately hastening a person's death, even by a few hours, is murder. Importantly, the court also held that even if the deceased had consented, this would not be a defence to the crime of murder. Hartmann was consequently convicted of murder. The court took into account the profound humanitarian circumstances of the case. Hartmann received a wholly suspended sentence. The judgment by the court in *Hartmann* confirmed the view that a humanitarian motive in ending the life of another person does not vitiate the unlawfulness of the conduct. It is also clear from the judgment that the court would not even consider explicit consent as a justification.

South Africa has seen significant social, political and legal changes since the decision in the *Hartmann* case in 1975. These changes prompted the South African Law Reform Commission (SALRC) to produce its 1999 'Report on Euthanasia and the Artificial Preservation of Life'. The Report recommends a statutory framework to deal with euthanasia. Legislation on euthanasia is yet to be debated and adopted by Parliament.[57] In the meanwhile developments in case-law is moving the debate forward. This is further explored below under 2.1.2.

2.1.2 Killing on request of the victim

In 2011 the question about the legality of assisted suicide (killing on request of the victim) was indirectly addressed by the court in the case of *S v Agliotti*.[58] The relevant charge simply stated that the accused did unlawfully and intentionally kill the victim, Roger Brett Kebble. In terms of the charge of murder, the court stated the well-known elements of the crime as follows: Murder is the unlawful and intentional causing of the death of another human being. The elements thereof are – (a) causing the death; (b) of another person; (c) unlawfully; and (d) intentionally. Murder may be caused through an act or omission that causes that death. The issue of assisted suicide (and euthanasia) arose because the prosecution alluded to the fact that the accused took part in an assisted suicide of the deceased (Kebble). It has to be said that this allegation did not form a cornerstone of the case for the state. The court addressed the issue at some length. From a doctrinal point of view it is worth taking note of some of these *obiter* remarks.

The court observed that one should not confuse or equate 'assisted suicide' with 'euthanasia'. The court noted that euthanasia normally takes place in a medical or clinical context. It often involves a terminally ill patient who 'either asks somebody, mostly a medical practitioner, to help him/her out of his/her misery by administering to that patient a fatal dose of something, or giving such patient medication or poisonous substance for the latter to end his/her life with'. Furthermore, the court also noted that euthanasia can be divided into active and passive euthanasia, as well as voluntary and involuntary euthanasia. The court then

---

56 *S v Hartmann* 1975 (3) SA 532 (C).
57 For a critical assessment see JV Larsen, 'Active euthanasia – potential abuse in South Africa: correspondence' [2011] 4 South African Medical Journal 211.
58 *S v Agliotti* 2011 (2) SACR 437 (GSJ).

proceeded to distinguish euthanasia from assisted suicide. The latter, according to the court, occurs when a person requests another person to kill him *by any means*.

From a legal comparative perspective, the court noted that both euthanasia and assisted suicide are to some extent regulated in comparative jurisdictions – which underscores the need for better regulation and legal certainty in South Africa. A cursory reading of the laws of the UK, Canada, Australia, the Netherlands and the US leaves one with the impression that, whereas assisted suicide is still criminalised and punishable, the position regarding euthanasia is more complex and nuanced – ranging from prohibition to progressive decriminalisation (the Netherlands, for instance).

With reference to South Africa, the court noted that the position is still, to a large extent, unclear and even confusing. And if one looks at case-law on these issues, the picture gets even more confusing. The general approach to these matters was summarised by the Supreme Court of Appeal in *Ex parte Die Minister van Justisie: In re S v Grotjohn*.[59]

It is not correct to view the judgment in *Grotjohn* as a general statement on the criminality of assisted suicide (or even euthanasia). The fact that the Supreme Court of Appeal accepted that (depending on the facts of the case) the act of assisting another to die can constitute the crimes of murder, attempted murder, or culpable homicide, should not be taken beyond that of a very general statement. The focus in the case was also on the element of causation, and not the element of unlawfulness. The moral and legal complexities and uncertainties surrounding the assisted suicide/euthanasia debate prompted the government to further investigate the matter, via the work of the South African Law Reform Commission – to which the court in *Agliotti* referred. The Commission considered a variety of viewpoints, including those in favour of and those opposed to euthanasia and/or assisted suicide as a matter of religious principle.

The conclusion in *Agliotti* was that in South Africa a person assisting any other person to commit suicide – let alone actually killing the suicide requestor – will be guilty of an offence. Consequently, anyone who conspires with, aids and/or abets another to commit suicide, albeit called assisted suicide, will be guilty of an offence. It is unfortunate that the court in *Agliotti* found it necessary to throw the euthanasia debate into the equation. The prosecution alluded to assisted suicide in the indictment. The moral context and the full factual matrix cannot possibly be equated with a typical euthanasia scenario. Even though the judge in *Agliotti* also distinguished between assisted suicide and the typical medical care scenario of euthanasia, the judge's understanding of the debate seems to be that all these matters are just two sides of the coin of one moral–legal question: should assisted suicide/euthanasia be allowed? The judge's conclusion regarding assisted suicide (no doubt informed by the factual matrix of the *Agliotti* case itself) is correct, as far as it goes. It is submitted that the question of euthanasia deserves an analysis in a different setting – not the kind of sensational, implicit criminal and morally dubious factual scenarios to which the judgment alluded to.[60]

More recently the debate about the lawfulness of assisted suicide and active euthanasia took yet another turn and gained considerable momentum and some concrete direction with the judgment in *Stransham-Ford v Minister of Justice and Correctional Services*.[61] This case concerned an urgent application by the applicant, who at the time was diagnosed with terminal stage four cancer. The applicant applied for a declaration by the court that he may request a medical practitioner to end his (the applicant's) life or to enable the

---

59 *Ex parte Die Minister van Justisie: In re, s v Grotjohn* 1970 (2) SA 355 (A).

60 For a critical assessment, see Gerhard Kemp 'Criminal Law' (2011) 4 Juta's Quarterly Review.

61 *Stransham-Ford v Minister of Justice and Correctional Services* 2015 (4) SA 50 (GP). See also Manyathi-Jele Nomfundo, 'Update on assisted suicide case' [2015] 554 De Rebus 23; Kemp (n 3) 139–140.

applicant to end his own life by the administration or provision of some or other lethal agent. Since the law as it stood at the time would cause potential criminal and/or civil liability for a medical practitioner who assisted an individual to commit suicide, or who caused such individual to die, the applicant requested the court to declare that the medical practitioner who provided or administered the lethal agent, shall not be held accountable and shall be free from any civil, criminal or disciplinary liability that may in the normal course of events arise from the administration or provision of such lethal agent to the applicant. Importantly, the application also requested the court to develop the common law by declaring the requested assisted suicide or euthanasia to be lawful and constitutional in the particular circumstances of this matter. Judge Fabricius observed that euthanasia and assisted suicide are complex issues. The judge therefore indicated that the issue will probably come before the Constitutional Court for the judges of that court to 'consider all relevant aspects'.[62] Having considered the facts and circumstances of the matter, comparative law, the recommendations of the South African Law Commission (Project 86), and relevant legal principles (notably various fundamental rights, including human dignity and freedom to bodily and psychological integrity), Judge Fabricius concluded that the applicant should be granted his request. The applicant was therefore granted the right to be assisted by a qualified medical doctor, 'who is willing to do so, to end his life, either by administration of a lethal agent or by providing the applicant with the necessary lethal agent to administer himself'.[63]

The judgment has implications for the scope of the common law crimes of murder and culpable homicide. Judge Fabricius declared as follows: 'The common-law crimes of murder or culpable homicide in the context of assisted suicide by medical practitioners, in so far as they provide for an absolute prohibition, unjustifiably limit the applicant's constitutional rights to human dignity, . . . and freedom to bodily and psychological integrity. . ., and to that extent are declared to be overbroad and in conflict with the said provisions of the Bill of Rights.'[64] It appears from the court order that the crimes of murder and culpable homicide in the context of assisted suicide by medical practitioners are not affected, except in so far as these crimes provide for an *absolute* prohibition. It appears that the elements of the crimes of murder and culpable homicide are certainly not affected by the acceptance of the lawfulness of assisted suicide in matters like the *Stransham-Ford* application, but the judgment does present a broadening of the *lawfulness* component, affecting the scope of the crimes and the emergence of a possible consent-based defence. The Constitutional Court will have to give further guidance on this sensitive issue. Ultimately, though, it should be Parliament that must thoroughly debate the merits of active euthanasia and preferably provide medical practitioners (and prosecutors) with the necessary legislative tools to deal with the issue of euthanasia in a lawful, compassionate and humane way.

The *Stransham-Ford* case illustrates the need to have a thorough debate about the legalisation of active euthanasia and assisted suicide. Indeed, *individual cases cannot reasonably establish the foundation of a policy that would have serious and widespread repercussions*. Parliament will have to take this debate further. A consequence of that may very well be the codification of the crimes of murder and culpable homicide, with appropriate provisions on the lawfulness of assisted suicide and active euthanasia.

---

62 ibid [1].
63 ibid [26].
64 ibid.

2.1.3 *Abortion*

Abortion was unlawful under common law. The defence of necessity was available when the life of the mother was in danger. Abortion was also permitted under limited circumstances in terms of the Abortion and Sterilization Act of 1975. After the adoption of South Africa's democratic Constitution of 1996 and the concomitant emphasis on human rights, which include specific protection of reproductive rights,[65] Parliament adopted the much more liberal Choice on Termination of Pregnancy Act.[66] This Act gives women a great deal of freedom to end pregnancies. Abortion may be performed with the informed consent of the woman concerned. The Act provides for specific procedures to be followed in cases where the woman is incapable to give consent. The Act is clear about the fact that only the woman's informed consent, and not the consent of any other person (including the father's) is required. Women under the age of 18 years (ie minors) also do not need the consent of their parents or guardians. The latter provision was challenged in *Christian Lawyers' Association v National Minister of Health*.[67] One of the submissions by the applicant was that the provision that gives minors the right to terminate pregnancies without the consent of parents or guardians of the minor mother involved, violates s 28 of the Constitution, which protects the rights of children as vulnerable persons. The argument was essentially that a child could not give an informed consent without the assistance and guidance of her parents or guardian. This argument was rejected by the court. It was held that informed consent could be given by a child under the age of 18 years. Where the child was not sufficiently mature to make an informed decision, the decision would at any rate not meet the statutory threshold for a valid consent.

For purposes of a lawful termination of a pregnancy it is important to distinguish between three different stages in the pregnancy:

- The first 12 weeks: The pregnancy may be terminated by a medical practitioner upon the request of the mother.
- Week 13 to (and including) week 20: The pregnancy may be terminated by a medical practitioner, after consultation with the mother. The procedure must be done for certain therapeutic,[68] eugenic[69] or humanitarian[70] grounds as set out in the Act.
- After week 20: The pregnancy may only be terminated because the mother's life is in danger or if the continued pregnancy will result in a severely malformed foetus. The decision to terminate the pregnancy cannot be made based only on the informed consent of the mother. The expert opinion of a medical practitioner, after consultation with another medical practitioner or a registered midwife, is required.[71]

---

65 Section 12(2)(a) Constitution of the Republic of South Africa 1996.
66 92 of 1996. For a critique of the Act (notably from a legality point of view) see Ferdinand Van Oosten, 'The Choice on Termination of Pregnancy Act: Some comments' [1998] 1 South African Law Journal 60, 72–76.
67 *Christian Lawyers' Association v National Minister of Health* 2004 (10) BCLR 1086 (T).
68 In this context: The mother's physical or mental health.
69 Especially where there is a substantial risk that the continued pregnancy may result in a severely physically or mentally handicapped baby.
70 This includes such grounds as where the pregnancy was the result of rape or incest. The socio-economic conditions of the mother may also play a role in the decision and may qualify as humanitarian grounds.
71 See further Burchell (n 1) 559–561; Kemp (n 3) 305–307.

2.2 Consent and non-fatal offences against the person

2.2.1 HIV and other communicable disease transmission

The Criminal Law (Sexual Offences and Related Matters) Amendment Act of 2007 does not include a provision on the deliberate exposure of a person to HIV or other communicable disease transmissions. An accused, knowing that he is HIV-positive and who had non-consensual sexual intercourse with another person, and who fails to inform the victim about his HIV status, is guilty of rape and attempted murder, according to case-law.[72] Some suggest that in cases of consensual and unprotected sexual intercourse and where one party deliberately withholds his HIV-positive status from a sexual partner, a conviction of rape or, alternatively, aggravated sexual assault, would be appropriate. This is so because the fraudulent non-disclosure of the HIV-positive status vitiates the required consent.[73] As a matter of logic the same would presumably apply to other sexually transmitted diseases, knowledge of which would also impact on a person's informed consent to sexual intercourse.

2.2.2 Medical treatment

In the normal course of events, adults with the necessary mental capacity can give informed consent to any medical treatment.[74] The National Health Act provides for substituted consent (consent by proxy) in situations where an adult person cannot give consent to medical treatment.[75] Another person may then give consent on such person's behalf. Section 7(1) of the Act provides as follows:

> Subject to section 8, a health service may not be provided to a user without the user's informed consent, unless
> (a) the user is unable to give informed consent and such consent is given by a person
>   (i) mandated by the user in writing to grant consent on his or her behalf; or
>   (ii) authorised to give such consent in terms of any law or court order;
> (b) the user is unable to give informed consent and no person is mandated or authorised to give such consent, and the consent is given by the spouse or partner of the user or, in the absence of such spouse or partner, a parent, grandparent, an adult child or a brother or a sister of the user, in the specific order as listed;
> (c) the provision of a health service without informed consent is authorised in terms of any law or a court order;
> (d) failure to treat the user, or group of people which includes the user, will result in a serious risk to public health; or
> (e) any delay in the provision of the health service to the user might result in his or her death or irreversible damage to his or her health and the user has not expressly, impliedly or by conduct refused that service.

In the case of a mentally ill patient, the Mental Health Care Act provides for the necessary consent requirements for medical treatment.[76] The Act provides for voluntary and involuntary

---

72 S v Nyalungu 2013 (2) SACR 99 (T).
73 Burchell (n 1) 226.
74 Kemp (n 3) 135.
75 61 of 2003.
76 17 of 2002.

care. As far as voluntary medical care is concerned, the Act provides that mentally ill persons may be able to consent to care, treatment and rehabilitation. The test of whether a person who has a mental illness is capable of giving informed consent, should be based on a clinical assessment.[77] Involuntary care is defined in the Act as 'the provision of health interventions to people incapable of making informed decisions due to their health status and who refuse health intervention but require such services for their own protection or for the protection of others and 'involuntary care, treatment and rehabilitation services' has a corresponding meaning'.[78]

A child of 14 years or older can give informed consent to medical treatment (excluding operations). The test is whether the child is sane and sober and otherwise mentally capable of making informed decisions.[79]

2.2.3 Sport injuries, 'horseplay', piercing

Voluntary participation in lawful sport and games implies 'consent to or voluntary assumption of the risk of bodily injuries incurred while the game is being played according to the rules'.[80] It should be noted that there is no requirement for a set of formal rules. Of course, most organised sport (including contact sport like boxing and rugby) has detailed rules governing all aspects of the game. In cases of friendly and informal 'horseplay' there will normally be explicit or implicit agreement on the limits of the game and on the common understanding that serious injury is to be avoided or not likely to be a risk. Consent to 'horseplay' will consequently qualify as a defence in cases of injury or harm.[81]

In organised sport, where games are governed by formal rules, the question is whether harm flowing from a violation of the rules of the game is also covered by consent. It appears that consent will apply to actions, although contrary to the rules of the game, that are still within the normal bounds of the given sport. For instance, when a rugby player causes injury to an opposing player because of a tackle that is contrary to the rules of the game, his action will still be lawful, provided there is no intention to assault and provided the action falls within the normal, anticipated and accepted risks of the game.[82]

Piercings, understood as a minor or trivial form of harm for aesthetic purposes, will generally be lawful. The principle is that a person may freely consent to physical injury (such as a body piercing) as long as the injury is not serious and does not produce substantial harm.[83] One can also note that in pluralistic societies like South Africa, piercings are often done not only for aesthetic or cosmetic reasons, but also in the context of cultural practices. The test will remain the same: where the practice concerned results or is likely to result in minor injury only, consent will negate the unlawfulness of the bodily harm. In cases where the injury produces actual, serious bodily harm, the consent will be no defence.[84] The issue is, of course, not the injury *per se*. It is a question of whether public policy warrants juristic recognition of the consent.[85]

---

77 Carstens and Pearmain (n 21) 901.
78 Section 1, 17 of 2002.
79 Carstens and Pearmain (n 21) 902.
80 Burchell (n 1) 220.
81 ibid.
82 ibid 220–221.
83 *McCoy* 1953 (2) SA 4 (SR); Kemp (n 3) 134.
84 *S v Sikunyana and others* 1961 (3) SA 549 (E); ibid 136–137.
85 See remarks by Burchell (n 1) 217.

2.2.4 Specific sexual practices involving infliction of harm

The underlying policy question regarding the validity of consent in the context of sport injuries and body piercing is also applicable in cases of sexual practices involving infliction of harm. If a person consents to be subjected to the infliction of actual physical harm (or the risk of such) by another person as part of sado-masochistic practices, the question is whether the consent will serve as a defence to the harm done. Individual autonomy, collective security and cultural diversity are some of the prominent policy considerations that will play a role in determining the lawfulness of consent to bodily harm for sexual practices.[86] It was pointed out above that the seriousness of the bodily harm inflicted is important, but not the only factor. Individual autonomy, privacy, and dignity are constitutional rights that inform the broader policy analysis.[87] At present there is no reported case-law in South Africa on consensual sexual practices involving the infliction of bodily harm, and whether consent in this context will be viewed as a defence. Commentators suggest that a nuanced, constitutionally and culturally sensitive approach should lead to a finding that strikes a balance between individual autonomy and collective welfare. Burchell writes that the 'criminal law, rather than the individual, is the final arbiter in the decision whether consent is defence to criminal liability or not'.[88]

2.3 Sexual offences

2.3.1 Absence of consent or use of force/threats

Section 1(2) of the Criminal Law (Sexual Offences and Related Matters) Amendment Act defines consent for purposes of the crime of rape as follows: '"consent" means voluntary or uncoerced agreement'. Section 1(3) of the Act provides for factors indicating that consent by the complainant is presumed to lack the requirements of consent as defined in s 1(2). These factors are:

(a) Where B (the complainant) submits or is subjected to such a sexual act as a result of –
   (i) the use of force or intimidation by A (the accused person) against B, C (a third person) or D (another person) or against the property of B, C or D; or
   (ii) a threat of harm by A against B, C or D or against the property of B, C or D;
(b) where there is an abuse of power or authority by A to the extent that B is inhibited from indicating his or her unwillingness or resistance to the sexual act, or unwillingness to participate in such a sexual act;
(c) where the sexual act is committed under false pretences or by fraudulent means, including where B is led to believe by A that –
   (i) B is committing such a sexual act with a particular person who is in fact a different person; or
   (ii) such a sexual act is something other than that act; or
(d) where B is incapable in law of appreciating the nature of the sexual act, including where B is, at the time of the commission of such sexual act –
   (i) asleep;
   (ii) unconscious;

---

86 ibid 216–217.
87 See *National Coalition for Gay and Lesbian Equality v Minister of Justice* 1999 (1) SA 6 (CC) on the importance of individual autonomy and privacy in South Africa's constitutional dispensation.
88 Burchell (n 1) 218.

(iii) in an altered state of consciousness, including under the influence of any medicine, drug, alcohol or other substance, to the extent that B's consciousness or judgement is adversely affected;

(iv) a child below the age of 12 years; or

(v) a person who is mentally disabled.

It is clear from the above statutory provisions that the use of force and threats, including the use of force and threats against third persons, may vitiate consent as a defence in sexual offences cases.

What is the impact of the revocation of consent during intercourse, after it was started consensually? In principle, consent should be regarded as a unilateral act. It can be withdrawn unilaterally (that is, at least until such time as the act commences).[89] Sexual intercourse presents a potential problem in this regard. Authority (such as the old case of *Handcock*) of dubious modern application holds that where a woman consents to have sex with a man and, after the commencement of the act, but before its completion, changes her mind and the man then refuses to desist and keeps going in order to reach climax, it will not be regarded as rape.[90] This view cannot be supported. Surprisingly, there is in South Africa no recent case-law on this issue and judgments such as *Handcock* will probably not find support in contemporary South African courts.

2.3.2 Evidentiary presumptions

On the topic of consent there is one presumption under common law, and now also provided for in the Criminal Law (Sexual Offences and Related Matters) Amendment Act, that is important to note. Under common law there was an irrebuttable presumption that a girl below the age of 12 years cannot give lawful consent to sexual intercourse. This presumption, now in statutory form, is no longer only applicable to girls and is applicable to any child under the age of 12 years. This presumption is, strictly speaking, not an evidentiary presumption. An irrebuttable presumption is a rule of substantive law. It directs a court 'to accept a situation as conclusively proved once certain (other) basics facts have been proved' (for instance, the age of the complainant).[91]

2.3.3 Mistake of fact about consent

The general principle is that 'the consenting person must be aware of the true and material facts regarding the acts to which he/she consents'.[92] The meaning of 'material facts' will be determined by the definition of the crime in question. Mistaken identity (*error personae*) is an example of a mistake of fact that impacts on the validity of consent in rape cases.[93]

---

89 Kemp (n 3) 144.
90 1925 OPD 147.
91 Pamela-Jane Schwikkard and SE van der Merwe, *Principles of Evidence* (2nd edition, Juta 2002) 34.
92 Snyman (n 4) 126. See also Burchell (n 1) 227.
93 *R v C* 1952 (4) SA 117 (O) 120–121; ibid 126.

2.4 Property offences and criminal damage

2.4.1 Place of consent in the offence structure

Consent in the context of crimes relating to appropriation of property may affect the unlawfulness of the appropriation. Consent and presumed consent (*negotiorum gestio*) may justify the appropriation of or damage to another's property. Where an owner consents to the accused's appropriation of or damage to the property (even where the accused is unaware of such consent, or where the accused thinks that no consent has been given) the appropriation or damage caused will not be unlawful.[94]

2.4.2 Mistaken belief in consent

Presumed consent (*negotiorum gestio*) was dealt with above under 1.3.2. It was noted that objective criteria apply when determining the existence of legitimate presumed consent. An unreasonable mistaken belief in the existence of consent will not be a defence.

---

94 Snyman (n 4) 484 (relying on Roman-Dutch authorities).

15
Australia

Mirko Bagaric

1 GENERAL ISSUES

1.1 Conceptual foundations

1.1.1 Philosophical and theoretical principles informing the law surrounding consent

There are nine jurisdictions in Australia (six states, two territories and the federal jurisdiction), each has its own criminal law. The main source of criminal law in three of the states (Victoria, New South Wales, South Australia) is the common law, which is derived from the UK. The criminal law in the other jurisdictions is based mainly in statute and, for this reason, they are referred to as the Code jurisdictions. The Criminal Codes in Queensland and Western Australia are the oldest and are similar. The Code in the Australian Capital Territory is based on the Commonwealth Code, which also informs aspects of the Northern Territory Code.

Despite the divergent sources of criminal law in Australia, there is considerable similarity in the way consent operates. This chapter focuses on the manner in which consent applies generally in the Australian criminal law, while highlighting any relevant or significant disparities.

Consent means agreement or, at least, permission. The concept of consent does not have a coherent role in Australian criminal law, stemming in part from the fact that Australian criminal law is devoid of an over-arching, conceptual framework. Moreover, the notion of consent does not have a (stand-alone) well-established doctrinal foundation. To the extent that consent has been subject to a meaningful degree of theoretical analysis, it is normally indirectly by reference to the broader ideals of autonomy and, to a lesser extent liberty, both of which underpin consent. Despite this, consent does figure prominently in the law concerning rape and assault.[1]

---

[1] The concept of autonomy has been defined in many ways. It has been treated as a synonym for freedom of the will, sovereignty, liberty and self-rule, or equated with self-knowledge, responsibility, dignity and integrity: see, for example, Gerald Dworkin, *The Theory and Practice of Autonomy* (Cambridge University Press 1986) 5–6; John Harris, *The Value of Life: An Introduction to Medical Ethics* (Routledge 1985) 195; John Finnis, 'Living Will Legislation' in Luke Gormally (ed), *Euthanasia, Clinical Practice and the Law*

The fundamental reason for the lack of coherency in the treatment of consent in Australian criminal law is that the criminal law does not itself have a clear and stable theoretical foundation. As Andrew Ashworth correctly notes, the criminal law is 'society's strongest form of official punishment and censure'.[2] Moreover, it is a 'fundamental ethical principle that we may not inflict pain or disgrace upon another without adequate justification'.[3] Thus, doctrinally the stigmatisation and punishment that are consequent upon a finding of guilt for a criminal offence require a moral justification. In order for an act to be deserving of blame and the deliberate infliction of punishment, it should breach an important norm or standard. Yet, Lord Atkin's observation in *Proprietary Articles Associations v AG for Canada* that morality and criminality are not co-extensive is correct.[4]

Breaches of numerous moral norms are not subject to criminal prohibition, such as lying and infidelity. Moreover, there are many acts that are morally unobjectionable but that are criminal offences in Australia, such as drug use, riding a bicycle without a helmet or parking in a non-parking zone. Despite this, Lord Coleridge's view that 'the absolute divorce of law from morality would be of fatal consequence' is also true.[5] Hence, in Australia there is a loose link between morality and the criminal law, however, the link is blurred by the fact that there is no express foundational moral theory that is endorsed by the Australian criminal justice system (or the broader community).

To the extent that there is a shared public morality in Australia, it is derived from a hybrid of normative principles, oscillating (seemingly arbitrarily) between a consequentialist ethic and deontological discourse (which focuses on observance of human rights). In abstract, deontological theories could create a considerable role for consent in the criminal law; however, no interest or right is absolute (even the right to life is subject to the right to self-defence), and deontological theories provide no clear answers to the limits of rights when they clash with other rights or the common good. And certainly, there has been no considered attempt to use the criminal law as a vehicle for protecting individual rights. The criminal law does protect a number of cardinal rights, such as the right to life, liberty, property and physical and sexual autonomy, however, they all have considerable exceptions (broadly based on consequentialist grounds), and neither the scope of the rights that are protected nor the exceptions have been developed by reference to rights discourse.

To the extent that individual rights are promoted by the criminal law, one of the most influential is closely connected with consent. It is the notion of liberty, which was most persuasively articulated by John Stuart Mill, as follows:

> The sole end for which mankind are warranted, individually or collectively, in interfering with the liberty of action of any of their number, is self-protection. The only purpose for which power can be rightfully exercised over any member of a civilised community, against his will, is to prevent harm to others. His own good, either physical or moral, is not a sufficient warrant. He cannot rightfully be compelled to do or forbear because it will be better for him to do so, because it will make him happier, because, in the opinion of others, to do so would be wise, or even right.[6]

(Linacre Centre for Health Care Ethics 1994) 167, 171. A common thread to emerge from these definitions is that autonomy is the capacity to live one's life as he or she chooses.

2 Andrew Ashworth, *Principles of Criminal Law* (2nd edition, Oxford University Press 1995) 16.

3 J V Barry, 'Morality and the Coercive Process' (1962–4) 4 Sydney Law Review 28, 29.

4 (1931) AC 324.

5 *R v Dudley and Stephens* (1884) 14 QBD 287.

6 John Stuart Mill, 'Utilitarianism' in M Warnock (ed), *Utilitarianism* (Fontana 1986) 135.

This concept has received some judicial endorsement in Australia. For example, Mason CJ and Brennan J stated:

> The right to personal liberty is . . . the most elementary and fundamental of all common law rights. Personal liberty was held by Blackstone to be an absolute right vested in the individual . . . he warned, 'of great importance to the public is the preservation of this personal liberty: for if once it were left in the power of any . . . magistrate to imprison arbitrarily . . . there would soon be an end of all other rights and immunities'.[7]

However, there are countless examples of encroachments on the virtue of liberty by the criminal law, such as the prohibition against the use of illicit drugs and the requirement to wear seat belts while driving.

Thus, the criminal law in Australia has a moral touchstone but not one that is coherent or obvious. This situation is not uncommon in a democracy where crime and sentencing is strongly influenced by populist sentiment. It is for these reasons that normative considerations such as consent have relevance in the criminal justice system but not in a manner that is necessarily principled and justifiable. This explains why some readers of this chapter will find the treatment of consent in the Australian criminal law to be inconsistent and, at times, curious. I now consider the specific role that consent has in the Australian criminal law system.

1.1.2 Influence of feminist and queer theory

Feminist theory has had a considerable influence on the role of consent in the criminal law, especially so far as the law relating to sexual offences and abortion is concerned. Women have the right to make decisions that preserve their physical and sexual integrity. Thus, as we shall see below, Australia has relatively liberal abortion laws that recognise the dominion that a woman has over her body.[8]

Moreover, considerable statutory changes have been made in the area of rape and sexual offences, which abolish antiquated criminal law defences, such as, that a husband cannot rape his wife,[9] and the view that continuation of sexual intercourse after consent has been withdrawn does not constitute rape.[10] Many of these changes have only been formulated in the past few decades. It was only in 1993 that the South Australian Court of Criminal Appeal in the *Case Stated by Director of Public Prosecutions (SA) (No 1 of 1993)*[11] noted that a trial judge's direction that consent obtained by a husband by 'rougher than usual handling' can constitute valid consent was a misdirection because it can give the impression that it is legitimate to obtain consent by force, against the will of the victim.[12] The matter has now been clarified by changes to the legal definition of consent which make it clear that in order for consent to be valid it must be totally free.[13] This approach has been reinforced by statutory changes that make it clear that a large number of types of threats, not only as to physical violence or force, can vitiate consent.

---

7 *R v Williams* (1986) 161 CLR 278, 292 (per Mason CJ and Brennan J).
8 See section 2.1.3, below.
9 The precise status of this doctrine as part of the common law of Australia has remained obscure: see, *SR v L* (1991) 174 CLR 379; *PGA v The Queen* [2012] HCA 21.
10 *R v Salmon* [1969] SASR 76; compare *Kaitamaki v The Queen* [1985] AC 147.
11 (1993) 66 A Crim R 259.
12 ibid.
13 See section 2.3 below.

The influence of the feminist perspective is also evident in relation to domestic violence laws. Domestic violence, which is usually perpetrated by men, is illegal in Australia pursuant to the general offence of assault. However, there was evidence that domestic violence was not as rigorously investigated by police or prosecuted as extensively as other cases of assault. Wide-ranging community education campaigns occurred to redress this failing.[14]

1.1.3 Definition of informed consent

As is discussed below, the concept of consent has an important role in relation to sexual offences and assault. In this context, consent is most commonly defined as 'free agreement'.[15]

1.1.4 Consent to risk or consent to outcome

Most activities carry the prospect of unforeseen outcomes that is reflected in the criminal law. Generally, it is consent to risk that is relevant; however, this is not the case in relation to activities that cannot be excused if the harm exceeds a certain level.[16]

1.1.5 Revocation of consent

Consent is never final and can always be withdrawn prior to the act in question. This stems from the underlying nature of autonomy, which entails that individuals should generally be free to define their own path. The non-binding nature of consent applies to all forms of offences to which consent is applicable, for example, rape and other types of sexual offences, dealings with property and even the right of a land owner to determine who can enter land.[17]

1.1.6 Ownership and limits of consent

Consent to the extent that it is relevant can only emanate from the person who has legal control and ownership of the relevant subject matter. Thus, individuals can consent to offences that relate to interference with their sexual or physical integrity. In relation to property offences, consent can only be given by people who own or control the objects. It is only the government that can consent to interferences with public legal interests.

1.2 Place of consent in the offence structure

All criminal offences can be broken down into a number of specific elements. For an accused to be guilty of a crime, every element must be established. Nearly all crimes have a combination of mental elements (known as the *mens rea*) and physical elements (known as the *actus*

---

14 Kerry Carrington, 'Domestic Violence in Australia – an Overview of the Issues' (*Parliament House of Australia*, September 2006). <http://www.aph.gov.au/about_parliament/parliamentary_departments/parliamentary_library/publications_archive/archive/domviolence> accessed 30 September 2015; Amanda George and Bridget Harris, *Landscapes of Violence: Women Surviving Family Violence in Regional and Rural Victoria* (Centre for Rural and Regional Law and Justice 2014); Prime Minister of Australia, 'National Awareness Campaign to Reduce Violence against Women and Children (Joint Press Release)' (*Parliament of Australia*, 4 March 2015) <https://minister.women.gov.au/media/2015–03–04/national-awareness-campaign-reduce-violence-against-women-and-children>.

15 See section 2 below.

16 See, for example, the discussion on horseplay below.

17 *Porter v Hannah Builders Pty Ltd* [1969] VR 673. In relation to sexual offences, see 2.3 below.

reus).[18] In addition to establishing each element of an offence, the prosecution must rebut each available defence.

Generally, consent (or the absence of it) is a part of the *actus reus* of an offence, but there is no strict rule to this effect. For example, as is discussed below, in the case of some assault offences, it operates as a defence.

1.3 Form of consent

1.3.1 Declared or implied

Consent can take a number of different forms. The most compelling and unequivocal is when it is declared (ie express). However, in some cases it can be implied, typically, when the event in question is a commonplace and largely unavoidable aspect of human activity, such as contact between people in a crowded bus or train. Voluntary participation in activities also implies consent to the types of contact that come within the scope of the norms or rules of that activity. Thus, individuals who participate in sporting activities consent to types of contact that are inherent and within the rule of the sporting activity.[19]

In most situations, consent is verbal, largely because many of the transactions and events which form the backdrop of criminal behaviour are informal human interactions. However, in formal settings when it is known in advance that there is likely to be a significant incursion into an individual's physical integrity or a transfer of property interests, consent normally occurs in a written form. Thus, patients typically sign a written document consenting to medical treatment and, in order for transfers in real property to occur, it is necessary for them to be facilitated by the written consent of the owner.

1.3.2 Presumed consent

Individuals generally have the right to make autonomous choices regarding their activities, hence, the law generally does not recognise the concept of presumed consent. The main exception to this, which is discussed further below, is in the medical domain where individuals who cannot express their consent are presumed to consent to life-saving or emergency medical treatment.

1.4 Capacity to consent

As noted above, consent means agreement. For this to occur, a person must have the capacity to understand the nature and character of the act.[20] Thus, as a general rule, adults can only consent to matters that are likely to have a long-term or significant impact on the physical or mental condition of a person.[21]

The association between intoxication and consent is complex. It is accepted that intoxication can impair judgment. However, the fact a person is intoxicated does not normally negate consent. This is especially pertinent in relation to sexual offences, where victims are assumed to be able to consent to sexual relations unless the extent of the intoxication is such that the person is not capable of freely agreeing.[22]

---

18 The exception being strict liability offences which have only *actus reus* requirements.
19 *Pallante v Stadiums Pty Ltd (No 1)* [1976] VR 331.
20 *Freeman v Home Office (No 2)* [1984] QB 524.
21 See further, the decision on medical treatment below.
22 See, for example, CC (NT), s 192(2)(c); Crimes Act 1958 (Vic), s 36(d); Criminal Code (Tas), s 2A(2)(h).

1.5 Consequences of mistaken consent

1.5.1 *Mistake*

As is noted above, most criminal acts require subjective wrongdoing on behalf of the defendant. It follows that if consent is an element of an offence or a defence, mistaken belief in the existence of a defence will normally operate to exculpate criminal liability.[23]

1.5.2 *Deception*

If consent is granted by a victim as a result of a misrepresentation or lie by the accused, this can (depending on the offence in question) vitiate the consent. In *R v Mobilio* the accused was a radiographer who inserted an ultrasound into the vagina of three women who consented after he had informed them it was a necessary medical procedure.[24] The referring doctors had not, in fact, requested such a procedure. The charges were ultimately quashed on the basis that even though the procedures were performed for the sexual gratification of the accused, the women consented to the very act that occurred and the accused's private motivation did not relevantly alter the essential nature of the act. This result has been overturned by legislation, and the effect of the changes is to accord greater importance for consent in relation to acts that impact on the sexual integrity of individuals.[25]

As noted below, consent is a paramount and determinative consideration in relation to property offences. It is in this context that deception also assumes its greatest significance. In relation to deception offences, there can be no crime when the complainant consents to the transfer or dealing with the property. However, the consent of the owner can be vitiated in a large number of ways, due to the relatively wide-ranging definition of deception and the circumstances in which it can occur. For example, s 81(4) of the Crimes Act (Vic) states:

> (4) For the purposes of this section, 'deception' –
>   (a) means any deception (whether deliberate or reckless) by words or conduct as to fact or as to law, including a deception as to the present intentions of the person using the deception or any other person; and
>   (b) includes an act or thing done or omitted to be done with the intention of causing –
>   (i) a computer system; or
>   (ii) a machine that is designed to operate by means of payment or identification – to make a response that the person doing or omitting to do the act or thing is not authorised to cause the computer system or machine to make.

Deception can occur by words or conduct and can be express or implied.[26] It can even relate to future events provided it misrepresents an existing fact such as one's present intention to do what was promised.[27]

The internet has resulted in new means for offenders to commit sexual offences, and, in particular, for them to groom minors. In Australia, such predatory conduct is a criminal offence. The consent of the child is no defence to such conduct, and it is only in limited

---

23 See section 2 below.
24 [1991] 1 VR 339.
25 See, for example, Crimes Act 1900 (NSW), s 61HA(5)(c); Criminal Law Consolidation Act 1935 (SA), s 46(3)(h); CA 1958 (n 22), s 34C(2)(i), s 38.
26 *DPP v Ray* [1974] AC 370.
27 *R v Lo Presti* (2005) 158 A Crim R 54; [2005] VSCA 259.

circumstances that a mistake by the accused can provide a defence to such conduct. For example, the Criminal Code 1995 (Cth) provides:

272.15 'Grooming' child to engage in sexual activity outside Australia
(1) A person commits an offence if:
   (a) the person engages in conduct in relation to another person (the child); and
   (b) the person does so with the intention of making it easier to procure the child to engage in sexual activity (whether or not with the person) outside Australia; and
   (c) the child is someone:
      (i) who is under 16; or
      (ii) who the person believes to be under 16; and
   (d) one or more of the following apply:
      (i) the conduct referred to in paragraph (a) occurs wholly or partly outside Australia;
      (ii) the child is outside Australia when the conduct referred to in paragraph (a) occurs;
      (iii) the conduct referred to in paragraph (a) occurs wholly in Australia and the child is in Australia when that conduct occurs. . . .

272.16 Defence based on belief about age
Offences involving sexual intercourse or other sexual activity with a child – belief that child is at least 16
(3) It is a defence to a prosecution for an offence against section 272.14 or 272.15 if the defendant proves that, at the time the defendant engaged in the conduct constituting the offence, he or she believed that the child was at least 16.

Thus, if a child deceives an accused that he or she is at least 16, this is a defence to this charge.

1.6 Mistake about consent

Where the absence of consent is an element of an offence, a belief in the existence of consent by the accused that is mistaken will negate the existence of this element. This is discussed further below in the context of sexual offences, property offences and assault.

2 SPECIFIC ISSUES

2.1 Consent and homicide offences

2.1.1 Mercy killings

In Australia, there is no formal definition of 'mercy killing'. However, normally the term is used to describe when a friend or family member intentionally kills the victim in circumstances where it is thought to be in the best interests of the victim.[28] Mercy killing can occur

---

28 Other definitions of mercy killing are in Law Reform Commission of Victoria, 'Murder: Mental Element and Punishment' (1984) Law Reform Commission of Victoria Working Paper No 8, 24. For a discussion on mercy killing, see Anthony Flew, 'The Principle of Euthanasia' in A B Downing and Barbara Smoker (eds), *Voluntary Euthanasia: Experts Debate the Right to Die* (Peter Owen 1986) 43.

in a number of relevantly different contexts. The key distinguishing features include whether the killing is done with the consent of the victim, and whether the death arises out of a positive act or an omission. The formal term used in Australia to describe killings that encapsulate all forms of mercy killings is euthanasia. This term is used in the next two subsections.

There are several categories of euthanasia.[29] Voluntary euthanasia is where the (typically) ill person has expressly manifested a desire to be killed. Voluntary active euthanasia refers to the taking of direct action, such as administering a lethal injection to kill someone who has expressed a wish to die.[30]

Voluntary passive euthanasia is to withhold or withdraw life-sustaining medical treatment from a patient with the intention of accelerating the patient's death at the patient's request.[31] As we shall see below, a distinction is often drawn between forms of passive euthanasia according to whether the treatment withdrawn is an 'ordinary' or 'extraordinary' means of prolonging life.[32]

In the next section, I discuss killing at the request of the victim. At this point, I focus on forms of euthanasia that are not performed at the request of the victim. There are two forms of euthanasia of this nature. Involuntary euthanasia is where the victim does not want to be killed but the accused believes that killing is in the best interests of the victim (for example, because the victim is very ill). Non-voluntary euthanasia is killing someone where he or she is either not in a position to have or to express any views on whether he or she would wish to be killed, for example, a person in an irreversible coma.[33] Conceptually, neither involuntary nor non-voluntary euthanasia can rely on many of the arguments that are customarily used to support voluntary euthanasia, such as respect for personal autonomy, and are almost universally condemned from the normative perspective.[34] Legally, they are both unlawful and constitute murder.

The only exception to this is non-voluntary passive euthanasia, where it is in the 'best interests of the patient'. In *Airedale NHS Trust v Bland*, the patient, then aged 17, was crushed in the 1989 Hillsborough football ground disaster.[35] He suffered irreversible brain damage and went into a permanent vegetative state with no hope of any improvement. At no time prior to the disaster had he indicated his wishes if he found himself in such a state. His father stated that his son would not want to be like that. After being in that state for over three years the family and hospital sought declarations that they might lawfully discontinue

---

29 An act which is closely associated with euthanasia is assisted suicide. This is where the ill person is aided in taking his or her life by another, for example, by being intentionally supplied with lethal drugs. In terms of outcome, this practice obviously has many similarities with euthanasia. The difference between active voluntary euthanasia and assisted suicide lies in who commits the last act. Their similarity lies in the involvement of another person to promote or bring about death. The key distinction lies in the fact that the patient maintains greater control of the procedure and hence there is greater regard for his or her autonomy and arguably less risk of abuse.

30 British Medical Association, *Euthanasia: A Report of the Working Party to Review the British Medical Association's Guidance on Euthanasia* (British Medical Association 1988) 3; Margaret Otlowski, 'Mercy Killing Cases in the Australian Criminal Justice System' (1993) 17 Criminal Law Journal 10.

31 William Cannon, 'The Right to Die' (1970) 7 Houston Law Review 654, 657.

32 T O'Donnell, 'Review of the Physician's Responsibility Toward Hopelessly Ill Patients' (1984) 51 Linacre Quarterly 351; David Louisell, 'Euthanasia and Biathanasia: On Dying and Killing' (1973) Catholic University Law Review 723, 730.

33 See, Jonathan Glover, *Causing Deaths and Saving Lives* (Pelican Books 1977) 191.

34 Although, see, James Rachels, *The End of Life: Euthanasia and Morality* (Oxford University Press 1986) 159, where he argues that many people have less difficulty accepting non-voluntary euthanasia than voluntary euthanasia – presumably because in cases of non-voluntary euthanasia the patient often has such a poor quality of life that it may seem to be in his or her best interests to not prolong life.

35 [1933] AC 789.

life-sustaining medical treatment, namely, artificial feeding and antibiotic drugs and, there-after, not provide treatment except for the sole purpose of enabling the patient to end his life with the least suffering. The removal of the nasogastric tube to provide artificial feeding and the discontinuance of artificial feeding were held to be omissions, rather than an act, thus it is a case of non-voluntary passive euthanasia.[36] The House of Lords upheld the decision of the Court of Appeal that it was lawful to discontinue the medical treatment.

2.1.2 Killing on request of the victim

In Australia, active voluntary euthanasia is unlawful and constitutes murder. The fact that the victim has consented to the killing is no defence. Consent of a victim is not a defence to death and, therefore, is not a basis upon which culpability can be avoided in cases of euthanasia. In 1992, Ognall J stated that there is an '*absolute* prohibition on a doctor purposefully taking life (emphasis added)'.[37] More recently, in 1993, the House of Lords in *Airedale NHS Trust v Bland*[38] confirmed that it is unlawful to take active measures to shorten the life of a terminally ill patient by directly intentionally killing the patient, 'even though that course is prompted by a humanitarian desire to end . . . suffering, no matter how great that may be'.[39] As Palmer notes 'If the acts done are intended to kill and do in fact, kill, it does not matter whether a life is cut short by weeks or months, it is just as much murder as if it were cut short by years.'[40]

To soften this strict approach, the courts often, at least partially, embrace the doctrine of double effect and maintain that while motive is irrelevant, intention is paramount. In *R v Adams* it was held that it is permissible to 'relieve pain and suffering even if the measure . . . incidentally shortens life'.[41] Even more pointedly, in *R v Cox* it was held that:

> if a doctor genuinely believes that a certain course [such as increasing the dose of anal-gesic] is beneficial to a patient . . . then even though he recognises that that course carries with it a risk to life, he is fully entitled, to nonetheless pursue it. If in those circumstances the patient dies, nobody could possibly suggest that . . . the doctor was guilty of murder or attempted murder.[42]

This approach effectively applies the doctrine of double effect.[43] The status of the doctrine was more recently endorsed by Walker LJ in *A Child (the conjoined twins case)*. In declaring

---

36 However, Sir Themes Bingham MR in the Court of Appeal, ibid 808, stated that since this had nothing to do with taking positive action to cause death it was not a case about euthanasia at all. And Hoffmann LJ, 856, stated that 'this is not a case about euthanasia because it does not involve any external agency of death. It is about whether, and how, a patient should be allowed to die'. These views fail to recognise passive euthanasia as a category of euthanasia.

37 *Cox* (n 38). In this case Dr Cox killed his terminally ill patient, and friend, who had expressed a wish to die by injecting her with potassium chloride (which has no therapeutic or analgesic effect) and was found guilty of murder. He was sentenced to a year in a jail, but the sentence was suspended. His employer, the Wessex Regional Health Authority, reprimanded him but did not bar him from continuing to practice medicine.

38 *Bland* (n 35).

39 ibid, 865.

40 H Palmer, 'Dr Adams Trial for Murder' [1957] Criminal Law Review 365.

41 ibid 365.

42 (1992) 12 BMLR 38, 39. See also, *Bland* (n 35) 867; *Auckland Area Health Board v Attorney-General* [1993] 1 NZLR 235, 248.

43 The doctrine provides that it is morally permissible to perform an act having two effects, one good and one evil, where the good consequence is intended and the bad merely foreseen, there is proportionality

that it was lawful to perform an operation that would certainly kill one conjoined twin, in order that the other could live, he stated that:

> The proposed operation would not be unlawful. It would involve the positive act of invasive surgery and Mary's death would be foreseen as an inevitable consequence of an operation which is intended, and is necessary, to save Jodie's life. But Mary's death would not be the purpose or intention of the surgery, and she would die because tragically her body, on its own, is not and never has been viable.[44]

In relation to passive voluntary euthanasia, (as is discussed below) patients are free to reject all forms of treatment and it is an assault to force a patient to undertake treatment against his or her wish. Hence, patient consent is determinative when it comes to the killing of a patient by an omission. Where a patient is not competent to indicate his or her wishes (because he or she is unconscious) then all necessary and appropriate treatment must be provided to him or her. The only exception relates to extraordinary treatment.[45] This can be withdrawn, even if it would result in the inevitable death of the patient if it is in the best interests of the patient, or the patient has signed an advanced directive.[46]

2.1.3 Abortion

Australia has relatively liberal laws in relation to abortion. The wishes of the woman are generally determinative and her consent to killing the foetus is lawful, so long as the abortion is necessary to preserve the woman from physical or mental danger, and the termination of the pregnancy is proportionate to the need to preserve the woman from danger.[47] To this end, the defence of necessity has been adapted to the context of abortion. This test has been interpreted broadly and there have been no prosecutions in Australian for unlawful abortions for several decades. Statutes in some jurisdictions enshrine the liberal approach to abortion.

For example, the Abortion Law Reform Law Act 2008 (Vic) enables a woman who is not more than 24 weeks pregnant to have an abortion without the need to provide reasons for her request.[48] After this period of gestation an abortion can only be provided if a doctor believes that an 'abortion is appropriate in all the circumstances',[49] including the relevant medical circumstances and the woman's physical, psychological and social circumstances.[50]

---

between the good and bad consequences, and those consequences occur fairly simultaneously. It is also sometimes contended that a further condition is that the act must not be intrinsically bad: see H T Engelhardt and J Kenny, 'Principle of Double Effect' in B Brody and H T Engelhardt (eds), *Bioethics: Readings and Cases* (Prentice Hall 1987) 160. However, given that the doctrine is commonly applied to very grave cases involving things such as the killing of innocent people and it is on the basis of the doctrine itself that such acts are sought to be justified, it begs the question of whether to make such a condition an internal part of the doctrine. See also, Thomas Nagel, *The View from Nowhere* (Oxford University Press 1986) 179, whose formulation of the doctrine of double effect essentially accords with the above.

44 [2000] 4 All ER 961.
45 Which includes feeding through an intravenous tube: *In Gardner, re BWV* [2003] VSC 173.
46 ibid.
47 *R v Davidson* [1969] VR 667.
48 Abortion Law Reform Law Act 2008 (Vic), s 4.
49 ibid, s 5(1).
50 ibid, s 5(92). Where an abortion is not carried out legally, the woman and other party assisting with the abortion is liable for a range of offences, including child destruction, abortion by another and supplying the means of abortion: see *Laws of Australia* [10.2.1360].

An abortion is a medical procedure and, hence, must be done with the consent of the woman. Where the individual is a minor, that is, younger than 18 years old, the consent can be provided by the parent or guardian unless the minor understands the nature of her request, in which case her consent is operative.

The morning-after pill is freely available in Australia. There is no requirement for a medical assessment or medical prescription for the pill. It is dispensed by pharmacists at the request of the woman.

2.2 Consent and non-fatal offences against the person

2.2.1 HIV and other communicable disease transmission

At common law, consent to sexual activities procured by fraud or non-disclosure of a communicable disease did not vitiate the consent.[51] However, statutory changes have altered this position. The changes come in two main forms. The first are generic offences that encompass conduct that threatens the well-being or life of other people, such as offences of 'conduct endangering life' and 'conduct endangering persons'.[52] Consent is a defence to reckless conduct endangering persons through the transmission of sexually-transmitted disease, but not in relation to the intentional infliction of such diseases.

In *Neal v The Queen,* it was held that:

> In our view, informed consent is capable of providing a defence to a charge of recklessly endangering a person with HIV through unprotected sexual intercourse, so long as the consent is communicated to the offender. It follows that, in order for the Crown to succeed in a prosecution for an offence of reckless conduct endangering a person with HIV through unprotected sexual intercourse, if the accused puts consent in issue, the Crown must prove beyond reasonable doubt that the complainant did not give informed consent to the risk or that the accused did not honestly believe that the complainant had given informed consent to the risk.
>
> It is different in the case of intentional infection of a complainant with HIV . . . We consider that the distinction between indifference to the risk of probable infection and intent that it should occur has a justifiable moral basis. As Lord Templeman said in *Brown*, in principle there is a difference between violence which is merely incidental to an activity and violence 'which is inflicted for the indulgence of cruelty'. As Judge LJ said in *R v Dica*, there is a similar distinction between the spreading of sexual disease which is merely incidental to consensual sexual intercourse and the intentional spreading of sexual disease through sexual intercourse. To adopt and adapt his Lordship's words, where the spread of sexual disease is merely incidental to sexual intercourse, the participants are not indulging in serious violence for the purposes of sexual gratification. They are simply prepared, knowingly, to run the risk – not the certainty – of infection, as well as all the other risks inherent in and possible consequences of sexual intercourse. Contrastingly, where sexual intercourse is engaged in with intent to spread sexual disease it is, as a matter of public policy, just as unlawful as consensual violent conduct causing serious physical injury.[53]

---

51 See *R v Clarence* (1889) LR 22 QBD 23 (holding that a wife's consent to intercourse with her husband was not vitiated by the husband's deception in failing to disclose that he was suffering from gonorrhoea).

52 See, for example, CC (NT) (n 22), *ss* 174B-H; CLCA 1935 (n 25), s 29; CA 1958 (n 22), ss 22–23. ibid.

53 [2011] VSCA 172, [72]–[73].

There are also specific offences aimed at targeting the deliberate spread of disease through sexual intercourse. For example, s 79 of the Public Health Act 2010 (NSW) states:

(1) A person who knows that he or she suffers from a sexually-transmitted infection is guilty of an offence if he or she has sexual intercourse with another person unless, before the intercourse takes place, the other person:

    (a) has been informed of the risk of contracting a sexually-transmitted infection from the person with whom intercourse is proposed, and

    (b) has voluntarily agreed to accept the risk. . . .

(3) It is a defence to any proceedings for an offence under this section if the court is satisfied that the defendant took reasonable precautions to prevent the transmission of the sexually-transmitted infection.

As is apparent from the above offence, consent is a cardinal consideration. It is permissible for individuals to have unprotected sex with HIV-positive people so long as they have full knowledge of the sexually-transmitted disease prior to engaging in sex.

2.2.2 Medical treatment

Surgery often involves the infliction of considerable pain and injury and carries a considerable risk of adverse side-effects, including death. Surgery, despite the immediate physical trauma that is often inflicted on the patient, normally has considerable benefits to the patient. It is in this context that the law is most liberal regarding the level of harm which can be excused, so long as the procedure is carried out with the consent of the patient. Patient consent provides a defence to all forms of harm, no matter how serious (including death), which arise out of surgery. As a community we accept that, on balance, it is desirable for surgical procedures to occur because they enhance patient well-being and are often necessary for the patient to survive a particular medical condition. Consent operates as a valid defence to surgical injury in relation to life-saving and life-improving surgery (such as to remove a tumour or carry out a heart by-pass procedure) and elective surgery. It also applies in relation to cosmetic surgery, which has no physiological imperative. In order for consent to be effective, the patient needs to be informed of the purpose of the procedure, the location of the surgery and the main risks.[54]

Where a person is unconscious, it is permissible for others to provide emergency treatment. The rationale for this is implied consent or the defence of necessity.

Consent applies not only in the positive sense to allow a medical procedure, but equally so in a negative sense to prohibit a medical procedure. Adults can refuse all medical procedures, even ones that are demonstrably in their best interests and ones that are life-saving. Administration of such procedures a patient has refused is illegal and constitutes battery. This is so even where the procedure is relatively minor and the benefit would be demonstrably immense.[55] This is an extreme example of the law upholding the right to individual autonomy. The common law principle is enshrined in legislation in several states.

In addition to patients expressly rejecting particular medical procedures, there is also legislation in most Australian jurisdictions enabling adults to make an advance directive refusing medical treatment if they are in a position where they are unable to refuse consent.[56]

---

54 *Rogers v Whitaker* (1992) 175 CLR 479.

55 ibid.

56 For example, see: Medical Treatment (Health Directions) Act 2006 (ACT), ss 7–9; Natural Death Act 1988 (NT), s 4 (this specifically provides for the right of a terminally ill patient to refuse medical treatment);

Children and the mentally impaired normally do not have the judgment to make their own decisions regarding medical treatment – parents normally assume the role. This applies to essential procedures and to non-essential minor procedures. For parental consent to be valid, the procedures must be in the best interests of the child.

Parental consent, however, is not always valid in relation to non-therapeutic major procedures. In such cases a court order may be necessary. The seminal case regarding the considerations that are relevant to medical treatment of the mentally impaired is *Secretary, Department of Health & Community Services (NT) v JWB and SMB* ('*Marion's Case*'), where the Court held that the paramount consideration is the best interests of the child.[57] In that case the High Court held that (only) the Family Court could authorise the sterilisation of a 14-year-old girl to prevent pregnancy. It held that this type of procedure went beyond the scope of the consent that could be given by parents because it was not medically essential and was invasive, irreversible and major surgery that carried a significant risk of being the wrong decision.

While full legal competence normally commences at the age of 18, there is no fixed age at which children can confer their own consent and hence negate parental consent. The point at which children can provide their own consent is when they can understand the proposed procedure and the risks and possible benefits involved.[58]

Superior courts have inherent jurisdiction to make orders concerning the welfare of children. Thus, where a person under the age of 18 makes a decision to reject treatment, which is demonstrably beneficial, particularly if it is likely to be life-saving, the court can order the treatment even if it is against the wishes of a child. Thus, in *Royal Alexander Hospital v Joseph*[59] a 15-year-old boy's rejection of life-saving blood products on religious grounds was not effective.[60]

2.2.3 *Sport injuries, 'horseplay', piercing*

In relation to sporting injuries, consent and intention are paramount considerations. A participant can consent to all levels of injuries so long as the intention of the person who inflicts the injury is to participate in the sport and not to intentionally cause injury. In *Pallante v Stadiums Pty Ltd*, the plaintiff brought an action against the organisers of a boxing contest for negligence in respect of injuries affecting his eyesight, which he sustained in the course of a professional boxing event.[61] The defendant argued that under common law doctrine, a person may not consent to the infliction of actual bodily harm. Thus, boxing amounted to an

---

Consent to Medical Treatment and Palliative Care Act 1995 (SA), s 7; Medical Treatment Act 1988 (Vic), s 5. In all other states (New South Wales, Queensland, Tasmania and Western Australia) the refusal to give consent for medical procedures is governed by common law.

57 [1992] HCA 15.

58 *Gillick v West Norfolk and Wisbech Area Health Authority* [1985] 3 All ER 402.

59 [2005] NSWSC 422.

60 There is now legislation in all states and territories which provides that minors are unable to validly refuse a blood transfusion if it is believed that such a transfusion is essential and the parents cannot be contacted, and at least two medical practitioners regard the transfusion as necessary to save the life of the minor: see Transplantation and Anatomy Act 1978 (ACT) Part 2, Division 2.5; Children and Young Persons (Care and Protection) Act 1998 (NSW), s 174; Emergency Medical Operations Act 1992 (NT), s 3; Transplant and Anatomy Act 1979 (Qld), s 20; CMTPCA 1995 (n 57), s 13(5); Human Tissue Act 1985 (Tas), s 21; Human Tissue Act 1982 (Vic), s 24; Human Tissue and Transplant Act 1982 (WA), s 21.

61 [1976] VR 331.

assault and the plaintiff's participation in an illegal activity prohibited him from recovering damages.

The Full Supreme Court of Victoria held that while one cannot generally consent to the infliction of actual bodily harm, the common law recognises an exception in the case of lawful sporting events which are not inherently dangerous to life or limb, and in which the infliction of actual bodily harm is reasonably to be expected under the rules – provided the participant's predominant intention does not become that of inflicting grievous bodily harm. If that does become the predominant intention, the lawful activities exception does not apply. Boxing is obviously a sport that envisages harm, but as the Full Supreme Court explained:[62]

> [1] in a spirit of anger or a hostile spirit and [2] with the predominant intention of inflicting substantial bodily harm so as to disable or otherwise physically subdue the opponent it may be an assault even though each of the contestants may have consented to the infliction of blows on himself.[63]

This same principle applies to other activities which are socially and culturally common-place. Thus, we see that practices such as tattooing, male circumcision and body-piercing are lawful so long as they are consensual and not undertaken with the intention to harm the individual. Less leeway is accorded to horseplay, such as induction or initiation activities at workplaces. There are not even informal rules associated with such practices and there is a considerable possibility that unintended consequences will occur. Accordingly, even consensual activities in this context are unlawful if they result in serious injury.[64]

2.2.4 Specific sexual practices involving infliction of harm

The main authority on the legality of sexual practices resulting in the infliction of harm remains the decision of the House of Lords in *R v Brown*.[65] In *Brown*, the accused were homosexuals who for a number of years willingly engaged in acts of sado-masochism in private locations. The police seized videotapes of the activities and charged the accused with assault occasioning actual bodily harm and unlawful wounding. None of the accused pressed for charges to be laid and there was no indication that the activities were non-consensual. In writing for the majority of the House of Lords, Lord Templeman stated that the question of whether consent should be recognised as a defence to a crime that involves occasioning actual or grievous bodily harm will depend on whether the perceived social utility of the activity outweighs any risks of harm emanating from it to such an extent as to render it a socially acceptable activity. Accordingly, Lord Templeman concluded that there were no ostensible social benefits in homosexual sado-masochism; to the contrary, his Lordship was of the view that the activities at issue involved nothing more than the deliberate infliction of violence for the gratification of the offender in circumstances where the acts were both injurious and dangerous to them. Lord Templeman held, therefore that under the particular circumstances of the case, consent was not a defence to the charges. In so holding, the House of Lords reaffirmed the general rule that a person cannot lawfully consent to the infliction of actual or grievous bodily harm unless the situation falls within one of the established exceptions.

---

62 ibid, 337.
63 See also, *McAvaney v Quigley* (1992) 58 A Crim R 457; *Abbott v The Queen* (1995) 81 A Crim R 55.
64 *Lergesner v Carroll* [1990] 1 Qd R 206, 219.
65 [1993] 2 All ER 75.

Some of the factors that the Court considered in deciding that an accused could not consent to the infliction of actual bodily harm included:

- whether the activity was undertaken in a controlled setting;
- whether the activity had the potential to morally corrupt others;
- whether the activity was unpredictable and dangerous;
- doubts about whether the victims actually consented;
- cultural considerations; and
- the possibility of the activity resulting in death or serious harm to those involved.[66]

Brown has been affirmed in a number of Australian decisions, where it has been held that consent in the context of sado-masochistic activities is a defence to bodily harm, but not really serious bodily harm (ie grievous bodily harm).

More tolerance has been accorded to the practice of branding. In *R v Wilson* it was held that it was lawful for a husband to brand his initials on his wife's buttocks.[67] The activity was held to be lawful by the Court on the basis that it was analogous to tattooing.

2.3 Sexual offences

2.3.1 Absence of consent or use of force/threats

There are large numbers of sexual offences committed in Australia. The most serious is rape, which, in essence, is sexual penetration without consent. Another commonly charged sexual offence is indecent assault, which covers acts of unwanted sexual contact that do not constitute penetration. For example, the Crimes Act 1900 (NSW) provides 'any person who assaults another person and, at the time of, or immediately before or after, the assault, commits an act of indecency on or in the presence of the other person, is liable to imprisonment for five years'.[68] All jurisdictions also have discrete statutory offences relating to sex with minors. Unlike sexual offences with adults, consent is never a defence to sexual acts with minors given the fact they are not of sufficient maturity to understand fully the nature of the act and considerable scope for exploitation of children.

In relation to sexual offences against adults, the absence of consent is an element of the offence. In this regard, consent means free agreement. In Victoria, consent means 'free agreement'.[69] In New South Wales and South Australia, the term is 'voluntary and free agreement'.[70] There are a number of factors that can vitiate consent. In most jurisdictions, they are set out in a non-exhaustive list in statute. The Crimes Act 1958 (Vic), states:

(1) For the purposes of subdivisions (8A) to (8D), consent means free agreement.
(2) Circumstances in which a person does not consent to an act include, but are not limited to, the following –
    (a) the person submits to the act because of force or the fear of force, whether to that person or someone else;

---

66 *Brown* has been affirmed in a number of cases: *R v McIntosh* [1999] VSC 358; *R v Stein* [2007] VSCA 300; *Neal v The Queen* [2011] VSCA 172.
67 [1996] 3 WLR 125.
68 See also, Crimes Act 1900 (ACT), s 92J; CA 1900 (n 25), s 61L; CC (NT) (n 22), s 188(1); Criminal Code (Qld), s 337(1); CC (Tas) (n 22), s 127; Criminal Code (WA), s 323; CA 1958 (n 22), s 39(2).
69 CA 1958 (n 22), s 34C.
70 CA 1900 (n 25), s 61HA; CLCA 1935 (n 25), s 46.

    (b) the person submits to the act because of the fear of harm of any type, whether to that person or someone else or an animal;

    (c) the person submits to the act because the person is unlawfully detained;

    (d) the person is asleep or unconscious;

    (e) the person is so affected by alcohol or another drug as to be incapable of consenting to the act;

    (f) the person is incapable of understanding the sexual nature of the act;

    (g) the person is mistaken about the sexual nature of the act;

    (h) the person is mistaken about the identity of any other person involved in the act;

    (i) the person mistakenly believes that the act is for medical or hygienic purposes;

    (j) if the act involves an animal, the person mistakenly believes that the act is for veterinary, agricultural or scientific research purposes;

    (k) the person does not say or do anything to indicate consent to the act;

    (l) having initially given consent to the act, the person later withdraws consent to the act taking place or continuing.[71]

As noted above, consent is never permanent and can be revoked at any time, including during the course of a sexual offence that was started consensually. This is a statutory adoption of the principle set out in *Kaitamaki v The Queen*.[72]

As noted above, force or threats vitiate consent. The nature of the threats that can vitiate consent is relatively wide and case-law indicates that it extends to threats of economic harm or humiliation. For example, in *R v G* the Court stated:

> To say to a woman that if she does not submit to sexual intercourse, videotapes of her having sexual intercourse would be published would plainly be a threat and any subsequent act of sexual intercourse induced by it would be rape.[73]

The courts have taken a relatively strict approach to the circumstances in which fraud can vitiate consent. In *Papadimitropoulos v The Queen* the accused lied to the complainant saying that they were married after they attended a Registry Office.[74] The complainant had sex with the accused based on this understanding. The court found that this did not vitiate consent because only fraud relating to the physical nature and character of the act or the identity of the person undercuts the reality of the consent. This position has been altered by statute in some jurisdictions.[75]

2.3.2 Evidentiary presumptions

There are numerous evidential presumptions relating to absence of consent. The presumptions are generally directed towards emphasising that consent must be absolutely free and that pragmatic realities such as the lack of overt resistance do not necessarily signify consent. A typical provision is s 46(3) of the Jury Directions Act 2015 (Vic), which states:

---

71 See, CA 1958 (n 22), s 34C. In New South Wales and South Australia, the term is 'voluntary and free agreement': CA 1900 ibid; CLCA 1935 ibid.

72 [1984] 2 All ER 435.

73 (Tas CCA, 25 June 1993).

74 (1957) 98 CLR 249.

75 For example, see CA 1900 (n 25), s 61HA (5). In Victoria, there is now a specific (less serious offence) that deals with fraud as to marriage: CA 1958 (n 22), s 57(2).

The prosecution or defence counsel may request that the trial judge –
(a) inform the jury that a person can consent to an act only if the person is capable of consenting and free to choose whether or not to engage in or allow the act; or
(b) inform the jury that where a person has given consent to an act, the person may withdraw that consent either before the act takes place or at any time while the act is taking place; or
(c) warn the jury that evidence of the following alone is not enough to regard a person as having consented to an act –
  (i) evidence that the person did not protest or physically resist; or
  (ii) evidence that the person did not sustain physical injury; or
  (iii) evidence that on any particular occasion the person consented to another act that is sexual in nature (whether or not of the same type) with the accused or with another person.

Directions of this nature are merely presumptions and, as a result, do not necessarily need to be adopted by a jury. Nevertheless, they serve a useful purpose in negating some flawed preconceptions that some jurors may have about the nature of consent.

2.3.3 *Mistake of fact about consent*

In order for an accused to be convicted of rape, or most sexual offences, he must be aware that the complainant was not consenting, or was reckless in that he was aware that the complainant might not be consenting to sexual penetration. If the accused is mistaken about the existence of consent it will negate this element. This reflects the fact that most crimes have a *mens rea* element and this is a subjective consideration. This rule in the context of rape and sexual offences was most prominently articulated in *Director of Public Prosecutions v Morgan*.[76]

The fact that belief in the existence of consent is a subjective test has raised concerns that it can be used as a basis for an accused to defeat sexual offence charges by simply asserting that in their mind they believed, albeit wrongly, that the complainant was consenting. While the accused can relatively readily make such an assertion, the reality is that if the objective circumstances are such that a reasonable person would not assume the existence of consent, a jury or judge is not likely to be swayed by the accused's assertion. This sentiment is reinforced by some statutory directions.

In South Australia, recklessness for the purpose of rape is defined pursuant to the Criminal Law Consolidation Act 1935 (SA) s 47 in the following terms.

For the purposes of this Division, a person is 'recklessly indifferent to the fact that another person does not consent to an act, or has withdrawn consent to an act, if he or she –
(a) is aware of the possibility that the other person might not be consenting to the act, or has withdrawn consent to the act, but decides to proceed regardless of that possibility; or
(b) is aware of the possibility that the other person might not be consenting to the act, or has withdrawn consent to the act, but fails to take reasonable steps to ascertain

---

76 [1976] AC 182. See also, *R v Saragozza* [1984] VR 187; *Getachew v The Queen* [2011] VSCA 164; *Wilson v The Queen* [2011] VSCA 328.

whether the other person does in fact consent, or has in fact withdrawn consent, to the act before deciding to proceed; or

(c) does not give any thought as to whether or not the other person is consenting to the act, or has withdrawn consent to the act before deciding to proceed.

In New South Wales, the *mens rea* for sexual assault without consent (Crimes Act 1900 s 61I), and the cognate offences of aggravated sexual assault (s 61J) and aggravated sexual assault in company (s 61JA), were codified in 2007. The primary offence in s 61I (which is the statutory counterpart to common law rape) provides that any 'person who has sexual intercourse with another person without the consent of the other person and who knows that the other person does not consent to the sexual intercourse' is guilty of an offence. Section 61HA narrows the circumstances if an accused can claim to believe in the existence of consent. It states:

(3) A person who has sexual intercourse with another person without the consent of the other person knows that the other person does not consent to the sexual intercourse if:

   (a) the person knows that the other person does not consent to the sexual intercourse; or

   (b) the person is reckless as to whether the other person consents to the sexual intercourse; or

   (c) the person has no reasonable grounds for believing that the other person consents to the sexual intercourse.

For the purpose of making any such finding, the trier of fact must have regard to all the circumstances of the case:

   (d) including any steps taken by the person to ascertain whether the other person consents to the sexual intercourse; but

   (e) not including any self-induced intoxication of the person.

Thus, we see that in New South Wales a belief in the existence of consent can no longer exculpate a rape charge unless the accused has a reasonable foundation for the belief. It is unclear whether, pragmatically, this will lead to different verdicts; however, it is desirable that the strict legal position coheres with the reality.

2.4 Property offences and criminal damage

People are free to do with their property as they wish; hence, consent is determinative of any action taken regarding their property. This includes the right to give away or even wantonly destroy their property.

2.4.1 Place of consent in the offence structure

The main property offences in Australia are theft (or stealing) and deception or fraud-related offences.

If property is acquired with the consent of the owner, there is no crime (since individuals are free to dispose of their property as they wish). The absence of consent could logically be an element of the offence or a defence. In most cases it is an element of the offence. Thus, s 134 of the Criminal Law Consolidation Act 1935 ('CLCA') provides (relevantly):

(1) A person is guilty of theft if the person deals with property –
    (a) dishonestly; and
    (b) without the owner's consent; and
    (c) intending –
        (i) to deprive the owner permanently of the property; or
        (ii) to make a serious encroachment on the owner's proprietary rights.

In other circumstances, consent is contained as an implied ingredient of another offence. For example, in Victoria, theft is committed in the following circumstances:

A person steals if he dishonestly appropriates property belonging to another with the intention of permanently depriving the other of it.[77]

Relevantly, the legislation provides that a person's appropriation is not dishonest:

(a) if he appropriates the property in the belief that he has in law the right to deprive the other of it, on behalf of himself or of a third person; or
(b) if he appropriates the property in the belief that he would have the other's consent if the other knew of the appropriation and the circumstances of it . . .[78]

In a similar manner, in Victoria the offence of criminal damage is defined as follows, pursuant to s 197 of the Crimes Act 1958:

(1) A person who intentionally and without lawful excuse destroys or damages any property belonging to another or to himself and another shall be guilty of an indictable offence and liable to level 5 imprisonment (10 years maximum).

A lawful excuse to destroying or damaging property is consent of the owner of the property.[79]

2.4.2 Mistaken belief in consent

Irrespective of whether consent is an express or implied element of an offence, it is a subjective inquiry, hence, a mistaken belief by an individual in consent to deal with the property is sufficient to obviate liability for theft or deception.[80] The relevant legal position is summarised in *R v Bedford*:

The sole ground of appeal complains that the trial judge removed from the jury's consideration the issue of claim of right.
    It has been pointed out that a claim of right can be based on an unfounded and unrealistic view. In *Walden v Hensler*, Brennan J referred to the common law view summarised by Stephen J, *History of the Criminal Law of England*:

---

77 CA 1958 (n 22), s 72.
78 ibid, s 73(2).
79 ibid, s 201.
80 *R v Salvo* [1980] VR 401.

Fraud is inconsistent with a claim of right made in good faith to do the act complained of. A man who takes possession of property which he really believes to be his own does not take it fraudulently, however unfounded his claim may be. This, if not the only, is nearly the only case in which ignorance of the law affects the legal character of acts done under its influence.

In the same case, Brennan J quoted, with approval, the following comments by Gibbs J (Stanley and Hanger JJ agreeing) in *R v Pollard*:

An accused person acts in the exercise of an honest claim of right, if he honestly believes himself to be entitled to do what he is doing. A belief that he may acquire a right in the future is not in itself enough.

. . . It is not to the point that the accused had no right to take the vehicle. If he had honestly believed that he was entitled to take it, or if the jury had a reasonable doubt whether he had such a belief, he should have been acquitted, however wrong his belief may have been, and however tenuous and unconvincing the grounds for it may seem to a judge.

In the light of these matters and the crucial role which a claim of right might play in deciding whether the element of dishonesty has been proved by the prosecution, care is necessary in deciding whether the issue should be left to the jury. In *R v Pollard*, Gibbs J underscored this consideration when he said:

1.1.1. It is well settled that a claim of right sufficient to relieve a person of criminal responsibility need only be honest and need not be reasonable (*Clarkson v Aspinall; Ex parte Aspinall* ([1950] St R Qd 79 at 89)); 'the fact that it is wrongheaded does not matter': *R v Gilson and Cohen* ([1944] 29 Cr App R 174 at 180). In *Rex v Bernhard* ([1938] 2 KB 264 at 270) the Court of Criminal Appeal said that a person has such a claim of right 'if he is honestly asserting what he believes to be a lawful claim, even though it may be unfounded in law or in fact'. At page 272 the court said:
"However strong and however well justified may be a judge's view that there is a preponderance of evidence against the defence of a claim of right, the question whether that defence is negatived by the evidence must be left as a question of fact to the jury".[81]

CONCLUSION

Self-determination is an important ideal, meaning individuals should be able to shape their own lives. This includes defining the interactions they have with other people, so far as matters over which they have dominion are concerned, including their physical and sexual integrity. Accordingly, consent is an important concept. This approach is generally observed in Australian criminal law. However, there are several notable exceptions. First, there is the general, albeit obscure, concept of public policy. This applies to limit the type of harm that people can allow to occur to their body. Thus, consensual killing or serious injury for 'no good reason' is a criminal act, no matter how enthusiastically a person consents to such conduct.

Fundamental principles of criminal law also operate sometimes to defeat the importance of consent. Thus, we see that accused who have a false belief in the existence of consent can avoid liability for some sexual and assault offences. The likelihood of this occurring is

---

81 (2007) 98 SASR 514; [2007] SASC 276.

diminished by statutory directions and legal presumptions that underscore the importance of an understanding relating to consent being based on reasonable grounds.

The realm of property offences is where consent has its greatest expressions. The importance of self-determination outweighs the importance of materialistic objects, hence, we see that consent is a defence to most property offences.

There are exceptions to all of these approaches – they are inevitable given the fragmented nature of Australian criminal law, which has nine separate jurisdictions. Some of these exceptions have been discussed. However, there is an overarching role of consent in Australian criminal law, which is set out in this chapter. The trend of law reform in this area suggests that consent will continue to evolve as an even more important ideal in Australian criminal law in the foreseeable future.

16

Germany

Kai Ambos and Stefanie Bock

1 GENERAL ISSUES

1.1 Conceptual foundations

1.1.1 Philosophical and theoretical principles informing the law surrounding consent

The unwritten, but commonly recognised,[1] defence of consent can be traced back to the ancient legal principle *'volenti non fit iniuria'*[2] – 'no wrong is done to one who consents'.[3] It is based on the notion that there is no need to protect a legal good (*Rechsgut*) against the will of its holder.[4] From a constitutional perspective, the defence of consent is an integral part of the right to autonomy and self-determination as enshrined in Article 2(1) of the German Basic Law (*Grundgesetz*).[5] As a rule, everyone is free to dispose of his own legal interests, which includes the right to waive protection and to consent to harmful acts.[6]

1　Kristian Kühl, *Strafrecht – Allgemeiner Teil* (7th edition, Vahlen 2012), s 9 marginal note [hereinafter: mn] 20; Rudolf Rengier, *Strafrecht Allgemeiner Teil* (6th edition, CH Beck 2014), s 23 mn 1; Henning Rosenau 'Vorbemerkungen zu §§ 32 ff. StGB' in Helmut Satzger, Wilhelm Schluckebier and Gunter Widmaier (eds), *Strafgesetzbuch Kommentar* (2nd edition, Carl Heymanns Verlag 2014) mn 31; also Thomas Weigend, 'Germany' in Kevin Jon Heller and Markus D Dubber (eds), *The Handbook of Comparative Criminal Law* (Stanford University Press 2011) 252, 271.

2　The *'volenti non fit iniuria'*-principle is attributed to the Roman jurist *Ulpian* (c 170–228 AD), Claus Roxin, *Strafrecht Allgemeiner Teil, Band I, Grundlagen. Der Aufbau der Verbrechenslehre* (4th edition, CH Beck 2006), s 13 mn 1; Kai Ambos, *Treatise on International Criminal Law – Volume I: Foundations and General Part* (Oxford University Press 2013) 387 with note 803.

3　English translation according to Vera Bergelson, 'The Defense of Consent' in Markus D Dubber and Tatjana Hörnle (eds), *The Oxford Handbook of Criminal Law* (Oxford University Press 2014) 629, 642.

4　Kühl (n 1), s 9 mn 23; Rosenau (n 1) mn 30; see also Markus D Dubber and Tatjana Hörnle, *Criminal Law – A Comparative Approach* (Oxford University Press 2014) 468.

5　Article 2(1) of the German Basic Law reads: 'Every person shall have the right to free development of his personality insofar as he does not violate the rights of others or offend against the constitutional order or the moral law'; translation according to: 'Basic Law for the Federal Republic of Germany' (*Juris*) <http://www.gesetze-im-internet.de/englisch_gg/> accessed 18 August 2016.

6　Kühl (n 1), s 9 mn 20; compare also BGH [Federal Supreme Court, hereinafter: BGH] Neue Juristische Wochenschrift [hereinafter: NJW] 1976, 1790, 1791.

1.1.2 Influence of feminist and queer theory

Feminist and queer theory heavily influences the recent discussion on the reform of the criminal law on sexual offences, which will be considered in more detail below (2.3.).

1.1.3 Definition of informed consent

Consent may be defined as a voluntary and informed agreement to an act, which fulfils the *actus reus* of a criminal offence. In order to be valid, it must meet the following prerequisites:[7]

- The consenting person must be entitled to dispose of the legal interests concerned (below 1.1.6.).
- The consenting person must have capacity to consent (below 1.4.).
- Consent must be given prior to the commission of the relevant act (below 1.1.5., 1.3.1.; on the special defences of presumed and hypothetical consent below 1.3.2. and 2.2.2.).
- Consent must be voluntary and informed, that is, it must be – at least in principle – free from error and force (below 1.5., with a particular view to medical treatments 2.2.2.).
- The defendant must know about the consent;[8] it is controversial, though, whether he must also be motivated by this knowledge.[9] Such an additional volitional threshold seems to be incompatible with the subjective elements of the offence, which only require that the defendant acts with intent; possible motives, and therefore the reasons why he performed the act, are irrelevant.[10]

1.1.4 Consent to risk or consent to outcome

In order to negate the wrongful result of the conduct (*Erfolgsunrecht*), the victim must – as a rule – consent to its outcome.[11] It is questionable if this also holds true for negligent crimes. In the classical textbook example, D offers to take V home. V accepts, although she realises that D is too drunk to drive safely. D causes an accident in which V is injured.[12] According to the prevailing opinion, D is not liable for causing bodily harm by negligence[13] because V

---

7 See, eg, Bernd Heinrich, *Strafrecht – Allgemeiner Teil* (4th edition, Kohlhammer 2014) mn 454; Urs Kindhäuser, *Strafrecht Allgemeiner Teil* (7th edition, Nomos 2015), s 12 mn 10.

8 Kühl (n 1), s 9 mn 41; Heinrich (n 7) mn 462; Theoder Lenckner and Detlev Sternberg-Lieben 'Vorbemerkungen zu den §§ 32 ff.' in Adolf Schönke and Horst Schröder (eds), *Strafgesetzbuch – Kommentar* (29th edition, CH Beck 2014) mn 51.

9 In this vein Hans-Heinrich Jescheck and Thomas Weigend, *Lehrbuch des Strafrechts Allgemeiner Teil* (5th edition, Duncker & Humblot 1996) 383; Rengier (n 1), s 23 mn 38; Johannes Wessels, Werner Beulke and Helmut Satzger, *Strafrecht Allgemeiner Teil* (45th edition, *Cf* Müller 2015) mm 567.

10 See Uwe Murmann *Grundkurs Strafrecht* (3rd edition, CH Beck 2015), s 25 mn 135; in the same vein Thomas Rönnau, 'Vorbemerkungen zu den §§ 32 ff' in Heinrich Wilhelm Laufhütte, Ruth Rissing-van Saan and Klaus Tiedemann (eds), *Leipziger Kommentar, Band 2, §§ 32 bis 55* (12th edition, De Gruyter 2006) mn 211. On the general discussion on the subjective elements of defences Kai Ambos and Stefanie Bock, 'Germany' in Alan Reed and Michael Bohlander (eds), *General Defences in Criminal Law – Domestic and Comparative Perspectives* (Ashgate 2014) 227, 228.

11 Roxin (n 2), s 13 mn 78; Gunnar Duttge, '§ 15' in Wolfgang Joecks and Klaus Miebach (eds), *Münchener Kommentar zum Strafgesetzbuch Band 1, §§ 1–37 StGB* (2nd edition, CH Beck 2011) mn 198; Volker Krey and Robert Esser, *Deutsches Strafrecht Allgemeiner Teil* (5th edition, Kohlhammer 2012) mn 670.

12 See, eg, Rudolf Rengier, *Strafrecht Besonderer Teil II. Delikte gegen die Person und die Allgemeinheit* (17th edition, CH Beck 2016), s 20 case 3.

13 Section 229 of the German Criminal Code [hereinafter: StGB].

was fully aware of the risks of drunk driving and deliberately decided to take them.[14] Critics of this view point out that V, even if she was aware of the danger, nevertheless hoped, that it would not materialise and thus had not consented to be harmed.[15]

Further difficulties arise from the fact that even the express and earnest request of the victim cannot exclude criminal liability for intentional killings.[16] This means that D does not have the power to dispose freely over her right to life.[17] According to some authors, this restriction of the right to self-determination applies only to intentional, but not to negligent killings.[18] The Federal Supreme Court argues, that for reasons of public policy and morals, D can, at least, not be allowed to consent to acts bringing her life into concrete danger.[19] The details are very controversial though.[20]

1.1.5 Revocation of consent

Consent must be declared before the respective act is committed and must continue to exist until it is completed. A subsequent approval does not relieve the perpetrator from responsibility.[21] Some minor offences, however, are only prosecuted upon request,[22] so that the victim may decide to spare the offender from criminal proceedings.[23] If the consent does not form part of a binding treaty,[24] it can be revoked freely.[25] From then on, the act becomes unlawful.[26]

1.1.6 Ownership and limits of consent

Consent can exclude the defendant's criminal responsibility only if the consenting victim is entitled to dispose exclusively of the legal interests concerned. Thus, the defence of consent is applicable only to offences against individual rights.[27] If, in contrast, the offence in question protects collective interests, then the individual's consent cannot have an exonerating effect since these interests do not fall within his authority to dispose. Collective interests belong to a collective entity, that is, normally the respective state or society, and thus cannot be disposed

---

14   Kühl (n 1), s 17 mn 82; Rengier (n 12), s 20 m 28–29; see also in the context of illegal car racing BGH Neue Zeitschrift für Strafrecht (hereinafter: NStZ) 2009, 148–149.
15   Lenckner and Sternberg-Lieben (n 8) mn 103; Duttge (n 10) mn 199; Krey and Esser (n 1) mn 674.
16   Section 216 StGB, in more detail *herein* 2.1.1.
17   Lenckner and Sternberg-Lieben (n 8) mn 37; Horst Schlehofer, 'Vorbemerkung zu den §§ 32 ff.' in Wolfgang Joecks and Klaus Miebach (eds), *Münchener Kommentar zum Strafgesetzbuch Band 1, §§ 1–37 StGB* (2nd edition, CH Beck 2011) mn 136.
18   ibid mn 136; Lenckner and Sternberg-Lieben (n 8) mn 104; Rengier (n 1), s 23 mn 32.
19   BGHSt [Entscheidungen des Bundesgerichtshofes in Strafsachen – Official Journal of Reportable Federal Supreme Court Decisions] 49, 166, 173; BGHSt 53, 55, 62–63; see also *herein* 2.2.3.
20   See only Kühl (n 1), s 9 mn 87–88; Rengier (n 1), s 23 mn 31–35; Krey and Esser (n 11) mn 671–676.
21   BGHSt 17, 359; Roxin (n 2), s 13 Rn 79; Michael Bohlander, *Principles of German Criminal Law* (Hart 2009) 86.
22   See, eg, s 247 StGB for 'theft from relatives or persons living in the same home'.
23   Roxin (n 2), s 13 mn 79; Rönnau (n 10) mn 171; Heinrich (n 7) mn 459.
24   Roxin (n 2), s 13 mn 72: V contractually allows his neighbour D to cut down a tree and therefore to destroy an object belonging to him. If V wants to revoke his consent to criminal damage (s 303 StGB), he has to annual or dispute the treaty; see also Lenckner and Sternberg-Lieben (n 8) mn 44.
25   Kühl (n 1), s 9 mn 32; Murmann (n 10), s 25 mn 125; Rengier (n 1), s 23 mn 22.
26   Bohlander (n 21) 86; see also Rönnau (n 10) mn 173.
27   On the restrictions of the right to self-determination following from s 216 StGB (killings at the request of the victim) and s 228 (no consent to acts which are incompatible with pubic moral) see *herein* 2.1.1, 2.1.1 and 2.2.3.

by an individual's decision alone.[28] In our drunken driving case, V may (if at all) consent to bodily harm, but not to the endangerment of traffic safety.[29] Even if V's consent relieves D from criminal responsibility for causing bodily harm by negligence, he still is liable for driving while under the influence of drink or drugs.[30]

Some offences protect individual and collective interests. According to s 315c StGB, for example, D commits the crime of endangering road traffic, if he drives a vehicle although due to consumption of alcoholic beverages he is not in a position to drive safely *and* thereby concretely endangers the life or limb of another person.[31] Section 315c StGB is a traffic offence as well as an offence against the person.[32] According to the Federal Supreme Court, consent of the endangered victim cannot exonerate the defendant because an individual has no right to dispose of the collective interests in traffic safety.[33] The contrary view stresses that a conviction for 'endangering road traffic' requires both, an abstract endangerment of traffic safety and a concrete endangerment of life and limb. Where the consent of the individual victim negates the wrongfulness of the latter, D can be liable only for drunk driving.[34]

1.2 Place of consent in the offence structure

German Criminal Law is based on a tripartite structure of crime distinguishing between offence definition (*Tatbestand*), general wrongfulness (*Rechtswidrigkeit*), and culpability in a normative sense (*Schuld*).[35] If an offence can only be committed against the will of the victim – as it is for example in the case of burglary, s 123 StGB,[36] or theft, s 242 StGB – lack of consent is a (negative) element of the crime.[37] In cases where the victim agrees to the respective conduct and its outcome, the *actus reus* lacks a definitional element (the lack of consent) and therefore is not fulfilled (*tatbestandsausschließendes Einverständnis*). With regard to all

---

28 BGH NJW 1970, 1380, 1381; Weigend (n 1) 271; Kühl (n 1), s 9 mn 27; also Ambos (n 2) 387.

29 See Rengier (n 12) and accompanying text.

30 Rengier (n 1), s 23 mn 11; also Weigend (n 1) 271. S 316(1) StGB provides: 'Whosoever drives a vehicle in traffic (Sections 315 to 315d) although due to consumption of alcoholic beverages or other intoxicants he is not in a condition to drive the vehicle safely shall be liable [. . .]', translation according to Michael Bohlander, *The German Criminal Code – A Modern English Translation* (Hart 2008) 196.

31 Translation according to Bohlander (n 30) 195–196.

32 BGH NJW 1970, 1380, 1381; Detlev Sternberg-Lieben and Bernd Hecker, '§ 315c' in Adolf Schönke and Horst Schröder (eds), *Strafgesetzbuch – Kommentar* (29th edition, CH Beck 2014) mn 1; Christian Pegel, '§ 315c' in Wolfgang Joecks and Klaus Miebach (eds), *Münchener Kommentar zum Strafgesetzbuch Band 5, §§ 263–358 StGB* (2nd edition, CH Beck 2014) mn 1; Rengier (n 12), s 44 mn 1.

33 BGH NJW 1970, 1380, 1381; concurring Martin Heger, '§ 315c' in Karl Lackner and Kristian Kühl (eds), *Strafgesetzbuch* (28th edition, CH Beck 2014) mn 32.

34 Sternberg-Lieben and Hecker (n 32) mn 41; Pegel (n 32) mn 114; Rengier (n 12), s 44 mn 19a. Endangering road traffic (s 315c StGB) is punishable by imprisonment not exceeding five years or a fine, drunk driving (s 316 StGB) by imprisonment not exceeding one year or a fine.

35 George P Fletcher, *Basic Concepts of Criminal Law* (Oxford University Press 1998) 101; Roxin (n 2), s 10 mn 13–26; Ambos and Bock (n 10) 227 with further references.

36 Rengier (n 12), s 30 mn 9; Rengier (n 1), s 23 mn 4; Weigend (n 1) 271. A burglary is committed by any person who 'unlawfully enters into the dwelling, business premise or other enclosed property of another' or 'remains therein without authorisation and does not leave when requested to do so', translation according to Bohlander (n 30) 110.

37 BGH NJW 2012, 1092; Rengier (n 1), s 23 mn 4; Bohlander (n 21) 83. A person commits a theft if he 'takes chattels belonging to another away from another with the intention of unlawfully appropriating them for himself or a third person', translation according to Bohlander (n 30) 160.

other offences, consent serves as a justificatory defence, that is, the act fulfils the offence definition, but is nevertheless regarded as lawful (*rechtfertigende Einwilligung*).[38]

1.3 Form of consent

1.3.1 Declared or implied

According to prevailing opinion, consent as a justificatory defence must be externally declared,[39] but not necessarily expressly.[40] Consent may be inferred from the acts of the victim.[41] Exceptionally, public or private law rules may require the use of a particular form. Non-compliance, however, will normally not affect the validity of the otherwise given consent. The case may be different where the formal requirements aim at protecting the victim against rash decisions.[42]

While the inner, silent approval of the victim cannot serve as a justification,[43] it negates the *actus reus* of an offence if lack of consent is a negative element of the respective crime. Take for example the so-called 'thief trap' cases, where the police marks an object, for example banknotes, with fluorescent powders, which leaves stains at the hands of all persons coming in contact with it, in order to prove D guilty of theft. That plan works only if D indeed takes away the object, that is, the police want him to do so. Accordingly, the *actus reus* of theft, which requires '*non-consensual* interference with another possession', is not fulfilled.[44] D is liable only for attempt.[45]

1.3.2 Presumed consent

Presumed consent is a well-recognised justification *sui generis*, which covers two different situations.[46] First, it is applicable in cases of emergency in which immediate action is required and a decision of the victim cannot be obtained in time.[47] Accordingly, Doctor D is justified in operating on the unconscious and badly injured V,[48] if a careful evaluation of all circumstances

---

38 Weigend (n 1) 271; Heinrich (n 7) mn 440; Murmann (n 10), s 25 mn 121–123; also Bohlander (n 21) 82. For a different view see Roxin (n 2), s 13 mn 2, who argues that consent of the victim always negates the *actus reus*.

39 BGH NJW 1956, 1106, 1107; Bohlander (n 21) 86; Heinrich (n 7) mn 457; Rengier (n 1), s 23 mn 21; Lenckner and Sternberg-Lieben (n 7) mn 43. For a different view see Wolfgang Joecks, '§ 223' in Wolfgang Joecks and Klaus Miebach (eds), *Münchener Kommentar zum Strafgesetzbuch Band 5, §§ 263–358 StGB* (2nd edition, CH Beck 2014) mn 76, who deems the inner, silent approval of the victim to be sufficient.

40 In particular with regard to medical treatment Oberlandesgericht [Higher Regional Court – hereinafter: OLG] Köln NJW 1978, 1690, 1691; Albin Eser, '§ 223' in Adolf Schönke and Horst Schröder (eds), *Strafgesetzbuch – Kommentar* (29th edition, CH Beck 2014) mn 43; also BGH NJW 1976, 1790, 1791.

41 Rönnau (n 10) mn 163; Lenckner and Sternberg-Lieben (n 7) mn 43; Kühl (n 1), s 9 mn 31.

42 Lenckner and Sternberg-Lieben (n 7) mn 43; Bohlander (n 21) 86.

43 BGH NJW 1956, 1106, 1107; Bohlander (n 21) 86; Rengier (n 1), s 23 mn 21; Lenckner and Sternberg-Lieben (n 7) mn 43. For a different view see Joecks (n 39) mn 76.

44 Dubber and Hörnle (n 3) 469.

45 Bayerisches Oberstes Landesgericht [Highest Regional Court of Bavaria – hereinafter: BayOblG] NJW 1979, 729; Rudolf Rengier, *Strafrecht Besonderer Teil II. Vermögensdelikte* (18th edition, CH Beck 2016), s 2 mn 67; also Lenckner and Sternberg-Lieben (n 7) mn 32b; Murmann (n 9), s 25 mn 125.

46 BGHSt 35, 246, 249; Kühl (n 1), s 9 mn 46; Bohlander (n 21) 88–89; Krey and Esser (n 11) mn 677.

47 Kühl (n 1), s 9 mn 46; Murmann (n 10), s 25 mn 145; Krey and Esser (n 11) mn 678.

48 On the qualification of medical treatment as 'bodily injury' in terms of, s 223 StGB *herein* 2.2.2.

indicates that V, if asked, would have consented.[49] In determining the hypothetical will of the victim, particular emphasis must be given to his previous statements, his individual wishes, concerns and moral concepts.[50]

Secondly, the defendant may rely on presumed consent, if the victim has no interest in the protection of his rights. D, who needs some change and takes out several coins from the purse of her friend V and replaces them by a 10 euro bank note, fulfils the *actus reus* of theft. Nevertheless, if she has no reason to assume that D has a special interest in these particular coins, her conduct is justified by presumed consent.[51]

The defence of presumed consent must be distinguished from the related, but very controversial, concept of hypothetical consent, which is discussed in the context of medical treatment. We will return to this point later.[52]

1.4 Capacity to consent

Consent is valid only if the victim possesses the necessary moral and mental maturity to understand the nature and consequences of the act directed against him.[53] The jurisprudence does not bind capacity to consent to the private law rules on contracting capacity or responsibility for tort with their fixed age limits, but focuses on the intellectual abilities of the individual victim.[54] For adults, that is persons over the age of 18, capacity to consent is presumed[55] unless concrete circumstances of the case, like mental illness[56] or a severe alcohol and drug intoxication, indicate that their reasoning powers were reduced.[57] The mere fact that a decision is unreasonable or irrational does not affect the validity of a given consent.[58] Depending on their individual maturity, even small children may consent to minor scuffles or the destruction of low-value objects.[59] As a rule, the older the minor is and the less severe the consequences of the respective conduct are, the more likely it is that the courts accept their consent as a valid defence.[60]

As long as children are incapable of consenting, it is for their legal representatives, normally the parents or legal guardians, to take the necessary decisions.[61] In doing so, they have to act in the best interest and welfare of the child.[62] If parents abuse their rights and, for example, refuse a potentially life-saving medical treatment for inappropriate reasons, their

---

49 Bohlander (n 21) 88; Kühl (n 1), s 9 mn 46; Murmann (n 10), s 25 mn 146.
50 BGHSt 35, 246, 249; BGHSt 45, 219, 221; Kühl (n 1), s 9 mn 47.
51 See also the similar case examples by Rengier (n 1), s 23 mn 56; Murmann (n 10), s 25 mn 146.
52 *Herein* 2.2.2.
53 BGH NStZ 2000, 87, 88; BayOblG NJW 1999, 372; OLG Hamm NJW 1983, 2095, 2096; Roxin (n 2), s 13 mn 85.
54 BGHSt 8 357, 358; BGHSt 12, 379, 382; BayOblG NJW 1999, 372; concurring Rosenau (n 1) mn 38; Lenckner and Sternberg-Lieben (n 7) mn 40; crit. as the application of different capacity standards in private and criminal law affect the unity of law Bohlander (n 21) 84; in detail on the discussion Heinrich (n 7) mn 465–467.
55 Roxin (n 2), s 13 mn 86; Rönnau (n 10) mn 194; Rengier (n 1), s 23 mn 16.
56 OLG Hamm NJW 1983, 2095, 2096; Lenckner and Sternberg-Lieben (n 7) mn 40; Dubber and Hörnle (n 3) 470.
57 BGH NStZ 2004, 204; BGH NStZ 2000, 87, 88.
58 Bohlander (n 21) 85; Lenckner and Sternberg-Lieben (n 7) mn 40; Rengier (n 1), s 23 mn 17; for a different view see BGH NJW 1978 1206 with critical analysis by Roxin (n 2), s 13 mn 86.
59 Rengier (n 1), s 23 mn 16. See also BayOblG NJW 1999, 372, that doubted that a 15-year-old boy can consent to be beaten up by three other teenagers in order be accepted as a new gang member.
60 Rönnau (n 10) mn 195; Bohlander (n 21) 85; Lenckner and Sternberg-Lieben (n 7) mn 40.
61 Bohlander (n 21) 85; Wessels, Beulke and Satzger (n 9) mn 554.
62 Schlehofer (n 16) mn 141; Kühl (n 1), s 9 mn 34; compare also Roxin (n 2), s 13 mn 92.

consent can be replaced by a decision of the guardianship court.[63] In a highly controversial case, the District Court of Cologne held in 2012 that parents of a four-year-old boy could not consent to a religiously motivated (not medically indicated) circumcision. The Court argued that the surgical removal of the prepuce is a severe and irreversible interference into physical integrity, which can only be lawful if based on an informed decision of the boy himself.[64] The Court's ruling was heavily criticised for disregarding Jewish traditions and practices, which finally led the German legislator to insert a new paragraph into the Civil Code, which allows under certain circumstances the religious circumcision of immature boys with the consent of their legal representatives.[65]

1.5 Consequences of mistaken consent

1.5.1 Mistake

Consent must be based on a voluntary and informed decision, that is, it must be free from error and force. This does not mean that all misconceptions of the victim are equally relevant. According to the prevailing view, only mistakes relating to the legal interests concerned, to its substance and the degree to which it is affected, render consent invalid.[66] If, for example, V allows D to operate on him, because he erroneously believes him to be a doctor, he does not foresee and understand the consequences of his actions.[67] The same holds true if V wants to write an email to his neighbour D, telling him, that he (V) does not allow D to cut down the tree on the property line, but accidentally omits the word 'not'.[68] In order to protect the legitimate interests of D, some authors argue that V's consent (albeit not fully informed) must nevertheless be considered valid in case D does not realise that V is mistaken and therefore acts in good faith.[69] Errors about accompanying circumstances and mistakes in motive are generally deemed irrelevant.[70]

1.5.2 Deception

With regard to mistakes caused by the defendant, some courts and scholars argue that fraudulently obtained consent is always invalid.[71] The convincing opposing view differentiates along the same lines described above.[72] Imagine that D promises to pay V 50 € if he donates

---

63 Roxin (n 2), s 13 mn 92; Lenckner and Sternberg-Lieben (n 7) mn 41e; Murmann (n 10), s 25 mn 126.

64 LG Köln NJW 2012, 2128.

65 Section 1631d BGB; for a critical assessment with a particular view to the constitutionality of s 1631d BGB see Jörg Scheinfeld, 'Erläuterungen zum neuen § 1631d BGB – Beschneidung des männlichen Kindes' in Onlinezeitschrift für Höchstrichterliche Rechtsprechung zum Strafrecht 2013, 268.

66 Rosenau (n 1) mn 40; Krey and Esser (n 11) mn 661; Wessels, Beulke and Satzger (n 9) mn 559; for a different view see Kindhäuser (n 7), s 12 mn 27.

67 Based on BGH NStZ 1987, 174; see also Bohlander (n 21) 86; Lenckner and Sternberg-Lieben (n 7) mn 46; Rosenau (n 1) mn 40.

68 Case based on Roxin (n 2), s 13 mn 111; compare also Lenckner and Sternberg-Lieben (n 7) mn 46; Rosenau (n 1) mn 40.

69 Kindhäuser (n 7), s 12 mn 31; Roxin (n 2), s 13 mn 111–112; for a different view see Lenckner and Sternberg-Lieben (n 7) mn 46.

70 Jescheck and Weigend (n 10) 383; Bohlander (n 21) 87; see also Murmann (n 10), s 25 mn 130; for a different view see Kindhäuser (n 7), s 12 mn 27.

71 OLG Stuttgart NJW 1982, 2266, 2267; Kindhäuser (n 7), s 12 mn 27; Heinrich (n 7) mn 469–471; Rengier (n 1), s 23 mn 33.

72 OLG Stuttgart NJW 1962, 62, 63; Lenckner and Sternberg-Lieben (n 7) mn 47; Rosenau (n 1) mn 40; Kühl (n 1), s 9 mn 37.

blood, although he knows that the aid organisation he is working for is insolvent.[73] D is fully aware that, and to what extent, his body will be harmed during the blood withdrawal. He merely erroneously expects to receive some payment in return. This mistake does not relate to the legal interest concerned, namely D's right to physical integrity, but only to the reasons why he allows D to encroach on it, ie his motive. D's consent is accordingly not vitiated.[74] The situation is more complicated though if the mistake in motive is so severe that it virtually excludes the victim's freedom of choice. Take the example of a mother who consents to a corneal transplantation because D pretends that this is the only way to save the eyesight of her son. In fact, D wants to sell the transplant on the black market.[75] Here again, V is fully aware of the physical impact and consequences of the medical operation. Nevertheless, she believes herself to be in a desperate situation, which leaves her no choice but to give up an eye. Her consent is not truly based on an autonomous decision and therefore can hardly relieve D from criminal responsibility.[76]

These principles on self-determination and autonomous decision-making apply only to consent as a justificatory defence. Consent as a negative element of the crime is understood in a more factual sense. Mistakes, even if caused by the defendant, do not affect its validity.[77]

1.6 Mistake about consent

The consequences of a mistake about consent depend on whether consent negates the offence definition or the wrongfulness of the act. In the former case, the defendant is unaware of a fact, which is a (negative) statutory element of the offence. Due to this mistake of fact, he acts without intent and – according to s 16(1) StGB[78] – is liable only for negligence, if applicable.[79]

Mistakes about the factual basis of a justificatory defence are treated slightly differently. In our tree-on-the-property-line case, for example,[80] D fulfils the *actus reus* of criminal damage by cutting down a tree belonging to V.[81] If one takes the view, that the typing error vitiates V's consent, the destruction of foreign property is not justified.[82] If, however, the facts were as D believed them to be, his act would have corresponded to the will of the owner. D did not want to infringe upon V's property rights, he – in other words – did not intentionally commit a wrong. Therefore, the majority opinion in German case-law and doctrine takes the view that in analogous applications of s 16(1) StGB D is not liable for intentional criminal

73 Case based on Roxin (n 2), s 13 mn 98.
74 Lenckner and Sternberg-Lieben (n 7) mn 47; Kühl (n 1), s 9 mn 37; see also Roxin (n 2), s 13 mn 99.
75 Case based on Roxin (n 2), s 13 mn 104.
76 Roxin (n 2), s 13 mn 104; in a similar vein Lenckner and Sternberg-Lieben (n 7) mn 47; crit. Heinrich (n 7) mn 471.
77 Heinrich (n 7) mn 471; Kühl (n 1), s 9 mn 44; crit. Roxin (n 2), s 13 mn 6.
78 § 16 (1) StGB reads as follows 'Whosoever at the time of the commission of the offence is unaware of a fact which is a statutory element of the offence shall be deemed to lack intention. Any liability for negligence remains unaffected', translation according to Bohlander (n 30) 41.
79 Heinrich (n 7) mn 450; Wessels, Beulke and Satzger (n 9) mn 549.
80 See (n 68) and accompanying text.
81 Section 303(1) StGB provides: 'Whosoever unlawfully damages or destroys an object belonging to another shall be liable [. . .]', translation according to Bohlander (n 30) 186.
82 See also the similar case by Heinrich (n 7) mn 463. As regards the defence situation, German criminal law opts for an objective *ex ante* test, which means that the situation must exist objectively and not only in the actor's mind, see Ambos and Bock (n 10) 227.

damage.[83] As this offence cannot be committed by negligence, D is not punishable at all. The distinction between direct and analogous applications of s 16 (1) StGB does not affect the criminal responsibility of the direct perpetrator, but may be relevant for third parties, because secondary participation is only possible in the latter case.[84]

2 SPECIFIC ISSUES

2.1 Consent and homicide offences

2.1.1 Mercy killings

As already indicated above,[85] the victim cannot validly consent to an intentional killing. Even his 'express and earnest request' does not relieve the defendant from criminal responsibility for murder, but only results in a mitigation of punishment (s 216 StGB)[86] or exceptionally an abstention from punishment.[87] Consequently, voluntary active euthanasia, that is, a direct act of killing, done with the consent of the victim and intended to end his suffering, is a criminal offence.[88] Assistance in an autonomous act of suicide, to the contrary, does not entail criminal liability.[89] This is due to the fact that (attempted) suicide itself is not a punishable act and secondary participation is accessory in nature and thus requires an intentional and unlawful principal offence.[90] The line between active euthanasia and assisted suicide is often difficult to draw. The decisive criterion is whether the victim controls the course of the event and can decide freely between life and death until the very last moment.[91]

Given the advances in intensive-care medicine and life-prolonging measures, the general prohibition of euthanasia is subjected to several exceptions. Palliative care, in

---

83 See, eg, BGH NStZ 2012, 272, 275 (with regard to self-defence); in particular with a view to consent Rönnau (n 10) mn 211; Heinrich (n 7) mn 463. The treatment of mistakes concerning the factual basis of a justificatory defence (*Erlaubnistatbestandsirrtum*), however, is very controversial; for more detail on the discussion Jescheck and Weigend (n 10) 462–467; Krey and Esser (n 11) mn 731–745; Kindhäuser (n 7), s 29 mn 11–26.

84 See Krey and Esser (n 11) mn 741–742; Heinrich (n 7) mn 1136–1141.

85 See above 1.1.4.

86 In more detail see 2.1.2.

87 See n 98 and accompanying text.

88 Hartmut Schneider, 'Vorbemerkung zu den §§ 211 ff.' in Wolfgang Joecks and Klaus Miebach (eds), *Münchener Kommentar zum Strafgesetzbuch Band 4, §§ 185–262 StGB* (2nd edition, CH Beck 2012) mn 100; Johannes Wessels and Michael Hettinger, *Strafrecht Besonderer Teil 1. Straftaten gegen Persönlichkeits- und Gemeinschaftswerte* (39th edition, Cf Müller 2015) mn 28; see also BGH NJW 1987, 1092; BGHSt 55, 191.

89 Bohlander (n 21) 184; Schneider (n 86) mn 32; Urs Kindhäuser, *Strafrecht Besonderer Teil 1. Straftaten gegen Persönlichkeitsrechte, Staat und Gesellschaft* (7th edition, Nomos Verlag 2015), s 3 mn 2.

90 In more detail Kai Ambos and Stefanie Bock, 'Germany' in Alan Reed and Michael Bohlander (eds), *Participation in Crime* (Ashgate 2013) 323, 326, 332. Note, that since December 2015 the commercial promotion of suicide is a punishable offence in terms of s 217 StGB.

91 See BGHSt 19, 135, 139–140; Kindhäuser (n 89), s 4 mn 9–10; crit. Murmann (n 10), s 23 mn 99. In more detail on the controversial discussion Hartmut Schneider, '§ 216' in Wolfgang Joecks and Klaus Miebach (eds), *Münchener Kommentar zum Strafgesetzbuch Band 4, §§ 185–262 StGB* (2nd edition, CH Beck 2012) mn 31–53; Albin Eser and Detlev Sternberg-Lieben, '§ 216' in Adolf Schönke and Horst Schröder (eds), *Strafgesetzbuch – Kommentar* (29th edition, CH Beck 2014) mn 11–11a.

particular medical treatment to reduce pain, which has the side effect of speeding the patient's death (indirect euthanasia) is considered permissible because the primary intention of the defendant is not to kill, but to comfort the patient.[92] Moreover, the Federal Supreme Court held in a fundamental ruling from 2010, that under certain circumstances even passive euthanasia by omission or active withdrawal of medical treatment can be justified.[93] The Court's reasoning is based on the notion that medical treatment against the will of the victim constitutes physical assault in terms of s 223 StGB.[94] The patient therefore has the right to refuse medical treatment in the first place, which implies that he also has the right to insist on the withdrawal of life-prolonging measures. Whether his wish for non-treatment is implemented by mere omission or a positive act like switching off life-support machines or disconnecting a feeding tube is deemed irrelevant.[95] In both cases, the defendant is relieved from criminal responsibility if the following three requirements are fulfilled:

- The patient suffers from a life-threatening disease, which, if untreated, results in death.
- The defendant withholds, withdraws or restricts medical treatment associated with this disease.
- The defendant acts with the (presumed) will of the victim.[96]

The courts' approaches towards passive and indirect euthanasia are convincing in so far as they respect the patient's right to self-determination at the end of his life. From a doctrinal point of view, this more liberal approach is nevertheless hard to reconcile with s 216 StGB and its underlying principle that no one can dispose of his own life.[97]

In a recent decision, the municipal court (*Amtsgericht*) of Köln found another interesting way to take into account the particularities of interfamilial mercy killings. It argued that the defendant who was guilty of killing his beloved, but fatally ill, father on his request (s 216), suffered so severely from the consequences of his act, that the imposition of a penalty would be clearly inappropriate.[98] Therefore, in extreme and very exceptional cases, the psychological situation of the perpetrator may justify an abstention from punishment.

---

92 See BGHSt 42, 301, 305; BGHSt 46, 279, 284–285; Bohlander (n 21) 183; Wessels and Hettinger (n 88) mn 31–33; also Albin Eser and Detlev Sternberg-Lieben, 'Vorbemerkungen zu den §§ 211 ff.' in Adolf Schönke and Horst Schröder (eds), *Strafgesetzbuch – Kommentar* (29th edition, CH Beck 2014) mn 26; in more detail Schneider (n 88) mn 104–113.
93 BGHSt 55, 191.
94 BGHSt 55, 191, 196–7; see also *herein* 2.2.2.
95 BGHSt 55, 191, 202.
96 Summary based on Rengier (n 12), s 7 mn 7b. In practice, the determination of the hypothetical will of the patient can be very difficult, in particular, if he has not made a formal living will, see in detail Eser and Sternberg-Lieben (n 92) mn 28b-28h.
97 In more detail Schneider (n 88) mn 106–113; see also Eser and Sternberg-Lieben (n 92) mn 28a; Rengier (n 12), s 7 mn 8; Murmann (n 10), s 21 mn 78–79.
98 Amtsgericht [hereinafter: AG] Köln Strafverteidiger 2015, 572. The Court based its ruling on s 60 StGB which reads 'The court may order a discharge if the consequences of the offence suffered by the offender are so serious that an imposition of penalties would be clearly inappropriate. This shall not apply if the offender has incurred a sentence of imprisonment of more than one year for the offence.' Translation according to Bohlander (n 30) 59.

2.1.2 Killing on request of the victim

A defendant, who intentionally kills another person, is normally liable to imprisonment of not less than five years.[99] If he is induced to kill by the express and earnest request of the victim, the penalty is reduced to imprisonment from six months to five years (s 216 StGB). The victim's wish to die is therefore not a full defence to homicide offences, but leads to a considerable mitigation of punishment if:

1 The victim requests to die. A request is more than mere consent. The victim must exert psychological influence on the defendant and induce him to kill.[100]
2 The request is express, that is unambiguous. An unequivocal gesture can be sufficient.[101]
3 The request is earnest, which presupposes a free, fully informed and reflected decision.[102]
4 The defendant is induced by the request. The victim's wish to die must be his guiding motive, the driving force behind his action.[103]

2.1.3 Abortion

According to s 218(1) StGB, a person who terminates a pregnancy is liable to imprisonment of not more than three years or a fine.[104] The offence can be committed by the doctor, who performs the abortion, other third persons, and the pregnant women herself.[105] Acts, the effects of which occur before the conclusion of the nidation, do not qualify as abortion.[106] Section 218(1) StGB thus does not cover the taking of the 'morning-after pill' or the use of intrauterine devices.[107]

The abortion offence aims at the protection of the unborn child,[108] which means, that – as a rule – consent of the pregnant woman cannot exempt the perpetrator from criminal responsibility.[109] In balancing the child's right to life against the mother's right to self-determination,

---

99 See s 212 StGB. Murder under specific aggravating circumstances (s 211 StGB) is punishable by life imprisonment.
100 BGH NJW 2005, 1876, 1879; Eser and Sternberg-Lieben (n 92) mn 6.
101 Eser and Sternberg-Lieben (n 92) mn 7; Murmann (n 10), s 21 mn 84; Wessels and Hettinger (n 88) mn 156; see also BGH NJW 1987, 1092.
102 BGH NStZ 2011, 340; BGH NStZ 2012, 85.
103 BGH NJW 2005, 1876, 1879; Eser and Sternberg-Lieben (n 92) mn 9; Murmann (n 10), s 21 mn 84.
104 Translation according to Bohlander (n 30) 148.
105 Albin Eser, '§ 218 StGB' in Adolf Schönke and Horst Schröder (eds), *Strafgesetzbuch – Kommentar* (29th edition, CH Beck 2014) mn 28–32; Walter Gropp, '§ 218a' in Wolfgang Joecks and Klaus Miebach (eds), *Münchener Kommentar zum Strafgesetzbuch Band 4, §§ 185–262 StGB* (2nd edition, CH Beck 2012) mn 37–41; Rengier (n 12), s 11 mn 10–15. The pregnant woman, however, benefits from a reduced sentencing scale (s 218(3) StGB: imprisonment of not more than one year or a fine) and an exemption from attempt liability (s 218 (3) StGB).
106 Section 218(1) StGB; translation according to Bohlander (n 30) 148.
107 Rengier (n 12), s 11 mn 7; in more detail Reinhard Merkel, '§ 218' in Urs Kindhäuser, Ulfried Neumann and Hans-Ulrich Paeffgen (eds), *Nomos Kommentar – Strafgesetzbuch* (4th edition, Nomos Verlag 2014) mn 13–16; Eser (n 105) mn 12–17.
108 Mekel (n 107) mn 7; Walter Gropp, 'Vorbemerkung zu den §§ 218 ff.' in Wolfgang Joecks and Klaus Miebach (eds), *Münchener Kommentar zum Strafgesetzbuch Band 4, §§ 185–262 StGB* (2nd edition, CH Beck 2012) mn 38; Wessels and Hettinger (n 88) mn 223; on the responsibility of the state to protect the life of unborn children Bundesverfassungsgericht (Constitutional Court) NJW 1993, 1751.
109 Eser (n 105) mn 34; Mekel (n 107) mn 135. Acting against the will of the pregnant women is an especially serious case of abortion punishable by imprisonment from six month to five years, s 218 (2) StGB.

however, s 218a (1) StGB provides that the offence of abortion is not fulfilled under three cumulative conditions:

1 the pregnant women requests the termination of the pregnancy and demonstrates to the physician that the she has received special counselling for pregnant women in a situation of emergency or conflict;[110]
2 the termination of the pregnancy is performed by a physician; and
3 not more than twelve weeks have elapsed since conception.[111]

In addition, a termination of pregnancy is justified, if it is necessary to avert danger to the life, physical or mental health of the pregnant women (medical indication) or if there are strong reasons to believe that the pregnancy was caused by rape or another sexual offence (criminological indication).[112] In all three cases, the doctor performing the intervention must act with the consent of the pregnant woman.[113] Courts tend to deny minors the right to take this decision on their own, because they believe that young girls generally lack the necessary maturity to understand the grave physical and psychological consequences of an abortion.[114] The prevailing view in doctrine argues for a more flexible approach, which takes into account the individual intellectual capacities of the respective minor.[115]

2.2 Consent and non-fatal offences against the person

2.2.1 HIV and other communicable disease transmission

An HIV-infection and comparable diseases constitute a negative pathological physical condition and a damage to health in terms of s 223(1) StGB.[116] If one takes the view that at least certain viruses qualify as noxious substances[117] or pose a danger to life,[118] a carrier intentionally

---

110 The details of the counselling are laid down in s 219 StGB. In particular, it must 'be guided by effort to encourage the women to continue the pregnancy and to open her to the prospects of a life with the child', translation according to Bohlander (n 30) 150.
111 Translation according to Bohlander (n 30) 148.
112 Rengier (n 12), s 11 mn 27; in more detail Walter Gropp '§ 218a' in Wolfgang Joecks and Klaus Miebach (eds), *Münchener Kommentar zum Strafgesetzbuch Band 4, §§ 185–262 StGB* (2nd edition, CH Beck 2012) mn 41; Albin Eser, '§ 218a StGB' in Adolf Schönke and Horst Schröder (eds), *Strafgesetzbuch – Kommentar* (29th edition, CH Beck 2014) mn 20.
113 Eser (n 105) mn 61; Reinhard Merkel, '§ 218a' in Urs Kindhäuser, Ulfried Neumann and Hans-Ulrich Paeffgen (eds), *Nomos Kommentar – Strafgesetzbuch* (4th edition, Nomos Verlag 2014) mn 16; compare also Gropp (n 112) mn 20. Consent of the father of the unborn child is not required, Eser (n 105) mn 62.
114 OLG Hamm NJW 1998 3424, 3245; AG Celle NJW 1987, 2307.
115 Merkel (n 113) mn 28; Gropp (n 112) mn 19; Eser (n 105) mn 61; in the same vein OLG Stuttgart NJW 1980, 646.
116 BGHSt 36, 1, 6; BGH NJW 1990, 129; BGH NStZ 2009, 34; Albin Eser '§ 223' in Adolf Schönke and Horst Schröder (eds), *Strafgesetzbuch – Kommentar* (29th edition, CH Beck 2014) mn 7. Note that already the HIV-infection itself constitutes a damage to the health, a progression to AIDS is not required.
    Section 223(1) StGB on 'Causing Bodily Harm' provides: 'Whosoever physically assaults or damages the health of another person, shall be liable to imprisonment not exceeding five years or a fine', translation according to Bohlander (n 30) 151.
117 Hans-Ulrich Paeffgen, '224' in Urs Kindhäuser, Ulfried Neumann and Hans-Ulrich Paeffgen (eds), *Nomos Kommentar – Strafgesetzbuch* (4th edition, Nomos Verlag 2014) mn 9; Eser (n 116) mn 7; Wessels and Hettinger (n 88) mn 268.
118 BGHSt 36, 1, 9; BGH NJW 1990, 129; Paeffgen (n 117) mn 40.

infecting another person may even be liable for 'causing bodily harm by dangerous means'.[119] It is commonly agreed that informed consent to sexual intercourse, and the risks associated therewith, may relieve the defendant from criminal responsibility. The reasons, however, vary. According to some authors, V who knowingly and voluntarily engages with the HIV-positive D and gets infected, was not harmed by another person, but deliberately decided to endanger herself. Consequently, already the offence definition of s 223(1) StGB, which does not cover self-inflicted injuries and damages, would not be fulfilled.[120] Others argue that V and D equally participated in sexual intercourse, so that D by infecting V has caused her bodily harm, but may be justified by her consent.[121] In any case, D is exonerated only if V makes a fully-informed decision, which presupposes that she knows about D's HIV+ status, the nature and severity of the disease and the infection risk.[122] Blind consent to sexual intercourse, as such, is not sufficient. How V gets the relevant information, is irrelevant. If she already knows that D is infected it is not necessary for him to explicitly disclose his disease to her.

2.2.2 Medical treatment

German jurisprudence assumes that medical treatment – even if performed *lege artis* – inflicts bodily harm on the patient. In order to act lawfully (and to avoid criminal liability), the physician therefore needs the (presumed) consent of his patient.[123] This approach puts an emphasis on the patient's right to autonomy and protects him from paternalistic, unwanted medical interventions.[124] In particular, consent is valid only, if the physician has advised the patient of the nature, consequences, side effects, risks and prospects of the proposed treatment and of appropriate alternatives.[125] The exact scope of the duty to disclose depends on the concrete circumstances of the case, like necessity and urgency of the intervention,[126] its experimental nature[127] and the seriousness of its consequences.[128] Failure to comply with

---

119 Section 224(1) StGB provides in its relevant parts: 'Whosoever causes bodily harm [. . .] by administering poison or other noxious substances [. . .] or [. . .] by methods that pose a danger to life, shall be liable to imprisonment from six months to ten years, in less serious cases to imprisonment from three months to five years', translation according to Bohlander (n 30) 224. In praxis, the main problems associated with HIV-cases are proof of causation (was the infection caused by the defendant or is it possible that the victim was infected elsewhere) and intention (not only if the defendant does not know that he carries HIV, but also if he receives antiretroviral drugs and therefor believes that he will not infect his sex partner), see Eser (n 116) mn 7 for further references.

120 BayObLG NStZ 1990, 81, 82; Hans-Ulrich Paeffgen, '§ 223' in Urs Kindhäuser, Ulfried Neumann and Hans-Ulrich Paeffgen (eds), *Nomos Kommentar – Strafgesetzbuch* (4th edition, Nomos Verlag 2014) mn 20; Wessels and Hettinger (n 88) mn 270.

121 Roland Helgreth, 'Aids – Einwilligung in infektiösen Geschlechtsverkehr' in NStZ 1988, 261, 262.

122 Paeffgen (n 117) mn 20; see also BGHSt 36, 1, 17; BayObLG NStZ 1990, 81, 82.

123 BGHSt 45, 219, 221; BGH NJW 2006, 2108; BGH NJW 2011, 1088; concurring Rengier (n 12), s 13 mn 15; for a different view see Wessels and Hettinger (n 86) mn 326, who argue that a medically indicated treatment which was performed *lege artis* and with the intent to heal, cannot be labelled as 'physical assault' or a 'damage to health' in terms of s 223 StGB; differentiating Eser (n 40) mn 31.

124 Dubber and Hörnle (n 3) 471; in the same vein Rengier (n 12), s 13 mn 17; Wessels and Hettinger (n 88) mn 558.

125 BGH NStZ 1996, 34; BGH NJW 2011, 1088; see also Krey and Esser (n 11) mn 669a.

126 BGH NJW 2006, 2108; see also Wessels, Beulke and Satzger (n 8) mn 376.

127 BGH NStZ 1996, 34; BGH NJW 2011, 1088.

128 Eser (n 115) mn 40d; see also BGH NJW 1976, 363, 364.

the information obligation vitiates the patient's consent and – as a rule – turns the medical treatment into a punishable offence.

These principles are undermined by the increasing recognition of the defence of hypothetical consent. According to this approach, medical interventions are justified, even though the physician has violated his duty to disclose, if the patient, if asked, would have consented.[129] In contrast to the defence of presumed consent,[130] hypothetical consent is applied in cases of non-emergency, where it was possible to obtain a valid and informed decision of the patient.[131] It therefore is criticised for violating patient autonomy.[132]

2.2.3 Sport injuries, 'horseplay', piercing

Injuries caused negligently in common sports like soccer or ice hockey may be seen as a realisation of a socially accepted risk, which does not give rise to criminal liability.[133] Boxing and other sports involving the intentional infliction of harm, to the contrary, require the – at least implied – consent of all participants. It covers only sport-specific risks, not injuries resulting from a gross breach of rules like an intentional 'blow below the belt'.[134] Moreover, s 228 StGB provides that the consent of the victim cannot justify the causation of bodily harm, if the harmful conduct violates public morals. The meaning and content of this provision, which obviously conflicts with the principle of autonomy, are far from clear.[135] Recent jurisprudence refrains from moral evaluations *sensu stricto* and considers in particular 'the scope of the physical injury and the degree of danger for the life and limb of the victim'; acts resulting in a concrete danger of death are generally deemed unacceptable for the legal order, the consent notwithstanding.[136] Consensual participation in high-risks sports with the inherent possibility of severe injury or even death is nevertheless possible, provided that they take place in a formal setting with adequate safety arrangements[137] and clear competition rules whose compliance is supervised by a neutral party.[138]

Similar considerations apply to horseplay, fistfights and brawls. They are not exempted from consent *per se*, but become incompatible with public morals when getting too dangerous.[139] With regard to fights between rivalling groups, recent decisions place an emphasis on the risk of an escalation. The Federal Supreme Court argued that a large number of participants makes

---

129 BGH Neue Zeitschrift für Strafrecht – Rechtsprechungsreport (hereinafter: NStZ-RR) 2004, 16; BGH NStZ-RR 2007, 340.
130 See 1.3.2.
131 Rengier (n 12), s 13 mn 19; Krey and Esser (n 11) mn 682.
132 Rengier (n 12), s 13 mn 19; Krey and Esser (n 11) mn 682; Wessels and Hettinger (n 88) mn 324.
133 Kühl (n 1), s 4 mn 48; in more detail Frank Schuster and Detlev Sternberg-Lieben, '§ 15' in Adolf Schönke and Horst Schröder (eds), *Strafgesetzbuch – Kommentar* (29th edition, CH Beck 2014) mn 214–215a.
134 Walter Stree and Detlev Sternberg-Lieben, '§ 228' in Adolf Schönke and Horst Schröder (eds), *Strafgesetzbuch – Kommentar* (29th edition, CH Beck 2014) mn 27; see also BGHSt 4, 88, 92; BGH NJW 2013, 1379, 1381.
135 In more detail Bernhard Hartung, '§ 228', in Wolfgang Joecks and Klaus Miebach (eds), *Münchener Kommentar zum Strafgesetzbuch Band 4, §§ 185–262 StGB* (2nd edition, CH Beck 2012) mn 15; Karsten Gaede 'Mit der Sittenwidrigkeit gegen Hooligangewalt – das Ende der "Dritten Halbzeit"?' (2014) Zeitschrift für Internationale Strafrechtsdogmatik 489, 490.
136 BGHSt 49, 166, 171, English translation by Dubber and Hörnle (n 3) 467; see also BGHSt 49, 166, 174; BGHSt 53, 55, 62; BGH NJW 2013, 1379, 1380.
137 BGHSt 4, 88, 92; Hartung (n 135) mn 35; see also BGH NJW 2013, 1379, 1381.
138 BGH NJW 2013, 1379, 1381; see also BayObOLG NJW 1999, 372, 373; Hartung (n 135) mn 35.
139 BGHSt 4, 24, 31–32; BayObOLG NJW 1999, 372, 373; Stree and Sternberg-Lieben (n 134) mn 32.

it difficult for the individuals involved to control the situation and that a heated atmosphere might easily lead the adversaries to exceed the limits of what was consented beforehand, if no special precautions are taken.[140] Due to the particularities of group dynamics, group brawls were found to be unacceptably dangerous, even if the single harming acts did not result in a concrete danger of death.[141] This extended interpretation of s 228 StGB is not uncontested and gives rise to crucial questions about the (social) function of criminal law and its relationship to the constitutionally guaranteed right to self-determination.[142]

Invasive beauty treatments like piercing and tattooing qualify as physical assault and damage to health in terms of s 223 StGB.[143] It is lawful only if based on valid and informed consent,[144] which presupposes that the piercer or tattooist has informed the client of the typical risks of the treatment.[145]

2.2.4 Specific sexual practices involving infliction of harm

No special rules apply to sexual practices involving infliction of harm. They are lawful, if conducted with the consent of all persons engaged. Note, that an act does not violate good morals in terms of s 228 StGB[146] merely because of a specific or 'abnormal' sexual motivation.[147] The boundaries of free consent are reached, however, if the respective sexual practice brings the victim into concrete danger of death.[148]

2.3 Sexual offences

2.3.1 Absence of consent or use of force/threats

Section 177 StGB on sexual assault and rape provides in its relevant parts:

(1) Whosoever coerces another person
 1 by force;
 2 by threat of imminent danger to life or limb; or
 3 by exploiting a situation in which the victim is unprotected and at the mercy of the offender, to suffer sexual acts by the offender or a third person on their own person

---

140 The Federal Supreme Court particularly pointed out that the adversaries have taken no measures to ensure that the opposing groups are equally strong and that heavily injured participants are not subjected to further attacks, BGH NJW 2013, 1379, 1382.
141 BGH NJW 2013, 1379.
142 Crit. for example Detlev Sternberg-Lieben 'Anmerkung' in *Juristenzeitung* 2013, 953; Gaede (n 135) 500.
143 Ulrich Schroth 'Die Einwilligung in eine nicht-indizierte Körperbeeinträchtigung zur Selbstverwirklichung – insbesondere die Einwilligung in Lebendspende, Schönheitsoperation und Piercing' in Winfried Hassemer, Eberhard Kempf and Sergio Moccia (eds), *In dubio pro libertate – Festschrift für Klaus Volk zum 65. Geburtstag* (CH Beck 2009) 719, 720; Kristian Kühl, '§ 223' in Karl Lackner and Kristian Kühl (eds), *Strafgesetzbuch* (28th edition, CH Beck 2014) mn 10.
144 Depending on their individual maturity, minors might need the consent of their legal representatives, see 1.4.
145 In detail Schroth (n 143) 739–741.
146 See (n 135) and accompanying text.
147 BGHSt 46, 166, 172, English translation by Dubber and Hörnle (n 3) 467; see also Roxin (n 2), s 13 mn 46; Gaede (n 135) 490.
148 See BGHSt 46, 166, 174, English translation by Dubber and Hörnle (n 3) 467: no valid consent to strangulation for a period of at least three minutes.

or to engage actively in sexual activity with the offender or a third person, shall be liable to imprisonment of not less than one year.

(2) In especially serious cases the penalty shall be imprisonment of not less than two years. An especially serious case typically occurs if

  1   the offender performs sexual intercourse with the victim or performs similar sexual acts with the victim, or allows them to be performed on himself by the victim, especially if they degrade the victim or if they entail penetration of the body (rape)...[149]

German law accordingly does not define sexual assault and rape as engaging in sexual activities without the consent of the victim, but requires an additional element of coercion, namely the use of force, a sufficiently qualified threat or the exploitation of a situation, which denies the victim a freedom of choice.[150] This restrictive approach leads to critical loopholes.[151] In a notorious case decided by the Federal Supreme Court in 2012, D performed anal sex with his wife V against her will. V was crying during the whole intercourse and begged D to let her go, but did not fight him, because she was afraid to wake her children. The Court of first instance convicted D for rape, but was overturned on appeal. The Federal Supreme Court argued, that D has not used coercive means and that the existence of a helpless situation (s 177[1] No 3 StGB) depends on whether D could have called for and received help from third persons.[152] Women's rights activists take this case as proof of the shortcomings of s 177 StGB and its incompatibility with international recognised human rights standards.[153] Not at least due to their criticism, the German Ministry of Justice recently proposed an extensive reform of the law on sexual crimes which will probably be implemented by the end of 2016.[154]

It follows from the coercion element of s 177 StGB that the defendant must act against the will of the victim. A free and informed consent to, for example, sado-masochistic sex practices negates the *actus reus*.[155] As usual, consent must continue to exist until the act is completed.[156]

---

149 Translation according to Bohlander (n 30) 132–133.
150 Bohlander (n 21) 201; see also Tatjana Hörnle, '§ 177' in Heinrich Wilhelm Laufhütte, Ruth Rissing-van Saan and Klaus Tiedemann (eds), *Leipziger Kommentar, Band 6, §§ 146 bis 210* (12th edition, De Gruyter 2010) mn 3; Joachim Renzikowski, '§ 177' in Wolfgang Joecks and Klaus Miebach (eds), *Münchener Kommentar zum Strafgesetzbuch, Band 3, §§ 80–184g StGB* (2nd edition, CH Beck 2012) mn 1.
151 In detail Tatjana Hörnle, 'Vor § 174' in Heinrich Wilhelm Laufhütte, Ruth Rissing-van Saan and Klaus Tiedemann (eds), *Leipziger Kommentar, Band 6, §§ 146 bis 210* (12th edition, De Gruyter 2010) mn 51.
152 BGH Strafverteidiger 2012, 534 with critical analysis by Joachim Renzikowski and Brigitte Sick 'Anmerkung' in NStZ 2013, 468.
153 See, eg, Deutscher Juristinnenbund/German Women Lawyers Association, 'Stellungnahme zur grundsätzlichen Notwendigkeit einer Anpassung des Sexualstrafrechts (insbesondere § 177 StGB) an die Vorgaben der Konvention des Europarats zur Verhütung und Bekämpfung von Gewalt gegen Frauen und häuslicher Gewalt (Istanbul-Konvention) von 2011' (*Deutscher Jurisinnenbund*, 9 May 2014) <http://www.djb.de/Kom/K3/st14–07/> accessed 18 August 2016. Notably, Article 34 of the Council of Europe Convention on preventing and combating violence against women and domestic violence (Istanbul Convention) defines rape as 'engaging in non-consensual vaginal, anal or oral penetration of a sexual nature' and thus opts – in contrast to the German law – for the pure 'absence of consent' model.
154 See Deutscher Bundestag, Drucksache 18/9097 of 6 July 2016. In particular, the German Federal Parliament proposes a new offence of sexual assault which merely presupposes that the perpetrator commits sexual acts against the will of the victim.
155 Renzikowski (n 150) mn 53; see also Hörnle (n 150) mn 55. Of course, consent is invalid if given under coercion.
156 See 1.1.5.

Consensually started sexual intercourse thus turns into sexual assault if V revokes her consent and is then coerced by D to suffer further sexual acts.[157]

2.3.2 Evidentiary presumptions

German criminal proceedings are marked by the principle of free evaluation of evidence. Judges consider and weigh all evidence presented at trial at their own discretion without being bound by evidentiary rules or presumptions.[158] In sexual cases, the degree of force necessary to overcome the resistance of the victim often is a decisive factor for proof that the defendant knew that he was acting against the will of the victim.[159]

2.3.3 Mistake of fact about consent

Mistakes about consent to sexual intercourse follow the general rules outlined above:[160] as absence of consent is a negative element of sexual assault and rape, D lacks the necessary intent if he mistakenly believes that V has consented to his sexual activities.[161] Notably, the exonerating effect of a mistake of fact does not depend on its reasonableness or unavoidability. Rather, German law accepts every factual misconception as a full defence, even the absurd.[162] Accordingly, the claim that the defendant believed that the resistance of the victim was only for show may lead to an acquittal for rape.[163] Depending on the circumstances of the case, however, the defendant may be liable for causing bodily harm by negligence.[164]

2.4 Property offences and criminal damage

2.4.1 Place of consent in the offence structure

Many property offences can only be committed against the will of the victim so that lack of consent is a negative element of the crime. Theft and robbery,[165] for example, require a non-consensual interference with another's possession.[166] In order to be liable for embezzlement, the defendant must *abuse* his position of power, which is not the case if he acts in mutual agreement with the principal.[167] The destruction of property in terms of s 303 StGB, to the

---

157 BGH NStZ 2003, 165, 166; Hörnle (n 150) mn 23; Renzikowski (n 150) mn 53.

158 Michael Bohlander, *Principle of German Criminal Procedure* (Hart 2012) 32; Uwe Murmann, *Prüfungswissen Strafprozessrecht* (3rd edition, CH Beck 2015) mn 36.

159 BGH NStZ 2002, 494; also BGH NStZ 1995, 230; Renzikowski (n 150) mn 59–60; Hörnle (n 150) mn 128.

160 See 1.6.

161 Renzikowski (n 150) mn 53; Hörnle (n 150) mn 125.

162 Hörnle (n 150) mn 125; Dubber and Hörnle (n 3) 474.

163 See BGH NStZ 1983, 71; BGH NStZ 2002, 494; detailed overview on the case-law by Renzikowski (n 150) mn 58–62.

164 Renzikowski (n 150) mn 62; see also BGH NStZ 2007, 218;

165 Robbery combines the offence of theft with elements of coercion. S 249(1) StGB provides: 'Whosoever, by force or threats of imminent danger to life or limb, takes chattels belonging to another from another with the intent of appropriating the property for himself or third person, shall be liable [. . .]', translation according to Bohlander (n 30) 163.

166 See 1.2. and 1.3.1.

167 BGHSt 3, 23, 24; BGHSt 50, 331, 343, s 266(1) StGB provides: 'Whosoever abuses the power accorded him by statute, by commission of a public authority or legal transaction to dispose of assets of another or to make binding agreements for another, or violates his duty to safeguard the property interests of another incumbent upon him by reason of statute, commission of a public authority, legal transaction

contrary, is not dependent on the defendant defying the will of the owner.[168] Consent thus does not negate the *actus reus*, but the wrongfulness of the act.

2.4.2 Mistaken belief in consent

If D mistakenly believes that he enjoys the consent of the victim, which in fact he does not, he is – by direct or analogues application of s 16 StGB – not liable for intent.[169] Since property offence generally cannot be committed by negligence, D is not punishable at all.

---

or fiduciary relationship, and thereby causes damage to the person, whose property interests he was responsible for, shall be liable [. . .]', translation according to Bohlander (n 30) 172.

168 Weigend (n 1) 271.

169 See 1.6.

17

Islamic law

Mohammad Hedayati-Kakhki

1 GENERAL ISSUES

Under Islamic law consent is not regarded as a defence unless an element of the crime is specifically negated by the consent of the victim. In these circumstances, providing certain conditions are satisfied, consent can be considered a complete defence. The victim must be capable of consenting to the action in law; therefore, for example, where sexual intercourse with a minor is concerned, consent provides no defence. Additionally, the victim must not be subject to duress or compulsion, but rather must consent freely and voluntarily. Consent must also not be obtained through fraudulent means. Under Islamic law any act that is carried out with an honest or mistaken belief that the individual is acting within the law is defensible. Consent will act as a complete defence in some cases, while in other circumstances it may only be accepted within certain limits,[1] or render the offender liable for a lesser crime.[2]

1.1 Conceptual foundations

Islamic law does not provide a specific definition of consent. However, when considering the various interpretations of consent based on the primary sources (Qur'an and Sunna) it could reasonably be defined as the voluntary assent of a mentally and legally capable individual to allow another person to act in a specific manner that infringes on their personal rights. The defence of consent becomes applicable where the injured party acquiesces to an act during or immediately before its commission; retrospective consent and/or subsequent forgiveness of the offender would not be regarded as a legal defence, rather a mitigating factor in certain crimes, which may result in a lesser sentence or the complete withdrawal of the prosecution.[3] Such consent may be clearly expressed or implied through various means.

---

1 Imran Ahsan Khan Nyazee, *General Principles of Criminal Law: (Islamic and Western)* (Lulu 2010) 155–156.
2 The victim's consent to sexual intercourse is a defence to the crime of rape, however the offender would remain liable under *zina*, which provides that any sexual relationship outside marriage is a crime.
3 Theft would not be punished by *hadd*, if the victim withdrew their allegation of theft before the execution of the punishment (eg amputation of a hand). This would not exclude the offender from being punished under *ta'zir* (lashes, imprisonment, fine, etc) principles.

Similar to the traditional interpretation of self-defence, the defence of consent is ordinarily regarded as justificatory in nature. However, in the context of the defence of duress it could be considered excusatory.

1.1.1 Philosophical and theoretical principles informing the law surrounding consent

There are a number of philosophical principles that underpin the law of consent. However, the extent to which the defence of consent is adhered to differs between jurisdictions, mainly due to varying interpretations of the primary sources of Sharia.

The Hanafi school of thought, for instance, places emphasis on personal liberty and demonstrates a reluctance to impose unwarranted restrictions upon this. Abu Hannifah, in particular, maintains that neither the community nor the government is entitled to interfere with the personal liberty of an individual, providing the individual has not violated the principles of Sharia law.[4] Hanafi principles appear to mirror the theory of liberalism in supporting the concept of individual autonomy, despite the fact that in some circumstances individuals will use said autonomy to make decisions that may not objectively be in their best interests.

In contrast, the Hanbali school seems to rely extensively on considerations of public interest. For example Imam ibn Hanbali issued a verdict compelling the owners of a large house to open their doors to the homeless, against their consent, and in the interests of improving society.[5] These same public policy considerations that feature so heavily in Hanbali teachings seem to suggest a more paternalist standpoint; consent will not be a viable defence where there is a good reason for society to want to limit activity that is relevant to *hadd* crimes, those in which the public interest is superior to the private rights of the individual. For instance, the Islamic approach to mercy killing is prohibitive, as this is in society's best interests in light of the Qur'anic significance of the sanctity of life, regardless of the consent of the individuals involved.

While these competing interpretations are but two of a host of different schools of thought, they aptly demonstrate some of the various philosophical principles that have shaped the creation of legislation across a number of Islamic jurisdictions.

1.1.2 Influence of feminist and queer theory

Within Islamic jurisdictions there is little official recognition of feminist and queer rights by the Qur'an and Sunna, which leave little room for interpretation. These sources promote a patriarchal society; while all human beings are respected by virtue of their humanity, men are always considered dominant.[6] For instance, subsumed into the concept of marriage is the implied consent of a wife to sexual relations and thereby the offence of rape within a marriage does not exist under Islamic law. As within other jurisdictions, feminists strongly criticise the imbalance between the sexes and the notion that anti-Islamic behaviour provides a legitimate provocation for sexual offences.

---

4 Mohammad Hashim Kamali, 'Law and Society: The Interplay of Revelation and Reason in the Shariah' in John L Esposito (ed), *The Oxford History of Islam* (Oxford University Press 1999).

5 ibid.

6 Rebecca Whisnant, 'Feminist Perspectives on Rape', *Stanford Encyclopaedia of Philosophy* (Fall edition, 2013) <http://plato.stanford.edu/entries/feminism-rape/#Con> accessed 3 May 2015.

Similarly, queer theory, as understood as a set of ideas based around the concept that gender identities are not fixed and do not determine who we are,[7] is not recognised under Sharia law as it is a fundamental principle that God created human beings as a 'male and female' and did so with a purpose.[8] The various different social identities, including homosexuality, hermaphroditism, and gender ambiguity to name but a few, that are subsumed within queer theory are not thought of as legitimate life choices within Islamic society. For instance, homosexuality is widely condemned within Sharia-based jurisdictions and often carries severe criminal penalty. Naturally, consent does not provide a defence to such offences, as they are regarded as crimes against God and it is in the public interest to prevent the spread of such practices that are considered contrary to your God-given identity. Resultantly, homosexual activity is condemned throughout the Islamic world; Afghanistan, Pakistan and the United Arab Emirates all prescribe lengthy prison sentences for consensual homosexual acts, whilst the death penalty is enforced in Iran, Yemen and Saudi Arabia.[9] Any suggestions from individuals of a queer or feminist perspective that consensual same-sex relationships should not be punished, due to the presence of consent as a legitimate defence, are largely ignored. The concept of conformity to the rules prescribed by God for your own gender remains paramount; and divine law cannot be overruled by academic theory or rights-based ideas put forward by a particular group.

Whilst acts of homosexuality are universally regarded as sinful by all schools of thought within Sharia, there are a minority of jurists who believe that while 'homosexuality is a grievous sin no legal punishment is stated in the Qur'an and it is not reported that Prophet Muhammad has punished anyone for the act; there is no authentic hadith reported from the Prophet prescribing a punishment for the homosexuals'.[10]

Despite this, there is a consensus amongst Sharia-based jurisdictions that homosexuality is illegal and that punishment should be prescribed by statute, the severity of which differs from jurisdiction to jurisdiction. For example, the Hanafite School that is currently used predominately in south and east Asia, maintain that no physical punishment is warranted; whilst the Hanabalites, a school of thought widely used in the Arab world, considers that severe punishment is necessary. The same cross-jurisdictional differences can be seen in the evidential requirements to prove the offence; for instance the Sha'fi and Shi'a Schools of thought, require a minimum of four adult male witnesses to prove homosexuality whilst the Hanafi School does not require such a strict standard of proof as they do not classify homosexuality as a *hadd* crime.[11]

In any case, the practices promoted by both feminism and queer theory are widely regarded to be illegal and anti-Islamic by their very nature, in a manner that goes to the core of the interests and values of Islamic society as a whole; there is no room for consent as a defence to such crimes.

---

7 David Gauntlett, 'Queer Theory' (*Theory.org.uk*) <http://www.theory.org.uk/ctr-que1.htm> accessed 13 June 2015.

8 Qur'an [49:13].

9 – –, 'Where is it illegal to be gay?' (*BBC News*, 10 February 2014) <http://www.bbc.co.uk/news/world-25927595> accessed 12 May 2015.

10 Mohamed El-Moctar El-Shinqiti, 'Threats to Behead Homosexuals: Shari'ah or Politics?' (*Islamic Research Foundation International Inc.*, 9 June 2008) <http://www.irfi.org/articles2/articles_2951_3000/Threats%20to%20Behead%20Homosexuals.HTM> accessed 5 August 2015.

11 J Leatham, 'Homosexual Practices in Individual Schools of Islam' (*Faithology*, 24 May 2013) <http://www.faithology.com/topics/homosexual-practices-in-individual-schools-of-islam> accessed 16 September 2015.

1.1.3 Definition of informed consent

In order to truly consent to an action, an individual must have a sound understanding of both the nature and quality of said action. Informed consent is generally defined as a clear voluntary agreement made by an autonomous person competent to make an intelligent decision about a proposed action. Such agreements should be based on sufficient deliberation and the provision of adequate and comprehensible information.[12]

Sharia law undoubtedly respects the underlying tenets of informed consent based on the above description and, in particular, there is a deep-rooted tradition in the observance and importance of personal autonomy. This is a fundamental aspect of consensual activity and has been shown to be particularly relevant in the context of medical treatment. The Qur'an clearly places emphasises on this point, by providing that 'the Lord declared man his viceroy on earth'.[13] Islamic scholars have found no difficulty in interpreting this message to mean that 'no one is entitled to dispose of the right of a human being without his permission'.[14] However, in practice this focus on personal autonomy has not translated into the doctrine of informed consent as widely interpreted among criminal lawyers.

In Saudi Arabia, 'prior to delivering medical treatment or carrying out an operative procedure, the legally competent patient's consent, shall be obtained', and 'the physician shall provide adequate explanation to the patient or his guardian on the nature of the medical treatment or operative procedure he intends to apply'.[15] However, these rules do not define an 'adequate explanation' or address the issue of decision-making, thereby demonstrating the difficulty of defining informed consent under Islamic law.

An important issue to be considered is the concept of personal autonomy within Islamic law, which consists of duties and obligations (eg with respect to an individual's right to seek treatment), as well as wider social responsibility for followers. Individual autonomy is thus subservient to the larger interest of the community while public interests take precedence over an individual's private considerations. That is to say, for a Muslim patient, absolute autonomy is exceptional, as the existence of feelings of responsibility towards God plays a paramount role in any decision made by the patient.[16] Additionally, any decision will be influenced by the teaching/*fatwa* of jurists within their social community, as well as the beliefs of the relatives, who would expect the patient to take into consideration relevant cultural principles when providing consent. Therefore, personal autonomy is restricted to the social norms and religious beliefs of the patient within their community.

---

12 Tom L Beauchamp, LeRoy Walters, Jeffrey P Kahn and Anna C Mastroianni, *Contemporary Issues in Bioethics* (5th edition, Wadsworth 1999); also: MY Rathor, 'The Principle of Autonomy as Related to Personal Decision Making Concerning Health and Research from an "Islamic Viewpoint"' (2011) 43 Journal of the Islamic Medical Association 28.

13 Qur'an [6:165].

14 S Aksoy and A Elmali, 'The core concept of the four principles of bioethics as found in Islamic tradition' (2002) 21(2) Medical Law 211.

15 Muhammad M Hammami and others, 'Patients' perceived purpose of clinical informed consent: Mill's individual autonomy model is preferred' (2014) 15(2) BMC Medical Ethics <http://www.biomedcentral.com/1472–6939/15/2> accessed 12 July 2015.

16 Samuel Packer, 'Informed Consent with a Focus on Islamic Views' (2011) 43(3) Journal of the Islamic Medical Association 215–218.

The nature of informed consent within Islamic teaching is also dependent upon the type of medical treatment proposed, eg a husband must be consulted in procedures regarding a woman's pregnancy.[17]

It must be noted that a basic foundation of Islamic law is to minimise the levels of harm to individuals and this has had a dramatic effect on the realisation of informed consent.

Consequently, Islamic law supports the doctrine of informed consent as it respects a person's dignity and freedom of choice; furthermore, it empowers spouses in consenting to issues relating to their wives' reproductive organs.

1.1.4 Consent to risk or consent to outcome

According to personal autonomy, an individual can voluntarily consent to the 'risk' of being unintentionally harmed; however, this principle does not apply when a person is subjected to 'inevitable' harm and deliberate violence. Therefore, a distinction must be made, between intentional and unintentional harm resulting from the action in which a person consents to take part. For example, when an individual freely takes part in sport, they consent to the associated unintentional risk of harm related to that activity. However, said person does not agree to any calculated intentional acts that would not ordinarily be expected to occur.

In the context of sexual offences, consent to risk is often accepted as a defence within some Islamic jurisdictions where sex segregation is a strict principle enforced within society. For instance, when a woman knowingly and voluntarily accepts a request by a man to accompany him to his residence without any legitimate reason (ie teaching, employment, etc), it is often held that she has in fact consented to the risk associated with joining him.[18]

With regards to rape, there is a clear difference between the circumstances where the victim voluntarily accepts an invitation putting herself in a potentially harmful situation; and where she is simply subjected to a random sexual attack. Even if it is accepted that the woman may have consented to the risk of being sexually exploited by accepting a date request, she certainly did not consent to the outcome of the action, namely, being raped. In such jurisdictions, the victim will nonetheless face punishment for entering into an illegitimate relationship (sexual or otherwise) outside marriage.

When considering the consent to risk in medical treatment, it is a well-founded principle of Islamic law that the doctor is obliged to fully disclose any risks attributable to the proposed treatment and ensure the patient clearly understands any risks, benefits and alternatives to the procedure. As in other jurisdictions, problems may arise where a patient undergoes treatment for a simple and straightforward procedure, for example treatment for a broken arm, but discovers the doctor has instead amputated his left leg contrary to his consent. Therefore consent will only be valid if it has been provided in respect of the relevant proposed treatment, otherwise criminal liability will be incurred.

In any case, a patient's religious beliefs and values must always be taken into consideration when honestly disclosing the risks associated with a medical procedure as this may affect a patient's decision to consent.[19]

---

17 Dana I Al Husseini, 'The Implications of Religious Beliefs on Medical and Patient Care' (MSc thesis, University of Pennsylvania 2011).

18 The case of Reyhaneh Jabbari in Iran is an example of how the prosecution view a woman's consent to risk through their behaviour.

19 Janine Leach (ed), 'Communicating risks of treatment and informed consent in osteopathic practice: A literature review and pilot focus groups' (University of Brighton 2011) <http://www.ncor.org.uk/wp-content/uploads/2012/10/communicating-risk.pdf> accessed 7 July 2015.

1.1.5 Revocation of consent

According to Sharia law, a person who provides consent to an act may equally revoke their consent at any time they wish, which effectively nullifies the original consent provided. Such revocation has an immediate effect, regardless of the way it is expressed. However, the timing of the revocation of consent in some instances may play an integral part in the defence of consent. For instance, if the revocation is expressed by a guardian during the performance of a surgery on a minor, this will not act as a barrier to effectively prevent the act, as doing so may cause further harm to the child.

The crime of kidnapping, however, provides a contrasting example; from the point an individual revokes their consent to continue to accompany another, the continuation of the act against the will of that person will be regarded as an offence of kidnapping as seen in the provisions relating to child abduction in Iran.[20]

In the context of assault and battery, if the victim withdraws their consent any subsequent harm caused would constitute an offence provided that the revocation was communicated effectively to the perpetrator. An exception to this is when a husband physically assaults his wife to correct her conduct to the level permitted by the Qur'an.[21]

This principle applies throughout Islamic jurisdictions, including the UAE; where the Supreme Court ruled that a man can beat his wife and children as long as he does not leave any physical marks; however, if it is proved that the husband 'has over-stepped his rights under Sharia' he may be punished.[22]

A revocation of consent may be heard in the case of separation or divorce, where the victim should effectively prove that by applying for divorce/returning to her father's home she in fact withdrew her initial consent to continue with the marriage. As mentioned above, the concept of marital rape is not recognised within Islamic jurisdictions. For instance, in Pakistan wives are deemed to have consented at the time of marriage to have sexual intercourse with their husbands as long as it does not cause harm to the wife.[23] Consequently, subsequent revocation of this consent will not have any legal effect so long as the marriage is still valid.[24]

1.1.6 Ownership and limits of consent

Islamic law differentiates between offences that are only regarded as a 'private interest' offence and those that hold a 'public interest' element. It is common among most Islamic law jurisdictions that the defence of consent will not be a valid defence if it is established that the harm caused by the act was serious enough to trigger public interest considerations, and committed without good cause.

---

20 Article 632, Iranian Penal Code.
21 Qur'an [4:34].
22 Becky Johnson, UAE 'Must Act' On Violence Against Women' (*Sky News*, 5 August 2014) <http://news.sky.com/story/1313121/uae-must-act-on-violence-against-women> accessed 10 September 2015.
23 Mehr Bano Langriall, 'Laws Against Rape in Pakistan' (*Human Rights Review*) <https://uclhumanrightsreview.wordpress.com/volume-ii/laws-against-rape-in-pakistan-a-minor-divide-questioning-the-debate/> accessed 6 September 2015.
24 The same principle is also enshrined in Ghana's Criminal Offences Act 1960, s 42(g) which stated that: 'a person may revoke any consent which he has given to the use of force against him, and his consent when so revoked shall have no effect for justifying force; save that the consent given by husband or wife at marriage, for the purposes of marriage, cannot be revoked until the parties are divorced or separated by a judgment or decree of a competent Court'.

With regard to the significance of the public interest element of an offence, consent is not a valid defence in *hadd* offences, as it is believed that they are prescribed in order to protect the public from any wrongdoing.[25]

Consent of the victim may act as a mitigating factor in *ta'zir* offence, if it relates to an offence containing both public and private interest elements. If the offence is only directed towards the victim with no public interest considerations, the consent of the victim may be accepted as a complete defence, depending upon the circumstances of the case. For instance, in a case of theft if it is proven that the thief actually took the property with the consent of the owner, no public interest element is engaged and therefore the owner's consent acts as a complete defence, the same can be seen in the offence of trespass. However, in the case of homosexuality, the consent of the parties will have no effect on the liability as the provisions are prescribed to protect the public from such acts which are considered sinful.

Considering the concept of assault within sporting activities, intentional and deliberate harmful acts of violence, which include immoral conduct, are not only a private interest matter but of concern to the public interest, as they violate the acceptable moral standards of society in general. When considering the limits to consent as a defence, within the scope of sexual offences, such as rape, consent may be void if the person providing the consent is under a particular age. In Pakistan for instance, under s 375 of the Pakistan Penal Code, a man is said to have committed rape despite a victim's consent if she is younger than 16 years of age.[26]

With regard to medical treatment, a fundamental principle of Islamic law dictates that only wrongful harms are subject to punishment, and not a mere harm-doing that is a possible consequence of medical treatment.[27]

Another limitation of consent is when it is obtained out of fear of pain or death. Under s 375 of the Pakistan Penal Code, a man will be guilty of rape if the consent to the sexual intercourse is obtained through putting a woman in fear of harm or death.

In summary, Islamic law places a fine line between consent given as an exercise of personal autonomy with no concern to the public and when the consequences of waiving such rights are so grave as to violate the individual's human dignity and bring wider harm to society, rendering any consent null and void as a defence.

1.2 Place of consent in the offence structure

Consent as a defence in Islamic criminal law may operate as a barrier to defeat the *actus reus* element of an offence, thus rendering an act lawful, and/or to undermine the malicious afore-thought attribute of the act negating the required *mens rea*. The defence of consent is not applicable to all crimes within Islamic jurisdictions and it can never be used for the offence of murder. However, in some circumstances, consent of the victim may disable an element of the offence; thus it will be accepted as a complete defence. For example, in the case of assault

---

25 These types of offences are regarded as crimes against God, with the punishment being prescribed by Allah, as stated within primary sources of Sharia.

26 An exception to this is a man having sexual intercourse with his wife as long as his wife is no less than 13 years of age.

27 Article 158 of the Iranian Penal Code states ' . . . committing conduct which is considered by law as an offense, shall not be punished in the following cases:

. . . (f) Every legitimate surgical or medical operation which is done by the consent of the patient or his/her parents or natural or legal guardians, or legal representatives, with due consideration given to technical and medical and governmental regulations. In emergency cases obtaining consent is not required.'

and battery, the consent of the victim to receive physical force renders the 'unlawfulness' of the act as 'lawful'.

In some jurisdictions, including Iran, if it is established that one party to the offence of *zina* was aware of the prohibition of this act, whilst the other was mistaken (for example, if the woman mistakenly believes that she is married to the other party), then 'only the knowing party shall be sentenced to the *hadd* punishment for *zina*'.[28] This provision is also applicable where it is proven that one party was forced to commit *zina*, and thus consent was not valid as the forced party did not hold the requisite *mens rea*.[29] In the case of rape, the *mens rea* for the offence includes forceful sexual intercourse with knowledge that the other party has not consented to the act. In such circumstances, whilst the perpetrator would be punished to the full extent of the law, the victim will not face liability for any offence against morality/decency due to the lack of *mens rea*.

In the case of criminal damage, the *mens rea* for the offence includes intentional destruction of another's property; thus if the defendant establishes that the act was performed with the consent of the owner, it will be accepted as a complete defence.

In assault and battery the consent may defeat the *actus reus* element of the act by providing the defendant permission to inflict harm for an agreed reason. Consent is a defence to the infliction of harm in the course of lawful sporting activities defeating the *actus reus* aspect of an act; however, from the point the act exceeds acceptable standards it will be regarded as unlawful and the initial implied consent from a victim will not be accepted as a defence.

1.3 Form of consent

The form of consent may vary depending upon the nature of the act and the method by which the intention of the consenting individual is disclosed. Consent may be provided expressly, impliedly from a person's actions/inaction (including the use of opt-out consent), or determined from the circumstances. For instance, if an individual provides his/her address and requests an emergency health service, consent to perform medical treatment on that person is implied from the request, regardless of whether a written consent form is signed beforehand. An individual's silence may be considered as implying consent to an action in particular circumstances; for instance in sexual offences while a woman 'crying out' indicates her resistance, her silence may imply her consent to the action.[30]

1.3.1 Declared or implied

Declared or express consent is when an individual provides clear and direct consent, usually in a verbal or written form, to authorise someone to perform a particular action. A declaration of consent may be implied if it is granted implicitly by an individual's actions and/or the facts of a particular incident. Consent may be implied if neither the law nor the parties require it to be expressed.

---

28 This is in accordance with Article 65 of the Iranian Penal Code which provides that if a woman or a man is aware of prohibition of the sexual intercourse whilst the other party is not aware and believes that this act is permissible for him/her, only the knowing party shall be sentenced to the *hadd* punishment for *zina*.

29 Eg Article 67 of the Iranian Penal Code stipulates that if the man or woman claims s/he has been forced to commit *zina*, the claim shall be accepted, provided that there is no proof to believe otherwise.

30 Hina Azam, *Sexual Violation in Islamic Law: Substance, Evidence, and Procedure* (Cambridge University Press 2015).

In Iran, the Islamic Penal Code governs the provisions of implied or written consent laying down specific rules for both. Causing harm without fulfilling the specific provisions of the Code would render that individual liable for an offence. Referring to medical treatment, a doctor must always receive consent from his patient before undertaking any form of surgery or performing any type of treatment. Such consents are normally informed and expressed by requiring the patient to sign a written declaration accepting the risk and consenting to the treatment prescribed. However, it could also be implied if the patient calls for medical assistance and an ambulance attends to provide him with such healthcare.

In Pakistan, a patient should provide express consent where the procedure entails risk or involves more than minor discomfort, except in situations of emergency.[31] However, where minor treatment is involved, consent may be implied from a patient's actions, for example booking an appointment for a blood test would be considered as implied consent for a nurse to take blood.

1.3.2 Presumed consent

Islamic legal systems regard the concept of 'presumed consent' as an assumption that a particular action would have been approved by a person or a party if permission had been sought.

In the context of organ donation, a presumed consent cannot be accepted if the patient did not express their wishes for organ donation during their lifetime. Muslim jurists are divided in their opinion as to whether it is possible for someone to provide consent for their organs to be transplanted to others after death. In Indonesia, the *ulama* believe that God is the sole owner of a person's organs thus they do not have the right to lend or sell them, or make any arrangements for their use after their death.[32] However, in Indonesia, consent to organ donation must be strictly in writing and the presumed consent will not be accepted as a defence;[33] this can be similarly seen in Turkish law (No 2238 of 3 June 1979).[34]

Under the Pakistan Code of Ethics of Practice for Medical and Dental Practitioners,[35] consent may be presumed if it involves an emergency situation where an unconscious patient's life is in danger, affording a practitioner the ability to save legally that person's life as consent is assumed in such circumstances.[36]

1.4 Capacity to consent

Consent must be a clear and voluntary declaration made by a competent individual who is of the requisite legal age, sound mind, and free will.

There are a number of circumstances where it may be held that an individual did not have the capacity to consent, due to the lack of appropriate understanding of the situation, rendering them incapable of making rational decisions resulting from their age or mental impairment.

---

31 Pakistan Medical and Dental Council, 'Code of Ethics of Practice for Medical and Dental Practitioners' (Deputy Controller, Stationery & Forms 2010) <http://www.pmdc.org.pk/LinkClick.aspx?fileticket=v5 WmQYMvhz4%3D&tabid=292&mid=845> accessed 17 September 2015.
32 The *ulama* are those jurists who are recognised as authorities of Islamic religious science.
33 Dariusch Atighetchi, *Islamic Bioethics: Problems and Perspectives* (Springer 2007) 173.
34 Alberto Abadie and Sebastien Gay, 'The Impact of Presumed Consent Legislation on Cadaveric Organ Donation: A Cross Country Study' (2004) NBER Working Paper No 10604 <http://www.nber.org/papers/w10604.pdf> accessed 17 September 2015.
35 PMDC Code of Ethics (n 31).
36 ibid.

Under Islamic law, the age of puberty (*bulug*) for a male is 15 years and nine years for a female. However in order to be able to comprehend the precise nature of the act he/she is consenting to, an individual must also reach the age of *rushd* (maturity).[37] This is an Islamic legal phrase that means that the person is capable to select the right path, act reasonably, be mentally and spiritually sound, and have the ability to make rational decisions or take the necessary steps to protect his affairs. Therefore, the consent is regarded as valid if it is provided by a person who has reached not only the age of puberty, but also the age of *rushd*.[38]

It is the rights of the guardians to decide for minors who have not yet attained the age of maturity, which is generally accepted as 18 years throughout the Muslim world.[39]

It is a basic principle of Islamic law that those who suffer from permanent mental impairment would be unable to form sufficient judgements or fully understand the ramifications of their decisions; their affairs would be presided over by a suitable guardian.

Those suffering from a periodical/partial mental impairment may be capable of consenting to a particular action provided the decision is made during a period of lucidity. The same can be said for those who are intoxicated by the effects of drugs or alcohol and are incapable of making rational decisions at the material time.[40]

Consent given by an individual during the time in which they are suffering from the effects of a substance would be null and void.

The above principles have been integrated into the Malaysian Penal Code (Act 574). Article 90 stipulates that consent is not considered valid by any section of this Code if:

- the consent is given by a person who, from unsoundness of mind or intoxication, is unable to understand the nature and consequence of that to which he gives his consent; or
- the consent is given by a person who is under 12 years of age.

Therefore in the majority of Islamic countries the age and mental soundness of the decision-maker is vital to any consideration of the validity of the consent given.

1.5 Consequences of mistaken consent

1.5.1 Mistake

An 'honest' but mistaken belief in a victim's consent may be accepted as a defence under Islamic law provided it can be established that the defendant did not have the *mens rea* required of the law in committing a particular offence, even though the *actus reus* element of the act was present. In determining the concept of mistaken consent, the capability of the victim to give valid consent remains a factor, as does the reasonableness of the perpetrator's mistake and the above-discussed principles as to the nature of the offence and its implications for the interests of wider society.[41]

---

37 Sayyid Muhammad Rizvi, *Marriage and Morals Islam* (Lulu 2014) Chapter 3(1).
38 Article 1210 of the Iranian Civil Code.
39 ibid.
40 Qur'an [4:43], 'O you have attained to faith! Do not attempt to pray while you are in a state of drunkenness.'
41 For instance, Kasani, Bada'I al-sana'I notes the opinion of Abu Hanifa and Abu Yusuf that cases of illegal sexual relationships based on mistaken identity may attract *hudud* liability as the offender could have enquired and established the identity of the woman he claims to have mistakenly believed to be his legitimate partner. Muhammad Mushtaq Ahmad, 'The Crime of Rape and The Hanafi Doctrine of Siyasah' (2014) 6(1) Pakistan Journal of Criminology 161–192.

The notion of mistaken consent has been enshrined into numerous statutes across the Islamic world. For instance, Article 79 of the Malaysian Penal Code (Act 574) states that an act undertaken by an individual due to a mistake of fact will not be an offence provided that, in good faith, he/she believed the act to be justified in law. Therefore the defence of consent would be accepted in such circumstances where the perpetrator acted in good faith and was genuinely mistaken as to the legitimacy of the act committed.

For instance, in sexual offences where a victim is duped into sexual relations with a man in the belief that their relationship is legitimate (ie they are married), the man will not escape liability for rape if he knowingly participates in sexual activity with the victim as consent is vitiated by her mistaken belief.

1.5.2 Deception

Within Islamic law, consent can be vitiated by fraud or deception in certain circumstances where an individual is deceived as to the identity of the offender or the nature and quality of the act committed.

As mentioned previously, for a valid consent it must be given freely by a legally competent individual, of sufficient maturity to consider and make a reasonable judgement in light of relevant known circumstances. However, that consent may be negated in circumstances: where a false representation (either by means of statement or conduct) pertaining to a matter of fact (as opposed to opinion or intention) has been knowingly or recklessly made with the intention to deceive; the individual has acted in furtherance of the intention to deceive; and the victim suffers a consequential harm. Silence, therefore, cannot constitute false representation; and the test is a subjective one.

Article 399 of the UAE Penal Code, reflecting general established legal principles of the Islamic law of deception, provides that consent obtained through fraudulent means will be invalid and the perpetrators will be subject to detention or a fine. The same can be said about adult grooming, where the adult in question has given consent to sexual activity as a result of deception.

1.6 Mistake about consent

Under Islamic law, mistake about consent can be a defence providing that certain conditions as to the nature of the offence and mistake are fulfilled. The provisions of the Malaysian Penal Code provide an appropriate illustration of the position of a mistaken offender under Islamic law.

According to Article 79 nothing is an offence that is done by any person who is justified by law, or who by reason of a mistake of fact and not by reason of a mistake of law in good faith believes himself to be justified by law in doing it. Guidance as to the definition of a 'reason to believe' is provided within Article 26, which stipulates that a person has a reason to believe a thing if he has sufficient cause to believe that thing, but not otherwise.

Additionally, Article 87 of the same code provides for consent as a defence to harm where death or grievous bodily harm is not caused; therefore an offender acting under the mistaken belief of consent provided for in Article 79 would have a valid defence for their actions.

2 SPECIFIC ISSUES

2.1 Consent and homicide offences

Assisted dying is the subject of significant debate amongst Muslim jurists on account of the varying interpretations promoted by different schools of thought. For instance the Hanafi's consider that consent in the case of homicide changes the offence from intentional homicide (*qatl 'amd*) to manslaughter (*shibh 'amd*), thereby acting as a mitigating factor, with the basis lying in doubt (*shubhah*) about the legitimacy of enforcing *hadd* punishment in such circumstance. They believe that where the victim has consented to his own death, *qisas* is waived.

Zufar, however, disagreed with this interpretation and advocated that consent does not amount to *shubhah* because it is not strong enough to amount to a material consideration undermining the provision of *hadd* for homicide. Similarly Maliki jurists maintain there is no *shubhah* in such circumstances, and *qisas* will still be imposed.

In contrast, the dominant opinion in both the Shafi'i and Hanbali Schools is that neither *qisas* nor *diyyah* is to be imposed in such circumstances. The killing of the individual with his consent becomes lawful, as it is the victim who has the right to personal autonomy that he can lawfully exercise. It is just like the destruction of his property. This school of thought would consider medically assisted suicide as lawful.[42] However the debate amongst these schools has not translated into a similar divergence in legislation amongst Muslim countries. Within the vast majority of these jurisdictions homicide committed with the consent of the victim is regarded as murder.

While consent to death would not be regarded as a defence to murder, it would be a mitigating factor where the victim's family forgive the perpetrator and provided him 'consent'. This cannot be regarded as a defence of consent, as it merely affects the punishment given to a homicide offender, with the family waiving their rights to *qisas*. According to Article 612 of the Iranian Penal Code such consent would result in a lesser punishment of the payment of blood money whilst the offender would continue to be punished for the public interest element of the crime by up to 10 years' imprisonment.

2.1.1 Mercy killings

Mercy killing, or 'euthanasia', is usually in reference to the situation in which an individual causes the death of another in order to end their suffering from an incurable illness. It is widely accepted within the Muslim world that euthanasia is forbidden. It is believed that the sanctity of life is a gift from God, in whose hands rests the decision as to its duration. According to the Qur'an, 'do not take life, which Allah made sacred, other than in the course of justice',[43] and 'no person can ever die except by Allah's leave and at an appointed term'; these provisions seemingly exclude suicide and euthanasia as permissible forms of death.[44]

There are also numerous hadiths providing examples of the circumstances in which the Prophet considered an individual to be interfering with the authority owed to God in respect of the time of their death; with reference to suicide:

Amongst the nations before you there was a man who got a wound, and growing impatient, he took a knife and cut his hand with it and the blood did not stop till he died. Allah said, 'My Slave hurried to bring death upon himself so I have forbidden him (to enter) Paradise.'[45]

It has been inferred from this that the taking of a life by another for the purposes of relieving someone's pain would similarly be prohibited. To this effect the Islamic Code of Medical Ethics, in its First International Conference on Islamic Medicine, explained that, 'mercy

---

42   Khan Nyazee (n 1) 155–156.
43   Qur'an [17:33].
44   ibid [16:61] and [3:145].
45   Sahih Bukhari 4.56.669.

killing, like suicide, finds no support except in the atheistic way of thinking that believes that our life on this earth is followed by void. The claim of killing for painful hope-less illness is also refuted, for there is no human pain that cannot be largely conquered by medication or by suitable neurosurgery. . . .'

Although the primary sources, along with supporting opinions, seem to be clear on the prohibition of mercy killing, there is room for flexibility when the termination of life is medically expedient through the withdrawal of treatment. While some Muslim scholars consider a do not resuscitate (DNR) order as a lesser form of euthanasia, and therefore not permitted under Islamic law, others believe that within a medical capacity the reality of the patient's prospect of recovery is fundamental to any course of action.

In support of the above notion, the Egyptian Scholar Sheik Yusuf al-Qaradawi commented in the context of a religious ruling that although euthanasia is the equivalent to murder, there are exceptions to this; for instance, a treatment that is deemed useless can be withheld.[46]

In reference to DNR orders, the aforementioned Islamic Code of Medical Ethics provided that 'it is futile to diligently keep the patient in a vegetative state by heroic means or to preserve the patient by deep freezing or other artificial methods. It is the process of life that the doctor aims to maintain and not the process of dying. In any case, the doctor shall not take a positive measure to terminate the patient's life.'[47] It is the process of life that the doctor aims to maintain and not the process of dying. In advocating this message Islamic jurists are clearly proposing that in certain situations it is possible to withdraw medical treatment, and consequently end a life.

Similarly the Islamic Medical Association of America (IMANA) considers mechanical life support as a temporary measure, and therefore deems the removal of life-support for patients in a permanently vegetative state (PVS) acceptable. However, the administration of medicine with the purpose of accelerating death is not authorised under Islamic law, as this could be considered euthanasia. In essence any positive action to cause the death of another is regarded as interfering with God's will, whereas inaction, or the removal of mechanical life-saving equipment, in certain situations is acceptable, as it could be considered to be leaving the patient in the hands of God.

The above Sharia principle has been enshrined into medical practice with a view to safeguard the lives of individuals. In most Islamic jurisdictions the physicians are duty bound to act in the interests of the patient with ultimate consideration given to the Sharia teaching that life belongs to God.[48]

2.1.2 Killing on request of the victim

As mentioned, under Sharia Law a person cannot harm or kill another, unless permitted in limited circumstances by the Qur'an (eg in the course of justice enforcing capital punishment); therefore, killing on the request of the victim is forbidden despite the absence of any specific wording referring to it. It seems to be the case that the principles of autonomy, which accords a certain respect to an individual's freedom to choose does not extend to scenarios such as killing on request of the victim, as this would amount to assisted suicide.[49] The same

---

46 Mehran Narimis, 'Euthanasia in Islamic Views' (2014) 2 European Scientific Journal 170.
47 Kiarash Aramesh and Heydar Shadi, 'Euthanasia: An Islamic Ethical Perspective' (2007) 6(5) Iranian Journal of Allergy, Asthma and Immunology 35.
48 Narimis (n 46).
49 As mentioned with reference to the hadith in which prophet Mohammad stated that the individual who commits suicide to relieve their pain, would not enter paradise; by analogy it is a great sin to assist someone to this effect.

verses of the Qur'an stating that life belongs to God and thus any form of homicide including mercy killing is prohibited, apply in the context of killing on the victim's request.

2.1.3 Abortion

The definition of abortion, as commonly agreed among Islamic jurisdictions, is the process of deliberately terminating a pregnancy, so no child is born. Although there are no specific provisions relating to abortion within the Qur'an, as stated above there is heavy emphasis on the sanctity of life.[50] Despite this, there has been serious debate surrounding the position Sharia law holds with respect to using abortion as a means of saving a mother's life.

The Afghanistan Criminal Code of 1976 provides strict principles in respect of abortion, prohibiting the termination of a pregnancy except in the circumstances to save the life of the mother. Therefore the performance of an abortion under Afghan law remains a criminal offence (except when saving a mother's life), even in situations involving rape. The above strict liability extends to medical negligence with Article 403(2) of the said Code stipulating that where, in the unfortunate circumstances of miscarriage being caused by the mistaken administration of a drug, the offender will nevertheless still be liable for punishment by a period of imprisonment and/or subject to a fine.[51]

In contrast, the Malaysian Penal Code (Act 574), at s 91 states that 'Causing miscarriage, except in cases exempted under section 312, is an offence independently of any harm which it may cause or be intended to cause the woman . . .'.

The above-mentioned s 312 provides an exemption for registered medical practitioners terminating a pregnancy in the best interests of the mother and her medical, physical and emotional well-being where the risk of injury is greater than if the pregnancy were terminated, based on their good faith medical opinion. Therefore, under Malaysian law, any other circumstances in which a termination is provided will amount to an offence punishable with a term of imprisonment, in addition to a fine.[52]

The consent of the patient plays a significant role in the punishment of offenders accused of unlawfully terminating pregnancies. Where a mother does not consent to an abortion the penalty for such an offence rises to a period of imprisonment of up to 20 years.[53] In Malaysia, therefore, termination of pregnancy is only justified in the circumstances where it is necessary to save the mother's life or to prevent significant injury to her, where the risk to her well-being is greater than that of the pregnancy being terminated.

The timing of any termination is also pertinent in most Islamic law jurisdictions. For instance Articles 99–101 of the Turkish Criminal Code permit abortion by a medical practitioner within the first ten weeks of pregnancy, provided a woman's consent is given.[54] However, if the termination of a pregnancy is conducted outside of this period, the perpetrator may be punished by no less than four years' imprisonment; this rises to ten years when consent of the patient is not obtained.

---

50 'Take not life which Allah has made sacred', Qur'an [6:151].
51 Article 403(2) Afghanistan Criminal Code 1976.
52 Section 312, Malaysian Penal Code (Act 574) which states that 'whoever voluntarily causes a woman with child to miscarry shall be punished with imprisonment for a term which may extend to three years or with fine or with both; and if the woman is quick with child, shall be punished with imprisonment for a term which may extend to seven years, and shall also be liable to fine.'
53 Please see s 313 (Causing miscarriage without woman's consent) and s 314 (Death caused by act done with intent to cause miscarriage. If act done without woman's consent) of the Malaysia Penal Code (Act 574).
54 Turkish Criminal Code 2004, Fifth Section, Articles 99–101.

The patient's consent to abortion would also constitute a criminal offence under Turkish law in its own right punishable by a sentence of one year's imprisonment and/or a punitive fine. The statue also specifically prohibits abortions by unauthorised individuals irrespective of consent being provided. This is punishable by up to two years' imprisonment.[55]

The law on abortion in Shi'a Iran, however, provides an interesting and slightly different approach to the above-mentioned examples. Iranian law regards the foetus's life as being divided into two stages; before the foetus is infused with life, and afterwards.[56] Therefore, under Iranian law, prior to the stage at which a foetus is considered to have a soul, an abortion is considered legal provided the mother's life is endangered from the pregnancy. According to the Shi'a interpretation of Islamic law, a foetus gains its soul after 16 to 18 weeks of pregnancy, and once a foetus reaches the stage of development where it is regarded as now having a soul; abortion becomes a criminal act, irrespective of whether the mother's life is at risk or her consent is obtained.

Where birth control is concerned, Sharia law has made a distinction between temporary reversible contraception and permanent irreversible contraception. The former category is largely permissible, with this general permission even extending to the morning-after pill in circumstances involving rape if taken immediately after the sexual assault.[57]

Permanent birth control however is widely discouraged on account of it preventing a couple from ever being able to have children, in conflict with the doctrine that the fundamental concept of marriage is procreation.[58] As a result many Islamic jurisdictions, such as Iran, have taken steps to criminalise sterilisation operations irrespective of the consent of any individuals involved.[59]

2.2 Consent and non-fatal offences against the person

As discussed in earlier sections, there are a number of non-fatal offences where consent may be used as a complete defence due to its fundamental importance of establishing the *mens rea* of the crimes. In assault and battery as long as the harm inflicted does not cause death or grievous bodily harm, the consent of the victim may be accepted as a defence as legislated for in Malaysia through Article 87 of its Penal Code.

The same can be seen in Nigerian legislation with reference to non-fatal offences. Article 53(1) states that 'no act is an offence by reason of the injury it has caused to the person or property of a person who, being above the age of eighteen years, has voluntarily and with understanding given his consent express or implied to that act'.

Other non-fatal offences against the person are also subject to the defence of consent provided that it satisfies all the legal requirements of a valid consent. These offences include,

55 ibid Article 99(4).

56 Farokhzad Jahani, 'Abortion in Iranian Law' (*Iran Persian Daily*, January 2004) <http://www.iran chamber.com/society/articles/abortion_iranian_law.php> accessed 30 September.

57 Ibrahim B Syed, 'Abortion' (*Islamic Research Foundation International*) <http://www.irfi.org/articles/articles_101_150/abortion.htm> accessed May 2015.

58 Taken from a Hadith recorded by Imam Abu Dawud, Imam an-Nasa'i and others quoted at: Shayk (Mufti) Muhammad Libn Adam, 'Contraception, Morning after and IVF' (*Central Mosque*) <http://www.central-mosque.com/index.php/Relationships/contraception-morning-after-and-surrogacy.html> accessed 17 September 2015.

59 Lizzie Dearden, 'Iran to ban permanent contraception after Islamic Cleric's edit to increase population' (*The Independent*, 11 August 2014) <http://www.independent.co.uk/news/world/middle-east/iran-to-ban-permanent-contraception-after-islamic-clerics-edict-to-increase-population-9662349.html> accessed 27 February 2015.

but are not limited to, acts of kidnapping, trespassing, releasing information contrary to data protection legislation, etc. In all of these situations where the concept of harm caused is undermined by the consent of the perceived victim, the defendant will be absolved from any criminal liability as no offence will be deemed to have been committed due to the lack of *mens rea*. Another example of consent being used as a defence in non-fatal offences against the person can be seen in Article 26 of the Turkish Penal Code, which stipulates that 'no punishment is given to a person acting under the consent of a person relating to a right disposable by that person'. Consequently, the scope of consent as a defence to various non-fatal offences is vast and therefore full analysis of all of these acts are outside of the remit of this chapter.

2.2.1 HIV and other communicable disease transmission

Generally, across Islamic jurisdictions, there is a strict approach taken towards those suffering from HIV or any other serious sexually transmitted diseases. It is even the case that in some jurisdictions such as Egypt and UAE, it is a criminal offence to be affected by one of these diseases where the offender would be arrested and imprisoned as a result of their illness. In any case, many Islamic countries regard HIV as taboo, due to connotations with sexual promiscuity and homosexuality, in addition to the growing association of the disease with drug addicts.[60]

Despite this, the discussion surrounding the defence of consent with relation to transmittable diseases can be focused on two major categories: (1) whether the disease was transmitted intentionally or unintentionally; and (2) whether the victim knowingly consented to sexual activity in spite of the disease (explicit or implied consent). Therefore, if an offender who is aware of his status knowingly and intentionally engages in sexual activity without informing the other party about the risks of being infected by the disease he/she has committed a criminal offence.

For instance s 23 of the Infectious Diseases Act 1977 in Singapore provides that any person who is aware that they are infected with HIV/AIDS is prohibited from engaging in sexual activity with another, unless prior to this activity the said individual has informed their prospective partner of the risk of contracting HIV/AIDS and, additionally, the other person voluntarily accepts this risk. This provision is equally applicable to those who have reason to believe that they may be infected with the disease.[61]

Where it is established that informed consent was not voluntarily provided prior to sexual activity by an uninfected person, the infected individual will have committed a criminal offence and will be liable for up to ten years' imprisonment and/or a significant fine. The criminalisation of such an act may be rooted in the concept that knowingly passing on HIV/AIDS is equivalent to homicide. Therefore, to avoid potential criminal liability an essential requirement is voluntary acceptance from another to engage in sexual activity, after being appropriately informed of any risk of infection; where this requirement has been fulfilled, consent may be relied upon as a defence to a prosecution under s 23.

Within the Arab world a number of Islamic rulings (*fatwa*) have regarded any form of intentional virus transmission to a healthy person as a 'forbidden act', which requires the imposition of a penalty based on the seriousness of the act and its impact on society.[62] To

---

60 Mohamed Nekhaira Al Dhaheri, 'The Impact of criminalising the transmission of HIV/AIDS in the United Arab Emirates' (PhD thesis, University of Sussex 2010).

61 Singapore Infectious Diseases Act 1977, Chapter 137, s 23(1) and (2).

62 ibid.

intentionally transmit such a disease, whether sexual or otherwise, is therefore regarded as a form of *Hiraabah* and corruption on earth in which the perpetrator is obligated to receive one of the penalties as cited in the Qur'an.[63]

2.2.2 *Medical treatment*

The nature of a doctor–patient relationship within Islamic law is both contractual and moral; however no clear distinction is made between doctors' moral and legal duties.[64] Islam strongly advises that human beings have a duty of care towards each other, as 'whoever saves one life, it is as though he has saved the whole of humanity'.[65] Sharia calls for people to contribute to alleviating human sufferings and pain by helping each other.[66]

Within the context of Islamic teaching a doctor's role is therefore prominent as he not only complies with his duty as a human being when medically assisting others, but also as part of his profession, in accordance with his legal obligations.

On a social scale, Islamic law considers an individual's access to medical treatment as a 'fundamental right'.[67] In some emergency situations, it may be necessary for a doctor to make a decision for his patient based on their experience and specialist knowledge. The principles of Sharia and the consensus of the Islamic jurists must also be taken into account when making a decision on a particular course of action. It is not permitted to perform certain medical treatments in conflict with Sharia principles. For example, bone marrow transplants and IVF treatment are subjected to various *fatwa* by Muslim jurists. As mentioned in previous sections, absolute individual autonomy is not possible within Muslim communities as the patients' consent is restricted by the various religious obligations and responsibilities as defined by Sharia for its followers.[68] Such obligations not only influence the consent provided by the patient, but also the decisions made by the doctor and the patient's relatives in the event they act on their behalf. There is a strong cultural belief and trust amongst patient's to follow the opinion of a medical practitioner as they are highly respected and trusted within the community.[69]

However, in order to safeguard the welfare of society and in the best interests of the public (*maslahah*), medical authorities acting on behalf of the state are tasked with regulating and monitoring the performance of the practitioners.[70]

Consent to treatment must be provided by either the patient or their legal guardian. In a situation where there is a disagreement between a husband and wife regarding a course of treatment for their child, the husband's opinion is preferred due to his status as a provider and protector of the family. Naturally, such an opinion must be medically supported by the relevant professionals otherwise it will not be regarded as being in the best interest of the child.

---

63 Nekhaira Al Dhaheri (n 60).
64 Kutaiba S. Chaleby, *Forensic Psychiatry in Islamic Jurisprudence* (The International Institute of Islamic Thought 2011).
65 Qur'an [Al-Maidah:32].
66 Islamic Religious Council of Singapore, 'Fatwa on Organ Transplants' (*Majlis Ugama Islam Singapura*) <http://www.officeofthemufti.sg/Fatwa/hota%282007%29%28eng%29.html> accessed 6 August 2015.
67 IMANA Ethics Committee, 'Islamic Medical Ethics: The IMANA Perspective' (2005) 37(1) Journal of the Islamic Medical Association 33.
68 Packer (n 16).
69 Somayeh Faghanipour, Soodabeh Joolaee, and Marzieh Sobhani, 'Surgical informed consent in Iran – How much is it informed?' (2013) 21(3) Nursing Ethics 1.
70 Islamic Religious Council of Singapore (n 66).

Of relevance to the defence of consent, Articles 59(2) of the Iranian Penal Code provides that the following acts shall not be considered an offence: 'every legitimate medical or surgical operation which is done by the consent of the patient . . .'. Furthermore, Article 60 of the same Code states that 'if a physician has obtained the consent of a patient or his/her guardian prior to treatment or operation, the physician is not liable for any loss of life . . .'. Similar provisions can be found within most other Islamic law jurisdictions.

2.2.3 Sport injuries, 'horseplay', piercing

The injuries caused as the result of a legitimate sport would not result in criminal liability under Islamic law so long as the harm was inflicted within the normal boundaries expected from that particular sport. It is accepted that any harm caused as the result of intentional application of force, within the customary rules of a particular game, is not considered as a criminal offence.[71] This is because, by participating in sport activities, an individual consents (expressly or impliedly) to the risk of harm resulting from these activities. Mere knowledge of the risk does not amount to implied consent but rather the person must genuinely appreciate the nature of the risk and consent to take that risk in an informative manner.[72] For a consensual bodily harm to be inflicted there must be a 'good reason' for causing such harm.

Under Article 53 of the Afghanistan Criminal Code, any act committed with good will for the purpose of exercising a right, shall not be considered a crime. Article 54 of the same Code states that acts committed in the course of sport games, provided they are exercised within the accepted rules and regulations of that sport, are considered an exercise of right.[73]

There are certain sporting activities that attract the attention of Muslim jurists who express conflicting views surrounding the legitimacy of the game. For instance, some Muslims scholars believe that boxing is prohibited in Islam due to the engagement of 'self-destructive behaviour' of the individual and the level of harm caused as the result, which is contrary to the teaching of the Qur'an and the practice of the Prophet Muhammad.[74] Despite these views, boxing is nonetheless lawful in most Islamic jurisdictions through the relevant domestic laws that are legislated based on a moderate approach to Islamic rules.[75]

The same rules apply to other lawful applications of force during the course of consensual activities including body piercing, tattooing and horseplay.

In some Muslim jurisdictions, such as Iran, conducting body piercing and tattooing is prohibited and thus the consent of the person receiving the service does not legitimise the action of the individual who performs the act.[76]

---

71 Kevin Heller and Markus Dubber (eds), *The Handbook of Comparative Criminal Law* (Stanford University Press 2011) 320.

72 Liaquat Ali Khan Niazi, *Islamic Law of Tort* (Research Cell, Cayal Singh Trust Library 2008).

73 UAE also follow the same principle in Article 53 of its Penal Code. It states that acts of violence which occur during sports within the limits prescribed for such sports, subject, however, to the rules of due care and caution.

74 Qur'an [5:195].

75 – –, 'Boxing in Islam' (*Opposing Views*) <http://people.opposingviews.com/boxing-islam-7161.html> accessed 6th August 2015.

76 Adam Withnall, 'Iran bans spiky haircuts, tattoos and use of sunbeds because they are signs of 'devil-worship' (*Independent*, 5 May 2015) <http://www.independent.co.uk/news/world/middle-east/iran-bans-spiky-haircuts-tattoos-and-use-of-sunbeds-because-they-are-signs-of-devil-worship-10226257. html?> accessed 23 September 2015.

2.2.4 Specific sexual practices involving infliction of harm

Consensual sexual harm from an Islamic perspective is considered within the general scope of causing harm (not resulting in serious injury or death) by consent. Therefore, in instances where a person consents to a specific harm, in whatever form, the offender will not be liable as long as the harm inflicted is neither serious enough to override the restrictions imposed by the Sharia for acceptable harm (public interest matter) nor exceeds the limits of the specified consent. An additional point to consider within Islamic jurisdictions is that if the sexual activities occurred outside of marriage, both parties may be liable for engaging in illegal relations before consideration is even given to the defence of consent for causing harm during an illegal activity. Within the context of marriage, any harm inflicted as the result of sexual practice is generally accepted so long as it is not severe enough as to warrant serious harm. The consent of the wife to any sexual activity is presumed upon her acceptance to enter into marriage.

2.3 Sexual offences

Within Islamic criminal law, consent on the part of the victim in the context of sexual offences is an important element when distinguishing between a voluntary sexual relationship (*zina*) and those occurring against the will of the victim (rape). The difference between the two is that in the case of *zina* both parties act on their own free will whereas, in an act of rape, one party forces the other into an act against their consent.[77]

An act of rape may also be established where the victim is unable to freely consent to the sexual activity due to their young age, mental status or unconsciousness, rendering them incapable of providing valid consent. Islamic jurists commonly agree that perpetrators of rape should receive *hadd* punishment (in the interests of the public) whilst the same punishment should not be applied to a victim of rape or those who voluntarily enter into a sexual relationship (*zina*).[78] Naturally, due to the lack of *mens rea* on the part of the victim in the case of rape, no punishment will be imposed against them under Sharia. In the case of consensual sexual relationships outside of marriage (*zina*), the marital status of the party may have an aggravating impact on the sentence, depending on the particular Islamic jurisdiction.[79]

2.3.1 Absence of consent or use of force/threats

In situations where a party does not consent to the act, or is forced into sexual intercourse, they will not be liable to any punishment, whether on the basis of rape or *zina* principles. There are reported instances (hadith) where a woman was forced to enter into sexual intercourse and the Prophet Mohammed did not impose any punishment on the victim based on her lack of consent.[80]

The same principle was also implemented during the period of the second Caliph (Umar) with reference to a thirsty woman who consented to sexual intercourse with a shepherd in return for water to save her life.[81]

---

77 Hina Azam, 'Rape' *Oxford Encyclopaedia of Islam and Law* (2013) <http://www.academia.edu/2083376/Rape_in_Islamic_Law_post-print_please_cite_accordingly_> accessed 14 April 2015.

78 ibid.

79 Whilst the punishment for illegal consensual intercourse for an unmarried man or woman is 100 lashes under the Islamic Penal Code of Iran (Article 88), if either of them are married at the time of the offence, he/she may face death by stoning as the appropriate punishment (Article 83).

80 Reported in Tirmizi, vol III (2007) 219.

81 Audah, Abd. Qadir, Al-Tashria'a Al-Jinai Al Islami, vol 11 (1987) 364–365.

It is therefore accepted under Islamic law that consent obtained by coercion or in a situation where the victims consents through fear of death or physical or psychological harm is not valid consent.[82]

Muslim jurists accept that not all submission to the sexual act should be considered as a consent, as women may doubt their ability to escape the situation or request help that may provoke the offender to cause them even greater harm. In such circumstances, women may decide that it is better to be raped than to lose their life at the hands of an assaulting party.[83]

Particular attention must be given to the victim's mind-set prior and during the act when establishing effective consent. For instance, if the victim initially consents to the act but revokes her consent during the intercourse, from the point of this declaration, the act will be regarded as rape. However, she may be punished for the crime of *zina* if she initially entered into the sexual activity freely and willingly.

2.3.2 Evidentiary presumptions

The general evidentiary requirements to establish a crime is applicable in the circumstances of sexual offences with particular weight given to the facts and circumstances of the case. This evidentiary requirement includes the testimony of witnesses, confession of the offender, circumstantial evidence including the knowledge of the judge obtained through various means (DNA testing, etc). Any physical marks on the victim associated with force would be taken into account when establishing whether she was in fact the subject of any sexual assault.[84] For instance, physical marks provided strong evidence of the victim's lack of consent in the case of *Bell Khan v The State*, in Pakistan when rejecting the defence of consent.[85]

In some jurisdictions, when a woman knowingly and voluntarily accepts to accompany a man to his place without any legitimate relationship or legal reason to justify such company (for instance, educational purposes), it is often presumed that she has in fact consented to any sexual relationship with that man thereafter.

2.3.3 Mistake of fact about consent

As is the case with other offences, an honest mistake of fact would be accepted as a defence including when such mistakes relates to the consent of the victim. Therefore, in the context of sexual offences, if the offender genuinely believes that the victim agrees to participate in the act, and there is no evidence to the contrary, his mistaken belief may be accepted as the *mens rea* element of the crime is affected by his misunderstanding of the facts.

For instance, in the case of *Allah Dad v Mukhtar Akhta* in Pakistan it was established that sexual intercourse between a man and a woman under a mistaken belief that they are married, would not amount to *zina* as their consent was influenced by their mistaken belief.[86] By the same analogy, if a woman enters into sexual relationship with a man in believing that

---

82 Mohamad Ismail Bin Hj. Mohamad Yunus, 'The Legal Status of Consent to Sexual Intercourse: An Islamic Dimension' (2002) Law Majalla 253.
83 ibid.
84 Mohamad Yinus (n 82).
85 (1995) NLR (SD) 535.
86 Similarly in *Mst. Basiran and Another v Muhammad Hussain* (1988) PLD (SC) 186, the Supreme Court held that if a man and a woman have good reasons to believe *bona fide* that they are husband and wife, the commission of intercourse under this belief cannot be held as 'wilful' commission of '*zina*'.

he is her husband, whilst the other is aware of the truth, only the man will be punished due to his knowledge of her mistaken consent.[87]

2.4 Property offences and criminal damage

Whilst the defence of consent is generally focused on crimes against the person, Islamic law recognises that in certain situations the victim's consent may negate an element of a crime against the property (*itlaf*) thereby absolving liability for the offence. The act must be conducted knowingly, deliberately and aggressively towards the property for the damage to be regarded as a criminal offence; therefore incidental destruction of property is not the subject of criminal proceedings.

When considering the crime of *Al-Sarqa* (theft), in the sense of an offence liable for hand amputation as the appropriate punishment (*hadd*), certain legal requirements must be fulfilled before the punishment is imposed. An essential element of this offence is that the theft is conducted without prior knowledge and/or the prior consent of the owner of the property.[88] Therefore, if the doer removes an item from a safe place with the prior consent of the owner (whether this be express or implied), the act will not be considered as a criminal offence. Similarly, in criminal damage or arson, if the defendant proves that the property was destroyed with the consent of the owner, in good faith, the defence will justify the action. An example of this can be found in Article 679 of the Iranian Penal Code, which provides that 'anyone who deliberately and unnecessarily kills ... someone else's halal-meat animal ... shall be sentenced to ninety one days to six months' imprisonment ...'. However, if it is established that a butcher killed the animal with the consent of the owner, no punishment will be imposed. Such offences usually violate the private right of the property owner rather than attracting the public interest; thus the prosecution will be ceased as soon as the defence of consent is established.

2.4.1 Place of consent in the offence structure

The consent of the owner undermines the *mens rea* element of an offence against property thereby justifying the actions of the defendant. For instance, in the case of theft, for the *mens rea* to be present, the offender must act in a dishonest manner with the intention to deprive the owner from their property (permanently or otherwise). Therefore, if the offender takes away someone's property with their consent and/or with the intention to return the item to the owner with no assumption of ownership right, the defence of consent will be successful in establishing that the *mens rea* element of the offence is not present. The *actus reus* attribute of the offence may also be undermined if the item is 'taken away' with the consent of the owner.

Of relevance to the *mens rea* requirement of an offence against property, Maliki requires not only intent to commit a crime but also knowledge of its illegality and the punishment. Therefore, if there is doubt about any aspect of the above elements, the crime cannot be proven. In the case of theft, Ibn al-Qasim states such an offence cannot be established when a father takes money from his son. This principle of doubt has been extended to include theft allegedly committed by spouses, servants who shared their master's house, and guests who stay in the owner's house. In all these scenarios, the consent of the owner and/or the permissibility to use the property creates doubt as to the existence of *mens rea*.[89]

---

87 Mohamad Yunus (n 82).
88 ibid.
89 Intisar A Rabb, *Doubt in Islamic Law: A History of Legal Maxims, Interpretations, and Islamic Criminal Law* (Cambridge University Press 2015) 165.

2.4.2 *Mistaken belief in consent*

An honest and genuine mistaken belief in consent will act as a defence to any crime against property. Therefore, if the offender truly believes that the owner of the property agrees to the action of the defendant, this will act as a complete defence depending upon the particular circumstances of the case. For instance, in a friendly relationship, a person may take away his friend's book from his library in order to read it and then return, on the mistaken belief that he is permitted to do so. In such a scenario, the doer's honest but mistaken belief in consent of his friend (even if his friend does not in fact consent to this) will be accepted as a defence as it negates the *mens rea* element (dishonesty) of the crime. The same can be said with reference to the offence of trespass where a genuine mistaken belief in the consent of the property owner would be accepted as a legitimate defence.

3 CONCLUSION

In summary, consent is not regarded as a defence within Islamic law. However, if it is established that an essential element of the offence is undermined by the consent of the victim, it will be regarded as a justificatory defence. It is a widely accepted principle across all Muslim jurisdictions that consent must be given voluntarily without coercion or deceit; that the consenting individual must have the capacity to understand the nature of the act they are consenting to; and that an individual must be fully aware of the issues relating to the said act. If all of these factors are present, the defence of consent will be accepted either as a complete defence or as a mitigating factor depending on the nature of the offence, acceptable limitations and prominence of the public interest aspects of the crime.

Consent is most commonly used as a defence in offences such as assault and battery, sporting events, medical treatment and sexual conduct. However, in each of these offences, certain criteria must be fulfilled before consent is considered as a valid and effective defence. While the foundation and underpinning basis for consent as a defence can be found within the primary sources of Islamic law, the varying approaches towards consent found within the respective legislature of Islamic countries are the result of contrasting interpretations of these sources based on the specific schools of thought that are prevalent within a particular state.

18

The Netherlands

Anne Postma

1 GENERAL ISSUES

1.1 Conceptual foundations

1.1.1 Philosophical and theoretical principles informing the law surrounding consent

First and foremost, it is important to note Dutch law approaches consent in a pragmatic rather than principled manner. Yet it is possible to identify some principles that have shaped the law as it stands.

Criminal law is public in nature: criminalisation of conduct primarily aims to protect public legal interests. Formerly, scholars used to emphasise this public character. In their approach very little room was left for a victim's consent to preclude criminal liability of an offender, as a criminal act necessarily infringes a public interest over which the consenting party has no authority (*beschikkingsmacht*).[1] In the course of time, the liberal value of self-determination, with its preference for minimal state intervention, has gained more weight. As a consequence, nowadays consent plays a more important role in the context of criminal law as a justification for certain conduct.[2] This is visible in both statutory law (for instance, special defences relating to termination of life on request of the patient and abortion) and case-law (consent forms a part of various special defences recognised by the Supreme Court). Now the question whether or not the victim has authority over the legal property (*rechtsgoed*) protected by a specific offence, is dealt with on a case-by-case basis.

It is important to note the prevailing view seems to be that consent in criminal law is an autonomous legal concept.[3] This means some aspects may differ from civil law. Arguably this is the case regarding capacity to consent, as will be outlined below. However, in many

---

1   TJ Noyon, *Het Wetboek van Strafrecht – verklaard door T.J. Noyon* (2nd edition, Wolters 1904) 22–23; WPJ Pompe, *Handboek van het Nederlandse strafrecht* (5th edition, Tjeenk Willink 1959) 10–11.

2   J Remmelink, *Mr. D. Hazewinkel-Suringa's Inleiding tot de studie van het Nederlandse Strafrecht* (15th edition, Gouda Quint 1996) 354; AG Silvis 5 July 2011, ECLI:2011:NL:PHR:BQ6690.

3   HA Demeersseman, *De autonomie van het materiële strafrecht* (Gouda Quint 1985) 413–414; Remmelink (n 2) 355.

contexts – for instance, consent concerning medical treatment or piercing – the criminal law notion of consent builds on specific regulation by civil law.

1.1.2 Influence of feminist and queer theory

Dutch literature and case-law do not refer to feminist and queer theory.

1.1.3 Definition of informed consent

There is no general definition of informed consent in statutory or case-law. Dutch doctrine, in contrast, offers some guidelines.[4] It is clear consent is valid only if it is given voluntarily, in absence of coercion, deception or mistake. In addition to voluntariness, a temporal restriction is deemed to be applicable: consent must be given prior to or during the conduct consented to. Approval after the offence is committed does not constitute valid consent.

In Dutch law the cognitive aspect of informed consent – to what degree does the consenting party need to know the nature and attendant risks of the form of conduct to which consent is given? – is not addressed as a general subject, and further elaborations on this topic are scarce. Yet concerning medical treatment, statutory law makes clear that as a rule informed consent relates to both the proposed treatment, and its expected consequences and inherent health risks.[5] However, it is unlikely consent to risks, and expected consequences of certain conduct, is also required in non-medical cases. As for sexual offences, like rape and sexual assault, it is assumed consent only relates to the specific consequences and the specific circumstances in which it is brought about.[6] Judged from this standard, sexual intercourse might only be consensual if the consenting party has knowledge of the identity of his sexual partner, the sexual partner's propensity to pass on HIV-infection, (non-)use of contraceptives and so on. In this view it will be necessary to distinguish material aspects (to which consent relates) from immaterial aspects (to which consent does not relate). Currently it is unclear if the aforementioned standard also applies to non-sexual offences and, if so, how material and immaterial aspects should be distinguished.

1.1.4 Consent to risk or consent to outcome

Dutch case-law does not explicitly distinguish between consent to infliction of harm (outcome) and consent to risk of harm (risk). This may be caused by the fact neither in civil law nor in criminal law is an injured party's 'risk-acceptance' and 'outcome-acceptance' recognised as legal concepts as such.[7] Except for crimes in which non-consent is an element of the definition, valid consent forms only a part of a broader special justificatory defence, such as the so-called 'sport and play-exception'. If accepted, such a defence negates the unlawfulness of the act. Consent is thus a necessary but not a sufficient condition for justification. As for these special defences, case-law rarely focuses on the aspect of consent. Yet, in particular in

---

4   GA van Hamel, *Inleiding tot de studie van het Nederlandsche strafrecht* (Belinfante 1927) 261; Demeersseman (n 3) 412–414; Remmelink (n 2) 354–355; AJM Machielse, 'Wetboek van Strafrecht: 10 Toestemming', in JW Fokkens, EJ Hofstee and AJM Machielse (eds), *Noyon/Langemeijer & Remmelink – Wetboek van Strafrecht* (Kluwer Navigator Collecties).

5   See section 2.2.2.

6   K Lindenberg, *Strafbare dwang: over het bestanddeel 'dwingen' en strafbaarstellingen van dwang, in het bijzonder art. 284 Sr* (Maklu 2007) 137–138.

7   See for civil law: HR (Supreme Court) 28 June 1991, ECLI:NL:HR:1991:ZC0300. See for criminal law: section 1.2.

the context of the 'sport and play-exception', some authors do explicitly refer to a victim's risk-acceptance.[8]

Keeping in mind this rather limited significance of consent taken alone, both modalities – consent to harm and consent to risk – can give rise to valid consent. The former comes to the fore in a range of activities implying consent to a particular kind of injury, such as medical treatment and decorative practices like piercing. Well-known examples of valid consent to risk are cases of inflicting harm during socially accepted sport or play; voluntary participation in such activities is deemed to imply acceptance of attendant risks.

1.1.5 Revocation of consent

Dutch criminal law does not contain a general rule on revocation of consent. Yet as for consent to medical treatment, it is clear given consent can be withdrawn. A similar approach follows from case-law on coercion-based sexual offences, from which can be derived that prior consent to engage in sexual intercourse is vitiated when one of the sexual partners revokes given consent during sexual intercourse.[9] It can be assumed the attitude of the victim *tempore delicti* is also of overriding importance outside the scope of medical treatment and sexual activity.

1.1.6 Ownership and limits of consent

The limits of valid consent are determined on a case-by-case basis: does the private interest of the consenting party outweigh any public interests that are at stake, in view of the offence involved and the circumstances in which harm is inflicted? If so, the consenting party is deemed to have authority over the legal property protected by the specific offence.[10] Due to this casuistic approach it is not possible to identify clear limits of consent. What follows below is a broad sketch of the position taken by Dutch law.

The interpretation of the offence concerned functions as a first yardstick for determining whether or not authority over a legal property may exist. This may have three outcomes. Firstly, it is conceivable that consent of a victim is regarded as irrelevant in view of the nature of the crime. For instance, it follows from parliamentary history and the offence description of Article 244 of the Dutch Penal Code (DPC) taken together that it is criminal to have sexual intercourse with a minor below the age of 12, regardless of given consent. Secondly, the opposite case is also possible: non-consent of a certain person is an (implicit) element of the crime. As for these offences, valid consent therefore prevents the offence description from being fulfilled. Such crimes can for instance be found in the context of the protection of private property. The same is considered to be true in the case of entering a home with the consent of the occupant (Article 138 DPC); giving permission to be insulted (Article 266 DPC); consent by a person aged 16 years and above to having sexual intercourse with another person (Article 242 DPC); or consent to the intentional infliction of pain or 'minor' bodily harm (Article 300 DPC).[11] This non-exhaustive catalogue illustrates with regard to certain legal interests – private property, inviolability of the home, a person's honour and reputation, and to a limited extent his sexual and physical integrity – the right of self-determination is

---

8 See section 2.2.3.
9 This topic will be elaborated on in section 2.3.1.
10 Remmelink (n 2) 354–355; C Kelk/F de Jong, *Studieboek materieel strafrecht* (5th edition, Kluwer 2013) 188.
11 See Machielse (n 4) 'Wetboek van Strafrecht: 10 Toestemming', 'Titel XVI Belediging' and 'art 300'; Kelk/ De Jong (n 10) 189.

of great weight; a victim's consent is giving otherwise criminal conduct a neutral character. Nevertheless, it will follow from s 2 that a person does not have absolute authority over his own life or body as for infringements on his physical or sexual integrity by another person.

The third possible outcome of offence interpretation lies between the aforementioned extremes. In that case the legislator has not made clear whether or not consent can play a justificatory role regarding the crime concerned. If it comes to that, which is mostly the case, acting on consent of the victim will only in specific circumstances exclude the unlawfulness of the act, namely if accepted as a non-statutory special defence by case-law (for instance the 'sport and play-exception').[12] Public interests, like public morality (*goede zeden*) and public order (*openbare orde*), arguably restrict the scope of these special defences. For instance, harm inflicted as a result of dangerous and socially condemned activities, like a consensual man-to-man street fight or Russian roulette, will not qualify for the sport and play-exception.[13]

1.2 Place of consent in the offence structure

Consent can exclude the unlawfulness of an act. The place of consent in the offence structure depends on the type of offence. Most offences have a tripartite structure. In such a case three stages of examination can be distinguished: subsequently examination of the offence description, unlawfulness of the act (*wederrechtelijkheid*) and blameworthiness of the offender (*verwijtbaarheid*).[14] This structure is followed, for instance, by the crime intentionally causing serious bodily injury to another person (Article 302 DPC). It can be seen the unlawfulness of the act and the blameworthiness of the offender are not part of the offence description. Both conditions are presumed to be fulfilled and need no proof accordingly. Exceptionally, unlawfulness or blameworthiness might be excluded by the acceptance of a corresponding defence (second and third stage of examination). Peculiarly, a successful defence will result in a 'discharge' (*ontslag van alle rechtsvervolging*); the defendant cannot be punished for a proven act. Only cases in which the fulfilment of an offence description is not proven, will lead up to an 'acquittal' (*vrijspraak*); no proof for the charge.

With a view to consent, the defence 'absence of substantive unlawfulness' is particularly relevant. This ground for justification was introduced by the Dutch Supreme Court, apparently being meant as a general defence.[15] In essence, the Supreme Court stated 'unlawfulness' contains a 'formal' and a 'substantive' aspect, and both must be fulfilled: in exceptional circumstances the commission of an offence (unlawfulness in a formal way) may still be justified (unlawfulness in a substantive way). As understood nowadays, in such cases justification is based on the fact that the specific act is in accordance with a certain standard outside criminal law (for example civil law), as a consequence of which the commission of the offence is not unlawful in a substantive way.[16] This category is best seen as a collection of various specific justifying grounds not classifiable under a statutory defence, including acting on consent in specific circumstances.[17] Well-known examples are the aforementioned 'sport and play-exception' and the 'professional conduct exception' (for instance acting in the capacity of a physician or

---

12 See section 1.2.
13 See for restrictions flowing from such public interests: Remmelink (n 2) 354–355; Machielse (n 4).
14 See for a more elaborative overview: E Gritter, 'The Netherlands' in A Reed and M Bohlander, *General Defences in Criminal Law: Domestic and Comparative Perspectives* (Ashgate 2014) 255 ff.
15 HR 29 February 1933, NJ 1933/918.
16 Remmelink (n 2) 344.
17 HD Wolswijk and G Knigge, *Ons strafrecht deel 1: het materiële strafrecht* (Kluwer 2015) 159.

artist).[18] It is important to keep in mind in such cases consent is a necessary but not a sufficient condition for justification. A classic example in this respect is a physician intentionally causing serious bodily injury to his patient in the course of a necessary medical treatment. In such a case the infliction of harm is lawful if the patient has consented to treatment and the physician has performed treatment in accordance with prevailing professional standards (*lege artis*). This explains that in Dutch law consent is merely addressed as an aspect of the justification brought about by the exercise of one's professional duties, and not as an independent topic.[19]

The outline above shows consent normally comes to play at the second stage of the examination. It was also mentioned that exceptionally 'non-consent' (implicitly) forms a part of the *actus reus* of the offence. Typically this will concern acts in which lack of consent is essential in giving otherwise morally neutral conduct a criminal character. For example, non-consent is an explicit element of the crime outraging public decency in a non-public place in the presence of another person against his will (Article 239(3) DPC). Presence of another person 'against his will' is giving otherwise neutral conduct a criminal character, whereas voluntary presence will lead to an acquittal.

1.3 Form of consent

1.3.1 Declared or implied

The question of what form of consent is required, is mainly addressed with regard to two contexts: first, cases in which the victim voluntary participates in social activity like sports and (horse)play and, second, cases in which the victim engages in medical treatment.

As for the former, the prevailing view in Dutch doctrine is that voluntary participation as such implies consent to attendant risks.[20] In the case of medical treatment, the issue of informed consent is regulated by civil law. This regulation is stricter in the sense that the patient must be informed about attendant risks explicitly. If that information is given, as a rule implicit consent as to the treatment and its risks suffices.[21] Special civil law regulation, contrastingly, raises the threshold for valid consent in case of termination of life on request of the patient and abortion. As a rule an oral request suffices in both procedures, but the interests at stake are deemed to be of such importance that they warrant a special decision-making procedure.[22]

1.3.2 Presumed consent

The topic of presumed consent is primarily addressed with a view to medical treatment. Consent may be presumed in two types of situations: emergency situations and in case of minor medical interventions.[23] It is unclear if the concept of presumed consent can play a role outside the medical context and, if so, in what situations.[24]

---

18 J de Hullu, *Materieel strafrecht: Over algemene leerstukken van strafrechtelijke aansprakelijkheid naar Nederlands recht* (6th edition, Kluwer 2015) 298.
19 ibid 357; Machielse (n 4).
20 The implied consent-approach is also taken in case of consent by proxy. See AG Silvis (n 2). Parents who let their child participate in a football match thus voluntarily expose their child to the risk of some pain or injury, which risk they are deemed to accept.
21 See section 2.2.2.
22 See section 2.1.2 and 2.1.3.
23 See section 2.2.2.
24 It seems reasonable to presume consent in cases of caretaking. See Demeersseman (n 3) 414. This type of case, however, is already covered by the general defence 'necessity' (Article 40 DPC).

1.4 Capacity to consent

The prevailing view seems to be that criminal law recognises an autonomous notion of 'capacity to consent'.[25] This means that this notion may deviate from the general rule in civil law about the competence to perform legal acts. Arguably, in criminal law it will generally be decisive whether or not the consenting party is in fact able to comprehend the implications of his or her consent.[26] This may include minors or adults under legal constraint, who are as a rule incompetent to perform legal acts according to civil law, or persons with a mental disorder. It must be judged from the specific circumstances of the case if the consenting party involved is in fact competent to give valid consent.

Although the general rule of civil law does not apply to criminal law, specific civil law provisions do. For instance, whether or not the consenting party has a capacity to consent to the intentional causing of bodily harm as a result of medical treatment or piercing (criminal law) must be derived from specific civil law regulations.[27] Therefore, although the capacity to consent is regarded as an autonomous notion, its scope is strongly influenced by civil law. This civil law influence is also visible in a case concerning consent by proxy. In this case two young boys had been circumcised by a physician on request of their father. At the time the father was sharing parental authority with his ex-wife and he knew that she was against this religiously motivated event. Because the mother's consent was lacking, the Court of Appeal convicted the father for premeditatedly and intentionally causing bodily harm to the boys (Article 301 DPC), which conviction was upheld by the Supreme Court.[28] Although neither the Court of Appeal nor the Supreme Court explicitly refers to civil law, the fact that consent of both parents was required derives from civil law regulation on parental authority (Article 7:465 (1) Civil Code).[29]

1.5 Consequences of mistaken consent

1.5.1 Mistake

Dutch doctrine states only in general terms that valid consent implies absence of coercion, deception or mistake.[30] It follows that errors by the victim are at least capable of negating consent. It remains unclear to what kind of mistakes the doctrine refers: mistake as to (an attribute of) the offender's conduct and/or his identity? Again, it seems that very much will depend on the specific circumstances of the case, such as the nature of the conduct at issue. For instance, a mistake by the victim as to the identity of the sexual partner seems far more important in the context of private sexual activity than in the context of sexual intercourse on a commercial basis. However, Dutch law does not offer clear guidance as to what kind of mistakes by the victim can vitiate consent.

1.5.2 Deception

The same general rule and reservations, as mentioned above, apply to cases in which the victim is deceived by the offender. Whether or not a vitiation of consent influences liability for the offence involved depends on the nature of that crime.

---

25 Demeersseman (n 3) 413–414; Remmelink (n 2) 355.
26 Demeersseman (n 3) 413–414.
27 See section 2.2.2 and 2.2.3.
28 HR 9 December 2014, ECLI:NL:HR:2014:3538.
29 AG Silvis (n 2).
30 See section 1.1.3.

This can be illustrated by two cases on rape, in which deception was related to the personal identity of the sexual partner.[31] In both cases the victim, who was half asleep, had given (implicit) consent to sexual intercourse with a person impersonating her sexual partner; both victims were having sex with men who pretended to be their boyfriend. It can be derived from both cases that in these circumstances impersonation vitiates consent. Lack of consent, as such, does not transform sexual intercourse into rape, as in Dutch law rape is a coercion-based crime. 'Coercion' requires awareness on behalf of the victim as to the involuntariness of her participation in sexual intercourse.[32] In the aforementioned cases this awareness was absent, due to which there was no criminal liability for rape.[33]

1.6 Mistake about consent

A mistake about consent by the offender is a form of mistake of fact. The legal implications depend on the place of the victim's consent in the offence structure. Generally a mistake will relate to consent as a special justificatory defence, such as an offender who intentionally damages private property whereas he wrongly believes to act on consent of the owner, or an offender who is intentionally causing pain to his sexual partner wrongly assuming she wants to be involved in BDSM. Dutch law treats mistakes of fact relating to defences – so-called 'putative defences' – as variations of the non-statutory excusatory defence 'lack of all culpability', which, if accepted, negates the blameworthiness of the offender. Under this general defence mistake of fact is accepted if two requirements are met: the offender in fact acted under mistake (factual mistake), the mistake is excusatory (excusable mistake). Whether or not an error is excusable requires an appreciation of the facts by the court.[34] An excusable mistake will lead to a discharge or an acquittal.[35]

Exceptionally a mistake about consent relates to intent. This is the case if the offence description requires intent as to the victim's non-consent. Rape, for instance, requires that an offender 'coerces' a victim to engage in acts comprising or including (non-penile) sexual penetration of the body (Article 242 DPC). This element of coercion implies conditional intent – which can be defined as 'consciously accepting the substantial chance of causing the consequence' – as to the involuntary involvement of the victim.[36] The offender's wrong belief about given consent to sexual intercourse can thus, without necessarily being excusable, give rise to an acquittal for intentional offences.

2 SPECIFIC ISSUES

2.1 Consent and homicide offences

2.1.1 Mercy killings

As a rule mercy killing – understood as intentional killing without the request of the victim – will give rise to liability for (premeditated) murder. The defendant may invoke a general defence like necessity (conflict of duties).[37] Not surprisingly, such an appeal will only very exceptionally be accepted.

---

31 HR 24 March 1998, ECLI:NL:HR:1998:ZD0980 and HR 14 February 2006, ECLI:NL:HR:2006:AU8042. See section 2.2.1 for another example in the context of HIV-cases.

32 J de Hullu, 'HR 24 March 1998, ECLI:NL:HR:1998:ZD0980' [1998] Nederlandse Jurisprudentie 1998/534 (case note); Lindenberg (n 6) 158–159, 185–186. Also see section 2.3.

33 In such a case the offender might nevertheless be held liable for a non-coercion based sexual offence.

34 De Hullu (n 18) 364–365.

35 This will be dictated by the offence structure, ie if the blameworthiness of the offender is part of the offence description (acquittal) or not (discharge).

36 See section 2.2.1.

37 Article 40 DPC.

A Supreme Court judgment of 2004 provides a good example.[38] In this case the defendant, a physician, had intentionally terminated the life of a comatose and terminal patient. His main reason for giving a lethal injection was that the patient found herself in an enduring humiliating state – she was uncared for, had bedsores and a very short life expectancy – which made the defendant fear that his patient would 'rot to death'. On the basis of these facts, he invoked necessity: ending a humiliating situation like that should take precedence over the duty not to commit a homicide offence. The Court of Appeal, however, denied necessity and convicted the defendant for premeditated murder under Article 289 DPC. This decision was upheld by the Supreme Court. It ruled that in cases of termination of life without a request of the victim, necessity can only be accepted if a patient is in a 'very urgent situation', thereby limiting the scope of necessity to very rare cases.[39]

2.1.2 Killing on request of the victim

The statutory regulation of killing on request restricts a person's right of self-determination. As part of this regulation, Article 293 (1) DPC makes punishable taking someone else's life at his explicit and serious desire. This crime is punished by a maximum of 12 years' imprisonment. Article 294 (2) DPC makes punishable assisting suicide, with a maximum penalty of three years' imprisonment at most. The rationale of both offences is protection of human life in general.[40] Both provisions, however, contain a special defence for physicians in the case of requests made by persons aged 12 years and above.[41] In such cases, terminating life, under Article 293 DPC, or assisting suicide, under Article 294 DPC, is justified, provided that a physician meets certain criteria of due care and reports the termination of life to the municipal coroner (Article 293(2) in conjunction with Article 294(2) DPC).

These criteria of due care, which are of most importance regarding consent, are laid down in Article 2 Termination of Life on Request and Assisted Suicide Act (*Wet toetsing levensbeëindiging op verzoek en hulp bij zelfdoding (WTL)*.[42] According to Article 2(1) WTL, a physician will have to: a) be convinced that the patient's request was made voluntarily and well-considered; b) be convinced that the patient's suffering is enduring and unbearable; c) inform the patient about the situation he is in, and about the prospects; d) be convinced, together with the patient, that no other reasonable solution is available; e) consult at least one other, independent physician, who has seen the patient, and who has given a written opinion on the aforementioned criteria; f) exercise due medical care when terminating the patient's life, or

---

38 HR 9 November 2004, ECLI:NL:HR:2004:AP1493.

39 See Y Buruma, 'HR 9 November 2004, ECLI:NL:HR:2004:AP1493' [2005] Nederlandse Jurisprudentie 217 (case note). The author suggests that this criterion may be fulfilled if, for instance, a terminal patient with lung cancer unexpectedly suffers from a massive pulmonary with a serious threat of immediate choking. In exceptional cases necessity can also be accepted concerning termination of life of severely disabled newborn children. See for an overview: J Dorscheidt, 'Levensbeëindiging bij pasgeborenen' (2015) 21 Nederlands Juristenblad 1001.

40 MS Groenhuijsen and F van Laanen, 'Euthanasia in the Broader Framework of Dutch Penal Policies' in MS Groenhuijsen and F van Laanen (eds), *Euthanasia in International and Comparative Perspective* (WLP 2006).

41 Minors below the minimum age are considered to be incapable of weighing their interests. See Kamerstukken II 1998/99, 26 691, no 3, 12.

42 WTL entered into force on 1 April, 2002. Before then, in exceptional cases necessity was accepted as a defence by the Supreme Court (see for example HR 27 November 1984, ECLI:NL:HR:1984:AC8615 and HR 21 June 1994, ECLI:NL:HR:1994:AD2122). Article 2 WTL is more or less a codification of case-law criteria (see De Hullu (n 18), 312).

assisting in his suicide.[43] The criteria under a) and c) are of particular importance concerning valid request. Taken together, both standards implicate that a physician's conviction must be grounded upon a patient's (oral or written) informed request. The standards of due care apply in an unaltered form to patients above the age of 18.

In two specific situations the criteria of Article 2(1) WTL are supplemented: firstly with respect to minors between the age of 12 and 18 who are reasonably able to weigh their interests, and secondly with regard to patients who are no longer able to express their will. With regard to minors, the law makes a further distinction. Minors from 16- to 18-years-old who are reasonably able to weigh their interests can validly request for termination of life themselves, parental consent is not required.[44] Article 2(3) WTL only formulates, in addition to the general due care criteria, that parents who have legal custody – in case of absence: a guardian – must be 'involved' in the decision-making. In the case of minors from 12 to 16 years old as a rule parental consent is required: under Article 2(4) WTL the parents (or guardian) must 'become reconciled' to the termination of life requested for. Nevertheless, absence of parental consent can be overruled by a physician, if the physician is convinced that continuation of enduring and unbearable suffering will accordingly be prevented.[45] As for patients who have lost their ability to express their will, the second specific situation, Article 2(2) WTL requires that the patient concerned has made his request to terminate life previously, when he was reasonably able to weigh his interests. As an additional safeguard, in such a case the request must have been written. In the case of minors from 12 to 16 years old, these standards are supplemented by the aforementioned parental consent and possibility to overrule (Article 2(4) WTL).

The above shows that the special defence under Article 293(2) DPC only applies, broadly stated, to physicians in the case of a valid request made by a person aged 12 years and above. Cases in which these standards are not met – for example cases in which a non-physician is involved in the termination of life – the general defence of necessity can be invoked instead. It is observed that necessity will only very rarely be accepted, since the aforementioned special defence is designed to demarcate typical circumstances in which both offences are justified.[46]

2.1.3 Abortion

The regulation of *abortus provocatus* is similarly structured as killing on request of the victim. As a rule, abortion is punishable under Article 296(1)–(4) DPC, although a special defence exists for physicians who act in accordance with certain due care criteria under Article 296 (5). If these standards are not met, a general defence – most likely necessity – can be invoked, but this will only very exceptionally be accepted.[47] The rationale of this statutory regulation is to safeguard an abortion practice with due care.[48] This regulation protects and delimits the

---

43   As translated by Groenhuijsen and Van Laanen (n 40).

44   Minors from 16 years up can validly consent to medical treatment according to the Civil Code. See section 2.2.2.

45   Kamerstukken II 1998/99, 26 691, no 3, 12.

46   De Hullu (n 18) 300; HR 9 November 2004, ECLI:NL:HR:2004:AP1493. See for an exceptional case in which assisting suicide by a non-physician was considered justified on the basis of necessity: Court of Appeal Arnhem-Leeuwarden 13 May 2015, ECLI:NL:GHARL:2015:3444.

47   Machielse (n 4) 'art 296'.

48   CPM Cleiren, 'Titel XIXA Afbreking van zwangerschap, inleidende opmerkingen' in CPM Cleiren, JH Crijns and MJM Verpalen (eds), *Tekst & Commentaar Strafrecht* (10th edition, Kluwer 2014).

pregnant woman's right of self-determination.[49] The delimitation plays a role at the level of both offence description and special defence.

As for the offence description, the basic offence, under Article 296 (1), makes punishable performance of a (medical) treatment where the offender knows or reasonably should expect that this treatment may result in termination of pregnancy. This crime is punished by a maximum of four years and six months' imprisonment. It is important to point out the limitation that flows from the requirement of 'pregnancy', meaning that a fertilised egg-cell must already have become implanted in the womb.[50] As a consequence, providing a morning-after pill – which prevents implantation – cannot trigger liability for Article 296, because the stage of pregnancy is not yet reached. Article 296(2)–(4) circumscribe aggravating circumstances: the maximum penalty is raised if the pregnant woman dies as a result of her treatment (six years); if she has not consented to her treatment (12 years); or if both consent is absent and the treatment turns out to be lethal for the woman (15 years). With regard to consent, it is assumed that in line with the regulation of termination of life on request of the victim, consent by proxy – for instance, if a pregnant woman is in a coma as a result of an accident – is invalid.[51]

Now I will turn to the special defence for physicians, under Article 296(5), and the role of consent therein. The aforementioned criteria of due care that need to be fulfilled, are laid down in the Abortion Act (*Wet afbreking zwangerschap (Wafz)*).[52] According to Wafz Article 5(1), abortion is only justified if the pregnant woman finds herself in an emergency situation that makes abortion inevitable, and if a careful decision-making procedure is followed. It is important to note that 'emergency situation' is related to psychological pressure, not physical harm.[53] The decision-making procedure shows that both the pregnant woman and the physician bear responsibility for the decision to terminate pregnancy.[54] Among other things, it holds that a request to perform abortion has to be made by the pregnant woman. Article 3(1) Wafz requires a period of at least five days to reconsider directly after. Furthermore, several duties rest on the physician: a duty to inform the pregnant woman about alternative ways to resolve her emergency situation; a duty to verify if she made and maintained her request both voluntarily and after careful consideration; and a duty to make sure that she is both aware of her responsibility for unborn life and aware of the implications of abortion for herself and her relatives, under Article 5 (2). Taken together, these requirements must safeguard that a decision to perform an abortion is well-considered.

Contrary to WTL, Wafz does not contain specific provisions with regard to requests of minors. As a consequence, the general provisions of the Civil Code about contracts on medical treatment are applicable.[55] This means that, as a rule, 'double consent' is required in case of minors between the age of 12 and 16; both the minor and her parents (or guardian) must consent to abortion. A refusal of parents or a guardian to do so, can be overruled if the minor still wants abortion after careful deliberation and the physician is of the opinion that abortion is in her interest.

---

49 ibid 'art 296'.
50 Machielse (n 4) 'art 296'.
51 Cleiren (n 48) 'art 296'.
52 Wafz entered into force on 1 November, 1984.
53 Commissie Evaluatie Regelgeving, *Evaluatie Wet afbreking zwangerschap* (ZonMw 2005) 37.
54 ibid 36–41.
55 See section 2.2.2.

2.2 Consent and non-fatal offences against the person

2.2.1 *HIV and other communicable disease transmission*

Dutch government policy focuses on the prevention of sexually transmissible diseases (STD) – including HIV – through the help of non-criminal means, like education and easy access to check-ups for high-risk groups. As for voluntary sexual activity, a basic principle of this policy is that sexual partners themselves bear responsibility for having safe sex.[56] Against this background it is understandable that Dutch criminal law does not contain a specific inchoate offence concerning a STD-positive person engaging in unprotected sex.[57]

However, attempted or completed transmissions of STD might give rise to criminal liability. The relevant case-law of the Supreme Court is eventually focused on (attempted) HIV infections in the context of grievous bodily harm under Article 302 DPC: may a person be held liable for intentionally causing serious bodily injury to another person (if he did in fact infect his sexual partner) or an attempt to do so (if his partner was not infected)? For a clear understanding of the matter, it is important to note that Dutch criminal law recognises several gradations of intent, ranging from wilful intent (*dolus directus*) to conditional intent (*dolus eventualis*). The latter is considered the lowest limit of intent, which also suffices for an attempt to commit an intentional offence. Conditional intent can be defined as 'consciously accepting a substantial chance of causing the consequence', that is in HIV cases by causing serious bodily injury to another person by transmission of HIV.[58] The case-law of the Supreme Court outlined below links up with cases where proof of conditional intent was questioned.

The Supreme Court has devoted four landmark decisions to these types of cases.[59] In all these cases an HIV-positive defendant and an HIV-negative victim voluntarily engaged in unprotected sexual intercourse, where the defendant knew that he was HIV-positive and the victim was unaware of his status. In the first two cases the Supreme Court quashed convictions for attempted murder (*HIV-I en II*), because in these cases sufficient proof of the 'substantial chance' that a HIV infection would kill the victim was lacking. Motivated by this, *HIV-III* and *IV* concern convictions for attempted (*HIV-III*) and completed grievous bodily harm (*HIV-IV*).

The last case not only differs from the former as for the actual HIV transmission, but also the defendant and the victim had had sexual intercourse in numerous instances and all the time the defendant had explicitly lied to the victim about his HIV status. Nevertheless this conviction was also quashed by the Supreme Court: although a HIV-positive person who engages in unprotected sexual intercourse creates 'a chance' to infect his sexual partner, this chance *per se* cannot be considered as 'substantial'. This will only be the case in 'special, risk-increasing circumstances'. Apparently, according to the Supreme Court, also the frequency of unprotected sexual intercourse in the underlying case of *HIV-IV* did not qualify for such a special circumstance. It is important to note that this delineation of 'substantial chance' – an element of conditional intent – is to a great extent driven by public health considerations.[60] In *HIV-IV*, for instance, the Supreme Court substantiates its interpretation by taking into

---

56 RIVM Rapport, 'Nationaal soa/hiv-plan 2012–2016: "Bestendigen en versterken"' (RIVM 2011) 2–12.
57 Kamerstukken II 2005, 29 800, no 157, 6.
58 See HR 25 March 2003, ECLI:NL:HR:2003:AE9049 (HIV-I).
59 HR 25 March 2003, ECLI:NL:HR:2003:AE9049 (HIV-I); HR 24 June 2003, ECLI:NL:HR:2003:AF8058 (HIV-II); HR 18 January 2005, ECLI:NL:HR:2005:AR1860 (HIV-III) and HR 20 February 2007, ECLI:NL:HR:2007:AY9659 (HIV-IV).
60 Y Buruma [2007] NJ 2007/313 (case note); De Hullu (n 18) 247–249.

account that bringing such HIV cases within the realm of criminal law might harm the interest of public health. That is to say the effect of criminalisation may be that people will refrain from HIV check-ups, which might result in an increase of the amount of HIV infections.[61] According to the prevailing view in literature, HIV cases as mentioned above will generally not be able to generate liability for an intentional offence, whether or not a victim consented to the unsafe character of sexual activity.[62]

2.2.2 Medical treatment

The infliction of harm caused by medical treatment is justified, provided that the treatment is exercised in accordance with prevailing medical-professional standards.[63] General provisions about contracts on medical treatment laid down in the Civil Code – enacted by the Medical Treatment Contract Act (*Wet op de geneeskundige behandelingsovereenkomst*) – form a part of these standards. It is within this framework that consent plays a role.[64]

The basic rule states that medical treatment must be based upon informed consent given by the patient involved (Article 7:448 (1–2) in conjunction with Article 7:450 (1) Civil Code). According to these provisions, the duty to inform that is placed upon the physician does not only relate to the proposed treatment, but – within reasonable limits – also to its expected consequences and inherent health risks. This basic rule in Article 7:447 Civil Code is applicable to patients aged 16 years and above.[65] In addition to this rule, civil law contains some special regimes. Firstly, for minors below 16 years of age. In case of minors aged between 12 and 16 years, as a rule consent is required both by the minor, and his parents or guardian (hereinafter subsumed under 'parents'). As an exception, the law discerns two situations in which parental consent is not required: if treatment is necessary to prevent serious detriment to the minor involved and, secondly, if the minor maintains his well-considered wish to be treated.[66] In case of minors aged below 12 years, as a rule only parental consent is required under Article 7:465 (1) Civil Code. Parental refusal to treatment can be overruled by the juvenile court under Article 1:264 Civil Code, in cases where treatment is necessary in view of the minor's health. Secondly, civil law also contains a special regime for patients aged 12 years and above who are reasonably not able to weigh their interests. In such cases, a legal representative has to give consent.[67] In all the aforementioned cases consent must be expressed, verbal or

---

61 See Kamerstukken II 2005, 29 800, no 157, 6–7.
62 Some authors take the view that in case of actual HIV transmission, liability for *negligently* causing serious bodily injury to another person (Article 308 DPC) remains possible, and is particularly warranted when given consent to unprotected sexual intercourse by a victim is caused by deception. See De Hullu (n 18) 248; Buruma (n 60). Contrary to intentional offences, crimes of negligence do not require an offender to 'contemplate' the (substantial) chance that the result will occur. Thus liability for negligent HIV transmission might arise when an offender often has had unprotected sex with various sex partners, irrespective of his awareness of his HIV status. Due to the fact that liability on the basis of negligence does not depend on such awareness, it would arguably not deter people from having HIV check-ups.
63 De Hullu (n 18) 357.
64 See Machielse (n 4); AG Silvis (n 2).
65 This is an exception to the general rule in Dutch law, which stipulates that minors below 18 years of age are regarded to be incompetent to perform legal acts (Article 1:234 Civil Code).
66 According to the memorandum in reply pertaining to the Medical Treatment Contract Act, *abortus provocatus* does not constitute prevention of serious detriment under Article 7:450 (2) Civil Code. See Kamerstukken II 1992, 21 561, no 11, 34.
67 In case of a patient aged 16 years and above: as a rule any previous and written refusals made when the patient was reasonably able to weigh his interest – for example a wish not to be reanimated – must be respected (Article 7:450 (3) Civil Code); 7:465 (2–3) Civil Code.

non-verbal. Consent, for instance, will be implied by offering one's arm after being informed about the coming injection.[68] Given consent can be withdrawn.[69]

As a rule legitimate medical care accordingly presupposes prior consent (by proxy). As noted previously, civil law acknowledges two cases in which consent can be presumed. First, if a victim who is unable to voice consent (for instance: due to unconsciousness) finds himself in an emergency situation calling for immediate medical treatment (for instance: the victim has lethal wounds as a result of a traffic accident). According to Article 7:466 (1) Civil Code, this treatment may take place 'without consent' of the victim. In fact this boils down to a rebuttable presumption that consent to treatment would be given if the victim would be able to express his will. This can be derived from the fact that as a rule a known prior expression of will, such as the patient's wish not to be reanimated, must be obeyed.[70] Secondly, consent can be presumed in case of futile medical treatments where an infringement of the patient's physical or mental integrity is hardly noticeable.[71]

2.2.3 Sport injuries, 'horseplay', piercing

Conduct that would otherwise be unlawful, might be lawful if it is performed in the course of a socially accepted sport or play.[72] There seems to be consensus in so far as manifestations of attendant risks – meaning risks related to the regular practise of the specific sport or play – are considered to be justified. According to some authors, this justification is based on the victim's risk acceptance; it can reasonably be assumed that participation in sport or play implies tacit acceptance of inherent risks.[73] The Supreme Court takes a similar stance, although it does not explicitly refer to risk acceptance. In its view participators in a sport or play 'have to expect to a certain extent dangerous conduct from each other provoked by the sport or play involved', which raises the threshold for unlawfulness (*wederrechtelijkheid*).[74] Both approaches more or less boil down to the same key question: is the dangerous conduct involved a manifestation of a foreseeable risk pertaining to a regular practise of the socially accepted activity (as a rule not unlawful) or is it regarded as a more or less detached event (as a rule unlawful)?

Case-law on this matter can be divided into two categories. The first category includes cases in which the dangerous act is performed during sport or play, but outside a situation of the game. Such a case will generally be regarded as a detached event, as was the case in a game of water polo during which two players jointly pushed an opponent under water for a while after she had scored a goal. This is clearly not dangerous conduct that one has to expect during water polo, but unlawful behaviour.[75]

---

68 CJJM Stolker, 'art 7:466' in JH Nieuwenhuis, CJJM Stolker and WL Valk (eds), *Tekst en Commentaar Burgerlijk Wetboek* (11th edition, Kluwer 2015).

69 ibid.

70 Kamerstukken II 1989–1990, 21 561, no 3, 12–14.

71 Article 7:466 (2) Civil Code; Stolker (n 68).

72 De Hullu (n 18) 356–357; Machielse (n 4).

73 Remmelink (n 2) 356; De Hullu (n 18) 356; Kelk/De Jong (n 10) 190.

74 HR 31 October 2006, ECLI:NL:HR:2006:AX9178; HR 22 April 2008, ECLI:NL:HR:2008:BB7087. See also Keijzer, 'HR 31 October 2006, ECLI:NL:HR:2006:AX9178' [2007] NJ 2007/79 and A-G Machielse, ECLI:NL:PHR:2008:BB7087. The Supreme Court had already taken a similar approach in case-law on tort law (onrechtmatige daad). See HR 28 June 1991, ECLI:NL:HR:1991:ZC0300.

75 District Court Almelo 22 October 2009, ECLI:NL:RBALM:2009:BK1065. Both players were convicted for joint perpetration of grievous bodily harm (Article 302 DPC).

The second category involves cases in which the dangerous act is performed in a situation of the game, and the sport or play concerned is or is not regulated by clear rules. If there are rules of the game, they function as a starting point for distinguishing 'lawful' from 'unlawful' conduct. This comes to the fore in a notorious case regarding gross misconduct during a football match between two professional teams.[76] During the match the victim was illegally tackled by an opponent, the defendant, as a result of which the victim became seriously injured. The Court of Appeal found that the defendant had run at high speed when he forcefully executed a 'flying' and 'straight-legged' tackle thereby causing a compound fracture of the victim's leg. The Court also took into consideration the applicable 'Guidebook for Referees' which stated that it is not allowed to execute a straight-legged tackle due to the risk of serious consequences for other players. Therefore, the Court of Appeal judged the defendant's tackle as a 'flagrant violation of the rules of football', which made the act 'unlawful'. On the basis thereof and because all the other elements of the crime were considered proven, the defendant was convicted for intentionally causing serious bodily injury to the victim (Article 302 DPC).[77] The conviction was upheld by the Supreme Court. Firstly, it brought to the fore that if a sport or play is regulated by clear rules – like football – these rules are of importance for 'determining the boundaries of unlawfulness'. It is clear that, in the view of the Supreme Court, as a rule conventional fouls do not give rise to unlawful conduct; after all, minor violations of rules of the game – such as late tackles – are expectable.[78] Due to this, a violation of rules will only very exceptionally be unlawful in the sense of criminal law, namely, according to the Supreme Court, if the 'specific rule-violation' and 'dangerousness of the act' taken together give rise to unlawfulness. In other words: in cases of disproportionate behaviour that goes far beyond regular play.[79] In the case at hand, the conduct of the defendant could be considered disproportionate, because his straight-legged tackle both flagrantly violated rules of the game and was very dangerous.

The approach of conduct relating to sport or play that is not regulated by clear rules does not seem to be very different, although an indication of expectable dangerous conduct can of course not be found in explicit rules.[80] Case-law on sport or play lacking clear rules is scarce. A well-known case in this regard is about a 'playful game' inside a building of a student association.[81] Regular members had tried to batter open an emergency exit by means of a 1,000 kilogram table, while committee members tried to prevent it. This event took place in a small room, with a lot of participants and most of them had imbibed (a lot of) alcohol. During the struggle a committee member was hit by the table and suffered two broken wrists. With a view to the 'sport and play exception', the defendant, who had played a part in the accident, claimed that he had not acted unlawfully. The Court of Appeal rejected his claim, primarily because this event could not be considered as a play or custom that was 'regularly' practiced by members of the association. In other words: it could not have been clear at all for the victim what dangerous conduct he could expect, due to which the exception is not applicable. The court convicted the defendant for joint perpetration of negligently causing serious bodily injury to the committee member under Article 308 DPC. This conviction was upheld

---

76 See HR 22 April 2008, ECLI:NL:HR:2008:BB7087. See for a similar case: HR 28 June 2011, ECLI:NL:HR: 2011:BQ4203.

77 As mentioned before: in Dutch law conditional intent suffices.

78 Keijzer (n 74).

79 Remmelink (n 2) 351–356–357; Kelk/De Jong (n 10) 192; De Hullu (n 18) 356.

80 Kelk/De Jong (n 10) 192; De Hullu (n 18) 356 and HR 22 April 2008, ECLI:NL:HR:2008:BB7087.

81 HR 31 October 2006, ECLI:NL:HR:2006:AX9178.

by the Supreme Court, thereby taking into account that 'the conduct was very dangerous, but the play was not demarcated by clear rules'.

As for piercing and tattooing, the law does not put restrictions on piercing or tattooing persons aged 16 years and above.[82] This is lawful, unless consent is lacking or these decorative practices are exercised contrary to prevailing professional standards.[83] Article 24 of the Commodities Act (Warenwet) and implementing regulation stipulate whether or not it is legitimate to pierce or tattoo minors below the age of 16 years. Article 24(1) sets forth that piercing earflaps is allowed.[84] For the rest, this provision restricts the right to self-determination with regard to this category of minors. The strictest approach is taken towards children below the age of 12: piercing (other than earflaps) or tattooing such a minor is prohibited, irrespective of consent (by proxy). A somewhat more relaxed approach is taken towards the category of minors from 12 to 16 years old: as a rule piercing or tattooing is regarded as lawful, provided that the minor is accompanied by his legal representatives – usually his parents – who must agree to the decorative practice concerned.[85] This general rule is limited by implementing regulation. It prohibits piercing or tattooing certain parts of the body, such as piercing genitals, or tattooing one's head.[86]

As for cases where consent is a relevant factor for lawfulness, the implementing regulation also safeguards that informed consent is obtained.[87] It does so, by placing a duty to inform upon the owner of a body piercing studio or tattoo parlour; prior to the decorative practice, written information about attendant risks must be given to the person being tattooed (and his legal representatives).

2.2.4 Specific sexual practices involving infliction of harm

Sexuality is considered to be primarily an individual responsibility. Nevertheless, Dutch criminal law sets certain limits for infringements on sexual integrity (sexual offences) and physical integrity (offences against the person). BDSM is a form of sexual activity that presupposes mutual consent between practitioners as to the physical constraints imposed.[88] BDSM as such is a (more or less) socially accepted phenomenon; consent to this form of sexual activity does not go against public morality.[89]

Yet BDSM practitioners do not have a *carte blanche* to do whatever they want. Although case-law on BDSM relating to offences against the person is scarce, the prevailing view in Dutch literature is that BDSM only provides a justification for minor infringements on physical integrity, like intentionally and unlawfully causing pain or minor bodily injury to another person (*mishandeling* under Article 300 DPC).[90] In such cases, the pain or injury imposed upon the victim is not unlawful as it is justified by given consent to this form of sexual activity. In contrast, if a specific BDSM practice creates a risk of serious bodily injury to another

---

82 See Kamerstukken II 2006, 30 173, no 14, 2.
83 See for case-law on lacking consent: HR 18 November 2014, ECLI:NL:HR:2014:3289.
84 Due to the minor's incompetence to perform legal acts, the minor's legal representative – normally his parents – must consent (Article 1:234 Civil Code). The legitimacy of piercing earflaps is probably rooted in the social acceptance of this decorative practice.
85 Article 24(2); see also Kamerstukken II 2006, 30 173, no 14, 2.
86 Article 10 Order in Council on Tattooing and Piercing (Warenwetbesluit tatoeëren en piercen).
87 Article 6 Ministerial Regulation on Tattooing and Piercing (Warenwetregeling tatoeëren en piercen).
88 See P Kruize and P Gruter, *Aan handen en voeten gebonden: Mis(ver)standen rond BDSM-scenes en de toereikendheid van zorg en recht* (Wetenschappelijk Onderozek-en Documentatiecentrum 2014), 9.
89 Machielse (n 4); Kelk/De Jong (n 10) 191; Kruize and Gruter (n 88) 117.
90 Machielse (n 4); Kruize and Gruter (n 88) 117.

person, the principle of self-determination is deemed to be outweighed by public interests that are at stake (like physical integrity of a human being and public morality). *A fortiori* the same is true when serious bodily injury or death actually occurs. For instance, quite recently the District Court of Limburg dealt with a case in which the victim was killed by the defendant during a consensual sex game.[91] The District Court found that, while the arms and legs of the late victim had been tied up and his mouth had been taped, the defendant had taken the victim's breath away by means of a rope. This eventually caused strangulation. The defendant was convicted for murder.

2.3 Sexual offences

2.3.1 Absence of consent or use of force/threats

In Dutch law, as a rule persons aged 16 years and above are regarded as capable of protecting their sexual integrity.[92] This means that sexual activity according to the free and independent will of such a person generally remains outside the scope of the sexual offences.[93] Therefore sexual crimes aim to protect 'the sexual integrity of persons who are, on a certain moment or in general, not capable to protect their sexual integrity'.[94]

Dutch sexual offences broadly speaking distinguish between two categories of crimes: coercion-based and non-coercion-based offences. Coercion-based sexual crimes penalise cases in which a victim has been compelled by the offender to undergo sexual acts. As for non-coercion based sexual crimes, criminal law takes a more patronising form: it is punishable to engage in sexual activity with vulnerable people incapable of preserving their sexual integrity, such as juveniles or (temporary) physically or mentally incapacitated persons (ranging from sleep to severe mental disabilities). Both the coercion-based and the non-coercion based offences cover two basic types of sexual acts. The first type is conduct comprising or including (non-penile) sexual penetration of the body; that is sexual intercourse and intrusions on sexual integrity of similar gravity.[95] If there are accompanying circumstances, these acts can give rise to the coercion-based offence 'rape' under Article 242 DPC or, in case of vulnerable people, non-coercion-based variants thereof under Articles 243–245 DPC. The second basic type encompasses 'indecent acts' not necessarily including penetration of the body. Whether certain conduct is in fact 'indecent', has to be judged from the prevailing 'social-ethical standards'.[96] Also this type of act is incorporated into both a coercion-based crime – sexual assault in Article 246 DPC – and non-coercion-based variants thereof (among others Article 247 DPC). Below the focus will be on the role of consent within the generic categories of coercion-based offences and respectively non-coercion-based offences.

Consent plays an important role within the scope of coercion-based sexual offences. As for coercion-based sexual offences, the Supreme Court defines 'coercion' as 'through a means of coercion intentionally causing the victim to undergo the sexual acts against his or her will'.[97] It is clear that consent negates coercion. Coercion requires more than non-consent of the

91 District Court Limburg 1 November 2014, ECLI:NL:RBLIM:2014:8406.
92 Note that there are various exceptions to this general rule, for instance in case of a minor below the age of 18 years who is in a position of dependence *vis a vis* the offender (Article 249 DPC).
93 Kamerstukken II 1988/89, 20 930, 5, 4–5.
94 ibid.
95 See HR 26 November 2013, ECLI:NL:HR:2013:1431.
96 Kamerstukken II 1988/89, 20 930, 5, 4–5.
97 See for example HR 16 October 2007, ECLI:NL:HR:2007:BA7650.

victim (involuntariness). It can be derived from case-law that 'coercion', applied to sexual intercourse, consists of the following elements:[98] it must have been reasonably inevitable for the victim to avoid engaging in sexual intercourse (relative inevitability),[99] the victim must have experienced his or her engaging in sexual intercourse as involuntary (victim's awareness of involuntariness), the offender's actions are the legal cause of the sexual intercourse (causality), the offender has used one of the four statutory means of coercion (use or threat of force and use or threat of non-violent acts,[100] not including deception), and, finally, the offender has conditional intent as to the aforementioned aspects of involuntariness, inevitability and the causal relation between his acts and the sexual intercourse (intent of the offender). This outline illustrates that non-consent to engage in sexual activity as such does not give rise to coercion. The same holds true for cases in which consent is revoked after the sexual intercourse was started consensually: more is needed than revocation of consent alone, for instance the continuation of sexual activity also needs to be relatively inevitable.[101] If consent is lacking but the inevitability test is not met – the victim did not resist, whereas resistance could reasonably be demanded in view of the means of coercion used by the offender – the offender might nevertheless be liable for a non-coercion based variant or the much less serious crime 'outraging public decency'.[102]

Non-coercion-based offences aim to protect a varied group of vulnerable persons, among others minors below the age of 16 years. These minors have a restricted right to sexual self-determination. This allows them to engage in sexual acts considered not of 'indecent' character, which has to be judged from the prevailing 'social-ethical standards' as mentioned before. Article 244 DPC makes clear that engaging in sexual intercourse with a child below the age of 12 is a criminal act, irrespective of the minor's consent and regardless of coercion. This kind of sexual activity is considered 'indecent' in and of itself. In other cases – such as sexual intercourse with a minor from 12–16 years old – it must be decided on a case-by-case basis whether or not the sexual activity has an 'indecent' character. In this regard, the Supreme Court has ruled that sexual acts might lack indecent character if there is both a 'small difference in age between the individuals', and, the sexual partners have 'voluntarily' engaged in those acts.[103] If a minor has not given prior consent to the sexual acts involved, these acts will indisputably be regarded as 'indecent'.[104]

The legal approach to victims of age who are (temporarily) incapable of preserving their sexual integrity – due to physical or mental incapacity – is similar to the aforementioned protection of minors below the age of 12. However, exceptionally consent might take away the unlawfulness of subsequent sexual activity. This follows from a judgment of the Supreme Court.[105] In this case the defendant was convicted by the Court of Appeal

---

98 Lindenberg (n 6) 132–190.

99 This will be the case if the victim resisted or, in absence of which, resistance could reasonably not be demanded in view of the means of coercion used by the offender. See HR 2 June 2009, ECLI:NL:HR: 2009:BH5725.

100 The latter is a broad category encompassing, among others, psychological pressure capable of compelling the victim and actually functioning as a means for coercion. See Lindenberg (n 6) 208–211; Machielse (n 4) 'art 242'.

101 See for instance: Court of Appeal The Hague 29 October 2007, ECLI:NL:GHDHA:2007:BB7107 (revocation of consent during sexual intercourse due to the nature of the intended acts).

102 Article 239 DPC; K Lindenberg, 'Zedendelicten en positieve verplichtingen' in J Gerards and C Sieburgh, *De invloed van fundamentele rechten op het materiële recht* (Kluwer 2013).

103 HR 30 March 2010, ECLI:NL:HR:2010:BK4794.

104 Lindenberg (n 102).

105 HR 15 June 1982, NJ 1983/153.

for having sexual intercourse with a woman who suffered from severe physical handicaps, whereas at the time of sexual activity the defendant knew that she was not able to resist due to her disability.[106] The defendant had claimed before the court that the woman had consented to sex, but the Court of Appeal had rejected this claim without further explanation. For this lack of explanation the conviction was quashed by the Supreme Court. It is derived from this decision that prior consent might justify engaging in sexual activity with a severely physically disabled person.[107] It is, however, far from clear in what circumstances consent provides a justification. For instance, it is debatable if a person of sound mind's prior consent to be engaged in sexual intercourse during sleep – sexual intercourse with an unconscious person is also protected by Article 243 DPC – provides justification for the following sexual conduct.[108]

2.3.2 Evidentiary presumptions

Statutory and case law on rape, sexual assault and variants thereof do not acknowledge irrebuttable presumptions. Two rather obvious rebuttable presumptions seem to exist within the framework of coercion-based offences.

Firstly, a judgment of the Supreme Court with respect to 'rape' shows an important rebuttable presumption regarding proof of intent as part of coercion: conditional intent as to the involuntary participation of the victim in sexual intercourse can generally be inferred from the use or threat of force as a means of coercion.[109] In the same judgment it is made clear that this presumption is rebuttable. The inference could, for instance, not be made in the underlying case. In that case the defendant had threatened to break the arm of his (former) girlfriend if she did not engage in sexual intercourse. However, the defendant and the victim had a relationship in which they alternately 'attracted and rejected each other', they had practised BDSM before and it was not entirely clear whether the relationship had already ended. Due to these exceptional circumstances, the Court of Appeal found that conditional intent as to involuntariness could not be proved. The acquittal for rape was upheld by the Supreme Court.

Furthermore, it seems to be accepted that non-consent of the victim can generally be inferred from resistance.[110] The mirror image – consent inferred from lacking resistance – does not provide an evidentiary presumption.[111]

2.3.3 Mistake of fact about consent

As mentioned above, the offender must have conditional intent as to the victim's non-consent. Mistake of fact thus negates intent. This is judged from the general standard for mistake of fact. In a general sense, there is little room for an intent-negating mistake, due to the wide scope of conditional intent.[112]

---

106   Article 243 DPC.
107   J de Hullu and JL van der Neut, *Zedelijkheidswetgeving in beweging* (Ars Aequi 1985), 100.
108   Rejected by Machielse (n 4) 'art 243', because such prior consent would go against public morality.
109   HR 16 June 1988, NJ 1988/156.
110   AG Knigge 31 May 2011, ECLI:NL:PHR:2011:BQ2491.
111   As this inference will (too) frequently be false, for example if non-resistance is motivated by avoiding bodily harm; ibid.
112   The judgment of the Supreme Court outlined in section 2.3.2 is an exceptional case.

2.4 Property offences and criminal damage

2.4.1 Place of consent in the offence structure

The unlawfulness of the act is an element of both theft (Article 310 DPC) and criminal damage (Article 350 DPC).[113] Theft requires, among other elements, 'unlawfully appropriating a good belonging wholly or partially to another person'. Criminal damage requires, among other elements, 'unlawfully damaging a good belonging wholly or partially to another person'. According to the prevailing view, for both crimes the element 'unlawfully' calls for proof of 'non-consent' of a person (partly) entitled to the good involved.[114] It follows that valid consent negates unlawfulness; in such a case the defendant will be acquitted accordingly.

2.4.2 Mistaken belief in consent

Theft requires wilful intent as to the unlawful character of the appropriation of a good. A mistaken belief in consent will accordingly negate wilful intent, resulting in an acquittal.

In cases of criminal damage, in contrast, the element of 'intent' is not related to the unlawful nature of damaging a good. Thus acting under mistaken belief in consent will take away neither intent nor the unlawfulness of that act (the entitled person has in fact not consented to the damage). In such cases the offence description will be fulfilled. As a result, the defendant will not be acquitted.[115] A mistaken belief can nevertheless lead to a discharge, provided that the mistaken belief is excusatory.[116]

---

113 Burglary (Article 311 DPC) and robbery (312 DPC) encompass theft.
114 See for instance Remmelink (n 2) 354.
115 See section 1.2.
116 See section 1.5.2.

19

New Zealand

Julia Tolmie

1 GENERAL ISSUES

1.1 Conceptual foundations

1.1.1 *Philosophical and theoretical principles informing the law surrounding consent*

Consent appears throughout the criminal law in New Zealand as a concept that demarcates criminal behaviour (assault, sexual violation and theft) from non-criminal behaviour (a hug, sex and a gift) in relation to particular violence and property offences. Consent is not defined in the legislation and whether it is present or absent largely tends to be treated as a factual issue for jury determination.

The theoretical principles that inform the law on consent in New Zealand are not particularly distinctive. The centrality of consent is founded in John Stuart Mill's notion of the sovereignty of the individual in matters that only impact on themselves.[1] Notions of autonomy and choice inform judicial definitions of consent – the need to ensure that a person is exercising free will and that they are sufficiently informed about what they are choosing for that choice to have cogency.[2] Thus, in *R v Annas*[3] the Court of Appeal said:

> To ensure the autonomy of the individual [consent] must be voluntary and deliberate. In order to be voluntary and deliberate it must not be coerced, that is, the decision to consent must be a function of the person's will, and not the will of some other person.[4]

The value of individual autonomy is balanced against public interest considerations that make certain activities of over-riding or minimal value. For example, a series of activities

---

1 'In the part which merely concerns himself, his independence is, of right, absolute. Over himself, over his own body and mind, the individual is sovereign': John Stuart Mills, *On Liberty* (Gateway Editions 1959).
2 In addition to being freely given, a valid consent requires a full understanding of the activity in question. *R v Adams* (NZCA, 5 September 2005): consent means 'a true, informed and voluntary decision which is given by a person who is in a position to make a rational decision about the sexual act in question.'
3 [2008] NZCA 534 (NZCA).
4 ibid [23].

are compulsory, regardless of the participant's non-consent.[5] Conversely, other activities are criminalised even when the complainant consents.[6]

1.1.2 Influence of feminist and queer theory

The influence of feminist theory can be seen in a number of practical reforms to sexual offences designed to avoid the use of sexist stereotypes by the jury to infer consent or the unreasonable assumption of consent by the defendant and the abolition of marital rape exemption. For example, s 44 of the Evidence Act 2006 provides that, in the absence of judicial permission, evidence cannot be given about the sexual experience of the complainant with anyone other than the defendant. It cannot be given about the sexual reputation of the complainant in any circumstances. In other words, evidence cannot be adduced to support an inference that the complainant must have consented because she consented (or had a reputation for consenting) to sexual activity with others. In relation to charges of sexual violation under s 128, as noted below, the defendant must have reasonable grounds for any honest belief in the complainant's consent.

The line between 'reluctant consent' and 'mere submission' (not consent) in relation to sexual violation has arguably shifted over recent years. A willingness to understand the female complainant as a legal subject with equal rights to self-determination may have informed that shift. Some of the older cases contain comments suggesting that appeal judges were happy with the concept of 'consent' given under a high degree of pressure, manipulation and dishonesty on the part of the defendant. For example, in *R v Cook*[7] the court was comfortable with 'a reluctant or even an unwilling consent or one produced by persuasion or by some fraudulent means or even by threats other than threats of bodily harm'.[8] These statements sit uncomfortably with the notion that consent must be a free and voluntary decision – that is, an expression of the complainant's will rather than that of the defendant.

One can contrast this with more recent decisions. For example, in *W v R*[9] the complainant had 'consented' to sex under a 'sustained and oppressive campaign' by the defendant directed at getting her to have sex with him. This included hundreds of demanding and threatening texts and blackmail (threats to share naked photos of the complainant with her family and employer). It was held that the defendant's actions made it inappropriate 'to describe what she did as a voluntary choice'. The court said that, although the complainant had other options (such as enduring the 'intensely humiliating experience' of having the photos disclosed), 'these were not options to be freely chosen by the complainant but options imposed on her by the appellant's criminal threats'.[10]

Queer theory has been significantly less influential in New Zealand (aside from the gender neutrality of sexual offences and abolition of the offence of sodomy). Sexual overtures by a man towards a woman are often considered to fall within the bounds of social tolerance even when they involve touching, so long as they are not persisted with if they meet with a negative

---

5 For example, compulsory assessment and treatment under the Mental Health (Compulsory Assessment and Treatment) Act 1992; compulsory examination and isolation in order to prevent the outbreak or spread of an infectious disease under the Health Act 1956; taking a bodily sample from a suspect for the purpose of criminal investigation into an indictable offence under the Criminal Investigation (Bodily Samples) Act 1995.

6 Below 1.1.6.

7 [1986] 2 NZLR 93 (NZCA).

8 ibid 97 [45]. See also *R v Herbert* (NZCA, 12 August 1998); *Adams* (n 2).

9 *W (CA190/12) v R* [2013] NZCA 316 (NZCA) [41].

10 ibid [43].

response.[11] However, it is arguable that these are more readily interpreted as indecent assaults or as raising legitimate fears of rape[12] when they come from a man towards another man.[13]

1.1.3 Definition of informed consent

Consent requires an understanding of the specific act that one is consenting to.[14] Traditionally in relation to sexual and non-sexual assaults only mistakes as to the nature of the act or the identity of the other person involved were considered sufficiently fundamental to vitiate the complainant's consent. Mirroring this, but less authoritative, is the suggestion that a fundamental mistake in relation to goods other than currency will vitiate an apparent consent to the passing of possession and/or title for the purposes of theft – that is, a mistake as to the identity of the transferee, or the identity or quantity of the thing delivered.[15] It follows that a failure to inform the complainant on these fundamental matters, if it results in a relevant mistake, will mean the complainant has not consented.

Sometimes an act is known by one party to be *riskier* than the other party realises. Still moot in New Zealand is whether the defendant is under an obligation in these circumstances to inform the other party of the risks. In *R v Lee (Yong Bum)*[16] Glazebrook J, speaking for the New Zealand Court of Appeal, said in *obiter* that:

> Normally, if the scope of the activity is understood by the person consenting, then the person will be assumed to have been consenting to any risks of that activity. Where, however, there is a known information imbalance about the risks involved between those giving and seeking consent it does not seem unreasonable to require the person seeking consent to correct that imbalance. This requirement may, however, be limited to cases where the risk is major because of the very serious consequences if it does eventuate (such as with unprotected sex and HIV).[17]

A contrary *obiter* opinion was expressed in *Barker v R*.[18] Hammond J said that 'the doctrine of informed consent as it [has] emerged in medical law is neither entirely straightforward, nor a pure articulation of what it is for consent to be authentic'. In his opinion the doctrine of informed consent raises significant doctrinal and practical difficulties that make

---

11 See, for example, *Peters v Police* (NZHC, 18 June 2007).
12 See, for example, *R v Ali* (NZHC, 21 July 2004).
13 See also *R v Sturm* [2005] 3 NZLR 252; (2005) 21 CRNZ 627 (NZCA) in which a man was charged with stupefying male complainants in order to facilitate the commission of sexual violations and other indecencies under, s 191. The male complainants were held to be not consenting to 'uncharacteristic' sexual activity after voluntarily taking disinhibiting drugs. They were conscious, had participated in the sexual activity and had returned on subsequent occasions to take drugs and participate in further sexual activity. It is possible to query whether charges would have been laid and the same factual conclusions reached if this was heterosexual activity. For example, in *Annas* (n 3) a teenager was sexually groomed by an older man whom she trusted and viewed as a confidant over an extended period of time. The court was not prepared to find that consent given in such circumstances was not a true consent.
14 In *R v Isherwood* (NZCA, 14 March 2005) [35], the Court of Appeal said that what will: 'always be essential for there to be a valid consent is that a complainant has understood her situation and was capable of making up her mind when she agreed to the sexual acts'.
15 *R v Illich* [1987] HCA 1 (HCA).
16 [2006] 3 NZLR 42; (2006) 22 CRNZ 568 (NZCA).
17 ibid [309].
18 [2010] 1 NZLR 235 (NZCA).

it inappropriate to introduce into the criminal law.[19] The consequences of breaching the criminal law are so onerous that people need to know clearly in advance what their legal obligations are so that they can comply with them.

While it is still moot as to whether informed consent is part of the criminal law, it exists in other areas of the law in New Zealand. The Code of Health and Disability Services Consumers' Rights provides those who are receiving a 'health service' with the right to be informed about the risks of any treatment options proposed by their health provider.[20]

1.1.4 Consent to risk or consent to outcome

Consent to an activity extends to harms that were intended or risked as a consequence of that activity.[21] It may not extend to harms that eventuated in fact, but were not foreseen or intended. However, accidental harms that do not result from criminal offending are unlikely to satisfy the requirements for a criminal offence.

As noted below, consent may be withdrawn as a defence to the infliction of grievous bodily harm that is intended or risked in some circumstances. However, consent to an activity is not withdrawn because it accidentally results in that level of bodily harm, even if this would have been foreseen by the reasonable person.[22] In *R v Lee* the Court of Appeal said that any other conclusion would mean that the defendant would lose the defence of consent because of harmful consequences that they neither intended nor knowingly risked.[23] Such an approach would be inconsistent with the fact that most serious offences of interpersonal violence require proof of subjective fault.

1.1.5 Revocation of consent

Whether a withdrawal of consent by the complainant results in a criminal offence depends on the nature of the activity that is being consented to. If the activity is a one-off event, and was validly consented to at the time that it occurred, then consent cannot be retrospectively revoked. On the other hand, if the activity is ongoing and consent is revoked at some point *during* that activity then, from that point in time, the *actus reus* and *mens rea* elements of the offence will be present. For example, a 'sexual connection', if not consented to by one of the parties involved, will amount to the offence of sexual violation.[24] Sexual connection is defined in s 2 of the Crimes Act 1961 (NZ) to include 'the continuation' of one of the forms of connection listed in the section.[25] It follows that if a person revokes their consent and their sexual partner is aware of that but continues with penetration or oral sex, then the offence of sexual violation occurs at that point.[26] Similarly a non-sexual assault can be on-going if it involves continual contact with the complainant's body.[27] Again, intentional continued contact once the defendant knows that the other person has revoked their consent is an assault. In relation to theft, possession can pass with the owner's consent. However, as long as ownership

---

19 See *R v Richardson (Diane)* [1999] QB 444 (UKCA), 450.
20 Right 7.
21 *Lee* (n 16) [312].
22 It is likely to be insufficient that the harm was simply intended or risked – it must also be caused: *R v Paice* [2005] 1 SCR 339; [2006] 3 WWR 38.
23 *Lee* (n 16).
24 Section 128, Crimes Act 1961 (NZ).
25 This is a codification of the common law: *R v Kaitamaki* [1980] 1 NZLR 59 (NZCA).
26 *R v Everson* (NZCA, 9 November 1995).
27 *Fagan v MPC* [1969] 1 QB 439; [1968] 3 All ER 442.

does not pass with possession and the owner is entitled to withdraw their consent to the use of their property, continued use once consent has been revoked, if it risks a change in the condition of the property, can amount to a theft.[28]

1.1.6 Ownership and limits of consent

In relation to the interpersonal violence offences, there is a point at which the level of physical harm that is inflicted on the victim is so severe, in the course of an activity that has so little social utility, that the defence of consent is withdrawn for public policy reasons. In other words, there are levels of harm in the course of particular activities that are criminalised even when they are consented to. In drawing this line New Zealand takes a strong stand in favour of personal autonomy and choice.

In *R v Lee*[29] the New Zealand Court of Appeal set out three tiers of harm – each attracting a different approach to the issue of whether the defence of consent is available on the facts.[30] At the first level, where the defendant intends or is reckless as to **actual bodily harm**, the consent of the victim is generally a defence. There are limited exceptions to this rule for certain categories of activities (described in *Barker*[31] as '*per se*' or 'across the board' exceptions). Presently only one activity falls within this exception. Once actual bodily harm is intended or risked, consent is not a defence to fighting (other than sparring matches or play fights and organised matches conducted with a referee according to established rules).[32]

At the second level, where **grievous bodily harm** is intended or risked, public policy factors might require the judge to withdraw the defence of consent from the jury.[33] Here, however, consent is not withdrawn on the basis of a *generic category of activity* but is withdrawn on the *individual facts of the case*, weighed in the context of *a number of competing values* – with an emphasis on the value of personal autonomy and thus a presumption in favour of consent being available as a defence.[34] In *R v Lee*[35] Justice Glazebrook said:

> the judge should take into account the right to personal autonomy, the social utility (or otherwise) of the activity, the level of seriousness of the injury intended or risked, the level of risk of such injury, the rationality of any consent or belief in consent and any other relevant factors in the particular case.[36]

If grievous bodily harm is intended, as opposed to risked, 'it will be rare for a court to accept that consent is available as a defence'.[37] The notion of social utility, like many of the other values employed in this analysis, is difficult to define. All consensual activities by definition must have

---

28 Section 219(1)(b), Crimes Act 1961 (NZ).
29 *Lee* (n 16).
30 The issue was whether consent was available as a defence to an assault that resulted in an accidental death in the course of an exorcism. The appellant was charged with manslaughter for causing death by an unlawful act, namely an assault: s 160(2)(a), Crimes Act 1961 (NZ).
31 *Barker* (n 18) 246.
32 Glazebrook J in *Lee* (n 16) [296], commented that, 'There may be other exceptions but these would be rare and Judges should be very wary of creating exceptions based on their own personal views of acceptable behaviour.'
33 It is not clear whether this is a bright line or a continuum. See *Ah Chong v R* [2016] 1 NZLR 445, [50].
34 Julia Tolmie, 'Consent to Harmful Assaults: The Case for Moving Away from Category Based Decision Making' (2012) 9 The Criminal Law Review 656.
35 *Lee* (n 16).
36 ibid [316]. See also O'Regan J in *Barker* (n 18) [136].
37 *Ah-Chong* (n33) [50].

some utility to a person who is genuinely consenting to them – even if the desires being gratified are not explicable to others. While some activities (like surgery) are easy to justify as having a widely agreed upon benefit to society – others (like boxing) are difficult to justify on any basis other than the fact that the majority tolerates them. The approach to social utility employed in *Lee* could be characterised as a 'human rights approach'.[38] Under this approach, even if it is not supported by a majority consensus, if an activity can be seen as the individual expression of a fundamental human right then it performs a useful social function. For example, in *Lee* the New Zealand Court of Appeal held that conducting ritual exorcisms is the manifestation of religious belief and therefore protected under s 15 of the Bill of Rights Act 1990 (NZ).[39]

At the third level, where **death** is intended by the defendant, then no defence of victim consent is available and there are no exceptions to this rule.[40]

In relation to property offences one of the significant limitations on the right of the owner to consent to the alienation of their property are any property interests others might have in that property. An owner is defined broadly in s 218(1) of the Crimes Act 1961 (NZ) to include a person who has possession or control of, any interest in, or the right to take possession or control of, the property. Section 218(2) makes it clear that an owner can commit theft against another owner. It follows that an owner who agrees to extinguish another person's property interest in their property, knowing that they do not have the right or authority to do so, can be guilty of theft under s 219(1)(b) notwithstanding that they own the property. Furthermore, a person in possession or control of the property can consent to someone else taking that property and the taking will not constitute theft, notwithstanding that the legal owner has not consented.[41]

1.2 Place of consent in the offence structure

In respect of those sexual and property offences where consent is significant, non-consent is set out in the legislation as an *actus reus* requirement.[42] This attracts a parallel *mens rea* requirement – an honest[43] or a reasonable[44] belief in consent by the defendant will mean that they lack the required *mens rea* for the relevant offence.

In contrast, the non-consent of the victim is not set out in the legislation as an *actus reus* element in relation to the non-sexual interpersonal violence offences.[45] However, the Court of Appeal in *Lee*[46] made it clear that victim consent is a common law defence that is preserved by s 20(1) of the Crimes Act 1961 (NZ) in relation to these offences.[47] One consequence that follows from consent being a defence, rather than an element of the offence, is that the defendant has the evidential burden of putting the victim's consent in issue before the Crown has

---

38 ibid [316].
39 ibid.
40 Section 63, Crimes Act 1961 (NZ).
41 ibid, ss 218(1)(a), 219(1). Although note that a subsequent dealing by the person who has taken possession with consent may amount to a theft under, s 219(1)(b) depending on their satisfaction of the *mens rea* requirements for theft.
42 For example, in relation to sexual violation, see ibid, s 128(2)(a), (3)(a). In relation to theft, see, s 219(1), (3).
43 ibid, ss 217, 219.
44 ibid, s 128.
45 For example, the definition of 'assault', in ibid, s 2, is silent on the issue of consent. It simply defines assault as the application of force to another's person (or the attempted or threatened application).
46 *Lee* (n 16).
47 This was confirmed in *Barker* (n 18). See also Fisher J in *Police v Bannin* [1991] 2 NZLR 237 (NZHC), 244.

the persuasive burden of disproving consent.[48] Technically it should also follow that *mens rea* on the part of the defendant may not be necessary – the mere fact that the complainant did not consent may mean that the defence is unavailable. However, as we shall see below, the courts have held that an honest belief by the defendant that the complainant is consenting is sufficient to raise the defence. The different approach taken in relation to non-sexual assaults appears to be the result of clumsy legislative drafting rather than any underlying difference in principle.

1.3 Form of consent

1.3.1 Declared or implied

The criminal law does not require any particular form of consent to bodily contact or the transfer of possession or ownership of property. Consent can be expressly communicated by words (oral or written) or conduct, or it can be implied. Issues of implied consent arise when a person voluntarily participates in activities – like contact sports – that necessarily risk the application of physical force to their person.

Where the victim has given implied consent by participating in an activity where physical contact will be part of the experience, the court must objectively determine the parameters of the consent. In *Lee*[49] the New Zealand Court of Appeal endorsed comments by the Saskatchewan Court of Appeal in *R v Cey*[50] to the effect that:

Ordinarily consent, being a state of mind, is a wholly subjective matter to be determined accordingly, but when it comes to implied consent in the context of a team sport, such as hockey, there cannot be as many different consents as there are players on the ice, and so the scope of implied consent, having to be uniform, must be determined by reference to objective criteria.[51]

The criminal law runs parallel to other bodies of law that do require particular forms of consent in respect of particular activities or the alienation of particular types of property. For example, the Code of Health and Disability Services Consumers' Rights creates an obligation to ensure that consent to a health care procedure is in writing if:

(a) The consumer is to participate in any research; or (b) The procedure is experimental; or (c) The consumer will be under general anaesthetic; or (d) There is a significant risk of adverse effects on the consumer.[52]

1.3.2 Presumed consent

New Zealand does not have a defence of 'presumed consent'. If it is necessary to do something to someone that is an offence without their consent (or without the permission of someone entitled to consent on their behalf) the defence of necessity must be invoked.[53] Section 61

---

48   Fisher J in *Bannin* ibid 245.
49   *Lee* (n 16).
50   (1989) 48 CCC (3d) 480.
51   ibid [28].
52   Right 7(6).
53   See Julia Tolmie, 'New Zealand' in Alan Reed and Michael Bohlander (eds), *General Defences in Criminal Law: Domestic and Comparative Perspectives* (Ashgate 2014) 281.

of the Crimes Act 1961 (NZ) provides a necessity defence specific to surgical operations performed with reasonable care and skill 'upon any person for his benefit, if the performance of the operation was reasonable, having regard to the patient's state at the time and to all the circumstances of the case'.[54]

1.4 Capacity to consent

The law determining who is entitled to make decisions on behalf of someone who may not be competent to make decisions on their own behalf is complex and located in multiple places. For example, s 16(2)(b) of the Care of Children Act 2004 (NZ) provides that legal guardians may determine for a child, or help a child to determine, whether they should undertake non-routine medical treatment. Once a child is 16 their consent to the donation of blood or any medical, surgical or dental treatment has effect as though they are adult.[55] Below the age of 16, however, children are not automatically disqualified from consenting. It becomes a matter of professional judgement as to whether the child is competent to make an informed decision or whether it is 'necessary or sufficient' to seek the informed consent of their guardian.[56] Under the Protection of Personal Property Rights Act 1988 (NZ) if a person is not able to make decisions for themselves the Family Court can appoint a welfare guardian to make such decisions. Alternatively, a person who anticipates a decline or loss of competence can provide someone else with a power of attorney to make decisions on their behalf.

At common law it is not possible to argue consent to activity if the victim was *incapable* of consenting because of their level of intoxication, youth or mental deficiency. Section 128A of the Crimes Act 1961 (NZ) has codified incapacity as a result of intoxication[57] or an intellectual, mental or physical condition or impairment in relation to the sexual offences.[58] Whilst youth is not mentioned as a source of incapacity in s 128A, it remains a source of incapacity at common law.[59] In addition, there are a raft of sex offences specific to children and young people where the consent (or non-consent) of the child or young person is irrelevant to criminal liability.[60]

Whether the complainant has been affected by alcohol or by an intellectual, mental or physical condition or youth to the point that they are not capable of consent requires a factual and normative judgement. It has been said that the complainant must be conscious of their circumstances, including what they are agreeing to,[61] and able to make a meaningful

---

54 Consent is not required in order to raise such a defence. In contrast consent is required under, s 61A, Crimes Act 1961 (NZ). In the medical context, if there is no person entitled to provide consent on behalf of a patient, a health provider is authorised under Right 7(4) of the Code of Health and Disability Services Consumers Rights to proceed with a medical treatment if it is in the 'best interests' of the patient, reasonable steps have been taken to ascertain the patient's views, and it has been concluded that 'the provision of the services is consistent with the informed choice' the patient would have made if they were competent or the 'views of other suitable persons who are interested in the welfare' of the patient have been taken into account.

55 Section 36(1), Care of Children Act 2004 (NZ).

56 ibid, s 36(3).

57 Section 128A (4), Crimes Act 1961 (NZ).

58 ibid, s 128A (5).

59 *Police v R* [2007] DCR 855 (NZDC).

60 Sections 132–134, Crimes Act 1961 (NZ).

61 *R v Foss* (1995) 14 CRNZ 1 (NZCA).

and rational choice as to consent.[62] In *Howard* it was said that there are three ways in which a vulnerable victim might not be able to consent.[63] These are where they:

- do not comprehend that the act was proposed or about to happen;
- have no understanding of the character of the proposed act (for example, that it is sexual); or
- are not able to appreciate that they can consent or refuse.[64]

The *Queen v Cox* held that the complainant must 'understand the significance of the act'.[65] 'Significance' implies more than the character of the act and extends to the weight or meaning of the act. For example, the weight and meaning of a sexual touching as opposed to the weight and meaning of a hug.

Traditionally the relevant time to examine the complainant's state of mind for the purposes of determining whether they were capable of consenting is the time of the alleged offending.[66] In *R v Sturm*[67] the court departed from this understanding in relation to incapacity as a result of intoxication, commenting that *how* the complainant came to take the intoxicating substance is relevant to whether or not they consented at the time of the sexual act, particularly where the intoxicating substances that they took are known to have a disinhibiting effect.[68] In *Sturm*[69] the court appeared to be influenced by the exploitative use of disinhibiting drugs by the accused, even in the 'more complex' circumstances where the complainant 'comes back and has voluntarily ingested drugs or alcohol knowing the likely effects and outcomes in terms of disinhibition and sexual behaviour'.[70] It rejected the traditional focus on the time of the sexual act as being no longer appropriate:

> with the advent and common availability of drugs which may induce uncharacteristic dis-inhibition in relation to sexual advances. In such cases an apparent consent may not be a true consent in that once the drug has taken effect on the mind of the person, the ability to form an informed and voluntary consent will have been impaired to a greater or lesser degree. On the other hand, drugs may have been voluntarily taken with awareness of, and acceptance of, the likelihood of disinhibited and otherwise uncharacteristic behaviour.[71]

A worrying aspect of this approach is that it invites scrutiny of the complainant's behaviour at a prior point in time. For example, a complainant's prior decision to become excessively intoxicated might be considered relevant to the issue of whether she consented to sexual activity whilst intoxicated. Commentators have argued that it is already extremely difficult to successfully prosecute defendants who take advantage of very intoxicated women.[72]

---

62 In *R v Isherwood* (NZCA, 14 March 2005).
63 [1965] 3 All ER 684.
64 See also *Moblilio* [1991] 1 VR 339, 351; (1990) 50 A Crim R 170, 182.
65 (NZCA, 7 November 1996), 8.
66 *Adams*, (n 2).
67 *Sturm* (n 13).
68 Building on *R v Isherwood* (NZCA, 14 March 2005).
69 [2005] 3 NZLR 252; (2005) 21 CRNZ 627.
70 ibid [45].
71 ibid [46].
72 See Jan Jordan, *The Word of a Woman? Police, Rape and Belief* (Palgrave MacMillan 2004), 84, 97–98, 114–118.

1.5 Consequences of mistaken consent

1.5.1 *Mistake*

At common law two types of mistakes by the complainant were considered to vitiate apparent consent that was given to physical contact, including sexual intercourse:[73] a mistake as to the identity of the other person or a mistake as to the nature of the act itself.[74] Section 128A(6)–(7) of the Crimes Act 1961 (NZ) codifies and extends the common law position in relation to the sexual offences, providing that a person does not consent to sexual activity if he or she allows it because he or she is mistaken about its nature or quality[75] or who the other person is.[76]

Historically a mistake as to identity was limited to mistakes where the victim thought they were interacting with a particular person but, in fact, it was another person.[77] Mistakes as to a person's status in the victim's life (for example a mistaken belief that they were married to the other person)[78] or their professional qualifications did not go to identity.[79]

Similarly a mistake as to the nature of the act was restrictively interpreted. This traditionally meant a mistake concerning the essential act itself – not encompassing the *risks* attached to the act.[80] Adding mistakes as to the 'quality of the act' to the list of mistakes that will vitiate consent to sexual contact has potentially broadened the types of mistakes that might qualify under this head. A number of cases successfully argued under this head involve situations where the complainant did understand the physical act they were agreeing to but was operating under the erroneous belief that they were undergoing a medical procedure[81] or a form of alternative healing[82] when, in fact, the defendant was sexually motivated. Whether mistakes as to the *risks* of an activity will result in a mistake as to the nature or quality of that *activity* when the risk is of sufficiently serious harm, or whether such a mistake will simply result in lack of consent to the *harm* (or exposure to the *risk of harm*), is still a moot question in New Zealand.[83]

1.5.2 *Deception*

The focus in New Zealand in relation to the interpersonal violence offences is on whether a relevant mistake was made by the complainant, rather than on whether the defendant played any role in inducing that mistake.[84] In most instances, however, the complainant will have made a mistake as to the nature and quality of the act or the identity of the other person

---

73 There has been a suggestion that a fundamental mistake in relation to the theft of goods other than currency will similarly vitiate an apparent consent – that is, a mistake as to the identity of the transferee, the identity or quantity of the thing being delivered: *Illich* (n 15). It is not clear if this is authoritative in New Zealand.

74 Such mistakes have to be honestly made by the victim – they do not have to be reasonable: *R v Murphy (No 2)* [1996] DCR 1002 (NZDC).

75 Section 128A (7), Crimes Act 1961 (NZ).

76 ibid, s 128A(6).

77 *Murphy (No 2)* (n 72).

78 *R v Papadimitropoulous* (1958) 98 CLR 249.

79 *R v Richardson (Diane)* [1999] QB 444 (UKCA).

80 *R v Clarence* (1888) 22 QBD 23.

81 *R v Ibrahim* (NZCA, 17 December 1998).

82 *R v Moffitt* (NZCA, 22 November 1993).

83 Below, 2.2.1.

84 See also *Richardson (Diane)* (n 79) 450.

because of the non-disclosure by the defendant of material facts or fraudulent assertions or misleading behaviour on their part. Whilst it may not matter *how* the complainant came about making the mistake it is important to demonstrate that the accused *knew* that the complainant was labouring under a relevant mistake when they consented. Otherwise there is no basis for finding that the defendant did not have an honest belief in their consent (including reasonable grounds for such a belief where these are required under s 128 of the Crimes Act 1961 (NZ)).

Many of the complex issues thrown up by deceptions practiced through the internet and recently developed forms of media have yet to be raised in the New Zealand context. Consistent with the fact that sexual offending involving underage victims does not require consent on the part of the victim are the grooming offences directed at underage victims – these are not dependent on establishing either deception by the defendant or a mistake on the part of the victim. Section 131B criminalises meeting or communicating with a person under the age of 16 and then later meeting them, travelling to meet them or persuading them to travel to meet, with the intention of committing a sexual offence against them.

In relation to property offences the position is somewhat different. Deception by the defendant, rather than the nature of the complainant's mistake, is central to a range of offences designed to fill gaps in the law on theft. Although certain fundamental mistakes may vitiate the passing of possession or title in relation to property other than currency,[85] in most instances a deception on the part of the defendant will not vitiate such consent for the purposes of theft.[86] However, s 240 of the Crimes Act 1961 (NZ) creates the offence of obtaining by deception or causing loss by deception. A deception is a knowing or recklessly false representation in a material particular, the breach of a duty to disclose a material particular with intent to deceive, or a fraudulent device, trick or stratagem used with intent to deceive.[87] Although it must be established that the false representation played a causal role in inducing the victim's consent to a property transaction it is not necessary to prove that they made any particular type of mistake.[88] In addition, there are a range of other offences criminalising certain types of deceptive transactions or deceptive behaviour by those in particular positions of responsibility.[89]

1.6 Mistake about consent

Mistakes by the defendant about the complainant's consent are analysed as a *mens rea* issue. Only in relation to the most serious offence of sexual violation under s 128 of the Crimes Act 1961 (NZ) does the defendant's mistake need to be reasonable. Here the requirement is that the defendant has 'reasonable grounds' for their belief that the complainant was consenting. The courts have held that this does not mean that the defendant had objective grounds for their subjective belief in consent. It means that 'a reasonable person in the shoes of the

---

85 *Illich* (n 15).
86 Section 219(3) expressly provides that a taking (theft dependent on the passing of possession:, s 219(1)(a)) 'does not include obtaining ownership or possession of, or control over, any property with the consent of the person from whom it is obtained, whether or not consent is obtained by deception'.
87 Section 240(2), Crimes Act 1961 (NZ).
88 *R v Bennitt* [1961] NZLR 452 (NZCA).
89 False statement by promoter (s 242); forgery (s 256); altering, concealing, destroying or reproducing documents with intent to deceive (s 258); using altered or reproduced document with intent to deceive (s 259); false accounting (s 260); counterfeiting public seals (s 261); counterfeiting corporate seals (s 262); possessing forged bank notes (s 263).

defendant' might have thought that the complainant was consenting.[90] As a result, the defendant's intoxication[91] and intellectual disability[92] are irrelevant to the issue of whether they had reasonable grounds for believing in consent.[93]

The defendant's belief in consent need only be honest in order to raise the defence of consent in relation to non-sexual offences.[94]

In relation to theft, an honest belief that there was consent from a person entitled to give such consent is also sufficient to avoid liability.[95]

2 SPECIFIC ISSUES

2.1 Consent and homicide offences

2.1.1 Mercy killings

It is murder to take action that accelerates a person's death – even if that person is terminally ill, in unbearable suffering and wishes to die – with either the intention of accelerating death or the knowledge that this is likely.[96] Assisting a person to kill themselves falls within the offence of assisting suicide.[97] There are two exceptions – the 'principle of double effect' and permissible omissions – both effectively confined to doctors.

The 'principle of double effect' holds that if a doctor's[98] primary purpose in administering treatment is pain relief for a terminally ill patient, and what is done is only what is 'reasonable and proper for that purpose', then the acceleration of death is a permissible side effect.[99]

Doctors are also permitted to deliberately accelerate a patient's death in certain circumstances by doing nothing, as opposed to acting. For example, they can withdraw life support from a patient when they have no duty to provide that support under s 151 (which requires a person who has a vulnerable adult in their care and charge to provide that person with 'necessaries'). In *Auckland Area Health Board v Attorney General*[100] Justice Thomas held that if life support is required to prevent, cure or alleviate a disease that endangers the life of a patient it might be a necessary. However if the patient is permanently insensate and unconscious with no chance of recovery then life support is not a necessary. He went on to hold that if there is no medical justification for continuing life support then this is a lawful excuse under s 160(2)(b) for withdrawal.

---

90 *Taniwha v R* [2010] NZSC 50 (NZSC); *R v Mustafa Can* [2007] NZCA 291 (NZCA); *R v Gutuama* (NZCA, 13 December 2001).

91 *R v Clarke* [1992] 1 NZLR 147 (NZCA).

92 *R v P* (1993) 10 CRNZ 250 (NZCA).

93 There is conflicting *obiter* on whether age can be a relevant consideration: *R v Mustafa Can* [2007] NZCA 291 (NZCA); *Police v R* (n 59).

94 *Lee* (n 16). See also *Solanki Devanand v R* (NZCA, 6 Sept 2005) [30]; *R v Nazif* [1987] 2 NZLR 11 (NZCA), 128; *Police v Bannin* (n 45) 244–245; *La Roche v New Zealand Police* (NZHC 5 July 2006), cf *Barker* (n 18).

95 Sections 217, 218, Crimes Act 1961 (NZ).

96 ibid, ss 160, 167.

97 ibid, s 179.

98 In *R v Martin* [2004] 3 NZLR 69 (NZHC) the court confined the defence of 'double effect' to doctors as they alone are qualified to prescribe the appropriate dose of pain relief.

99 *R v Seales* [2015] NZHC 1239 (NZHC), [106].

100 [1993] 1 NZLR 235 (NZCA).

In *R v Seales*[101] there was an unsuccessful challenge under ss 8[102] and 9[103] of the Bill of Rights Act 1990 (NZ) to the laws on homicide and assisted suicide in cases where a person wants to die, has a terminal illness and is in intolerable suffering. Relying on the interpretation given to similar provisions in the Canadian Charter of Rights and Freedoms, Lucreatia Seales argued that the criminal law forces a terminally ill person to take their life prematurely for fear of being incapable of doing so when the suffering gets too bad, denies people the right to liberty (to make decisions concerning their bodily integrity and medical care) and the right to security of person (leaving them to endure intolerable suffering).[104] The court rejected this interpretation of the relevant provisions, holding that medically assisted euthanasia would require legislative reform.

2.1.2 Killing on request of the victim

Section 63 of the Crimes Act 1961 (NZ) provides that a person cannot consent to 'the infliction of death upon himself'; and, if any person is killed, the fact that he gave such consent shall not affect the criminal responsibility of any person who is party to the killing'. However, s 63 only applies when death is intentionally inflicted.[105] This would mean that a person can consent to activities where either death is risked or serious harm is risked and death results (so long as the defence of consent is not withdrawn on public policy grounds as set out in *Lee*).[106] If the activity that results in death is not unlawful because the defence of consent is available, then it will not be an 'unlawful act' for the purposes of culpable homicide under s 160(2)(a) and cannot amount to murder or manslaughter. A non-culpable homicide is not a criminal offence.[107]

2.1.3 Abortion

Section 182(1) of the Crimes Act 1961 (NZ) creates the offence of 'killing an unborn child'. This criminalises causing 'the death of any child that has not become a human being in such a manner that [the defendant] would have been guilty of murder if the child had become a human being'. Section 183 creates the offence of 'procuring an abortion by any means'. An abortion is the 'destruction or death of an embryo or fetus after implantation'. It is not clear when a foetus becomes an unborn child. All we can say, based on the current case law, is that this occurs after the first trimester of pregnancy[108] and before 26 weeks' gestation.[109]

---

101   *Seales* (n 99).
102   Section 8 of the Bill of Rights Act 1990 (NZ) sets out the right not to be deprived of life except on such grounds as are established by law and are consistent with the principles of fundamental justice.
103   Section 9 of the Bill of Rights Act 1990 (NZ) sets out the right not to be subjected to torture or to cruel, degrading, or disproportionately severe treatment or punishment.
104   *Carter v Canada* [2015] SCC 5 (SCC).
105   *Lee* (n 16) [312]; *Seales* (n 99) [93].
106   ibid.
107   Section 160(4), Crimes Act 1961 (NZ).
108   *Woolnough* [1977] 2 NZLR 508 (NZCA).
109   *R v Henderson* [1990] 3 NZLR 174 (NZCA). This transition might occur at the point of viability (around 20 weeks' gestation).

The morning-after pill is not covered by either offence. The pill is available over the counter at pharmacies and correctly taken within three days of intercourse. Given, that the average time for implantation after conception is seven to ten days, the morning-after pill is not an abortion and nor does it involve the killing of an unborn child.

The consent of the pregnant woman is not a defence to the offences in ss 182 and 183; however there are necessity defences specific to those offences directed at preserving her life and/or health. For example, s 187A provides that for pregnancies of not more than 20 weeks gestation, a defence to s 183 is available if the 'continuance of the pregnancy would result in serious danger (not being danger normally attendant upon childbirth) to the life, or to the physical or mental health, of the woman or girl'.[110]

Whilst abortion is only available in the limited circumstances of necessity set out in the legislation, in practice it is available on demand in New Zealand prior to 20 weeks gestation so long as the procedures set out in the Contraception, Sterilisation and Abortion Act 1977 are followed.[111]

Section 38 of the Care of Children Act 2004 (NZ) provides that a female child of *any* age can agree to or refuse a termination of pregnancy and her decision will 'have the same effect as if she were of full age'. Parental consent is not required.

2.2 Consent and non-fatal offences against the person

2.2.1 HIV and other communicable disease transmission

Despite the doubts expressed by Justice Hammond in *Barker*, there are several New Zealand cases suggesting that consent to the *risk of HIV infection* during unprotected intercourse needs to be informed.[112] In *R v Mwai*[113] a man who infected several women by having unprotected consensual sex with them without disclosing his HIV status was convicted under s 188(2) of causing grievous bodily harm with reckless regard for another's safety. He was also convicted under s 145 of criminal nuisance, on the basis that he omitted to discharge a legal duty knowing that his failure would endanger the life, safety or health of an individual. Under s 156 there is a duty on persons in charge of dangerous things (seminal fluid infected with the HIV virus) to use reasonable care. Both offences criminalise the transmission, or exposure to the risk of transmission, of the HIV virus, rather than the sex act itself. Consent cannot be argued as a defence to these provisions unless the complainant was informed of the risk or it was reduced (for example, by the use of a condom). In *Lee*, Glazebrook J confined the informed consent requirement to those cases where the risk is 'major because of the very serious consequences if it does eventuate'.[114] Given that the use of a condom does not remove the risk of serious consequences, but does reduce the likelihood of those consequences occurring, the remoteness of the risk must also be a matter that goes to a consideration of whether it is 'major'.

In *KSB v ACC* the defendant, who had consensual unprotected intercourse, was convicted of criminal nuisance under s 145 on the basis that he had exposed his sexual partner to the

---

110 Section 187(1)(a), Crimes Act 1961 (NZ). In the case of a pregnancy of *more* than 20 weeks gestation, the standard is higher: s 187A(3).

111 See *Bayer v Police* [1994] 2 NZLR 48 (NZCA), 52; *Right to Life NZ Inc v The Abortion Supervisory Committee* [2012] NZSC 68 (NZSC), [25].

112 *Barker* (n 18).

113 [1995] 3 NZLR 149.

114 *Lee* (n 16).

risk of HIV infection without disclosing that risk and obtaining her consent.[115] She had not contracted HIV but had developed post-traumatic stress disorder as a result of her exposure to the virus. Cover for mental injury under the Accident Compensation Act 2001 (NZ) is only available where the claimant has been the victim of a serious offence – it is not available for victimisation under s 145 but is available for sexual violation under s 128. The Court of Appeal held that she had experienced sexual violation because deception as to HIV status (given the associated risk of serious harm) goes to the very nature of the sexual act. There-fore she had made a fundamental mistake that vitiated her consent to sex. Cover under the Accident Compensation Act 2001 is available for sexual violation even when there can be no criminal conviction – for example, because the defendant lacked *mens rea*, but where to the complainant it was a non-consensual act with all of the corresponding harms. This is because the Act is focused on victim recovery rather than the moral wrongdoing of the defendant. It follows that the decision in *KSB v ACC* was made in the civil context and the court did not express an opinion on whether the same conclusion should be reached in the criminal context.[116]

2.2.2 Medical treatment

By analogy with *Mwai*[117] and *Lee*, a failure to inform a patient that particular medical treat-ment carries a 'major' risk could result in criminal charges in respect of any harm that even-tuated. However, this issue has yet to arise in the criminal law.[118] As noted above, there is an obligation to inform patients of the risks involved in medical treatment under the Code of Health and Disability Services Consumers' Rights.[119]

A medical procedure that involves the intentional or reckless infliction of grievous bodily harm is vulnerable to having the defence of consent withdrawn on the facts (although the presumption in favour of allowing the defence, in relation to reckless harm, would need to be overturned).[120] This might occur in respect of a procedure that carried a high risk of seri-ous harm, had minimal social utility and involved a vulnerable victim: for example, cosmetic surgery carrying a high risk of disfigurement in respect of an underage victim.

2.2.3 Sport injuries, 'horseplay', piercing

As noted above, if grievous bodily harm is risked or intended in the course of an activity the defence of consent is vulnerable to being withdrawn on the facts (although the presumption in favour of allowing the defence, in relation to reckless harm, would need to be overturned).[121]

Whilst violence that exceeds the limits of implied consent regularly occurs in contact sports, criminal prosecutions in New Zealand are generally not laid.[122] Instead, discipline is left to the governing sporting body and the disciplinary systems of the various codes of

---

115 [2012] NZCA 82 (NZCA).
116 ibid.
117 *Mwai* (n 113).
118 *Lee* (n 16).
119 Right 7.
120 *Lee* (n 16). Above 1.4.
121 ibid. Above 1.4.
122 Paul Farrugia, 'The Consent Defence: Sports Violence, Sadomasochism, and the Criminal Law' (1996–1999) 8 Auckland University Law Review 472, 484; Jayne Francis, 'What is barbaric behavior?' (1997) Criminal Law Journal 121; David Gendall, 'New Developments: Increasing scope for lawyers in the sports arena' (July 1997) LawTalk 4, 5–6.

sport.[123] It is possible to debate whether this is the right approach to take. For example, it gives those with athletic prowess immunity from prosecution in respect of behaviour that in another context would attract criminal consequences. It also arguably sets a bad example – by modelling that violence will not attract criminal consequences. On the other hand criminal prosecution is a clumsy form of social regulation that has harmful consequences and, if other systems of social regulation are effective, then arguably it is preferable to use them.

2.2.4 Specific sexual practices involving infliction of harm

Only if sexual activities involving SM, bondage or branding intend or risk grievous bodily harm is the consent of the complainant potentially unavailable as a defence to criminal charges. For this to occur, the strong value given to personal autonomy, at least in cases of reckless harm, would have to be outweighed on the facts by factors such as the particular activity in the circumstances having negligible social utility, risking a high level and degree of harm and/or involving a vulnerable party.[124]

In *Barker*[125] Justice Glazebrook, in dissent, proposed a generic category of activity in respect of which the defence of consent is automatically withdrawn once actual bodily harm is intended or risked: 'By analogy with the Crimes Act provisions on sexual conduct with those under 16 … scarification when done in a sexual context (but not otherwise) on a child who is under 16'.[126] The majority disagreed. Justice O'Regan said that the 'generic exceptions' were not intended to apply to situations 'as specific as that envisioned by Glazebrook', a point somewhat contradicted by the fact that fighting has always been fractured into subsets of lawful and unlawful fighting – depending on whether it takes place according to rules and in the presence of a referee or for motivations that are likely to minimise the risk of harm to participants or without these features.[127]

2.3 Sexual offences

2.3.1 Absence of consent or use of force/threats

The offences of sexual violation[128] and indecent assault criminalise sexual behaviour that is performed without consent.[129] There is no requirement that consent be affirmatively expressed if it is to be taken as present.[130] A positive definition of consent would require the defence to point to something that represented a clear communication of agreement by the complainant. It would not be enough (as it currently is) that the complainant had done or said nothing to indicate that they did *not* consent.

Section 128A(2) provides that a person does not consent to sexual activity if they allow it because of force or the threat or fear of force applied to themselves or some other person. Just as

---

123   See David Gendall, 'New Developments: Increasing scope for lawyers in the sports arena' (1997) 480 LawTalk 14; Paul Farrugia, 'The Consent Defence: Sports Violence, Sadomasochism, and the Criminal Law' (1997) 8 Auckland University Law Review 472, 486.
124   *Lee* (n 16).
125   *Barker* (n 18).
126   All three judges (including the minority) thought that scarification did not constitute a generic exception to the rule allowing consent as a defence to the intentional or reckless infliction of actual bodily harm. This is because it had a useful social function as an exercise of personal or tribal identity.
127   *Barker* (n 18) 260.
128   Section 128, Crimes Act 1961(NZ).
129   ibid, s 135.
130   But see *Ah-Chong* (n 33) [53]–[55].

the consent of the complainant is entirely subjective – it is for them to give or withhold without the need to justify their decision – so their subjective fear of force is sufficient to negate consent. There is no need to prove the complainant's fear is reasonable or that any force is threatened.[131]

The sexual act that can form the foundation of a sexual violation charge – penetration of genitalia by an object or body part or oral sex – includes the continuation of such behaviour.[132] This means that continuation with knowledge that consent has been revoked will amount to an offence.

A range of offences criminalise sexual behaviour, even if consented to, that takes place in circumstances that are considered to be inherently coercive. Examples are where the consent of the victim is extracted by certain kinds of non-violent threats,[133] where there is a family relationship with the victim,[134] where the victim is underage[135] or has a significant impairment that makes them vulnerable to exploitation.[136]

2.3.2 Evidentiary presumptions

Section 128A sets out a range of specific circumstances where allowing sexual activity does not constitute consent to that activity.[137] Most are codifications of the common law and some have been discussed elsewhere in this chapter.[138] These examples are inclusive but not definitive and there will be other factual situations where a person may have allowed sexual connection but has not consented because their free will is overcome by the coercive nature of their circumstances.[139]

Section 128A(1) provides that 'a person does not consent' just because he or she does not protest or offer physical resistance to the activity. This means non-consent may be apparent from the broader circumstances in which the sexual activity takes place even in the absence of dissent. Non-consent can also, as illustrated by *R v Daniels*, be consistent with the complainant providing some assistance to the assailant (in this case assisting him to insert his penis into her vagina).[140] Nevertheless, the Court of Appeal has said that a jury is still entitled to infer consent from a failure to protest verbally or resist physically.[141] Section 28A(1) simply means that if: 'the jury accepted the complainant's evidence that she did

---

131   *R v Brewer* [1994] 2 NZLR 229 (NZCA).

132   Above 1.1.5. See the definition of 'sexual connection' in, s 2, Crimes Act 1961 (NZ).

133   ibid, s 129A. The relevant threats are: the threat of a serious criminal offence that does not involve the application of force; the threat of an accusation or disclosure that will seriously damage someone's reputation; or the threat to make improper use of a power or authority arising out of an occupational or vocational position or a commercial relationship.

134   Incest, ibid, s 130; sexual connection with a dependant family member, s 131.

135   ibid, ss 132, 134.

136   ibid, s 138: Obtaining consent by exploiting a significant intellectual, mental or physical impairment that impairs a person's capacity to understand the nature of sexual conduct or decisions about sexual conduct, appreciate the consequences of decisions about sexual conduct or communicate those decisions.

137   Note that there are also evidentiary exclusions (s 44, evidence of sexual experience of complainant in sexual cases; s 88 restriction on disclosure of complainant's occupation in sexual cases) and jury directions (s 127, delayed complaints or failure to complain in sexual cases) particular to sexual offending set out in the Evidence Act 2006.

138   Above 1.4, 1.5.1, 2.3.1.

139   Section 128A(8), Crimes Act 1961 (NZ), provides that, 'This section does not limit the circumstances in which a person does not consent to sexual activity'.

140   [1986] 2 NZLR 106 (NZCA).

141   *R v S* (NZCA, 19 September 2002); *R v Kim* [2010] NZCA 106 (NZCA); *R v Rakau* [2011] NZCA 180 (NZCA).

not in fact consent, then lack of protest or physical resistance did not convert absence of consent into consent'.[142] This view can be contrasted with that of the majority in *Ah-Chong* who interpreted s 128(1) to mean that 'consent requires some positive or affirmative words or conduct'.[143]

Section s 128A(3) provides that a person does not consent if they are asleep or unconscious. The simple factual issue is whether the person is asleep or unconscious and, if so, they are not consenting to any sexual connection that takes place or continues at that point.[144] Nonetheless, it was held in *R v S* that the defendant may still lack *mens rea* if they have a reasonable belief in consent.[145]

2.3.3 Mistake of fact about consent

The offences of sexual violation and indecent assault have different *mens rea* standards. Sexual violation (including rape) requires the accused to have reasonable grounds for any mistaken belief in their sexual partner's consent.[146] The courts have held that this does not mean that the court should look at whether the defendant had objective grounds for their subjective belief in consent. It means that 'a reasonable person in the shoes of the defendant' might have thought that the complainant was consenting.[147]

For the offence of indecent assault, by way of contrast, consent is a defence.[148] An honest mistake about the other persons consent is a sufficient foundation on which to base such a defence.[149]

2.4 Property offences and criminal damage

2.4.1 Place of consent in the offence structure

Part 10 of the Crimes Act 1961 (NZ) contains a series of offences relating to the use, transfer or destruction of property. Victim non-consent in most instances is part of the offence structure. In other words, it must be established as an *actus reus* requirement and the accused must have an accompanying *mens rea*. For example, theft under s 219 of the Crimes Act 1961 (NZ) consists of either taking property without the consent of the person in possession or, having come into possession of that property, using or dealing with it without the consent of the owner. Such an act must be performed 'dishonestly and without claim of right'.

2.4.2 Mistaken belief in consent – Definition of honesty

'Dishonestly' is defined in s 217 of the Crimes Act 1961 (NZ) in relation to the property offences to mean 'done or omitted without a belief that there was express or implied consent to, or authority for, the act or omission from a person entitled to give such consent or authority'. In other words, an honest belief in consent is sufficient to negate the offence – reasonable grounds are not required.

---

142 *R v S* ibid.
143 *Ah-Chong* (n 33) [53].
144 *Rakau* (n 140).
145 [2015] NZHC 801.
146 Section 128, Crimes Act 1961 (NZ).
147 *Taniwha v R* [2010] NZSC 50 (NZSC); *R v Mustafa Can* [2007] NZCA 291 (NZCA); *R v Gutuama* (NZCA, 13 December 2001), *R v Clarke* [1992] 1 NZLR 147 (NZCA).
148 Above 1.2.
149 Above 1.6; *Lee* (n 16).

20

United States of America

Vera Bergelson*

1 GENERAL ISSUES

1.1 Conceptual foundations

1.1.1 *Philosophical and theoretical principles informing the law surrounding consent*

Consent is a power to change the normative relations between the consent-giver and others. By giving consent, a person releases others from certain obligations they used to have with respect to that person and gives them the privilege, power or immunity to do what they could not legitimately do before. In some cases, consent operates to prevent the commission of a crime: it 'turns a rape into love-making, a kidnapping into a Sunday drive, a battery into a football tackle, a theft into a gift, and a trespass into a dinner party'.[1] And yet there are many examples of conduct that remains wrongful despite its consensual nature. Homicide, riot, bribery, and bigamy are among those.

The Model Penal Code ('MPC') explains this incongruity; 'consent is given defensive effect by the law when it is logically relevant either to negative a prescribed element of the offence or to preclude the occurrence of the harm or evil that the law defining the offence seeks to prevent'.[2] Accordingly, consent precludes conviction of theft because the objective of theft law is to protect property rights against unauthorised infringement. Being a waiver of rights, consent negatives the unauthorised character of the infringement and precludes the harm and evil of theft. But consent is powerless to preclude the harm or evil of homicide, riot, bribery or bigamy where the objectives of the law go beyond the interests that may be asserted by an identifiable victim.

* I would like to thank my research assistants Siobhan Kinealy and Nicole Perez for their invaluable help in researching and editing this paper.

1 Heidi M Hurd, 'Blaming the Victim: A Response to the Proposal that Criminal Law Recognize a General Defense of Contributory Responsibility' (2005) 8 Buffalo Criminal Law Review 503, 504. *See generally* Wesley Newcomb Hohfeld, *Fundamental Legal Conceptions* (Walter Wheeler Cook ed, Yale University Press 1923).

2 Model Penal Code § 2.11 cmt 1 (1980) 395.

1.1.2 Influence of feminist and queer theory

The feminist and queer jurisprudences have contributed to the debate about the role of consent in criminal law, most notably the law of rape. The main issue in that debate has been whether consent ought to serve as the demarcation line between the morally (and legally) acceptable and unacceptable sexual conduct.

The liberal feminist theorists have challenged the traditional definition of rape that required the use of force by the perpetrator and resistance by the victim. In contrast, the liberal feminist theorists focused not on the force or resistance but on the consensuality of sexual conduct. They have argued that *any non-consensual* sex – including non-violent sex between dates, cohabitants or spouses; sex imposed upon unconscious, intoxicated or mentally incapacitated victims; and sex coerced through implied threats of future violence, or of a non-violent violation of rights – should be criminally punishable.[3] As a corollary, according to the same theorists, *any consensual* sex should be neither criminalised nor disapproved of by society at large.

The views of liberal feminists have played a significant role in reforming sexual assault laws all over the United States. For example, commenting on its revised rape statute, a New Jersey court observed that the new provisions were formulated by a coalition of feminist groups assisted by the National Organization of Women National Task Force on Rape.[4] Today, a growing number of American jurisdictions criminalise all instances of non-consensual intercourse, even though this departure from the traditional force requirement still remains in the minority.[5]

In contrast, the liberal feminist position regarding permissibility of *any consensual* sexual conduct has been much less influential. Even though in *Lawrence v Texas*, the United States Supreme Court held that a Texas statute prohibiting homosexual sodomy was unconstitutional in so far as it applied to the private conduct of two consenting adults, courts have been reluctant to expand this holding to other sexual consensual relationships.[6] In the years that followed, the *Lawrence* decision has been unsuccessfully invoked in the context of consensual adult incest, polygamy, and sado-masochism.[7]

The liberal feminist views have prompted criticism not only from the right (the defenders of the traditional rape model) but also from the left (the representatives of radical feminism and queer theory). Drawing upon Marx's critique of consensuality in labour relations, radical feminists argued that in the sexual sphere, no less than in the economic, 'consent' is not a meaningful marker between autonomy and coercion.[8] West recalls how, beginning in the 1980s, 'radical feminists in law and outside of law, but most forcefully MacKinnon, have argued in various ways that the sharp line drawn by liberals between consensual and

---

3 Robin West, 'Sex, Law and Consent' in Franklin Miller and Alan Wertheimer (eds), *The Ethics of Consent: Theory and Practice* (Oxford University Press 2009).

4 *State in the Interest of MTS* 609 A 2d 1266, 1274 (NJ 1992).

5 Michelle J Anderson, 'Negotiating Sex' (2005) 78 Southern California Law Review 101, 103.

6 *Lawrence v Texas* 539 US 558, 578 (2003).

7 See, for example, *State v Van* 688 NW 2d 600, 615 (Neb 2004) (ibid, 'did not extend constitutional protection to *any* conduct which occurs in the context of a consensual sexual relationship' but only to such that does not involve injury to a person or abuse of an institution protected by law); *Bronson v Swensen* 394 F Supp 2d 1329, 1334 (D Utah 2005) ('[T]his court cannot hold that *Lawrence* can be read to require the State of Utah to give formal recognition to a public relationship of a polygamous marriage'); *Beard v State* 2005 Tenn Crim App LEXIS 568, 6 (Tenn Crim App June 7 2005) ('[I]ncestuous relationships are not protected by our state constitution and the *Lawrence* decision in no way alters our holding . . .').

8 Catherine A MacKinnon, *Toward a Feminist Theory of the State* (Harvard University Press 1989).

non-consensual sex falsifies the degree of coercion imposed upon women by men in our ordinary sexual lives'.[9]

According to the radical feminist view, sex is never free from coercion. The coercion may come from various sources: direct threats, social and economic pressures as well as the sexualised and pornographic culture that forces women to go along with the demands on their sexual autonomy. Morgan, for example, has argued that rape occurs any time when sexual intercourse has not been initiated by the woman, out of her own genuine affection and desire. She wrote:

> How many millions of times have women had sex 'willingly' with men they didn't want to have sex with? ... How many times have women wished just to sleep instead or read or watch the Late Show? ... Most of the decently married bedrooms across America are settings for nightly rape.[10]

Whereas radical feminists criticised the liberal emphasis on consent because it could lead to under-criminalisation of consensual yet exploitive sexual conduct, the queer theorists criticised the same because it could lead to over-criminalisation of sex. For example, Halley has argued that in a culture that is overtly hostile to sexual variation and sex itself, claims of non-consensual sex, ie rape, are often the product of a 'sex panic', rather than an actual assault.[11] According to Halley, the accusation of rape often comes from the woman's confused and guilty feelings about sex. The woman calls sex rape in order to negate any possible suggestion that she may have enjoyed it. In the same spirit, Kennedy suggested, in the wake of the Lewinsky–Clinton scandal, that in the world of sexuality such liberal banalities as consent, choice, and autonomy are not particularly important.[12] According to Kennedy, unconstrained sex is of such great hedonic value that it simply should not be sacrificed to legal niceties.[13]

1.1.3 Definition of informed consent

The doctrine of informed consent has been particularly relevant in the context of physician–patient relationship. The doctrine, which requires physicians to obtain the informed consent of their patients before initiating treatment, is of fairly recent origin. Historically, patients were not supposed to have much say in their medical treatment. The American Medical Association ('AMA') in its 1847 Code of Ethics maintained that patient 'obedience ... to the prescriptions of their physician should be prompt and implicit. They should never permit their own crude opinions ... to influence their attention to their physicians.' This approach to the doctor–patient relationship persisted until the first half of the twentieth century when the development of medical science and technology opened to the physicians various treatment

---

9 Robin West (n 3) 7; see also Catherine A MacKinnon, *Feminism Unmodified* (Harvard University Press 1988) 81–93; ibid 146, 174.

10 Robin Morgan, *Going Too Far: The Personal Chronicle of a Feminist* (Random House 1977) 165–66.

11 Janet Halley, 'Sexuality Harassment' in Catherine A MacKinnon and Reva B Siegel (eds), *Directions in Sexual Harassment Law* (Yale University Press 2003) 182, 193–98; see also Janet Halley (writing under the name Ian Halley), 'Queer Theory by Men' (2004) 11 Duke Journal of Gender Law & Policy 7, 52; Janet Halley, 'The Politics of Injury: A Review of Robin West's "Caring for Justice"' (2005) 65(1) Harvard Journal of the Legal Left (Unbound) 92.

12 David Kennedy, 'The Spectacle and the Libertine' in Leonard V Kaplan and Beverly I Moran (eds), *Aftermath: The Clinton Impeachment and the Presidency in the Age of Political Spectacle* (NY University Press 2001) 279, 289.

13 Robin West (n 3) 15.

strategies, each with benefits and risks that a competent adult patient would want to consider. Those changes set the stage for an increased respect for patient autonomy. As Justice Cardozo formulated in *Schoendorff v Society of New York Hospital*:

> Every human being of adult years and sound mind has a right to determine what shall be done with his own body; and a surgeon who performs an operation without his patient's consent commits an assault for which he is liable in damages.[14]

To avoid this liability, however, all that the physician needed was the most perfunctory, bare consent of the patient.[15] The landmark case which rejected the 'bare consent' standard and held that a physician had a duty to disclose all facts necessary for the patient to make intelligent decisions was *Salgo v Leland Stanford Jr. University Board of Trustees*.[16] In further cases, courts held that the appropriate standard of disclosure should be judged by what a reasonable patient would want to know.[17]

By the end of the twentieth century, the importance of informed consent was recognised by the law and medical professional organisations alike. The current AMA's Code of Medical Ethics provides that the patient 'has the right to receive information from physicians and to discuss the benefits, risks, and costs of appropriate treatment alternatives',[18] and that the patient 'should make his or her own determination on treatment'.[19]

1.1.4 Consent to risk or consent to outcome

American criminal law largely disregards the difference between consent to the inevitable and deliberate harm and consent to the mere risk of harm.[20] For example, in *In re JAP*, a group of eighth graders played the game of 'passout', the object of which was for one player to make a fellow player faint.[21] JAP grabbed his friend around the neck and proceeded to choke him for a few seconds until that boy lost consciousness and fell on the ground. The victim suffered a few facial lacerations and chipped teeth. By the time of the trial, all his injuries had been treated and healed. Nevertheless, the juvenile court concluded that JAP had engaged in delinquent conduct by committing aggravated assault, an offence that required finding of 'serious bodily harm'.[22]

On appeal, the *JAP* court concluded that a rational juror could determine that the act of choking presented a substantial risk of death; thus the 'serious harm' element of the charged offence was established. What the court apparently overlooked was that, under the state law, a 'serious injury' was defined as an *injury* that created a substantial risk of death, not merely

---

14 *Schoendorff v Society of New York Hosp* 105 NE 92, 93 (NY 1914).
15 'Battery actions in the medical context have been limited to situations where the physician did not gain consent for his or her actions or greatly exceeded the scope of that consent, for example, operating on the wrong limb'. *Yoder v Cotton* 758 NW 2d 630, 637 (Neb 2008).
16 *Salgo v Leland Stanford Jr. Univ Bd of Tr* 317 P 2d 170, 181 (Cal Ct App 1957).
17 Brian J Warren, 'Pennsylvania Medical Informed Consent Law: A Call to Protect Patient Autonomy Rights by Abandoning the Battery Approach' (2000) 38 Duquesne Law Review 917, 923.
18 AMA Council on Ethical and Judicial Affairs, *Code of Medical Ethics* (American Medical Association 2014–2015) 10.01(1).
19 ibid 8.08.
20 See, for example, MPC (n 2) § 2.11(2).
21 *In re JAP* No 03–02–00112-CV, Tex App LEXIS 7374 (2002), 3.
22 ibid 12–13.

an *activity* that created such a risk.[23] Otherwise, following the court's logic, a driver who exceeded the speed limit and was stopped by the police before he had a chance to get into any accident would be automatically guilty of causing serious injuries to his passengers even though none of them have suffered a scratch.

Ironically, even though the court could have been mistaken in finding the infliction of 'serious harm', it was nonetheless correct in denying JAP the defence of consent: under the state statute, just like under the MPC, consent may be a defence only if 'the conduct did not *threaten or inflict* serious bodily injury'.[24] So, the very threat of serious harm (which arguably has not materialised) made JAP's friend's consent to the game ineffective.

1.1.5 Revocation of consent

The issue of revoked consent may arise in different contexts but it has gained most attention in recent years in connection with post-penetration rape. Post-penetration rape usually means a situation in which both parties have initially consented to sexual intercourse, but, at some point during the act, one party has communicated to the other that he or she no longer consents to the intercourse and wishes to terminate it. Despite this request, the other party continues the intercourse for some time against his or her partner's will.[25] May this person be convicted of rape? The answer used to be 'no'.[26] One court opined:

> The essence of the crime of rape is the outrage to the person and feelings of the female resulting from the nonconsensual violation of her womanhood. When a female willingly consents to an act of sexual intercourse, the penetration by the male cannot constitute a violation of her womanhood nor cause outrage to her person and feelings. If she withdraws consent during the act of sexual intercourse and the male forcibly continues the act without interruption, the female may certainly feel outrage because of the force applied or because the male ignores her wishes, but the sense of outrage to her person and feelings could hardly be of the same magnitude as that resulting from an initial nonconsensual violation of her womanhood.[27]

More recently, however, a number of courts have criticised that reasoning as based on archaic and outmoded social conventions and ruled that a defendant is guilty of forcible rape if, 'during apparently consensual intercourse, the victim expresses an objection and attempts to stop the act and the defendant forcibly continues despite the objection'.[28] Currently, one state (Illinois) criminalises post-penetration rape by statute and seven more states (Alaska, California, Connecticut, Kansas, Maine, Maryland, and Minnesota) achieve the same result

---

23 See Vernon's Tex Penal Code Ann § 1.07(a)(46) (2005), (serious bodily injury is an 'injury that creates a substantial risk of death or that causes death, serious permanent disfigurement, or protracted loss or impairment of the function of any bodily member or organ').

24 ibid 10 (emphasis added).

25 Amanda O Davis, 'Clarifying the Issue of Consent: The Evolution of Post-Penetration Rape Law' (2005) 34 Stetson Law Review 729.

26 See, for example, *State v Way* 254 SE 2d 760, 762 (NC 1979); *Battle v State* 414 A 2d 1266, 1270 (Md 1980).'

27 *People v Vela* 218 Cal Rptr 161, 165 (Cal Ct App 1985).

28 *In re John Z* 60 P 3d 183, 185 (Cal 2003); see also State v Robinson 496 A 2d 1067, 1070–71 (Me 1985); *McGill v State* 18 P 3d 77, 84 (Alaska Ct App 2001); *State v Siering* 644 A 2d 958, 963–64 (Conn App Ct 1994); *State v Bunyard* 133 P 3d 14, 29 (Kan 2006), overruled in part by *State v Gaither* 156 P 3d 602, 612 (Kan 2007).

by judicial decisions.[29] A few other courts appear to follow, without explicitly holding that rape can occur after penetration.[30] The only state that has considered the issue and still maintains that intercourse after withdrawal of consent is not rape is North Carolina.[31]

The central question for those courts that recognise the offence of post-penetration rape is how quickly a reasonable person should obey the request to stop. In *In re John Z*, the defendant argued that the act of sexual intercourse arouses a male's primal urge to reproduce; it is therefore, 'unreasonable for a female and the law to expect a male to cease having sexual intercourse immediately upon her withdrawal of consent. It is only natural, fair and just that a male be given a reasonable amount of time in which to quell his primal urge.'[32] The court rejected the 'primal urge' defence and opined that the defendant's failure to withdraw for four or five minutes after the victim's first request was not reasonable.[33] Similarly, the Appellate Court in *State v Bunyard* held that, '[w]hen consent is withdrawn, continuing sexual intercourse for five to ten minutes is not reasonable and constitutes rape'.[34] The Supreme Court of Kansas, however, opined that it is up to the jury to determine whether the time between withdrawal of consent and the interruption of intercourse was reasonable.[35]

1.1.6 Ownership and limits of consent

Pursuant to the MPC and state laws, consent precludes what otherwise would be the victim's right violation, with one exception: consent to physical harm may serve as a defence only when the injury or its risk is (i) not serious; (ii) a reasonably foreseeable hazard of participation in a lawful athletic activity; or (iii) a result of a recognised form of medical treatment.[36] The reasons cited in support of this limitation on the victim's authority to consent usually are that, when the victim incurs serious injury or death, not only the victim's private interests are harmed but also those belonging to the state (including military, economic, socio-political, and moral).[37]

Consent is also ineffective in the following circumstances: (1) when consent is given by a person who is not legally entitled to do so (for example, when a stranger 'consents' to the removal of another's property); (2) when consent is induced by force, duress or deception (see 1.5.2.); and (3) when consent is given by a person who, by virtue of youth, mental disease or intoxication, is legally incompetent to authorise the conduct charged to constitute the offence.[38] When consent is required for a medical procedure on a person who is legally incompetent to give it, a surrogate decision-maker must speak for that person. A medical ethicist explains:

> There is a specific hierarchy of appropriate decision makers defined by state law ... If no appropriate surrogate decision maker is available, the physicians are expected to

---

29 Sarah O Parker, 'No Means No ... Sometimes: Developments in Postpenetration Rape Law and the Need for Legislative Action' (2013) 78 Brooklyn Law Review 1067, 1068–69.
30 David Kennedy (n 12) (citing decisions from Pennsylvania, New Mexico and South Dakota).
31 *Way* (n 26).
32 *John Z* (n 28) 187.
33 ibid.
34 *State v Bunyard* 75 P 3d 750, 756 (Kan Ct App 2003).
35 *Bunyard* (n 28) 49.
36 MPC (n 2) § 2.11(2). For further discussion, see section 2.2 below.
37 See Vera Bergelson, 'The Right To Be Hurt. Testing the Boundaries of Consent' (2007) 75 George Washington Law Review 165.
38 MPC (n 2) § 2.11(3)(a).

act in the best interest of the patient until a surrogate is found or appointed. In rare circumstances, when no surrogate can be identified, a guardian ad litem may have to be appointed by the court.[39]

Young children lack the capacity to give informed consent; for them, their parents can provide informed *permission* for treatment. Adolescents can provide informed consent either if they are emancipated or under specific statutes. For example, they may consent to treatment of sexually transmitted infections (in all states; some statutes, however, require the minor to be of a certain age); to contraceptives (in almost a half of all states); and to prenatal care (in approximately two-thirds of states).[40] In addition, some states allow 'mature minors' to consent to medical treatment, including the matters of sexual and reproductive health, mental health, and substance abuse.[41]

1.2 Place of consent in the offence structure

Consent of the victim may exonerate the perpetrator in two sets of circumstances: one, when it negatives an element of non-consent required by the definition of the offence, and two, when it prevents the infliction of the harm or evil that the criminal statute seeks to prevent.[42] In the first case, consent leads to the failure of proof defeating the charges of such offences as rape, theft or kidnapping. In the second case, consent serves as an affirmative defence to what otherwise would be a criminal act. For example, consent to a boxing match may shield its participants from criminal liability for assault and battery.

About a quarter of all US jurisdictions explicitly recognise the general defence of consent by their statutes[43] whereas other jurisdictions have incorporated the concept of consent in the Special Part of their penal codes, making non-consent an element of an offence or providing for the defence of consent with respect to specific crimes.[44] Where the statute does not explicitly mention consent, case-law usually explains in what circumstances consent of the victim may function as a defence.

---

39 Jessica De Bord, 'Informed Consent' (*Ethics in Medicine, Univ of Wash School of Med*, 7 March 2014) <http://depts.washington.edu/bioethx/topics/consent.html> accessed 22 August 2015.

40 – –, 'Minor Consent to Medical Treatment Laws' (*National District Attorneys* Association, January 2013) <http://www.ndaa.org/pdf/Minor%20Consent%20to%20Medical%20Treatment%20%282%29.pdf> accessed 08 September 2015.

41 The mature minor doctrine is an American term for the statutory, regulatory, or common law policy accepting that an unemancipated minor patient may possess the maturity to choose or reject a particular health care treatment, sometimes without the knowledge or agreement of parents, and should be permitted to do so: *West's Encyclopaedia of American Law: Volume 8* (2nd edition, West Group Publishing 1998) 47. Fourteen states permit mature minors to consent to general medical treatment either in all or a range of restricted circumstances. Doriane Lambelet Coleman and Philip M Rosoff, 'The Legal Authority of Mature Minors to Consent to General Medical Treatment' (2013) 131(4) Pediatrics 786.

42 MPC (n 2) § 2.11.

43 See, for example, Ala Code § 13A-2–7 (2005); Colo Rev Stat § 18–1–505 (2004); Del Code Ann tit 11 §§ 451–453 (2001).

44 See, for example, 720 Ill Comp Stat 5/12–17 (2002) ('It shall be a defence to any offence under [sexual crimes sections] of this Code where force or threat of force is an element of the offence that the victim consented').

1.3 Form of consent

1.3.1 Declared or implied

The distinction between declared and implied consent stems from a more basic question: what is *consent*? Is it one's inner thoughts (attitudinal consent) or one's actions as a manifestation of acquiescence (expressive or performative consent)? For example, in prosecutions for rape, what should determine the presence or absence of consent – the victim's state of mind or the victim's actions and words?

The choice between these two models is often relevant in interpreting sexual assault statutes. The MPC and traditional state law seem to prefer the attitudinal model.[45] On the other hand, newer sexual assault statutes tend to require communication of consent.[46]

In the medical field, consent has always been understood as expressive rather than attitudinal. For example, the patients may not give physicians consent to surgery without communicating their acquiescence, orally or in writing. A medical ethicist explains:

> All health care interventions require some kind of consent by the patient, following a discussion of the procedure with a health care provider. Patients fill out a general consent form when they are admitted or receive treatment from a health care institution. Most health care institutions . . . also have policies that state which health interventions require a signed consent form. For example, surgery, anaesthesia, and other invasive procedures are usually in this category.
>
> For a wide range of decisions, explicit written consent is neither required nor needed, but some meaningful discussion is always needed. For instance, a man contemplating having a prostate-specific antigen screen for prostate cancer should know the relevant arguments for and against this screening test, discussed in lay terms.[47]

There is some controversy as to the ethical sufficiency of standardised forms, especially when the 'health literacy' of the patient is questionable, 'Signatures, let alone ticks in boxes, may have legal weight, but they lack ethical weight, and often do not provide evidentiary weight that genuinely informed consent has been given.'[48]

In certain limited circumstances, a physician may proceed without a patient's declared consent. If a person is at a serious risk of death or injury but unconscious, or otherwise unable to give explicit consent, consent to give aid or medical treatment is implied.[49] Implied consent may be inferred from the patient's action of seeking treatment or some other act manifesting a willingness to submit to a particular course of treatment.[50]

---

45 See, MPC (n 2).

46 See, for example, Fla Stat §794.011(1)(a) (2015).

47 Jessica De Bord (n 39).

48 Neil C Manson and Onora O'Neill, *Rethinking Informed Consent in Bioethics* (1st edition, Cambridge University Press 2007) 190–91.

49 Gregory S Sergienko, 'Assumption of Risk As a Defense to Negligence' (2006) 34 W St U L Rev 1, 27–28 (observing that 'the precedent for an implied consent is so strong that, in an emergency, an unconscious person will ordinarily be held to have given consent to an operation and even implied to have agreed to pay for it, even though the operation does not lead to a beneficial result').

50 *Yoder* (n 15) 636.

1.3.2 Presumed consent

In the United States, the issue of presumed consent has been under consideration primarily in connection with organ donations. Starting in the late 1960s, many states have adopted presumed consent statutes that allowed retrieval of tissues or organs (including hearts, lungs, livers and kidneys) from dead persons who came under the custody of coroners or medical examiners. Pursuant to those statutes, coroners and medical examiners could authorise the donation of the tissues and organs as long as they were not aware of an objection by the deceased or a family member.

While potentially very effective,[51] presumed consent statutes were controversial from the start. Objections against them ranged from concerns about exploiting minorities, to respecting religious and cultural beliefs, to issues of spending and individuals' rights.[52] Several constitutional challenges were brought to courts by relatives of the deceased persons whose corneas or organs were taken without consent. However, the courts found no due process violation and upheld the statutes.[53] The Uniform Anatomical Gift Act ('UAGA') of 1987 also recommended the presumed consent standard for the donation of any organ or tissue from cadavers under the custody of coroners or medical examiners.[54] At one time or another, more than two-thirds of all states adopted presumed consent statutes.

The favourable treatment of presumed consent began to change in the 1990s, after a federal Appellate Court opined that taking corneas from cadavers without family members having some opportunity to be heard on the matter may violate the procedural due process of the Fourteenth Amendment.[55] In light of constitutional uncertainty, the drafters of the new, 2006 UAGA eliminated the provision for presumed consent.[56] In the years that followed, the 2006 UAGA was endorsed by numerous medical organisations and adopted by the overwhelming majority of states, most of them eliminating presumed consent entirely and only a few retaining it, primarily for corneas.[57]

1.4 Capacity to consent

Certain groups of people are deemed legally incompetent to give valid consent. Among those are developmentally disabled, mentally ill (oftentimes, these two categories are jointly referred to as 'mentally defective'), severely intoxicated, and minors. The question of capacity to consent frequently comes into play in connection with sexual offences.

---

51 David Orentlicher writes, 'Georgia adopted its cornea retrieval statute in 1978, and the number of cornea transplants in the state jumped from 25 in 1977 to 1000 in 1984. Florida enacted its statute in 1977, and cornea transplants increased from 500 in 1975 to 3000 in 1984. Texas saw an increase from an average of 215 cornea transplants a year to more than 1,300 transplants a year after adopting its statute in 1977'. David Orentlicher, 'Presumed Consent to Organ Donation: Its Rise and Fall in the United States' (2009) 61 Rutgers Law Review 295, 302.

52 Kenneth Gundle, 'Presumed Consent for Organ Donation: Perspectives of Health Policy Specialists' (2004) 3 Stanford Undergraduate Research Journal: Medical Anthropology 28.

53 See, for example, *Tillman v Detroit Receiving Hosp* 360 NW 2d 275, 277 (Mich Ct App 1984); *Ga Lions Eye Bank v Lavant* 335 SE 2d 127, 128–29 (Ga 1985); *State v Powell* 497 So 2d 1188, 1190–94 (Fla 1986).

54 Unif Anatomical Gift Act § 4 (1987).

55 *Brotherton v Cleveland* 923 F 2d 477, 482 (6th Cir 1991). Similar concerns were expressed a decade later by another federal Appellate Court. *Newman v Sathyavaglswaran* 287 F 3d 786 (9th Cir 2002).

56 Rev Unif Anatomical Gift Act § 8 (2006).

57 – –, 'Anatomical Gift Act' (*Uniform Law Commission*, 2006) <http://uniformlaws.org/Act.aspx?title=Anatomical+Gift+Act+%282006%29> accessed 8 September 2015; David Orentlicher (n 51) 300–01.

(i) Mental deficiency

Some states invalidate people's consent if, at the time of the sexual activity, they are 'mentally defective', ie unable to comprehend the distinctively sexual nature of the conduct or are incapable of understanding or exercising the right to refuse to engage in such conduct.[58] Other states have similar provisions but do not define who is considered 'mentally defective'.

Lately, a number of jurisdictions have made an effort to revise their sexual assault statutes so as not to ban completely people with intellectual disabilities from engaging in consensual sex. A recent case involving former Iowa legislator Rayhons brought attention to the question of whether Alzheimer's patients may continue sexual relationships with their long-term partners. Rayhons, 78, was prosecuted for allegedly having sex with his wife suffering from Alzheimer's when visiting her at a nursing home. He was eventually found not guilty of sexual abuse but it was not clear what determined the jury's verdict. A lawyer commented: 'They may have concluded that Donna was able to consent, despite her Alzheimer's, or they may have decided that prosecutors hadn't provided enough evidence that Rayhons had sex with his wife after being told not to.'[59]

(ii) Intoxication

All states impose liability for rape on the perpetrators who have sex with persons who are completely unconscious, and practically all states impose the same liability when the perpetrators have sex with persons who are severely incapacitated (even though not unconscious) by drugs or alcohol given to them without their knowledge by the perpetrators. However, many rape statutes do not impose liability if the victim was in an incapacitated condition short of complete unconsciousness due to someone else's actions.[60] The MPC is particularly restrictive: it imposes liability for rape only when (i) the defendant administered the intoxicant; (ii) without the victim's knowledge; and (iii) 'for the purpose of preventing resistance'.[61]

It is especially hard to obtain conviction when the victim's intoxication (short of complete unconsciousness) is a result of their own choice to drink. In *State v Haddock*, the defendant was convicted of rape under a statute that prohibited sexual intercourse with a person who, due to an act committed upon that person, was substantially incapable of appraising the nature of his or her conduct or resisting the act.[62] The conviction was reversed because the incapacity was caused by the victim's own actions. About two-thirds of American jurisdictions have similar restrictions. The wisdom of those restrictions has been challenged, particularly in light of the reported numbers of sex crimes on college campuses. One analysis has revealed that 'in student populations, up to 81% of incidents can involve drinking on the part of the victim'.[63]

---

58   *State v Olivio* 589 A 2d 597, 599 (NJ 1991).

59   Sarah Kaplan, 'Former Iowa legislator Henry Rayhons, 78, found not guilty of sexually abusing wife with Alzheimer's' (*The Washington Post*, 23 April 2015).

60   Sanford H Kadish and others, *Criminal Law and Its Processes: Cases and Materials* (9th edition, Aspen Publishers 2012) 380–81.

61   MPC (n 2) § 213.1(1)(b).

62   *State v Haddock* 664 SE 2d 339 (NC Ct App 2008).

63   Sharon Cowan, 'The Trouble With Drink: Intoxication, (In)Capacity, and the Evaporation of Consent to Sex' (2008) 41 Akron Law Review 899, 904–05.

(iii) Age

Another set of questions involving legal competence has been raised in connection with the age of consent. In the United States, for the purposes of medical treatment, in most states it is 18.[64] For sexual activities, it is set between 16 and 18, depending on the jurisdiction. Some states provide an exception (the so-called 'Romeo and Juliette' exception) from criminal liability for sexual intercourse with a minor if the partners are of relatively the same age (the difference usually may not exceed four to five years). Yet, those states are still in the minority.[65]

The story of Genarlaw Wilson has been often cited as an illustration of the harshness of the existing laws regulating sexual behaviour of minors: the young man was sentenced to a mandatory ten-year sentence for having had consensual oral sex with a 15-year-old girl when he was 17. Wilson's sentence was eventually changed from a felony to a misdemeanor and the young man was released from prison but not before he had already served two years of his sentence.[66]

1.5 Consequences of mistaken consent

1.5.1 Mistake

Victims may grant consent (i) out of mistaken fear that they (or others) will be physically harmed unless they submit or (ii) under a mistaken belief about (A) the nature of the act; (B) the identity of the person to whom consent is given; or (C) some other attending circumstances.

With respect to mistaken fear, courts have generally held that consent is invalid only if the victim's fear was reasonably grounded, and 'generated by something of substance'.[67] As one judge explained, the complainant in a rape case 'may not simply say, "I was scared," and thereby transform consent or mere unwillingness into submission by force'.[68]

Other mistakes (listed under (ii) above) have been treated the same way as mistakes stemming from deception (see 1.5.2.), specifically – mistakes about the nature of an act always destroy consent; mistakes about the identity of the person to whom consent was given sometimes destroy consent; and mistakes about other, collateral circumstances (a person's social status, job prospects, other benefits and setbacks) almost never destroy consent.

1.5.2 Deception

Almost all American jurisdictions distinguish between deception that involves the nature of the act (fraud in the factum) and deception that involves some collateral matter (fraud in the inducement). The former vitiates consent; the latter does not.[69]

---

64 Norman M Goldfarb, 'Age of Consent for Clinical Research' (2008) 4(6) Journal of Clinical Research Best Practices 1.

65 See Sandra Norman-Eady, Christopher Reinhart and Peter Martino, 'Statutory Rape Laws by State' (2003) US Department of Health & Human Services OLR Research Report 2003-R-0376 <https://www.cga.ct.gov/2003/olrdata/jud/rpt/2003-r-0376.htm> accessed 8 September 2015.

66 Brenda Goodman, 'Georgia Supreme Court Hears 2 Appeals in Teenage Sex Case' (*The New York Times*, 21 July 2007).

67 *State v Rusk* 424 A 2d 720, 733 (Md 1981) (Cole J dissenting). At least one court has held, however, that conviction can be sustained where the victim's fear was unreasonable but the perpetrator was aware of that fear and took advantage of it. *People v Iniguez* 872 P 2d 1183, 1188 (Cal 1994).

68 *Farrar v United States* 275 F.2d 868 (DC Cir 1959) *opinion amended* (1960).

69 Ronald N Boyce, Donald A Dripps and Rollin M Perkins, *Criminal Law and Procedure* (12th edition, Foundation Press 2013) 1079.

This distinction was crucial in *Boro v Superior Court*, in which the defendant lied to the victim that she had a life-threatening disease, which could be cured by her having sexual intercourse with a donor who had been injected with a 'serum'. The victim consented under the mistaken belief that otherwise she would die.[70] The defendant was prosecuted on several charges, including rape. That charge failed, however, as the court held that fraud in the inducement did not vitiate consent. The court characterised the defendant's lies as fraud in the inducement because the deception related not to the fact of the sexual intercourse but merely to the incentive for having that intercourse.

In the aftermath of *Boro*, California's rape provision has been revised and today the victim is considered to be 'unconscious of the nature of the act' when she was not aware of the 'essential characteristics of the act due to the perpetrator's fraudulent representation that the sexual penetration served a professional purpose when it served no professional purpose'.[71]

Another area of rape law in which the distinction between fraud in the factum and fraud in the inducement has been quintessential is impersonation of a husband (or in some later cases boyfriend). Jurisdictions have been split on how such impersonation should be characterised. A court explained:

> Some courts have taken the position that such a misdeed is fraud in the inducement on the theory that the woman consents to exactly what is done (sexual intercourse) and hence there is no rape; other courts . . . hold such a misdeed to be rape on the theory that it involves fraud in the factum since the woman's consent is to an innocent act of marital intercourse while what is actually perpetrated upon her is an act of adultery.[72]

The MPC has followed the traditional approach that impersonation of a husband vitiates consent but it classifies it not as rape but as gross sexual imposition, a felony of a lower degree. At the same time, the MPC has added to the list of prohibited actions two more kinds of deception: (1) inducing the victim to enter a void marriage by deceiving her as to the defendant's eligibility to marry; and (2) staging a mock marriage to create the false supposition that the couple are man and wife.[73]

1.6 Mistake about consent

Where non-consent is an element of an offence, the effect of the perpetrator's mistake regarding the victim's consent is governed by the culpability requirements of that element of the offence (see *State v Kelly* discussed in 2.4.2.). Where consent serves as an offence-specific defence, the results of the defendant's mistakes vary depending on the language of the specific provision. Where consent is a general defence, which precludes the harm or evil of the offence, the perpetrator's mistake about the fact or effectiveness of consent 'will with a few exceptions cause the loss of the defence'.[74] The perpetrator is more likely to retain the defence if the mistake is about the effectiveness of the victim's consent (due to the victim's youth, mental disease or defect, or intoxication) and not the fact of consent.[75] The MPC disregards

---

70 *Boro v Superior Court* 210 Cal Rptr 122 (Cal Ct App 1985).
71 Cal Penal Code § 261(a)(4)(D).
72 *Boro* (n 70).
73 MPC (n 2) § 213.1 cmt 7(b).
74 Paul H Robinson, *Criminal Law Defenses: Criminal Practice Series* (Thomas West 1984) para 66(h), 318.
75 ibid.

mistaken consent as a defence only if the victim is legally incompetent to grant consent *and* 'manifestly unable or known by the actor to be unable to make a reasonable judgment'.[76]

The distinction between the inculpatory (when non-consent is an element of an offence) and exculpatory (when consent is a defence) functions of consent is often ignored by courts in sexual assault cases. Thus, even when a statute lists non-consent as an element of sexual assault and punishes only those defendants who act recklessly, knowingly or purposely with respect to each element of the offence, the defendant's honest but unreasonable mistake about his partner's consent does not usually protect the defendant.[77] The absolute majority of states give weight only to an honest *and reasonable* mistake.[78] Moreover, a small number of states disregard even a reasonable mistake about consent in sexual assault cases.[79]

2 SPECIFIC ISSUES

2.1 Consent and homicide offences

2.1.1 Mercy killings

Mercy killing is the act of putting a person to death for reasons of compassion. In the United States, mercy killing – consensual or not – is considered murder. In a well-publicised case, *Michigan v Kevorkian*,[80] the state prosecuted Dr Kevorkian for administering a lethal injection to a former racecar driver who, due to the Lou Gehrig's disease, was no longer able to move, eat, or breathe on his own. Even the patient's family had accepted his choice to escape the suffering and indignity of the slow demise.[81] But not the trial court or the Appellate Court: the former convicted Dr Kevorkian of second-degree murder, and the latter affirmed the conviction.[82]

This prohibition of mercy killing has one narrow exception: in the states of (i) Oregon, Washington, Vermont (by voter referendum or legislation), and (ii) Montana, and New Mexico (by judicial decisions), terminally ill patients may end their lives through the voluntary self-administration of lethal medications, expressly prescribed by a physician for that purpose.[83]

For example, under the paradigmatic Death With Dignity Act, adopted in Oregon, the person who seeks such a prescription must: (i) be terminally ill and have six months or less to live; (ii) make two oral and one written requests for assistance in dying; (iii) convince two physicians that he or she is sincere and not acting on a whim, under depression, and that the

---

76 MPC (n 2) § 2.12(3)(b); see also Me Rev Stat Ann tit 17-A, § 109(3)(B) (1983).

77 See, for example, *Hes v State* 20 P 3rd 1121 (Alaska 2001).

78 See, for example, *State v Oliver* 627 A 2d 144 (NJ 1993).

79 *Commonwealth v Simcock* 575 NE 2d 1137, 1142–43 (Mass App Ct 1991) ('a belief that the victim consented would not be a defence even if reasonable'); see section 2.3.3.

80 *People v Kevorkian* 639 NW 2d 291, 298 (Mich Ct App 2001).

81 ibid.

82 ibid 296.

83 ibid. – –, '"Death with Dignity" Laws by State' (*FindLaw*) <http://healthcare.findlaw.com/patient-rights/death-with-dignity-laws-by-state.html> accessed 23 August 2015. It is expected that many more states will adopt some forms of Death with Dignity laws in the near future. In September 2015, California lawmakers passed legislation modelled after Oregon's law. The legislation is now waiting an approval of California Gov Jerry Brown, who has yet to indicate his position on the matter. M Martinez, 'California lawmakers send assisted-suicide bill to governor' (*CNN*, 12 September 2015) <http://www.cnn.com/2015/09/12/us/california-assisted-suicide-legislation> accessed 30 October 2015.

decision is voluntary; (iv) be informed of 'the feasible alternatives', including, but not limited to, comfort care, hospice care, and pain control; and (v) wait for 15 days.[84]

2.1.2 *Killing on request of the victim*

Killing on request of the victim is treated the same way as consensual mercy killing, ie usually considered murder. However, the victim's request is taken into account at the sentencing stage of a criminal trial. Presently, approximately half of all states and the federal government recognise either the victim's participation in the crime or consent to the criminal conduct, or both, as a mitigating factor.[85]

The victim's consent to homicide is also a mitigating factor for capital sentencing purposes in the absolute majority of death penalty jurisdictions that list statutory mitigating factors.[86] The MPC comments that in the situation of a mercy killing, 'the defendant's homicidal act may not have occurred had the victim not consented to it. [In that case], the conduct of the victim in bringing about his own death deserves consideration as a mitigating factor in assigning a death sentence.'[87]

2.1.3 *Abortion*

The current judicial interpretation of the US Constitution is that women have a legal right to abortion but that right may be restricted by the state. For example, many states require parental notification for minors seeking abortion.[88] The Supreme Court has upheld those laws, provided that they do not effectively give the parents a veto power over their daughters' right to abortion, and provided that parental notification is not mandated in every instance, without creating exceptions for minors who are sufficiently mature to make the abortion decision on their own, or those for whom an abortion would be in their best interests.[89] A statute that prohibits an abortion from being performed without the consent of the putative father is unconstitutional.[90]

The laws regulating minors' access to contraceptives differ from state to state. Almost half of states explicitly allow all minors to consent to contraceptive services without parental permission. Another half of states permit minors to consent to contraceptive services if certain conditions are met (for example, being married, being a high school graduate or reaching a certain age; having been pregnant before; demonstrating maturity; or receiving a referral from a specified professional, such as a physician or member of the clergy).

Pursuant to a 2013 federal Appellate Court's decision, emergency contraception known as the 'morning-after pill' can be sold over the counter to minors.[91] The US Department of Justice, in a sharp reversal of its earlier policy, has decided not to appeal that ruling.

---

84 The Oregon Death with Dignity Act, Or Rev Stat § 127.800 *et seq.* (1994).
85 See Vera Bergelson, 'Victims and Perpetrators: An Argument for Comparative Liability in Criminal Law (2005) 8 Buffalo Criminal Law Review 385, 436.
86 See James R Acker and Charles S Lanier, 'In Fairness and Mercy: Statutory Mitigating Factors in Capital Punishment Laws' (1994) 30 Criminal Law Bulletin 299, 320–21.
87 MPC (n 2) § 210.6 cmt 6(b).
88 Maya Manian, 'The Irrational Woman: Informed Consent and Abortion Decision-Making' (2009) 16 Duke Journal on Gender Law & Policy 223, 250–51.
89 William H Danne, Jr., 'Validity, construction, and application of statutes requiring parental notification of or consent to minor's abortion' (2000) 77 ALR 5th 1, 2a.
90 See *Doe v Rampton* 366 F Supp 189 (D Utah 1973); *Rothenberger v Doe* 374 A 2d 57 (NJ Super Ct Ch Div 1977).
91 *Tummino v Hamburg* 936 F Supp 2d 162 (EDNY 2013).

2.2 Consent and non-fatal offences against the person

2.2.1 HIV and other communicable disease transmission

According to the recent publication of the Centers for Disease Control and Prevention, currently, 24 states have general laws that criminalise exposure to sexually transmitted infections and communicable diseases.[92] In addition, 33 states have one or more HIV-specific criminal laws. Those laws vary state by state. Some target people who have HIV/AIDS and fail to disclose their status to their partners before a sexual encounter; others address needle sharing; yet others cover blood, organ or semen donation. Sentences vary too: 18 states impose sentences up to ten years; seven impose sentences between 11 and 20 years; and five impose sentences of greater than 20 years.[93]

In most of the states that penalise intentional or reckless transmission of HIV, informed consent of the person exposed to infection either exempts the conduct from the definition of the offence or serves as an affirmative defence.[94] That under-criminalisation of consensual exposure to HIV may be seen as a problem in the context of practices known as 'bug-chasing' and 'gift-giving', which involve 'bug-chasers' (HIV-negative men) who actively seek out infection by having unprotected sex with infected partners ('gift-givers'). According to a source, this practice is the cause of 25% of all new infections among American gay men.[95] These statistics have been questioned, but even if they are not entirely accurate, there is a general consensus that 'bug-chasing' and 'gift-giving' present a problem for the gay community.[96]

However, over-criminalisation of HIV-related risks has been seen by many as a much greater problem than under-criminalisation. In a 2015 position paper on the criminalisation of HIV, sexually transmitted infections, and other communicable diseases, the Infectious Diseases Society of America and the HIV Medicine Association observed that many HIV-related criminal statutes are outdated and include excessive incarceration sentences for behaviours that pose little to no risk of HIV transmission. The paper urged state policy-makers to refrain from enacting laws that criminalise infectious disease transmission and revise their existing criminal laws.[97]

2.2.2 Medical treatment

The MPC and state laws either exclude from the scope of the offence or provide an affirmative defence for the consensual use of force by a physician administering to a patient a 'recognised form of treatment'.[98] What form of treatment is deemed 'recognised' and what

---

92 J Stan Lehman and others, 'Prevalence and Public Health Implications of State Laws and Criminalize Potential HIV Exposure in the United States' (2014) 18(6) AIDS and Behavior 997–1006.

93 ibid.

94 American Civil Liberties Union, 'State Criminal Statutes on HIV Transmission' (*ACLU Foundation: Lesbian & Gay Rights Project Aids Project,* 2008) <https://www.aclu.org/state-criminal-statutes-hiv-transmission> accessed 23 August 2015.

95 Gregory Freeman, 'In Search of Death' (*Rolling Stone,* 6 February 2003).

96 Amanda Weiss, 'Criminalizing Consensual Transmission of HIV' (2006) University of Chicago Legal Forum 389, 389–90.

97 IDSA and HIVMA, 'Infectious Diseases Society of America (IDSA) and HIV Medicine Association (HIVMA) Position on the Criminalization of HIV, Sexually Transmitted Infections and Other Communicable Diseases' (*The Centre for HIV Law & Policy,* 2015) <http://www.hivlawandpolicy.org/sites/www.hivlawandpolicy.org/files/HIVMA-IDSA-Communicable%20Disease%20Criminalization%20Statement%20Final.pdf> accessed 23 August 2015.

98 MPC (n 2) § 3.08(4). Such treatment is also justified (a) with respect to a minor or incompetent when authorized by a parent or guardian; and (b) in emergency when no one capable of consent is available and a reasonable person would have consented to the treatment. ibid.

is merely experimental have been interpreted differently in different times and by different courts. Sometimes, judicial characterisation depends on the 'regulatory status of a product or the novelty of a procedure, while in other instances an established product or procedure may become experimental simply because a research protocol aims to investigate its use'.[99] A few courts have invalidated – as unconstitutionally vague – state statutes that criminalised certain medical procedures characterised as 'experimental'.[100]

The existing boundaries of 'recognised' and 'not-recognised' medical treatments are not always consistent. For example, a woman who carries a breast cancer gene may choose to have a preventive mastectomy.[101] Such a radical surgery is considered to be controversial in medical literature: there is little proof that, for purposes of cancer prevention, it is superior to less extreme and disfiguring alternatives.[102] For women with 'familial breast cancer syndrome', a condition indicating a high risk for developing breast cancer,[103] the main advantage of the surgery is that it helps to relieve chronic stress and anxiety over the substantial likelihood of developing the disease.[104]

Yet no amount of stress or anxiety legitimises an elective surgery on a patient with Body Integrity Identity Disorder ('BIID'), a rare ailment whose victims seek to become amputees.[105] The limited statistics seem to indicate that, if BIID patients succeed in their pursuit, their quality of life improves dramatically.[106] A surgeon who agrees to perform such an amputation, however, opens himself up to criminal liability because his patient's consent is legally invalid.[107] The BIID patients often compare themselves to those suffering from Gender Identity Dysphoria ('GID'), describing the common experience as 'being trapped in the wrong body'.[108] The law, however, treats the two groups very differently: the GID patients can consent to a sex change operation, which often involves removal of healthy sexual organs, whereas the BIID sufferers cannot consent to amputation of an arm or a leg. Rejected by the medical community, some BIID sufferers turn to self-help or illegal practitioners in order to achieve their goal – the amputation of unwanted limbs:

> In May of 1998 a seventy-nine-year-old man from New York travelled to Mexico and paid $10,000 for a black-market leg amputation; he died of gangrene in a motel. In October 1999 a mentally competent man in Milwaukee severed his arm with a homemade guillotine, and threatened to sever it again if surgeons reattached it. That same

---

99 Lars Noah, 'Informed Consent and the Elusive Dichotomy between Standard and Experimental Therapy' (2002) 28 American Journal of Law and Medicine 361, 377.

100 See *Jane L v Bangerter* 61 F 3d 1493, 1500–02 (10th Cir 1995), rev'd on other grounds sub nom *Leavitt v Jane L* 518 US 137 (1996); *Margaret, s v Edwards* 794 F 2d 994, 999 (5th Cir 1986) ('The whole distinction between experimentation and testing, or between research and practice, is . . . almost meaningless in the medical context').

101 See, for example, Jane E Brody, 'Personal Health: Why Cancer-Free Women Have Breasts Removed' (*New York Times*, 5 May 1993).

102 Lane D Ziegler and Stephen S Kroll, 'Primary Breast Cancer After Prophylactic Mastectomy' (1991) 14 Journal of Clinical Oncology 451, 453.

103 ibid 452.

104 See Mal Bebbington Hatcher, Leslie Fallowfield and Roger A'Hern, 'The Psychosocial Impact of Bilateral Prophylactic Mastectomy' (2001) 322 British Medical Journal 76, 76.

105 – –, 'When It Feels Right to Cut Off Your Leg' (*Geelong Advertiser*, 4 July 2005) 15.

106 ibid.

107 But see Tim Bayne and Neil Levy, 'Amputees by Choice: Body Integrity Identity Disorder and the Ethics of Amputation' (2005) 22 Journal of Applied Philosophy 75, 84–85.

108 Carl Elliot, 'A New Way to Be Mad' (*The Atlantic*, December 2000) 73–74.

month a legal investigator for the California state bar, after being refused a hospital amputation, tied off her legs with tourniquets and began to pack them in ice, hoping that gangrene would set in, necessitating an amputation. She passed out and ultimately gave up. Now she says she will probably have to lie under a train, or shoot her legs off with a shotgun.[109]

To what extent all these restrictions are justified is a question open for debate. On the one hand, the liberal tradition with its emphasis on personal autonomy opposes criminal limitations on the decision-making power of rational adult citizens if their choices do not directly harm others. On the other hand, concerns over the rationality of certain choices, particularly those involving grave and irreversible injuries, support the intuition shared by many that not every experimental medical procedure should be permitted.

2.2.3 Sport injuries, 'horseplay', piercing

The MPC, as well as state laws, provides an exception from the rule prohibiting consensual bodily injury for 'the conduct and the injury [that] are reasonably foreseeable hazards of joint participation in a lawful athletic contest or competitive sport or other concerted activity not forbidden by law'.[110] The very participation in such an activity manifests one's consent.[111]

To determine whether this exception applies to a particular set of facts, courts seek to determine whether (i) the defendant's conduct 'constituted foreseeable behaviour in the play of the game'; and (ii) the injury occurred as a 'by-product of the game itself'.[112] In *State v Floyd*, for example, a fight broke out during a basketball game and the defendant, who was on the sidelines, punched and severely injured several opposing team members. The court denied the defence because the statute 'contemplated a person who commits acts during the course of play, and the exception seeks to protect those whose acts otherwise subject to prosecution are committed in furtherance of the object of the sport'.[113]

In contrast with legitimate athletic competitions, such activities as duelling, 'horseplaying' or hazing can never benefit from the defence of consent.[114] A court pointed out that difference:

When faced with the question of whether to accept a school child's consent to hazing or consent to a fight, or a gang member's consent to a beating, courts have declined to apply the defence. Obviously, these cases present 'touchings' factually distinct from 'touchings' occurring in athletic competitions.[115]

It should be noted, however, that, unlike criminal law, the law of torts may recognise consent of the victim in the examples above. For example, in *Hellriegel v Tholl*, a teenage boy had challenged three of his friends to try to throw him into a lake. As a result the boy was seriously injured. In a civil action, the court held that the boy's consent was a valid defence for his friends against the charge of battery.[116]

---

109   ibid 73.
110   MPC (n 2) § 2.11.
111   ibid cmt 2.
112   *State v Shelley* 929 P 2d 489 (Wash Ct App 1997).
113   *State v Floyd* 466 NW 2d 919 (Iowa Ct App 1990).
114   *People v Lenti* 253 NYS 2d 9 (NY Cnty Ct 1964) (hazing).
115   *Shelley* (n 112).
116   *Hellriegel v Tholl* 417 P 2d 362 (Wash 1966).

Almost every state has laws addressing some aspect of body art. At least 38 states have laws restricting body piercing and tattooing of minors. Seventeen states prohibit tattooing of minors regardless of parental consent, while three states do so for body piercing.[117]

2.2.4 Specific sexual practices involving infliction of harm

Practically every case involving consensual sado-masochistic encounters ended with the sadist participant's conviction of assault. Such conviction necessitated the finding of 'serious' harm suffered by the masochist participant, and making that finding was never a problem for a court.[118] In *State v Collier*, for instance, the victim's injuries consisted of 'a swollen lip, large welts on her ankles, wrists, hips, buttocks, and severe bruises on her thighs'.[119] The defendant was convicted of assault resulting in a serious injury, and the Appellate Court agreed, even though, as the dissenting judge pointed out, the inflicted bodily harm did not constitute a serious injury within the meaning of the state statute.[120]

The MPC and some state penal codes include physical pain in the definition of 'bodily harm'.[121] In *State v Guinn*, for example, the defendant was convicted of inflicting 'serious physical injury' in the course of a sexual encounter.[122] There was no evidence that the victim 'ever required any medical attention or suffered any wounds of any sort'.[123] Yet the Appellate Court sustained the assault conviction, reasoning that the sado-masochistic paraphernalia the defendant used must have caused serious physical pain – the candle wax was 'hot and it stung' and the nipple clamps were 'tight and cutting' – and 'serious physical pain' satisfied the definition of 'physical injury'.[124] Naturally, under a statute of this type, almost any sado-masochistic encounter automatically qualifies as criminal.

Some defendants have attempted to use the statutory exception for the 'other concerted activity not forbidden by law' as a defence in prosecution for consensual sado-masochistic sex, yet all those attempts failed.[125] In *State v Collier*, for example, the court held that the legislature did not intend to include sado-masochistic activity in the list of 'sport, social or other activity' under the Iowa Code.[126] Even in a rare instance when a court feels compelled to give weight to the victim's consent, it still tends to reiterate the traditional rule. In *People v Jovanovic*, for example, New York Appellate Court opined:

> Indeed, while a meaningful distinction can be made between an ordinary violent beating and violence in which both parties voluntarily participate for their own sexual

---

117 Michael Csere, 'Body Piercing and Tattooing of Minors' (2013) US Department of Health & Human Services OLR Research Report 2013-R-0231 <https://www.cga.ct.gov/2013/rpt/2013-R-0231.htm> accessed 23 August 2015.
118 See MPC (n 2) § 2.11 cmt 2 (acknowledging that the 'iniquity of the conduct involved' tends to affect judicial assessment of the seriousness of the harm). The Commentary notes that the MPC provision does not explicitly foreclose resort to such judgments, though the envisioned emphasis is on the amount of injury itself. ibid.
119 *State v Collier* 372 NW 2d 303, 304 (Iowa Ct App 1985).
120 ibid 309 (Schlegel J dissenting).
121 See, for example, MPC (n 2) § 210.0(2); Wash Rev Code § 9A.04.110(4)(a) (2004) ('"Bodily injury," "physical injury," or "bodily harm" means physical pain or injury, illness, or an impairment of physical condition').
122 *State v Guinn* No 23886–1-II, 2001 Wash App LEXIS 502 (Wash Ct App, 30 March 2001).
123 ibid 34.
124 ibid.
125 MPC (n 2) § 2.11.
126 See *Collier* (n 119) 307.

gratification, nevertheless, just as a person cannot consent to his or her own murder, as a matter of public policy, a person cannot avoid criminal responsibility for an assault that causes injury or carries a risk of serious harm, even if the victim asked for or consented to the act.[127]

One other way for a court to disregard consent in the sado-masochistic context has been through declaring the consent irrational, and thus invalid. In *People v Samuels*, for example, the defendant was convicted of aggravated assault for whipping an apparently willing victim in the course of the production of a pornographic movie. The case was complicated by the fact that the victim could not be found to confirm his consent. However, the court dismissed the very possibility of such consent, saying, 'It is a matter of common knowledge that a normal person in full possession of his mental faculties does not freely consent to the use, upon himself, of force likely to produce great bodily injury.'[128]

2.3 Sexual offences

2.3.1 Absence of consent or use of force/threats

Historically, non-consensual intercourse in the absence of force or threat of force constituted a crime only in limited circumstances (for example, when the victim was legally incompetent). Today, a growing trend in the United States is to criminalise all instances of non-consensual intercourse. The new rule, however, remains in the minority. The vast majority of states still 'require both the defendant's force and the victim's non-consent before an act of sexual penetration becomes a felony'.[129]

The key question in this regard has been how to define force. For most courts, it means only physical force or threat of physical force. Additionally, such physical force may not be the force inherent in all sexual penetration but 'physical compulsion necessary to overcome the resistance of the victim'.[130] Other jurisdictions have been less restrictive in their definition of force – those extend the offence of rape or sexual assault to situations in which consent is obtained by duress, coercion or extortion.[131] Pennsylvanian legislature went even further and defined forcible compulsion (an element of the offence of rape) as compulsion by use of 'physical, intellectual, moral or psychological force, either express or implied'.[132]

2.3.2 Evidentiary presumptions

Most jurisdictions continue to presume consent to sex in the absence of some expression of unwillingness (verbal or physical). In some of those jurisdictions, verbal resistance alone does not provide sufficient evidence of non-consent ('no means yes'),[133] whereas in others, verbal

---

127 ibid. Consequently, the court ignored the basic logic and did both: (a) reiterated that consent of the victim may not serve as a defence to the charge of assault and (b) reversed the defendant's assault conviction because the trial judge had improperly excluded evidence indicating the victim's consent.

128 *People v Samuels* 58 Cal Rptr 439, 447 (Cal Ct App 1967).

129 Michelle J Anderson (n 5) 1403. Only 14 states punish nonconsensual intercourse in the absence of force as a felony, and eight more punish it a as misdemeanor. See Michelle J Anderson, 'All-American Rape' (2005) 79 St John's Law Review 625, 629–30.

130 *Gibbins v State* 495 SE 2d 46, 48 (Ga Ct App 1997).

131 See Sanford H Kadish (n 60) 359.

132 *MTS* (n 4).

133 Sanford H Kadish (n 60) 377.

objection creates an irrebutable presumption of non-consent. A judge in *Commonwealth v Lefkowitz* opined that, 'when a woman says 'no' to someone[,] any implication other than a manifestation of non-consent that might arise in that person's psyche is legally irrelevant, and thus no defence'.[134]

In addition, the law retains the notion of what may be called generalised consent, or presumed consent. A scholar explains:

> The notion of generalised consent exists in rape law to the extent that consent to prior sexual intercourse either indicates consent to subsequent intercourse or suggests a greater likelihood that the defendant reasonably believed the victim consented to the later encounter. This notion effectively creates a presumption of consent to sexual intercourse on any specific occasion that the victim must somehow negate.[135]

Marital exemption from prosecution for rape provides an example of such presumed consent. Even though it no longer exists in its absolute form, nearly half of all states retain qualified versions of the exemption. For instance, 20 states either implicitly or explicitly exempt spouses from prosecution for sex offence charges if the complainant spouse was mentally incapacitated or physically helpless at the time of the assault.[136]

The notion of presumed consent may also apply to non-marital sexual relationships. Most states include an exception from their 'rape shield' laws (the laws that restrict admission of evidence of the rape victim's sexual past), which allows for such evidence if it covers prior sexual conduct between the defendant and the victim, thereby making previous consent presumptively relevant to the determination of present consent or of reasonable belief in consent.[137]

2.3.3 *Mistake of fact about consent*

To be convicted of rape, an actor must act with the culpability that reaches at least the level of recklessness and, more often, knowledge or purpose.[138] While states uniformly require that this mental state accompany the sexual conduct and the use of force, there is no similar consensus as to whether it must also accompany the element of non-consent. Most American jurisdictions permit the defence of mistake regarding the victim's consent only if such mistake is honest and reasonable;[139] a few states permit the defence when the mistake is honest but unreasonable; and a few states convict regardless of whether the defendant's mistake be reasonable or not as long as the complainant does not consent and the defendant knows that he is engaging in the sexual conduct through force.[140]

The mismatch between the prevailing low level of culpability as to the victim's consent (negligence and sometimes even strict liability) required for conviction and the resulting

---

134 *Indian Valley Golf Club Inc v Long Grove* 481 NE 2d 277, 282 (Ill App Ct 1985).
135 – –, 'Acquaintance Rape And Degrees Of Consent: "No" Means "No," But What Does "Yes" Mean?' (2004) 117 Harvard Law Review 2341, 2342.
136 ibid.
137 ibid.
138 Rosanna Cavallaro, 'Criminal Law, A Big Mistake: Eroding the Defense of Mistake of Fact about Consent in Rape' (1996) 86 Journal of Criminal Law & Criminology 815, 818–19.
139 See, for example, *Oliver* (n 78).
140 See, for example, *State v Reed* 479 A 2d 1291 (Me 1984); *Commonwealth v Williams* 439 A 2d 765 (Pa Super Ct 1982); *State v Houghton* 272 NW 2d 788 (SD 1978).

steep punishments has been criticised by some scholars as harsh and inconsistent with the principles of criminal law.[141] Others defended the current law explaining:

> Rape is different from other crimes in a way that justifies severe potential penalties even when liability is based solely upon negligent conduct [because] male self-deception about whether a woman has consented . . . is morally worse than ordinary forms of criminal negligence.[142]

2.4 Property offences and criminal damage

2.4.1 Place of consent in the offence structure

Consent is universally recognised as a ban on criminal conviction of property offences (for example, theft, criminal mischief, unlawful entry, burglary). In some jurisdictions, non-consent is an element of the offence; thus, the presence of consent leads to the failure of proof. In other jurisdictions, consent is viewed as a defence; here, consent functions to preclude 'the harm or evil sought to be prevented' by the offence.[143]

Under the MPC, all property offences include an element of unlawful taking, thus consent of the owner defeats the requirement of 'unlawfulness' and results in the failure of proof. In addition, the MPC provides for the affirmative defence of claim of rights, which applies, among other circumstances, when the defendant (i) acted under an honest belief that he had the right to take the property; or (ii) took the property exposed for sale with the intent to pay for it or with a reasonable belief that the owner, if present, would have consented to the taking.[144] Most states limit the application of the claim-of-rights defence described in (i), particularly with respect to self-help. The presumed consent defence described in (ii) is recognised in the minority of the US jurisdictions.[145]

2.4.2 Mistaken belief in consent

When non-consent is an element of the offence, the effect of the defendant's mistake about the owner's consent to taking, using or destroying the property depends on the culpability requirements of the offence. If the required culpability is purpose, knowledge or recklessness, any honest (even unreasonable) mistake would shield the perpetrator from liability. Consider *State v Kelly*, in which the defendant was convicted of larceny for removing fireplace mantels from two unoccupied houses and selling them to an antique dealer. The defendant had acted pursuant to an agreement with Bradley whom he believed to be the owner of the houses. In fact, Bradley merely co-owned the houses with his estranged wife who did not give consent to the removal of the mantels. On appeal, Kelly's conviction was reversed, the Appellate Court opining that one who takes property in good faith honestly believing that he has the

---

141 See Michael Vitello, 'Punishing Sex Offenders: When Good Intentions Go Bad' (2008) 40 Arizona State Law Journal 651, 667–74.

142 Andrew E Taslitz, 'Willfully Blind: On Date Rape and Self-Deception' (2005) 28 Harvard Journal Law & Gender 381, 387–88.

143 MPC (n 2) § 2.11(1).

144 MPC (n 2) § 223.1(3).

145 Paul H Robinson (n 74) para 109(b), (c).

authority to do so lacks the intent to steal required for larceny and, therefore, is not guilty even though his mistaken belief was unreasonable.[146]

In contrast, when consent is considered a defence, the language of a particular provision determines at what level of *mens rea* the perpetrator may be exonerated. For example, the presumed consent defence (see 2.4.1.) succeeds only when the defendant's mistake about the owner's consent is reasonable.[147]

---

146 *State v Kelly* 338 SE 2d 405 (W Va 1985).
147 MPC (n 2) § 223.1(3).

21
Turkey

R Murat Önok

1 GENERAL ISSUES

1.1 Conceptual foundations

1.1.1 Philosophical and theoretical principles informing the law surrounding consent

The legal justification for granting validity to consent attracts different opinions. According to one view, consent is a corollary of the right to self-determination, which refers, in the Constitutional law sense (Article 17), to a person's right to freely develop his/her own personality.[1] When a person is granted a right to full disposal over certain legal interests, he/she can choose, in connection with a concrete situation, to relinquish the abstract legal protection granted by the State over such rights.[2] This understanding may be said to reflect the German-oriented 'Social Value Theory' according to which the validity granted to consent is premised on law policy thoughts.[3]

Others rely on 'the theory on waiver of rights': a person who has been given the right to dispose over a right may also voluntarily choose to waive such right.[4]

The 'legal transaction' theory also has its supporters; consent authorises the violation of a given right creating a legal transaction as penal law attaches legal consequences to such declaration.[5]

---

1   Meral Ekici Şahin, *Ceza Hukukunda Rıza* (Oniki Levha 2012) 53; Hakan Hakeri, *Ceza Hukuku: Genel Hükümler* (18th edition, Seçkin 2015) 356; Mahmut Koca and İlhan Üzülmez, *Türk Ceza Hukuku Genel Hükümler* (7th edition, Seçkin 2014) 274; Hamide Zafer, *Ceza Hukuku Genel Hükümler Ders Kitabı* (4th edition, Beta 2015) 312.
2   Hakeri ibid 356.
3   Kayıhan İçel, *Ceza Hukuku Genel Hükümler* (6th edition, Beta 2014) 354.
4   Nur Centel, Hamide Zafer and Özlem Çakmut, *Türk Ceza Hukukuna Giriş* (8th edition, Beta 2014) 313; Bahri Öztürk and Mustafa Ruhan Erdem, *Uygulamalı Ceza Hukuku ve Güvenlik Tedbirleri Hukuku* (14th edition, Seçkin 2014) 233.
5   Sulhi Dönmezer and Sahir Erman, *Nazari ve Tatbiki Ceza Hukuku* (11th edition, Beta 1997) mn. 743; Timur Demirbaş, *Ceza Hukuku Genel Hükümler* (10th edition, Seçkin 2014) 318; Osman Yaşar, Hasan Tahsin Gökcan and Mustafa Artuç, *Yorumlu-Uygulamalı Türk Ceza Kanunu – vol I* (Adalet Yayinevi 2010) 679.

Finally, some authors argue that where conduct is consented to, there is no social benefit justifying state intervention through penal sanctions.[6]

1.1.2 Influence of feminist and queer theory

It does not seem that queer theory has, so far, had any influence on the Turkish penal law of consent. As for feminist theories, efforts have mostly focused on crimes committed against sexual liberty, and on the meaning of 'consent' to rape in particular. Discussions about sex crimes are discussed further below.

However, NGOs dealing with women's rights have achieved important successes in the process of drafting the new Turkish Penal Code, which entered into force on 1 January 2005. The following achievements deserve mention:[7]

- Adultery was not criminalised.
- Sexual crimes were considered to violate the personal rights ('sexual integrity') of the victim, and no longer 'public morality' and 'family order', as was the case with the previous penal code of 1926.[8]
- The definition of rape now specifically covers oral penetration.[9]
- The relevant provisions no longer refer to patriarchal values such as chastity, pudicity, or modesty.[10]
- Marital rape was specifically criminalised.[11]
- The provision on the discontinuation of criminal proceedings or revocation of punishment if the perpetrator married the victim no longer exists.[12]
- Forced genital examination was criminalised (which is important in connection with unconsented 'virginity' tests).[13]

1.1.3 Definition of informed consent

TPC Article 26(2) provides that no punishment shall be imposed in respect of any act committed as a result of the consent expressed by the concerned person with regard to a right over which he is fully entitled to dispose of.

The application of the provision is subject to the following conditions:

- The person expressing the consent must have legal capacity to do so.
- Consent must be explicitly declared or implicitly manifested.

---

6 Nevzat Toroslu, *Ceza Hukuku Genel Kısım* (18th edition, Savaş Kitap ve Yayınevi 2012) 176; Doğan Soyaslan, *Ceza Hukuku Genel Hükümler* (6th edition, Yetkin 2014) 369.

7 Yeşim Arat, 'Feminist Hukuk' (2006) 9 Kadın Araştırmaları Dergisi 64; Handan Eslen Ziya, 'Türk Ceza Kanunu Değişiminde Kadın Aktivistler: Bir Lobicilik Hikayesi' (2012) 15(1) Journal of Sociological Research 141. For further info refer to Pınar Ilkkaracan, 'Reforming the Penal Code in Turkey: The Campaign for the Reform of the Turkish Penal Code from a Gender Perspective' (*Institute of Development Studies*, 9 January 2007) <http://www.ids.ac.uk/ids/Part/proj/pnp.html> accessed 8 September 2015.

8 For extensive info refer to Türkan Yalçın Sancar, *Türk Ceza Hukukunda Kadın* (Seçkin 2013) 97–101.

9 ibid 194.

10 ibid 103.

11 Previously, the Court of Cassation only viewed forced anal penetration to constitute a crime, which was however, not rape, but 'ill-treatment of family members' – a minor crime (for example Criminal Court (4th Chamber), judgment of 19 December 1990, no 5557/7044). For extensive info refer to Sancar (n 8) 107.

12 ibid 132.

13 ibid 125–129.

- Consent must regard a right which the person is fully and freely entitled to exercise. In other words, consent only applies to those legal values at the disposition of the individual.

Hence, consent may be defined as 'the approval or acceptance, by a person who has capacity to express consent, of a conduct which may imperil or cause damage to his/her legally protected value/interest over which the legal order has granted the person a right to disposal'.[14]

Informed consent is discussed within the framework of medical treatment. The Court of Cassation has relied on Article 26 of the Regulation on Physicians' Ethics to explain the meaning of the term.[15] Accordingly, the patient must be informed of all of the following:

- the patient's health condition and diagnosis;
- the method, chance of success and duration of the suggested treatment;
- risks entailed for the patient's health by the treatment;
- the method of administration of prescribed drugs and their potential side effects;
- the problems caused by the illness in case of failure to approve the suggested treatment; and
- possible treatment alternatives and risks.

In addition, the information provided must be appropriate to the cultural, social and psychological condition of the patient, and information must be provided in a way that is understandable to the patient. The burden of proof on all the above issues lies with the physician or the hospital.[16]

1.1.4 Consent to risk or consent to outcome

This is not a matter that has been discussed at length, but the answer will depend on whether the crime in question is an intentional or a negligent one, and on whether its definition merely requires a given conduct or further requires a typical result to occur.[17]

As regards intentional crimes, if the legal definition requires a given damage to occur, the person giving consent must know of the conduct and of the result: where the legal definition of the crime entails a typical result, consent must cover such result.[18]

If there is an intentional crime that merely requires the endangerment of the protected legal interest, the person giving consent must know of the danger in question when consenting to the conduct.[19] In similar vein, where the crime only requires a prohibited conduct, consent must be directed at the performance of the typical act.[20] Hence, in these cases, consent is given to the typical act that entails danger to the protected legal interest.

As regards negligent crimes, most of the time consent will be inapplicable: although consent is given to the act that is in violation of the objective obligation of diligence and attention, the actual result originating from such conduct is initially unclear, and a person cannot be accepted to consent to an unknown result.[21]

---

14 Ekici Şahin (n 1) 7.
15 Court of Cassation (13th Law Chamber), judgment of 9 April 2014, no 30822/10772.
16 Court of Cassation (13th Law Chamber), judgment of 16 January 2014 (17487/794). However, this rule is valid for civil lawsuits.
17 Ekici Şahin (n 1) 125.
18 ibid 131.
19 ibid 125.
20 ibid 132.
21 ibid 129.

1.1.5 Revocation of consent

Consent must be expressed before or during the conduct that constitutes a crime.[22] Consent may be revoked during the execution of the conduct in question. Hence, if an act has been previously authorised, but consent has been withdrawn during its execution, there is no valid consent that justifies acts subsequent to the revocation.[23] Obviously, acts committed prior to the withdrawal of consent retain their validity. For example, in case of entering someone else's residence with permission, once the person is asked to step out, he/she has to, otherwise he/she has violated the inviolability of domicile (TPC Article 116). However, in this case, the Court of Cassation requires the person to be granted a reasonable time to leave the premises.[24]

Consent may not be revoked after the conduct has been completed. An exception to the right to revoke consent may only be accepted where it is no longer possible to interrupt, or put an end to the conduct that has already commenced, as in the case of a passenger who has voluntarily boarded a plane that has already taken off.[25] Where consent has been granted through a private law agreement, and the conduct foreseen in the agreement is being executed, a valid revocation may not always be possible.[26]

In addition, with regard to medical interventions, the Regulation on the Rights of the Patient (Article 24(6)) provided that revocation of consent to an operation that is under way was only possible where there was no medical prejudice.[27] This was the case where suspension of the intervention created a clear and irreversible medical disadvantage in terms of the patient's life or health.[28] In April 2014 this provision was deleted. Article 25 states that the patient may refuse or ask for the suspension of a treatment.

1.1.6 Ownership and limits of consent

Consent may only be expressed by the owner of the legal interest protected by the norm in question.[29] Hence, the conduct over which consent is being expressed is decisive. A person may only express consent to conduct that harms or imperils a protected legal value over which he/she has an absolute right to disposal (Article 26(2)).[30]

Thus, the crime in question must be protecting legal interests of an individual nature.[31] Whether this is the case will depend on the nature of the crime in question. For example, with regard to violations of the inviolability of residence; Article 116(3) provides that in case of a household any family member, and where a residence or workplace is shared any of the sharers, can give consent. However, consent should be given for a 'legitimate purpose'. For example, where the husband invites a stranger to his home to have sex, the

---

22 Dönmezer and Erman (n 5) mn. 751; İçel (n 3) 358.

23 ibid 751; Ekici Şahin (n 1) 180; M.Emin Artuk, Ahmet Gökcen and A Caner Yenidünya, *Ceza Hukuku Genel Hükümler* (8th edition, Adalet Yayınevi 2014) 439; İçel (n 3) 358; Demirbaş (n 5) 321; Hakeri (n 1) 363.

24 Court of Cassation (2nd Chamber), judgment of 7 February 2007, no 15780/1371.

25 Ekici Şahin (n 1) 182.

26 ibid 182.

27 Hakeri (n 1) 363.

28 R Barış Erman, *Tıbbi Müdahalelerin Hukuka Uygunluğu* (Seçkin 2003) 123. It was argued that this provision was in violation of the Constitution (Ekici Şahin (n 1) 185).

29 Dönmezer and Erman (n 5) mn. 745; İçel (n 3) 355; Centel, Zafer and Çakmut (n 4) 313; Toroslu (n 6) 181.

30 'Legal interest' in lieu of 'right' would have represented a better formulation (Ekici Şahin (n 1) 11).

31 Artuk, Gökcen and Yenidünya (n 23) 434; İçel (n 3) 354; Öztürk and Erdem (n 4) 234; Koca and Üzülmez (n 1) 274.

stranger would be held responsible for violation of inviolability of domicile *against the wife*. However, the husband would not be considered to have committed a crime. With regard to minors who have achieved the age of 15 and live with their parents, their consent (invitation to the household) is also legitimate as long as they have full mental capacity. However, the Court of Cassation has wrongly decided otherwise, and held that a crime is committed *against the parents*, in cases where boyfriends have been invited in without knowledge of the parents.[32] These decisions are criticised, in that, even where the purpose is to engage in sexual intercourse, such conduct cannot be regarded as an 'illegitimate' action against the parents.[33]

Where a crime protects more than one legal interest (eg robbery), all those whose rights are at stake must have consented.[34] Where multiple interests are protected, and only one (or some) of these are disposable by the owner of the right, consent will not justify the act, even if the primary legal interest protected by the crime is disposable by the person concerned.[35]

Where the holder of the right has full capacity, consent expressed by a proxy is considered either generally invalid,[36] or only valid with regard to crimes against property.[37] Obviously, consent given by the owner of the legal interest at stake may be communicated by a third person, including a proxy.[38]

In relation to private legal persons, consent may be expressed by the organ entitled to represent that entity.[39]

With regard to children and those under tutelage, the legal representative may only express valid consent to medical interventions, and certain acts concerning property rights.[40] Hence, in principle, only the child is entitled to express consent where there is a strictly personal right involved.[41]

Where the child has no capacity to consent, it is argued that parents may only consent to medical treatments and some types of property-related crimes.[42]

In cases of persons of unsound mind, it is usually the guardian appointed by the court that will express such consent, although a court decision may also be occasionally required.[43]

Even where individual rights are at stake, consent may only be given to specific acts, and not in the abstract and/or generally for the indeterminate future. Hence, a general waiver of a given legal interest is not permissible. Such consent would be in violation of the individual right to self-determination enshrined in Article 17 of the Constitution, and of the

---

32 Court of Cassation (2nd Chamber), judgments of 16 April 2007, no.1548/5557, 28 March 2007, no 408/4461 and 26 February 2009, no 15021/9143.

33 D Tezcan, MR Erdem and RM Önok, *Teorik ve Pratik Ceza Özel Hukuku* (11th edition, Seçkin 2014) 476.

34 Ekici Şahin (n 1) 114.

35 ibid 119.

36 Dönmezer and Erman (n 5) mn. 745; Toroslu (n 6) 182; Centel, Zafer and Çakmut (n 4) 314; Demirbaş (n 5) 319; Soyaslan (n 6) 373; Zafer (n 1) 313; Yaşar, Gökcan and Artuç (n 5) 683.

37 İçel (n 3) 356. Compare Öztürk and Erdem (n 4) 236.

38 İçel (n 3) 356; Centel, Zafer and Çakmut (n 4) 314; Yaşar, Gökcan and Artuç (n 5) 683.

39 Öztürk and Erdem (n 4) 236; Yaşar, Gökcan and Artuç (n 5) 680.

40 Ekici Şahin (n 1) 165.

41 Artuk, Gökcen and Yenidünya (n 23) 439.

42 Demirbaş (n 5) 319.

43 ibid. An example is abortion performed on a mentally-ill woman (Article 6 of the Law no 2827 on Population Planning).

prohibition to relinquish or to unlawfully or unethically[44] restrict fundamental liberties, laid down in Article 23(2) of the Turkish Civil Code.[45]

Generally speaking, consent may be expressed with regard to the following crimes committed against:

- property rights, unless otherwise indicated by law;[46]
- personal honour,[47] unless otherwise indicated by law;[48]
- individual liberties;[49]
- sexual freedom, unless otherwise indicated by law;[50]
- the protection of private life.

On the other hand, consent shall not constitute a justification for the following crimes:

- international crimes;
- crimes committed against life;
- certain instances of crimes committed against bodily integrity. There seems to be concurrence about the fact that consent may not justify permanent and grave damages (such as mutilation), or acts which endanger life.[51] However, the reasoning differs. The classical approach argues that every individual has duties towards his country, the society, and his family, and he cannot reduce himself to a condition where he cannot fulfil such duties.[52] A more modern approach argues that consent is based on the right to freely develop one's identity, and this also constitute the permissible limit of consent: if the act in question is not apt to allow such development, and, on the contrary, is likely to limit such possibility, consent is not valid.

> The exact consequence of either approach is not clear. However, it is argued that crimes against bodily integrity may be justified by consent only where the crime in question is prosecutable upon complaint.[53] Others argue that this criterion shall not be treated

---

44 The precise meaning of this criterion (that consent shall not be in violation of ethics) is unclear. It is argued that in order to avoid subjective interpretations, one should not take into consideration judgment values based on individual views or general social beliefs, but rules of conduct which comply with the ideal of a 'democratic social order' (Erman (n 28) 138; Ekici Şahin (n 1) 221).

45 Artuk, Gökcen and Yenidünya (n 23) 435.

46 An exception is constituted by TPC Article 170: in case of damage to property, consent of the owner will justify the conduct as regards damage to property, but the perpetrator may still be held liable for intentionally endangering public safety where the damage caused is capable of creating panic, fear or anxiety in the public, or capable of endangering the life, health, property of the public.

47 A minority view opines that a person may not validly consent to acts harming his honour (İçel (n 3) 358). However, the writer seems to confuse the distinction between honour and human dignity.

48 For example, insulting a public official due to his duty (Article 125(3)(a)) is prosecutable *ex officio*. In reality, consent would be invalid because public interests are also at stake.

49 However, 'consent searches' are not allowed under Turkish Law (Zafer (n 1) 317) as determined by the Supreme Administrative Court (judgment of 13 March 2007, no 6392/948).

50 An example is Article 104 concerning the punishment of consensual sexual relationship with minors who have completed the age of 15.

51 Other writers refer to 'serious damage' in general (Koca and Üzülmez (n 1) 275) or 'permanent weakness' (Toroslu (n 6) 178).

52 Dönmezer and Erman (n 5) mn. 758; Toroslu (n 6) 179; Artuk, Gökcen and Yenidünya (n 23) 437; Hakeri (n 1) 369; Soyaslan (n 6) 371. For an even more restrictive stance refer to Centel, Zafer and Çakmut (n 4) 316.

53 Artuk, Gökcen and Yenidünya (n 23) 437; İçel (n 3) 360; Centel, Zafer and Çakmut (n 4) 317.

as decisive, what matters is whether the individual's disposal over a certain right serves the free development of his/her personality within the boundaries established by law.[54]

- crimes that protect legal interests belonging exclusively or partly to the society or the state. Some examples are crimes committed against public health (such as drug offences), crimes committed against the family order (such as polygamy or altering the lineage of the child), crimes committed against the reliability and functioning of the public administration (such as embezzlement and bribery), crimes committed against the judiciary (such as calumny and perjury), crimes committed against the constitutional order and its functioning (such as assassination attempts against the president).

1.2 Place of consent in the offence structure

The wording of Article 26(2) is neutral as to the legal qualification of consent as it merely states that the person acting upon consent shall not be punished.[55] Academic writings make a dual distinction between consent acting as a justification, and consent eliminating the 'typicity' of the conduct (that is, causing the conduct not to fall within the legal definition of the crime).

If there is a ground justifying the act, there is no criminal wrong in the first place. As consent is considered to eliminate the unlawfulness of the act, a legitimate consent renders an act lawful. That is why the new Penal Code speaks of consent of 'the person concerned', rather than consent of 'the victim', which was the term previously used in academic writings and judicial decisions. The idea, as stated in the official explanation of Article 26, is that there can be no 'victim' in case of legitimate consent, since there has been no wrongful conduct that causes unjust harm.[56] Hence, Article 26(2), as stated in the official explanation of the provision, constitutes a justification.[57]

Exceptionally, consent may also eliminate the 'typicity' of the conduct, in other words, it may mean that the conduct in question does not fit into the definition of any criminal offence. According to academic writings, this is the case *only*[58] when the legal definition of a criminal offence specifically requires the conduct to be unlawful[59] (or, more specifically, unconsented[60]),[61] or it is possible by way of interpretation to conclude that the typical conduct must manifest itself in the absence of consent.[62]

---

54 Koca and Üzülmez (n 1) 276.

55 Ekici Şahin (n 1) 9.

56 Artuk, Gökcen and Yenidünya (n 23) 432. For the view that there is no such term see Zeki Hafızoğulları and Muharrem Özen, *Türk Ceza Hukuku Genel Hükümler* (5th edition, Yayıncılık 2012) 252.

57 Toroslu (n 6) 175; Hafızoğulları and Özen (n 56) 251; Soyaslan (n 6) 368; Zeynel Kangal, 'Ceza Hukukunda Varsayılan Rıza' (2011) C.XV(4) Gazi Üniversitesi Hukuk Fakültesi Dergisi 224. Confirmed by the Court of Cassation (5th Criminal Chamber), judgment of 16 April 2007, no 3496/2859.

58 As opposed to some German writings which accept that consent always eliminates the typicity of the conduct (Koca and Üzülmez (n 1) 271).

59 An example may be found in Article 109 on deprivation of liberty, which reads 'Any person who unlawfully deprives a person of his freedom to go to, or to remain in, a particular place. . .'.

60 Typical examples may be found in Article 116 concerning violation of the immunity of residence ('A person who enters an individual's residence or its associated buildings without consent. . .') and Article 141 on theft ('Any person who takes another's removable property from its place, without the consent of the individual in whose possession it is, in order to derive benefit for himself or a third party. . .').

61 Artuk, Gökcen and Yenidünya (n 23) 433; Öztürk and Erdem (n 4) 233–234.

62 Ekici Şahin (n 1) 89; Koca and Üzülmez (n 1) 270.

Only one author argues[63] that the lack of consent *always* constitutes a 'negative element' (of the criminal offence) hence representing one of the material elements of the crime.[64] According to this understanding, knowledge about the fact that a justification does not apply to the conduct is part of criminal intent.[65]

The above dual distinction is very important, as shall be seen below, in the application of the provisions concerning mistake. Furthermore, where consent eliminates typicity, there is no need, as opposed to consent which acts as justification, to enquire whether the consenting person has capacity to consent,[66] or whether the perpetrator is aware of the existence of such consent.[67]

1.3 Form of consent

1.3.1 Declared or implied

Whereas there is no clarity in Article 26 itself, academic writings[68] and the Court of Cassation concur that consent may be expressed explicitly or implicitly.[69] Implicit consent exists where a person who has the will to authorise a certain act does not explicitly state it but displays such will through his conduct.[70]

Consent may be expressed orally or in writing.[71] Exceptionally, in cases of 'major chirurgical operations' written consent is required by Article 70 of the Law no 1219 which regulates medical practices. Furthermore, where the patient is rejecting treatment, he/she must be informed about the consequences of withholding treatment, and this notification must be certified in writing (Article 25 of the Regulation on the Rights of the Patient). However, it is argued that, if consent does exist, the fact that it is not in written form may lead to private law liability, but not to criminal responsibility.[72] The exception is Article 90 TPC, which requires consent to human experimentation be in written form to constitute a justification.

In any case, consent must derive from free will, and should not have been impaired by the use of force, threat or deceit.[73] Finally, consent cannot retroactively justify a criminal conduct.[74]

1.3.2 Presumed consent

This doctrine has particular importance with regard to medical interventions, although it may also apply to any other crime.

---

63 İzzet Özgenç, *Türk Ceza Hukuku Genel Hükümler* (10th edition, Ankara 2014) 346–347.
64 This monist approach must be rejected since the Penal Code, apart for providing a general justification in Article 26(2), explicitly refers to the lack of consent in defining certain crimes (Ekici Şahin (n 1) 84, 86).
65 Özgenç (n 63) 347.
66 Ekici Şahin (n 1) 73; Hakeri (n 1) 358.
67 However, consent must have been expressed (Ekici Şahin (n 1) 173).
68 Dönmezer and Erman (n 5) mn. 749; İçel (n 3) 357; Centel, Zafer and Çakmut (n 4) 314; Öztürk and Erdem (n 4) 237; Demirbaş (n 5) 320; Soyaslan (n 6) 374; Hafızoğulları and Özen (n 56) 253.
69 Court of Cassation (11th Chamber), judgment of 6 February 2008.
70 Hakeri (n 1) 372.
71 Artuk, Gökcen and Yenidünya (n 23) 439; Centel, Zafer and Çakmut (n 4) 314; Öztürk and Erdem (n 4) 237.
72 Barış Erman, *Tıbbi Müdahalelerin Hukuka Uygunluğu* (Seçkin 2003) 124; Ekici Şahin (n 1) 178.
73 İçel (n 3) 358; Centel, Zafer and Çakmut (n 4) 315; Demirbaş (n 5) 320; Yaşar, Gökcan and Artuç (n 5) 682.
74 İçel (n 3) 357; Centel, Zafer and Çakmut (n 4) 315; Öztürk and Erdem (n 4) 237; Demirbaş (n 5) 321.

While academic writings generally recognise the doctrine of presumed consent,[75] the legal qualification of this institution is open to debate: while it is widely regarded as a justification,[76] some regard it as a manifestation of 'permitted risk' (*erlaubtes Risiko* in German) based on the social adequacy of the conduct,[77] while others regard it as falling in-between consent and necessity.[78] The Court of Cassation has also occasionally relied on presumed consent, however, mistakenly spoken of 'implicit consent' instead.[79]

Presumed consent may only enter into play where it is not possible to obtain the consent of the person concerned.[80] To accept the existence of presumed consent, the judge must determine that had the person, who has the right to consent, known the situation it was strongly probable that he/she would have consented to the act in question.[81]

Consent may be presumed when the perpetrator's aim is to protect the legitimate interests of the person concerned.[82] However, the legal interest sought to be protected must be greater than that harmed by the intervention.[83] The conduct must be in conformity with the presumed will of the holder of the right. Where the perpetrator acts with such subjective belief, which, however, later turns out to be incorrect, he shall still benefit from presumed consent as long as the above conditions have been complied with.[84]

As regards medical treatment, the intervention will be justified if it can be said that the patient would have consented to it had he/she not been incapacitated.[85]

When the bearer of the right to consent has previously made an express statement, there is no possibility to have recourse to this doctrine, even where the conduct aims at safeguarding that person's interests.[86] Hence, so-called 'hypothetical' consent is viewed negatively: where the doctor has the chance to have recourse to the patient's will, but does not, it is not possible to justify the act by arguing that had he done so, the patient would have most likely consented.[87] However, in such case, the objective imputability of the result to the perpetrator may be called into question.[88]

1.4 Capacity to consent

Capacity to consent is assessed independently from the rules on legal capacity laid down by the Civil Code.

---

75 Artuk, Gökcen and Yenidünya (n 23) 440; Centel, Zafer and Çakmut (n 4) 314; Öztürk and Erdem (n 4) 238; Demirbaş (n 5) 320; Hakeri (n 1) 371; İçel (n 3) 357; Zafer (n 1) 321; Ekici Şahin (n 1) 223; Yaşar, Gökcan and Artuç (n 5) 683. However, some authors argue that consent may not be presumed (Özgenç (n 63) 361) or that this term is an 'invented' notion borrowed from private law, and that other justifications (such as exercise of a right) or excuses shall be relied upon is such cases, Koca and Üzülmez (n 1) 278.

76 Ekici Şahin (n 1) 241.

77 T Zeynel Kangal, *Ceza Hukukunda Zorunluluk Durumu* (Seçkin 2010) 195; Öztürk and Erdem (n 4) 238.

78 Hakeri (n 1) 371.

79 Refer to ibid 372–373 for examples.

80 Kangal (n 57) 231; Ekici Şahin (n 1) 225; Demirbaş (n 5) 321.

81 Hakeri (n 1) 371; Centel, Zafer and Çakmut (n 4) 314.

82 Artuk, Gökcen and Yenidünya (n 23) 440.

83 ibid 419; İçel (n 3) 357.

84 Öztürk and Erdem (n 4) 238.

85 Çakmut, 211.

86 Artuk, Gökcen and Yenidünya (n 23) 440.

87 Kangal (n 57) 225–226; Ekici Şahin (n 1) 254; Öztürk and Erdem (n 4) 239.

88 Kangal (n 57) 226.

The mentally ill may not express consent.[89] Those who are not 12 years of age are also deemed incompetent,[90] as are those under the influence of substances which eliminate or decisively reduce their capacity to comprehend.

However, with regard to certain crimes, the lawmaker may adopt a different threshold: an example is trafficking in human beings (Article 80), where minors have no capacity to express consent. Similarly, where the victim has not reached 15 years of age, he/she cannot express valid consent to sexual intercourse.[91]

With regard to minors over 12 years of age, each case demands a specific analysis: it must be determined that the minor is able to comprehend the meaning and consequences of the legal interest at stake, and of waiving legal protection thereof.[92] In fact, this may be taken as the general rule as regards any child, of any age.[93]

However, the specific criminal offence in question will be decisive. For example, with regard to deprivation of liberty, the Court of Cassation requires the minor to have reached the age of 15 to be able to validly express consent.[94] In fact, some authors believe that this age limit is generally applicable to all crimes,[95] unless the law or the case-law has determined otherwise.[96] This is because children who have reached 15 years of age are deemed to possess mental capacity (Article 31(2)).[97] However, as explained above, it is a better approach not to make categorisations based merely on age, but to make an assessment on a case-by-case basis.[98]

1.5 Consequences of mistaken consent

1.5.1 Mistake

Where consent acts as a justification, any mistake by the victim in expressing consent will vitiate and invalidate this declaration of consent.[99] In fact, some authors argue that where consent is not declared seriously, it is also not valid.[100]

However, some authors argue that mistake (or even deceit) does not invalidate consent when it is not related to the legal interest over which consent is being expressed.[101]

---

89 Centel, Zafer and Çakmut (n 4) 313.

90 ibid.

91 In fact, even where the minor is 16 or 17, 'conventional' sexual intercourse (normal or anal penetration) will fall into Article 104 (sexual intercourse with a minor), which is prosecutable upon complaint. It is generally accepted that, where the will of the parents contradict that of their child, the minor's will is decisive on the issue of complaint.

92 Ekici Şahin (n 1) 135; Centel, Zafer and Çakmut (n 4) 313; Öztürk and Erdem (n 4) 236; Koca and Üzülmez (n 1) 276.

93 Dönmezer and Erman (n 5) mn. 747; Ekici Şahin (n 1) 150.

94 Grand Chamber, judgment of 11 March 2008, no 5–253/52.

95 Artuk, Gökcen and Yenidünya (n 23) 435; Demirbaş (n 5) 320.

96 An example is Article 234(3) which punishes to keep a child who has run away from home (without informing, or obtaining the consent of his legal guardian) without notifying the parents or competent authorities, even if the child has consented.

97 However, there is a mandatory reduction for their punishment.

98 İçel (n 3) 356; Toroslu (n 6) 182; Centel, Zafer and Çakmut (n 4) 313.

99 Dönmezer and Erman (n 5) mn. 750; Toroslu (n 6) 183; Artuk, Gökcen and Yenidünya (n 23) 438; İçel (n 3) 358; Centel, Zafer and Çakmut (n 4) 315; Öztürk and Erdem (n 4) 237; Hakeri (n 1) 358; Demirbaş (n 5) 321; Soyaslan, (n 6) 375; Koca and Üzülmez (n 1) 277.

100 Dönmezer and Erman (n 5) mn. 750; Toroslu (n 6) 183; Soyaslan (n 6) 375; Ekici Şahin (n 1) 185.

101 Ekici Şahin (n 1) 202, Hakeri (n 1) 364 (an example given by the author is where a person accepts to donate blood in the wrong belief that he will be remunerated).

1.5.2 Deception

The majority view is that any deceit will always invalidate consent.[102] The matter has rather been discussed in connection with specific offences, such as rape. The previous penal code provided for a criminal offence (Article 423) where the victim lost her virginity as a result of sexual intercourse procured by a false promise of marriage, whereas there is no such provision in the new penal code. Hence, it is debated whether a false promise of future marriage, given to a woman to convince her to accept sexual intercourse, invalidates such consent, leading to liability for rape. The majority opines in the negative,[103] although the reasoning differs:

- One view is that a false promise of marriage is a form of deceit that does not directly affect the legal interest protected by the provision on rape; hence, the consent is considered valid.[104]
- Some argue that a restrictive approach is required as regards the meaning of deceit in the framework of rape.[105]
- Another view relies on the fact that such promise is not apt to eliminate the victim's resistance, hence the perpetrator cannot be held responsible for rape.[106]
- Finally, a minority view argues that the perpetrator can be held responsible for rape because consent must be legitimately obtained: deception exists in all cases where a misleading action has led to obtaining a consent that would not have been provided in the absence of such deceitful action.[107]

Furthermore, there may be cases where 'deception' constitutes an aggravating circumstance of the crime, thus, *a fortiori*, invalidating consent (an example is Article 109 on deprivation of liberty).

1.6 Mistake about consent

The legal consequence of the wrong belief by the offender about the existence of consent depends on whether, in connection with the specific criminal offence, consent constitutes a justification or it eliminates the typicity of the conduct.

Where there is no consent but the perpetrator wrongly believes in the contrary, the following distinction applies:

- In the case of consent as a justification, TPC Article 30(3) applies: 'Any person who is inevitably mistaken about the existence of circumstances concerning grounds excluding or reducing criminal responsibility shall benefit from such mistake.'[108] Thus, if the mistake is inevitable, no criminal responsibility arises. If the mistake was not inevitable, there are different views.[109] According to one view (theory on negative elements of typicity), this mistake negates intent, thus the first paragraph of the article shall apply, and the

---

102 Dönmezer and Erman (n 5) mn. 750; Soyaslan (n 6) 375; Ekici Şahin (n 1) 203; Yaşar, Gökcan and Artuç (n 5) 682.
103 Refer to Tezcan, Erdem and Önok (n 33) 332 for references.
104 Hakeri (n 1) 358; Ekici Şahin (n 1) 92.
105 Fahri Gökcen Taner, *Cinsel Özgürlüğe Karşı Suçlar* (Seçkin 2013) 132.
106 Yaşar, Gökcan and Artuç (n 5) 3241.
107 Tezcan, Erdem and Önok (n 33) 332.
108 Unless otherwise indicated, the translations are the author's own.
109 This refers to the perpetrator's lack of guilt in being mistaken.

perpetrator may only be held responsible if the act amounts to a crime that can be punished when committed negligently.[110] According to another view (strict guilt theory), this mistake precludes culpability, but the conduct is still intentional and unlawful, therefore the perpetrator shall be held responsible for the crime, but the mistake shall be taken into account, according to Article 61 of the TPC, in the determination of the sentence.[111]

- Where consent eliminates the typicity of the conduct, Article 30(1), regulating mistake in the legal elements of the criminal offence shall apply: 'Any person who, in the execution of the act, does not have knowledge of the material elements in the legal definition of the crime, is not deemed to have acted with intent.' As a consequence, it is irrelevant whether the perpetrator was at fault or not in his/her incorrect belief – he/she is considered not to have acted intentionally. As a result, the perpetrator may only be punished for a negligent crime, if the negligent conduct constitutes a crime. To give an example, if a student is invited to room no 169 in Dorm building A, and due to his carelessness, he walks into room no 196 in that building, he cannot be held criminally responsible since Article 116 on violation of the immunity of residence can only be committed intentionally. However, at the time of the previous penal code, the Court of Cassation held the author responsible where the consent was only apparent and not genuine: A woman whose husband was in Germany for labour was called on the phone on 15 successive days by the perpetrator who asked her to engage in sexual intercourse. The woman apparently accepted, but only to call to police to make sure that they caught the man, who was later arrested in the yard of the woman's house. The Court of Cassation, wrongfully, held the man responsible for Article 116.[112]

The exact opposite scenario is where consent exists, but the perpetrator is unaware of it:

- In case of consent acting as justification, the perpetrator shall not benefit from a consent of which he is unaware,[113] and it is argued that he should be held responsible for attempted crime.[114] However, the majority defends that grounds for justification are 'objective' in nature: their actual existence suffices for the perpetrator to benefit from it.[115]
- In the case of consent that eliminates the typicity of the conduct, the provisions on 'impossible attempt' shall apply.[116] Depending on the theory adopted regarding the consequences of impossible attempt, some argue that this will lead to lack of criminal responsibility, while others argue that the perpetrator can be held responsible for attempt.

---

110 Artuk, Gökcen and Yenidünya (n 23) 531; Özgenç (n 63) 431; Koca and Üzülmez (n 1) 287; Hakeri (n 1) 376; Devrim Güngör, *Ceza Hukukunda Fiil Üzerinde Hata* (Yetkin 2007) 72; Kangal (n 77) 365, 369.

111 For the understanding of this view see Koca and Üzülmez (n 1) 283 and Kangal (n 57) 366. Compare V Ö Özbek, M N Kanbur, K Dogan, P Bacaksiz and I Tepe, *Türk Ceza Hukuku Genel Hükümler* (5th edition, Ankara 2014) 421 (the authors find this view acceptable but unjust); Güngör ibid 70.

112 Grand Chamber, judgment of 29 May 1995, no 4–146/170. However, at that time there was no provision similar to Article 30(1).

113 Artuk, Gökcen and Yenidünya (n 23) 439; Öztürk and Erdem (n 4) 239; Özbek and others (n 111) 291; Koca and Üzülmez (n 1) 253.

114 Compare RB Erman, *Yanılmanın Ceza Sorumluluğuna Etkisi* (PhD thesis, Istanbul University 2006) 390–2 (the writer argues that in case of the objective existence of a justification, one may speak of 'impossible crime', hence the perpetrator cannot be punished at all).

115 Dönmezer and Erman (n 5) mn. 696; Demirbaş (n 5) 266; Centel, Zafer and Çakmut (n 4) 283, Soyaslan (n 6) 357; Kangal (n 57) 203; Güngör (n 110) 63; Ekici Şahin (n 1) 176. Refer to Tuğrul Katoğlu, *Ceza Hukukunda Hukuka Aykırılık* (Seçkin 2003) 81 for extensive debate.

116 In the same direction Ekici Şahin (n 1) 176.

2 SPECIFIC ISSUES

2.1 Consent and homicide offences

2.1.1 Mercy killings

There is no specific regulation on the matter of mercy killings. However, since an individual is not granted a right to dispose over his/her own life, such consent would be irrelevant, and the perpetrator would be held responsible for intentional homicide (Article 81). The motive of the perpetrator may be taken into account by virtue of Article 61(1)(g) concerning the individualisation of the penalty. However, this would have no practical effect since the punishment for Article 81 is life-time imprisonment, and Article 61(1) bears on the determination of the punishment when there is a lower and upper limit prescribed by law.

2.1.2 Killing on request of the victim

The above considerations also apply to this case. Euthanasia has led to particular debates. The Draft Penal Codes of 1989 and 1997 incorporated a provision on euthanasia that required, *inter alia*, the 'insistent request' of an incurable patient, and provided for a lenient sentence (one to three years). This provision was later dropped.

Academic writings draw a distinction between active, passive and indirect euthanasia.[117] It is unanimously accepted that active euthanasia amounts to intentional homicide, and that indirect euthanasia does not constitute a crime.[118] There is debate as to whether passive euthanasia shall be treated as intentional homicide. The majority opines in the negative,[119] while some authors, usually based on the doctor's position of guarantorship, which imposes a legal obligation to prevent the patient's death, consider such inaction to also amount to intentional killing by omission (Article 83).[120]

2.1.3 Abortion

TPC Article 99 regulates in detail uterine evacuation carried out by persons other than the carrier. The structure of the regulation is as follows:

- In the first ten weeks of pregnancy, the carrier is free to have an abortion performed. However, if the person carrying out such operation is not a competent doctor, that person shall be punished.
- After the initial ten weeks, only 'medical necessity' may excuse an abortion. Where there is no such necessity, consent of the carrier is irrelevant, and abortion will lead

---

117   Active euthanasia refers to conduct that is aimed at ending the life of a terminal patient. Passive euthanasia refers to all omissive conduct that encompasses a failure to provide medical treatment, thus leading to a patient's decease. Indirect euthanasia refers to medical treatment aimed at decreasing suffering, but which has the collateral effect of shortening a patient's life.

118   Refer to Tezcan, Erdem and Önok (n 33) 153 for references. In fact, in most cases, this will constitute 'premeditated' murder, which carries a punishment of 'aggravated life-time imprisonment'. Compared to a normal life term, the required time to become eligible for conditional (early) release is longer, and the rules on the enforcement are harsher.

119   Refer to Ekici Şahin (n 1) 276–282.

120   İçel (n 3) 361; Tezcan, Erdem and Önok (n 33) 154; Zafer (n 1) 316; Yaşar, Gökcan and Artuç (n 5) 681. Also see Centel, Zafer and Çakmut (n 4) 319 and Artuk, Gökcen and Yenidünya (n 23) 437 who draw no distinction between different types of euthanasia in concluding that this does not constitute a justification under Turkish Law.

to the punishment of both the carrier, and the person who performs the operation (Article 99(2)).

- Exceptionally, if pregnancy is the result of a criminal offence committed against the carrier, uterine evacuation may be performed until the end of the twentieth week of pregnancy (Article 99(6)).[121]

It is the provision of Article 99(6) that leads to debate: how is it to be determined that pregnancy is the result of an offence committed against the consenting carrier? It may be said that there is unanimity as to the fact that a finalised court judgment as to the existence of such crimes cannot be required since it would take too long to obtain such a determination. Also, a mere statement by the carrier should not suffice to accept that the pregnancy has resulted from a crime suffered. Hence, it may be said that the visiting doctor's medical opinion, based on the statement of the consenting carrier, shall be decisive.[122]

With regard to the 'medical necessity' exception, the majority seems to opine that the consent of the carrier is still to be sought. However, others argue that in the application of Article 99(2) the consent of the carrier is not required.[123]

As for consent in the first ten weeks of pregnancy, minors are also competent to make such declaration as long as they understand the meaning and consequences of such statement.[124] Since this is a strictly personal decision, it is argued that parents (and legal guardians in general) are not competent to invalidate the consent expressed by such minor, or to authorise abortion despite the lack of consent by such minor.[125]

Similarly, the use of 'morning-after' pills by the woman, even if she is a minor, is authorized. In fact, even if such pill is administered by another person in the lack of the woman's consent, it would not fall under Article 99 since that provision only applies to interventions against the foetus, which would require implantation ('nidation')[126] to have taken place. Such conduct could constitute intentional wounding (Article 86) against the mother.

2.2 Consent and non-fatal offences against the person

2.2.1 HIV and other communicable disease transmission

There is no legal provision with regard to any obligation for partners to disclose to each other health information, including being HIV-affected. The issue is discussed within the framework of the crime of intentional wounding (Article 86). The legal definition of said crime

---

121 The legal qualification of the consent in this provision is open to debate: it is regarded by some as a justification, by some as a ground precluding wrongfulness (Özgenç (n 63) 360) and by others as a personal ground excluding punishment (refer to Tezcan, Erdem and Önok (n 33) 315). Further compare Özbek and others (n 111) 295 who argue that consent eliminates the typicity of the conduct.

122 Refer to Tezcan, Erdem and Önok (n 33) 315–316 for the debate. However, some argue that it is unfair to expect the doctor to form an opinion on this point (Ekici Şahin (n 1) 354; Yener Ünver, 'Hekim ve Hasta Haklarının Ulusal ve Uluslararası Hukuk Açısından Konumlandırılması' (2007) 2(1) Ceza Hukuku Dergisi 213; Serap Keskin Kiziroğlu, 'Gebeliğe Son Verilmesi, Sterilizasyon, Kastrasyon Gibi Tıbbi Müdahalelerin Türk Hukuku Bakımından Değerlendirilmesi' (Sağlık Hukuku Sempozyumu 2007) 216.

123 Refer to Tezcan, Erdem and Önok (n 33) 312 for the different views.

124 Özbek and others (n 111) 296.

125 ibid.

126 That is the stage of pregnancy at which the conceptus adheres to the wall of the uterus. Usually, it requires at least six days after ovulation.

comprises the impairment of health, and the transmission of HIV falls under this rubric, even where AIDS is later not developed.[127]

The more difficult situation is when the HIV-infected partner does not disclose this information, but uses contraceptives, which, however, fail to protect the other partner from infection. In this case, rather than relying on consent, it would be fair to say that intent (direct or indirect) does not exist.[128]

Where the partner has informed the other about being infected, and the partner has consented nonetheless, the victim has 'voluntarily assumed the risk', and the result (the transmission of HIV) is not 'objectively imputable' to the perpetrator.[129] However, authors that reject the validity of consent to potentially life-threating conduct, and that do not rely on criteria of imputability when establishing the existence of a causal link, may argue that the partner should be held responsible.

As for doctors, it is argued that the HIV-positive patient's relatives should be notified, and that such action would not be in violation of Article 136 concerning unlawful diffusion of personal data.[130] There is no regulation on the matter, though.

2.2.2 Medical treatment

The first discussion is whether the lawfulness of a medical intervention is based on the exercise of a right by the doctor,[131] or the consent of the patient, with the majority inclined to rely primarily on the former.[132] The distinction is important in that those relying on the exercise of a right usually do not require consent where the intervention aims at treatment (therapy).[133]

In addition, the legal meaning of consenting to a medical operation has been discussed with regard to the crime of intentional wounding (Article 86). Some argue that a successful operation conducted in accordance with medical rules eliminates the typicity of the conduct since such action cannot be qualified as inflicting bodily harm on, or damaging the health of, the patient. Others argue that, in any case, all medical interventions fulfil the material elements of intentional wounding, hence actual or presumed consent of the patient is required to eliminate the unlawfulness of the act.[134]

The Regulation on the Rights of the Patient (Article 24) requires consent by the patient, or by his legal guardian where he/she is a child or under guardianship.[135]

In order for consent to be valid, it must be an informed one: the patient must have been informed about the purpose, scope, consequences and the possible risks of the operation as well as possible adverse consequences in case of failure to operate.[136]

---

127 Tezcan, Erdem and Önok (n 33) 210. In fact, an aggravating circumstance will also apply: causing an incurable illness to the victim (Article 87(2)(a)).

128 Tezcan, Erdem and Önok (n 33) 210.

129 Tezcan, Erdem and Önok (n 33) 210, fn. 39.

130 Özgenç (n 63) 356, fn. 582.

131 In this direction Dönmezer and Erman (n 5) mn. 729; İçel (n 3) 348; Centel, Zafer and Çakmut (n 4) 332; Artuk, Gökcen and Yenidünya (n 23) 416; Öztürk and Erdem (n 4) 230; Demirbaş (n 5) 310; Hafızoğulları and Özen (n 55) 253.

132 Çakmut (n 85) 121–122; Hakeri (n 1) 374.

133 See, for example, Demirbaş (n 5) 311 who, in this case, only seeks that the intervention is conducted in compliance with required medical standards.

134 Erman (n 114) 47, 77.

135 Where the parents fail to consent to the prejudice of the child's benefit, it is possible to obtain a court order authorising the intervention.

136 Çakmut (n 85) 225; Artuk, Gökcen and Yenidünya (n 23) 418; Centel, Zafer and Çakmut (n 4) 332. With regard to the content of the duty to inform refer to Erman (n 114) 99.

Further conditions are that the doctor be competent with regard to the particular intervention,[137] that there be 'medical indication' (medical or social necessity in performing the intervention), and that the intervention be performed in accordance with required medical standards.[138] Where the last condition has not been fulfilled, the doctor may be held responsible, as the case may be, for a negligent or intentional crime whereas failure to comply with any of the other conditions will lead to liability for an intentional crime.[139]

The newly amended Article 24(7) of the Regulation allows the performance of medical interventions absent consent under exceptional circumstances, such as where it is not possible to obtain the patient's consent and his/her life is under threat.[140] In such case, the intervention would be justified under the rules on 'exercise of a right' (Article 26(1) TPC).[141]

In addition to the above conditions, the least risky method must be employed in performing the intervention,[142] and intervention may only be performed where its probable result is not expected to cause graver consequences than the failure to perform it (prohibition to increase the risk).[143]

Exceptionally, the law does not require the consent of the patient in certain instances where public health interests are at stake. This is the case with Law no 1593 on Public Health and Hygiene, which allows the vaccination of the passengers and crew of ships, to prevent the infection of Turkish ports with epidemics (Article 49). In addition, according to Article 103 of the same law, those infected with syphilis, gonorrhoea and chancroid are under an obligation to undergo treatment, and shall be compelled to do so in case of refusal (Article 107). Law no 1593 (Articles 88, 90) also obliges persons to get a smallpox vaccination.[144]

Another exception to the consent requirement is with regard to force-feeding of inmates on hunger/death strikes, provided that a doctor determines that they are unconscious or under life-threatening conditions (Article 82(2) of the Law no 5275 on the Execution of Punishment and Security Measures). Obviously, the way force-feeding is administered must be compliant with human dignity and medical standards, otherwise a violation of Article 3 of the European Convention on Human Rights may arise.[145]

---

137 The exception is where urgent medical attention is required, in which case general practitioners are also required to act (Artuk, Gökcen and Yenidünya (n 23) 421). In addition, interventions performed by persons lacking the required competence may be treated under the rules on necessity (Centel, Zafer and Çakmut (n 4) 331; Özgenç (n 63) 361).

138 Hakeri (n 1) 374.

139 ibid 375.

140 Ministry of Health, 'Hasta Haklari Yönetmeliğinde Değişiklik Yapilmasina Dair Yönetmelik' (2014) 28 994 Resmî Gazete <http://www.resmigazete.gov.tr/eskiler/2014/05/20140508–3.htm> accessed 8 September 2015.

141 Özgenç (n 63) 357.

142 For a conviction based on the performance of an unnecessary operation coupled with the failure to inform the patient about less invasive methods, see the Court of Cassation (12th Criminal Chamber), judgment of 20 January 2015, no 7841/710.

143 Özgenç (n 63) 363.

144 Refer to Özgenç (n 63) 356, fn. 582 for details.

145 Article 3: 'No one shall be subjected to torture or to inhuman or degrading treatment or punishment'. As determined by the European Court of Human Rights in *Case of Ciorap v Moldova* App No 12066/02 (ECtHR, 19 June 2007) a measure which is of therapeutic necessity from the point of view of established principles of medicine cannot, in principle, be regarded as inhuman and degrading. The same applies to force-feeding when aimed at saving the life of a person on hunger-strike. The medical necessity must nevertheless have been convincingly shown, the procedural guarantees complied with and the manner in which the force-feeding was carried out must not have exceeded the threshold of the minimum level of severity under Article 3.

Where parents or guardians do not consent to an intervention that is necessary from the medical viewpoint, and the time required to obtain an order from the court would imperil life, or one of the vital organs, there is no consent requirement (Article 25 of the Regulation on the Rights of the Patient). Where there is no such danger, the relevant rules of the Civil Code (Articles 272, 431) shall apply, and a court order must be obtained.[146]

Finally, there are specific rules governing certain types of medical interventions:

- Law no 2238 regulates consent with regard to the taking, keeping and transfer of organs and tissues. With regard to transfer from living persons, only those who are sound of mind and who are 18 years of age may provide organs and tissues (Article 5 of the Law). Informed consent may be given orally or in writing; however, a document indicating the existence of consent must be drawn up in the presence of two witnesses, and approved by a physician (Article 6 of the Law).[147]
- Article 90 TPC regulates in detail the conditions required for a valid consent to human experimentation (para 2 applies to adults, and para 3 applies to minors). In both cases, consent must be written. In case of minors, consent must be obtained by the child as well as both parents.

2.2.3 Sport injuries, 'horseplay', piercing

Consent to acts such as piercing or having a tattoo done is considered legitimate since they would constitute instances of simple wounding.[148] A further argument may be the 'social adequacy' of such acts, which would eliminate their unlawfulness.[149] In connection with this view, it is also argued that such 'insignificant' instances do not require the intervention of criminal law since it cannot be argued that any protected legal interest has been violated.[150]

With regard to horseplay ('pranks'), presumed consent may justify the act. However, where the victim is not consenting, the provisions on intentional wounding are applicable since the motive of the perpetrator does not constitute an element of the legal definition of the offence. To give an example, where the victim is being hit in his back with a baton for the purpose of filming this prank, the perpetrator knows that he is inflicting physical pain on the victim, thus the requisite mental element (intent) is established.[151] Hence, theories such as implied or presumed consent, social adequacy or criminal insignificance of the act must be employed.

As regards sports injuries, the overwhelming majority opines that the criterion is whether the disciplinary rules applicable to a given sport activity have been respected or not.[152] However, a different view argues that violation of a rule governing the conduct of play does not suffice: by consenting to participate to a sport activity, the person in question creates an area of 'permitted risk' that covers not only conduct that complies with the rules of the game, but also conduct that is connected with the run of the play, even if the conduct is in violation of such rules.[153] This is the case when the injury is the result of a conduct that is part of the game

---

146 Artuk, Gökcen and Yenidünya (n 23) 419.
147 Demirbaş (n 5) 314.
148 Hakeri (n 1) 369.
149 Circumcision for religious reasons is given as an example (Öztürk and Erdem (n 4) 241).
150 Hakan Hakeri, 'Ceza Hukukunda Önemsiz Hareketler' (2007) 69 Türkiye Barolar Birliği Dergisi 55, 92–93; Ekici Şahin (n 1) 292.
151 Tezcan, Erdem and Önok (n 33) 212.
152 See, *inter alia*, Dönmezer and Erman (n 5) mn. 735; İçel (n 3) 352; Demirbaş (n 5) 317; Artuk, Gökcen and Yenidünya, (n 23) 431.
153 Tezcan, Erdem and Önok (n 33) 214.

action, and the resulting injury, may be deemed a 'normal' consequence of the risks inherent in the game. To give an example, where a defender tackles from behind a striker who is bearing down on goal, but misses the ball and brings down the opponent, thereby causing a penalty and being red carded, this is not a criminal offence even if the mistimed tackle caused a distortion to the opponent's ankle. However, if the perpetrator has violated the principle of good faith, and has knowingly caused damage by intentionally disrespecting the physical integrity of the opponent, this is a crime. For example, if there is a scuffle between players during which one elbows the other, this would be a crime.

2.2.4 Specific sexual practices involving infliction of harm

The issue of sado-masochist practices has been debated in the context of crimes against bodily integrity.

One view argues that where sexual partners have full legal capacity (in terms of age and mental condition), there would be no crime – the only issue would be to determine if both partners' consent was genuinely the product of free will.[154]

The classical view, however, believes that the decisive criterion is the same that applies to consent over bodily integrity: was there a risk of permanent and severe damage, or a threat to life? If the answer is in the positive, there is no valid consent.[155]

According to a more radical view, 'sadistic' practices may never draw a valid consent.[156]

Furthermore, it is also argued that if the permitted conduct violates 'human dignity', the consent is invalid, although no guidance is provided as to the exact content of this criterion.[157]

2.3 Sexual offences

2.3.1 Absence of consent or use of force/threats

While a minority opines that consent to sexual practices eliminates the typicity of the conduct,[158] the majority regards consent as a justification.[159]

Where consent is obtained through the use of force or threat, it is not considered valid. In any case, it is also argued that the proof of material or moral violence (or deceit) is not required since what matters is if the act of a sexual nature has been consented to or not.[160] In other words, lack of consent suffices. However, Article 103 on sexual exploitation of minors specifically seeks recourse to the use of force or threat, deceit or other ground affecting the will, when the victim is 15 years of age, and is capable of comprehending the meaning and consequences of the sexual act.

The definition of threat in this context in is open to debate. The Court of Cassation holds that the harm threatened must be more severe than the harm suffered by consenting to the sexual act.[161] Some authors argue that this is a wrong approach to the matter: the decisive

---

154   ibid 274.
155   Ekici Şahin (n 1) 117. However, consent would eliminate the application of the provisions on sexual crimes (Taner (n 105) 168).
156   Artuk, Gökcen and Yenidünya (n 23) 440; Toroslu (n 6) 183; Soyaslan (n 6) 375.
157   Refer to Tezcan, Erdem and Önok (n 33) 274 for citations.
158   Ekici Şahin (n 1) 89; Hakeri (n 1) 357; Taner (n 105) 162.
159   Refer to Tezcan, Erdem and Önok (n 33) 328, 341 for references.
160   Taner (n 105) 115; Sancar (n 8) 201.
161   Grand Chamber, judgment of 17 October 2000, no 5–196/201; in the same direction (5th Criminal Chamber), judgment of 23 May 2011, no 2970/4134. In one instance, a woman was induced into having

criterion is whether the threatened harm has caused the victim to consent to an act that he/she would not have otherwise permitted.[162]

As regards the use of force, academic writings argue that it suffices that the potential resistance of the victim was, even if in part, broken down in order to achieve sexual conduct. It is not required that the victim fought back constantly and spryly to the limit of her possibilities, nor does it matter that he/she did not call for help or suffer any injuries.[163]

Where the consenting person lacks mental capacity, the Court of Cassation holds the perpetrator responsible for the relevant sexual offence where it can be proved that the perpetrator knew or *might have known* of the victim's condition.[164] This approach is criticised in that it seems to imply that sexual intercourse with a mentally ill person is a crime *per se*.[165]

With regard to sexual practices, it is accepted in academic writings that where consent is revoked during engagement in sexual acts, the perpetrator will be held responsible in case of carrying on such acts.[166] Hence, consent must exist throughout the performance of sexual acts. In addition, consent must also cover the way in which the sexual act is performed (eg if permission is granted for normal sexual intercourse, engaging in unconsented anal intercourse will constitute rape).[167]

Finally, as regards sexual harassment (where there is no physical contact), the Court of Cassation relies on consent to justify written messages of a sexual nature where messages of similar nature have been previously reciprocally sent.[168]

2.3.2 Evidentiary presumptions

The Court of Cassation is usually attentive to the application of the *in dubio pro reo* principle. However, the Chamber that deals with sexual offences has developed a presumption in favour of the victim: if she has no reason to commit calumny against the perpetrator, and if there is no inconsistency in her statements throughout the proceedings that may cast doubt on her sincerity, such statements are considered to be true.[169] This presumption is open to criticism in that the Court premises it on the disturbing belief that a woman who suffers a sexual crime partly loses her 'chastity', which is precisely the reason which leads to suicides and 'honour killings' perpetrated by family members, as well as silence and lack of cooperation with investigating authorities on part of the victims.[170]

Even more important, news reports seem to indicate that *local* courts often acquit the accused when there is no clear physical evidence of forced conduct. This is caused by the wrong approach to equate failure to oppose resistance to having consented to the sexual act.[171]

---

sexual intercourse through the perpetrator's menace that he would have informed her family of a sexual intercourse entertained by that woman with another man. The Court of Cassation decided that this did not qualify as a threat (Court of Cassation, judgment of 17 September 1986, no 3383/3557).

162 Tezcan, Erdem and Önok (n 33) 331. Also see Taner (n 105) 128.
163 Tezcan, Erdem and Önok (n 33) 330; Taner (n 105) 123; Sancar (n 8) 201.
164 Grand Chamber, judgment of 20 December 2011, no 5–230/273.
165 Taner (n 105) 165.
166 Tezcan, Erdem and Önok (n 33) 329.
167 ibid.
168 Court of Cassation (14th Chamber), judgment of 27 October 2011, no 7732/1479.
169 See, *inter alia*, the Court of Cassation (5th Chamber), judgments of 9 February 2010, no 697/714 and 20 October 2009, no 2958/11746.
170 For further examples of lamentable masculine approaches by the High Court see Sancar (n 8) 209.
171 Sancar (n 8) 202.

2.3.3 Mistake of fact about consent

There is no specific sexual offence-related standard that applies to mistake of fact about consent. General principles apply.

2.4 Property offences and criminal damage

2.4.1 Place of consent in the offence structure

As already mentioned above, with regard to theft (Article 141), lack of consent is required by the definition of the provision, which makes lack of consent a negative material element of the offence. Hence, where consent exists, the conduct is no longer typical. In other property offences consent constitutes a justification unless lack of consent is a negative element of the nature of the conduct.[172]

2.4.2 Mistaken belief in consent

The distinction explained above between mistake concerning consent as a justification, and mistake concerning consent as part of the nature of the conduct also applies here. To give examples, in case of theft, consent concerns the typicity of the conduct, as the legal definition of the offence requires, as a material element, the lack thereof. Hence, where the perpetrator acts in the wrong belief that consent exists, Article 30(1) will apply, and he/she will not be held responsible since theft may only be committed intentionally.

In case of theft of things of minor value, TPC Article 145 provides for a mitigating circumstance or, exceptionally, for no punishment by taking into account the way the crime was committed and its characteristics. In the previous penal code there was no such provision, and in a case where a few apples had been stolen from a tree in the victim's garden, the Court of Cassation had decided that there was no crime as 'customs and traditions' allowed for such action.[173] This approach led to criticism in that 'custom' may not act as a justification; rather, one may speak about presumed consent or social adequacy of the act.[174] Today, Article 145, which is premised on the idea that where the 'content of wrongfulness' of the conduct is minimal, it does not justify criminal intervention and punishment, may be applied.

---

172 An example is Article 163(3), concerning benefiting without payment from services such as electrical energy, water and natural gas.
173 Grand Chamber, judgment of 26 October 1987, no 6–406/499.
174 Tezcan, Erdem and Önok (n 33) 587.

22
France

Dimitrios Giannoulopoulos and Raphaële Parizot

1 GENERAL ISSUES

1.1 Conceptual foundations

1.1.1 *Philosophical and theoretical principles informing the law surrounding consent*

Comparative law observers hoping to find assistance, in French law, with definitional problems pertinent to the law of consent are most likely to be disappointed, as no statutory text provides a definition. In relation to criminal law more specifically, no attempt is made to define the consent of the victim, perhaps in terms similar to those used in the 'groundbreaking' definition of consent introduced under s 74 of the Sexual Offences Act 2003 in England and Wales.[1] Perhaps it is not surprising that French law has shied away from defining consent, in the light of the experience of English criminal law at least, where 'the concept has proved notoriously difficult to define'[2] and where the concept of consent remains today highly vague and contestable despite the statutory definition.[3] In the absence of such a definition in France, criminal law scholarship and criminal jurisprudence were called upon to fill the void. Viewing the public interest as the alpha and omega of criminal law, these have taken as their starting point that, contrary to the maxim *volenti non fit injuria*, individual consent does not neutralise criminal liability. Two illustrations of this are: the prostitute's consent does not vitiate the charge for an offence of controlling prostitution for gain;[4] and the consent of the general assembly does not vitiate the director's liability for

---

1 Celia Wells and Oliver Quick, *Lacey, Wells and Quick – Reconstructing Criminal Law* (4th edition, Cambridge University Press 2010) 515.
2 Jonathan Herring, *Criminal Law* (Palgrave 2015) 99.
3 Andrew Ashworth and Jeremy Horder, *Principles of Criminal Law* (7th edition, Oxford University Press 2013) 352.
4 Article 225–5 French Penal Code.

an offence of misusing company assets for personal use, *abus de biens sociaux*.[5] In principle, consent does not constitute a defence in French criminal law.[6]

However, we must take note of two important developments that have the capacity to qualify this principle. The first is the proliferation of criminal offences aimed to prevent harm to individual interests (as opposed to protecting the public interest).[7] Individuals can, in principle, freely dispose of such interests neutralising the effect of relevant criminal law prohibitions. In recent years French criminal law has, with mounting frequency, started extending its protective net beyond archetypal individual interests – such as property and bodily integrity – to individual interests it has long ignored or taken little interest in (such as private life and sexual autonomy) thus increasing the role of individual consent as a precondition to setting the criminal law and criminal process in motion.[8] Even if in these cases the absence of consent is seen as part of the *actus reus* rather than a criminal defence *per se*, the fact remains that consent is becoming more central to the application of criminal law offences in France as in other countries.[9]

The incessantly growing number of exceptions applying to violations of bodily integrity offers a second, and more direct, illustration of this phenomenon. Aesthetic surgery, experimentations[10] and sterilisations for contraceptive reasons are a few examples of violations of

---

5 Article L 241–3 French Code of Commerce.

6 See generally Philippe Conte and Patrick Maistre du Chambon, *Droit pénal général* (7th edition, Armand Colin 2004) n 277; Xavier Pin, *Droit pénal général* (6th edition, Dalloz 2014) n 213; Jean Pradel, *Droit pénal général* (20th edition, Cujas 2014) 601. See also Antoun Fahmy Abdou, *Le consentement de la victime* (Coll Bibliothèque de sciences criminelles 1971); Amane Gogorza, 'Faute de la victime et responsabilité pénale' (2009) Revue pénitentiaire et de droit pénal 265; Xavier Pin, *Le consentement en matière pénale* (Coll Bibliothèque des sciences criminelles 2002); Xavier Pin, 'La théorie du consentement de la victime en droit pénal allemand – Eléments pour une comparaison' (2003) Revue de science criminelle et de droit pénal comparé 259; Xavier Pin, 'Le consentement à la lésion de soi-même en droit pénal' (2009) Droits 83, n 49; Philippe Salvage, 'Le consentement en droit pénal' (1991) *Revue de science criminelle et de droit pénal comparé* 699.

7 This new emphasis on individual interests has been facilitated in France by the restructuring of the Penal Code. Whilst under the Napoleonic Code of 1810, the 'special part' opened with the section on the offences against the public interest, under the new Penal Code, in force since 1994, the 'special part' now first deals with offences against the person, then property offences and it is its final part that looks at offences against the state, the nation and public order offences.

8 It is important to note the victim has exclusive ownership of the action that is needed for the initiation of a criminal prosecution in relation to such offences, depriving the prosecution service from the ability to do so where the victim does not consent to such a procedural outcome. To take the example of the offence punishing violations of the right to private life, Article 226–6 of the Penal Code provides that 'criminal proceedings may only be initiated on the complaint of the victim, his legal representative or the legal successor to his rights'.

9 On the question of whether the *absence* of consent is an element in the offence or the *presence* of consent constitutes a criminal defence, with specific reference to sexual offences, see Ashworth and Horder (n 3) 320.

10 See Article 223–8 French Penal Code which provides that 'carrying out or causing biomedical research to be carried out on a person without having obtained the free, informed and explicit consent of the person concerned, or of those who have parental authority for him or of his guardian or any other person, authority or organisation appointed to consent to or to authorise the research in the cases provided for under the provisions of the Code of Public Health is punished by three years imprisonment and a fine of €45,000' and which also states 'the same penalties are applicable where the biomedical research is practised after the consent has been withdrawn'. Article 223–8 provides for an exception where 'the examination of someone's genetic characteristics' or 'his identification by his genetic fingerprints [are] carried out for scientific research purposes'.

bodily integrity where consent vitiates liability for conduct that might otherwise amount to a violent offence against the person.[11] In such cases, the French principle of the inviolability of the human body loses its force, and the presence of consent legitimates interference with the latter.[12] The French position on this matter is beginning to transform from a principled rejection of consent as a means allowing the individual to dispose of his bodily integrity[13] to a position much more in line with the principle of self-determination emerging from the jurisprudence of the European Court of Human Rights (ECtHR).[14]

1.1.2 Influence of feminist and queer theory

French jurisprudence and academic literature does not engage meaningfully with the influences of feminist and queer theory.

1.1.3 Definition of informed consent

For a finding of informed consent in French law three conditions must be fulfilled. First of all, consent must have been given prior to the commission of the offence, which explains why, when a public order offence has been committed, the victim cannot stop the prosecution service from bringing charges against the defendant, even where the victim has waived the right to bring a civil action.[15]

Secondly, the person giving consent must be deemed capable of understanding the effect of the consent that he is giving. Mental disability and young age can vitiate any consent that may have been given. Sexual offences against children are a characteristic example. French law operates a distinction between non-consensual child sexual activity and consensual child sexual activity.[16] In both cases it is sexual activity with a minor under 15 years of age that is punishable, but to a different degree and different labelling applies. Non-consensual sexual activity is punishable by the offence of 'sexual aggression' (*agression sexuelle*),[17] whereas the less serious offence of sexual assault with a minor (*atteinte sexuelle*) is committed where

---

11 See Article L. 2123–1 Code of Public Health.

12 See Article 16–1 of the French Civil Code which provides that '[e]veryone has the right to respect for his body. The human body is inviolable. The human body, its elements, and its products may not form the object of a patrimonial right'.

13 See eg the '*stérilisés de Bordeaux*' case, where the *Cour de cassation* held that the consent of the interested parties to a sterilisation procedure was not giving them the right to violate the public interest in respecting bodily integrity. Cass crim, 1 juillet 1937, *Recueil Sirey*, 1938, 1, 193.

14 *Pretty v United Kingdom* [2002] ECHR 423. See generally Muriel Fabre-Magnan, 'Le domaine de l'autonomie personnelle. Indisponibilité du corps humain et justice sociale' (2008) Recueil Dalloz 31; Diane Roman, '"A corps defendant". La protection de l'individu contre lui-même' (2007) Recueil Dalloz 1284.

15 Article 2 French Code of Criminal Procedure.

16 On the issue of the absence of consent by children, see generally Renée Koering-Joulin, 'Brèves remarques sur le défaut de consentement du mineur de quinze ans victime de viols ou d'agressions sexuelles' in Jean Pradel, *Le droit pénal à l'aube du troisième millénaire. Mélanges offerts à Jean Pradel* (Cujas 2006) 389; Delors Germain, 'Le consentement des mineurs victimes d'infractions sexuelles' (2011) Revue de science criminelle et de droit pénal comparé 817.

17 Article 222–22 French Penal Code: 'Sexual aggression is any sexual assault committed with violence, constraint, threat or surprise'. If the sexual aggression is a rape (aggression with penetration) against a minor under the age of 15 years, it is punished by 20 years' criminal imprisonment (Article 222–23 and 222–24 French Penal Code); if it is a sexual aggression other than rape against a minor under the age of 15 years, it is punished by seven years' imprisonment and a fine of €100,000 (see Article 222–27 and 222–29 French Penal Code).

it can be proven the child consented.[18] In other words, French law treats consent in child sexual offences as a factor that can potentially mitigate the heinousness of the offence, with the important caveats that no violence, threat, constraint or deceit (*surprise*) has been present (the conditions, in other words, that trigger criminal liability for non-consensual activity with persons aged 15 and over) and that a presumption of the absence of consent from the part of the child does not apply. The absence of consent may be presumed as a result of the age difference between the child and the perpetrator or the authority the latter may exercise over the victim.[19] English law, in contrast, does not place any significance on the issue of consent where children under the age of 13 are involved in sexual activity,[20] arguably with a view to protecting them 'from themselves as well as from others who are minded to prey upon them'.[21] Where the child is 14 or 15 years old the defendant will escape criminal liability if the prosecution fails to demonstrate that he did not reasonably believe that the child was 16 or over.[22] There is notable convergence with French law on this point; defendants will escape criminal liability for sexual activity with a child if reasonable belief that the child was 15 or over is demonstrated in court, especially where the physique of the child lent support to such a belief. A notable divergence between French and English law (other than the one-year difference in the age from which consensual sexual activity ceases to be unlawful; 15 in France, 16 in England and Wales) is that the former limits criminal liability for consensual sexual activity with children only where the defendant is aged 18 or over.[23] This means that in France children under 18 who engage in consensual sexual activity with each other do not commit a criminal offence, a position much more in line with respecting individual autonomy and changing sexual attitudes among teenagers than the position adopted in England. In England and Wales, much depends on how far the prosecution service may be prepared to go when investigating child sexual offences, but this does not change the fact that children can be prosecuted for innocent sexual activity that may be considered perfectly compatible with modern social mores.[24] The fact that mouth-to-mouth kissing between consenting 15-year-olds is theoretically punishable with five years' imprisonment speaks for itself. A recent House of Lords judgment, upholding the conviction for rape of a 15-year-old boy who had had sexual intercourse with a consenting 12-year-old girl (who had even told the defendant she was 15) provides a good illustration of the risks inherent in punishing consensual sexual activity between children.[25]

The third and final condition for a finding of informed consent is that consent has been freely given. Certain offences make explicit reference to this condition. For example, the

---

18 See Article 227–25 French Penal Code which states that '[t]he commission without violence, constraint, threat or surprise of a sexual offence by an adult on the person of a minor under fifteen years of age is punished by five years' imprisonment and a fine of €75,000'.

19 Article 222–22–1 French Penal Code introduced with the Law of 8 February 2010. See generally S Detraz, 'L'article 222–22–1 du code pénal à la lumière de la jurisprudence' (2015) Droit pénal étude 24.

20 See ss 5–8 Sexual Offences Act 2003.

21 *Corran* [2005] EWCA Crim 192 [para 6].

22 See ss 9–12 Sexual Offences Act 2003.

23 This condition was introduced with the New French Penal Code of 1994, which departed from the position that every sexual activity with a child under 15 was punishable even where the act had been committed by another underage person. In practice, prosecutions were rare, but this does not change the fact that French law was until 1994 susceptible of punishing innocent sexual activity between children, exactly in the way that English law is susceptible of doing so today.

24 See generally John R Spencer, 'The Sexual Offences Act 2003: (2) Child and Family Offences' [2004] Criminal Law Review 347, 360.

25 *R v G* [2008] UKHL 37; [2009] 1 AC 92 (HL).

actus reus of the offence of experimenting upon human beings is complete where biomedical research upon a person has been undertaken in the absence of a 'free, informed and explicit consent'.[26] Other offences only implicitly require free and informed consent, such as 'sexual aggressions' that are committed where there has been 'violence, threat, constraint or surprise'; in other words, situations naturally vitiating the consent of the victim.[27]

1.1.4 Consent to risk or consent to outcome

Criminal law scholarship in France has not theorised the distinction between consent to risk and consent to outcome. On the question of consenting to risk, some commentators give the example of withdrawing money from cash points where there are insufficient funds in the account. In such cases where the transaction has not been automatically blocked, the bank is seen as having consented to the *risk* of an account holder with insufficient funds withdrawing money from the cash-point. The bank cannot then object that it has not consented to the transaction, and criminal law cannot interfere.[28] Similarly, the example most often cited in relation to consent to outcome is that of consenting to interference with bodily integrity in the context of medical operations performed for therapeutic reasons.[29] Certain commentators consider on more paternalistic grounds that in these cases doctors are relieved of criminal liability not because of the consent of the patient, but because the law specifically authorises interference with a patient's bodily integrity in his best interest and subject to respecting the conditions specifically set by relevant legislation.[30]

1.1.5 Revocation of consent

A revocation of consent only carries significance, from the point of view of criminal law, when it has happened *prior to* the criminal act. When consent has been revoked *after* the act, it has no retroactive effect, with revocation being seen as a form of regret that raises no issues of criminal liability for the perpetrator. More perplexing is the question of what happens when consent has been revoked *during* the act, notably in cases of sexual activity where one of the parties continues to sexually touch or penetrate the other party notwithstanding revocation of the initial consent. There is no jurisprudence, and no high level analysis from French criminal law doctrine, on this matter. This seems to be the result of taking a pragmatic approach, considering that the problems inherent in proving the exact point when consent may have been withdrawn under such circumstances do not lend themselves to abstract

---

26 Article 223–8 French Penal Code. For example, a doctor was found guilty of this offence in a case where it was established that he had undertaken biomedical research upon a patient that was significantly weakened who was in no position to give a 'free, informed and explicit consent', and which in addition had not been obtained in writing or any other way. See Cass Crim 24 février 2009, *Recueil Dalloz* 2009, 2087, note P-J Delage).

27 See Agathe Lepage and Haritini Matsopoulou, *Droit pénal spécial* (Presses Universitaires de France 2015) n 423.

28 Xavier Pin, *Le consentement en matière pénale* (Coll Bibliothèque des sciences criminelles 2002) n 217.

29 According to Article 16–3 French Civil Code, '[t]here may be no infringement of the integrity of the human body except in case of medical necessity for the person or exceptionally in the therapeutic interest of another' and '[t]he consent of the person concerned must be obtained beforehand, except when his condition necessitates a therapeutic intervention to which he is not able to assent'.

30 See, eg, Jean Pradel and Michel Danti-Juan, *Droit pénal spécial* (6th edition, Cujas 2014) n 45. See also Michel Danti-Juan (dir), *Les orientations actuelles de la responsabilité pénale en matière médicale* (Travaux de l'Institut de sciences criminelles de Poitiers 2013), notably Bruno Py 'La dimension exonératrice des causes d'irresponsabilité pénale', 133–151.

theorising of any sort. In other words, and from the point of view of a comparison with English law, French law appears reluctant to engage with the situation examined in *Kaitamaki v R* and *Graeves*, which established the principle that a man can be guilty of rape if he does not withdraw his penis when his partner withdraws her consent.[31]

1.1.6 Ownership and limits of consent

Certain criminal offences are not constituted at all where the 'victim' consents. This is where the protected interests can be freely disposed of. Property is the characteristic example here: theft,[32] extortion,[33] and blackmail, all provide illustrations of such offences.[34] If we take the example of theft, there is no fraudulent appropriation of property where the owner has voluntarily transferred property to another person, including where this is due to a mistake not caused by the person who appropriates the property. The person who mistakenly receives property he is not entitled to will not be liable for theft even if he knowingly retains it.[35] This is in stark contrast to the position adopted in England under s 5(4) of the Theft Act 1968 and following *AG's Reference No 1 of 1983*.[36] These allow for the conviction of a person who receives property by another's mistake and has no intention to make restoration of that property, which 'in effect creates an offence of theft by omission . . . subtly stretching doctrinal margins'.[37]

1.2 Place of consent in the offence structure

In cases where, for the commission of a criminal offence, an act against the will of another individual is required (for example, an act of violence or threats or fraud) and where that individual can dispose of the interest protected by the criminal offence (for example, property or private life), consent can neutralise the criminal offence. In such cases, the existence of consent means that the required elements of the *actus reus* are not present. Consent is not seen as a defence.

Where the criminal offence protects an interest that the individual cannot dispose of (for example, the human body), consent has no effect save in exceptional circumstance provided by statute, such as Article 16–3 of the French Civil Code which provides that:

> [t]here may be no infringement of the integrity of the human body except in case of medical necessity for the person or exceptionally in the therapeutic interest of another. The consent of the person concerned must be obtained beforehand, except when his condition necessitates a therapeutic intervention to which he is not able to consent.[38]

---

31 See *Kaitamaki v R* [1985] 1 AC 147; *Graeves* [1999] 1 Cr App R (S) 319.

32 Article 311–1 French Penal Code: 'fraudulent appropriation of a thing belonging to another person'.

33 Article 312–1 French Penal Code: signature, commitment, renunciation, revelation of a secret, handing over of funds, securities or of any asset obtained 'by violence, by the threat of violence or constraint'.

34 Article 312–10 French Penal Code: signature, commitment, renunciation, revelation of a secret, or the handing over of funds, valuables or any asset obtained 'by threatening to reveal or to impute facts liable to undermine a person's honour or reputation'.

35 There is constant jurisprudence on this point. See eg Cass crim, 31 août 1899, *Recueil périodique Dalloz*, 1902, 1, 331.

36 [1985] QB 182.

37 Wells and Quick (n 1) 400.

38 See also supra 1.1.4.

1.3 Form of consent

1.3.1 Declared or implied?

Even if consent must be expressly given and unambiguous, a specific form for giving consent is not in principle required. There are some notable exceptions, particularly in relation to medical operations. Article 226–25 of the French Penal Code, in combination with Article 16–10 of the French Civil Code, requires express consent to be obtained in writing before a person undergoes an examination of his genetic characteristics.[39] In some cases, where the person consents to suffering grave harm, even consent obtained in writing might not be enough. For instance, where the individual concerned wants to donate organs while still alive, consent must be given 'before the president of the court of first instance or another magistrate designated by [the latter], who ensures that consent is freely given and informed and that the donor conforms to the conditions' set by the relevant legislation.[40]

1.3.2 Presumed consent

Presumptions of consent operate in relation to various offences in French criminal law. For example, where audio-visual recordings take place in the sight and with the knowledge of the persons concerned and without their objection (although they were in a position to object), it is presumed that the recordings were made with the consent of these persons and no violation of the right to privacy has been committed.[41] A similar presumption applies to the removal by doctors of bodily organs from a dead person, for therapeutic or scientific reasons, where the person has not previously objected to such a medical operation.[42] France operates an opt-out system, whereby anyone who has not registered to opt out of donating an organ, will be presumed to have consented. Consent to such operations is not presumed in England, where individuals wishing to donate must join the national donor register or where the donor's family give their consent if the donor has not done so in life. Interestingly, Wales has now adopted a position of deemed consent similar to that adopted in France; individuals who have not registered a clear decision to opt out of being a donor will be treated as having no objection to doing so.[43] *Prima facie* breaches of medical confidentiality may also be cured, where a court concludes that the patient would have necessarily consented to the doctor revealing the medical information to the prosecution service.[44] The court may draw the

---

39 According to Article 226–25 of the French Penal Code: 'The study of the genetic characteristics of a person for purposes other than medical purposes or scientific research, or their study for medical purposes or scientific research without having obtained the person's prior consent pursuant to the conditions set out under article 16–10 of the Civil Code, is punished by one year's imprisonment and a fine of €15,000'. Article 16–10 of the French Civil Code provides that '[a]n examination of the genetic characteristics of a person may only be undertaken for medical purposes or for scientific research. The express consent of the person must be obtained in writing before the carrying out of the examination, after the person has been duly informed of its nature and its purpose. The consent shall specify the purpose of the examination. It may be revoked at any time without any formality.'
40 Article L 1231–1 French Code of Public Health.
41 Article 226–1 French Penal Code.
42 (n 40).
43 See Human Transplantation (Wales) Act 2013. The new legislation comes into effect from 1 December 2015.
44 See eg Cass crim 8 mars 2000, *Droit pénal*, 2000, n100, obs M Véron.

presence of consent from the circumstances of the case. Article 226–14 of the French Penal Code defines that breaches of professional secrecy are

> not applicable to the cases where the law imposes or authorises the disclosure of the secret, but also . . . to a doctor who, with the consent of the victim, brings to the knowledge of the public prosecutor instances of cruelty or deprivation, either physical or psychological, that he has observed in the exercise of his profession that cause him to believe that physical, sexual or psychological violence of any sort, has been committed.

Legislation introduced in 2007 now removes the issue of the victim's consent from consideration where the victim is a minor. The victim is presumed to consent to the doctor reporting to the police physical, sexual or psychological violence that he may have observed in the exercise of his profession.[45]

1.4 Capacity to consent

The capacity to consent in French criminal law is linked with the capacity to understand. This is an issue for the appreciation of the judge except in cases where there is a presumption of absence of consent (see above 1.1.3).

1.5 Consequences of mistaken consent

1.5.1 Mistake

In these hypotheses where the presence of consent means the *actus reus* elements of the offence are absent and the offence has not been committed, a finding of mistaken consent will reintroduce the qualification of the act as a criminal offence. Impersonation in sexual offences, for instance, is seen as a case of mistaken consent generating criminal liability. There will be other scenarios where mistaken consent is still a consent. We can take the example of a cash point mistakenly dispensing a larger sum of money than the one requested or the example of a petrol pump that mistakenly charges the customer a lower sum.[46]

1.5.2 Deception

French criminal law gives particular attention to cases where the defendant has deceived another person in order to obtain his consent, by providing for special criminal offences addressing these situations. For example, impersonating another person in order to have sexual intercourse qualifies as 'viol par surprise'.[47]

---

45 See generally Bruno Py, 'Le secret professionnel et le signalement de la maltraitance sexuelle. L'option de conscience : un choix éthique' (2012) *Archives de politique criminelle* 'Violences sexuelles' 71.

46 See, eg, Pradel and Danti-Juan (n 30) n 862; Lepage and Matsopoulou (n 27) n 655.

47 Article 222–23 French Penal Code. We can take the example of a case from the end of the nineteenth century, where an individual had entered the bedroom of a woman, who was still asleep and whose husband was away, and had sexual intercourse with her while she was under the impression that she was having sexual intercourse with her husband. See Cass crim 25 juin 1857, *Recueil Sirey*, 1857, 1, 711. See also Cass crim 18 octobre 2006, pourvoi n 06–85924; Crim 21 février 2007, pourvoi n 06–88791.

1.6 Mistake about consent

Where a defendant mistakenly believes the victim has consented, *mens rea* is not complete and the defendant is not liable for any harm inflicted. To the English observer, French law thus still appears to operate, with regards to sexual offences more specifically, at the level of the *DPP v Morgan* honest belief in consent test. This test was struck into oblivion with the Sexual Offences Act 2003, which substituted an objective test for the subjective *DPP v Morgan* test, with the intent of tackling the perennial problem of proving the absence of consent in trials for sexual offences. Despite consent remaining an inherently complex issue even after the Sexual Offences Act 2003, the importance of this reform for the English law on sexual offences cannot be underestimated and presents French criminal law with a ready-made solution to a continuing problem. Analysis of relevant jurisprudence reveals that French criminal courts continue to place emphasis on the attitude of the victim – the defendant's perception of the attitude of the victim – rather than that of the defendant, being indifferent as to whether the defendant has taken the reasonable steps required to ascertain the complainant's consent.[48]

2 SPECIFIC ISSUES

2.1 Consent and homicide offences

2.1.1 Mercy killings

Euthanasia qualifies as murder or *assassinat* (premeditated murder) in French law.[49] The consent of the victim is taken into consideration only at the sentencing stage. The position of French law on this subject has considerably evolved with the Law of 22 April 2005 on the rights of patients and the end of life,[50] which, without having authorised euthanasia or assisted suicide, now allows doctors to interrupt life support, according to a strictly regulated procedure, if it would be unreasonable to continue with it. In its recent judgment in *Lambert v France*, the Grand Chamber of the ECtHR found that French legislation was compatible with Article 2 of the Convention, in a case where the Council of State (*Conseil d'État*) had authorised the termination of life support for a patient who had been in a permanent vegetative state for

---

48 The Cour d'assises du Haut-Rhin (21 avril 1959, *Recueil Dalloz*, 1960, 369) held that an acquittal to a charge of rape can be based on a finding that the defendant was mistaken or could have been mistaken about the consent of the victim, leading him to erroneously consider that her resistance was not serious or real. See also Cass crim 20 octobre 1999, n 98–88079, which placed emphasis on the argument that the defendant could have considered the attitude of the complainant as an invitation to engage in sexual activity. See generally Audrey Darsonville, 'Viol' (2012) Répertoire pénal Dalloz n 40–41; Pradel and Danti-Juan (n 30) n 775; Lepage and Matsopoulou (n 27) n 432; Catherine Le Magueresse, 'Viol et consentement en droit pénal français. Réflexions à partir du droit pénal canadien' (2012) Archives de politique criminelle 223.

49 See generally Françoise Alt Maes, 'Le respect de la dignité au centre des pratiques et de la loi sur la fin de vie' (30 May 2006, *Gazette du Palais*) n 150; Philippe Conte, 'Le code de la santé publique et le choix de mourir exprimé par le malade: scène de crime à l'hôpital' in Françoise Alt-Maes, *Les droits et le Droit. Mélanges dédiés à Bernard Bouloc* (Dalloz 2007) 229; Bruno Py, 'Le médecin et l'agonie' in *La mort et le droit* (Presses universitaires de Nancy 2010) 207; Jean Pradel, 'La Parque assistée par le droit. Apports de la loi du 22 avril 2005 relative aux droits des malades et à la fin de vie' (2005) Recueil Dalloz 2106; Agathe Prothais, 'Notre droit permet plus qu'il n'interdit en matière d'euthanasie' (2011) Droit pénal n 5; Cédric Ribeyre, 'Le droit pénal et la fin de vie' (2014) Revue pénitentiaire et de droit pénal 63.

50 Loi n 2005–370 du 22 avril 2005 relative aux droits des malades et à la fin de vie.

seven years.[51] In this area, there is significant divergence between the law in theory and the law in action. Anecdotal evidence suggests that, though consent is not recognised in theory as a valid defence, instances of euthanasia or assisted suicide are rarely punishable in practice, as juries in mixed tribunals (*Cours d'assises*) are often overtly sympathetic to defendants who find themselves confronted with such tragic circumstances. The recent *procès Bonnemaison* – in which the *Cour d'assises* imposed upon the defendant, a doctor, a suspended sentence of two years' imprisonment, in a case where he had been charged with the murder of seven patients – offers a stark illustration. A legal columnist for *Le Monde* offered the view that the jurors and professional magistrates in this case gave particular weight to the fact that the families of two of the deceased publicly expressed their support for the doctor when giving evidence in court, as well as to the fact that the family of only one of the victims was represented as a civil party in the process.[52]

2.1.2 Killing on request of the victim

Where there is a killing on request of the victim, consent is irrelevant and is again taken into consideration only at the sentencing stage. This is an issue that has received very little attention from either jurisprudence or criminal law theory in France.

2.1.3 Abortion

The consent of a woman who is having an abortion is indispensable for the legality of the relevant medical operation; otherwise an unlawful interruption of pregnancy will have been committed. This is a serious offence, punished by a maximum imprisonment of five years and a fine of €75,000.[53]

2.2 Consent and non-fatal offences against the person

2.2.1 HIV and other communicable disease transmission

The act of intentionally concealing one's HIV status before engaging in unprotected sexual intercourse, with the consequence of transmitting HIV, is qualified by the Cour de cassation as an administration of a noxious substance that causes harm upon the physical integrity of a person.[54] French law seems to be aligned with English law in that respect; as *EB*,[55] *Konzani*[56] and *Dica*[57] establish, a failure to disclose a sexually transmitted disease vitiates consent to the risk of being infected with such a disease and suffering bodily harm (even if it does not vitiate consent to the act of sexual intercourse itself) and so the perpetrator can be held liable for inflicting bodily harm. Contrary to English law, French law does not at all examine the issue

---

51   *Lambert et autres contre France*, App No 46043/14 (ECtHR, 5 June 2015).

52   Pascale Robert-Diard, 'Procès Bonnemaison : un verdict rendu la main tremblante' (24 October 2015, Le Monde.fr) <http://prdchroniques.blog.lemonde.fr/2015/10/24/proces-bonnemaison-un-verdict-rendu-la-main-tremblante/> accessed 18 December 2015.

53   Article 223–10 French Penal Code.

54   Cass Crim 5 oct 2010, *Bull crim*, n 147, *Revue de science criminelle et de droit pénal comparé* 2011, 101, obs Y Mayaud. See also Cass Crim, 10 janvier 2006, *Bull crim*, n11; *Recueil Dalloz* 2006, 1096; *Droit pénal* 2006, 30, obs M Véron; *Revue de science criminelle et de droit pénal comparé* 2006, 321, obs Y Mayaud.

55   [2006] EWCA Crim 2945.

56   [2005] 2 Cr App R 14.

57   [2004] Crim EWCA Crim 1103. See generally Matthew Weait, 'Criminal Law and the Sexual Transmission of HIV: *R v Dica*' (2005) 68 Modern Law Review 121.

from the viewpoint of the victim and consent, but rather from that of the defendant and his intention to inflict physical harm. This intention is deduced from the defendant's knowledge of their carrying the sexual disease and concealing the fact from the victim.

2.2.2 Medical treatment

The very essence of the medical profession consists of acts that interfere with the bodily integrity of patients and that could in principle qualify as violent offences against the person,[58] or as the offence of administering noxious substances.[59] A medical licence to practice related operations, coupled with the consent of the patient and the therapeutic nature of such operations, relieves doctors of criminal liability. The consent of the patient does not suffice in itself to relieve the doctor of criminal liability, when performing an operation prohibited by law. Conversely, doctors can exceptionally disregard the lack of consent from the part of the patient and perform medical operations particularly where the patient is facing a life-threatening situation.[60] This hypothesis has been tested in the challenging scenario of Jehovah witnesses refusing a blood transfusion; the *Conseil d'État* and French criminal law doctrine clearly accept that, in life threatening situations, doctors can bypass the patient's lack of consent.[61]

2.2.3 Sport injuries, 'horseplay', piercing

French criminal law appears reluctant to interfere in areas where the conduct in question is part of the cultural fabric, such as 'violent' sports or piercings. Whether the conduct is within the rules of the game is decisive as to whether the person who suffers harm in the process can be taken to have impliedly consented to the risk of such harm being inflicted. Deliberately transgressing the rules of the game or demonstrating particular animosity towards other participants can trigger the perpetrator's criminal liability for violent offences against the person. The nature of the game is also of critical importance; the more violent the game (boxing is a classic example) or the more it involves physical contact (such as rugby or football), the less likely it is that criminal liability for the infliction of physical harm will be upheld.[62] It is naturally interesting to correlate the French position with the detailed analysis undertaken by the English Court of Appeal in *Barnes* as to the factors relevant to whether conduct has gone beyond the rules and practice of the game, reaching the required threshold to be criminal. The 'type of the sport, the level at which it is played, the nature of the act, the degree of force used, the extent of the risk of injury, the state of mind of the defendant' are all factors that the Court of Appeal considers are 'likely to be relevant in determining whether the defendant's actions go beyond the threshold'.[63]

---

58 Those, for example, punished under Article 222–7 French Penal Code.
59 Article 222–15 French Penal Code.
60 Consent is in principle required by Article L 1111–4 French Code of Public Health.
61 See Conseil d'Etat, 26 octobre 2001, n 198546, which held that 'doctors who proceed to blood transfusions in order to save the life of a patient against his own wishes do not commit a mistake that can engage the responsibility of the State'. See also generally Bruno Py, 'La dimension exonératrice des causes d'irresponsabilité pénale' in Michel Danti-Juan, *Les orientations actuelles de la responsabilité pénale en matière médicale* (Travaux de l'Institut de sciences criminelles de Poitiers 2013) 133–151.
62 See generally Alain Lacabarats and Jean-Michel Pastor, 'Sport et activités physiques' (2010) Répertoire pénal Dalloz n 132.
63 *Barnes* [2014] Crim EWCA 3246 para 15. See generally Hazel Hartley, *Sport, Physical Recreation and the Law* (Routledge 2009).

2.2.4 Specific sexual practices involving infliction of harm

The question of criminal liability for sado-masochistic acts causing bodily harm and, more specifically, the question of whether the consent of the 'victim' relieves the participants from criminal liability, has not so far generated any jurisprudence in France. The jurisprudence of the ECtHR on this matter recognises the individual autonomy-based principle that 'the ability of every person to lead his life in the way that he chooses can also include the ability to give himself over to activities that are perceived as being physically or morally harmful to his person'.[64] The ECtHR accepts, at the same time, that the prosecution and conviction of individuals engaging with such conduct can be 'necessary in a democratic society for the protection of health' within the meaning of accepted interference with the right to privacy,[65] a position that Ashworth and Horder convincingly describe as 'a considerable disappointment to those who expected [the Court to adopt] a rights-based approach'.[66] Against this backdrop of trying to balance individual autonomy with the public interest in the protection of health and moral values, we can turn to French commentators like Fabre-Magnan who emphasise the level of the harm inflicted as a key factor for conducting this delicate balancing exercise. Fabre-Magnan notes that

> [t]he fact that a person consents to being a victim should not be able to excuse every harm upon his physical integrity, every torture and barbaric behaviour, and possibly even murder; this is so even if it is demonstrated that the person consents and even gets sexual gratification [from this behaviour] (the definition of masochism). The consent of the victim is not a defence that can erase all criminal offences, even if Law in certain contexts tolerates minor harms upon the bodily integrity of another person.[67]

This position can be contrasted with the House of Lords' condemnatory remarks of all homosexual sado-masochistic conduct – regardless of the level of harm inflicted – in the infamous *Brown* case, which categorically rejected consent as a defence available to those engaging with such conduct.[68] Murphy locates 'a good deal of old-fashioned paternalism' in Lord Templeman's majority opinion[69] that '[s]ociety is entitled and bound to protect itself against a cult of violence', that 'pleasure derived from the infliction of pain is an evil thing' and '[c]ruelty is uncivilised'.[70] The two other majority opinions by Lord Lowry and Lord Jauncey provide further support to the view that the House of Lords' 'overwhelming distaste for the defendants' activities' has underpinned the controversial jurisprudential outcome reached in

---

64 *KA et AD contre Belgique*, App Nos 42758/98 and 45558/99 (ECtHR, 17 February 2005) para 83, citing *Pretty v United Kingdom*, App No 2346/02 (ECtHR, 29 April 2002) para 66.

65 *Laskey v United Kingdom* (1997) 24 EHRR 39, para 50.

66 Ashworth and Horder (n 3) 327.

67 Muriel Fabre-Magnan, 'Le domaine de l'autonomie personnelle. Indisponibilité du corps humain et justice sociale' (2008) Recueil Dalloz 31.

68 *Brown* [1994] 1 AC 212.

69 P Murphy, 'Flogging Live Complainants and Dead Horses: We May No Longer Need to Be in Bondage to *Brown*' [2011] Crim LR 758, 760. Gurnham similarly points out that 'the speech of Lord Templeman . . . is particularly notable for his moral rhetoric on sado-masochism'. David Gurnham, 'Legal Authority and Savagery in Judicial Rhetoric: Sexual Violence and the Criminal Courts' (2011) International Journal of the Law in Context 177 at 125. See also Amy Kerr, 'Consensual Sado-Masochism and the Public Interest: Distinguishing Morality and Legality' (2014) 2 North East Law Review 51.

70 *Brown* (n 68) 237.

this case.[71] French observers will not find much support for an equality-driven and rights-based approach in the majority opinions in *Brown* or the highly inconsistent Court of Appeal cases that followed in its footsteps, for that matter.[72] On the other hand, it will be instructive for them to look at Lord Mustill's dissenting opinion in *Brown*. In emphasising that sado-masochistic conduct falls within a realm of 'private morality' that criminal law should not interfere with, Lord Mustill's opinion would provide a far more reliable compass for French criminal courts if they were to venture into this complex area of inherently conflicting values.[73] In fact, French criminal law's apparent unwillingness to interfere might be more in keeping with changing sexual attitudes[74] and the fashionably idiosyncratic view that consensual sado-masochistic conduct 'has moved from sexual subculture to normal bedroom antics'.[75]

2.3 Sexual offences

2.3.1 Absence of consent or use of force/threats

The concept of consent is nowhere more central to the application of criminal law than in the area of sexual offences. With the exception of child sexual offences,[76] consent is the distinguishing factor between sexual activity indifferent to criminal law and unlawful sexual activity triggering a response from the criminal justice system.[77] Article 222–22 of the French Penal Code, which provides the general framework for the punishment of sexual assaults and other sexual offences (*agressions sexuelles*), takes the absence of consent as one of the elements of the *actus reus*, even if the article makes no explicit reference to consent. Article 222–22 requires that the sexual activity in question has been the result of 'violence, constraint, threat or surprise' from the part of the defendant. In accordance with the principle of legality, the prosecution must demonstrate the presence of at least one of these conditions to establish that the sexual activity has taken place without the consent of the victim.[78] Where, in addition to one of these conditions, there is 'penetration', the offence of rape will have been committed.[79] One might go as far as read into Article 222–22 a presumption of the presence of consent every time there is sexual activity. To rebut it the prosecution must demonstrate that the sexual activity in question derived from one of the conditions

---

71 Ashworth and Horder (n 3) 325.

72 See *Wilson* [1996] 2 Cr App R 241; *Emmett* (1999) *The Times* 15 October.

73 *ibid* 273.

74 Murphy observes that 'time and public *mores* have moved on since *Brown* [was decided in] 1994': Murphy (n 61) 760.

75 Richard Easton, 'Fifty Shades of *Brown*' (2015) Solicitors Journal 159 (10 March 2015), available at <http://www.solicitorsjournal.com/comment/fifty-shades-brown> 18 December 2015.

76 See above 1.1.3.

77 On sexual offences, see notably the 2012 volume of the *Archives de politique criminelle* dedicated to 'Violences sexuelles'; Audrey Darsonville, 'Viol' (2011) Rép pén Dalloz n 20; Valérie Malabat, 'Infractions sexuelles' (2002) Rép pén Dalloz n 24; Michèle-Laure Rassat, 'Agressions sexuelles', *Jurisclasseur Pénal Code*, 'Art. 222–22 à art. 222–33–1', fasc 20, 2014 (mise à jour 2015).

78 See Cass crim 17 sept 1997, *Bull crim* n 302; Cass crim 21 octobre 1998, *Bull crim* n 274; Cass crim 17 mars 1999, *Bull crim* n 49. In its decision of 8 July 2005, the *Cour de cassation* specified that, unless the prosecution make reference to one of these conditions, the *actus reus* has not been constituted. Cass Assemblée plénière 8 juillet 2005, *Bull crim* n 1 décision.

79 Article 222–23 French Penal Code.

mentioned above.[80] Here we note considerable divergence with the English law on sexual offences, where proof of the absence of consent is not linked to specifically enumerated situations, giving courts much wider latitude when defining the conditions from which the absence of consent may be deducted. In fact, conditions like 'violence', 'constraint' or 'threat', which only serve to allow the prosecution to meet its burden of proof in French criminal trials for sexual offences, go as far as to reverse the burden of proof in English criminal trials.[81] Where there is impersonation (surprise), the gap is even wider, as this will trigger an irreversible presumption of the absence of consent in English law (while in French law, it will only serve to allow the prosecution to meet its burden of proof).[82] French commentators read in this construction of the law of consent a prioritisation of the presumption of innocence, which does not sit well with the modern English approach to the law of sexual offences.[83] Driven by a seemingly urgent need to increase conviction rates, the Sexual Offences Act 2003 strengthened the position of the prosecuting party in trials for sexual offences.[84] This was achieved by making the absence of consent easier to prove, including through the introduction of presumptions of absence of consent (and not just rebuttable presumptions) regardless of the threats for the presumption of innocence likely to derive therefrom.[85]

Far more striking in the eyes of English law observers will be the central position that violence and the use of force still appear to have in the statutory construction of sexual assault, rape and other sexual offences in France, as is made evident by the conditions that Article 222–22 restrictively enumerates. McEwan comments critically – in relation to continued stereotypical cultural understandings of sexual behaviour in England and Wales obstructing fairer outcomes for female victims – that '[c]omplainants have been mortified to be told that their bruises are not severe enough for the case to go forward or to be asked in cross-examination, "Why did no one hear screams?"'.[86] An impressionistic first view of Article 222–22 might exercise a similar effect upon those looking from outside, especially upon English observers versed in *Olugboja*'s long-standing distinction between consent and submission.[87] They might be forgiven for thinking Article 222–22 could be oblivious to the possibility that far more delicate powers may be at work. When the victim submits (as opposed to consents) to sexual advances made by the defendant, the absence of violence or injury does not mean the complainant has consented,[88] and 'the dividing lines in such circumstances between real

---

80 For a critique of this position see Catherine Le Magueresse, 'Viol et consentement en droit pénal français. Réflexions à partir du droit pénal canadien' (2012) *Archives de politique criminelle* 223.

81 See the evidential presumptions of Article 75 Sexual Offences Act 2003.

82 See the conclusive presumptions of Article 76, *ibid*.

83 See notably Françoise Desprez, 'Preuve et conviction du juge en matière d'agressions sexuelles' (2012) *Archives de politique criminelle* 'Violences sexuelles' 45.

84 See eg Home Office, *Setting the Boundaries: Reforming the Law on sex Offences* (July 2000).

85 See generally Jenny McEwan, 'Proving Consent in Sexual Cases: Legislative Change and Cultural Evolution' (2005) 9 *International Journal of Evidence & Proof* 1, 20. With regards to the rebuttable presumptions of, s 75 Sexual Offences Act 2003, McEwan notes that its effect 'will be, in a small number of cases, to impose an evidential burden unfairly on the accused. Where, on proof of a basic fact, another fact is *prima facie* presumed to exist, the task faced by the prosecution is significantly reduced. It places pressure on the accused to enter the witness box'. On the, s 76(1)(a) conclusive presumption, McEwan also discusses a scenario where 'there is potential conflict . . . with the presumption of innocence in Article 6 of the European Convention on Human Rights', 21.

86 McEwan *ibid* 2, citing Jessica Harris and Sharon Grace, *A Question of Evidence: Investigating and Prosecuting Rape in the 1990s* (Home Office 1999) 21 and Beverly Brown, Michel Burman and Lynn Jamieson, *Sex Crimes on Trial: The Use of Sexual Evidence in Scottish Courts* (Edinburgh University Press 1993) 183.

87 *Olugboja* (1982) QB 320, 332.

88 McEwan (n 85) 2.

consent on the one hand and mere submission on the other may not be easy to draw'.[89] To speak like Tadros, the French and English positions on sexual offences and the law of rape more specifically can, at first sight, be contrasted on the basis of whether 'the focus is primarily on the will, or rather consent, of the victim, relegating force to a subsidiary role'; French law seemingly adopts a violence-based approach while English law defines rape around consent.[90]

When we begin to explore jurisprudential extrapolations of Article 222–22 of the French Penal Code, a different picture emerges. We must start with the essential observation that French criminal courts enjoy a wide discretion when determining whether particular conduct comes under the ambit of one of the four conditions required by this article for criminal liability for sexual assault to be established. As Desprez argues, judges use their *intime conviction* (the principle of free evaluation of proof)[91] to avoid the perils that a potential narrow reading of these conditions might generate for the effective prosecution of sexual offences.[92] The concepts of violence and constraint, for instance, have been interpreted as including situations where the victim may have put up very little resistance or not put up any resistance at all, as a result of the imbalance of power between the two parties, and more importantly situations where the victim has been psychologically coerced into submitting to the defendant.[93] In fact, since a 2010 reform,[94] the concept of 'constraint' is seen as deriving both from the use of force and the exercise of psychological pressure,[95] and extends to situations where the victim has suffered from a particular vulnerability including a state of intoxication.[96] Moreover, different levels of 'threat' may suffice for the sexual assault to be committed, from very serious threats – for example where a weapon has been used –[97] to less serious cases of verbal abuse.[98] Finally, a variety of meanings are given to the concept of 'surprise'; it may pinpoint a particular vulnerability of the victim or the aggressive character of a stratagem employed by the defendant[99] or may refer to cases of impersonation.[100] A case-by-case approach, which looks at the circumstances of each case separately to ensure maximum flexibility, is seen as the guiding principle here.

---

89 *Olugboja* (n 87).

90 Victor Tadros, 'Rape without Consent' (2006) 26 Oxford Journal of Legal Studies 515, 516.

91 Valérie Dervieux, 'The French System' in Mireille Delmas-Marty and John R Spencer (ed), *European Criminal Procedures* (CUP 2002) 233.

92 Desprez (n 83) 51.

93 Cass crim 8 juin 1994, *Bull crim* n 226; Cass crim 27 novembre 1996, pourvoi n 96–83954. See *ibid* 51. The approach taken with *Olugboja* in English law may be finding accommodation here, though it remains very problematic that the Court's inquiries revolve around the complainant's 'resistance' (or her ability for resistance) in the first place.

94 Loi n 2010–769 du 9 juillet 2010 relative aux violences faites spécifiquement aux femmes, aux violences au sein des couples et aux incidences de ces dernières sur les enfants.

95 See Article 222–22–1 French Penal Code.

96 Cass crim 18 décembre 1991, pourvoi n 91–85607; Cass crim 18 octobre 2006, pourvoi n 06–85924; Crim 21 février 2007, pourvoi n 06–8879. See Desprez (n 83) 52.

97 Cass crim 19 janvier 2005, pourvoi n 04–86303; Cass crim 13 juin 2007, pourvoi n 07–82499. See Desprez (n 83) 55.

98 Cass crim 23 octobre 2002, pourvoi n 02–85715. See Desprez (n 83) 56.

99 Cass crim 18 octobre 2006, pourvoi n 06–85924; Crim 21 février 2007, pourvoi n 06–88791 (in both cases there was a finding of 'surprise', while in the second case there was also a finding of 'constraint' deriving from the fact that the defendant had taken advantage of the victim who had been intoxicated). See Desprez (n 83) 60.

100 Cass crim 25 juin 1857, *Recueil Sirey*, 1857, 1, 711: the defendant had impersonated the husband of the victim.

From this point of view, the differences between the French and English approaches to consent in sexual offences may be less substantial than first acquaintance suggests. The scope of inquiries on the absence of consent may have, in reality, shifted towards an approach not too dissimilar from that adopted in England with *Olugboja* originally and, more recently, with the Sexual Offences Act 2003.

2.3.3 Mistake of fact about consent

See above 1.5. and 1.6.

2.4 Property offences and criminal damage

2.4.1 Place of consent in the offence structure

See above 1.2.

2.4.2 Mistaken belief in consent

See above 1.5.

CONCLUSION

An important conclusion stemming from this brief overview of consent in French criminal law is the surprising lack of normative and jurisprudential analyses of the concept of consent there. With certain notable exceptions, French criminal law seems reluctant to prioritise consent, thus depriving from the state the power to intervene to protect the public interest. Consent is not recognised as a general defence vitiating criminal liability for the infliction of harm. Any jurisprudential inroads into this principle are pursued in a piecemeal fashion, through a casuistic approach not typical of Continental legal systems; there is no grand theory of consent. This is true of English criminal law too, though one can also observe the beginnings of developing a more systematic approach towards dealing with issues of consent; the provisions of the Sexual Offences Act 2003 provide a good illustration. In fact, the high level of engagement of English appellate jurisprudence with issues of consent that are also prevalent in the French legal system provides French law with an interesting opportunity to rethink some of the most complex issues surrounding this topic. However, as the troubled life of *Brown* and its progeny demonstrates – or continuing challenges surrounding the issue of consent in sexual offences for that matter – French law should treat English appellate jurisprudence with caution. There are interesting lessons to learn and complications to avoid, and the same is true if we look for such comparative lessons from the other side of the Channel.

23
Spain

Mario Maraver Gómez and Manuel Cancio Meliá

1 GENERAL ISSUES

1.1 Conceptual foundations

1.1.1 *Philosophical and theoretical principles informing the law surrounding consent*

In Spanish criminal law, the victim's consent is generally considered to be grounds for a defence against criminal liability. Although Article 20 of the Penal Code (PC) does not mention it among the general defences, legal scholars consider it a supra-legal defence, deriving from the political principles inspiring the legal system, such as the principles of *freedom* or *personal autonomy*. Article 1 of the Spanish Constitution (SC) stipulates that freedom is a supreme value in the legal system and Article 10 SC provides that dignity of the individual, inviolable rights that are inherent, and the free development of personality are the foundation of political order and social peace.[1]

The importance afforded to freedom and personal autonomy means, *inter alia*, that it is necessary to take into account a person's will to determine to what extent his own interests should be protected by criminal law. As a general rule, it is understood that the person's interests should not be protected against or aside from his will.[2] We take a *liberal* conception as a reference, which understands that criminal law fundamentally serves to protect freedom and individual interests, unlike a *statist* conception, whereby criminal laws serve fundamentally to protect the interests of the state.[3] Respect for individual freedom means recognising a person's freedom to dispose of his own legally protected interests and, therefore, the possibility of consent operating to exclude criminal liability.

Nevertheless, this recognition is not absolute. It is accepted that an individual's free disposal of his own legally protected interests and the effectiveness of consent can be subject to some limitations. In general terms, leaving aside cases in which the decision does not really

---

1 Enrique Casas Barquero, *El consentimiento en el Derecho penal* (Universidad de Córdoba 1987) 54–55; Jacobo López Barja de Quiroga, *El consentimiento en el Derecho penal* (Dykinson 1999) 12–13; María José Segura García, El *consentimiento del titular del bien jurídico en Derecho penal* (Tirant lo Blanch 2000) 112 ff.
2 Segura García, *El consentimiento del titular del bien jurídico en Derecho penal* (n 1) 112–115.
3 ibid 26–27.

concern a person's own legally protected interests, but rather affects third parties (*harm principle*), the limitations to consent can be justified from various points of view:

1 Firstly, certain limitations are proposed to ensure that the person who consents, really does so freely. In particular, the person should have *capacity*, in the sense of being capable of making his own decisions. From this standpoint, consent would not be accepted from persons who lack comprehension, are coerced or are unaware of the consequences of their decision. These limitations are proposed from a standpoint sometimes referred to as *soft paternalism*, although actually they can be deduced from the very concept of freedom. According to a Kantian concept of freedom, this approach is sometimes taken further, requiring additionally that consent be *rational*. In contrast to a Millsian concept of freedom, which values free decision without taking into account the content of the decision, a Kantian concept of freedom considers that decisions are only free when they are autonomous, that is when they derive from a person's capacity to act according to normative reasons. What those reasons are does not matter as much as the fact that the decision complies with a normative reasoning scheme defined by the individual himself.[4] This could be seen as an approach akin to *hard paternalism* to the extent that it implies preventing the individual from making imprudent or irrational decisions against his own interests. However, in fact it does not stray from the liberal views, since it does not go so far as to deny an individual's freedom to dispose of his legally protected interests. It is more a sort of *procedural paternalism* that seeks to provide guarantees to consent so that it reflects a really autonomous decision.[5]

2 Secondly, some limits to consent are proposed when the legally protected interest under threat is deemed more important than the freedom of the holder to dispose of it. In some cases, the need to reject the disposal of legally protected interests considered particularly important, such as life or physical integrity, is stressed, while in other cases proposals are made to limit the effectiveness of consent in crimes against a person's dignity, this being an interest that cannot be waived in any case. These are the limitations supported by so-called *hard paternalism*, which does not question individual title to certain legally protected interests, but which does propose limiting free disposal of the same in the interests of the individual himself.[6]

3 Thirdly, some limits to consent can be justified by *communitarian* reasons, in order to respect the prevailing moral values in society. Sometimes it is understood that these values should be respected because they are important in themselves and other times to stabilise the fundamental norms of society and avoid undesirable situations in the future.[7] Thus, for example, in this regard the irrelevance of consent in assisted suicide could be justified by the desire to avoid situations in which, for some reason, a person is pressurised to opt for suicide instead of addressing his situation in another way. From a similar point of view, it is argued that not all decisions freely adopted by the legal interest holder should be judged favourably. How society assesses consent can take into

---

4 Julian Savulescu, 'Autonomía, buena vida y elecciones controvertidas' in Mendoza Buergo, *Autonomía personal y decisiones médicas: cuestiones éticas y jurídicas* (Civitas 2010) 35 ff.

5 Ulfried Neumann, 'Problemas actuales de la eutanasia en Derecho penal' in Mendoza Buergo ibid 295–296.

6 Regarding the different types of paternalism in this context see Tomás-Valiente Lanuza, 'Autonomía y paternalismo en las decisiones sobre la propia salud' in Mendoza Buergo ibid 64 ff.

7 From a critical point of view, compare Alfonso Ruiz Miguel, 'Autonomía individual y derecho a la propia muerte' in Mendoza Buergo ibid 246–247.

account very different aspects, such as the reasons for which this decision was made or the seriousness of the injury caused, for example.[8]

As we can see, once we accept that consent constitutes general grounds for a defence against criminal liability, problems arise when it comes to determining its true scope. The limitations proposed are not only very different from a political and moral point of view, but also vary according to the legally protected interests affected. For this reason, in the end, consent usually has a different scope and requirements, depending on the criminal offence in question. Not surprisingly, the Spanish legislator has not provided a general regulation of consent and the Spanish courts have avoided stating an opinion on this matter in very general terms. The scope of consent as a defence against liability can only be determined by looking at the regulation of the different criminal offences in the so-called Special Part of the Penal Code.

In any event, some judgments of the Spanish Constitutional Court (CC) and some recent legislative reforms reveal the growing importance placed upon an individual's freedom to dispose of his legally protected interests, even interests as important as life or health.

In this respect, two judgments of the CC are usually cited, which, although denying the right to die or to decide freely on one's own death, hold that feeding or medical treatment cannot be imposed against a person's will, even when necessary to guarantee life or health.[9] It is thought that imposing such measures would be contrary to the right to self-determination over one's body and thus also contrary to the right to life and physical and moral integrity provided in Article 15 SC. Hence, the will or consent of the legal interest holder is not effective *vis a vis* 'active' conduct, putting his life or health at risk, but it is *vis a vis* 'passive' conduct, discontinuing life-saving treatment.

The duty to respect a patient's freedom to accept or reject any treatment has become a general principle in medicine. This general principle, expressly recognised in Article 5 of the Oviedo Convention of 4 April 1997[10] and in Article 3.2 of the Charter of Fundamental Rights of the European Union of 18 December 2000, is also provided in Law 41/2002, of 14 November governing patient autonomy and rights and obligations regarding clinical information and documentation (LPA).[11] Article 2.2 LPA provides that: 'Any intervention in the area of health requires, as a general rule, the patient or user's prior consent.' This demonstrates that the *principle of freedom* or *autonomy* takes precedence over the *principle of benefit*. The freedom of the individual to take decisions about medical treatment is recognised, even if the decisions are prejudicial to life or health. This has two important consequences in criminal law: on the one hand, patient consent may serve as a defence to criminal liability of whoever discontinues medical treatment; on the other hand, a doctor may be subject to criminal proceedings for imposing medical treatment on a patient against his will.[12]

---

8 Enrique Peñaranda Ramos, 'El consentimiento en las lesiones' in Miguel Bajo Fernández, *Compendio de Derecho Penal, Parte Especial, I* (Ramón Areces 2003) 366; Pablo Guérez Tricarico, 'Consentimiento' in Fernando Molina Fernández, *Memento Penal* (Francis Lefevre 2015) 214–215.

9 One is STC 120/1990, of 27 June, in which force feeding of terrorist prisoners on hunger strike was discussed, and the other is STC 154/2002, of 18 July, in which the possible liability of some Jehovah's witnesses was assessed for not convincing their 13 year old son, also a Jehovah's witness, to accept a blood transfusion which could have avoided his death.

10 Convention for the Protection of Human Rights and Dignity of Human Being with regard to the Application of Biology and Medicine (Convention on Human Rights and Biomedicine).

11 [2000] OJ C346/01.

12 See below 2.2.3 for more details on this question.

All in all, an individual's freedom to dispose of his own legally protected interests has been gaining increasing recognition. Even though this freedom of disposal is not absolute, it does have sufficient scope to be generally recognised. If we review criminal offences that protect individual legal interests, we can see that consent provides a complete defence against criminal liability in the majority of them (freedom offences, property-related offences, privacy offences, those against honour...). Even in cases of criminal offences that protect legal interests traditionally considered inalienable, such as life or health, consent leads to a considerable mitigation of the punishment, as well as allowing certain 'passive' injuries, derived from withdrawal of a treatment. Only a few criminal offences, such as the crime of exploitation of the prostitution of others, openly negate the relevance of consent. Therefore, we can conclude that consent acts as a general exoneration, subject to certain limitations. This, therefore, accords with Ulpian's principle, contained in the Digest, in that '*nulla iniuiria est, quae in volentem fiat*', summed up in the aphorism '*volenti non fit iniuria*'.[13]

1.1.2 Influence of feminist and queer theory

Feminism, as well as queer theory and other emancipatory theories, has enriched the debate about the scope of consent, drawing attention to some limitations that can derive from discriminatory situations suffered by women and other groups. Using a critical analysis of the purely formal understanding of consent as a starting point, these theories highlight the need to take into account the material situation or the social context of the person giving consent. Thus, specifically considering the situation of women, feminism opens up the possibility of limiting the scope of consent from two perspectives. On the one hand, from the personal freedom point of view, by referring to specific types of coercion women may suffer, which are not the same as those generally suffered by men, but which similarly limit their personal autonomy. On the other hand, from the perspective of society's values, by warning of the danger that certain practices, which, even if consented to, contribute to replicate or strengthen the domination system we are seeking to avoid. In criminal law, these considerations have been the main focus of the debate about the scope that should be afforded to consent in two types of criminal offence, fundamentally, those related to *prostitution* and *gender-based violence*.

As far as prostitution is concerned, there is an intense debate, even in feminist circles, as to whether or not criminal sanctions should apply when the person consents to engage in prostitution. For a large number of legal scholars, proponents of the so-called *abolitionist* theory, consent is not a sufficient reason to exclude the wrongfulness of the conduct. It is arguable whether a person who decides to engage in prostitution makes that decision autonomously, not only because the decision reflects a situation of need or desperation, but also because, according to some more conservative approaches, such a decision is completely irrational and essentially incompatible with freedom. Conversely, prostitution constitutes, in any case, an attack on a person's dignity that also reinforces the reification and exploitation of women by men, thus contributing to maintaining the system of patriarchal domination.[14] This abolitionist approach, criticised by part of another branch of the feminist movement, is reflected to some extent in the Spanish Penal Code (PC), which, while not directly imposing criminal

---

13 Beatriz Escudero García-Calderón, *El consentimiento en Derecho Penal* (Tirant lo Blanch 2014) 29.
14 About abolitionist theories see María Luisa Maqueda Abreu, *Prostitución, feminismos y derecho penal* (Comares 2009) 14 ff.

sanctions on the prostitute or her clients, does penalise the exploitation of the prostitution of others, even when the person engaging in prostitution consents (Article 187.1 PC).[15]

As far as gender-based violence is concerned, there is discussion about the importance to be afforded to the woman victim's will, both from the procedural as well as from the strictly substantive point of view.[16] In criminal law, the main problem in offences of gender-based violence (Articles 148.3°, 153 and 173.2 PC) arises because, as well as the actual criminal punishment, an obligatory accessory restraining order must be imposed (Article 57.2 PC), which is not infrequently breached with the consent or actions of the victim herself. Once the Constitutional Court admitted the constitutionality of this provision by Judgment 60/2010 of 7 October, discussion centred on whether this regulation should be changed, *de lege ferenda*, to take into account the abused woman's will. While some feminist standpoints deny the existence of valid consent in these cases or defend a paternalist stance to protect the woman's safety, there are also other feminist views which stress the need to make the criminal system more flexible allowing the woman to manage the situation and putting an end to a widely held dismissive view that abused women are necessarily incapable of acting rationally.[17]

1.1.3 Consent to risk or consent to outcome

When referring to consent as grounds for exemption from liability, we generally think about consent to the harmful outcome. When the Penal Code provides a reduction in the criminal punishment for murder or bodily harm in cases of assisted suicide (Article 143) or consent to bodily harm (Article 155), or when it acknowledges that consent excludes criminal liability in certain offences, it is referring to cases in which the legal interest holder consents to the criminal outcome being produced.

This means that the person who consents has a clear understanding of what the outcome of the offender's actions will be and consents to it. Certainly, consent is given to a dangerous action prior to the outcome occurring, but it also includes the harmful outcome that could be expected from that dangerous action. This is the crucial aspect. If the person consents to a particular dangerous action, but does not know about or does not consent to the outcome that may result from it, there is consent to the risk, but not consent to the outcome.

Consent to risk can also be relevant to limit or exclude criminal liability, but it operates differently and also has different consequences. Its validity does not follow directly from the relevance afforded to consent to the outcome. In offences against life or integrity, for example, it can also have an exonerating effect, but in other offences such as crimes against intimacy or sexual freedom, for example, it does not have any exonerating or liability limiting effect.

By taking part in a dangerous act, the legal interest holder assumes part of the responsibility for the possible harmful outcome. If a harmful outcome ensues, consent to the risk makes it possible for the outcome to be attributed to the victim, sometimes even excluding attribution to the perpetrator. For example, this could occur if a person freely accepted to ride on a motorcycle with someone, in an illegal race. If there was an accident, the outcome could possibly be attributed to the victim, completely exonerating the driver from liability. The criminal punishment would not be mitigated, as in assisted suicide, instead it would be

---

15   This rule corresponds with Article 1 of the United Nations Convention for the Suppression of the Traffic in Persons and of the Exploitation of the Prostitution of Others (adopted 21 March 1950, entered into force 25 July 1951) 96 UNTS 271.

16   Compare generally Elena Larrauri Pijoan, *Mujeres y sistema penal* (BdeF 2008) 167 ff.

17   Maqueda Abreu, 'La violencia de género. Entre el concepto jurídico y la realidad social' (2006) 2 Revista Electrónica de Ciencia Penal y Criminología 1, 9–10; ibid 195–198.

understood that the criminal act (*actus reus*) had not been committed. Cases of consent to risk are dealt with, ultimately, in the same way as cases that affect the determination of so-called 'objective imputation'.[18] The will of the consenting individual is not as relevant as that person's assumption of certain responsibility for his own behaviour.[19]

1.1.4 Revocation of consent

It is generally recognised that consent can be revoked.[20] Consent is only effective in so far as it represents a voluntary act disposing of a legally protected interest. If the individual changes his mind and revokes consent, the initial consent is cancelled and loses its effectiveness completely.

For revocation to be effective, it must be expressed outwardly.[21] If the individual does not express it in some way, it can be understood that either there is no actual revocation or that, in any case, the offender incurs an unavoidable mistake about the existence of consent, which leads to the same results.[22]

1.1.5 Ownership and limits of consent

Consent does not exclude criminal liability in all cases. Two important limitations stem from the very concept and basis of this legal institution, beyond those relating to requirements and form that consent must comply with. There are indeed two types of offence in which consent in not effective. One concerns crimes protecting legal interests that are not *individually owned* and the other relates to crimes protecting individually owned legal interests that are *inalienable*.

Traditionally, a distinction is drawn between offences protecting *individual legal interests*, belonging to a person (for example crimes against life, health or physical integrity, freedom, sexual freedom, honour, privacy or property), and offences in which *collective legal interests* belonging to the state or the community are protected (for example crimes against the socio-economic order, the environment, public health, the administration of justice or the tax authority). Consent, as a manifestation of individual freedom, can only be effective in offences that protect individual legal interests. Individuals can only dispose of the interests they hold.[23]

---

18 According to this legal doctrine (accepted by case-law), any offence consisting of the production of an outcome must contain two unwritten elements: a) creation of a non-permitted risk; b) realisation of this risk in the outcome. In cases where the victim exposes himself to danger (for example, when he consumes an illegal drug supplied by another) the person responsible for co-causing the outcome is deemed not to have produced a non-permitted risk (that is to say, in the example, there would be an offence of drug trafficking, but not of homicide) since it comes within the scope of the preferential responsibility of the legal interest holder; Compare principally Manuel Cancio Meliá, *Conducta de la víctima e imputación objetiva* (2nd edition, JM Bosch Editor 2002) 284. Compare also Mir Puig, *Derecho Penal, Parte General* (10th edition, 2015 Repertor) 517; Diego-Manuel Luzón Peña, *Lecciones de Derecho Penal, Parte General* (2nd edition, Tirant lo Blanch 2012) 6.
19 Cancio Meliá, *Conducta de la víctima e imputación objetiva* ibid 261 ff.
20 José Cerezo Mir, *Curso de Derecho penal español, Parte General, II, Teoría jurídica del delito* (6th edition, Tecnos 2004) 329, with more references.
21 Segura García, *El consentimiento del titular del bien jurídico en Derecho penal* (n 1) 139.
22 See below 1.6.
23 Cerezo Mir, *Curso de Derecho Penal español* (n 20) 326; Mir Puig, *Derecho Penal, Parte General* (n 18) 520; Luzón Peña, *Lecciones de Derecho Penal, Parte General* (n 18) 369–370.

Consent has a general, but not unlimited, effectiveness in offences that protect individual legal interests. The greater the importance afforded to individual freedom, the wider the effectiveness of consent, but it rarely amounts to absolute effectiveness. Restrictions are placed in respect of certain legal interests, considered *inalienable* for paternalist or communitarianist reasons.[24] The effectiveness of consent is excluded, or at least limited, in offences protecting inalienable legal interests. For example, this is the case in offences against life (Article 137 *et seq* PC) or health (Article 147 *et seq* PC) and offences that fundamentally protect a person's dignity, such as the exploitation of the prostitution of others (Article 187.1.2º PC). Where life or health are concerned, the victim's consent allows a considerable reduction of the criminal punishment (Articles 143 and 155 PC), but does not exempt the offender from criminal liability.[25] This limitation is sometimes justified by the greater importance of these interests in comparison to freedom and other times by the risks that could arise, for example, from individuals taking a decision hastily or under some type of pressure. In the criminal offence of abortion, the consent of the pregnant woman implies exemption from liability in some cases, but more generally only limits it (Article 45 PC), thereby demonstrating that the legally protected interest in this case is not totally alienable, in part, precisely, because it includes interests that are not solely held by the pregnant woman.

1.2 Place of consent in the offence structure

There is no article in the Spanish Penal Code providing a general regulation of consent. Nevertheless, it is understood to be general grounds for exempting liability because it is mentioned in many specific criminal offences and also because there is a tendency to think that it operates generally in all offences that protect alienable legally protected interests, by virtue of the principle of freedom and personal autonomy.

From this starting point, a discussion about the legal nature of consent arises. A significant number of legal scholars maintain a 'differentiating theory'. Under this theory consent constitutes '*absent element grounds*' in some offences, meaning a lack of distinctive criminal elements; in other offences it constitutes '*justification grounds*' meaning that the characteristic elements of the crime are satisfied but there is a lack of unlawfulness.[26] In offences that require that the criminal conduct be carried out against the will of the victim or without the victim's consent, consent would amount to a lack of a distinctive criminal element. This is the case, *expressly*, in offences such as non-violent theft (Article 234 PC), breaking and entering (Article 202 PC), sexual abuse (Article 181 PC) or discovery and disclosure of secrets (Article 197 PC) and *impliedly* in offences such as duress (Article 172 PC), unlawful imprisonment (Article 163 PC) or kidnapping (Article 164 PC). In other offences, in which the legally protected interest is more independent from the holder's will, consent would constitute grounds for justification and would give rise to a lack of unlawfulness. This is the case in some forms of bodily harm offences (Article 147 PC), principally, or in criminal damage (Article 263 PC). However, in recent years a 'unitarian theory' has been gaining acceptance among legal scholars, which maintains that, in any event, consent prevents us from considering that all distinctive elements of the crime have been satisfied, without needing to find

---

24 Casas Barquero, *El consentimiento en el Derecho penal* (n 1) 93–95; López Barja de Quiroga, *El consentimiento en el Derecho penal* (n 1) 11.

25 See also below 2.1 and 2.2 on this question.

26 Casas Barquero, *El consentimiento en el Derecho penal* (n 1) 34–38; Cerezo Mir, *Curso de Derecho Penal español* (n 20) 326–334; Gonzalo Quintero Olivares, *Parte General del Derecho Penal* (Aranzadi Thomson Reuters 2010) 504–505; Luzón Peña, *Lecciones de Derecho Penal, Parte General* (n 18) 371–375.

a justification. The idea is that consent prevents actual harm to the legal interest protected by the offence.[27] When there is consent, conduct is either lawful or criminally irrelevant. It has even been considered as grounds to exclude attribution of the criminal outcome to the offender ('objective imputation').[28]

However, regarding the offence of bodily harm, it is usual to differentiate according to the type of injury. There are some types in which consent is deemed to exclude the legal relevance of the conduct, without the need to resort to a justification. Thus, there are doubts whether injuries that are *socially appropriate* (such as those which occur when taking part in sport or sado-masochistic practices and injuries that occur in the field of medicine, for example) constitute an offence against health and they are considered, not only justified, but totally lawful conduct. Nevertheless, there are other types in which it is thought that the defining elements of the crime are satisfied, but that they are justified. This is the case of organ transplants, sterilisation and sex-reassignment surgery, which expressly provide the possibility of consent completely excluding liability (Article 156 PC) and not only reducing it, as occurs with the remaining consensual injuries (Article 155 PC).[29]

In any event, this is essentially a theoretical argument with very few practical consequences, specifically in respect of consent. Both interpretations lead to the conclusion that the act is not criminally unlawful. Frequent attempts have been made to impose more or fewer requirements regarding the form consent should take based upon the different nature of the offence. However, it is not clear whether such differences in requirements, from one offence to another, should depend on the nature of the consent. We could also maintain that this should depend on the greater or lesser importance of the legally protected interest or the greater or lesser seriousness of the offence.

1.3 Form of consent

1.3.1 Declared or implied

Except in cases in which a specific form of consent is expressly required, it can be given in any manner. The so-called 'legal transaction theory', which maintains that the form of consent should be the same as that required by private law to enter into legal transactions, contrasts with the so-called 'direction of will theory', which considers that it is sufficient that consent in fact exists. However, the majority of legal scholars in Spain are proponents of the so-called 'intermediate theory' or 'conciliatory theory', for which it is important that consent is expressed and can be recognised in some way.[30]

27 Beatriz de la Gándara Vallejo, *Consentimiento, bien jurídico e imputación objetiva* (Colex 1995) 95; Enrique Bacigalupo Zapater, *Principios de Derecho Penal, Parte General* (5th edition, Akal 1998) 199 ff; López Barja de Quiroga, *El consentimiento en el Derecho penal* (n 1) 8–9; Segura García, *El consentimiento del titular del bien jurídico en Derecho penal* (n 1) 61–67, 91–106; Polaino Orts, 'Alegato a favor de un tratamiento jurídico-penal unitario para los casos de acuerdo y consentimiento como causas de atipicidad' (2004) 82 Cuadernos de Política Criminal 163, 197.
28 de la Gándara Vallejo, *Consentimiento, bien jurídico e imputación objetiva* (n 27) 109; Mir Puig, *Derecho Penal, Parte General* (n 18) 518; José Miguel Zugaldía Espinar, *Lecciones de Derecho Penal, Parte General* (Tirant lo Blanch 2015) 254.
29 Peñaranda Ramos, 'El consentimiento en las lesiones' (n 8) 368–369; Manuel Cancio Meliá, 'Lesiones' in Fernando Molina Fernández, *Memento Penal* (Francis Lefevre 2015) 816–818.
30 Casas Barquero, *El consentimiento en el Derecho penal* (n 1) 60–61; López Barja de Quiroga, *El consentimiento en el Derecho penal* (n 1) 17; Segura García, *El consentimiento del titular del bien jurídico en Derecho penal* (n 1) 137. Compare also, although highlighting the possibility of arriving at the same

The perpetrator of the harmful conduct must know that the legal interest holder has consented. If there is consent, but it has not been expressed in any way or, if expressed, it has not come to the attention of the perpetrator, it will not completely relieve him of criminal liability. In this case it can be understood that there is no 'wrongful outcome', but there is still a 'wrongful action', so that punishment could be for attempt.[31]

In general, no specific form of consent is required in any offence. Nevertheless, in the field of medicine, certain procedures expressly require consent in writing. Article 8.2 of Law 41/2002 on Patient Autonomy states that consent must be in writing for surgical operations, diagnostic and invasive therapeutic procedures and, in general, for all procedures that imply risks or serious complications to the patient's health.

1.3.2 Presumed consent

When consent cannot be obtained, nor requested from the person's representatives, so-called 'presumed consent' is permitted. It is generally accepted that presumed consent is a valid substitute for actual consent and likewise excludes liability.[32]

Two requirements must be met: 1) it is not possible to obtain the legal interest holder's permission – or that of his representatives, when permitted – and 2) an emergency makes it necessary to carry out the conduct which could constitute a criminal offence. Thus, for example, if someone enters a neighbour's house in the neighbour's absence to repair a broken pipe, or in cases of medical procedures on unconscious patients.

These cases can be distinguished from a *necessity defence* because the harm averted does not have to be greater than the harm caused by the criminal conduct. It is sufficient if one can presume that the legal interest holder would have consented to the conduct if he could have done so. The important thing to bear in mind is the person's likely will, regardless of objective evaluations of the interests at stake, even regardless of whether the presumed consent turns out to be irrational or detrimental to the interest holder. It is only necessary for there to be reasons to believe that this could actually be the person's will.[33] If there are reasons to believe otherwise, it would not be possible to rely on presumed consent and one could only resort to other justification grounds, based on necessity, if the required conditions are met.[34]

Presumed consent should not be confused with *consent by proxy*, which is actual consent given by another person when it is impossible for the legally protected interest holder to give it. Nor should it be confused with *hypothetical consent*, which is sometimes raised in cases where though consent would be possible to obtain, for some reason, it has not been. In these cases, some scholars consider that, at least in some fields such as medicine, if one can be convinced

---

conclusion requiring knowledge of the consent, Escudero García-Calderón, *El consentimiento en Derecho Penal* (n 13) 183–192.

31 Compare below 1.6.

32 Casas Barquero, *El consentimiento en el Derecho penal* (n 1) 103; Norberto de la Mata Barranco, 'El consentimiento presunto ante comportamientos realizados en interés propio' in Jesús María Silva Sánchez (ed), *Política criminal y nuevo Derecho penal: libro homenaje a Claus Roxin* (JM Bosch Editor 1997) 399; López Barja de Quiroga, *El consentimiento en el Derecho penal* (n 1) 18–19; Segura García, *El consentimiento del titular del bien jurídico en Derecho penal* (n 1) 148–149; Escudero García-Calderón, *El consentimiento en Derecho Penal* (n 13) 212 ff.

33 Casas Barquero, *El consentimiento en el Derecho penal* (n 1) 104–108; López Barja de Quiroga, *El consentimiento en el Derecho penal* (n 1) 20.

34 López Barja de Quiroga, *El consentimiento en el Derecho penal* (n 1) 20; Segura García, *El consentimiento del titular del bien jurídico en Derecho penal* (n 1) 153.

that the person would have consented, it is also possible to take this hypothesis into account to exclude the 'wrongful outcome' and apply penalties only for attempt.[35]

Questions have been raised about the possibility of accepting presumed consent when the person who engages in the harmful conduct acts directly for his own benefit. Allowing presumed consent in such a case would risk giving rise to abusive situations, and consequently some scholars propose its application be rejected in these cases.[36]

1.4 Capacity to consent

The PC does not usually specify who has capacity to consent. Most legal scholars understand that a person has capacity if he is capable of understanding the meaning and scope of the consent. Legal capacity, as required in other areas of law, is not necessary for an individual's will to be valid. In criminal law it is sufficient for an individual to have a natural comprehension capacity.[37]

A person may lack legal capacity to deal with his property, but still give consent thereby excluding criminal liability. The transaction in this case may be unlawful, but it will not necessarily give rise to criminal liability.[38]

It is not generally necessary for a person to be of a certain age. It is sufficient if he can understand the significance of his conduct. The legislator has, however, expressly provided a minimum necessary age for some offences. Thus, for bodily harm and for organ transplants, sterilisations and sex reassignment surgery, consent is invalid if given by a person under 18 years of age or by someone declared to be lacking capacity (Articles 155 and 156 PC). For crimes against sexual freedom, it is understood that there is no valid consent if the person is under 16 years of age (Article 183.1 PC).[39]

In a medical context, for consent to be valid, it is also considered sufficient if the patient has natural comprehension capacity. He could be a minor or even lacking legal capacity. What is important is that the patient can understand the scope of the procedure. Because the issues affected are deemed extremely personal, consent is sought to respect the patient's will to the maximum extent possible. Only when the patient lacks this capacity, can resort be made to his legal representatives or relatives (Article 9.3 Law 41/2002 of 14 November on Patient Autonomy). In any event, consent given by proxy must always be in the patient's interest, respecting his personal dignity and involving the patient in all that is possible (Article 9.5 Law 41/2002 of 14 November on Patient Autonomy).[40]

A person may lack capacity to consent either permanently (minority, illness or disability), occasionally or temporarily (intoxication, loss of consciousness or temporary mental disorder).

When capacity is lacking, the representatives or relatives can give consent for the benefit of the legal interest holder, except when expressly precluded by the law, as is the case, for example, in organ transplants, sterilisations and sex-reassignment surgery (Article 156.1º

---

35 For further detail regarding this type of consent, see Escudero García-Calderón, *El consentimiento en Derecho Penal* (n 13) 277–348.

36 Segura García, *El consentimiento del titular del bien jurídico en Derecho penal* (n 1) 152–153.

37 López Barja de Quiroga, *El consentimiento en el Derecho penal* (n 1) 14–16; Cerezo Mir, *Curso de Derecho Penal español* (n 20) 329; Mir Puig, *Derecho Penal, Parte General* (n 18) 522–523; Luzón Peña, *Lecciones de Derecho Penal, Parte General* (n 18) 387–388.

38 Escudero García-Calderón, *El consentimiento en Derecho Penal* (n 13) 153–155.

39 See below 2.3 for more detail on this question.

40 Guérez Tricarico, 'Consentimiento' (n 8) 216–217.

PC). An exception is made in the case of sterilisation of persons with severe mental impairment, for whom authorisation can be given by a judge, in the person's interests, at the request of their legal representative, after hearing the Public Prosecutor and with a prior report of two specialists (Article 156.2° PC).

1.5 Consequences of mistaken consent

Consent is valid to the extent that it represents a free and voluntary decision of an individual. Therefore, consent given by a person lacking capacity or under duress, by means of violence or intimidation, is not considered valid.[41]

In principle, apart from cases of duress, the reasons for which consent are given are not taken into account. Except when the possible reasons are expressly limited by law, consent can be given at a price or even for illegal purposes. However, there is an express exception in the case of offences causing bodily harm and in organ transplants, sterilisations and sex-reassignment surgery, where consent must be spontaneous and cannot be obtained for a price or reward (Articles 155 and 156 PC).[42]

1.5.1 Mistake

Several doubts arise concerning mistake related to consent, which is not mentioned in the Penal Code. When referring to consent in a specific criminal offence, the Penal Code simply requires that consent be valid. In principle, one might think that when the person giving consent is mistaken, consent is vitiated because he is not fully aware of what he is doing and, therefore, he is not taking a free decision. However, legal scholars consider that not all cases of mistake render consent invalid or ineffective.

For example, it is often said that *mistake in the declaration* (which occurs when someone wishes to declare or express his will and, by mistake, says something different) does not render the consent ineffective. In these cases, what actually occurs is that the person who interferes with or attacks the legally protected interest is mistaken, believing he has the victim's consent, when in fact it is lacking.[43] It cannot be said that there is valid consent, but the consequences are similar, because if the other person makes an unavoidable mistake, criminal liability will similarly be excluded.[44]

On the other hand, it is understood that *mistake in the object, scope, form or dangerousness* of the interference or attack to which consent is to be given does vitiate consent. The person should, at least, be fully aware of what he is consenting to.

However, *mistake as to the identity* of the offender is not always considered relevant. Except in cases where identity has been a deciding factor in giving consent, mistake as to the identity of the person does not invalidate consent. If someone thought that doctor A was going to carry out the operation and finally it is done by doctor B, it cannot be argued that his initial mistake invalidates the consent. It would be a different matter if the reason – or one of the reasons – why he accepted the procedure was precisely because doctor A was going to carry it

---

41   Casas Barquero, *El consentimiento en el Derecho penal* (n 1) 77–78; Segura García, *El consentimiento del titular del bien jurídico en Derecho penal* (n 1) 143–144.

42   Casas Barquero, *El consentimiento en el Derecho penal* (n 1) 99; Cerezo Mir, *Curso de Derecho Penal español* (n 19) 330; Escudero García-Calderón, *El consentimiento en Derecho Penal* (n 13) 180–181.

43   Luzón Peña, 'El consentimiento en Derecho penal: causa de atipicidad, de justificación o de exclusión sólo de la tipicidad penal' (2010) 18 Revista General de Derecho Penal 32.

44   Compare below 1.6.

out. Likewise, the identity of the person to whom consent is given can be a deciding factor for some criminal offences, such as those against privacy. Therefore, it is difficult to give just one answer about the relevance of the identity of the person who threatens the legally protected interest. It depends on its greater or lesser importance in the will-forming process expressed in the consent.

1.5.2 Deception

Special problems arise in cases where the person is deceived as to the *motives* that lead him to give consent. In principle, these cases of mistake are considered irrelevant and do not vitiate consent.[45] For example, it would not be relevant if someone consented to sexual relations with a person who had lied about his amorous intentions or if someone consented to his property being damaged after having been deceived about its true value.

In particular, mistakes as to the price to be given in exchange for consent are considered immaterial – in cases where a price or reward is permitted: for example, when a person promises to give an amount of money to another in exchange for being allowed to go into his house or for consenting to sexual relations, later breaking the promise. This mistake as to the motives or reasons for which someone makes the decision are considered to be criminally immaterial except when they give rise to the criminal offence of fraud, which is only punished when the victim's economic assets are affected.

However, the relevance of mistake is admitted when a person is deceived about a situation of need in order to force him to perform an altruistic act or to rescue someone, for example, if a person is deceived about the need to donate an organ to a third person.[46]

The debate about the relevance of mistake as to motives is an open debate and legal scholars have different opinions. Actually, it seems difficult to deny the relevance of this type of mistake in general terms, since clearly it can influence a person's will just as much as any other type of mistake. What is important, as with other types of mistake, is to evaluate the importance of the mistake in the will-forming process manifested in the consent and the legal relevance that such mistake could have depending on the legal interest protected.[47]

1.6 Mistake about consent

The offender's mistake about the consent given by the legal interest holder is also relevant. This mistake can be of two types.

1 First, the offender may wrongly believe the victim has consented. In this case, there is a mistake as to the defining elements of the offence. It is a *mistake of fact* as to the elements of the crime and not as to the legal assessment of the facts. According to most legal scholars, a mistaken belief as to the non-existence of a defining criminal element (the person does not know that he is causing death) is on a par with mistaken belief as to the existence of a fact excluding the illegal character of the conduct (the person thinks consent has been given or that he is being attacked, in the case of self-defence: mistake of fact). In these cases the mistake negates the *mens rea*. If the mistake is unavoidable

---

45 Casas Barquero, *El consentimiento en el Derecho penal* (n 1) 86.

46 Segura García, *El consentimiento del titular del bien jurídico en Derecho penal* (n 1) 145.

47 Compare, in this sense, opting for a differing solution, Luzón Peña, 'El consentimiento en Derecho penal' (n 43) 20–35; Escudero García-Calderón, *El consentimiento en Derecho Penal* (n 13) 170–179.

there will be no criminal liability whatsoever, but if it is avoidable it will still be possible to apply penalties for the crime of negligence.[48]

2 Secondly, the offender could believe that the victim has not given consent when in fact he has. There are two possible solutions in this case: a) either we consider that, since the subjective element is missing, the justification is not complete and, therefore, the act should be punished, although the punishment would be reduced – which presupposes treating the consent as a defence of justification; or b) we consider that, in so far as consent exists, it does not give rise to a 'wrongful outcome' and the act should be punished as if it were an attempt.[49] Both solutions are accepted by legal scholars and both imply the same mitigation in punishment according to the regulation of the Penal Code.

2 SPECIFIC ISSUES

2.1 Consent and homicide offences

2.1.1 Mercy killings

There are no specific provisions for cases in which the perpetrator ends another person's life moved by feelings of compassion when not at the victim's request. In any case, this could be considered a mitigating factor.

2.1.2 Killing on request of the victim

The crime of homicide or murder does not apply, under any circumstances, when death occurs at the victim's request, provided the victim is responsible and conscious of what he is doing. If it is a case of assisted suicide, the PC describes this conduct as aiding and abetting in the commission of suicide (Article 143.3 PC: 'if such cooperation were to reach the point of death ensuing'), reducing the term of imprisonment very significantly compared to homicide (from 10 to 15 years to 6 to 10 years). When death occurs at the request of the victim in the context of euthanasia (Article 143.4 PC: 'in the event of the victim suffering a serious disease that would unavoidably lead to death, or that causes permanent suffering that is hard to bear'), the term of punishment imposed is reduced to 18 months to 6 years.

2.1.3 Abortion

Since the enactment of Organic Law 2/2010, on sexual and reproductive health and termination of pregnancy, Spain has had a system based on time limits (allowing abortion in the first 14 weeks of pregnancy) if the pregnant woman consents to the abortion. This voluntary termination of pregnancy necessarily requires prior express written consent of the pregnant woman (express consent not being necessary in cases of immediate and serious risk to her physical or psychological integrity and when it is impossible to obtain it [OL 2/2010 Article 13]). The current Conservative parliamentary majority has given up amending this legislation – contrary to its election manifesto – so we can assume that this regulation will not change. Nevertheless, a constitutional challenge, lodged by the Conservatives, when they were in the opposition, is still pending at the Constitutional Court.

---

48 Zugaldía Espinar, *Lecciones de Derecho Penal, Parte General* (n 28) 255.
49 Cerezo Mir, *Curso de Derecho Penal español* (n 20) 330–331; Mir Puig, *Derecho Penal, Parte General* (n 18) 526–526; ibid 255.

The political controversy surrounding this offence, which had hitherto centred on a choice between a conditions-based system (which applied before 2010) and a time-limit system, has recently shifted to focus on the specific question of whether minors, specifically those of 16 and 17 years of age, have capacity to consent. In accordance with the general rules set out in the LPA, minors of 12 to 16 years of age must be consulted on any therapeutic measure, and anyone over 16 can decide on it exclusively. However, a different regime applies for termination of pregnancy. OL 2/2010 provided a system in which consent was shared between the 16- or 17-year-old and her legal representatives, this requirement being dispensed with when there was a situation of conflict. Nevertheless, very recently, the legislator has opted to require that the consent of the pregnant minor be accompanied by that of her parents or legal representatives in all cases (by Organic Law 11/2015 of 21 September, to strengthen the protection of minors and women with judicially modified capacity in voluntary termination of pregnancy).

The so-called 'morning-after pill' is not considered a means of abortion, but rather an emergency anti-contraceptive measure, so there are no specific requirements concerning consent.

2.2 Consent and non-fatal offences against the person

2.2.1 In general

As regards bodily harm offences, there are various situations in which consent of the victim is relevant in one way or another: a) injuries consented to by the victim (Article 155 PC); b) injuries caused in organ transplants, sex-reassignment surgery and sterilisation (Article 156 PC).[50]

In the first situation there is a general (mitigation) rule, while the second sets out certain cases in which liability is exempted (as justified). It should be understood that this regulation refers to cases of consented injuries inflicted by another, excluding all other types of secondary participation in self-harm, since there is no express criminal liability attached to different forms of participation, as is the case in Article 143 PC. Therefore, the boundary between self-harm and harm inflicted by another becomes crucial.

(a) The general rule is set out in Article 155 PC, which states 'In bodily harm offences, if the consent has been validly, freely, spontaneously and expressly given by the victim, a punishment that is lower by one or two degrees will be imposed. Consent granted by a minor or incapacitated person in special need of protection will not be valid.'

The requirements for consent to be valid (for this provision to come into play) are: a) it has been given freely (free from duress or threat); b) it is spontaneous (some contend that this appears to exclude a proposal made by another for a price or reward, while others require the initiative to come from the interest holder himself, which seems more appropriate taking into account the express wording); c) it is express and current. The mitigating rule contained in Article 155 PC, as a general solution in cases of consent, was an amendment introduced in the current Penal Code, following a stormy legislative passage. It has been subject to severe criticism since it seems to remain in no-man's-land, on the road to recognition of the relevance of autonomy of will. It should be noted that there are various points of view when proposing an interpretation of the Article 155 PC rule. From the autonomy of will perspective, a number of scholars reject mere mitigation of liability, understanding

---

50 See about the following Cancio Meliá, 'Lesiones' in Molina Fernández, *Memento Penal* (n 29) 816–818.

that the legal interest holder's will should allow third parties to intervene interfering with his own health, thus excluding an essential element of the offence: it would be an inappropriate way to recognise the scope afforded (constitutionally) to autonomy of will provided in Article 10 SC (free development of personality). Therefore, apart from rejecting the rule in accordance with this approach, an interpretation should be sought, above all, allowing its application to be excluded. Conversely, there are scholars who essentially agree with the legislator and believe the application of the rule should not be restricted to any type of harm. This is because it would be necessary to establish a general prohibition against third persons interfering adversely in the health of others, although consent of the injured person should be taken into account, by means of a reduction in the punishment. In this respect, mention is made of the 'multidimensional' nature of the legally protected interest, made up both of the physical bodily basis and of the holder's autonomy. Finally, a third approach seeks to find an interpretation giving a reasonable sense to the regulation, a sense that does not impose a mitigation solution in all cases. From this perspective, Article 155 PC should apply only in cases of serious injuries (PC Articles 149 and 150), that is to say, serious and permanent injuries, since objectively there are certain types of consented behaviour excluded from criminality as society considers them normal. In other words, there are cases in which consent (for example: informed consent in medical treatment – see below) or elements of the objective imputation theory (self-exposure to danger) exclude the injuries as elements of the crime, thus shutting the door to the application of the Article 155 PC mitigation rule. Mitigation would reflect a paternalist approach, where it does apply, considering that the injuries are of an irreversible nature and seriously affect the legally protected interest. Therefore, less serious cases should be excluded from the application of this rule. In conclusion, the last option seems most appropriate. Even without elaborate theoretical arguments, it seems clear that the application of the Article 155 PC mitigation rule would lead to a punishment that can hardly be referred to as such and consequently it only applies, in fact, to cases aggravated by the magnitude of the outcome (PC Articles 149 and 150).

The only existing case in which the rule has applied in practice, as far as one can see, concerned sado-masochistic practices causing permanent injuries – although conviction was under CP Article 148.1o.[51] Generally, we should not lose sight of the fact that, as mentioned above, it is within the scope of bodily harm offences that different versions of a dogmatic institution ('consent to the risk'; 'participation in self-exposure to danger', 'attribution of liability to the victim') have been developed within the framework of the theory of objective imputation (and have been assumed by case-law), which exclude the elements of a criminal offence from the conduct of the person who takes part in the self-harming behaviour, together with the legal interest holder, on the basis of the preferential competence of the holder who assumes responsibility for himself. Thus, injuries occurring while engaging in sport or taking part in an illegal, dangerous competition are not deemed to constitute an offence of bodily harm, within the framework of the general rules, unless they cause permanent and very serious injuries.

(b) Article 156 provides that 'validly, freely, spontaneously and expressly given consent shall exempt from criminal liability in cases of organ transplants undertaken in accordance with the law, sterilisations and sex reassignment surgery, carried out by a surgeon, unless consent is vitiated, or obtained for a price or reward, or when the person consenting is a minor or absolutely lacks capacity to give consent, in which

---

51 STS 5 June 2002 (A 4080).

case consent of such persons or of their legal representatives will not be valid. Sterilisation of persons, who cannot, in any way, give the consent referred to in the previous paragraph, shall not be punishable when authorised by a judicial body, provided they are exceptional cases in which there is a serious conflict between the legally protected interests, so that the prevailing interest can be upheld, all in accordance with the provisions of civil legislation.'

The first cases do not pose problems: under the system of values established in the Constitution, these are cases in which the legal system recognises the worthiness of the underlying motives: free development of personality in core areas (sterilisation; sex-reassignment surgery) and solidarity (organ transplants). The situation is more complex in the case of sterilisation of incapacitated persons needing special protection since autonomy is not the only value to be taken into account and this explains the special precautions applicable in this case. The previous regulation in this respect has now been replaced by OL 1/2015, the underlying reasons for this not being very clear. In this regard, one cannot see the sense of substituting the reference to an incapacitated person for the vague concept of a 'person who is not in any way in a position to give consent', which evidently reduces legal certainty in this area. We could think – as did one of the reports of the competent bodies on the pre-legislative texts recommending the previous wording be maintained – that it is a generic restriction on the possibility of sterilisation for reasons not explicitly stated (perhaps of an ideological nature). This is suggested by the removal of the mention of the incapacitated person's interests, replacing it with an indeterminate reference to legal interests in serious conflict, as if these did not belong to an incapacitated person anyway, and existed in the abstract, without considering the interest of the person in question. Thus, before making this amendment to the procedure, giving rise to great uncertainty, it would have been desirable to have established the rules in civil legislation first (in this respect, see the first additional disposition of OL 1/2015); at the very least, it would have been essential to have maintained the reference to the incapacitated person's overriding interest, which should take precedence in a free and secular system, over and above essentialist perceptions of what is good in itself, in accordance with some transcendental order of values.

2.2.2 HIV and other communicable disease transmission

The problem of HIV transmission through sexual contact has been addressed on several occasions in case-law. All the cases in which criminal proceedings have been brought concern stable relationships where the carrier (consciously) had hidden the fact he was a carrier from his partner and had engaged in risk practices. Mere transmission of HIV has been held by the courts to amount to a serious injury (causing a serious illness (Article 149 CP)) it not being necessary for AIDS to have developed.[52] From existing case-law, it can be inferred *sensu contrario* that transmission, once the partner has been informed, would amount to a 'self-inflicted danger', not subject to punishment.

2.2.3 Medical treatment

As stated above, the crucial statute in this field – containing the essential provisions of the doctor–patient relationship – is now a law referring, precisely, to patient autonomy (LPA

---

52 See Judgments of the Supreme Court of 18.11.1991; 28.1.1997; Judgment of the Audiencia Provincial de Santa Cruz de Tenerife (Sección 2ª) of 20.1.1996 (the latter two in respect of the same case).

41/2002; although there are also laws corresponding to the autonomous regions). The principle of autonomy is the hub of the entire regulation and proclaims itself the key element of the whole normative system.[53] Accordingly, the following are basic principles (Article 2 LPA):

1 A person's dignity, respect for his autonomy of will and his privacy shall guide all activities aimed at obtaining, using, filing, safe-keeping and transmitting information and clinical documentation.

2 All actions within the scope of health require, in general, the prior consent of patients or users. The consent must be obtained once the patient has received sufficient information and shall be given in writing in the events provided for by law.

3 The patient or user has the right to decide freely between clinical options available, once he has received proper information.

4 All patients and users have the right to refuse treatment, except in the cases determined by law. Denial of treatment must be noted in writing.

As mentioned above, this is based on the Oviedo Convention on Biomedicine (ratified by Spain in 1999) which provides, in this respect, that any intervention can only be carried out after the person concerned has given free and unequivocal consent. The person shall be given appropriate information beforehand as to the purpose and nature of the intervention as well as its consequences and risks (Article 5).

On the operational level, the LPA defines informed consent as the free, voluntary and conscious agreement of a patient, stated in the full use of his faculties, after receiving proper information, so that an action concerning his health can be undertaken (Article 3). In general, the basic requirements of consent are that it is given prior to the intervention, that the person has capacity to dispose of the legally protected interest in question and that he understands the terms of what he is consenting to.

Evidently, what is most relevant in this respect is the configuration and effects of vitiated consent, that is, the cases in which consent is considered invalid, legally non-existent and therefore insufficient to eliminate the wrongfulness of the intervention in its scope. We can leave aside duress or violence as vitiating factors, and consider only the lack of (informed) consent either through lack of necessary information or lack of capacity to consent. As regards the former, the physician is the guarantor of the patient receiving the information (Article 4.3 LPA). In accordance with the majority of scholars, it can be said that the absence of information will be relevant when it refers directly to the legally protected interest, on the one hand, or affects the necessity of the intervention – that is to say the global sense – of the medical treatment in question, on the other hand. As a result, the failure to supply the necessary information can open the door to the doctor's criminal liability. It is not the patient's responsibility to obtain the information; he can be assured that it will be supplied by the guarantor, the doctor who is treating him.

It seems clear that capacity to consent is an especially relevant area in healthcare: an ill patient – and this is particularly the case in the ever-growing sector of the population suffering from chronic illnesses at advanced ages – can easily present characteristics that call into question his capacity to consent.

---

53 See about the following Manuel Cancio Meliá, 'Autonomie und Einwilligung bei ärztlicher Heilbehandlung. Eine Skizze aus spanischer Perspektive' in Bernd Schünemann and Christian Jäger (ed), *Festschrift für Claus Roxin zum 80. Geburtstag* (Walter de Gruyter 2011) 507–522.

The duty to supply the information lies with the physician responsible for the patient (Article 4.3 LPA; although Article 5.3 refers to the 'attending physician', it should be understood that it is the physician responsible for the patient, defined as the professional in charge of coordinating assistance and main interlocutor – Article 3), although, all healthcare professionals who treat the patient have a duty to supply information in their respective areas. Nevertheless, in practice there may be many healthcare scenarios in which there is no such 'physician responsible' because the treatment is undertaken jointly by a medical team. Since autonomy is the guiding principle of all medical practice, it can be said that the primary purpose of any information process is to help the patient take decisions in accordance with his system of values (Article 4.2 LPA).

The minimum content of this information refers to the aim, nature, risks and consequences of undertaking, or not, the planned therapeutic procedure. It should be stressed that the physician must adapt the information so that it is comprehensible and suited to the needs of the patient (Article 4.2 LPA). The physician must also decide when the patient should not receive the information – in which case it must be made available to persons tied to the patient, when he lacks the capacity to understand the information due to his physical or mental state (Article 5.3 LPA). What could be referred to as the intensity of the information – its degree of detail and scope – should accord with the urgency (if relevant), the necessity of the procedure (the lesser the necessity – in voluntary medicine for example, in cosmetic surgery – more detail is required), and the characteristics of the patient (his lifestyle and other particular circumstances); again, it is a question of helping the patient to exercise his autonomy. As regards the form of consent (as provided in Articles 8.2 and 3 LPA and of fundamental importance when it comes to evidence), it can be oral consent as a general rule. However, written consent is required for surgical operations, invasive procedures in general and for all procedures that imply risks or drawbacks having a notable and foreseeable negative repercussion on the patient's health. The informed consent document must include 'sufficient information'. The regulation of the information also foresees cases in which, for therapeutic reasons, it is precisely not advisable to inform the patient; in this case, the physician can exercise the 'power' to carry out the treatment without information, and, therefore, without consent. This hypothesis, sometimes called 'therapeutic privilege' – following the Anglo-Saxon terminology – is defined as a state of therapeutic necessity (Article 5.4 LPA):

> The patient's right to health information can be limited by the accredited existence of a state of therapeutic necessity. Therapeutic necessity can be understood as the power of the physician to act professionally without informing the patient in advance, when the patient's knowledge of his own situation could cause serious harm to his health, due to objective reasons. Should this situation arise, the physician must make a motivated note of the circumstances in the clinical record and must communicate his decision to members of the patient's family or to persons tied to him for *de facto* reasons.

Finally, the predominance of autonomy leads in some cases precisely to the patient rejecting the information: any person has the right not to be informed and this must be respected (Article 4.1 LPA). The patient's right to ignore therapeutic information is limited by the interests of the patient's own health and by the therapeutic demands of the case (Article 9.1 LPA). It seems clear that the physician responsible is the person who must decide in which specific cases to waive the right to information.

2.3 Sexual offences

(a) As mentioned above, since the enactment of OL 1/2015, consent of any person under 16 years of age is generally irrelevant and any sexual contact is, in principle, a criminal offence (Article 183.1 PC).[54] With this new age limit for irrelevance of consent in cases of abuse, the necessary exclusion clause is especially significant. This has been included in Article 183 quater PC, to avoid criminalising sexual conduct between peers – that is, between adolescents or young people or very young adults and persons under 16 – in which there has not been undue influence, and, therefore, abuse. In this respect, the new Article 183 quater PC provides that 'freely given consent by a person under 16 years of age excludes criminal liability' for the applicable offences 'when the perpetrator is a person close in age and degree of development and maturity to the minor'.

> The main problem that arises with regard to this clause is its lack of precision. The two elements the provision requires cumulatively, proximity in age and in degree of maturity, are not sufficiently defined. The legislator has not followed comparative law models that have opted to establish a specific age difference to avoid legal uncertainty, and, once more, has just copied the terms of Article 8.1 of Directive 2011/93/EU slavishly, failing again to take into account that this norm does not contain a proposal for elements of a criminal offence, but rather intends to set out material common denominators. Clearly, this uncertainty is even more worrying in a procedural system such as the Spanish one, which allows private or popular prosecution of criminal offences (unlike neighbouring countries, in which, in principle, it is up to the public prosecutor to bring the action and the prosecutor's judgement acts as a filter to weed out cases that do not appear to merit prosecution). Moreover, a first initial investigation is undertaken by an investigating court with the burden imposed on the person initially subject to the investigation (imagine a relationship between a young woman of 15 years 11 months and a young man who has just turned 18, which the parent or guardian considers should be criminally prosecuted and acts accordingly).

(b) As regards the general rules relating to consent and its proof, typical elements of violence and intimidation are common in sexual offences.[55] In these offences it is worth stressing – in a matter half way between the concept of violence/intimidation and its proof – that there is consolidated case-law to the effect that resistance of the victim is not an element of the offence, while the violence or intimidation of the offender is. There has been a departure from previous case-law (in former times when it was a matter of the woman's 'honesty'), which initially required considerable resistance, later requiring reasonable resistance, but now establishing the victim's will to the contrary will suffice. Obviously, this does not change at all the fact that physical proof of the victim's resistance is very relevant as evidence of lack of consent and use of violence. According to this approach to intimidation, the traditional issue of formal resistance to preserve a woman's honesty (*vis haud ingrata*) now appears in a completely different light: aside from exotic and unusual sexual contexts, these days a man can never assume that a woman's 'no', regardless of how advanced the approach

---

54 See about the following Cancio Meliá, 'Delitos contra la libertad e indemnidad sexuales' in Molina Fernández, *Memento Penal* (n 29) 978–983.

55 ibid 964–968.

between them may be, means anything other than a refusal. Thus, the possibility of alleging a mistake in these cases is considerably reduced: 'From the legal point of view, what is truly important in rape is to know the rapist's decided intention and to know the means employed in his physical or moral attack. Since the former doctrine regarding resistance offered by the victim, requiring it to be momentous, has already been abandoned, then considering serious resistance to be sufficient, later defining it as reasonable resistance, sometimes even not requiring the characteristics of a defensive attitude at all which may only put the woman's life in danger, without having any legal effect'.[56]

> In this regard, the victim's resistance is not a necessary element of the *actus reus* of rape. Therefore, times in which the main object of the evidentiary debate concerned the injuries the offender had inflicted on the victim, proving there had been resistance, are a thing of the past: the fact that the accused does not use force on his victim in a manner that causes visible injuries is not an element that questions her resistance to the aggressor.

(c) As we can imagine, evidentiary problems deriving from many sexual offences are particularly relevant in practice. The victim's statement is frequently the only incriminating evidence – logically so, taking into account the most frequent factual situations in these offences. There is settled case-law, in this respect, to the effect that the testimony of the victim may be sufficient to rebut the presumption of innocence, defence lawyers often alleging non-observance of this presumption in this type of offence. For this purpose, the credibility of the victim's version of events must necessarily be assessed. The Supreme Court has summarised three elements to undertake the assessment:[57] a) absence of subjective lack of credibility: there should be no relationship between the accused/victim or complainant, which could lead to the inference that there was a motive of resentment, hostility or any other type, thus depriving the testimony of the necessary validity to generate this subjective state of certainty on which judicial decisions essentially rest. In this respect, such resentment or hostility cannot be deemed to exist when those feelings derive or originate precisely from the attack on the victim's property or person at the hands of the accused; b) credibility of the testimony (which is not actually such, in so far as the victim can be a party to the proceedings); the testimony must have certain objective peripheral corroboration, making it valid evidence. In short, what is essential is to determine the actual existence of a fact; c) persistence in the incrimination. This must be prolonged in time, plural, unambiguous and without contradictions.

---

56 Judgment of the Supreme Court of 16.5.1995.
57 See Judgments 23.5.2002; 2.1.1996; 21.7.2003; 19.7.2013.

24
Sweden

Petter Asp and Magnus Ulväng

1 GENERAL ISSUES

1.1 Conceptual foundations

1.1.1 Philosophical and theoretical principles informing the law surrounding consent

The basic importance of consent[1] is – in Sweden as in most other jurisdictions – explained by the *volenti non fit injuria* maxim (to a willing person no harm is done).[2] This principle is of importance at many different levels of the criminal law system: at the level of criminalisation (as a reason for not criminalising), at the level of application or interpretation of proscriptions (many proscriptions contain implicit or explicit references to non-consent) and as a reason for justifying otherwise criminal behaviour. Behind the principle lies an (essentially liberal) idea of self-determination: the individual has the right to dispose of his or her own interests. It is clear that the state does not leave everything in the hands of the individual. Therefore, in addition to the consent given by the individual, two additional 'yes's' have to be added if consent is to be of relevance in a criminal law context.[3]

First, in order for the consent to make a difference, it must be considered an expression of self-determination. This means that the law will deny the effect of 'consent' given under certain circumstances; for example a 'yes' given under threat or under the influence of deception will not constitute valid consent. See, for example, sections 1.2. and 1.5. below.

Secondly, should consent make a difference it must concern an issue to which the law allows the consenting person to consent. This means that the law will generally deny the possibility to consent to certain types of acts; this applies, for example, to acts causing serious

---

1 There is a limited number of books that deal with questions of consent. The most important texts are Petter Asp, Magnus Ulväng and Nils Jareborg, *Kriminalrättens grunder* (Iustus förlag 2015) 226–236, and Nils-Olof Berggren and others, 'Brottsbalken. En kommentar' (Zeteo 2015), under Chapter 24 s 7. Of special importance is the preparatory works that are found in Swedish Government Official Reports (SOU) 1988:7 (see especially 99–124 and 205–206) and Government Bill to Parliament (proposition) 1993/94:130 (see especially 37–44 and 72–73).

2 See, for example, Asp ibid 226.

3 See Petter Asp, *Sex och samtycke* (Iustus förlag 2010) 90 f.

harm to the person. As a result, a person can under no circumstances consent to being shot to death, tortured etc.

1.1.2 Influence of feminist and queer theory

It would be difficult to argue that feminist or queer theory should have directly influenced the concept of consent as it is applied in law. The structure of consent, as it is currently regulated in Chapter 24 s 7 of the Criminal Code, has in essence been the same for a considerable time, long before it was codified in 1994. Feminist theory has contributed to development in certain areas, for example when it comes to sexual offences, both by emphasising the importance of consent, and by questioning what could be called the 'liberal paradigm'. This has been done both by questioning whether consent is always the right concept to build upon when constructing offences, and by questioning the meaning of consent in a world of inequalities.[4] Indirectly this has led to broader acceptance that the traditional point of departure, ie that there is no harm where there is consent, is not a god-given truth. This has contributed to our understanding according to which consent is 'empty' in the sense that one must always decide when consent is valid and how much harm one can consent to.[5] In other words such theory has indirectly contributed to an understanding according to which the starting point (once again, that there is no harm where there is consent) can always be called into question.

1.1.3 Definition of informed consent

If consent is to be considered a justification under Chapter 24 s 7 of the Criminal Code, the act of consent has, among other things, to be given by a capable person and with knowledge of the relevant circumstances: ie if the person giving consent is deceived with regard to, or not informed about, relevant factors, the consent given will not be valid.[6] Thus, consent according to Swedish law presupposes that the person has a somewhat correct understanding of the relevant factors. It is not necessarily easy to say which factors are relevant in this sense, ie there is no clear definition of what constitutes informed consent. Generally speaking, one can say that the person consenting has to know what he or she is consenting to and the consequences of his or her consent. This means, for example, that consent cannot explain the permissibility of all forms of medical treatment: in some cases the patient does not have the ability to undertake a rational assessment of the risks.

When consent negates the prerequisites of a specific offence, non-informed consent may be considered enough in some circumstances. In such cases there is, however, normally another offence that can be applied and that builds upon deception or misuse of a superior position. For example, permission to take an object excludes responsibility for theft.[7] However, if permission has been obtained through deception this may constitute fraud; fraud consists of deceiving another into performing an act causing economic harm to that person and profit for another.[8]

---

4 See, for example, Kerstin Berglund, *Straffrätt och kön* (Iustus förlag 2007) who, among other things, tries to make a distinction between individual autonomy (which according to Berglund forms the point of departure for criminal law today) and individual integrity (which can be constructed from a feminist view on mankind).
5 See section 1.1.1.
6 See Asp (n 1) 229 f. and Berggren and others (n 1).
7 See the Swedish Criminal Code Chapter 8 s 1.
8 ibid Chapter 9 s 1.

1.1.4 Consent to risk or consent to outcome

Under Swedish law, one can, in principle, consent both to the exposure to risk and to actual harm. However, since consent can, under the general section in Chapter 24 s 7 of the Criminal Code, justify an act only if the act having regard to the circumstances is *defensible* (see section 1.2. below), the possibility to consent to harm is, generally speaking, much more limited than the possibility to consent to risk. Acts including the imposition of harm will, more often than acts including the mere exposure to risk, be considered to be indefensible. Thus, the presence of consent to risk for bodily harm will, in most cases, exclude liability for causing danger of bodily harm (ie the act will, generally speaking, be considered defensible if there is consent). Conversely, should the harm actually occur the act will be considered defensible only as long as the harm is not too severe (one can consent to pain and bruises, but not to serious bodily harm).

The Supreme Court has, nevertheless, indicated that there might be limits to the possibilities to consent to risk-taking or exposure to danger.[9] It is very unclear in which situations one would not be able to legally consent to a risk or danger. It is reasonable to assume that the cases where one cannot consent to a risk will be cases in which the risk is very substantial and relates to matters of life and death.

1.1.5 Revocation of consent

One precondition for there to be valid consent is that the consent exists from the time when the act is performed (when it starts) and (if the act is ongoing) until the act ends.[10] Consequently, consent can be revoked as long as the act continues. The law does not require the revocation to be done in a certain way (ie there are no formal requirements), but if the revocation is not communicated, this may of course lead to a situation in which the perpetrator thinks that he or she still has consent (see section 1.6. as regards putative consent).

The only exception to the rule that one can revoke consent concerns situations where the consent has been given by entering into a binding (private law) agreement.

Consent given after the act (ratihabition) is, in principle, irrelevant, though it may be a reason for the victim not to report the offence to the police.[11]

1.1.6 Ownership and limits of consent

Generally speaking, the sole person who can give consent is the bearer of the interest that is protected by the proscription in question. As regards offences against persons this means that the victim is the one that can give consent (within the limits set by the requirement that the act performed with consent must be defensible; see the general description of this defence in section 1.2. below). According to the Parental Code, the persons who are responsible for a child (normally the parents) can consent on behalf of the child to certain acts that otherwise would be proscribed. This is of special importance when it comes to medical treatment.

As regards offences directed at public interests there is normally no one who is competent to give consent. This means that consent is normally without importance when it comes to offences directed against public interests.

---

9 Swedish Supreme Court Case NJA 2004 p. 176.
10 See Asp (n 1) 229 and Berggren and others (n 1).
11 ibid.

1.2 Place of consent in the offence structure

Consent can be of relevance in the offence structure in (mainly) two ways.

First, non-consent is in many instances a prerequisite for fulfilling the offence description. For example, the offence of theft presupposes that something is taken 'without permission', which means that presence of consent will negate the offence description of theft.[12] Similarly the offence of rape by means of coercion will be negated by the presence of consent since the offence description requires that the victim is forced to have sex by means of violence or threats.[13]

Secondly, there is a general justificatory ground based on the idea of consent. Consent as a justification is regulated in Chapter 24 s 7 of the Swedish Criminal Code. It reads as follows:

> An act committed by a person with the consent of some other person towards whom it is directed, constitutes a crime only if the act, having regard to the injury, violation or danger which it involved, its purpose, and other circumstances, is indefensible.

The section presupposes, if there is to be a justification, (1) that there is valid consent and (2) that the act committed with consent of the victim is defensible.

Consent is valid if it is (1a) present during the whole act; (1b) given by someone who has the authority to dispose of the interest affected; (1c) given by someone who has the capacity to understand the meaning and consequences of consenting; (1d) given by 'free will' and with knowledge about the relevant circumstances; and, (1e) meant as a serious expression of consent.[14]

Consent may also be a factor to take into account when justifying conduct under the unwritten exceptions referred to by the term social adequacy. Social adequacy can, under Swedish law, be described as the unwritten exceptions needed for the purpose of explaining the lawfulness of an act in cases where the act does fulfil the prerequisites of the offence in question and where there is no (other) applicable justification. It can be seen as a safety valve, which can be used for avoiding the conclusion that an act constitutes an offence in cases where this is clearly unintended by the legislature. The connection to consent is established by the fact that in some cases social adequacy is of importance only if there is consent. For example, circumcision of a child for religious reasons (traditions etc) and without any pain reduction has, in a Supreme Court ruling, been considered to be justified with reference to social adequacy.[15] A precondition for this conclusion was, of course, that the circumcision was made with the consent of the parents (now this area of law has been regulated so the decision has lost most of its former importance; however, the principle is basically the same).[16]

The interplay between consent and social adequacy can in these situations be understood in different ways. One can say that consent may, at times, be of relevance for the application of the unwritten exception of social adequacy, ie that it is social adequacy that is effective while consent is merely a precondition. It could, alternatively, be argued that it is the rule on consent in Chapter 24 s 7 that is effective, and that the principle of social adequacy merely dispenses with some limitations that would otherwise apply. Normally it is, for example, not

---

12 See the SCC (n 7) Chapter 8 s 1.
13 ibid Chapter 6 s 1 subs 1.
14 See Asp (n 1) 227, Berggren and others (n 1), NJA 2013 p. 397.
15 NJA 1997 p. 636.
16 See the Act (2001:499) on the circumcision of boys.

possible to consent to the type of harm that is connected to circumcision without pain reduction; however, since the behaviour is strongly rooted in culture and religion, the threshold is somewhat raised.

1.3 Form of consent

1.3.1 Declared or implied

The general point of departure is that consent as a justificatory factor does not have to be communicated. This applies to the rule on consent in Chapter 24 s 7 (ie it can be used in situations when there is a silent/non-communicated consent). Thus, a person who actually consents to something without communicating it will thereby create a justification (if the conditions for valid consent are at hand and the act committed by the perpetrator is defensible).[17] In theory, the person who gets beaten by another person can consent silently, thereby justifying the act of the other person. This principle would not be very important in practice if there were a requirement of knowledge as to the justifying circumstances on the part of the perpetrator (since the perpetrator will normally not know about the existence of a non-communicated consent); however, the general rule, when it comes to justifications, is that they can be invoked by the perpetrator irrespective of their actual knowledge of them. It is enough that it is established that the justificatory circumstances existed 'objectively' or 'in fact'.

The principle of silent consent applies not only when it comes to consent as a justification, but also when it comes to consent as an explicit or implicit prerequisite under the different offence descriptions. Accordingly, a silent consent in relation to a theft will negate responsibility for theft etc. As regards sexual offences, it has been proposed, in both a legislative inquiry[18] and through academic discourse, that consent must always be required to be communicated (in some way).[19] The main reason for this position has been that there is as regards sexual offences, (slightly simplified) a strong connection between the disrespect of the self-determination of the person and the relevant intrusion of the protected interest (in a way that is not necessarily the case as regards other offences). Further, it has been argued that it should not, in situations where it is clear that consent has not been communicated, be a question whether the victim actually silently consented (despite being forced etc).

There is no requirement that consent should be given in a specific form. One can consent by saying yes, by nodding or by otherwise indicating consent. In some cases one may be required to fill in a form of consent (for example, by companies providing risky activities), but such a form merely provides proof that an act of consent was performed at a certain time. It is not in itself constitutive for there being consent.

1.3.2 Presumed consent

Presumed (or hypothetical) consent is not accepted as such.[20] Only actual consent is a basis for justification. However, presumed consent can still play a role when assessing whether an act can be considered unlawful or not. For example, presumed consent can be of importance for justifying medical treatment in an acute situation where the actual consent of the person

---

17 See Asp (n 1) 227 and Berggren and others (n 1).
18 Swedish Government Official Report, 'Sexual Crimes Legislation: The Evaluation and Reform' (SOU) 2010:71.
19 Asp (n 3) 118–121 .
20 See Asp (n 1) and Berggren and others (n 1) under the heading.

cannot be obtained due to unconsciousness. It can also be of importance as a reason for considering minor property offences as being socially adequate. For example, a person borrowing the lawn mower of a neighbour who could be presumed to be consenting, but has not actually consented, does not necessarily commit an offence (despite the fact that the rule on consent in Chapter 24 s 7 of the Criminal Code cannot be applied due to the lack of actual consent and despite the fact that there are no other explicit justifications applicable).

1.4 Capacity to consent

Consent as a justification under Chapter 24 s 7 of the Criminal Code presupposes that the consent is given by someone who has the ability to understand the meaning and the consequences of consenting. Consent given by someone who is very young or is mentally ill may be invalid. The invalidity of the consent cannot be directly connected to any specific age or diagnosis. One must in each and every case make an assessment of whether the person consenting has the ability to make a rational assessment and actually exercise his or her self-determination in the case in question. In NJA 1974 p. 614 the Supreme Court found that a five-year-old girl did not have the capacity to consent to unlawful deprivation of liberty in a way that would exclude liability.[21] As indicated above in section 1.1.6, parents can, to a certain extent, consent on behalf of their children to different acts that would otherwise constitute an offence against the child.

1.5 Consequences of mistaken consent

1.5.1 Mistake

Should there be a justification under Chapter 24 s 7 of the Criminal Code, the consent has to be given with knowledge of relevant circumstances, ie if the person giving consent is deceived, or not informed, about relevant factors, the consent given will not be valid. It is not necessarily easy to say which factors are relevant in this sense. Generally speaking the person consenting has to know what he or she is consenting to and the consequences of his or her consent. In most cases a mistake must be seen as relevant (making the consent invalid) if it concerns a circumstance that is of such importance to the consenting person that he or she would *not have consented*, had he or she known how things really were.

1.5.2 Deception

As indicated in the previous section deception in relation to relevant circumstances invalidates any consent given. In this regard it does not matter whether the lack of knowledge about the relevant circumstances is due to deception or whether the person consenting is simply not informed.

In this context it should be emphasised that as regards sexual offences consent will, generally speaking, be an issue that decides whether or not the offence description is fulfilled, and not an issue of justification (see above section 1.2.). At present the question of deception will be dealt with when assessing whether the perpetrator has improperly misused the fact that the victim was in a particularly vulnerable position. If, for example, a person participates in sex due to the fact that the person mistakenly believes that a second person who has entered a bed (in the dark) is his or her partner, the question will be whether the perpetrator has improperly misused the vulnerable position of the victim. Thus, deception is one factor that may put the victim in a vulnerable position.

---

21   See the SCC (n 7) Chapter 4 s 2, NJA 1974 p. 614.

1.6 Mistake about consent

The *mens rea* requirement means, according to Swedish law, that the perpetrator has to have intent not only in relation to the elements of the offence description (for example, that he or she has inflicted pain to another person), but also in relation to the *absence of justifications*.[22] The latter requirement means that if a person believes that the circumstances were such that the act would have been justified, had the circumstances been such as he or she believed them to be, then the person cannot be convicted for an offence requiring intention. This means that a person cannot be convicted of an offence requiring intention if:

1 the person wrongly believes that consent was actually given, and
2 the person does not do more than what would have been 'defensible' had his or her beliefs been correct.

In such a case the intent requirement is not fulfilled: the person realised that he or she inflicted pain on another person, but believed that the circumstances were such that his or her act would have been justified (ie the person does not have intent in relation to the fact that he or she inflicts pain under circumstances where this is not justified). There is no requirement of reasonableness as regards the mistake. Unreasonable mistakes may exclude liability for intention (though, the unreasonableness of a mistaken belief may, of course, be one factor among others when considering whether the person actually was mistaken as regards the existence of consent or just claims that he or she was mistaken).

If the person due to lack of intent in relation to the absence of justifications (consent in this case) cannot be convicted of an intentional offence, it might be possible to convict the person for a negligence offence. This presupposes the existence of such an offence as regards the act in question (such an offence does not exist when it comes to the infliction of pain) and that the person in question was negligent in believing that consent was given (ie it is required that one can say that the person ought to have realised that there was no consent given).

When non-consent is a factor that is a prerequisite for an offence requiring intent, an (honest) mistake on the part of the perpetrator will exclude liability for the offence. In these cases there will be no need to make an assessment whether the act was defensible having regard to the mistake. This follows from the principle that the intent should 'cover' the elements of the offence. However, if there is an offence of negligence, this may of course, apply if the mistake is negligent.

2 SPECIFIC ISSUES

2.1 Consent and homicide offences

2.1.1 *Mercy killing (and killing on request)*

Mercy killing is not accepted as a defence in Swedish law. Neither is the victim's consent relevant to the question of criminal liability for anyone who takes the life of another person. This follows from the requirement that the act performed with consent has to be defensible (and killing is never considered to be defensible). Nevertheless, if a crime was occasioned by strong human compassion, this will be taken into consideration as a mitigating circumstance, which can affect the labelling of the crime (compare murder/manslaughter). Mercy killings are often considered to display such compassion and are usually treated much more

---

22 See, as regards this kind of mistakes, Asp (n 1) 344 ff.

leniently at sentencing. Whether other forms of killing on request deserve extenuation is an open question.

Just as with every other form of intentional killing relevant for criminal law, responsibility for mercy killings or killings on the victim's request presuppose that the person subject to criminal evaluation is considered to be the perpetrator (or co-perpetrator); ie the *actus reus* requirements must be fulfilled. Since suicide is not criminalised in Swedish law, the rules on complicity are not directly applicable in cases where someone aids or abets someone who himself commits suicide. It could therefore be said that if someone has not committed the offence himself, then criminal responsibility is *prima facie* excluded. However, there are a number of possibilities for holding someone responsible for someone else's death although he or she is not the perpetrator *stricto sensu*. The most obvious example is perhaps killings caused through omission, for example a protection guarantor who intentionally fails to prevent a person (for whom he has responsibility) from killing himself or omits to distribute life-essential medicine to a patient in need (and who cannot administer this him- or herself).

The boundary between non-criminal complicity in deliberate suicide and killing at the victim's request is sometimes very subtle, for example when someone (B) wants to kill themselves, but is unable to due to paralysis, and therefore persuades someone else (A) to perform the act. If A, for example, administers morphine tablets to B, who is terminally ill and B then swallows them, it is likely that this falls within the non-criminalised area (aiding someone's lawful suicide). Alternatively, if A helps B to swallow the pills, for example, by massaging his throat, the outcome might be the opposite.

It should be noted that no one has a right to get help to die. Such a right is considered contrary to the basic right to life. Meanwhile there is constitutional protection for everyone against enforced physical interference. It is easy to imagine situations where these two interests come in conflict. The individual's desire to self-determine his life has largely been respected, although the reasons for him wanting to die – rather than submitting to certain medical treatments for example, blood transfusion) – may appear to be irrational to most other people. Sometimes there is an obligation for others (doctors, nurses, etc) to intervene.

As regards the possibility for doctors to lawfully shorten a life, the law is in several respects ambiguous. Nevertheless, it is clear that it is sometimes permissible. The basic principles in this context are the following. Measures whose sole purpose is to cause the death of a patient are never allowed (not even at the patient's request). However, measures that cannot cure but still alleviate, are to be undertaken although they will ultimately kill the patient, as long as reasonable grounds for doing this exists (for example, for the sake of the patient or his family).

This still leaves a space for doctors to lawfully undertake some measures (by act or omission) that will hasten death. Although there is reason to believe that a patient's life may be shortened, a doctor can lawfully take measures in the following cases:

(i) If life-support measures serve no reasonable purpose, the doctor should be considered to have the right not to treat a patient (so-called passive euthanasia). Freedom from responsibility for crimes of omission may often be motivated by the failure of the act to represent an unacceptable risk (omitting certain acts does not change the risk).

(ii) Where there is no other way to achieve a substantial care goal (usually avoiding pain), a doctor should have the right to undertake a measure that as a side-effect hastens death; for example, administering morphine. In many of these cases there is no question of a controlled killing, but merely a permissible risk in relation to an uncontrolled effect (death).

From what has been said, it is obvious that there is a subtle line between the taking of measures that *cause* death and the taking of measures that only *hasten* death. Prosecutors encounter similar problems when it comes to proving, in retrospect, what actually caused death in a specific case. Without doubt, there are many cases where the medical treatment has either facilitated death, or hastened it, in such a way that it meets the requirements of murder or manslaughter.

2.1.2 *Killing on request of the victim*

See section 2.1.1.

2.1.3 *Abortions*

According to Swedish law, a woman has a right to terminate a pregnancy if termination takes place within 18 weeks from when the child was conceived. The National Board of Health and Welfare can in special circumstances grant exemptions from this rule, for example if the foetus is suffering from severe disease or malformation or the mother's life is endangered by the pregnancy.

The mother has to make a specific request for an abortion; ie consent from the mother is presumed. Age is not relevant to this question. A girl of minor age who becomes pregnant has the same right to terminate the pregnancy as an adult. This right is absolute.

The foetus has no specific standing or legal rights until it is born (life is considered to begin when the mother goes into labour or the child is being delivered through a caesarean). Consent from any other person, including the father or any guardian of the mother, is also not required. This is only of practical relevance during the first 18 weeks when the mother has the prerogative to decide if she wants to end the pregnancy.

The state has no general authority to determine which pregnancies ought – or ought not – to be terminated. One could, however, imagine some exceptions. If the mother for example, suffers from severe illness and her life is endangered and lacks the capacity to request an abortion, a doctor could take the decision to terminate the pregnancy, despite the absence of explicit consent. This follows from general rules on justification (for example, necessity, rules and standards for measures in healthcare etc).

An abortion must be performed according to the rules in the Act (1974:595) on abortions. Whoever, without being authorised to practise medicine, intentionally performs an abortion on another will be convicted of *illegal abortion*. Any consent from the mother (to an illegal abortion) is irrelevant in this respect.

2.2 Consent and non-fatal offences against the person

2.2.1 *HIV and other communicable disease transmissions*

A person infected with HIV, or another similar serious sexual transmittable disease, will often expose a partner to the risk of transmitting the disease. Whether such risk-taking is unlawful or not depends on many different circumstances.

Both the quality and the quantity of the risk are relevant for such assessment. The more undesirable a consequence is (death, severe illness etc), the less risk-taking is necessary in order to make the risk-taking unlawful. The relatively low risk of transmitting HIV infection through unprotected sexual intercourse has consistently been deemed sufficient for responsibility.[23] Infected persons who have sexual intercourse with unknowing partners are regularly convicted for *creating danger to another*.[24] However, the low risk of transmission, and achievements made in the medical field when it comes to treating HIV infections, have meant that this attitude in courts has been questioned.

As explained above (see section 1.1.4), there is a rather broad margin for accepting risk-taking as lawful as long as the parties act with consent and are fully aware of the risks. In cases of transmitting the HIV infection, the risk is rather low. Consensual intercourse between persons, where one of them is infected by HIV, can be lawful. What makes an otherwise unlawful act (risk-taking) permitted is consent from the victim.

Accepting a risk (of harm) is nevertheless not the same as accepting a harm that follows from the risk-taking. If the result of unprotected consensual sexual intercourse is that the infection is transmitted, then the importance of an inherently valid consent (to risk-taking) ceases to be of importance for the question of criminal liability. Since the risk-taking, *ipso facto*, is unlawful, the question of whether the deed (as such) can be justified or not depends on the assessment of defensibility. Taking a risk might be deemed defensible (or rather *not indefensible*) if the harm does not occur, while actual transmission of the disease is deemed unlawful (because such a consequence is deemed indefensible). This difference in assessment is explained by the fact that a potential victim can only give valid consent to minor harms (or risks) but not to more severe ones. An HIV-infected person who actually transmits the disease to a consenting partner is criminally liable for *causing bodily injury or illness*.[25]

Should a victim as a consequence of the unlawful deed (transmitting the disease) later develop AIDS, and ultimately die from this, the offender will normally not be liable for any crime that requires intent, eg (attempted) *murder* or *manslaughter*. This is not because the act is in any sense justified, but instead explained with reference to the fact that the sequence of events is misaligned with the offence description (compare '(attempt to) take the life of another'). Whether the offender could be convicted for reckless or negligent *causing another's death* is an open question.[26] Normally there are practical reasons for why he or she cannot be convicted or even tried in a court of law (compare statutes of limitation, *ne bis in idem* etc). Consent from the victim is of no relevance to this question.

2.2.2 *Medical treatment*

Interventions by physicians and other healthcare professionals often involve significant risks for another's life or health. Medical interventions of various kinds – especially operations – regularly meet the definition of *assault, unlawful coercion or molestation*.[27] To what extent such actions are justified is an open question and the law is to a considerable extent still ambiguous.

Risk-taking in medical treatment may always be considered permissible if the act is carried out in accordance with what is accepted scientific knowledge and proven experience (*lex artis medici*). What counts as acceptable risk-taking often follows from provisions forwarded by authoritative standards and instructions issued by, for example, the National Board of Health

---

23 See NJA 2004 p. 176 (n 9).
24 See SCC (n 7) Chapter 3 s 9.
25 See SCC (n 7) Chapter 3 s 8. If intent to the actual transmission of the disease is at hand, this might also constitute assault under Chapter 3 s 5.
26 ibid Chapter 3 s 7.
27 See ibid Chapter 3 ss 5 and 6, and Chapter 4 s 4.

and Welfare or general doctrines of medicine. To a large extent, this applies in situations where the physician, or other staff, cause physical damage through the treatment.

Medical treatment is normally carried out with the consent of the patient. Although interventions of this kind often include higher risks than what a person really can consent to, the deed is still allowed (as lawful risk-taking) as long as it is done in accordance with science and proven experience. It is not necessary to justify the treatment with reference to justificatory circumstances (ie consent, necessity etc). The treatment is normally allowed because different standards apply to actions carried out within the context of medical treatment compared to ordinary life. It is clear that the area of discharge from liability is considerably higher concerning measures in healthcare than in other areas. Justification is offered because of the many and obvious benefits of medical treatment.

In situations where the treatment not only involves enhanced risk-taking but also harm caused by controlled actions (for example surgical incisions, anaesthetising of a patient etc), it becomes necessary to find a justification for the act that meets the requirements of an offence description. Since there is no real risk-taking involved (the harm is instead controlled by the actor), it becomes dogmatically impossible to say that the treatment is lawful because the 'risk-taking' is acceptable. In situations of this sort it becomes necessary to find a justification for causing the relevant harm involved. This is usually done with reference to *consent* from the patient or by applying the law on *necessity*.[28]

What represents the most difficult situations is when a patient either resists the recommended treatment or lacks the necessary capacity to understand what interventions the treatment involves (ie when there is no valid consent).

In situations where there is a direct threat to the patient's life, the possibility to invoke necessity is not excluded by the fact that the person threatened does not wish to be saved. The law on necessity can justify several forms of coercive treatment of a person (surgery, coercive feeding, and various forms of life support). As long as the physical violation is not to be deemed *indefensible*, this applies at least in situations where the patient lacks the capacity to give valid consent, but also – to some extent – in cases where the patient resists treatment. But there is still an open question – what does indefensible mean?

Proper respect for the individual's autonomy would as a rule exclude allowing interventions against decisions made by competent persons (ie conscious patients opposing the measure in question). Thus, as a general rule, if possible, consent should be obtained. But what if no such consent is given? What is at jeopardy is the interest of the person's right to self-determination. The (doctor's) duty to protect and save lives conflicts with the (patient's) right to self-determination. The admissibility of an action that takes place without valid consent is therefore dependent on how the expression 'physical violation' is interpreted, as well as on what is deemed (in)defensible in emergency situations.

If there is no direct threat to life, but 'only' a threat of non-fatal injuries, the assessment becomes even more difficult. The general rule on necessity applies here also. As explained above, interventions in emergencies can become unlawful if the action is indefensible. When assessing whether or not an act is defensible, consideration should be given to the character of the danger at hand, to the harm caused to other interests and to the circumstances in general. In cases of (risk of) non-fatal injuries, the value of the protected interest is relatively less than in situations where there is a direct threat to someone's life. This affects the balancing of

---

28 ibid Chapter 24 ss 4 and 7.

interests. The harm, or the negative value, brought about by the act (violating a person's right to autonomy) must, on balance, be such as is required to trigger criminal law.

Regarding the unconscious patient, there are reasons to investigate whether consent can be presumed, something that one usually can. From experience, it can be assumed that someone who has attempted suicide does not oppose health care. The reverse may apply to, for example, people who for religious reasons refuse a blood transfusion. To the extent courts want to use the legal figure of 'hypothetical consent', the assessment must be concrete, ie refer to the individual concerned. Otherwise, one easily ends up in a situation where all the interventions scrutinised are deemed reasonable (ie would be accepted by 'sane' people) and considered non-coercive. Thus, the legal protection emphasised in the constitution would become illusory.[29]

Exceptions from what has been said above must be made regarding children who oppose a procedure. In such cases, the guardian's attitude is crucial for the assessment. If the child refuses treatment, the guardian may nevertheless give valid consent to proceed with the measures taken. This follows from the fact that it may be a criminal offence under the Criminal Code Chapter 3 to fail to ensure that a child gets proper medical attention. If the guardians oppose treatment of the child, medical staff might refer to justificatory rules on necessity. In contrast, for less invasive procedures, there are no reasons for not accepting a child's consent to any procedures (although the guardians oppose this).

2.2.3 Sport injuries, 'horseplay' and piercing

Sport activities (organised or not) as well as playing games etc often create dangerous situations and can in some cases result in casualties. Participation in such activities often raises the question of whether the game 'itself', or the fact that the contender voluntarily participates in the exercise (ie consent), has any effect on the possibility to ascribe criminal responsibility to the one causing the harm. The answer is yes. But it all depends on what kind of harm, risk-taking or activity that is scrutinised. Nevertheless, an absolute condition for any acceptable standard of justification (because of some sort of relevant consent) is that the risk-taking refers to persons who voluntarily participate in the exercise of the sport.

In order to make sense of the doctrinal position on harm caused by sport activities, etc it is necessary to separate situations where the game/exercise is organised in some way from more spontaneous activities (while exercising a sport/game etc). More precisely: it is of great importance if the harm was caused by some conduct that is thought to be within the 'rules of the game' or not.

For all *organised sports* there are rules, some of which assume the character of safety standards. From a criminal law point of view such safeguards can be regarded as relatively valuable standards for assessing acceptable behaviour. Whoever is taking the necessary safety measures – in accordance with the regulations and other standards applicable in the field – is therefore, *a priori*, within the admissible area.

Many sports – for example football, wrestling, ice hockey and rugby – are conducted in a way where it is normal for rule violations to occur and that these sometimes lead to injury. There are many examples, where tackles and the like meet the requirements of the offence description of for example assault, unlawful coercion, molestation etc. Nevertheless, acts of this sort rarely constitute an offence; they are considered to be 'part of the game'. Participants are aware of the risks or consequences, and they willingly take part in the risky game, thus expressing some sort of consent (which is not the same as accepting harm of a more serious

---

29   See the Instrument of Government Chapter 2 s 6.

kind in an individual case). The general idea is that a risk taken through a 'natural' rule infringement is to be regarded as permissible. Regarding gross rule infringements – in conflict with the general standards of the activity – there are no reasons to accept the risk-taking as permissible. This obviously applies in cases where the violation was done with intent to cause harm (for example, fistfights in a hockey game).

In *non-organised sport*, as well as for (horse)play, the assessments are more difficult. Partaking in games or playing in tangible forms (with rough consequences) belongs to basic human needs (at least at some ages). This leaves a rather wide margin to accept various forms of risk-taking. When no norms of relevance could serve as guidelines for acceptable behaviour (ie lawful risk-taking), the border between acceptable and unlawful behaviour may be significantly lower than in organised sports.

In the absence of a specific standard that makes risk-taking permitted, one must consider if an otherwise criminalised act may nonetheless be permitted on the grounds of justification – ie some sort of consent from other participants. What makes this complicated is that consent to partake in a game or some other form of activity involving risks, does not mean that a potential victim has consented to the actual realisation of the risks in question.

The possibility to render a certain form of risk-taking permissible with reference to the 'rules of the game' does not nearly cover all types of deeds that take place in ordinary life. Breaking the rules of the game is often part of the game. Since many of these activities are considered to have great social value – organised or not – and represent mass phenomena, the state therefore has an interest in limiting criminal liability, although these activities will inevitably lead to injuries, harms etc. Some sort of justification, which stretches further than the standards of what is considered lawful risk-taking, is, in other words, needed. Otherwise, civil life in the area of recreation and exercise would be more or less paralysed. (The alternative would be to either ban many types of sports or to prosecute everyone who creates harm within these kinds of activities.)

Anyone who *voluntarily* participates in activities of this sort is presumed as having consented to all acts of violence etc that stay within the rules of the game. Nevertheless, the regulation on consent cannot solve this problem since there usually is no (expressly or hypothetically) given consent. A *general* – more or less unwritten – *rule for justification* applies in Swedish law, granting exoneration in cases where the rules of the game have been broken, but the behaviour is still within 'the idea of the game'. For example, a football player, who, during a match takes hold of another player in violation of the rules of the game, is not guilty of unlawful coercion or molestation. Similarly, anyone who, during a football match, in the battle for the ball, deliberately kicks the leg of an opponent in the course of the game, thereby causing not insignificant pain, is not liable for minor assault (even if football rules prohibit such kicks).

Wilful acts of violence against officials and spectators are, of course, never acceptable. The same may be said to apply to violence that takes place without any connection to the game. Exception from a rule of justification is made for intentional and more serious offences. (Should a player intentionally break a bone on an opponent, he or she is obviously guilty of assault.)

Simplistically summarised it could be said that it is possible to separate (i) violence that occurs during sports practice that is to a large extent accepted, from (ii) violence exercised directly connected to the game that is partially exonerated (it takes place in the 'heat of the battle'), and a third category consisting of (iii) violence unrelated to the game, which is treated as any other form of assault or coercion.

The question that remains to be answered is what role the general justificatory rule on consent (in the Criminal Code Chapter 24 s 7) serves. The easy answer is – not much. Most cases of endangerment or causing of harm that occur within sports etc are dealt with as either a question of whether the risk-taking is considered unlawful or not, or as a question of whether the general exclusion rule (covering harms caused by voluntary partaking in sports) applies.

2.2.4 Specific sexual practices

Sexual acts with sado-masochistic elements (bondage etc) frequently meet the requirements of assault, gross assault, unlawful coercion, molestation etc. The question is whether it ought to be taken into consideration that the harm has been caused from (sexual) consensual activities.

It is clear that certain types of assault or coercion with consent are allowed and others are prohibited. The circumstances that must be considered in determining whether consent should make a breach of the law permissible, are primarily the actual injury caused by the act, the danger of further injury, the offender's purpose and the social value of the deed. It is vital to have reasonably clear boundaries for responsibility. Special emphasis is placed on the type of injury involved.

According to the preparatory works, consent can make an otherwise unlawful deed allowable and therefore tolerated if the type of injury would be labelled as *minor assault* or at the most *assault*. Causing of harm that meets the requirements of minor assault (minor pain, bodily harm etc) always excludes responsibility if the victim has given her consent.

Whether assaults, uses of force etc that cause more than minor injuries or illness can be permissible is more difficult to say. Substantial weight should be given to the purpose of the act, as well as how plausible it is that the victim, having given her consent, later regrets this. Reference to precedents and practice in courts show it is rather difficult to find any examples where it appears clear that consent excludes liability.

There may be cases where an act of a specific nature causes greater harm (than minor bodily harm, pain etc) but in which the circumstances still are such that consent from the victim should result in a discharge. Consensual sexual activities of a complex nature – like the above mentioned – belong to this category, something that is partially explained by the fact that courts are in need of a relatively simple rule. As for wilful causing of relatively minor injuries or illness during acts of, for example sadism, masochism, bondage (including intimate piercing, tattoos) etc, consent is arguably rendered relevant as long as the harm involved does not meet the requirements of gross assault. Thus, there is probably a somewhat greater scope for accepting consent as relevant in cases where sexual acts of such a nature as discussed above cause bodily harm or coercion.

2.3 Sexual offences

2.3.1 Absence of consent or use of force/threats

The Swedish law on sexual offences is not built on consent as such, but the idea has been to capture situations of non-consent by describing situations where consent is not present.[30] Consequently, the law criminalises forcing someone to have sex by means of violence or threats, to improperly take advantage of someone's especially vulnerable position, to seriously misuse someone's dependence etc. According to the preparatory works the reference to a person's 'especially vulnerable position' includes cases where the victim does not say 'no'

---

30 See NJA 2004 p. 176 (n 9) 231. See also Madeleine Leijonhufvud, *Samtyckesutredningen* (Thomson 2008) and Asp (n 3).

due to fear and cases where the victim is deceived about which person the victim is having sex with or about the sexual nature of the act (for example, when a person is the subject of medical examination and the doctor performs a sexual act). The level of violence required in cases of force is set very low. All in all, this means that Swedish law in practice covers most conceivable cases in which there is sex without consent. It could be argued that there still might be cases of non-consent that are not covered by the legislation. For example, if a person makes it clear that he or she does not consent but also makes it clear that he or she will not make any attempt to resist (but just expects his or her 'no' to be respected) it would be hard to convict a person who disrespects the 'no'. It could be argued that it would be of value for normative reasons to make it clear that it is non-consent that is the ratio behind the legislation.

As regards the offence of forcing someone to have sex by means of violence or threats, the presence of consent will negate the prerequisites of the offence (if there is consent to sex the person will not have been forced to have sex). As regards the offences of taking advantage of someone's especially vulnerable position or dependence, the fulfilment of the required factors are such that they will make the consent that might be given invalid; ie the conclusion that there has been improper abuse of a vulnerable position equals (in principle) the conclusion that there has been no valid consent.

Recently, in October 2016, a legislative inquiry has presented a proposal for new legislation on sexual offences, the main idea being that it should build on non-consent, but that the law should provide clear guidance as regards what constitutes non-consent.

2.3.2 Evidentiary presumptions

There are no presumptions in play other than those that may be used when assessing evidence. For example, the fact that someone who is in a certain position normally understands x and y, can be taken as a reason to conclude that the perpetrator has understood x and y (unless there is reason to conclude otherwise).

2.3.3 Mistake of fact about consent

As regards sexual offences, non-consent is, as indicated above, an implicit part of the offence description. If a person believes that there is consent when such consent negates the offence description this will, due to the general intent requirement, negate the required intent.[31] There is no specific standard for sexual offences: the relevant issue is whether the person actually (honestly) was mistaken. Accordingly, there is no correspondence in Swedish law to the idea of 'reasonable belief' often seen in common law jurisdictions. Unreasonable belief will be dealt with as a case of negligence (which is at present not criminalised when it comes to sexual offences in general; as regards statutory rape it is enough with negligence in relation to the fact that the victim was underage).[32]

2.4 Property offences

2.4.1 Place of consent in the offence structure

One might expect that the rule on consent in the Criminal Code Chapter 24 s 7 would be of great importance to property offences. However, this is not the case. As explained above,

---

31 See above, section 1.6. *in fine.*
32 See SCC (n 7) Chapter 6 s 13.

consent sometimes becomes relevant as a factor that negates the prerequisites of the offence description in question.

When determining which form of consent is relevant in such a context, it is thought to be justified to accept lower requirements than the ones imposed under the general exemption rule. This is, for example, the case regarding consent to what would otherwise be a theft; it is not excluded that a person lacking in legal capacity may provide the relevant consent, thereby making the taking of property lawful. When 'force' constitutes part of a property crime description (for example, robbery), it may well be that this prerequisite is not fulfilled because of a given consent that does not entirely satisfy the requirements mentioned above. If A, for example, agrees to B taking some property that A either owns or is in possession of, then the *taking* is lawful. A has the right to dispose of the property as he likes. If he chooses to accept this change in possession, then this (different) form of consent negates the prerequisite of 'without permission'.

What has been said so far applies not only to the types of crime where the word 'unlawfully' is especially mentioned in the offence, but also to other crimes requiring a certain effect on an interest which the potential victim disposes of. See, by way of comparison:

- Theft:[33] – 'A person who without permission takes what belongs to another. . .',
- Inflicting damage/vandalism:[34] – 'destroys or damages property. . . to the detriment of another's right thereto',
- Breach of trust of trust and authority abuse (for example, breach of faith committed by an agent against his principal):[35] – 'A person who, by reason of a position of trust. . . abuses his position. . .'.

The only property offences in which an application of the Criminal Code Chapter 24 s 7 specifically could be relevant appears to be receiving (handling of stolen goods) and certain crimes against creditors under the Criminal Code Chapter 11.[36] The latter would be without significant practical importance.

2.4.2 Mistaken belief in consent

Many of the legal-technical terms that are found in the offence descriptions of property offences relate to situations where some sort of consent from the potential victim could be of relevance. If a person mistakenly believes that he owns a thing he has taken, the question arises whether he intentionally has taken 'what belongs to another'.

Mistakes concerning the legal concepts are normally irrelevant for the assessment of responsibility. Ignorance of law is no defence. The *mens rea* requirements are fulfilled as long as the offender understand what he does (ie that he takes goods and thereby gets into a position where he is in sole possession of this or if he, by his *taking*, cuts of someone else's possession to the goods).

Nevertheless, mistake of facts is by no means immaterial to the assessment of guilt, although these are caused by the perpetrator's miscomprehensions of concepts like 'possession' and

---

33 See ibid Chapter 8 s 1.
34 ibid Chapter 12 s 1.
35 ibid Chapter 10 s 5.
36 ibid Chapter 9 s 6.

'ownership' etc. As said above, many terms regarding property offences have a special legal meaning that does not always correspond with how the term is used in general language. If the offender's classification of his actions is not reasonably legally correct, he has often not understood the implications of his act. This is especially true if the legal terminology has become part of common parlance, but where it is not certain that the term publicly has the same defined meaning as it has in the legal-technical sense. According to the practice in courts, error and ignorance regarding 'ownership', 'consent to taking of property' etc exclude intent if the mistake relates to either of the prerequisites of the offence description. Thus, a person who wrongly assumes that all things found in a forest or in public places are abandoned, or that the owners will never be able to come back and find it, wrongly believes that the removal is lawful. Consequently there is no intent to the prerequisite of taking 'without permission'; the perpetrator thinks he has a consent handed down from legislation.

This is also true in situations when the offender believes he has consent from the person who, for example, owns, possesses or has been entrusted with the goods in question. For example, if someone is under the misapprehension that a neighbour is willing to lend his lawn mower to anyone in need of it, and therefore takes and uses it, he lacks the necessary intent for dispossession 'without permission'. He thought he had the necessary consent to make it lawful.

Index

435